AFTER THE BERLIN WALL

The history and meaning of the Berlin Wall remain controversial, even three decades after its fall. Drawing on an extensive range of archival sources and interviews, this book profiles key memory activists who have fought to commemorate the history of the Berlin Wall and examines their role in the creation of a new German national narrative. With victims, perpetrators, and heroes, the Berlin Wall has joined the Holocaust as an essential part of German collective memory. Key Wall anniversaries have become signposts marking German views of the past, its relevance to the present, and the complicated project of defining German national identity. Considering multiple German approaches to remembering the Wall via memorials, trials, public ceremonies, films, and music, this revelatory work also traces how global memory of the Wall has impacted German memory policy. It depicts the power and fragility of state-backed memory projects, and the potential of such projects to reconcile or divide.

HOPE M. HARRISON is Associate Professor of History and International Affairs at the George Washington University. The recipient of fellowships from Fulbright, the Wilson Center, and the American Academy in Berlin, she is the author of *Driving the Soviets up the Wall* (2003), which was awarded the 2004 Marshall Shulman Book Prize by the American Association for the Advancement of Slavic Studies, and was also published to wide acclaim in German translation. She has served on the National Security Council staff, currently serves on the board of three institutions in Berlin connected to the Cold War and the Berlin Wall, and has appeared on CNN, the History Channel, the BBC, and Deutschlandradio.

AFTER THE BERLIN WALL

Memory and the Making of the New Germany, 1989 to the Present

HOPE M. HARRISON

The George Washington University

CAMBRIDGE
UNIVERSITY PRESS

CAMBRIDGE
UNIVERSITY PRESS

University Printing House, Cambridge CB2 8BS, United Kingdom

One Liberty Plaza, 20th Floor, New York, NY 10006, USA

477 Williamstown Road, Port Melbourne, VIC 3207, Australia

314–321, 3rd Floor, Plot 3, Splendor Forum, Jasola District Centre,
New Delhi – 110025, India

79 Anson Road, #06–04/06, Singapore 079906

Cambridge University Press is part of the University of Cambridge.

It furthers the University's mission by disseminating knowledge in the pursuit of
education, learning, and research at the highest international levels of excellence.

www.cambridge.org
Information on this title: www.cambridge.org/9781107049314
DOI: 10.1017/9781107278899

© Hope M. Harrison 2019

First published 2019

Printed in the United Kingdom by TJ International Ltd. Padstow Cornwall

A catalogue record for this publication is available from the British Library.

Library of Congress Cataloging-in-Publication Data
Names: Harrison, Hope Millard, author.
Title: After the Berlin Wall : memory and the making of the new Germany, 1989
to the present / Hope M. Harrison.
Description: Cambridge ; New York, NY : Cambridge University Press, 2019. |
Includes bibliographical references and index.
Identifiers: LCCN 2019014879| ISBN 9781107049314 (Hardback) |
ISBN 9781107627406 (Paperback)
Subjects: LCSH: Collective memory – Germany. | Germany – History – Unification,
1990 – Historiography. | Berlin Wall, Berlin, Germany, 1961–1989 – Historiography. |
National characteristics, German. | Germany – Politics and government – 1990–
Classification: LCC DD290.24 .H37 2019 | DDC 943.088–dc23
LC record available at https://lccn.loc.gov/2019014879

ISBN 978-1-107-04931-4 Hardback
ISBN 978-1-107-62740-6 Paperback

In Memory of Manfred Fischer,
whose work to preserve the memory
of the Berlin Wall remains an inspiration
and
For Mary G. Leferovich,
whose love, generosity, and support
as my aunt are unsurpassed

CONTENTS

FIGURES

ACKNOWLEDGMENTS

This book represents many years of work, and I am deeply grateful to the many people and institutions in the United States and Germany who have helped me along the way. The opportunity offered by the city of West Berlin to join a group of Harvard and Stanford graduate students on a trip to Berlin in November 1989 was a life-changing one, since we landed in Berlin on the morning of November 10, less than twenty-four hours after the Berlin Wall had been pushed open. Being there to soak up the extraordinary atmosphere in Berlin for ten days was in some sense the beginning of this book. Many of the people and institutions listed below enabled me to return to Berlin countless times after that, including for major anniversaries of the rise and fall of the Wall.

For twenty years, the George Washington University has been my professional base, and I cannot imagine nicer colleagues at my two GW homes, the Elliott School and the history department. At the Elliott School, former deans Harry Harding and Michael Brown and current dean Reuben Brigety have been generous supporters of me and my work, including by providing funds from an anonymous donor for Strategic Opportunities for Academic Reach (SOAR) that were essential to many of my trips to Berlin. At the Elliott School's Institute for European, Russian, and Eurasian Studies (IERES), current and former directors Peter Rollberg, Henry Hale, and Jim Goldgeier have made IERES a wonderful, interesting place to be and have also provided funding for research assistants. My colleagues in the history department, including several who also work on memory issues, have offered inspiration as well as helpful comments on my work. I am particularly grateful to former department chairs Ron Spector, who hired me, and Bill Becker who gave me good advice at a crucial moment. GW's Office of the Vice President for Research helped in the final stages of this work with a grant from its Humanities Facilitating Fund.

Research fellowships from several institutions have provided the greatest gift of time to work on this project, starting with a semester at the American Academy in Berlin when Gary Smith was the director. The American Academy is paradise on earth for a scholar, especially one whose research is based in Berlin. The entire staff of the Academy was so welcoming and helpful, including: Gary Smith; Paul Stoop who oversaw the academic aspects of the fellowship program and introduced me to many people useful for my research; Yolanda Korb the librarian who procured all sorts of essential research materials for me; Marie Unger who oversaw the logistical aspects of the fellowship, offered friendship and good advice on swimming pools and other things; and Reinold Kegel, the Academy's chef, who made every meal a treat, especially the inventive Berlin Wall-related meal he created the evening I presented my work. I was quite fortunate that the Academy paired me with Hans-Otto Bräutigam to be my "mentor." We had many fascinating conversations about German history and grappling with the GDR past, delightful meals, and an unforgettable trip around several of Berlin's historic cemeteries.

A Fulbright fellowship to spend the 2009–2010 academic year in Berlin, coinciding with the twentieth anniversary of the fall of the Berlin Wall, was incredibly important for this book. I am so appreciative of all that Rolf Hoffmann and Reiner Rohr of the German-American Fulbright Commission did to facilitate my research. I spent the year at the Federal Foundation for Reappraising the SED Dictatorship (*Bundesstiftung zur Aufarbeitung der SED-Diktatur*), which was the perfect place to be. I am deeply grateful to Anna Kaminsky for hosting me and to Rainer Eppelmann, Ulrich Mählert, Ruth Gleinig, Jens Hüttmann (who has since moved elsewhere), Sabine Kuder, Robert Grünbaum, and the librarians Sylvia Kubina and Maria Jung. Ruth Gleinig was so gracious to share her office and many conversations with me, thus beginning a long-lasting friendship. I was very lucky that Helena Finn was the minister-counselor for public affairs at the US embassy in Berlin that year and sent me around the country to speak about my research, helping me to learn a lot along the way. Her colleague Manfred Stinnes was also very helpful.

The Center for Contemporary History (ZZF) in Potsdam, just outside of Berlin, has hosted me several times for visits or talks, and I am happy to thank the previous co-director, Konrad Jarausch, and the current co-director, Martin Sabrow, as well as Hans-Hermann Hertle for their hospitality, interesting conversations, and comments on my work – as well as for their answers to my many questions about German approaches to the Wall and the East German past.

Several stints at the Woodrow Wilson International Center for Scholars in Washington, DC, especially for the year-long fellowship program in 2013–14, have been of essential importance for this book. The staff there make me feel as if the Wilson Center is my "home away from home" in DC when I am not at GW. Words cannot express how grateful I am to Rob Litwak for his support of my work and his friendship. Rob represents all that is so special about the Wilson Center. The staff go out of their way to assist visiting scholars, and it is a pleasure to thank them: Kim Conner and Arlyn Charles in fellowships; Janet Spikes and Michelle Kamalich at the library; Krishna Aniel for her work in finding fantastic research interns; and Maria-Stella Gatzoulis in event planning. It was wonderful to be a part of the Center's History and Public Policy Project led by my dear friend Christian Ostermann with great help from Chuck

Kraus and Pieter Biersteker. Thanks also to Center President Jane Harman and to Mike van Dusen as well as to Lindsay Collins, Chuck Brown, Howard Watkins, the IT staff, and all the others who make the Wilson Center such a fantastic place to work. The writing group several of us formed in the 2013–14 scholars program was very inspiring, and I treasure the friendship it led to with Amal Fadlalla who happily was in the office next to mine. We have talked about our books and much else ever since.

I have been graced with several stellar research assistants. The Wilson Center paired me up at different times with two German research assistants, Julian Wettengel and Jannis Jost, both of whom went way beyond anything I could have ever expected. Julian found some very helpful sources for me in DC and then (with GW funding over the summer after Julian and I had both left the Wilson Center) gave me invaluable aid by conducting research in several archives in Berlin. Jannis's work made all the Wilson Center scholars wish they had him working for them. His wide-ranging research, sophisticated thinking, and discussions with me about my work were immensely helpful. Thomas Pennington and Brian Pollock worked with me for shorter periods at the Wilson Center and I am grateful to them as well. I also want to thank my research assistants at GW: Chance Williams, Alexandra Cantone, and Raabia Shafi. Raabia was a master's student in history and was the first to show me what a really great research assistant can do. I will never forget her research, her analysis of her findings, and her probing questions to me about my work, all of which led to many long, fruitful discussions and then to a close friendship in the years to come.

This book has benefited from discussions with colleagues at many institutions and at conferences in the USA, Germany, and beyond; including at the Washington History Seminar, the Association for the Study of Nationalities, the German Studies Association, the American Institute for Contemporary German Studies, the Association for Slavic, East European, and Eurasian Studies, the German Historical Institute, Georgetown's BMW Center (thanks to Eric Langenbacher), George Mason's School for Conflict Analysis and Resolution (thanks to Karina Korostelina), Bowdoin College (thanks to Jill Smith), the University of Waterloo (thanks to Gary Bruce), St. Antony's College Oxford (thanks to Anne Deighton), the international history department at the London School of Economics (thanks to Piers Ludlow), the Institute for German Studies at Birmingham University (thanks to Sara Jones), the history department at the University of Heidelberg (thanks to Detlef Junker, Edgar Wolfrum, Birgit Hofmann, and Katja Wezel), and the Public History Program at the Free University of Berlin (thanks to Andreas Etges who was still there at the time before moving to Munich). Jay Winter and Jeff Olick are both inspirations in the field of memory studies, and I am grateful for their comments on my work or the advice they each gave me at different points.

Christian Seeger's decision to publish my first book, *Driving the Soviets up the Wall*, in German translation as *Ulbrichts Mauer* with Proplyäen Verlag on the occasion of the fiftieth anniversary of the erection of the Wall in 2011 offered the fascinating opportunity for my research to become part of the debates about how to remember the Wall. Three years later, Anna Slafer's request that I write a blog for the International Spy Museum about my attendance at events in Berlin marking the twenty-fifth anniversary of the fall of the Wall provided the chance to put down my thoughts about that anniversary in real time. Both experiences proved to be very helpful for the present book.

Since they are so central to the story told in this book, I have had many conversations with people who were or are connected to the Berlin Wall Memorial, the Berlin Wall Supporters' Association or the Reconciliation parish over the years, including Manfred Fischer, Axel Klausmeier, Günter Schlusche, Maria Nooke, Rainer Just, Rudolph Prast, Gerhard Sälter, Gabriele Camphausen, Helmut Trotnow, Leo Schmidt, and most recently with Thomas Jeutner. I cannot thank Axel Klausmeier enough for his seemingly infinite willingness to answer my many questions and for hosting me several times, especially for the launch of *Ulbrichts Mauer*. I owe a special thanks to Rainer Just who spent a great deal of time with me in the fall of 2018 answering my questions, especially since tragically Manfred Fischer could no longer do so, and finding pictures for me to use in this book. Manfred Wichmann and Caroline Knopke were also very helpful in tracking down pictures for me to use. Sarah Bornhorst provided me with transcripts of interviews conducted for the Berlin Wall Memorial, and Thomas Jeutner kindly granted permission for me to consult his interviews before the transcripts were finalized.

For helping me track down photographs, I am grateful to Florian Weiss and Bernd von Kostka at the Allied Museum, Carolin Kohl at Kulturprojekte Berlin, and Christoph Ochs at the Robert-Havemann-Gesellschaft.

I deeply appreciate the time all of my interviewees gave me in person (sometimes for several hours) and in follow-up conversations by email when I needed it. Rainer Klemke rivals only Axel Klausmeier for his friendly readiness to answer my questions. I am also very grateful to him for inviting me to a variety of events connected to remembering the Wall and for granting me access to his files on the Berlin Senate's "Master Plan for Commemorating the Berlin Wall."

For a scholar who thrives on dialogue with others, there is nothing as helpful as having others read my work and discuss it with me. Christian Ostermann, Kelly Smith, Jens Schöne, Eric Langenbacher, Susan Pearce, and an anonymous reviewer for Cambridge University Press read all or part of previous drafts of this book. At the moment I needed it most and when they were both very busy themselves, both Christian Ostermann and Kelly Smith read the entire manuscript and offered invaluable advice and reassurance. Christian did the same thing for my first book, and I feel so lucky that he continues to be my "first reader." I always learn from our discussions about German history. I am fortunate to have such generous colleagues and friends in Christian and Kelly.

Years of my engagement with the history and commemoration of the Berlin Wall and the Cold War have led to invitations to serve as a member of the Berlin Wall Memorial Supporters' Association, the Advisory Council of the Allied Museum in Berlin, the International Advisory Council of the BlackBox Cold War Exhibit at Checkpoint Charlie, Berlin, and the Advisory Council of the Point Alpha Foundation in Geisa, Germany. The views expressed in this book are solely those of the author and do not necessarily reflect the views or opinions of these organizations.

I am delighted to thank everyone at Cambridge University Press who has made the publication of this book possible, starting with Michael Watson who commissioned the book, read early chapters, always made me feel his enthusiasm, and proved to be very patient waiting for me to finish. My thanks also go to my editor Liz Friend-Smith and to Ruth Boyes in production.

Friends and family have stood beside me throughout the process of researching and writing this book. Maggie Paxson and Charles King are simply extraordinary in the general love, support, and concrete help they have given me on this project. From discussing the deepest issues I have grappled with in this book (and sometimes even helping me see them more clearly), to offering advice on my choice of words, to singing to me or cooking for me, they humble me with their capacity to give and to think. Maggie was even my first guide into the literature on collective memory. Other dear friends have brightened my days in so many ways: Maria-Stella Gatzoulis; Devin Reese, Hal Cardwell and their children/my godchildren Camila, Owen, and Guy; Marsha Danzig; Raabia Shafi; Annie Hershberg; Teresa Gallina and Leopoldo Nuti; and Vlad Zubok. Friends in Berlin who feel like family have given me places to stay for many years: Claudia Wilhelm; Angelika and Lothar Wilker; Heike and Manfred Görtemaker; and Beate and Johannes Tuchel. They are a big part of the reason that I love Berlin.

My father and stepmother, Robert and Linda Harrison, and my aunt, Mary G. Leferovich, have heard all about this book for a long time, and I know they are very happy it is finally finished! Their enthusiasm and support has meant a great deal to me. My father remains my favorite traveling companion to Berlin, and our regular conversations about Berlin and the *Ostsee* sustain us between visits. My Aunt Mary, as all my friends call her too, has done everything humanly possible to step in and offer a mother's love since I lost my mother, her sister. Aunt Mary occupies a very special place in my life and my heart, and I hope that dedicating this book to her demonstrates how profoundly grateful I am for all that she has given and continues to give to me.

I also dedicate this book to the memory of Manfred Fischer whose tireless, persistent, and creative efforts to preserve the memory of the Berlin Wall – and pieces of the Wall itself – remain an inspiration. I wish I had met him sooner, but I am so glad I did meet him.

ABBREVIATIONS AND GERMAN TERMS

Alltagsleben, everyday life

Alternative für Deutschland (AfD), Alternative for Germany

ARD, First German Television

Aufarbeitung der Geschichte, grappling with history

Beirat, Advisory Board or Council

Berliner Mauer, Berlin Wall

Brandenburger Tor, Brandenburg Gate

Bundesbeauftragte für Kultur und Medien (BKM), Federal Commission/er on Culture and Media (refers to both the institution and the person running it)

Bundesbeauftragte für Stasi Unterlagen (BStU), Federal Commission/er for Stasi Records (refers to both the institution and the person running it)

Bundesgerichtshof (BGH), Federal Court of Justice

Bundesstiftung zur Aufarbeitung der SED-Diktatur (*Stiftung Aufarbeitung*), Federal Foundation for Reappraising the SED Dictatorship

Bundestag, Federal German Parliament

Bundeszentrale für politische Bildung (BpB), Federal Agency for Political (or Civic) Education

Bündnis 90, Alliance 90

Bürgerbüro, Citizens' Office

Central Investigation Office for Governmental and Organized Criminality (ZERV)

Christian Democratic Union (CDU)

Christian Social Union (CSU)

Demokratische Aufbruch, Democratic Awakening

Deutsches Historisches Museum (DHM), German Historical Museum

Dominostein, domino

Erinnerungskultur, memory culture

Erinnerungspolitik, memory policy

Federal Republic of Germany (FRG), West Germany, 1949–1990, or united Germany, 1990–present

Fenster des Gedenkens, Window of Commemoration

Fest der Freiheit, Festival of Freedom

Free Democratic Party (FDP)

Freie Deutsche Jugend (FDJ), Free German Youth (GDR communist youth group)

Freiheitsmahnmal, Freedom Memorial

Freiheits- und Einheitsdenkmal, Freedom and Unity Monument

Gedenkkonzept, commemorative plan

Gedenkpolitik, commemoration policy

Gedenkstätte, memorial (generally refers to a site and the organization administering it)

Gedenkstätte Berliner Mauer (GBM), Berlin Wall Memorial

Gedenkstättenkonzeption, plan for memorials

German Democratic Republic (GDR), East Germany

Gesamtkonzept, master plan

Geschichtspolitik, history policy

Grenzer, border soldier(s)

Grundgesetz, Basic Law/constitution of FRG

Grüne, the Green Party

Hinterlandmauer, the rear part of the Berlin Wall, the first obstacle an East German would come to, as opposed to the forward Wall, the external part facing West Berlin

Kampfgruppe gegen Unmenschlichkeit (KgU), Action Group against Inhumanity

Konzept, plan

Kristallnacht, Night of Broken Glass, November 9, 1938

Lernort, site of learning

Lichtgrenze, border of light

Die Linke, the Left Party (successor to the SED and PDS)

Mahnmal, memorial or monument (in the sense of warning or admonishing, not celebrating)

Mauer, Wall

Mauergrundstücksgesetz, law on property at the (former) Wall

Mauerweg, Wall trail

National Defense Council of the GDR (NVR)

Nationale Volksarmee (NVA), National People's Army of the GDR

Neue Bundesländer, new federal states (the former GDR)

North Atlantic Treaty Organization (NATO)

Ostalgie, nostalgia for the East (the GDR)

Ostpolitik, policy toward the East initiated by FRG Chancellor Willy Brandt

Party of Democratic Socialism (PDS), successor to SED and predecessor to the Left Party (*die Linke*)

Platz, square

Politische Bildung, Political (or Civic) Education

Radweg, bicycle trail

Republikflucht, flight from the Republic (trying to escape from the GDR)

Schiessbefehl, order to shoot

Schreibtischtäter, perpetrators who sit at desks issuing orders

SM-70, splinter mine, mounted on external fence along GDR border with FRG

Social Democratic Party (SPD)

Sozialistische Einheitspartei Deutschland (SED), Socialist Unity Party of (East) Germany

Staatskapelle, Berlin State Orchestra

Stasi, Staatssicherheitsdienst, the GDR's secret police

Stiftung Berliner Mauer (SBM), Berlin Wall Foundation

Union der Opferverbände kommunistischer Gewaltherrschaft (UOKG), Union of Victims' Associations of Communist Tyranny

United Nations Educational, Scientific and Cultural Organization (UNESCO)

Unrechtsstaat, unjust state or state without rule of law

Verein, association

Vergangenheitsbewältigung, coming to terms with the past

Verharmlosung, belittling or downplaying

Versöhnungsgemeinde, Reconciliation Church Community

Versöhnungskapelle, Chapel of Reconciliation

Versöhnungskirche, Church of Reconciliation

Vertriebene, expellees

Volkskammer, East German Parliament

Volkspolizei, VoPos (People's Police of GDR)

Warsaw Pact, Soviet bloc counterpart to NATO

ZDF, Second German Television

~

Introduction: The Berlin Wall and German Historical Memory

Thirty years after the fall of the Berlin Wall on November 9, 1989, people around the world still remember the joyous drama of that night and the days and nights that followed. Even at a time before smartphones and Twitter helped people experience an event together, the surprise opening of the Berlin Wall was viewed by millions on television sets and splashed across headlines around the globe. For Berliners and Germans, dramatic days followed that would change their lives and their country.

When the Wall fell, nineteen-year-old Georg[1] had just begun his compulsory military service in the National People's Army (NVA). Born and raised in a small town in East Germany where he had learned how to milk cows at a collective farm, he was assigned for his eighteen-month service to the one unit of the NVA based in East Berlin, the Friedrich Engels Guard Regiment. The regiment's duties were to stand guard at the central Monument to Victims of Fascism and Militarism (the *Neue Wache* on the main thoroughfare of the city, Unter den Linden) and at military installations in East Berlin, as well as to serve as the honor guard at official state visits. Georg just wanted to get his military service done as soon as possible without any problems and go on with his life. Yet, now, in the early days of November, living at the regimental barracks in the heart of East Berlin, just blocks from the Berlin Wall and the Brandenburg Gate, he could hear the shouts of demonstrators on the streets outside and grew increasingly anxious.

The young draftee and his colleagues were given no information about what was going on and were not allowed to read the newspapers or listen to the radio. They were not armed with guns nor had they been trained to use firearms, although they had been trained to march with goose steps in front of the *Neue Wache*. The only people in the unit who had access to a radio were those on duty on each floor of the barracks. As fate would have it, Georg had floor duty on the night of November 9, his ninth day in the army.

---

[1] Georg's name has been changed to grant him anonymity. Interviews with author, November 9, 2014 and June 25, 2018. All translations from German to English in this book have been done by the author.

1

Early that evening, before Georg was sitting by the radio, Politburo member Günter Schabowski had declared at a press conference that there were new regulations for travel to the West. These had previously been extremely restrictive for people of working age, generally granting permission to travel to West Berlin or West Germany only for the funerals, weddings, or major birthdays of close family members; one of the many points of complaint of increasingly large groups of East German protestors. Schabowski announced that the regime was now considering allowing East German citizens to "travel wherever they want to" without the previously necessary justifications and also that they had just decided earlier that day that people who wanted to "permanently leave" the GDR could now do so at any border crossing point, including in Berlin. The new regulations for those seeking to emigrate would take effect "immediately, without delay," in Schabowski's memorable words. The fact that Schabowski had misread his briefing documents and that, actually, the borders were not supposed to be totally open and people still needed to obtain a visa to leave, was lost.[2]

Georg had heard rumors in the barracks about Schabowski's press conference and remained at his floor post by the radio listening closely, with some confusion and growing trepidation. As the evening wore on, he heard reports that his fellow East German citizens were making their way to checkpoints on the border in droves and that, as of around 11:30 p.m., the first border crossing at the Berlin Wall was opened to free movement at Bornholmer Strasse, less than three miles directly north of where he was sitting.[3] The nineteen year old grew increasingly worried, wondering, "Holy shit, what kind of a situation will I be in now?" Just after midnight, the East German authorities gave in to the crush of their citizens at the border and opened all the checkpoints to West Berlin (Figure 1). Two of the checkpoints, at Invalidenstrasse and at Checkpoint Charlie, were just over a mile away from Georg's barracks, to the northwest and southwest respectively. In the dark early morning hours, Georg and his regiment were given orders to prepare to move out. They were armed with batons and packed onto trucks. They had no idea where they were going, nor what their mission would be on this dark, cold November night. Would they be ordered to use force against their fellow citizens? Would they be attacked by their fellow citizens for representing the East German authorities, Georg worried.

---

[2] Hans-Hermann Hertle, "The Fall of the Wall: The Unintended Dissolution of East Germany's Ruling Regime," *Bulletin 12/13*, Cold War International History Project (Fall/Winter 2001), pp. 131–40. See also Mary Elise Sarotte, *The Collapse: The Accidental Opening of the Berlin Wall* (New York: Basic Books, 2014).

[3] For a description of the events at Bornholmer Strasse through the eyes of Harald Jäger, the leader at the East German checkpoint for the key hours, see Gerhard Haase-Hindenberg, *Der Mann, der die Mauer öffnete: Warum Oberstleutnant Harald Jäger den Befehl verweigert und damit Weltgeschichte schrieb* (Munich: Wilhelm Heyne Verlag, 2007). See also Sarotte, *The Collapse*, pp. 136–47.

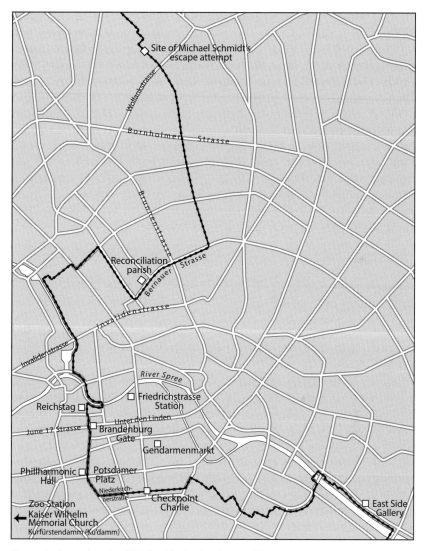

Figure 1 Central path of Wall with checkpoints and key sites

He did not have to wonder for long about where they were headed as the trucks stopped less than a mile later in front of the Brandenburg Gate – or, from the western perspective, behind the Gate. They were ordered to form a human chain just in front of the eastern fence marking the perimeter of the Berlin Wall restricted zone. Georg and the other new draftees had not even taken the military oath yet, and they were suddenly deployed at the front line in Berlin at the greatest symbol of the divided city, the Brandenburg Gate.

Enthusiastic crowds had been flocking to the Brandenburg Gate from both West and East Berlin since the borders had been opened a few short hours earlier. The Gate stood in the middle of Berlin and straddled the main East-West thoroughfare, which had been cut off by the building of the Berlin Wall in 1961. Located in the Berlin Wall death strip and surrounded by no-man's-land, the Gate had for decades been out of reach of everyone but the East German border soldiers. Now, in the middle of the night between November 9 and 10, more and more people made their way from both west and east to the Brandenburg Gate. This was also the only location where the Berlin Wall had a broad, flat area on top so that people could actually stand on it. All other sections of the Wall featured a rounded top, which made it impossible to stand on and difficult even to grasp onto by hand, a construction design meant to hinder escape attempts. Buoyed by enthusiasm and in some cases by alcohol, people hoisted each other up to reach the top of the nearly twelve-foot Wall. The Wall at the Brandenburg Gate seemed to offer the perfect place for celebrating Berliners to gather, some of them hammering away at the Wall and removing small pieces.

Concerned by the damage to their well-constructed border and with the growing chaos surrounding the Gate, the East German authorities tried to gain control of the situation by directing the border soldiers to urge the revelers to get down and leave the area or, when that did not work, by forcing the revelers down by the use of water cannons. The officers and soldiers on duty there were faced with West Berliners trying to come over the Wall from the West into the East and by East Berliners entering the secure zone of the Brandenburg Gate from the East, walking en masse right past the armed guards, and using ladders or even climbing on top of the water cannons to get up onto the Wall to join the others. In response, the border troops based in Berlin were put on alert and all possible units were ordered to deploy to the Brandenburg Gate.[4] Although Georg's guard regiment was not part of the border troops, it was based only a few blocks from the Gate and it would take some time for other backup forces to get through the chaos of the city, so he and his regiment were ordered to go to the Gate.

By 5 a.m., more than 600 border officers and soldiers, police, and other units had secured the area around the Brandenburg Gate between the Wall and the eastern security perimeter where Georg and his colleagues joined police-men in a human chain. The East German authorities ended the state of alert. Yet it was difficult to stop the people partying on top of the Wall. As soon as the border soldiers would coax them down, new people eager to celebrate would

[4] Hans-Hermann Hertle, *Chronik des Mauerfalls: Die dramatischen Ereignisse um den 9. November 1989*, 11th expanded ed. (Berlin: Ch. Links, 2009), pp. 176–84.

arrive and climb up, especially once daylight broke on November 10.[5] The state of alert was repeated on the night of November 10–11, and Georg remained on duty at the Gate for nearly forty-eight hours, alternating between standing at his post in the defense chain at the eastern perimeter of the Brandenburg Gate and resting in the truck.

On one of the occasions when the East German authorities had removed revelers from the area around the Gate and things were relatively quiet, Georg took the chance to do what so many others wanted to do: he walked through the Brandenburg Gate. Thinking, "I'll probably never have this chance again," Georg strode through one of the portals of the massive stone structure. He saw the external Berlin Wall ahead of him, lit up by security spotlights from the eastern side and television lights from the western side. Just the day before, he could have never imagined he would be there, and he had no idea what would happen next. He turned and walked back rather nervously to his position guarding the eastern side of the Gate.

Deployed there, as part of the human security chain, Georg and the others were fully visible to everyone. During the day, a constant stream of tourists on bus tours kept going by taking pictures of them, and people yelled at them day and night: "You Stasi pigs!" and "Open the Gate!" It was hard to stand there and take it all. Georg felt immensely grateful when a woman in the crowd yelled back, "Shut up! It could be my son standing there." It was a much-needed psychological boost for the nineteen-year-old country boy suddenly thrust into the center of national and international politics: at least someone had empathy for his situation.

When crowds again massed at the Brandenburg Gate on the night of November 10–11, things were less peaceful than the night before. Some of the revelers threw Molotov cocktails over to the eastern side and threatened the border troops, who responded with strong bursts from their water cannons. The West Berlin police chief, Georg Schertz, feared that if someone was injured or perhaps even killed, the situation could really escalate. He proposed to the East German security forces that they direct border guards to stand on the Wall, thus preventing the masses of regular citizens from climbing up there. Schertz would then deploy police vans and a chain of policemen to guard the western side of the Wall, thereby protecting the East German border guards and the Wall. This was all in place by noon on November 11, with around 300 unarmed border soldiers standing on top of the Wall and the West Berlin police in front of them.[6] The following night the West Berlin police and East German border guards worked together to create a new border crossing point, just south of the Brandenburg Gate at Potsdamer Platz, so as to relieve the pressure at the Gate.[7]

[5] Ibid., pp. 185–86, 216.
[6] Ibid., pp. 250–55.
[7] Ibid., pp. 259–61.

East Germany ended the state of alert of the military forces on November 11 and that night Georg's unit returned to its barracks. Georg breathed huge sighs of relief and wondered how things would develop. By the end of the following month, conscripts were given the option of carrying out the rest of their service period in the civilian sphere, but they had to find their own posting. Georg called a well-connected friend of his mother and begged her, "Get me out of here as soon as possible! Please do anything you can." In the meantime, he carried out his duty guarding military buildings in East Berlin. Less than three months later, his mother's friend came through with a suitable placement. He returned to his village about fifty miles from Berlin and worked at a kindergarten, changing diapers, mowing the lawn, pulling weeds, and feeling very grateful.

Two young East German musicians, Robert and Petra, experienced the fall of the Wall very differently than Georg did.[8] On the evening of November 9, they were out having dinner with friends at the Gendarmenmarkt, just outside of the concert hall where Robert played in the orchestra of the East German opera house, the *Staatsoper*, and only a few blocks from the Brandenburg Gate. As the evening went on, they kept hearing more and more sirens and saw many people on the streets. They vaguely wondered what was going on, but they were tired after a long day and went home to sleep. Only when they woke up the next morning did they learn what they had missed the night before! They decided right away to visit West Berlin. In their early twenties and with Petra nearly nine months pregnant, they expected the Wall would close again soon and wanted to seize the chance while they could to visit the West. Even if only in utero, they wanted their child to experience West Berlin.

They followed the rules and headed to their local police station to request permission to visit West Berlin. As they approached the police station, however, they saw that the line of people waiting to do the same thing snaked around the entire city block. Someone on the street told them: "Just go to the border; I've heard they're letting people pass through." So they headed to Friedrichstrasse, the central train terminal for movement between East and West Berlin, complete with its own border facilities and guards. The train station was packed with people who had the same idea. Robert wondered whether Petra was up to dealing with it all. Yes, she assured Robert, she was.

In order to shield Petra and her large stomach, Robert enlisted others in the crowd at Friedrichstrasse to join him in forming a human cordon around Petra. They inched their way slowly through the masses in the station and after what seemed like hours they made it through the unusually lax border facilities at the station and onto the famous platform B, the place to board trains headed west. Robert and Petra moved with the crowd through the doors of the train for the final stage of their journey toward West Berlin's central Zoo Station. The

---

[8] The names of Robert and Petra have been changed to protect their anonymity.

elevated S-Bahn train tracks crossed over the Berlin Wall, fully visible below, and through the Tiergarten forest; the train deposited the happy, astonished passengers in the heart of downtown West Berlin within a matter of minutes. Their first stop was a bank (with another long line of fellow citizens) so that each of them could claim their 100 deutsche marks "welcome money." The next stop was a place to eat where Petra could also sit and restore her energy.

Robert and Petra wandered around West Berlin for hours, looking at the shops, the streets, the colorful neon lights, and the people, before deciding it was time to head home. The S-Bahn was so full with other East Germans arriving in West Berlin or trying to get back home that they had to walk back to the nearest border entry point to reenter East Berlin. It turned out to be a long walk that brought them to the Checkpoint Charlie crossing point, normally only for use by non-Germans and particularly by members of the Allied Powers in Berlin: the United States, United Kingdom, France, and the Soviet Union. Yet, as with so much else since the previous night, everything was different. Robert and Petra made their way, again with masses of other people, through the checkpoint and eventually back to their apartment in East Berlin.

The next day, Petra wrote a note to their as yet unborn child, describing their November 10 adventure in case it was never to be repeated. When their daughter, Laura, was born in early December, the note was put into her scrapbook on a page for "major milestones in my life" so far. Years later, when Laura was old enough to understand and in fact was studying in what had been West Berlin, Petra would take out the scrapbook and tell her about that day.

* * *

On the night of November 9–10, the Wall was instantly transformed from a hated and feared edifice into a symbol of the triumph of freedom. The fall of the Wall became a touchstone of global memory. For many, it reflected our better selves; a world where people came together instead of being pulled apart, where freedom prevailed, where walls were brought down instead of built up. It gave people hope that other obstacles could come tumbling down as well.

In Germany itself, within months of the fall of the Wall, the East German communist regime collapsed, and Germany was united less than a year later on October 3, 1990. East Germany's main backer, the Soviet Union, ceased to exist the following year, and the Cold War was over. Robert would now travel with the *Staatsoper* and orchestra all over the world. Laura would eventually spend a summer working as an intern in Australia. Georg would enroll at Berlin's Humboldt University, taking classes in English just a block or two from where his guard barracks had been. He interrupted his studies to spend a year in London improving his English and working as an intern at a German bank. Georg returned to Humboldt to study history and English and went on to become a historian. Like Petra, Robert, and Laura, he has traveled far and wide since unification.

Since the fall of the Berlin Wall, only its memory remains – and the pieces of it that people took or bought. Many people were so moved by the peaceful demise of the seemingly permanent Berlin Wall that they rushed to Berlin to see "history in the making." The chance to break off a piece of the Wall and to take it home as "my own piece of history" was an added bonus. But what does it mean to "own" a piece of history – both in the sense of locating history in a specific material object, like the Wall, and in the sense of making the past your own, extrapolating its meanings for the present? These issues are at the center of this book.

Visitors from around the world come to Germany's capital city to see the Berlin Wall. They search Berlin for pieces of the iconic Wall, surprised there is not more to see. When visitors find the few remaining pieces of the Wall, they touch them, turn toward their friends holding a camera or smartphone and smile for the picture, keeping their hand firmly on the Wall. Touching the Wall makes them feel that they too are somehow part of its history.[9] They have the feeling – "I was there!" – albeit only after the Wall was removed as a deadly state border.

Many people who come to see and touch the Wall know little in detail about the history of the Wall. They just know that it is famous – or infamous. They often do not realize that the Berlin Wall was in fact not just one wall but an external and internal wall with a layer of obstacles in between, including armed guards with an order to shoot people trying to escape. This "death strip" was far more forbidding than a look at the few surviving remains of the Berlin Wall indicates. As Rainer Klemke, a long-time senior official of the Berlin Senate's department of cultural affairs, puts it: "The Wall was like a living, dangerous polar bear, and only the fur is left."[10]

For years after the fall of the Wall, visitors struggled to get a sense of how it felt when the city was divided by the Wall – and to do this at a place with original pieces of the Wall still standing. The desire to get rid of the Wall was stronger than the sense that some of it should be kept as a reminder. Even if Germans were reluctant to be reminded of the brutality of the Wall, an outsider might assume that united Germany would quickly establish the fall of the Wall as a central event to be remembered and celebrated, to be "owned." As this work will demonstrate, however, it would take twenty years for German leaders and many others to embrace this part of their history and to remember the Berlin Wall in the public sphere. Along the way, there would be an intense battle over the relative weights of the Nazi and communist periods in German memory policy and over the right balance in commemoration between what some Germans call the "negative" and the "positive" moments in their twentieth-century history.

---

[9] Polly Feversham and Leo Schmidt, *Die Berliner Mauer Heute/The Berlin Wall Today* (Berlin: Verlag Bauwesen, 1999), p. 128.

[10] Rainer Klemke, "Between Disappearance and Remembrance: Remembering the Berlin Wall Today," in Anna Kaminsky, ed., *Where in the World Is the Berlin Wall?* (Berlin: Berlin Story Verlag, 2014), p. 253.

Debates about whether and how to remember the Berlin Wall (its rise and fall and the twenty-eight years it stood in between) would become caught up in these broader battles and would exert significant influence on them.

This book traces and analyzes the multiple German approaches to the historical memory of the Berlin Wall since 1989. It focuses on official, public memory in public spaces seen and experienced by millions of people, although personal and private approaches to memory are included when they influence the public process. This work also examines connections between the German contest over the memory of the Berlin Wall and German identity in the twenty-first century.[11]

Germany and the Berlin Wall

For twenty-eight years, Germans killed Germans for trying to escape over the Berlin Wall. This German structure became a worldwide symbol for repression, communism, and the Cold War itself. In 1952, Kremlin chief Joseph Stalin had closed East Germany's border with West Germany so as to stop East Germans from fleeing to West Germany. This left Berlin – more than 100 miles inside communist East Germany – as the only place in Germany with free movement between East and West. East German leader Walter Ulbricht desperately wanted to close this "loophole," and for years he pressed for Soviet backing to do so. The attraction of West Berlin as an island of capitalism and democracy in the midst of the communist German Democratic Republic (GDR) was too great a threat to Ulbricht's hard-line regime. Berlin, however, was under Four Power control by the Soviets, Americans, British, and French, making any unilateral move there risky. Stalin had tried to cut off Western access to Berlin with the Berlin Blockade in 1948–49, but the West had responded with the airlift. Stalin's successor, Nikita Khrushchev, had tried to push the West out of West Berlin by demanding it be transformed into a demilitarized "free city" in the fall of 1958, but the West refused to withdraw.

Ulbricht grew increasingly frustrated with Khrushchev's temporizing in the late 1950s and early 1960s. The East German leader was concerned that refugees, especially those with higher levels of education and skills, continued to stream from East to West via West Berlin. Whole towns were bereft of doctors due to this brain drain, and factories had trouble meeting production targets with so many of their workers leaving. Ulbricht started to clamp down on movement between East and West Berlin, and the Soviets repeatedly reprimanded him for taking "unilateral actions on the borders of Berlin" without their knowledge or assent. Finally, in July 1961, in the wake of a failed summit meeting between

---

[11] Earlier versions of some of the concepts developed in this book can be found in Hope M. Harrison, "The Berlin Wall and its Resurrection as a Site of Memory," *German Politics and Society* 29, no. 2 (Summer 2011), pp. 78–106; and Harrison, "From Shame to Pride: The Fall of the Berlin Wall through German Eyes," *The Wilson Quarterly*, November 4, 2014.

Khrushchev and President John F. Kennedy, with more than 1,000 East Germans fleeing every day, and Ulbricht warning of the impending collapse of his state, Khrushchev gave in to Ulbricht's calls to close the border in Berlin.[12]

At midnight on the night of August 12–13, East German police and construction troops suddenly began sealing off the nearly 100-mile border around West Berlin so that East Germans could not access the city from East Berlin or from the surrounding East German countryside. Streets, subway stations, waterways, and families were cut in two. In the following days, particularly dramatic scenes took place at Bernauer Strasse where people jumped out of their windows (sometimes with East German soldiers trying to stop them) on the East Berlin side of the street toward the sidewalk below, which was in West Berlin. If they were lucky, they landed in the huge nets held by West Berlin firemen.

To close the border, East German troops used barbed wire at first and within days began to replace it with cement bricks. Then they topped this with broken pieces of glass or barbed wire to make it difficult to climb over. They created a whole border strip, which would become known in the West as the death strip (Figure 2), with external and internal walls, guard towers, guard dogs, signal fences, anti-vehicle obstacles, bright lights, and armed guards who were ordered to shoot at would-be escapees.[13] People were forced to move out of houses in the death strip, for example on the eastern side of Bernauer Strasse, and the houses were boarded up and eventually destroyed. The East German leaders wanted the border guards to have full visibility in the Berlin Wall border zone, with a clear line of sight of potential moving targets running toward West Berlin.

Trying to cross the border without permission ("flight from the Republic" or *Republikflucht*) was labelled a crime. Those who were caught doing so were, in the best case, imprisoned or, in the worst case, killed. Many people constructed tunnels under the Wall, such as at Bernauer Strasse.[14] Some made it out; others were captured. Tens of thousands of East Germans would be imprisoned for attempting or being suspected of planning *Republikflucht* in Berlin or elsewhere along the borders. Nearly 140 people would be killed at the Berlin Wall and hundreds more would be killed for attempting to leave the GDR at other points along the border.[15] Sometimes people who escaped to the West were captured by

---

[12] Hope M. Harrison, *Driving the Soviets up the Wall: Soviet-East German Relations, 1953–1961* (Princeton: Princeton University Press, 2003).

[13] Patrick Major, *Behind the Berlin Wall: East Germany and the Frontiers of Power* (New York: Oxford University Press, 2010); and Hans-Hermann Hertle, *The Berlin Wall – Monument of the Cold War* (Berlin: Ch. Links, 2007).

[14] Maria Nooke, ed., *Mauergeschichten von Flucht und Fluchthilfe. Begegnung mit Zeitzeugen* (Berlin: Ch. Links, 2017); Klaus-M. von Keussler and Peter Schulenburg, *Fluchthelfer: Die Gruppe um Wolfgang Fuchs* (Berlin: Berlin Story Verlag, 2015); and Greg Mitchell, *The Tunnels: Escapes Under the Berlin Wall and the Historic Films the JFK White House Tried to Kill* (New York: Crown, 2016).

[15] Hans-Hermann Hertle and Maria Nooke, eds., *The Victims at the Berlin Wall, 1961–1989: A Biographical Handbook* (Berlin: Ch. Links Verlag, 2011); and Pertti Ahonen, *Death at the*

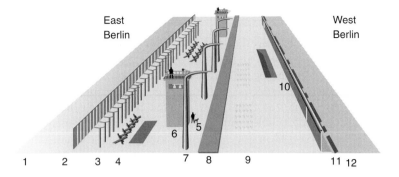

East
Berlin

West
Berlin

1   Markings announcing restricted border zone
2   Internal concrete Berlin Wall, the *Hinterlandmauer*
3   Electrified wire fence connected to alarm in tower
4   Long steel spikes in metal netting and other obstacles on ground
5   Armed guards and guard dogs on ground and runs for guard dogs
6   Guard tower with armed guards
7   Flood lights
8   Patrol road for guards
9   Sand strip (to notice footprints, including of guards)
10 Anti-vehicle ditch
11 External concrete Berlin Wall topped with rounded tube
12 Border to West Berlin

Figure 2 Diagram of Berlin Wall death strip

the East German secret police (the Stasi) and brought back to the GDR and imprisoned. Thousands reported to the Stasi about people they suspected were

Berlin Wall (New York: Oxford University Press, 2011). For the 327 victims documented thus far at the inner-German border, see Klaus Schroeder and Jochen Staadt, eds., *Die Todesopfer des DDR-Grenzregimes an der innerdeutschen Grenze 1949–1989: Ein biografisches* (Frankfurt am Main: Peter Lang, 2017). In addition to people killed at the Berlin Wall and the inner-German border, an estimated further 200 were killed at the northern border at the Baltic Sea and up to 300 were killed trying to escape from other Soviet bloc countries to the West. Thus, in total approximately 1,000 people were killed due to the East German border regime. Andreas Conrad, "327 Tote an innerdeutscher Grenze," *Tagesspiegel*, 7 June 2017. In 2018, Schroeder and Staadt's calculations of the number of people killed at the inner-German border were found to be inflated. Research by rbb (Rundfunk Berlin-Brandenburg) found problems with at least 50 of the supposed 327 cases of deaths at the border, including cases of border officers taking their own lives and even a former Waffen-SS soldier who had been executed in Moscow. Gabi Probst, "Zahl der Toten an innerdeutscher Grenze vermütlich falsch," rbb, November 6, 2018; and Alexander Fröhlich, "Umstrittene Studie zu Mauertoten 'nicht verfügbar'," *Tagesspiegel*, November 8, 2018.

planning to escape. Border guards who stopped fleeing citizens, dead or alive, were rewarded with medals, promotions, and/or money.[16]

Each time someone escaped, the authorities tightened up whatever aspect of the border had been too weak. In the years between 1961 and 1989, the East German regime kept "perfecting the border" to make it more and more impenetrable. The first two "generations" of Berlin Wall border fortifications were composed of barbed wire and then hollow concrete blocks and concrete slabs with barbed wire on top, coupled with wooden guard towers. Additional layers of obstacles were deployed in 1962, including metal fences and anti-vehicle barriers, as the East German authorities began to increase the depth of the border in their desperate effort to prevent people from fleeing. The third generation featured prefabricated concrete slabs for the Wall and concrete guard towers, making it harder for people to escape and easier for guards to do their job in stopping any such attempts. Viewing a demonstration area for this third edition of the death strip in 1965, Defense Minister Heinrich Hoffmann expressed cold admiration: "The Wall and border fence are very cultural. The Wall is very appealing, especially due to pipe on top. Cannot be overcome by a single person, and it is still difficult to do so with the help of a second person or other means."[17]

The East Germans introduced a fourth generation in the 1980s called "Border Wall 75." Even more durable than the third generation Wall, this version with its L-shaped construction featured vertical pieces of high-performance, prefabricated concrete Wall that were nearly seamlessly connected together and painted white to look smooth, modern, and unthreatening. Indeed, a design criterion for this new generation of Wall stipulated that it should have "[a]n appearance appropriate for the capital of the GDR," which did not want its increasingly successful quest for international legitimacy in the 1970s harmed by the appearance of a brutal border.[18] This was very important to the GDR leaders who seemed to care more about the view they presented to the West with this westernmost external part of the Berlin Wall fortifications than about satisfying the needs and desires of their own citizens, not least their desire to move freely.[19] Indeed, the smooth, canvas-like appearance of this external Wall inspired many in West Berlin to paint pictures and messages with varying levels of artistic and political content, many of them quite critical of the East German regime and its border.[20]

[16] Ahonen, *Death at the Berlin Wall.*
[17] Leo Schmidt, "The Architecture and Message of the 'Wall'," *German History and Politics* 29, no. 2 (Summer 2011), p. 68.
[18] Ibid., p. 72.
[19] Ibid., pp. 71–76.
[20] Heinz J. Kuzdas, *Berliner Mauer Kunst. Mit East Side Gallery* (Berlin: Espresso, 1990/ 1998); and Annette Dorgerloh, Anke Kuhrmann and Doris Liebermann, *Die Berliner Mauer in der Kunst: Bildende Kunst, Literatur und Film* (Berlin: Ch. Links, 2011).

When the dramatic events of November 9, 1989 occurred, East German military designers were in the midst of planning for a fifth generation high-tech "Wall 2000" augmented by infrared sensors, laser tripwires, high-frequency cables, microprocessors, and seismic sensors, including underwater microwave and vibration detectors for locations where the border went through water such as in rivers and lakes in and around Berlin. Military planners in the 1980s were frustrated that they lacked the sufficient know-how to produce, or money to buy, the necessary technology to make this fifth-generation Berlin Wall a reality. Hence, plans for implementation kept receding further into the future.[21]

The border regime itself represented a significant drain on the already strained state budget. While the personnel and materials comprising the border cost 610 million East German marks in 1970, the annual costs rose to 990 million marks in 1983 and 1.2 billion marks in 1989.[22] Astonishingly, in 1989 economists assessing the border troops found that "each arrest at the border cost 2.1 million marks," arriving at this figure after "divid[ing] the costs for the border by the number of arrests."[23] Yet the leaders believed their regime depended on maintaining the Berlin Wall, a conviction that would be confirmed by the rapidity of the regime's collapse after the toppling of the Wall.

Between 1961 and 1989, hundreds of thousands of East Germans were involved in supporting the Berlin Wall, from the political, military, and Stasi leaders who gave the orders, to the border soldiers who implemented them (these alone numbered 50,000), the military research and development experts, the Stasi officials who oversaw posts at the border, the construction workers tasked with fixing and perfecting the Wall, the doctors who dealt with those who were wounded or killed at the Wall, and all the informants. It took many, many people in the GDR to maintain the Berlin Wall as the deadly bulwark it was. Blame cannot easily be directed elsewhere.

To younger Germans now, it seems impossible to believe that their parents' generation lived with and tolerated the Wall and all it meant. How was it possible for a city of three and a half million people to be divided by a lethal border? How could it be that people were killed for trying to go from East Berlin to West Berlin or were imprisoned for trying? Furthermore, why was Germany home to two authoritarian styles of rule in the twentieth century; the Nazi regime for thirteen years and then the communist regime in the eastern

---

[21] Wolfgang Rathje, *"Mauer-Marketing" unter Erich Honecker. Schwierigkeiten der DDR bei der technischen Modernisierung, der volkswirtschaftlichen Kalkulation und der politischen Akzeptanz der Berliner "Staatsgrenze" von 1971–1990*, 2 vols. (Berlin: Ralf Gründer Verlag, 2006), vol. 1, pp. 798–846; Schmidt, "The Architecture and Message of the 'Wall'," p. 76; and Gerhard Sälter, "Die Sperranlage, oder: Der Unendliche Mauerbau," in Klaus-Dietmar Henke, ed., *Die Mauer. Errichtung, Überwindung, Erinnerung* (Munich: Deutscher Taschenbuch Verlag, 2011), p. 137.

[22] Rathje, *"Mauer-Marketing,"* p. 935.

[23] Hertle, *The Berlin Wall*, p. 97.

part of Germany for over forty years? The Wall reminds Germans of these uncomfortable questions, which could not be covered up by its peaceful fall.

With the Wall representing a living, often painful memory and embodying powerful competing meanings ranging from imprisonment to liberation, after German unification there was no straight path forward for treating it as a now defunct part of German history. Initially the main impulse was to tear it down and move on, focusing on the intensive practical work of uniting East and West Berlin and Germany, even as tourists continued to flock to Berlin (as they still do) hoping to see the Wall. Only gradually would a public debate develop about whether the Berlin Wall should be remembered or not and then about what exactly should be remembered: The decision to build it in 1961 so as to prevent East Germans from fleeing to the West? Living with the Wall for the next twenty-eight years and what that meant to both East and West Germans? Telling the stories of the people who were killed at the Wall? Explaining and celebrating the fall of the Wall in 1989? All of this? None of this? And should parts of the Berlin Wall be preserved or not?

Coming to terms with the history of the Berlin Wall is a complicated endeavor for Germans. No one wants to assume responsibility for what became a worldwide symbol of repression. Some former East German leaders and their supporters blame the Russians. Others blame the more abstract "Cold War" for the Wall and division of Berlin and Germany. Some maintain that the Berlin Wall actually stabilized the situation in the center of Europe and the Cold War, keeping the two sides separated and preventing crises over East German refugees from triggering a broader conflict. Others argue that East Germany was only policing its sovereign borders, a normal act for any state. Some former border guards insist they were "just following orders." For many Germans the Wall and division were forms of punishment for Nazi crimes and for World War II. On the other hand, some, particularly without family or friends on the other side of the Wall, hardly felt affected by it, especially if they lived in West Germany. Many got used to it in one way or another. Most felt powerless to do anything about the Berlin Wall. The memory of the Wall is a troublesome subject.

The ongoing process of uniting East and West Germany has impacted debates about the memory of the Wall. Unlike the other post-communist countries in Central and Eastern Europe, which could confront the past (or not) as they wished, the sixteen million citizens of the GDR had no independent ability to come to terms with the dark parts of their communist past, such as the brutality of the Berlin Wall and the ubiquity of the Stasi, since their country ceased to exist and was fused into the Federal Republic. Moreover, former West Germans have dominated the political, legal, and other hierarchies in the united Federal Republic (Chancellor Angela Merkel being a notable exception), with former East Germans for a long time exerting less control over debates about historical memory and everything else. Thus, as Aleida Assmann has observed, the East Germans engaged in a double transition away from communism with its memory culture and into West Germany with a very different memory culture.[24] Discussions about the Berlin Wall and the East German past accordingly have sometimes had the effect of prolonging a sense of division instead of fostering unification. As the dominant discourse in united Germany has characterized East Germany as an *Unrechtsstaat* (a "state without the rule of law" or an "unjust state") and a "dictatorship," many former East Germans feel this condemns the lives they lived in the GDR. This discourse, combined with the difficult transition many in the East have endured since unification, has inspired on the part of some (particularly older East Germans) a certain nostalgia (*Ostalgie*) for the GDR and a sense of alienation within united Germany.

Yet discussions about the memory of the Wall and the GDR have highlighted not just East-West differences, but also divergent approaches within the former East, such as between former opponents and supporters of the regime and its Wall. People who were victims of the regime want to see more attention given to those who were killed at the Wall and more financial and other support from the state for those who were persecuted in the GDR. They view the Wall in the context of measures the GDR leaders took to repress their citizens. It does not help that many people who held positions in the former East German regime (such as in the military or the Stasi) receive a relatively good state pension in united Germany, whereas people who tried to escape or otherwise opposed the regime and were imprisoned in the GDR receive a much lower "victim's" pension if they receive one at all. Those who served at the Wall often focus their memories more on the technical aspects of the border and their jobs at the front line of the Cold War or try to avoid discussing the Berlin Wall. Some of them also remember their fear of being faced with the decision of whether to shoot a would-be refugee or not.

German History, Collective Memory, and Memory Activists

Sociologists, anthropologists, historians, literary theorists, and others have long drawn connections between national identity, history, and collective memory. How nations remember their past – what they choose to mark or to ignore – says much about what they value, how they see themselves in the present, and who they want to be in the future. As Maurice Halbwachs first formulated and many scholars have elaborated upon since, memory is not just personal; it also has a social or collective aspect.[25] What we learn or

---

[24] Aleida Assmann, *Das neue Unbehagen an der Erinnerungskultur* (Munich: C. H. Beck, 2013), pp. 110–11.

[25] Maurice Halbwachs, *On Collective Memory*, ed., trans., and with an intro. by Lewis A. Coser (Chicago: University of Chicago Press, 1992).

"remember" about history comes significantly from our social environment –
our family, school, town, or nation. Collective memory is derived from religious
traditions, national holidays, textbooks, museums, memorials, commemorative
ceremonies, and other such public phenomena. Yet historical memory is not the
same as history itself. As Aleida Assmann, following in the footsteps of
Halbwachs and others, has emphasized, "memory must be represented" since,
in the absence of a time machine, a "simple retrieval of the past into the present is
not possible."[26] The way history is represented depends very much on the mores
and methods of the present and can result in the "suspension of differences
among the past, present and future."[27]

Which parts of the past are worthy of memory or commemoration? The
answers are often quite contentious, as has been the case with the Berlin Wall.[28]
Furthermore, what or, more to the point, *who* fuels the narrative on display in
public representations of the past? The individuals I call memory activists are a
key link between personal memory and collective memory. Memory activists
push for more public attention to some part of the past or lobby for a different
emphasis on that past. They may be regular citizens whose personal memory is
different from the prevailing social memory or they may be historians, museum
or memorial directors, journalists, religious representatives, politicians, or
others who have strong views on history and how it is portrayed.[29]

Much is at stake here, ranging from personal memory and self-image (particularly if it is recent history, as the Wall is for millions of Germans), to the funding
of a memorial site, the passage of laws, the declaration of a national holiday, and
most broadly the legitimacy of the nation as a whole.[30] Emotions can run high on
issues related to historical memory – as demonstrated by recent debates about
confederate monuments in the United States, the Holocaust in Poland, or the

---

[26] Aleida Assmann, *Das neue Unbehagen*, p. 206.

[27] Ibid., p. 210.

[28] On the contested aspects of collective memory, see Jeffrey K. Olick and Joyce Robbins,
"Social Memory Studies: From 'Collective Memory' to the Historical Sociology of
Mnemonic Practices," *Annual Review of Sociology* 24 (1998), pp. 105–140.

[29] Other scholars who have written about "memorial entrepreneurs," "agents of memory,"
or "memory activists" include Jennifer Jordan, *Structures of Memory: Understanding
Urban Change in Berlin and Beyond* (Stanford: Stanford University Press, 2006); Vered
Vinitzky-Seroussi, *Yitzhak Rabin's Assassination and the Dilemmas of Commemoration*
(Albany: State University of New York Press, 2009); Elizabeth Jelin, *State Repression and
the Labors of Memory* (Minneapolis: University of Minnesota Press, 2003); Jenny
Wüstenberg, *Civil Society and Memory in Postwar Germany* (New York: Cambridge
University Press, 2017); and Anna Saunders, *Memorializing the GDR: Monuments and
Memory after 1989* (New York: Berghahn, 2018). See also Peter Carrier, *Holocaust
Monuments and National Memory: France and Germany since 1989* (New York:
Berghahn Books, 2005), whose book centers on the work of memory activists even if he
does not use this term.

[30] Margaret Macmillan, *Dangerous Games: The Uses and Abuses of History* (New York:
Modern Library, 2010).

accepted way to view World War II in Russia. While individual memory activists may or may not be motivated by politics, their work to direct public attention to parts of the past often eventually requires political support to gain access to long-term funding and to the power of the state to disseminate information – as is the case in Germany. Hence, politics and politicians may become involved in the process of supporting a certain memory about history, some more aware than others of their power thereby to shape collective memory.

Germany has a particularly strong tradition of taking the remembrance of the past seriously. Indeed, as Brian Ladd has observed, the Germans "may lead the world in agonized self-examination" of their history.[31] This began with West German grappling with the Nazi past and has continued in united Germany.[32] The importance attached to confronting dark chapters in their history – taking on what Wulf Kansteiner terms "collective symbolic guilt"[33] – is meant to atone and compensate for the past and to demonstrate that Germans have changed.[34] For Germans, a key part of what they call their "democratic memory culture" means openly facing up to the past.[35]

On the fortieth anniversary of the German surrender to the Allies in World War II – May 8, 1985 – West German President Richard von Weizsäcker gave a speech that marked a watershed in the approach to the Nazi past, making him a particularly influential memory activist. He called on Germans to accept responsibility for the Holocaust and spoke at length of the need to "look truth straight in the eye." He argued that, "Remembering means recalling an occurrence honestly and without distortion so that it becomes a part of our very beings."[36] What is now considered normal

---

[31] Brian Ladd, *The Ghosts of Berlin: Confronting German History in the Urban Landscape* (Chicago: University of Chicago Press, 1997), p. 39.

[32] Major scholarly works on Germany's grappling with the Nazi past include Charles Maier, *The Unmasterable Past: History, Holocaust, and German National Identity* (Cambridge: Harvard University Press, 1997); Jeffrey K. Olick, *The Sins of the Fathers* (Chicago: University of Chicago Press, 2016); Bill Niven, *Facing the Nazi Past: United Germany and the Legacy of the Third Reich* (New York: Routledge, 2002); James E. Young, *The Texture of Memory: Holocaust Memorials and Meaning* (New Haven: Yale University Press, 1993); Konrad Jarausch, *After Hitler: Recivilizing Germans, 1945–1995* (New York: Oxford University Press, 2008); and Aleida Assmann, *Der lange Schatten der Vergangenheit: Erinnerungskultur und Geschichtspolitik* (Munich: C. H. Beck, 2006).

[33] Wulf Kansteiner, *In Pursuit of German Memory: History, Television, and Politics after Auschwitz* (Athens: Ohio University Press, 2006), p. 4.

[34] For a different approach, see Jeffrey K. Olick, *The Politics of Regret: On Collective Memory and Historical Responsibility* (New York: Routledge, 2007).

[35] Deutscher Bundestag, ed., "Schlussbericht," in *Materialien der Enquete-Kommission "Überwindung der Folgen der SED-Diktatur im Prozeß der deutschen Einheit,"* Band 1 (Baden-Baden: Nomos Verlag, 1999), p. 587.

[36] "Speech by President Richard von Weizsäcker during the Ceremony Commemorating the 40th Anniversary of the End of War in Europe and of National-Socialist Tyranny on 8

regarding intensive German contrition for the Holocaust was forty years in the making.

Von Weizsäcker told his fellow countrymen that "the genocide of Jews is unparalleled in world history." Furthermore, Germans of the time could not justifiably plead ignorance: "Whoever opened his eyes and ears and sought information could not fail to notice that Jews were being deported." Only the top leaders knew the details of the plans to annihilate the Jews, "but every German was able to witness what his Jewish compatriots had to suffer" and most found "ways of shunning responsibility, looking away, keeping mum." This terrible history must be remembered or it could be repeated. The West German president emphasized that Germans who lived through the Nazi period, as he did, must educate young Germans about the history of the Holocaust and World War II and their lessons. He spelled out very clearly the lessons for how Germans should treat minorities, their neighbors, and so many others: "do not let yourselves be forced into enmity and hatred of other people, of Russians or Americans, Jews or Turks, of alternatives or conservatives, blacks or whites." Von Weizsäcker also declared that Germans should see that "May 8 was a day of liberation. It liberated all of us from the inhumanity and tyranny of the National-Socialist regime." Thus, the day of German surrender was actually a good day. Germans should look back on the day not primarily as a defeat, as had been the view for forty years, but as a new start on the path to democracy. This view has held ever since.

In East Germany, on the other hand, the leaders of the ruling Socialist Unity Party (SED) had always insisted that the West German "capitalists and imperialists" were the heirs to the Nazis, not the East Germans who had been communist anti-fascists and essential in the resistance to the Nazi regime.[37] This view changed only in 1990. The first and last freely elected East German parliament, the Volkskammer, voted unanimously on April 12, 1990 to accept joint responsibility with West Germany for Nazi crimes by paying reparations to Jewish survivors and their heirs, establishing relations with Israel, and fostering Jewish religion, culture, and traditions in Germany.[38]

May 1985 at the Bundestag, Bonn," www.bundespraesident.de/SharedDocs/Downloads/DE/Reden/2015/02/150202-RvW-Rede-8-Mai-1985-englisch.pdf?__blob=publicationFile. On the Holocaust and Nazi crimes, Raul Hilberg, *The Destruction of the European Jews*, 3rd ed. (New Haven: Yale University Press, 2003); Richard J. Evans, *The Third Reich in History and Memory* (New York: Oxford University Press, 2015); Daniel Johan Goldhagen, *Hitler's Willing Executioners: Ordinary Germans and the Holocaust* (New York: Knopf, 1996); and Timothy Snyder, *Black Earth: The Holocaust as History and Warning* (New York: Tim Duggan Books, 2015).

[37] Jeffrey Herf, *Divided Memory: The Nazi Past in the Two Germanys* (Cambridge: Harvard University Press, 1997).

[38] Gemeinsame Erklärung der Volkskammer, April 12, 1990, www.ddr89.de/ddr89/vk/vk_Erklaerung.html.

By the time of unification, the conviction that they must deal with the Nazi past had been deeply drilled into West Germans and had begun among East Germans. Hence the priority for German memory policy was the Holocaust. The most widely discussed approach of the new united German government to Holocaust commemoration involved erecting a Holocaust memorial. In 1992, the Berlin Senate approved a central location near the Brandenburg Gate as the site for such a memorial, and in 1999 the Bundestag gave the architect Peter Eisenmann the go-ahead to begin construction. The completed Monument to the Murdered Jews of Europe was dedicated on May 8, 2005, the fiftieth anniversary of the defeat of Nazi Germany and features 2,711 stelae in the form of very large blocks of different sizes. Many find it reminiscent of a cemetery. Located just steps from the Brandenburg Gate, the massive monument in the heart of the city is the most visible expression of the many steps united Germany has taken to remember and atone for the Holocaust.[39]

Most nations focus on remembering and celebrating positive things from their past and use this as a way to foster a sense of pride and belonging as a nation. Yet Germans have been unique in centering their historical memory and national identity on negative aspects of their past, particularly the Holocaust.[40] While they cannot change what happened in the past, they can affect their own sense of self-worth as individuals and legitimacy as a nation by how they handle this past. Facing dark parts of the past means having what the Germans call an active "history policy" (*Geschichtspolitik*). There are multiple, interrelated aspects of this.

First, *Geschichtspolitik* involves describing what exactly happened, telling the history as thoroughly as possible without shirking. The results of a 2018 survey demonstrated that 88 percent of Germans believe that knowledge about the Nazi period is part of being German.[41] Accordingly, Germans have launched countless historical investigations into what happened to victims and perpetrators during and right after the Nazi period, giving names and faces especially to the victims but also to the perpetrators.[42] They have also preserved concentration camps to show exactly where the crimes against humanity were committed, believing that authentic sites are important aids to memory and understanding. Second, *Geschichtspolitik* means demonstrating

---

[39] Niven, *Facing the Nazi Past*, pp. 194–232.

[40] Assmann, *Das neue Unbehagen*, pp. 78, 208.

[41] "Deutsche fühlen besondere moralische Verantwortung – aber keine Schuld," *Frankfurter Allgemeine Zeitung*, February 13, 2018.

[42] See, for example, the respective investigations of the roles of the Foreign Ministry and the Justice Ministry in the Third Reich and afterwards: Eckart Conze, Norbert Frei et al., *Das Amt und die Vergangenheit: Deutsche Diplomaten im Dritten Reich und in der Bundesrepublik* (Munich: Karl Blessing Verlag, 2010); and Manfred Görtemaker and Christoph Safferling, *Die Akte Rosenburg: Das Bundesministerium der Justiz und die NS-Zeit* (Munich: C. S. Beck, 2016).

contrition, such as through policies of restitution toward victims and their families, commemorative ceremonies, and memorials (e.g., the memorials in Berlin to the Jewish, homosexual, Sinti and Roma, and euthanasia victims of the Nazis). Third, facing this history requires drawing lessons from it, explaining why it is still relevant, and making sure young people are taught about it, as von Weizsäcker emphasized. The main lesson Germans draw from the Nazi period is that "never again" (*nie wieder*) should Germans allow such crimes to occur and that they must be vigilant in countering racism, violence, and an excessive concentration of power and must defend democratic values of inclusiveness, liberty, the rule of law, and nonviolence.[43]

Practicing this kind of responsible *Geschichtspolitik* helps construct a certain German historical narrative and national identity that essentially argues: *We were bad then and did terrible things. Although we are good now, we still have the potential for bad. Hence, we must keep the memory of our brutal past alive to make sure that current and future generations do not repeat this history.* While the motivation for this approach is largely internal, the Germans also know that others are watching them for any sign of their former destructive domestic or foreign policies. They are eager to prove to themselves that they are different than the Nazis (doing the right thing now since their ancestors did not) and also to reassure others.[44]

Remembering the past is so important in Germany that Germans have multiple terms related to *Geschichtspolitik*: memory policy (*Erinnerungspolitik*); remembrance or commemoration policy (*Gedenkpolitik*); memory culture (*Erinnerungskultur*); coming to terms with or mastering the past (*Vergangenheitsbewältigung*); and working through the past (*Aufarbeitung der Geschichte*). Complicating the matter somewhat, *Politik*, as in *Geschichtspolitik, Erinnerungspolitik,* or *Gedenkpolitik* means both "policy" and "politics." Thus, *Geschichtspolitik*, for example, can mean either "history policy" in a more neutral way or the more charged "politics of history." It has become a widely accepted part of German political culture that political leaders must speak about the past and must have a history/memory/remembrance policy. Indeed, one of Chancellor Angela Merkel's speechwriters had this as part of his portfolio, and a commitment to an appropriate *Erinnerungspolitik* is generally a part of government coalition treaties at both the federal and state

---

[43] Aleida Assmann, *Der europäische Traum. Vier Lehren aus der Geschichte* (Munich: C. H. Beck, 2018), esp. pp. 38–56; and Lily Gardner Feldman, "Commemoration in Comparison: Germany's Comprehensive and Complex 'Culture of Remembrance'," in Daqing Yang and Mike Mochizuki, eds., foreword by Akira Iriye, *Memory, Identity, and Commemorations of World War II: Anniversary Politics in Asia Pacific* (Lanham: Lexington Books, 2018), pp. 141–55.

[44] See the comments in the Bundestag about Germany's neighbors and the world watching how it deals with both the Nazi and communist pasts. Deutscher Bundestag, ed., "Schlussbericht," in *Materialien der Enquete-Kommission* (1999), p. 589.

levels.[45] In addition, political parties such as the CDU and SPD generally have certain historians they rely on for advice regarding *Geschichtspolitik*.

The increasingly popular, right-wing *Alternative für Deutschland* (AfD) party is critical of Germany's "cult of guilt" about the Nazi past and focuses on a more "positive" sense of nationalism, albeit an ethnic German, Christian, anti-Muslim nationalism.[46] Since the AfD's entry into the Bundestag following the 2017 elections, this has led other parties to redouble their efforts to deal "appropriately" and "responsibly" with both the Nazi and communist pasts.[47]

The ethos of confronting German history has permeated society, from museums and universities to newspapers, television, and radio. It is not uncommon for a radio listener to hear, for example, a woman with a sexy voice advertising a three-day TV series on the start of World War II in between an ad for toothpaste and the announcement of an upcoming street fair. In addition, for Germans, civic education – what they call *politische Bildung* (political education) – is closely related to historical memory and includes both remembering the past and learning from it. The Federal Agency for Civic Education (*Bundeszentrale für politische Bildung*, BpB), and its affiliated *Landeszentrale für politische Bildung* (LpB) in each German state, have a strong emphasis on history and memory in their activities and publications. Another institution, the Federal Foundation for Reappraising the SED Dictatorship (*Bundesstiftung zur Aufarbeitung der SED-Diktatur*), created nearly a decade after the fall of the Berlin Wall, is particularly clear about its educational mission with its motto: "memory as mandate" (*Erinnerung als Auftrag*).

The West German focus on confronting the Nazi past continued after unification and was joined by many East Germans wanting to make up for lost time in atoning for the crimes of the Holocaust. As Aleida Assmann observed, "memory of the Holocaust was the negative founding myth of reunited Germany."[48] A researcher in the mid-2000s examining German approaches to the East German past often faced criticism for not focusing on the "more important," much more destructive Nazi past instead. Yet after unification, there was also a more recent difficult past to confront. The history of the SED

---

[45] See for example, "Ein neuer Aufbruch für Europa. Eine neue Dynamik für Deutschland. Ein neuer Zusammenhalt für unser Land," Koalitionsvertrag zwischen CDU, CSU und SPD, Berlin, March 12, 2018, pp. 167–68.

[46] Amanda Taub and Max Fisher, "Germany's Extreme Right Challenge Guilt over Nazi Past," *New York Times*, January 18, 2017; and Maria Fiedler, "Alexander Gauland und der 'Vogelschiss'," *Tagesspiegel*, June 2, 2018.

[47] Bündis 90/Die Grüne Parliamentary Group, Fraktionsbeschluss, "Für eine verantwortungsbewusste Erinnerungskultur: Wissen ausbauen und für die Zukunft lernen," May 4, 2018. See also the Bundestag debate about "Demokratie und Erinnerungskultur in Deutschland angesichts rechtsextremischer Angriffe," Plenarprotokoll 19/15, February 23, 2018, pp. 1289–1307.

[48] Aleida Assmann, *Das neue Unbehagen an der Erinnerungskultur*, p. 67.

regime, its secret police, and lethal border provided an additional sense of a nation, or partial nation, of perpetrators. Germans asked themselves again and again: *How could it be that Germany produced two dictatorships in the twentieth century?*

This work will illustrate that the legacy of the German process of dealing with the Holocaust has had important, sometimes contradictory, influences on how German officials and others have gone about dealing with the East German communist past, including the Berlin Wall. In the years since unification, some in both East and West have maintained that nothing in *Geschichtspolitik* is more important than dealing with the Holocaust past and that nothing should get in the way of this or compete with it, such as dealing with a second difficult past and a second set of perpetrators and victims. The very mention of both regimes – the Nazi and SED – in one sentence, such as references to "the two German dictatorships of the twentieth century,"[49] has been seen by many in Germany, and not just Jewish Germans, as a dangerous equivalence that does not recognize the uniquely terrible nature of the Holocaust. Others, however, have argued that it is an obligation of modern Germany to deal with *all* difficult parts of German history, including the killing of people at the Berlin Wall. Indeed, adding a second dark period in the contemporary German past on top of the first, more profoundly atrocious past, makes some Germans feel a deeper sense of urgency about the need to deal with the communist past, to get German memory policy, *Erinnerungspolitik*, right the second time after taking so long to get it right the first time after World War II.[50]

---

[49] Two Bundestag Commissions of Inquiry on "the SED dictatorship" in the 1990s used the wording "two German dictatorships of the twentieth century," and the wording was the subject of much debate in the 2000s about updating the federal guidelines for memorials. See Chapter 3 and Chapter 6 for elaboration.

[50] Soon after the March 1990 elections in the GDR, Bärbel Bohley declared that the newly democratic Volkskammer "will not constitute democracy if we do not deal with our past and its questions." She insisted: "If history is not confronted, we repeat here all that was connected in West Germany after 1945 to the survival of former Nazis in the state apparatus – and not just there. We do not want to wait twenty years for our '68 the way you [in West Germany] did." "Damit sich Geschichte nicht wiederholt: Keine Stasi-Mitarbeiter in die neue Volkskammer," *taz*, March 22, 1990, p. 10, cited in Anne Sa'adah, *Germany's Second Chance: Trust, Justice, and Democratization* (Cambridge: Harvard University Press, 1998), p. 67. Bundestag member Rainer Eppelmann argued in 1992 that lawmakers must examine the East German past and learn from it so as "not to be in the stupid position of a child who opens the hot oven door for the third time and burns his fingers painfully once more." Der Deutsche Bundestag, ed., "Debatte des Deutschen Bundestages am 12. März 1992," in *Materialien der Enquete-Kommission, "Aufarbeitung von Geschichte und Folgen der SED Diktatur in Deutschland," Band 1* (Baden-Baden: Nomos Verlag, 1995), p. 27.

Commemoration in Germany

The heart of this book is an examination of the contentious German undertaking of moving some of the *Erinnerungspolitik* spotlight from the Holocaust
to, first, another set of German victims – those who were killed at or suffered
because of the Berlin Wall – and second, to the "positive" history, as many call
it, of the toppling of the Wall and the East German "peaceful revolution." The
foundations of this study rest on two pillars: the memory activists who pushed
for certain memories to be highlighted; and the format whereby the memory
was disseminated or performed, such as commemorative events hosted by
public figures, including political leaders, particularly on important anniversaries of the rise and fall of the Wall. As Jeffrey Olick has pointed out,
"Commemoration is a way of claiming that the past has something to offer
the present, be it a warning or a model."[51] For many Germans, the memory of
the Berlin Wall offers both: a warning about the dangers of engaging in
thinking and policies that lead to the erection of walls, and a model of the
peaceful toppling of a wall.

People, groups, and nations have long felt the need to connect the present
with the past, to understand their place in time. A historical sense of where they
and their ancestors have come from provides them with a sense of identity.
Public commemoration of the past began centuries ago, in religious contexts
with the Jews commemorating the exodus from Egypt and Christians commemorating the resurrection of Christ with rituals, and in more secular
contexts with ancient Greeks building and inscribing their temples with
information about their history.[52] In modern times, nations have commemorated key events and individuals deemed to have played an essential role in
their history, whether they be wars, revolutions, political leaders, cultural
icons, or martyrs. Indeed, John Gillis observes that, "In the nineteenth century
nations came to worship themselves through their pasts, ritualizing and commemorating to the point that their sacred sites and times became the secular
equivalent of shrines and holy days."[53] This can also be seen in contemporary
commemorations of the Berlin Wall.

A particular form of commemoration that focuses on anniversaries of
historical events offers an important opportunity to reflect on the past for
political leaders and historians alike. For centuries Germany has marked key
historical anniversaries of people and events with ceremonies (as well as with

[51] Jeffrey K. Olick, "Genre Memories and Memory Genres: A Dialogical Analysis of May 8,
1945 Commemorations in the Federal Republic of Germany," *American Sociological
Review* 64 (June 1999), p. 381.
[52] Jan Assmann, *Das kulturelle Gedächtnis. Schrift, Erinnerung und politische Identität in
frühen Hochkulturen* (Munich: C. H. Beck, 1992).
[53] John R. Gillis, ed., *Commemorations: The Politics of National Identity* (Princeton:
Princeton University Press, 1994).

scholarly and popular publications), and this has only increased over time, as it has in other countries, fueled by the opportunities of digital media.[54] Indeed, nearly every major anniversary celebration in Germany now has a website dedicated to it. Martin Luther and the launch of the Reformation with his ninety-five theses were probably the original models of a person or event to be celebrated for their foundational roles in modern German history. In northern Germany, major commemorations of Martin Luther commenced in 1617 with the centenary of the posting of his ninety-five theses, which began the Reformation, and continued in 1817, 1917, and 2017.[55] Germans also celebrated Luther's birth (1483) with significant ceremonies in 1883 and 1983.[56] Since the inauguration of wide-ranging commemorations of Luther, major German writers and composers such as Johann Wolfgang von Goethe (in 1899 and 1999)[57] and Ludwig van Beethoven (in 1870, 1952, 1977, and 2020)[58] have also been the beneficiaries of such celebrations on the anniversaries of their birth or death. As we shall see, Beethoven and his music have come to be closely associated with the fall of the Berlin Wall, and his music has frequently been performed at anniversary ceremonies commemorating this event. Moreover, the federal government declared in 2013 that preparing for the 250th anniversary of Beethoven's birth in 2020 was "a national task."[59]

In the past half-century and especially in recent years, contemporary Germany has held major commemorations of anniversaries connected to the

---

[54] Jörg Arnold in the forum on "Anniversaries," *German History* 32, no. 1 (2014), p. 81.

[55] Achim Landwehr, "Mein jahr mit Luther: Thesen zur Geschichtskultur," meinjahrmitluther.wordpress.com/category/thesen-zur-geschichtskultur/.

[56] Peter Burke, "Co-memorations. Performing the Past," in Karin Tilmans, Frank van Vree and Jay Winter, eds., *Performing the Past: Memory, History, and Identity in Modern Europe* (Chicago: Amsterdam University Press, 2012), p. 107; and Thomas A. Brady's remarks in the forum on "Anniversaries," *German History* 32, no. 1 (2014), p. 84. See also Angela Merkel, "Speech given by Federal Chancellor Dr. Angela Merkel in Lutherstadt Wittenberg on 31 October 2017 on the occasion of the 500th anniversary of the Reformation," October 31, 2017.

[57] Tim Grady in the forum on "Anniversaries," *German History* 32, no. 1 (2014), p. 80.

[58] David B. Dennis, *Beethoven in German Politics, 1870–1989* (New Haven: Yale University Press, 1996), pp. 32–36, 196; Beate Kutschke, "The Celebration of Beethoven's Bicentennial in 1970," *The Musical Quarterly* 93, nos. 3–4 (Fall/Winter 2010), pp. 560–615; and Elaine Kelly, "Late Beethoven and Late Socialism," in *Composing the Canon in the German Democratic Republic: Narratives of Nineteenth Century Music* (New York: Oxford University Press, 2014), pp. 144–90. The year 2020 will mark the 250th anniversary of Beethoven's birthday, and Germany's Beethoven Anniversary Society (*Beethoven Jubiläums Gesellschaft*), together with the cultural authorities in Bonn and the German government, are planning a Beethoven year from December 16, 2019–December 17, 2020. There is already a website dedicated to it: www.lvbeethoven.de/en/beethoven-2020. Rick Fulker, "Highlights of the Beethoven Anniversary Year 2020 Announced," *Deutsche Welle*, March 9, 2018.

[59] Federal government coalition treaty, "Deutschlands zukunft gestalten: Koalitionsvertrag zwischen CDU, CSU und SPD," November 27, 2013, p. 92.

Holocaust and the two World Wars, memories of violence and aggression perpetrated by Germany. These commemorations reflect a widespread sense of contrition for the past and a feeling of obligation to demonstrate this contrition and to learn from the mistakes of the past. Dates connected with key events in the Holocaust and the beginning and end of the two World Wars have been singled out and remembered in large and small ceremonies throughout the country nearly every year; as most recently in 2019 with the eightieth anniversary of the German invasion of Poland launching World War II (September 1, 1939), and in 2018 with the eightieth anniversary of the Night of Broken Glass, *Kristallnacht* (November 9, 1938) and the centenary of the end of World War I (November 11, 1918).

Anyone who spends much time in Germany could easily conclude that the Germans have an "anniversary mania," or "anniversaryitis" as Achim Landwehr calls it,[60] with memories of the (usually painful) past emanating almost nonstop from television sets, theaters, museums, politicians, and scholars, particularly around significant anniversaries. Indeed, the Germans have recently taken to celebrating certain anniversaries for an entire year instead of just on one day or for a week or month surrounding a certain day. These anniversaries celebrated over the course of a year, however, tend to involve more positive memories, such as the twentieth or twenty-fifth anniversaries of the fall of the Berlin Wall in 2009 and 2014, the 500th anniversary of the Reformation in 2017, or the 250th anniversary of Beethoven's birth in 2020, although remembering the centenary of World War I in Germany (and elsewhere in Europe) also involved many commemorations over four years between 2014 and 2018. Joining the government in highlighting major anniversaries, hotels, stores, book publishers, and the media seek to capitalize on the festivities.[61]

Germany is not the only country to mark significant historical anniversaries more frequently and intensively than previously. Many countries in East Asia held extensive commemorations of the seventieth anniversary of the end of World War II in 2015. In examining these commemorations, Daqing Yang and Mike Mochizuki coined the term "anniversary politics" to refer to the political motivations propelling national leaders to devote attention to an anniversary as well as the consequences of this attention.[62] Yang observes that anniversaries offer "a special opportunity – a calendrical megaphone so to

---

[60] Landwehr, "Mein Jahr mit Luther: Thesen zur Geschichtskultur."

[61] Ibid.; the comments by the participants in the forum on "Anniversaries," *German History* 32, no. 1, pp. 79–100; and Thomas Welskopp, "Die Magie der Zahl: Zu Theorie und Praxis von Julibäen und Gedenktagen in Geschichtsmuseen," Herbsttagung der Fachgruppe Geschichtsmuseen im Deutschen Museumsbund vom 15. bis 17. November 2014 in Bielefeld, www.museumsbund.de/wp-content/uploads/2018/05/2014-2-welskopp-gedenk tage.pdf.

[62] Yang and Mochizuki, eds., *Memory, Identity, and Commemorations*, p. xix.

speak – to broadcast messages to both domestic and external audiences through a variety of commemorative activities."[63] These messages are meant to unite the nation around a particular view of the past, a particular narrative of collective memory. For decades, German political leaders have been guided by a sense of anniversary politics, particularly in marking anniversaries of the Holocaust, but more recently as well in their commemorations of the rise and fall of the Berlin Wall.

To counteract the simplification and politicization of the past that often takes place when states sponsor anniversary commemorations, the historian Jörg Arnold has outlined what he sees as the role historians should play. He recommends that historians "draw on historical evidence. . .to provide historical depth to the anniversary moments, . . .show the complexity and contingency of the past, [and]. . .historicize memory by identifying the memory communities and their respective politics, tracing the narratives, symbols and commemorative practices."[64] These practices can challenge the state-sponsored narratives put forth on anniversaries. This is precisely what this study seeks to do regarding German *Erinnerungspolitik* on the Berlin Wall. Arnold observes that "anniversaries tend to crystallize the past around iconic events."[65] The rise and fall of the Berlin Wall were precisely such iconic events, and this book will illustrate how they have become the subjects of German anniversary politics in an effort to affect collective memory and redefine national identity.

Most work on historical memory focuses on grappling with memories of trauma, such as the Holocaust. But in the case of the Wall, historical memory concerns both the trauma for many of the Wall's existence and the joy for many of its fall. This book is one of the first studies to offer an in-depth examination of a case of joyful historical memory, taking up the challenge made in a special issue of the journal *Memory Studies*, "Memories of Joy," that "memory studies needs to pay more attention to the role of joyful and positive types of memory."[66]

Commemorative ceremonies marking anniversaries (and the increasing media attention to them) are one of the main methods for disseminating collective memory. Scholars such as Paul Connerton and Jan Assmann have argued that taking part in such rituals (or witnessing them on television) deepens or even creates certain memories of the past as well as narratives connected with those memories. Assmann distinguishes between communicative and cultural forms of collective memory, whereby the former occurs during the lifetime of people who experienced what is remembered as they tell

---

[63] Daqing Yang, "China: Meanings and Contradictions of Victory," ibid., p. 15.

[64] Arnold in the forum on "Anniversaries," p. 86.

[65] Ibid.

[66] Tea Sindbaek Andersen and Jessica Ortner, "Introduction: Memories of Joy," *Memory Studies* 12, no. 1 (February 2019), p. 5.

others about their experience and memory and the latter occurs among later generations who did not experience the history themselves.[67] For Assmann, rituals serve to "institutionalize the circulation of myths" about the past and thus "to maintain the identity system of the group."[68] In the case of Germany since 1989, both the communicative and cultural forms of collective memory of the Berlin Wall exist simultaneously, since the population is comprised of people who lived with the Berlin Wall and have personal memories of it and people who were born after the Wall was toppled and thus learn about it from others. This book will examine how various memory activists, most of whom experienced the Wall when it stood, have worked to fashion a certain collective memory of the Wall. It will also investigate the integration of memory activists and their narratives into commemorative rituals, particularly those occurring on anniversaries.

When Halbwachs formulated his concept of collective memory more than seventy years ago, he had a vision of a united, "collective," approach to the past holding people and groups, even nations, together.[69] Others studying the subject since have observed that commemorations, including on historical anniversaries, can also have the opposite effect. As the interviewers for the *German History* journal put it to a group of historians in a forum dedicated to anniversaries, "Anniversaries have the potential to generate or reanimate competing antagonistic narratives subscribed to by opposing memory communities."[70] Similarly, Peter Burke notes that the very process of "performing the past" in commemorating it can "often reveal cracks or even fissures in the community" and how people see the past. The very effort by some to put forward a certain historical narrative can result in a backlash from others who do not agree with that narrative, giving rise to "counter-narratives," "counter-memories," and "wars of memory."[71] This work will show the ways that anniversaries related to the history of the Berlin Wall have both helped to solidify a certain historical narrative but have exposed some counter-narratives as well.

It will also discuss the tension in German *Erinnerungspolitik* between memory of the Holocaust and memory of the Berlin Wall, which has been accentuated by a historical coincidence of dates: both the fall of the Wall and the Night of Broken Glass (*Kristallnacht*, when the Nazis attacked Jewish homes, synagogues, businesses, and cemeteries) occurred on November 9, albeit the former in 1989 and the latter in 1938. The violence perpetrated against Jews on *Kristallnacht*, including murder, marked a significant turn in Nazi policies toward what would become the Holocaust. An earlier Nazi

[67] Jan Assmann, *Das kulturelle Gedächtnis*.
[68] Ibid., p. 143.
[69] Halbwachs, *On Collective Memory*.
[70] Forum on "Anniversaries," *German History* 32, no. 1 (2014), p. 84.
[71] Burke, "Co-memorations. Performing the Past," p. 108.

association with November 9 dates from 1923 when Hitler and his National Socialist allies staged a march through Munich. The march was part of a failed coup attempt, the so-called Beer Hall Putsch, to take over the Bavarian state government as a preliminary step toward dislodging Germany's parliamentary democracy known as the Weimar Republic. These Nazi associations with November 9, particularly *Kristallnacht*, are the main reason this day was not made into a national holiday in Germany after 1989 and have impacted German celebrations of the fall of the Wall ever since.

While Germans themselves are the key actors examined in this book, they are not the only ones important in influencing German memory policy on the Wall. International interest in the Berlin Wall, drawing on the global memory of the Wall, has also played an important role.[72] Tourists and political leaders from outside Germany travel to Berlin wanting to see remnants of the Wall and participate in commemorative events, particularly on key anniversaries of the fall of the Wall.[73] External interest has been used by German memory activists to justify more support for the memory of the Wall and has also influenced how Germans have remembered the Wall.

This book focuses primarily on people who pushed to remember the Berlin Wall in a public way. It is much less the story of people who wanted or needed to forget. The book also does not offer a close examination of the commercial aspects of Wall commemoration, such as the economic motives of various individuals or institutions or even the city of Berlin[74] for preserving memory and pieces of the Wall or selling souvenirs connected to the Wall, although they will be touched upon. These related and interesting topics will hopefully be studied by others.

The present work explores the evolution of "anniversary politics" and more generally *Erinnerungspolitik* in Germany connected to the Berlin Wall since 1989, focusing on memory activists, the narratives they have developed, and the rituals they and public officials have engaged in. This book offers a close examination of how German leaders and others have commemorated milestone anniversaries of the rise and fall of the Berlin Wall and draws connections between these celebrations and the nature of national identity in united Germany, thus historicizing the German collective memory of the Berlin Wall.

---

[72] On global memory, see Aleida Assmann and Sebastian Conrad, *Memory in a Global Age: Discourses, Practices and Trajectories* (New York: Palgrave Macmillan, 2010); and Paul Williams, *Memorial Museums: The Global Rush to Commemorate Atrocities* (New York: Berg, 2007).

[73] On historical tourism, see Duncan Light, "Gazing on Communism: Heritage Tourism and Post-Communist Identities in Germany, Hungary and Romania," *Tourism Geographies* 2, no. 2 (2000), pp. 157–76.

[74] Berlin is both a city and a state. In order to distinguish it from the federal government, however, this book will refer to the Berlin government as a municipal one.

This study utilizes the methods of the historian, such as archival research, as well as the methods of the sociologist, such as interviews and participant observation. Since historical memory of the Berlin Wall is reflected in many different ways in Germany, this book relies on a wide-ranging group of sources. These include the author's interviews with nearly 100 officials, heads of memorials and museums, journalists, historians, and other memory activists involved in coming to terms with the history of the Berlin Wall; attendance at events connected with anniversaries of the rise and fall of the Wall; guidelines for memorial and monument design competitions; exhibits and exhibit catalogues; press coverage and debates; speeches by political leaders; parliamentary debates; national and state prize competitions and winners related to East German history; policy papers and records, including from the Berlin interagency Working Group on Commemorating the Berlin Wall;[75] and films, novels, exhibits, and memoirs related to East Germany and the Wall.

[75] The author was an invited observer for several years to the Arbeitsgruppe Erinnerung an die Berliner Mauer run by Rainer Klemke and granted access to related materials.

1

Divergent Approaches to the Fall of the Wall

With the toppling of the Berlin Wall and soon thereafter the East German SED regime, Horst Schmidt wanted to make sure "the murderers" at the Wall would pay for what they had done. His twenty-year-old son Michael had been killed on December 1, 1984 while trying to escape across the Berlin Wall. When the Wall fell, Horst and his wife Dorothea "could not feel anything of the excitement...they would have felt without Michael's tragic death. I kept thinking that only about 200 yards from the place where Michael was hit by the bullet of a murderer, there was now a border crossing that anyone could easily pass through."[1] Horst Schmidt set out to get justice for his son, or at least what semblance of it he could, given that nothing could bring back his son. His goal was to have the border soldiers who killed Michael tried in court.

The vast majority of Berliners and Germans, however, were eager to move on and leave the Wall and the division of the city and country in the past. For Berliners who had lived with the Wall for twenty-eight years, there was a strong urge to get rid of the Wall, which despite its peaceful opening, had long been associated with danger. A sort of evil spirit hung over it. As is often the case in countries with violent pasts, most people wanted to forget this difficult period of their history. Others were enthralled by the peaceful toppling of the Wall and wanted their own piece of what now felt like an enchanted structure, miraculously transformed from an edifice of fear into one of joy, hope, and freedom.

The focus in Berlin, especially for political leaders, was on rebuilding the center of the city, looking forward not back. Thus, most of the Wall was torn down very quickly to make way for new developments – government buildings for the capital to move from Bonn to Berlin, shopping centers, apartments – in the long barren stretch of what had been the death strip. There was much work to do to rebuild the center of the city and to redevelop much of the eastern part of it. The demands of the present and future were louder than concerns from the past.

---

[1] Horst Schmidt, "Kaltblütiger Mord. Bericht des Vaters von Michael Schmidt, 1991," www .chronik-der-mauer.de/todesopfer/171662/horst-schmidt-kaltbluetiger-mord-bericht-des-vaters-von-michael-schmidt-1991.

"Die Mauer muss weg!"

"The Wall must go!" was one of the demands of East German citizens in the fall of 1989, as a groundswell of opposition to the GDR regime developed and people took to the streets inspired by Soviet leader Mikhail Gorbachev's reforms and those in neighboring Poland. Tired of the strictures of communism, pressure to conform, widespread surveillance by the secret police, and the lack of freedom to choose their own career path or their national leaders, people wanted change. The Wall was the most visible reflection of the repressive nature of the SED, preventing people from visiting the West without special permission, which the vast majority of citizens were denied, since their leaders feared they would not return. Once the Wall was breached on November 9, those East German leaders never fully regained control of the border or the country.

Popular pressure moved the government to open up more and more holes in the Wall to allow people to go back and forth between East and West Berlin, at the Brandenburg Gate and many other places. In late December, the East German regime decided that instead of focusing on creating specific new openings in the Wall, it should tear down the whole thing. GDR border troops began the wholesale removal of the Wall between the Brandenburg Gate and Checkpoint Charlie to the south of it in March, and in April they started to dismantle the signal fence, an essential part of the border that had tripped a signal to alert the border guards when someone touched it. In June the troops moved to the area north of the Brandenburg Gate. A month later, more than 100 streets along the Wall had been reopened.[2]

On October 3, 1990, the GDR ceased to exist and was absorbed into the Federal Republic of Germany, consigning the Berlin Wall to history and with much of it already removed. Although some East German politicians and civic activists had sought to slow down the quickly accelerating drive for unification on West German terms and preserve parts of a significantly reformed, more democratic East German socialist system, the majority of the people had lost patience with any East German "experiments" and wanted a clean break with the regime and its Wall. By the end of November, the inner-city Wall had been removed, and by the end of 1991, the Wall, fence, and other barriers that had comprised the death strip around the outskirts of Western Berlin had also been

---

[2] On the dismantling of the Berlin Wall, see Polly Feversham and Leo Schmidt, *Die Berliner Mauer heute/The Berlin Wall Today* (Berlin: Verlag Bauwesen, 1999); Gerhard Sälter, *Mauerreste in Berlin. Relicts of the Berlin Wall*, 2nd revised ed., trans. Mariamne Fields (Berlin: Verein Berliner Mauer Gedenkstätte und Dokumentationszentrum e.V., 2007); and Wolfgang Rathje, *"Mauer-Marketing" unter Erich Honecker. Schwierigkeiten der DDR bei der technischen Modernisierung, der volkswirtschaftlichen Kalkulation und der politischen Akzeptanz der Berliner "Staatsgrenze" von 1971–1990*, 2 vols. (Berlin: Ralf Gründer Verlag, 2006).

dismantled. Ultimately, less than two miles of various sections of the Wall would be preserved in their original locations. Nothing would be left in key central areas like the Brandenburg Gate, the Reichstag, and Checkpoint Charlie – precisely the areas where people wanted it removed at first and would regret the removal years later.

The process of dismantling the Wall was further stimulated by the countless "Wall peckers" from Germany and far beyond who came to Berlin to take pieces of the infamous and now defunct Wall as souvenirs. The fall of the Wall seemed like magic to many people, and thousands and thousands of Wall peckers flocked to Berlin to get their own piece of it. After all, it is unusual for a major world event to be centered on an object, especially one that would be removed as a consequence. The physical nature of the Wall had long contributed to its photogenic and telegenic qualities and these only increased with its opening, making it even more of a magnet than it had been already. Many people around the world viewed the Berlin Wall as the icon of the Cold War and now suddenly and astonishingly it had been toppled overnight without any bloodshed. It made them want to drop everything and go to Berlin to celebrate and imbibe the magic of the moment.

Holding in one's hand – or even owning – a piece of what represented such contrasting evil and joy was quite spectacular. It made people feel good to have a piece of the Wall. They could look at it and experience the sense of elation and wonder elicited by the fall of the Wall. Instead of the helpless feeling the existence of the Wall and the Cold War had provoked, many people in Germany and around the world now felt empowered and optimistic. If the Berlin Wall could fall, other good things could happen too – for themselves, their family, their country, or even their own business. For many, the fall of the Wall seemed to signal the end of the messiness and violence of history and the herald of a new age.[3]

In the months and years to come, tourists, businesses, national governments, international organizations, schools, and other institutions from around the world would take or buy small pieces or whole segments of the iconic Wall to display.[4] Memory of the Wall was a global, not solely German phenomenon, and pieces of the Wall would end up in countries all over the world.

---

[3] The fall of the Wall gave added support to Frances Fukuyama's argument in "The End of History?" *The National Interest*, no. 16 (Summer 1989), pp. 3–18. For the lesson German leaders drew from 1989 that "history was over," see Thomas Bagger, "The World According to Germany: Reassessing 1989," *The Washington Quarterly* 41, no. 4 (Winter 2019), pp. 53–63.

[4] For a detailed look at where pieces of the Wall have ended up, see Anna Kaminsky, ed., *Where in the World Is the Berlin Wall?* (Berlin: Berlin Story Verlag, 2014). The first German edition of the book was published in 2009 for the twentieth anniversary of the fall of the Wall. An expanded German version in 2014 matches the 2014 English version.

To the surprise of many Germans who did not want any reminders of the Wall, others did and were willing to pay for them. The nearly bankrupt East German regime realized it could sell pieces of it, which it soon did, in direct transactions or at auctions.[5] The first offer to buy pieces of the Wall came in to the East German government already on November 10, 1989 from a business-man in West Germany's Bavaria. The US and British governments also inquired with the GDR embassies in Washington and London about buying some pieces. An American coin dealer offered $50 million for the whole thing. An Austrian Wall enthusiast was willing to pay DM500,000 for some pieces of the Wall at Potsdamer Platz. A Japanese company offered $185,000 for one segment near the Brandenburg Gate. In light of this international interest, the East German minister for foreign trade, Gerhard Beil, made the case that while it might seem ironic to sell parts of what the GDR regime had officially termed the "anti-fascist protective barrier" to the capitalists in the West, it could actually bring in some much needed hard currency. Prime Minister Hans Modrow agreed in December, and the council of ministers gave their seal of approval in January 1990, decreeing that the foreign ministry would oversee the process. The latter then contracted with the import-export firm Limex to proceed with selling pieces of the Wall. In late January, they chose a well-known section of the Wall with graffiti along Waldemar Strasse in Kreuzberg. Under cover of darkness, with guards making sure no one intervened, troops removed fifty pieces of the Wall. More segments were removed elsewhere.[6]

Hagen Koch, a cartographer employed by the Stasi for decades until resigning in 1985, was hired by the GDR's Institute for Historical Preservation a week before the fall of the Wall and then, in 1990, given the job of overseeing the demolition of the Wall. Koch advised the GDR govern-ment on which segments of Wall should be preserved in place (such as at Bernauer Strasse), which should be sold off (as the East German economic and political leaders wanted), and which should be given as gifts.[7] In August 1961, the twenty-one-year-old Koch had been ordered to draw a white line on the street to mark the border to make sure the construction crews were building the Berlin Wall in the right place – and not trespassing on West Berlin territory. In 1989–90, he was deeply involved in efforts to preserve some remnants of the Wall, document its history (using many files he had "acquired"

---

[5] On selling pieces of the Wall, see Ronny Heidenreich, "From Concrete to Cash: Turning the Berlin Wall into a Business," ibid., pp. 268–81; Anna Kaminsky, "Remembering the Wall since 1990," ibid., pp. 28–29; and Rathje, *"Mauer-Marketing,"* vol. 1, pp. 874, 880, 884, 887, 893–94, 903–904, 908, 915–16, 919, 923–24.

[6] Heidenreich, "From Concrete to Cash," pp. 268–70.

[7] See for example the letter from Koch, acting on Prime Minister de Maizière's orders, to the head of the border troops on August 20, 1990, with a detailed list of institutions in Germany and around the world that should be given a piece of the Wall for no charge. Rathje, *"Mauer-Marketing,"* vol. 2, p. 1770.

over the years to create his "Berlin Wall Archive"), and decide which pieces to sell, such as the section of Wall on Waldemar Strasse.[8]

The most sought-after pieces of Wall were those with graffiti on them. Yet what was sold was not always with the original graffiti and sometimes featured paintings that had been commissioned *after* the fall of the Wall to make these segments of the Wall more likely to attract high payments. Other pieces had the painting touched up. In West Berlin, the Lelé Berlin company represented Limex in marketing the Wall to private individuals, companies, and galleries. The East German regime decided to justify the sale of the Wall by declaring it would use the proceeds for "assisting public health in the [GDR]" where "funds are urgently needed" due to "inadequate supplies of material, instruments, hospitals, etc.," as the catalogue for an auction in June in Monaco declared. Two doctors from East Berlin's most prestigious hospital, the Charité, signed their names to the foreword in the catalogue in which they asked: "Is it right to sell this symbol of freedom as a showpiece? After much thought and consideration we have decided that it is good and proper to sell the Wall and convey the profits to those who have suffered because of it." The acknowledgments in the catalogue, rather too cheekily, thanked the GDR's Berlin border troops for "their unusual and committed service" in helping procure the pieces of the Wall to be auctioned off.[9]

Peter Goralczyk was in charge of historic preservation in the GDR. He, like Hagen Koch, argued that some of the Wall should be preserved as a historical artifact and that some of it should be sold off. With regard to the former, Goralczyk acted to protect some pieces from destruction or sale on the day before German unification by declaring them historic landmarks. Looking back years later, he felt that it was "the West Berlin historical preservation office which exerted the main pressure to preserve the Wall. They had more distance from it than we did. And they picked places along the Wall where it seemed likely it could survive the craziness of 1989–90, such as Niederkirchnerstrasse and Invalidenfriedhof."[10] Given the widespread national and international interest in the Berlin Wall, Goralczyk and his colleagues, together with officials from other parts of the government, also had many discussions about who exactly owned the Wall and thus who could sell it. Was it the government, which of course had constructed it? Or did the Western graffiti artists own the pieces they had painted, as some of them

---

[8] Interview with Peter Goralczyk, March 22, 2010; Katja Iken, "Der Mauermann," *Spiegel Online*, November 9, 2007; and Edmund L. Andrews, "The Wall Berlin Can't Quite Demolish," *New York Times*, August 13, 2001.

[9] Maitre Marie-Therese Escaut-Marquet, *Die Mauer. The Berlin Wall Special Auction, Saturday June 23, 1990, 12.00 Hours, Monte Carlo Hotel Metropole Palace*. Organized by Galerie Park Palace and Lelé Berlin Wall (Berlin: Elefanten Press, 1990).

[10] Interview with Peter Goralczyk, March 22, 2010.

claimed, demanding royalties from the sales? The GDR government decided that it owned the Wall and thus could sell it.[11]

Consequently, Goralczyk found himself in the unlikely position in the summer of 1990 of leading the delegation to the uber-capitalist city of Monte Carlo to oversee the auctioning off of eighty-one segments of the Wall to the highest bidders. Given that each piece weighed 2.6 tons, transporting them was quite a costly undertaking. The collection included pieces of Wall from the Brandenburg Gate, Potsdamer Platz, Kreuzberg, and elsewhere. Unbeknownst to the buyers, some pieces had been painted specifically for the auction. The "evening was a success," as Goralczyk observed, netting the GDR about DM2 million. Yet only some of that money or other profits from sales made by Lelé Berlin or Limex made it to the needy people in East German hospitals. A portion of the profits went to the government and artists (after many of the artists filed lawsuits), but some of the money disappeared as well.[12]

As the historian Ronny Heidenreich describes, in the process of dismantling the Wall, East German troops, as well as East and West German companies, sometimes sold pieces on their own, pocketing the profits for themselves. American and British troops also helped remove the Wall (Figure 3) and sent some segments home to military and other museums. Indeed, sixty tons of the Wall were shipped to the United States in the two weeks after November 9. Three American companies received contracts to market pieces, and sales began on board the USS *Intrepid* in Manhattan in February 1990.[13] While these all involved large complete segments of the Wall, an entrepreneurial German, Volker Pawlowski, had the idea to set very small pieces of the Wall in plastic cases and also to affix them to postcards. These are still available in just about every souvenir shop in Berlin today – complete with the spray paint on them added in Pawlowski's workshop.[14]

Sections of the Berlin Wall can be found in more than fifty countries around the world, on all seven continents, and at more than 140 sites. Indeed, there are now more pieces of the Wall on display around the world than there are for the public to see in Berlin.[15] The United States is the country with the largest share, since so many Americans felt a connection to the fall of the Wall and believed that US policies during the Cold War played a significant role in bringing down the Wall, not least with Ronald Reagan's call to "tear down this Wall!" (albeit more

[11] Ibid.

[12] Heidenreich, "From Concrete to Cash;" and interview with the artist Kani Alavi, January 14, 2010.

[13] Ibid. For more on the Berlin Wall at the USS *Intrepid* in New York City, see en.the-wall-net.org/new-york-city-ny-5/. For pieces of the Wall at other sites in Manhattan, see ephemeralnewyork.wordpress.com/2011/09/08/a-chunk-of-the-berlin-wall-on-53rd-street/.

[14] Heidenreich, "From Concrete to Cash"; and Ben Knight, "Chipping Away at Berlin Wall Souvenir Myths," *thelocal.de*, October 19, 2009.

[15] Kaminsky, ed., *Where in the World Is the Berlin Wall?*

Figure 3 British troops dismantling the Wall, October 29, 1990
Source: Photographer: H. Pastor. Archive, Allied Museum Berlin, from British Ministry of Defence, Public Information Office Berlin.

than two years before it actually happened).[16] Of the original 54,000 concrete segments of the Wall,[17] what was not taken, sold, kept as a memorial, or stored to give away as a gift, was ground up and reused to construct roads and buildings. Many years after the demolition of the Wall, so-called (yet unlikely) authentic pieces are still being sold to tourists wanting their own piece of the Berlin Wall.[18]

Joyful Memory: The Fall of the Wall and Beethoven

In a country steeped in a deep sense of classical culture and with many world-renowned composers among their forebears, Germans often turn to classical

---

[16] Anne Elizabeth Moore and Melissa Mendes, "How Two-Thirds of the Berlin Wall Ended up in the U.S.," *Wilson Quarterly* (Fall 2014). While the United States does have the highest number of pieces of the Wall outside of Germany, it is an exaggeration to say that it has two-thirds of the Wall. On Ronald Reagan's speech, see "Remarks on East-West Relations at the Brandenburg Gate in West Berlin," June 12, 1987.

[17] Kaminsky, "Remembering the Wall since 1990," p. 29; and Heidenreich, "From Concrete to Cash," p. 269.

[18] Giero Schliess, "Why the Berlin Wall Is Still a Big Business," *Deutsche Welle*, August 12, 2016. Visiting the Checkpoint Charlie Museum in 2018, one could watch through a glass window an employee painting small pieces of Wall for sale.

music to express the importance of an occasion. The fall of the Wall was no exception, and in 1989 Ludwig van Beethoven was the overwhelming favorite. Beethoven himself had been an advocate of freedom and democracy in Germany, particularly when he was first inspired by the French revolutionary ideas of liberté, equalité, and fraternité, and then when he sought to promote resistance to Napoleon and his military forces who had fought all the way to Berlin during the Napoleonic Wars. The fact that Beethoven wrote many of his beautiful works after he had gone deaf makes him even more of an admired figure, and his music has long been performed on special occasions in Germany.[19]

While countless people were expressing their joy over the fall of the Wall by taking or buying pieces of it or by joining the crowds of onlookers watching as it was dismantled, some celebrated by attending a concert of Beethoven's music. Indeed, performing Beethoven's music would develop into a regular part of the ritual of celebrating the toppling of the Wall in the years to come. In November 1989, the conductor and pianist Daniel Barenboim was working on a recording in West Berlin with the Berlin Philharmonic Orchestra. The day after the Wall opened, Barenboim and the orchestra decided they wanted to do something to mark the occasion. On Sunday November 12, the maestro conducted the orchestra in a free concert for East Germans in the (West) Berlin Philharmonic Hall (see Figure 1). The all-Beethoven concert featured the composer's First Piano Concerto and his Seventh Symphony. As the program notes to the Sony Classical CD of the concert observed, "the dance-like buoyancy" of the two works was a perfect fit for the feelings unleashed by the fall of the Wall. Among the musicians were some who had escaped from the GDR in the months before the Berlin Wall was erected and later joined the Philharmonic.[20] They, as well as others in the orchestra, had friends and family in the East and were just as excited by the turn of events as people on the streets and in their audience.

Only concertgoers with an East German identity card were permitted to attend the November 12 event.[21] Many East Germans had slept in their cars

---

[19]   On the longstanding use of Beethoven in German politics, see David B. Dennis, *Beethoven in German Politics, 1870–1989* (New Haven: Yale University Press, 1996). German political leaders from the Kaisers through the Nazis and East and West Germans treated Beethoven and his music differently, with each adopting their own views of what he and his music stood, as Leonard Bernstein would in 1989. On the East German treatment of Beethoven, see Elaine Kelly, "Beethoven and the Berlin Wall," *Oxford University Press Blog* (November 9, 2014).

[20]   Program notes, Berliner Philharmoniker, Daniel Barenboim, *Das Konzert: November 1989*, Sony Classical CD, 1989, pp. 4, 6.

[21]   Catherine Hickley, "Coalition Builds to Celebrate 20th Anniversary of Berlin Wall's Fall," *Washington Post*, November 8, 2009; and Kate Connolly, "I'll Always Associate Beethoven's 7th with the Fall of the Wall," *Independent*, November 9, 2009. A CD of Barenboim's free concert of November 12, 1989 was released later that year by Sony as *Das Konzert: November 1989.*

overnight in the parking lot of the Philharmonic, and those who came on foot started lining up at the door around 4 a.m. for the 11 a.m. concert. The normally rule-abiding staff of the concert hall admitted far more people than legally permitted. The hall "was packed to the rafters," and in violation of all fire codes people were even allowed to sit on the floor in the aisles.[22] The combination of the excitement on the streets of Berlin and Beethoven's music created a profoundly emotional atmosphere for both the musicians and the audience. One of the hornists remembers that he did not dare look into the eyes of anyone in the audience lest he be so moved that he would be unable to play. The orchestra members heard the weeping and sniffling as the over-whelmed East Germans listened to Beethoven.[23] As one East German attendee said, Beethoven's was the "best possible music for marking this occasion." Another observed that the selection of Beethoven's Seventh Symphony was perfect because "it is a happy piece for a happy event...[with] something of a carnivalesque feeling to it."[24]

The first movement of the symphony builds and builds, with the violins and others ascending note by note up the scale like the people climbing up onto the Wall. The second movement begins quietly and deeply in the low registers with an unrelenting five-note theme, later joined by the upper strings and woodwinds creating an intensely lyrical melody. The same five-note theme repeats with different instruments playing together, then separately, then together again, ascending in volume and emotion, becoming more and more persistent and grand. It is not hard to imagine it expressing the increasing urgency of the East German people calling for change and the opening of the Wall. The third movement steps up the pace and the final movement can only be described as jubilant. The audience erupted in applause at the end of the symphony and showered the orchestra with flowers.

After the concert, an older woman accompanied by a young man came to see Maestro Barenboim backstage. She gave the conductor a bouquet of flowers and told him a very personal story. Thirty years earlier, her husband had taken their infant son and moved to the West, leaving the woman behind. Her efforts to find her son failed as long as the Wall stood. Then, the day before the

---

[22] For information on the 1989 concert, see "Konzert zum 'Fest der Frieheit' am Brandenburger Tor: Daniel Barenboim und die Staaatskapelle Berlin spielen Wagner, Schönberg, Beethoven und Goldmann," *KlassikInfo.de*, www.klassikinfo.de/NEWS-Single.54+M50c8a9c6214.0.html.

[23] For interviews with members of the Berlin Philharmonic about the concert on November 12, 1989, see "The Fall of the Berlin Wall: Memories of Musicians of the Berliner Philharmoniker," Berliner Philharmoniker Digital Concert Hall, November 7, 2014.

[24] Interviews conducted by David B. Dennis at the Berlin Philharmonic's concert on November 12, 1989, Dennis, *Beethoven in German Politics*, p. 199. I am grateful to Judson Scott for his help in analyzing the scores of the Beethoven pieces discussed in this chapter.

concert, her son came to find her in East Berlin. Attending the concert was part of their reunion celebration.[25]

The most famous of Beethoven's many well-known works and the one most closely associated in Germany with celebrating the fall of the Wall is his Ninth Symphony with its glorious "Ode to Joy" finale.[26] Named a UNESCO world heritage work, the melody from the "Ode to Joy" movement is used as the anthem of the European Union and of NATO. The fourth movement of the symphony is based on Friedrich Schiller's poem "Ode to Joy" and features lyrics that seemed particularly fitting for the fall of the Wall: "Joy, beautiful spark of the gods/...your magic reunites/what custom strictly divided./All people become brothers."

The conductor and composer Leonard Bernstein performed Beethoven's Ninth in both East and West Berlin over Christmas in 1989 and changed the "Ode to Joy" to "Ode to Freedom." He announced: "I believe this is a heaven-sent moment when we should sing the word 'Freedom' whenever the score reads 'Joy.'...And I believe that Beethoven would have given us his blessing. Let freedom live!"[27]

Bernstein arranged for musicians and singers from both parts of Germany and from the Four Powers who had occupied Germany after World War II (the New York Philharmonic, the Kirov Theater Orchestra, the London Symphony Orchestra, and the Paris Orchestra) to participate in the concerts. In a break from tradition, a children's choir from the Dresden Philharmonic was included with the adults as though looking forward to a future where they would grow up in a Germany no longer divided. The concerts were held on December 23 in the (West) Berlin Philharmonic Hall and then on Christmas morning in the (East) Berlin Schauspielhaus. The Wall at the Brandenburg Gate had been opened on December 22, 1989 in a ceremony with West German Chancellor Helmut Kohl and East German Prime Minister Hans Modrow, adding even more to the euphoric atmosphere in Berlin. Bernstein himself had gone to see the new opening in the Berlin Wall and to chisel off a piece.

There were large screens and loudspeakers set up outside the concert halls for both performances of Beethoven's Ninth, and the maestro's Christmas concert was televised live in Germany and broadcast to more than twenty countries. In West Berlin, instead of setting up the viewing party outside the Philharmonic, the concert organizers decided to go where the hundreds of thousands of East

[25] Interview with Daniel Barenboim, "The Berliner Philharmoniker's 1989 Concert Celebrating the Fall of the Berlin Wall: Memories of Daniel Barenboim," Berliner Philharmoniker Digital Concert Hall, November 7, 2014.

[26] Kerry Candaele released a documentary film on Beethoven's Ninth in 2013, *Following the Ninth*. Daniel M. Gold, "The Ode Heard Round the World: 'Following the Ninth' Explores Beethoven's Legacy," *New York Times*, October 31, 2013.

[27] Citation from the concert program, Dennis, *Beethoven in German Politics*, p. 202.

Germans were that weekend: in the heart of West Berlin's shopping district along the Kurfürstendamm next to the Kaiser-Wilhelm Memorial Church at Breitscheidplatz.[28] An East German couple who watched the concert on the screen there enthused, "you couldn't find a more appropriate work for this festive occasion than the Ninth Symphony because it expresses our present feelings of joy."[29] In East Berlin, the viewing party was directly outside of the Schauspielhaus at the Gendarmenmarkt, the center of which is occupied by a statue of Schiller, the author of the "Ode to Joy" poem.

The four-movement Ninth Symphony is full of all the best that music has to offer: quiet, lyrical moments and grand, dramatic passages where the musicians play with full force. The first minute of the first movement alone offers all of this. Beethoven's directions to the musicians at multiple points in the piece are to play with "majesty" (*maestoso*). Needing nearly an hour and a half of playing time, the piece is a monumental work. The singers must sit patiently waiting through the first three movements: the magnificent first movement with its many highs and lows; the dance-like, buoyant second movement; and the slow and achingly beautiful third movement. The final movement begins with a furious burst of sound, becomes quiet and then continues with increasing urgency. It is clearly working up to some sort of climax, and the first-time listener must wonder: will the climax be dark and violent or glorious and sweet?

This question was one the East Germans on the streets had been asking themselves for weeks as they called for change in the fall of 1989, and with the opening of the Wall, they had their answer. Beethoven's answer would be similar, although not immediately. In the final movement of Beethoven's Ninth on Christmas morning, with a dark burst of sound at the opening, followed by calmer passages, it was not certain where the "Ode to Freedom" was leading. Then the cellos and basses quietly took up the famous melody, joined by the violas and bassoons in a countermelody, and finally by the violins on top. The beautiful tune then danced around the orchestra, here with the violins, there with the cellos, and then with the whole orchestra together growing louder, then softer, as Bernstein smiled while keeping time with his baton. As the music suddenly got fast and darkly furious again, the baritone soloist rose from his chair on the stage in the ornate concert hall and sung out at full volume: "Oh friends, not these

---

[28] On Bernstein conducting Beethoven's Ninth Symphony in East and West Berlin over Christmas 1989, see the recording (with English subtitles) of the concert in East Berlin's Schauspielhaus, December 25, 1989 as well as interviews with Bernstein and others, www .youtube.com/watch?v=IInG5nY_wrU. See also AP, "Upheaval in the East: Berlin; Near the Wall, Bernstein Leads an Ode to Freedom," *New York Times*, December 25, 1989. Bernstein's "Ode to Freedom" concert was released on CD by Deutsche Grammophon in 1990 and by Medici Arts on DVD, accompanied by a short documentary film, for the twentieth anniversary in 2009.

[29] Dennis, *Beethoven in German Politics*, p. 202.

tones! Rather, let us raise our voices in more pleasing/And more joyful sounds!" Instead of the traditional "*Freude!*" ("Joy!") that comes next in Schiller's poem, the baritone sang "*Freiheit!*" ("Freedom!") and launched into the melody of the piece. "All people become brothers/Where your gentle wing rests." With that, the long patient chorus at the back of the stage and in the balcony above the orchestra joined their voices to his and sang the "Ode to Freedom" chorale. Bernstein could not help himself and sang along at times as well.

A reporter from the *Neue Osnabrücker Zeitung* at the concert in the Schauspielhaus wrote: "many in East Berlin shed tears unashamedly. A young woman next to me gave up trying to save her makeup. Even Bernstein and the musicians, overwhelmed by...the profundity of the moment, played with an intensity, a fervor, as if they were hugging the world." And when the final "Ode to Freedom" chorus ended, there was "One moment of silence: and then all people jumped jubilantly from their seats and fell into one another's arms."[30] Bernstein embraced the concertmaster with a big hug, bade the musicians to rise, and turned to face the cheering and whooping audience. The audience both inside and outside the Schauspielhaus stayed on their feet applauding and shouting out "Bravo!" for nearly fifteen minutes, their faces beaming with happiness as the performers took bow after bow. Someone handed Bernstein a Berlin flag, which he waved while continuing to receive bouquets of flowers from grateful members of the audience. Clearly no one wanted the experience to end.

The jubilant Ninth Symphony expressed, better than any words, what it meant to many Germans that the Wall had fallen. Beethoven's work would be performed again and again in the years following 1989, first in the Schauspielhaus on October 2, 1990 as part of East Germany's last official ceremony before unification at midnight and later to mark the twentieth and twenty-fifth anniversaries of the fall of the Wall in 2009 and 2014. In 2009, the Berlin Sinfonietta would play the Ninth at the Schauspielhaus in October, and on November 9, 2009, Berlin's Rundfunk Symphony Orchestra would play the third movement at the Berlin cathedral. In 2014, for the twenty-fifth anniversary of the fall of the Wall, Barenboim and the *Staatsoper* would perform the "Ode to Joy" at the Brandenburg Gate on November 9, while the Berlin Philharmonic would play the whole symphony in the Philharmonic Hall and then in Warsaw, Prague, and Budapest.[31] By pairing this music with commemorations of the fall of the Wall, Barenboim, Bernstein, Sir Simon Rattle,

---

[30] Klaus Adam, "Freiheit schöner Götterfunken: Bernstein mit der Neunten in West- und Ost-Berlin," *Tagesspiegel*, December 25, 1989, cited in Dennis, *Beethoven in German Politics*, p. 203.

[31] On Beethoven and other music performed for the twenty-fifth anniversary of the fall of the Wall, see Hope M. Harrison, "Reflections from the Berlin Wall: Twenty-Five Years Later," blog, International Spy Museum, Washington, DC, November 6–12, 2014, blog. spymuseum.org/reflections-from-the-berlin-wall-25-years-later/.

and other conductors acted as memory activists, highlighting and remembering the joy of the moment.

Beethoven composed one other work that has also been closely connected with the fall of the Wall: his only opera, *Fidelio*. Set in a state prison in late eighteenth-century Spain, it is the story of a woman (Leonore) dressing up as a man (Fidelio) to liberate her husband (Florestan) who has been imprisoned unjustly by the tyrannical governor of the state prison system (Pizarro). Astonishingly, one month *before* the fall of the Wall, a production of *Fidelio* premiered in the East German city of Dresden with a set designed to mimic the Berlin Wall. When the curtain in the Semperoper went up on Act I, which is set in the courtyard of the state prison, the audience gasped. They were faced with a fence topped with barbed wire at the front of the stage, a guard tower in the middle of the stage toward the rear, and tall walls on three sides of the stage topped with what looked like the Berlin Wall's floodlights all around it. It also bore a distinct resemblance to the Stasi prison at Bautzen forty miles away to which many of the protestors on the streets of Dresden were taken in the fall of 1989.[32]

There was no mistaking the intention of the brave (or foolhardy, if things had turned out differently) East German director, Christine Mielitz. At a time when there were large daily demonstrations on the streets of Dresden, in the Theaterplatz right outside the opera house, at the main train station, and elsewhere, many of which had escalated to violence with the police and resulted in arrests, the opera reflected what was happening in their own lives in the GDR. Indeed, members of the opera house and the audience had to pass through a chain of policeman to enter the Semperoper in early October due to the dramatic confrontations between demonstrators and police on the streets.

Fidelio had been the first opera performed in Berlin after World War II, underlining the liberation of the Germans from the Nazi dictatorship. In the spring of 1989, Christine Mielitz had persuaded Dresden's cultural and political authorities that the opera should be performed in October for the fortieth anniversary of the founding of the GDR and to mark the bicentennial of the French Revolution. As she later recalled, none of the authorities "dared to ban Beethoven."[33] She did not share with them her view that, "The piece is

---

[32] "Mielitz' 'Fidelio'-Inszenierung zum letzten Mal in der Semperoper," *Musik-in-Dresden*, April 28, 2010.

[33] Moray McGowen, "*Fidelio* and *Faust* in the German 'Wende' of 1989/90," in Lorraine Byrne, ed., *Goethe: Musical Poet, Musical Catalyst*. Proceedings of the Conference hosted by the Department of Music, National University of Ireland, Maynooth, March 26 and 29, 2004 (Dublin: Carysfort Press, 2004), p. 129. On the production of *Fidelio* in September 1945, see "Today in history: Beethoven's opera 'Fidelio' in Berlin, 1945," *People's World*, September 4, 2015.

contemporary, it concerns us all. . .We cannot be cowardly; we must say what we must say. Nothing should be swept under the carpet."[34]

The "Prisoners' Chorus" is a focal point of the opera. Leonore dressed as Fidelio persuades the prison director, Rocco, to let the prisoners out of their cells into the courtyard for some fresh air. She assumes her husband will be among them, not knowing that he is alone in the dungeon, starving and in chains. As the prisoners came out into the courtyard at the *Semperoper*, facing the audience through the fence and barbed wire, they started to sing, first quietly and just a few of them and then all of them, increasing in volume, about their joy at being outside breathing in the fresh air: "Oh what joy to breathe freely/in the open air! . . ./Hope softly whispers to me:/ 'We shall be free, we shall find peace'/Oh heaven! Freedom! Oh, what joy!/Liberty, can you return?" As they all raised their voices and their hopes, one of them warned: "Speak low! Be careful!/Ears and eyes are on us!" All the prisoners joined in singing this warning, looking out at the audience. One of the members of the choir, Klaus Milde, remembers that he had a lump in his throat and tears in his eyes and that others must have been in the same state. Yet they somehow sang, as a reviewer observed, "with tonal beauty and evenness" instead of with quivering voices.[35]

When the "Prisoners' Chorus" ended at the premiere on Saturday October 7, 1989, the audience members rose to their feet, erupting in spontaneous applause even though it was not the finale. Just as the prisoners wanted freedom and not to be watched all the time, East Germans in Dresden and elsewhere wanted the same. More and more of them were resisting the power of the GDR regime and feared imprisonment. Choir member Andreas Heinze remembered enduring "a sense of underlying fear and tension" for weeks during the rehearsals due to the incredible coincidence of the themes of the opera and reality on the streets.[36] Of the standing ovation, Heinze recounted afterwards: "Usually applause starts, gets louder and then quiets down. But in this case, it stayed loud and for us it continued for a really long time, since we kept to our roles and stood there like stones, not knowing what would happen. We were really scared and it was certainly a form of protest by the people against the current political situation, against the circumstances."[37] Klaus Milde also recalled: "The latent danger that we might have to stop the performance hung in the air the entire time." He was relieved when "the audience sat down again – thank god – after the lengthy applause."[38] The applause that greeted the "Prisoners' Chorus" on the following

---

[34] Michael Cookson, "After Nearly Thirty Years Mielitz's *Fidelio* Still Looks Contemporary and Fresh," *Seen and Heard International*, May 5, 2018.

[35] Klaus Milde, "Eine Oper wird politische Realität: Wiederaufnahme des 'Fidelio'," *Semper Magazin* 8 (June 4, 2012).

[36] "Die Wende in Dresden: Im Oktober 1989 steht die DDR kurz vor dem Bürgerkrieg," *3sat.online*, April 21, 2009.

[37] Ibid.

[38] Klaus Milde, "Eine Oper wird politische Realität."

night lasted for so long that it "nearly interrupted the evening," as Martin Walser wrote for *Die Zeit*. There was even applause in the box for the East German leaders, occupied that night by the party chief of Dresden (who would soon become the East German prime minister), Hans Modrow.[39]

Once the audience was seated again, the opera continued and moved toward its climax in the dungeon where Florestan was held. Leonore/Fidelio and prison director Rocco dug a grave for Florestan, whom prison governor Pizarro planned to murder. As Pizarro approached Florestan with a dagger, Leonore/Fidelio rushed to her husband covering his body with hers and telling Pizarro he must kill her first. She announced that she was in fact a woman and Florestan's wife. Just then a minister (Fernando) from the king arrived, recognized his old friend Florestan and set him free (this is an opera after all). Shortly thereafter, Fernando announced an amnesty for all the prisoners. In the Dresden production, the wives who came to collect their husbands from prison were dressed in contemporary garb like the members of the audience. The opera ended with everyone singing of joy and praising Leonore for her courage.[40]

The standing ovation at the end of the opera went on and on. Once they finally left the stage, a good number of the singers, musicians, and staff of the Semperoper as well as many from the audience went back out onto the streets to join in the demonstrations, perhaps a little more hopeful than they had been before seeing *Fidelio*.

The second night of the production may be more famous than the first because of the long-lasting implications of the fact that Modrow was attending the opera instead of being reachable by phone in his office during the demonstrations that night. A demonstration in front of the opera house in the Theaterplatz was violently dispersed earlier in the day on Sunday October 8 with 150 people arrested, including members of the Semperoper. Things reached a head again later in the evening in the pedestrian district on Prager Strasse between the Theaterplatz and the central train station when police surrounded around 1,500 protestors.[41] At the head of the lines of protestors was the twenty-nine-year-old Chaplain Frank Richter from Dresden's Catholic *Hofkirche*. He saw that ahead of them approaching the central train station, the police had closed off the street and were lined up carrying shields and clubs and wearing helmets. The side streets were closed off too. Chaplain Richter knew that demonstrators were regularly surrounded, arrested, taken off to prison and beaten up. He thought to himself, "don't let yourself be forced into this, try at least to talk to the policemen." Meanwhile, demonstrators were calling out, "No violence!" ("*Keine Gewalt!*")

---

[39] Martin Walser, "Kurz in Dresden: Einige Szenen aus dem deutschen Frühling im Herbst," *Zeit*, October 20, 1989. See also Dr. med. Ingrid Straßberger, "Fidelio zum 40. Jahrestag," *Ärzteblatt Sachsen* 9 (2014), p. 375.

[40] Lyrics from Fidelio as translated in the libretto of the Warner Classics CD, *Beethoven/Barenboim: Fidelio* (1999).

[41] McGowen, "*Fidelio* and *Faust* in the German 'Wende' of 1989/90," pp. 128–30.

Richter took another Catholic chaplain with him and they crossed the "no-man's- land" between the demonstrators and police to find the officer-in-charge. Initially none of the police would speak to Richter, but eventually a young man in civilian clothes came forward. Officer Detlef Pappermann was a member of the special forces of the People's Police (*Volkspolizei*, VoPos). Richter suggested that Pappermann call the mayor to come talk to the people and keep things peaceful. Seeing that the police were far outnumbered by the demonstrators, Pappermann thought "talking is not a bad idea" and left for a few minutes to call his boss – not the mayor. Meanwhile, Richter decided it was advisable to organize a group of people to represent the protestors in talks with the mayor and to come up with a list of demands. He climbed up onto a fountain and called for ten volunteers. When fifty came forward, he and his colleague chose a diverse group from among them – young and old, a worker, an academic, and others. Although there were twenty-three people, they later would be called the *Gruppe der 20* (Group of 20). Next, the chaplain called out to the crowd that they should come up with a list of demands for the mayor. The first demand yelled out was, "Freedom to travel!" The chaplain made a list of eight demands, which also included free elections, the right to demonstrate, peaceful dialogue and – reminiscent of the plot of *Fidelio* – the release of political prisoners.

Pappermann's call to his boss set off a flurry of deliberations among the military and political leaders in Dresden about what to do. Should they call Berlin? Should they call Modrow? Mayor Berghofer did in fact try to reach Modrow, but he was at the opera and thus Berghofer made the decision without him: he sent word that he would meet with the demonstrators on the following morning. Pappermann returned to the scene in the pedestrian zone and conveyed the mayor's agreement to a meeting. Dresden's Bishop, Johannes Hempel, used a megaphone to tell the crowd the good news: in the morning of October 9, the *Gruppe der 20* would meet with the mayor and in the evening, the results of the discussion would be disseminated to the citizens through the churches. As Pappermann remembers it, Hempel then turned to him and asked, "And now?" Pappermann responded: "'Now we will go home.' And everyone went home. Policemen walked with demonstrators to their cars, people talked." Violence was averted.

The meeting with the mayor took place the next day, and there was cooperation between the police and the people at the demonstration later that day and in the days and weeks following. The lesson of dialogue from Dresden on October 8 spread to Leipzig the next day when a demonstration of 70,000 people took place peacefully in spite of widespread expectations the authorities would crack down.[42] What came to be known as the "peaceful

---

[42] Robert Ide, double interview with Chaplain Frank Richter and Officer Detlef Pappermann, "Das Wunder von Dresden – warum die Revolution friedlich blieb," *Tagesspiegel*, October 8, 2014.

revolution" had a significant beginning on October 8 in Dresden and October 9 in Leipzig. One month later the Berlin Wall was toppled.

Mielitz's production of *Fidelio* would be performed many times afterwards in united Germany, mirroring and in some sense reenacting what had been performed by real people in East Germany in the fall of 1989. The production was reprised in 2004 and 2009 for the fifteenth and twentieth anniversaries of the peaceful revolution and the fall of the Wall and on many other occasions. For the tenth anniversary in 1999, Barenboim and the *Staatsoper* released a recording of their own version of *Fidelio*.[43] For the twenty-fifth anniversary, the final scene of *Fidelio* was performed at the national commemorative ceremony in Berlin in the same hall (the former Schauspielhaus, renamed the Konzerthaus) where Bernstein had led Beethoven's Ninth on Christmas Day in 1989.[44] The story of *Fidelio* was integrated into the ritual of marking the fall of the Wall.

Memory on Trial

A very different sort of reenactment of the history of the Berlin Wall took place in courtrooms in Berlin and beyond after unification in the form of criminal trials of those responsible for the order to shoot at the border (*Schiessbefehl*) and its implementation. Horst Schmidt got his wish in bringing to trial the two border soldiers who had killed his son Michael.

As with the removal of the Wall, many Germans felt that the trials would help bring closure – punishing the perpetrators and securing justice for the victims or their survivors. Of course, for those who had lost a loved one, closure would not be so easy.[45]

Particularly in the first cases against former border soldiers (*Grenzsoldaten* or *Grenzer*), family members, such as Horst Schmidt, of those killed at the Wall had initiated the proceedings in the final months of the GDR's existence. Public prosecutors took up the cases in united Germany, as the last East German parliament (the Volkskammer) and the unification treaty had specified that GDR state crimes would continue to be investigated and brought to trial in united Germany.[46] Evidence to build the cases came from vast numbers of documents from the former GDR and FRG.

---

[43] *Beethoven/Barenboim: Fidelio*, Warner Classics CD (1999).

[44] Alison Smale, "On a Memory-Filled Date, the Fall of the Berlin Wall Stands Front and Center," *New York Times*, November 9, 2014.

[45] For detailed information on people killed at the Berlin Wall, see Hans-Hermann Hertle and Maria Nooke, eds., *The Victims at the Berlin Wall 1961–1989: A Biographical Handbook* (Berlin: Ch. Links Verlag, 2011).

[46] Roman Grafe, *Deutsche Gerechtigkeit. Prozesse gegen DDR-Grenzschützen und ihre Befehlsgeber* (Munich: Siedler, 2004), p. 15.

By May 1991, Berlin's public prosecutor had already started 153 investigations and had named thirty-eight *Grenzer* in cases of murder at the border.[47] In September 1991, Berlin created the Central Investigation Office for Governmental and Organized Criminality (ZERV) regarding the former GDR to oversee the process. The Chief Public Prosecutor and head of ZERV was Christoph Schaefgen. Since his office was overwhelmed with the caseload and Berlin did not have the resources, Berlin's Senator for Justice, Jutta Limbach, persuaded the federal government to hire more lawyers. Eventually she was given funding for about sixty lawyers. Given the obvious need for training in Federal German jurisprudence, these lawyers came from the former West Germany. Most of them did not want to remain long away from home in Berlin and generally stayed at ZERV for only about two years, which complicated its overwhelming task.[48]

Between 1991 and 2004, more than 500 *Grenzer* and their military and political superiors were accused and often found guilty of manslaughter, attempted manslaughter, complicity to manslaughter, and other related charges for the deaths of individuals at the Berlin Wall and at the inner-German border.[49] Ultimately the courts held former officials throughout the entire chain of command to account, including not just the border soldiers at the bottom of the chain but also regimental commanders, the commander in chief of the border troops and his deputies, the leadership of the Ministry of Defense (the Kollegium), members of the National Defense Council (NVR, composed of civilian and military leaders), and the Politburo (the top political leaders). As it turned out, these trials were the primary way that leaders of the former GDR would be judged in the public eye: by charging them with killing people at the border. Thus, in these trials the Berlin Wall came to represent, in some sense, the whole former East German regime. It was the one place where former East German citizens (and their lawyers) could confront the former leaders publicly and face-to-face for what they had done.

The trial of the two *Grenzer*, Uwe Hapke and Udo Walther,[50] for killing the twenty-year-old Michael Schmidt (Figure 4) when he tried to escape across the Berlin Wall began in mid-December 1991 after much effort by his father, Horst. It was the second such trial, following in the footsteps of the trial of the four *Grenzer* involved in killing Chris Gueffroy, who had been the last

---

[47] "Sie wirft Schatten bei Nacht," *Spiegel*, May 27, 1991.

[48] Grafe, *Deutsche Gerechtigkeit*, p. 18.

[49] Hansgeorg Bräutigam, "Die Toten an der Berliner Mauer und an der inner-deutschen Grenze und die bundesdeutsche Justiz," *Deutschland Archiv* 37, no. 6 (2004), December 14, 2004, p. 975; Grafe, *Deutsche Gerechtigkeit*, pp. 308–9; and Clemens Vollnhals, "Die Strafrechtliche Ahndung der Gewalttaten an der innerdeutschen Grenze," in Klaus-Dietmar Henke, *Die Mauer* (Munich: dtv, 2011), pp. 249–50.

[50] Hertle and Nooke, eds., *The Victims at the Berlin Wall*, pp. 399–402. See also the testimony of Michael Schmidt's father: Horst Schmidt, "Kaltblütige Mord," 1991.

victim shot at the Berlin Wall in 1989 and whose mother Karin had worked so hard to seek justice.[51] Horst and Dorothea Schmidt were there in the court-room for the first day of the trial seven years after their son had been killed on December 1, 1984. His mother would subsequently stay at home to spare herself the pain, but Horst would continue to attend this trial and others afterwards. Horst testified at the trial and has written about what brought his son Michael to try to escape.

At the time of Michael's attempted escape, Horst's own father lived in West Berlin, and the GDR regime refused to grant Horst permission to visit his father for his eightieth birthday in June 1984. Michael was very upset by this, feeling it was not right to stop a son from seeing his father on his birthday, especially at such an advanced age.[52] A short time later, when military officials attempted to persuade Michael to carry out his compulsory military service at the border, his opposition to the East German regime and desire to leave the country apparently "escalated to blind hatred." He reportedly told his military interviewers in no uncertain terms that he would not "shoot unarmed people in the back." Michael was practically thrown out of the room by the military officer who had been interviewing him.[53]

In the wake of this confrontation, Michael spoke to his parents about wanting to file an application to emigrate – the only way to legally leave the country. The authorities rarely approved such applications (especially for a young person of working age) and Michael and his family would likely suffer during the long process of waiting for the probable rejection of his application. Michael's brother had just begun his studies at the university, and this was generally the kind of "privilege" denied to individuals (or their family members) who were not viewed as supportive of the regime, a category into which Michael and his family would fall if he applied to emigrate. In the fall of 1984, Michael's parents asked him to wait a year or two longer before filing the application. Michael, however, seems to have decided he could not wait any-more. Instead, he would try to get out on his own. He spoke with at least one friend about trying to escape and vowed he would carefully prepare a plan to do so.[54]

---

[51] A. James McAdams, *Judging the Past in Unified Germany* (New York: Cambridge University Press, 2001), pp. 30–35; and Pertti Ahonen, *Death at the Berlin Wall* (New York: Oxford University Press, 2011), pp. 255, 259–61.

[52] Horst Schmidt, "Vater eines Maueropfers. 'Sie morden wieder auf Befehl'," in Roman Grafe, ed., *Die Schuld der Mitläufer: Anpassen oder Widerstehen in der DDR* (Munich: Pantheon, 2009), pp. 148–49.

[53] Ibid., and Horst Schmidt, "Kaltblütiger Mord," 1991, p. 1.

[54] Information on the lead up to Michael Schmidt's escape attempt and what happened on the night of December 1, 1984 and in the days afterwards is drawn from Horst Schmidt, "Kaltblütiger Mord," 1991, pp. 1–5; Hertle and Nooke, eds., *The Victims at the Berlin Wall*, pp. 399–401; and "Wir machen alles gründlich," *Spiegel*, June 24, 1991, p. 81.

Figure 4 Photograph of Michael Schmidt (center with rose in front), *Fenster des Gedenkens*, Berlin Wall Memorial
Source: Hope M. Harrison.

Michael worked as a carpenter for a construction company, and some of his work sites were at buildings on the edge of the restricted zone approaching the Berlin Wall border area. From the roof of one of these buildings, he had gained a good sense of the composition of the border installations – at least the parts he could see. The back courtyard of one of the buildings was closed in by the internal Wall of the border strip, the so-called *Hinterlandmauer*. On the night of Friday November 30, Michael went to a disco in the Pankow district of Berlin with some friends, talked constantly about wanting to leave the GDR, drank more than usual, and departed the disco a while later with a woman (whose identity remains hidden to this day). They made their way to one of the warehouses Michael's company used in the border area and got two ladders. They brought the ladders over to the *Hinterlandmauer*. The woman seemed to have second thoughts and left Michael on his own.

Michael used one ladder to climb over the *Hinterlandmauer* at just past 3 a.m. He must have thrown the other ladder over, because he also had a ladder to climb over the signal fence inside the border strip. In the process, however, Michael triggered a signal wire, and a border soldier yelled out for him to stop. Michael kept the ladder with him, running with it toward the final barrier as warning shots rang out. Two *Grenzer* started shooting at him as Michael put up the ladder against the final external Wall and made his way up it. He had just grabbed the top of the Wall to pull himself over and jump down into West Berlin when he was hit by bullets in his back and knee. The two soldiers, Hapke and Walther – now on trial in December 1991 – fired more than fifty shots at Michael. He and the ladder fell to the ground.

Hapke and Walther ran over to him. Hapke was agitated and demanded of Michael, "What kind of shit are you pulling?" Michael answered weakly, "I guess you guys got me after all." Three other soldiers quickly arrived on the scene and dragged the bleeding yet still alive Michael to a nearby military vehicle and brought him to a watchtower where he was hidden from sight. West Berlin police officers and members of the French military whose sector of West Berlin bordered the area had in fact watched the aftermath from a raised platform.[55] Klaus-Dieter Baumgarten, head of the border troops and Deputy Minister of Defense, later warned Defense Minister Heinz Hoffmann that, "It cannot be ruled out that enemy forces…saw the use of firearms and that projectiles landed on West Berlin territory."[56]

Once the *Grenzer* had moved "the border violator," no one gave Michael any first aid in spite of his pleas for help. They merely covered him with a blanket. A paramedic vehicle (not an ambulance) from a military hospital forty-five minutes away (not the nearest hospital) finally arrived. Michael was delivered to a hospital more than two hours after he had been shot. There, doctors began an emergency operation but Michael Schmidt died at 6:20 a.m. as a result of the gunshot to his back that caused massive bleeding when it punctured his left lung.

Knowing none of this, Michael's parents were distraught, wondering where their son was and unknowingly being misled by the Stasi, as was Stasi practice with family members of someone who was killed while trying to escape. Western news reports on Saturday December 1 that an escape attempt, presumed to be fatal, had occurred the night before near where Michael worked made them fear the worst. It did not help their mood that December 1 was celebrated in the GDR as Day of the Border Troops, and the newspapers, television, and radio were filled with praise for all who served at the border.[57] Michael's father went to the police and the nearby hospitals asking for information and got none. The police dissuaded him from filing a missing person's report on December 1 and 2, reassuring him that a young man not coming home after a Friday night out was not the most unusual thing.

---

[55] Hertle and Nooke, eds., *The Victims at the Berlin Wall*, p. 400.
[56] "Sie wirft Schatten bei Nacht," *Spiegel*, May 27, 1991, p. 22.
[57] See Honecker's letter to the border troops printed on the first page of *Neues Deutschland* and reprinted in Grafe, *Deutsche Gerechtigkeit*, p. 222. Grafe counterposes this with a reprint of a West Berlin newspaper headline from December 2, 1984, "Wall-Murder: Refugee Died in Hail of Bullets" (*Mauer-Mord: Flüchtling starb im Kugelhagel*), p. 223.

On Monday December 3, Horst went so far as to ask someone at the criminal police office whether his son had been involved in the incident at the Wall over the weekend. He was told not to believe Western media and that nothing remotely harmful had occurred that weekend at the Wall. Horst still insisted that he be allowed to file a missing person's report. He initially felt hopeful that GDR authorities were on the case the next day, Tuesday December 4, when he went to the family doctor and learned that someone from the criminal police had come by to get some of Michael's records. Horst's sense of relief that the authorities were trying to find his son was short-lived.

That evening, two Stasi men appeared at the Schmidts' house and announced that they were taking the couple to the chief military prosecutor's office. There, a Stasi man, a certain Herr Cras, began interrogating Michael's parents, while Horst kept asking where their son was. Eventually the chief military prosecutor told them, after nearly four days of not knowing whether their son was dead or alive, that Michael had been shot when he tried to breach the border and that "in spite of all medical efforts," he had died. The prosecutor said the *Grenzer* "acted in self-defense."

The following day, December 5, Cras met with Michael's parents again and insisted they must deny all "rumors" about a death at the Wall and whether it was Michael or not. They must tell no one and certainly not the Western media. If they did not comply, Cras made it clear that their older son would not be allowed to continue his university studies. Cras also wanted to organize Michael's funeral. His parents refused, but Cras showed up at the funeral on December 10 along with various other plainclothes agents, many of them armed as they had been in their deployment near the house for days.[58] Michael's colleagues who came to the funeral were followed by the Stasi afterwards and his boss was reprimanded for bringing the whole work crew to the funeral.

Seven years later, in the juvenile chamber of the Moabit Criminal Court in Berlin, the border soldiers Uwe Hapke and Udo Walther were put on trial for killing Michael Schmidt. Walther had been twenty years old when he had fired the shots and was considered a minor in a criminal case. Hapke had been twenty-three. Before examining their actions on December 1, 1984, the court investigated their backgrounds.[59] Walther had lived in an orphanage until he was two years old when he was taken in by foster parents who then formally

[58] Horst Schmidt, "Kaltblütiger Mord," 1991, pp. 1–5; Hertle and Nooke, eds., *The Victims at the Berlin Wall*, pp. 399–401; and "Wir machen alles gründlich," *Spiegel*, June 24, 1991, p. 81.

[59] Details of the personal backgrounds of Walther and Hapke are contained in the verdict of the Berlin District Court from February 5, 1992: "Lfd. Nr. 2. Erschießungs eines flüchtenden DDR-Bürgers-Fall M.-H. Schmidt. Erstinstanzliches Urteil des Landgerichts Berlin vom 5.2.1992, Az. (518) 2 Js 63/90 KLs (57/91)," in Klaus Marxen and Gerhard Werle, eds., *Strafjustiz und DDR-Unrecht: Gewalttaten an der deutsch-deutschen Grenze, Dokumente,*

adopted him when he was six. His father was a butcher and his mother a veterinarian. Walther had learning problems and was better at practical undertakings than more abstract studies, as he said. He wanted to be a car mechanic but did not have good enough grades, so he trained to be a butcher like his father. Both Walther and Hapke joined the communist organizations common for each age group in the GDR starting with the Young Pioneers, although only Walther joined the SED.

Walther married in 1983 and began his military service that same year. He signed up for a three-year term, as military recruiters generally pressed draftees to do, instead of just the required eighteen months. Walther wanted to work eventually as an auto mechanic for the VoPos and erroneously assumed he would be assigned to the VoPos for his military service. Instead, he was deployed to the border. The nineteen-year-old believed at the time that defending the border was necessary and justified, as he told the judge. He also became a "community informer" for the Stasi, reporting on any comments by colleagues that might indicate they were not "trustworthy" and might be planning to escape. He had six months of training as an NCO, which included weapons training with a Kalashnikov. In April 1984 he was deployed to Border Regiment 33 at the Berlin Wall, arriving there seven months before Hapke did.

Hapke grew up spending more time with his grandmother than his parents, since they were occupied with their jobs as a telecommunications technician and a saleswoman. A good student, Hapke was trained as an electrician. His father was an SED member, but did not press his son to follow the party line. Hapke married in 1983. The following year for his compulsory military service he was assigned to the border troops without being asked. He resisted pressure to agree to a three-year term. Hapke spent six months in a border training regiment, including learning to use an AK-47, and then was deployed to Border Regiment 33 at the Wall in November 1984.

As border soldiers, Hapke and Walther had political education training twice a month where political officers stressed the importance of defending the border against imperialists from the outside and traitors from the inside. They were also told about *Grenzer* who had been killed at the border and in whose memory their barracks and rooms were named. Like all *Grenzer*, Hapke and Walther received Kalashnikovs for their use at the border. Walther had fired his before December 1, but Hapke had not. Walther was a very good shot and had received his shooter's cord to display on his uniform before December 1, 1984. Hapke received his shooter's cord in 1985.

The trial of Hapke and Walther was held between December 1991 and early February 1992. The defendants described their side of the events of

Band 2/1. Teilband, compiled by Toralf Rummler and Petra Schäfter (Berlin: De Gruyter Recht, 2002), pp. 105–9.

December 1, 1984. Both were on duty in a guard tower when Walther first saw Schmidt climbing over the *Hinterlandmauer*. The leader of the pair on duty, Walther ordered Hapke to go down and stop the person trying to escape. Walther fired warning shots from the tower, while Hapke scrambled down to the ground and yelled at Schmidt to stop. As Schmidt ran with his ladder toward the outer Wall, Hapke ran after him. When Schmidt put his ladder up against the Wall, Hapke was approximately 120 yards away. He stood still, leaned against the Wall to steady himself, aimed at Schmidt's calves and fired at least twenty-five shots in five seconds as Schmidt started up the ladder. From up in the tower more than 150 yards away, Walther fired at least twenty-seven shots aimed at Schmidt's legs. When Schmidt had reached the top of the ladder and had one hand on top of the Wall, both Hapke and Walther fired again.

Hapke's shot hit Schmidt in the knee and Walther's hit him in the back. Schmidt and the ladder fell to the ground, and the two *Grenzer* ran over to him. As Hapke testified, when he approached Schmidt not moving on the ground, he had the feeling he, Hapke, had done something wrong, a feeling that grew afterwards and became a certainty.[60] Walther, on the other hand, made it clear he was not one for much self-reflection.[61] They both assumed that the "border violator" had been injured but did not make any effort to ascertain this or to help him.

Other *Grenzer* and their superiors quickly arrived on the scene. Hapke and Walther were instructed to make sure the Wall was secure where Schmidt had tried to climb over it and then to proceed to the command tower for an inspection of their weapons and an inventory of how many shots they had fired. Back at the regiment's base, they would turn in their AK-47 submachine guns and be taken in to the Stasi for questioning. At the base, they were praised for their actions, awarded a "Medal for Exemplary Border Service," and given a significant pay bonus of 200 East German marks. Their superiors "were very satisfied with us" for preventing a "border violation." The soldiers were not told that Schmidt died and they each were soon transferred to other units not serving directly at the border, as was the norm to limit discussions about killing refugees. Afterwards, Hapke did not wear his medal, since he felt "it was covered in blood," and Walther apparently only wore his because his superior told him to.[62]

---

[60] Details of what happened on the night of December 1, 1984 are contained in the full text of the verdict, ibid., pp. 110–12. Excerpts of the verdict can be found at www.chronik-der-mauer.de/todesopfer/171661/urteil-des-landgerichts-berlin-in-der-strafsache-gegen-udo-w-und-uwe-h-auszuege-az-2-js-63–90-fall-michael-schmidt. See also Hapke's testimony at the Border Troops trial on January 19, 1996, in Grafe, *Deutsche Gerechtigkeit*, pp. 85–88.

[61] Gisela Friedrichsen, "Wer so auf Menschen schießt," *Spiegel*, January 27, 1992, p. 43.

[62] In addition to the details of the border soldiers' testimonies in the verdict, esp. pp. 111–13, see also Hapke's later testimony in the Border Troops trial of January 19, 1996 in Grafe, *Deutsche Gerechtigkeit*, pp. 87–88.

When interrogated at the 1991–92 trial about whether they intended to kill the would-be escapee, the former *Grenzer* said that they did not want to kill him but knew that it was possible that their actions could have that result. They stressed that they had an order, which they considered binding, to prevent any escape. Also, as Hapke testified, "if we didn't shoot we would be transferred or demoted."[63] Accordingly, instead of starting with single targeted shots as was prescribed, they skipped this and fired short rounds of shots in a sustained manner, to make sure Schmidt could not escape, knowing that this would increase the likelihood of both hitting him and doing so with a deadly shot. The defense lawyers stressed the justifiability of the border troops defending their state border "as every state has the right to do." On the question of why they thought Schmidt was trying to escape, neither Hapke nor Walther saw him as a criminal, saboteur, or spy, the typical epithets used by GDR officials to refer to "border violators." Instead, Walther assumed Schmidt "wanted to find his luck in the West" and Hapke thought he just wanted to get out of the GDR and could not find another way.

In spite of the fact that their defense lawyers tried to portray them as "politically indoctrinated," that did not seem to be the case, at least not in Horst Schmidt's view. Both former *Grenzer* said in court that they had watched West German television at home and that even secretly in the barracks they had sometimes listened to Western stations on a portable radio. Thus, they clearly had access to information beyond what was provided by SED indoctrination and might have been in a position to view the situation at the border with a more critical eye. Michael's father noted this as well as the fact that they "never apologized" to him, although "they had many chances" during the trial.[64]

Judge Ingeborg Tupperwein read out the verdict on February 5, 1992. Walther and Hapke were found guilty of joint manslaughter and given sentences of eighteen months and twenty-one months, respectively. The judge, however, suspended both sentences due to "a variety of circumstances [justifying] a milder sentence," such as their indoctrination within the military and their positions at the bottom of the chain of command. Judge Tupperwein relied, as many subsequent trials would, on the March 1982 East German Border Law. Paragraph 9 of this law, "general provisions," stated that the border could generally only be crossed at official crossing points and with the required documents. Paragraph 17 on "border violations" covered "all actions directed against the inviolability of the state borders." Paragraph 18 detailed "the responsibilities of state organs" at the border, whereby the border troops were required "to preserve the inviolability of the state borders." Finally, Paragraph 27 detailed provisions for "the use of firearms" by members of the border troops, noting that the "use of firearms" was "the most extreme

---

[63] Ibid., p. 88.
[64] Roman Grafe's interview with Horst Schmidt after the trial in 1992, ibid., p. 302.

measure of violence to be used against people." It further advised that "when using firearms, the life of individuals is to be preserved if possible."[65] Details of the judge's reasoning for her verdict and that of the Federal Court of Justice (*Bundesgerichtshof*, BGH), which upheld the verdict, will be analyzed later following a discussion of the Wall trials of senior officials.

For Horst Schmidt, the trial of the soldiers who had killed his son had been "downright shock therapy." He never expected the defense lawyers would continue to "follow the SED line" that, "the Wall was absolutely fine. . . .A sovereign state can defend its borders as it wants. . . .Period." In Herr Schmidt's eyes, justice had not been done for his son. The German courts, he observed, were quite "severe on property related issues," giving, for example, property in the East back to previous owners from the West, but on "matters of health and life, it was one mitigating circumstance after another." Furthermore, he certainly did not see evidence of the indoctrination Judge Tupperwein had referred to as one of those mitigating circumstances. As far as he could tell from what Hapke and Walther said during the trial, "they shot, so that they wouldn't have any problems. Then there would be no demerits for the border company."[66]

After the trials of border soldiers for killing their sons at the Berlin Wall, Horst Schmidt, Karin Gueffroy, and other family members of those killed at the border would go on to act as joint plaintiffs in the trials of senior military and political officials whose orders the *Grenzer* were carrying out. Indeed, several of the senior officials were already imprisoned at the same compound in Moabit where the trials had been held. The public prosecutor's office had begun gathering information on these former officials before the *Grenzer* trials started. The general public had been critical during the first two trials, arguing that the courts were making the lower-level border soldiers the scapegoats and letting their superiors off the hook. The importance of bringing to trial the *Schreibtischtäter* (perpetrators who sat at their desks) who were behind and above the *Grenzer* was seen as paramount. The term *Schreibtischtäter* had long been used to refer to the Nazi leaders who presided over the Holocaust, and now prosecutors, members of the press, and others would use the term to refer to the East German military and political perpetrators responsible for issuing the orders that resulted in deaths at the Berlin Wall and the inner-German border.[67]

Less than two months after German unification, German authorities issued an arrest warrant – on November 30, 1990 – for the former leader of the SED and of the National Defense Council (NVR), Erich Honecker, in connection

---

[65] Gesetz über die Staatsgrenze der Deutschen Demokratischen Republik vom 25. März 1982, www.verfassungen.de/de/ddr/staatsgrenze82.htm.

[66] Grafe's interview with Horst Schmidt after the trial, in Grafe, *Deutsche Gerechtigkeit*, p. 302. See also Horst Schmidt, "Sie morden wieder auf Befehl," pp. 149–50.

[67] "'Wir machen alles gründlich.' Die Todesgrenze der Deutschen (I): Schreibtischtäter aus Wandlitz," *Spiegel*, June 24, 1991.

with murders at the border. Instead of turning himself in, Honecker and his wife were under Soviet protection at a Soviet military hospital outside of Berlin, where doctors were treating what seemed to be liver cancer. In March 1991, the Honeckers were flown from a Soviet military base outside Berlin to Moscow. In mid-May, the Berlin public prosecutor's office issued a nearly 800-page indictment charging Honecker and other members of the top-ranking NVR, including former East German Defense Minister and Politburo member Heinz Kessler, with indirect complicity to manslaughter.[68] Just as Honecker had fled to Moscow, so German authorities suspected that Kessler planned to do the same. Kessler and his wife had booked flights for a two-week trip to the Soviet Union from May 22 to June 4. While they were visiting their son and grandchildren outside of Berlin beforehand, however, the police seized the opportunity to search Kessler's house in Berlin-Karlshorst. They carted away stacks of documents and changed the locks, leaving a note saying that Kessler could pick up the new keys at the police station. When a neighbor alerted Kessler that it seemed that someone had "broken into his house," he returned home and went to get the keys at the police station. Instead, Kessler was arrested on charges of incitement to manslaughter for deaths at the Wall.[69]

In mid-May, three other members of the NVR were arrested and imprisoned in Moabit as well: former East German Premier Willi Stoph, Fritz Streletz (chairman of the NVR from 1971 to 1989 and deputy Defense Minister and Chief of the Army's General Staff from 1979 to 1989), and Hans Albrecht (deputy chair of the NVR and SED chief in the city of Suhl). The NVR investigation started with sixty-eight cases of people killed at the border, but in the interests of not dragging the trial out for multiple years and necessitating the hiring of even more lawyers, it ultimately focused on four cases from the 1980s, including that of Michael Schmidt. The Border Troops trial of 1995–96 would focus on twenty-one cases: eleven who had been killed, including Michael Schmidt; and ten who had been injured. The Politburo trial of 1996–97 would start with over 100 cases (in which Michael Schmidt was case number sixty-three) and ultimately focus on the same four cases as the NVR trial, including Schmidt. Limiting the cases was no doubt upsetting for family members of those killed who did not get their chance in court to confront the *Schreibtischtäter*, but on the other hand it shortened the time to wait for their possible imprisonment.

In July 1992, Moscow extradited Honecker back to Germany where he was incarcerated in Moabit with the others. The NVR trial began on November 12, 1992, with Horst Schmidt in attendance as a joint plaintiff. The public prosecutors had many documents that tied the NVR leaders (and later the leaders of

---

[68] McAdams, *Judging the Past in United Germany*, p. 35.
[69] "Sie wirft Schatten bei Nacht," *Spiegel*, May 27, 1991, pp. 19–20; and Heinz Keßler, *Zur Sache und zur Person: Erinnerungen* (Berlin: edition ost, 1996), pp. 331–32.

the border troops, the Kollegium of the Ministry of Defense, and the Politburo) to orders to use deadly force at the border. Particularly important was the twenty-page protocol of the May 3, 1974 session of the NVR at which the leaders "fully supported" Honecker's insistence that "border violations must absolutely not be permitted" and that "a perfect firing field must be preserved" in the border zone so that soldiers would have an uninterrupted line of fire to shoot at people trying to escape. Honecker decreed: "As before, firearms are to be used ruthlessly against efforts to break through the border, and the comrades who use their firearms successfully are to be commended."[70] An order to the border troops in 1976 declared further that "provocateurs attacking the border installations must be destroyed."[71]

In addition, the all-important *Schiessbefehl* (Order 101, the order to shoot) was renewed annually by Defense Minister Kessler and passed down the chain of command as Orders 80, 40, and 20 via Deputy Minister of Defense and Chief of the Border Troops Klaus-Dieter Baumgarten, his deputy Erich Wöllner, the Northern, Central (at the Berlin Wall), and Southern Border Commanders, and the regimental commanders to officers who finally passed it on as verbal injunctions to the border soldiers each day before their guard duty. These orders generally stated that the border troops must "arrest or destroy border violators," if necessary "with the first shot."[72]

These and other directives agreed to by the Politburo and NVR members would serve as key incriminating evidence against the leaders in the trials of the NVR, the Kollegium of the Ministry of Defense, the border troops, and the Politburo. In the case of the Politburo, only three former members remained healthy enough to make it through the whole trial: Egon Krenz, Günter Schabowski, and Günther Kleiber. Krenz had been a Politburo member and the Central Committee secretary for security issues since 1983, deputy chair of the State Council since 1984, and succeeded Honecker as the SED leader in mid-October 1989. Schabowski had been a Politburo member since 1984 and the SED chief in East Berlin since 1985. In the drama of 1989, Schabowski is best known as the SED spokesman who mistakenly announced at the international press conference on the evening of November 9, 1989 that the Berlin Wall was open "immediately, without delay." Kleiber joined the Politburo in

---

[70] "Sie wirft Schatten bei Nacht," *Spiegel*, May 27, 1991; and "Wir machen alles gründlich," *Spiegel*, June 24, 1991. The latter contains a summary of the protocol of the May 3, 1974 NVR conference.

[71] "Wir machen alles gründlich," *Spiegel*, June 24, 1991, p. 77.

[72] See for example the documents used to convict Egon Krenz in the Politburo trial, in Klaus Marxen and Gerhard Werle, *Strafjustiz und DDR-Unrecht: Gewalttaten an der deutsch-deutschen Grenze, Dokumente, Band 2/2, Teil 3* (Berlin: Walter de Gruyter, 2002), pp. 723–24; Grafe, *Deutsche Gerechtigkeit*, p. 58; and "Mit dem 1. Schuß treffen," *Spiegel*, September 1, 1997, pp. 42–43.

1984, the NVR in 1988, and had long held important positions overseeing parts of the economy.

From the testimonies of the defendants and other witnesses and the arguments made by the lawyers, prosecutors, and judges at the trials, a variety of views of the Berlin Wall emerge. The first and probably more widely held view was that the border regime had been inhumane and violated human rights. Therefore, those responsible for upholding the lethal character of the border were criminals and must pay a price for the deaths and injuries they caused, starting with those who pulled the trigger and going up the chain of command. Family members of those killed, prosecutors, and many in the general public held this view. As the mother of Chris Gueffroy insisted: what the border soldiers did to her son "was murder."[73]

Another approach, one taken in the trials by nearly all the senior political and military leaders and their defense lawyers, was that the GDR as a sovereign state (and recognized as such by the international community and West Germany) could police its border as it saw fit, however brutal others might think it was. There were two kinds of argument made about why it was necessary to have a particularly strong regime at the border. The first, in the words of Politburo member Horst Dohlus, "was to prevent the hemorrhaging of the GDR." As he noted, even "applications to emigrate...were often not approved, since otherwise the GDR would have soon been empty," something the family of Michael Schmidt knew all too well.[74] Gerhard Lorenz, who had been the deputy chief of the border troops and director of political adminis-tration, explained while on trial that, "The border regime and limitation of freedom of movement were acts of self-defense of the GDR...which...had the right to implement the necessary regulations for its ongoing existence. The endangering of the GDR by a systematic hemorrhaging could not be accepted."[75] Similarly, Robert Unger, one of the defense lawyers in the Politburo trial, declared to Karin Schmidt (no relation to Michael Schmidt) whose husband was killed at the Wall: "It is my strong conviction that there is no personal blame for what happened here. The people in the GDR had no other way to secure the border, the GDR had to be preserved."[76]

Indeed, as historical documents show, the East German leadership under Walter Ulbricht, Honecker's predecessor, ordered the border closed and for-tified in 1961 to stop the massive exodus to the West of East Germans that had reached crisis proportions in the summer of 1961 with more than 1,000 people

---

[73] "Aufspüren, festnehmen, vernichten," *Spiegel* 33 (1990) August 13, 1990, p. 36.

[74] Horst Dohlus's testimony at the Politburo trial, May 9, 1996, in Grafe, *Deutsche Gerechtigkeit*, pp. 129–30.

[75] Gerhard Lorenz's testimony at the Border Troops trial, August 30, 1996, ibid., p. 171.

[76] Defense lawyer Dieter Wissgott during the closing arguments at the Politburo trial, August 4, 1997, ibid., p. 234.

leaving every day.[77] As Ulbricht, whose initiative it had been to build the Wall told his Soviet counterpart, Nikita Khrushchev: "It is not possible that a socialist country such as the GDR can carry out a peaceful competition with an imperialist country such as West Germany with open borders."[78] When the Wall fell twenty-eight years later, East Germans again streamed to the West, even when it became clear that East and West Germany would be united. Thus, the argument that East Germany could only survive with the Wall was a well justified one.

Former chief of staff at the Central Border Command of the Berlin Wall, Günter Bazyli, did not believe that the deadly border regime was meant just to save the GDR in general. The aim was more specific in his view. He told the judge in the Politburo trial that the leaders of the border troops had suggested to the Politburo that "border violations" could be prevented by adding more soldiers instead of having the soldiers shoot so much. The Politburo members rejected this proposal, since, in Bazyli's view, their main goal was to stay in power, and they believed that their "fear of a mass exodus" could best be countered by the *Schiessbefehl*.[79] Bazyli further declared: "Everyone could see that we imprisoned the people" with brutal methods.[80]

At several points in the trials, the defendants were questioned about whether in fact, as Bazyli pointed out, the East German leaders could have prevented people from escaping by less brutal methods, namely by means short of shooting them. Prosecutors and lawyers asked Krenz, Baumgarten, Streletz, and some of the *Grenzer* whether they could have used many more dogs and soldiers – with the *Grenzer* perhaps even wearing sneakers to help run after border violators, as Hanns-Ekkehard Plöger the lawyer for the joint plaintiffs in the Politburo case, suggested[81] – and built the Wall higher so they could have captured the refugees alive. Krenz answered Plöger: "A further deployment of more personnel would not have been possible."[82] Presumably this was due to the financial and political costs this would have entailed. But these costs were also involved in the use of firearms. During the Border Troops and Politburo trials, Streletz confirmed that he had complained to Baumgarten

---

[77] "Fluchtbewegung aus der DDR und dem Ostsektor von Berlin – Juni bis August 1961," www.chronik-der-mauer.de/material/178763/fluchtbewegung-aus-der-ddr-und-dem-ostsektor-von-berlin-juni-bis-august-1961.

[78] See Ulbricht's letter to Khrushchev on September 15, 1961, cited in Hope M. Harrison, *Driving the Soviets up the Wall: Soviet-East German Relations, 1953–1961* (Princeton: Princeton University Press, 2003), pp. 220–21.

[79] Günter Bazyli's testimony at the Politburo trial, February 27, 1997, in Grafe, *Deutsche Gerechtigkeit*, p. 201.

[80] Ibid., p. 183.

[81] Hanns-Ekkehard Plöger's questioning of Krenz at hearing at BGH, October 27, 1999, ibid., pp. 250–51.

[82] Krenz's response to Plöger's questioning during Politburo trial on July 24, 1997, ibid., p. 229.

about "the unreasonably high expenditures of ammunition"[83] used by the *Grenzer* with their frequent sustained firing instead of single shots.[84] The financial costs were too great. Streletz reported that Krenz had regularly complained to him about this: "When will you stop it with [so much] shooting at the border?"[85] Chief Justice Monika Harms at the BGH in November 1999 confirmed the prosecutor's contention that, "Securing the border was possible without needing to resort to deadly gun shots."[86]

The second line of argument adopted in the trials by former East German officials and their lawyers about the justifiability of the stringent border policy was that the borders between East and West Berlin and East and West Germany were at the center of the Cold War, which could turn hot at any time. Thus they needed to maintain "control" and "stability" at the border, including by shooting people trying to escape. When Chief Justice Josef Hoch in the Politburo trial expressed skepticism about this line of reasoning, Krenz insisted: "It was about the question of war and peace. . . .If you changed the border regime, you had to bear in mind that you could bring your country into a world war. . . .What the court is demanding of us is that we should have risked involving GDR citizens in a war" by changing the brutal practices at the border.[87] As Krenz told the media in August 1997, "The border is being downplayed as an internal German or inner-city border. But it was a border between two worlds. . . .The border between the Warsaw Pact and NATO was a restricted military zone. Every state in the world shoots under such circumstances."[88]

In stressing how dangerous the Cold War was and the location of Germany and Berlin at the front line, some of the defendants expressed their rather disingenuous seeming "sympathy" for the "many victims of the Cold War on *both* sides of the border" (emphasis added), among whom they included those killed at the Berlin Wall. This was hardly a consolation to Horst Schmidt and others.[89] Streletz portrayed the people who were killed and injured at the border as "tragic victims of the Cold War."[90] Yet these "tragic victims" were

---

[83] Streletz's response to Chief Prosecutor Bernhard Jahntz during the Politburo trial on August 26, 1996, ibid., p. 168.

[84] Streletz's testimony at the Border Troops trial, May 17, 1996, ibid., p. 128.

[85] Streletz's answer to Jahntz during the Politburo trial on August 26, 1996, ibid., p. 168.

[86] Chief Justice Monika Harms's oral arguments for conviction, BGH, November 8, 1999, ibid., p. 252.

[87] Krenz, Politburo trial, July 24, 1997, ibid., p. 227.

[88] Conversation between Egon Krenz and constitutional law expert Wolfgang Seiffert, "Grenze zwischen zwei Welten," *Spiegel*, August 18, 1997, p. 36. Kessler and Streletz elaborated on this argument years later in their book, *Ohne die Mauer hätte es Krieg gegeben* (Berlin: edition ost, 2011).

[89] For statements by Baumgarten, Heinz Ottomar Thieme, and others to this effect, including Judge Boss's verdict in the NVR trial, see Grafe, *Deutsche Gerechtigkeit*, pp. 31, 46, 59, 142.

[90] Streletz's closing statement at the NVR trial, September 14, 1993, ibid., p. 29.

not without blame in the opinion of these former officials since, as Heinz-Ottomar Thieme, the former director of training for the border troops, put it, "these people behaved against the laws of the GDR and knew about the risk of illegal movement at the border." Baumgarten reminded the judge that the border "was clearly marked, so people were warned."[91] This was the kind of remark that caused Horst Schmidt to view the trial as "shock therapy."

Blaming "the Cold War" seemed to deflect blame away from the defendants. Although it is true that one cannot understand the Berlin Wall without understanding the broader Cold War context, it is also true, as a public prosecutor in the Border Troops case maintained, that, "The 'Cold War' didn't kill any fleeing GDR citizens. They were killed by people, by members of the Border Troops who acted as they did because of political education, propaganda and a chain of orders for which the accused share responsibility."[92] Hence the need for the trials in a state such as the Federal Republic of Germany governed by the rule of law.

Within the "don't blame us, blame the Cold War" argument, defendants took two specific approaches, one blaming "the imperialist" West Germans and the other blaming the Soviets. Before Honecker was found to be too sick with liver cancer to stand trial and was allowed to leave to join his wife and daughter in Chile in early 1993 (where he would die the following year), the former East German leader declared at the NVR trial that the Wall was actually the result of West Germany's Cold War against the GDR. Krenz later claimed in the Politburo trial that, "The FRG had an interest in deaths at the border, it organized such incidents." Likewise, Baumgarten argued in the Border Guards trial that the "FRG mass media" with its "false recommendations" not to recognize the GDR borders kept inspiring people to try to escape.[93] There were in fact people in the FRG, so-called escape helpers, who did try to get East Germans out, but they hardly wanted those people to be killed in the process.[94] When people were killed at the border, West German politicians and media did use those instances as opportunities to criticize the GDR regime.[95] Yet saying, as the defense lawyer Frank Osterloh did at the Border Troops trial, that

[91] Thieme's statement at the Border Guard trial, June 11, 1996, ibid., p. 142, and Baumgarten's statement in the trial, November 3, 1995, ibid., p. 60.

[92] Statement by public prosecutor Klaus-Jochen Schmidt at the Border Troops trial, August 9, 1996, ibid., p. 164.

[93] Statements by Honecker, Krenz, and Baumgarten, ibid., pp. 27, 226, and 132–33, respectively.

[94] Maria Nooke, ed., *Mauergeschichten von Flucht und Fluchthilfe: Begegnung mit Zeitzeugen* (Berlin: Ch. Links, 2017); Burkhard Veigel, *Wege durch die Mauer: Fluchthilfe und Stasi zwischen Ost und West*, 3. *Auflage* (Berlin: Edition Berliner Unterwelten, 2011); and Ahonen, *Death at the Berlin Wall*, pp. 99–103.

[95] Ibid., pp. 32, 41.

the FRG made "efforts to have as many deaths at the border as possible to blame on the GDR" went too far for the court and many observers.[96]

The other line of the "don't blame us, blame the Cold War" approach was to insist that on the communist side of the Cold War, the Soviets not the East German leaders called the shots, including and especially at the border. Indeed, in negotiating the final treaties on German unification the West German Interior Minister Wolfgang Schäuble was surprised that Gorbachev had not insisted on assurances that the East German leaders and other representatives of the regime would be granted immunity from prosecution.[97] For his part, Chancellor Kohl thought it would have been easier to move forward with the ongoing process of unification if Honecker had stayed in Moscow and not been extradited to Germany.[98] The German courts, to say nothing of the survivors of people killed or injured at the Wall, thought differently though and Gorbachev did not raise the issue before unification. The defendants in the Wall trials and their lawyers focused on highlighting Soviet influence and thereby downplaying the role of the East Germans in the brutal border regime.

Krenz's defense lawyer, Robert Unger, asserted in his closing statement at the Politburo trial in August 1997 that: "All fundamental decisions on security issues were made by the Soviet Union alone."[99] Krenz himself most memorably declared: "Ronald Reagan came to West Berlin in 1987 and did not call out, 'Honecker or Krenz, open this Wall!' He said: 'Gorbachev, open this Wall!'"[100] Judge Friedrich-Karl Föhrig in the Border Troops trial also adopted some of this line of reasoning in his verdict that Baumgarten and others serving in the border troops did not have full control over the border and that significant responsibility lay with "supranational bodies like the Warsaw Pact and with the big brother the Soviet Union."[101]

Historically and in the light of some of the conflicting testimony in the trials, this argument, "don't blame us, blame the Soviets for the deadly border regime" does not hold up well. The Soviets resisted the pleas, demands, and

---

[96] Defense lawyer Frank Osterloh's statement at the Border Troops trial, August 27, 1996, in Grafe, *Deutsche Gerechtigkeit*, p. 169.

[97] Interview with Wolfgang Schäuble, Berlin, May 26, 2004.

[98] Interview with Helmut Kohl, Berlin, February 11, 2004.

[99] Defense lawyer Robert Junger's closing statement at the Politburo trial, August 4, 1994, in Grafe, *Deutsche Gerechtigkeit*, pp. 233–34. See also Krenz's statement at the Politburo trial, March 7, 1996, ibid., p. 115; Streletz's testimony in the Politburo trial on July 8, 1996, ibid., p. 149; and Baumgarten's remarks during the Border Troops trial, July 12, 1996, ibid., p. 151.

[100] Conversation between Egon Krenz and constitutional law expert Wolfgang Seiffert, "Grenze zwischen zwei Welten," *Spiegel*, August 18, 1997, p. 36; and Edmund L. Andrews, "Ex-East German Chief Gets 6 years for Deaths at Wall," *New York Times*, August 26, 1997.

[101] Judge Föhrig's verdict in the Border Troops trial, September 10, 1996, in Grafe, *Deutsche Gerechtigkeit*, p. 325.

unilateral policies of East German leader Walter Ulbricht to close the border in Berlin for nearly eight years until they acquiesced in the summer of 1961. It was Ulbricht who wanted to do this to preserve his regime; it was not forced on him by the Soviets. Once the East Germans began sealing the border and constructing the Berlin Wall on August 13, 1961, the Soviets were very critical of East Germans shooting too readily and frequently at the border and instructed Ulbricht that this must be stopped.[102]

Honecker oversaw matters concerning the new border regime, and subsequently ousted and succeeded Ulbricht in 1971. As former Soviet ambassador Valentin Falin testified at the NVR trial, Soviet leaders "Brezhnev and Gorbachev often asked Honecker if the deaths at the border could be avoided. There were some discussions at lower levels too. Each time, the East Germans said that the border regime was their responsibility [and that t]he deaths were unavoidable if unfortunate."[103] Obviously, it was in Falin's interest to deflect blame from the Soviet regime onto the East German leaders, but some of the testimonies given by the defendants in the trials also countered the claim that the Soviets bore sole responsibility for the character of the border.

A prime example of East German room for maneuver on their border policy was Honecker's decision to remove the SM-70 splinter mines on the inner-German border in 1984. These horrendous devices had been deployed on the inner-German border (although not at the Berlin Wall) in the early 1970s as part of the ongoing effort to "perfect" the border without having to pay for more *Grenzer*. In addition to the landmines sitting just under the surface of the ground, the SM-70s were mounted at three different heights on the external fence, the final part of the "death strip" before reaching West German territory. They were self-triggering and filled with 110 grams of TNT. When someone breached a signal wire approaching them, he or she would be sprayed with a high velocity cone of more than eighty sharp-edged steel fragments, generally leading to a gruesome death.[104] When the East German economy worsened in the 1980s and Honecker needed more financial aid from West Germany, he decided to remove the SM-70s as a sign of goodwill toward the West. Honecker informed the Politburo of his decision in May 1984.

As Streletz described at the Politburo trial in July 1996, Defense Minister Hoffmann was apparently surprised by the decision and had no idea whether it "had been discussed with the friends" in Moscow. So he quickly sent Streletz to

---

[102] Harrison, *Driving the Soviets up the Wall*, pp. 212–13.

[103] Testimony of Valentin Falin at the NVR trial, spring 1993, in Grafe, *Deutsche Gerechtigkeit*, p. 29.

[104] Gordon L. Rottman, *The Berlin Wall and the Intra-German Border, 1961–89* (Oxford: Osprey Publishing, 2008), p. 21; and "Urteile im letzten Mauerschützenprozeß," *Frankfurter Allgemeine Zeitung*, November 9, 2004.

Moscow in June. Streletz (who reported regularly to the Stasi on Soviet officials and on his senior East German colleagues, including Hoffmann and NVA Chief Kessler, who was then Chief of the General Staff of the army[105]) met with Marshal Viktor Kulikov, Commander in Chief of the Warsaw Pact. Streletz told Kulikov about the "political decision" to remove the SM-70s. Kulikov reported that "his superiors were astounded" but agreed as long as there "would be no cutbacks in the military security of the border."[106] Since the SM-70s were pointed inwards at fleeing East Germans, their deployment would have had no bearing on defending the GDR and the Warsaw Pact from a NATO attack. Thus at East German, not Soviet instigation, the SM-70s were removed.

Also at the Politburo trial, former Politburo member Günter Kleiber expressed his belief that they probably could have changed the practice of shooting at the border under Gorbachev without any problem, something Krenz's lawyer contested.[107] In his verdict in the Politburo trial, Chief Justice Josef Hoch clearly agreed with Klieber and argued: "The accused still contributed to the deaths of refugees when Gorbachev had long ago said that every state in the Warsaw Pact must decide for itself how it would construct socialism. . . .Until the end, refugees were shot because the SED leadership held strong to the border regime."[108] The East German leaders made exceptions to the *Schiessbefehl* during state visits, holidays, and other big events so as not to face any potential uproar if someone was killed at the Berlin Wall while a foreign leader or an important international group was visiting Berlin. As Judge Föhrig said in his verdict in the Border Troops trial, "If it was politically opportune, soldiers were not permitted to shoot anymore."[109] Thus, the GDR leaders did have the capacity to modify the border regime.

In spring 1989, after Chris Gueffroy was killed trying to escape across the Berlin Wall, Honecker finally ended the *Schiessbefehl*. During the Politburo trial, Judge Hoch questioned former NVR chief Streletz about this. Streletz hesitated, no doubt aware that he was about to put a hole in the "don't blame us, blame the Soviets" defense, but then went on to recount his conversation with Krenz on April 3, 1989. As Streletz described it, the West had used "the tragic incident with Mr. Gueffroy" in February to unleash a "massive hate campaign" against the GDR. Krenz (second in importance only to Honecker) called Streletz, instructing: "What we need at the border is calm, order and reason. . . .If possible make sure there is no shooting at the border." Streletz

---

[105] Grafe, *Deutsche Gerechtigkeit*, pp. 33–35.
[106] Streletz's testimony at the Politburo trial, July 11, 1996, ibid., p. 151.
[107] Kleiber in Politburo trial, December 2, 1996, ibid., p. 196.
[108] Chief Justice Josef Hoch's oral verdict in the Politburo trial, August 25, 1997, ibid., pp. 238–39.
[109] Judge Föhrig's verdict in the Border Troops trial, September 10, 1996, ibid., p. 328.

then passed this on verbally.[110] Clearly the GDR leaders could and did modify the *Schiessbefehl* if and when they found it desirable.

While the representatives of the former East German military and political structures were on trial over killings at the Wall, there was a sense from all sides, especially and angrily expressed by the defendants and their lawyers, that the trials were about far more than just the deadly border regime and were really meant to indict the whole former East German regime and maybe even all forty years of East German history. Hence the accused often defended themselves in very broad terms, as Krenz defiantly asserted during the trials: "I have no reason to say that my life I lived in the GDR was wrong."[111] Günter Gabriel, the chief of technology, armaments, and border installations (such as the SM-70s) for the border troops insisted: "[I have been] put on trial only because I lived in the GDR and consciously did my duty.... .I remain convinced that I made an active contribution to the preservation of peace."[112] The defendants felt the trials were an effort to exact "victor's justice." Baumgarten maintained: "This is a collective charge not just against the six generals of the Border Troops. . .but the juridically-veiled politically settling of accounts with the GDR."[113] Krenz told the court: "I am charged because I took part in an anti-capitalist alternative on German soil."[114] Kessler declared: This is an effort to "criminalize people who thought differently."[115]

Of the three Politburo members on trial, only Krenz was linked to the 1984 killing of Michael Schmidt, due to the timing of Krenz's membership on the Politburo. He addressed Michael's father during the trial: "I must say that it really aggrieves me to have the father of a victim sitting across from me and I can only say to him that we could not have done anything [about the border regime].... .I did what I could. I couldn't do more." This of course ignored all the evidence to the contrary. Former border troops chief Baumgarten similarly addressed Horst Schmidt during the Politburo trial, albeit in a more back-handed way: "I can't undo what has happened and also not the fact that your son was in the border area where it was expressly forbidden to go." An observer watched Schmidt "fight back tears of rage."[116]

After the fall of the Wall, Horst Schmidt had "often stood in front of the memorial that was erected for [Michael] on Nordbahn Strasse, and I thought

[110] Streletz's testimony at the Politburo trial, August 8, 1996, ibid., p. 161.

[111] Statement of Krenz at the BGH, October 27, 1999, ibid., p. 252.

[112] Testimony of Günter Gabriel in the Border Troops trial, August 1996, ibid., p. 171.

[113] Baumgarten reading joint statement in the Border Troops trial, November 3, 1995, ibid., p. 59. See also Baumgarten, *Erinnerungen: Autobiographie des Chefs der Grenztruppen der DDR* (Berlin: edition ost, 2008), pp. 241–43, 256–57, 261–62.

[114] Testimony of Krenz in the Politburo trial, February 19, 1996, in Grafe, *Deutsche Gerechtigkeit*, p. 110.

[115] Testimony of Kessler in the NVR trial, September 14, 1993, ibid., p. 29.

[116] Krenz at the Politburo trial, July 24, 1997, ibid., p. 227; and Baumgarten at the Politburo trial, June 5, 1997, ibid., p. 221.

about his terrible death and about how many mostly young people had to die at this damn Wall so that a gang of decaying bigwigs could stay in power as long as possible."[117] Now he was faced with these former "bigwigs" defending themselves. He was particularly incensed when Krenz's lawyer, Dieter Wissgott, declared that instead of being guilty regarding the deaths of people at the border, Krenz was a "national hero" for not calling up military force to stop the toppling of the Wall, following, as Wissgott said, in the footsteps of the courageous group of opposition leaders who attempted to assassinate Hitler on July 20, 1944.[118]

When the lawyer for Horst Schmidt and the other joint plaintiffs, Hanns-Ekkehard Plöger, asked Krenz why no one "gave medical aid to Michael Schmidt" as he lay there wounded and asking for help, Krenz responded: "I am no medical expert...according to the regulations, life was to be saved....I am not a murderer."[119] Herr Schmidt himself confronted Baumgarten on the witness stand at the trial: "[My son] could have been saved. Who is responsible for this lawless situation at the border?" Baumgarten told Schmidt that the delay in bringing his son to a hospital was "due to human error."[120]

Plöger declared in his closing statement at the Politburo trial in July 1997 that the accused were collectively guilty even if they wore "neckties instead of weapons."[121] He ended his statement by reading Horst Schmidt's lengthy, emotional account, "Cold Blooded Murder," of all that Michael and the family were put through during the 1980s until the fall of the Wall, from Michael's desire to leave, the horror of learning Michael had been killed in his attempt to escape, the Stasi pressure and cover-up afterwards, and their lives since without their younger son, whose "sacrificial death contributed to the eventual fall of the Wall of Shame." As Herr Schmidt told a reporter, even thirteen years after Michael was killed, "I still feel the grief....[N]ot a day goes by when I don't think about him...The wound has a little scab, but it hasn't healed. And it will never be healed."[122]

Schabowski observed in his own closing statement that Horst Schmidt's account was "the most depressing document of the trial." When comparing

[117] Horst Schmidt, "Kaltblütiger Mord," 1991.

[118] Grafe, *Deutsche Gerechtigkeit*, p. 234. The judge's verdict in the case of Krenz did in fact take into account his non-use of force to reduce the sentence. Ibid., p. 245.

[119] Krenz at the Politburo trial, July 24, 1997, ibid., p. 229.

[120] Statements by Baumgarten at the Politburo trial, July 5, 1995, ibid., p. 221.

[121] Closing argument by Hanns-Ekkehard Plöger, the representative for the joint plaintiffs in the Politburo trial, August 14, 1994, ibid., p. 237; and Horst Schmidt, "Kaltblütiger Mord," 1991.

[122] Dietmar Jochum, "Das war ein gesetzlosen Haufen, die ganzen Grenzsoldaten. Interview mit Horst Schmidt, Nebenkläger im Politbüro Prozeß," *TP-Presseagentur*, April 21, 2016. Although the interview was apparently published in 2016, it was clearly carried out in 1997, near the end of the Politburo trial and also, as Horst Schmidt says, thirteen years after his son Michael was killed.

Schmidt's words to his "own memories of the last years of the GDR," Schabowski commented, "[t]here is only one possible conclusion: When you sense that a feeling for the individual, human, adverse effects of a policy has been lost, you must either take a stand against this or resign," neither of which Schabowski had done of course, although he expressed much regret and remorse during the trial.

In spite of the often vehement statements made by the accused and their lawyers about their innocence, the members of the Politburo, the NVR, and the Defense Ministry Kollegium, as well as the leaders of the border troops and many of the *Grenzer* were found guilty of direct or indirect manslaughter, complicity to manslaughter, or attempted manslaughter. For three cases of indirect perpetration of manslaughter, Schabowski and Kleiber were each sentenced to three and a half years in prison. For his role in the indirect perpetration of manslaughter of Michael Schmidt and three others, Krenz was sentenced to six and a half years in prison. He was arrested immediately. Horst Schmidt was appalled by the "paternalistically mild" sentences.[123]

In the Border Troops trial, Baumgarten was sentenced to six and a half years in prison for his role in the manslaughter of eight people (including Michael Schmidt) and the attempted manslaughter of five others. Other senior officials in the border troops were given sentences of three to five years. The biggest sentence for an official in the Wall trials was given to former Defense Minister Kessler in the NVR trial: seven and a half years. NVR chief Streletz received five and a half years, and Hans Albrecht received five years and one month. The Defense Ministry Kollegium members received sentences of around three years. None of the former leaders served their full terms in prison, with most being released after completing two-thirds of their sentence due to their advanced age and low likelihood of repeating their crimes. By 2004, fifteen years after the fall of the Wall, they had either died or been released from prison.[124]

As was the case with the two border soldiers who shot Michael Schmidt, most of the *Grenzer* were given suspended sentences. The longest prison term a border soldier received was ten years in a case from 1965 when a commander of the border troops fired thirty shots at a would-be escapee who had already surrendered.[125] The court cases ended in 2004 with trials of three more Politburo members (charged with complicity to manslaughter by negligence, by not undertaking actions to make the border more humane)[126]

[123] Grafe, *Deutsche Gerechtigkeit*, p. 242. The quote from Schabowski is from ibid., p. 238.
[124] After serving their time, the ever-unrepentant Kessler, Streletz, Baumgarten, and their wives were invited by the then-Cuban Defense Minister Raoul Castro for a four-week vacation in 2000 to help them recover. They repeated their Cuban vacations in the following two years. Baumgarten, *Erinnerungen*, pp. 332–33.
[125] Hertle and Nooke, eds., *The Victims at the Berlin Wall*, pp. 197–99.
[126] "Krankheit oder Schuldspruch," *Stern*, August 6, 2004; Hansgeorg Bräutigam, "Die Toten an der Berliner Mauer und an der inner-deutschen Grenze und die

and four engineer officers of the border troops (charged with complicity to manslaughter and attempted manslaughter) involved in key aspects of the deadly border, particularly the installation and maintenance of the SM-70s at the inner-German border.[127] The Politburo members were convicted, but two received suspended sentences and one received no punishment. The military defendants were found guilty but not given any sentence. Since 1991, nearly 500 people were tried in more than 240 trials. Around one-third were found innocent. Half of those convicted received suspended sentences.

While the prosecutors and joint plaintiffs such as Horst Schmidt wanted clear recognition of guilt and long sentences for the accused in the Wall trials and the defendants wanted vindication that they could not have behaved differently, the justifications given in the verdicts shared aspects of both and hint at the complicated reality of the history of the Berlin Wall. An examination of verdicts given by both the Berlin District Court and the BGH in the Michael Schmidt case demonstrates this. In essence, the courts ruled on the two border soldiers Hapke and Walther: yes, they were clearly guilty of manslaughter for multiple reasons; but there were also important extenuating and surrounding circumstances that required the judges not to view the behavior of the accused in a vacuum. One could say that the judges were arguing that there were multiple layers of the history of the Berlin Wall and what took place there and a simple pinpointing of blame was difficult.

Judge Tupperwein in Berlin and the justices at the BGH went into great detail about the documentary, testimonial, and forensic evidence making clear the guilt of Hapke and Walther. In contrast to the trial of border soldiers who had killed Chris Gueffroy where the judge had notably declared that the East German border regulations "deserved no obedience," since the "preservation of life" was more important than any law,[128] Judge Tupperwein focused more on ways in which she believed Hapke and Walther had broken East German laws. In particular, instead of doing the minimum of what would likely have stopped Schmidt's escape (and what according to the 1982 GDR Border Law was supposed to come first after a warning shot), namely firing single targeted shots at his legs, they both fired bursts of sustained shots at him. Walther and Hapke knew beforehand that this would increase the risk of killing the would-be escapee. Second, once their shots had in fact stopped Schmidt and he was lying on the ground without moving and clearly injured,

bundesdeutsche Justiz," *Deutschland Archiv* 37, no. 6 (2004), December 14, 2004, pp. 969, 973–75; and Grafe, *Deutsche Gerechtigkeit*, p. 256.

[127] "Urteile im letzten Mauerschützenprozeß," *Frankfurter Allgemeine Zeitung*, November 9, 2004; and Eike Frenzel, "Die Grenze des Rechtsstaats," *Spiegel*, November 7, 2014.

[128] Rainer Frankel, "Tötung im Interesse der Obrigkeit," *Zeit*, January 24, 1992; and Ahonen, *Death at the Berlin Wall*, pp. 258–59.

neither of them did anything to help save his life.[129] Both the Berlin
Court and the BGH argued, similar to the Gueffroy case, that "the right
to life is the highest of all rights" and that the accused had learned in
school that "orders which were against human rights did not need to be
followed." The Border Law provisions also spoke of the need "to spare
life."

Third, as added by the BGH in its verdict, "[u]nlike those who were given
an order just before shooting, the accused had a certain room for maneuver
due to the sudden appearance of the escapee which meant they had to rely on
themselves only." Thus, they were "not just the accomplices of those who
issued the orders."[130] This was the essential argument in this case. After all, not
all guards fired under such circumstances. In the case of the murder of
Gueffroy at the Berlin Wall, one of the *Grenzer* had not fired, although he
had ordered his partner to shoot. When asked during his later testimony why
he himself as the guard leader did not shoot, he answered, "Because I was too
much of a coward." The judge responded, "Then one can only wish that you
will remain a coward for the rest of your life. If everyone had been this way, we
would not be sitting here today."[131]

In the case against Hapke and Walther, the judges in Berlin and the BGH
maintained, as Horst Schmidt no doubt had in mind regarding the "Cold
Blooded Murder" of his son, that the accused were guilty of brutal, unneces-
sary, and immoral action at the Wall, which caused the death of Michael
Schmidt. The BGH verdict "agreed with the [Berlin District Court] that the
murder of an unarmed refugee by sustained fire under the given circumstances
was an act of such horror and beyond any reasonable justification that it was
obviously an attack against the elementary injunction not to commit murder
even for an indoctrinated person without any further understanding."[132]

Yet the judges' justifications for their verdicts and sentences did not stop
there. They also argued, as Hapke and Walther and others further up the chain

---

[129] For Judge Tupperwein's reasoning in her verdict on the case of Walther and Hapke's
killing of Michael Schmidt, see "Lfd. Nr. 2. Erschießungs eines flüchtenden DDR-
Bürgers-Fall M.-H. Schmidt. Erstinstanzliches Urteil des Landgerichts Berlin vom
5.2.1992, Az. (518) 2 Js 63/90 KLs (57/91)," in Marxen and Gerhard Werle, eds.,
Strafjustiz und DDR-Unrecht, esp. pp. 109–16, 130–32. See also "Schlichte Gemüter,"
Spiegel, October 19, 1992, p. 65.

[130] "Lfd. Nr. 2. Erschießungs eines flüchtenden DDR-Bürgers-Fall M.-H. Schmidt.
Revisionsurteil des Bundesgerichtshofs vom 3.11.1992, Az. 5 StR 370/92," in Marxen
and Werle, eds., *Strafjustiz und DDR-Unrecht*, p. 153. The full texts of the verdicts of the
Berlin District Court on February 5, 1992 and the BGH on November 3, 1992 are also
contained in this volume.

[131] Testimony of the border soldier Mike Schmidt (no relation to Michael Schmidt who was
killed at the Wall) from the Chris Gueffroy case at the Border Troops trial, March 8,
1996, in Grafe, *Deutsche Gerechtigkeit*, p. 121.

[132] Ibid., p. 154.

of command believed, that there was more to understanding what happened on December 1, 1984 and on other similar occasions. The judges pointed to many extenuating circumstances that led to their decision to suspend the sentences they gave Walther and Hapke. These included more personal circumstances: both of the accused made extensive confessions; regretted what they had done; were upstanding members of society with jobs, wives, and children; and the circumstances under which the crimes were committed had ceased to exist with the fall of the SED regime and the unification of Germany, making it highly improbable that they would repeat the crime. Broader political, social, military, and international circumstances also played a role, starting with the intense pressure in the GDR to conform in general and specifically for the *Grenzer* "at the bottom of the societal and military hierarchy."

Expecting them to have countermanded the military orders and political atmosphere, "especially on such an explosive matter as the *Schiessbefehl* would only have been possible with rare civic courage and under the acceptance of fear of being spied on, criminal punishment and detrimental effects on a future career," as the Berlin verdict stated.[133] The BGH noted that as far as the judges knew, there were no cases in the GDR of "people in positions of responsibility in politics, leadership of the troops, law, [or] science making public an opposition to killing at the border. No trials were carried out against [border] guards."[134] Furthermore, the judge argued, "the crime did not come from self-interest or criminal energy but from circumstances over which they had no influence, such as the political and military confrontation in divided Germany, the particular conditions in the former GDR, and with this in mind certainly [also] the uncritical willingness of the accused to follow an order that was unlawful."[135] Thus, the BGH found that it was not really fair to ask Walther and Hapke to have done more than all these other people "who had a much broader overview and a more differentiated education" had done.[136] The BGH concluded that the two defendants "were to a certain degree also victims of all the circumstances associated with this border."[137]

In sum, the defendants were both perpetrators and victims of the regime at the Berlin Wall. This message from the trials did not fully satisfy anyone, and certainly not Horst Schmidt, but it may have come closest to reflecting the complicated history of the Wall.

While Schmidt campaigned for a detailed memory of what the Berlin Wall had entailed, wider German society in the 1990s and into the 2000s was in fact

---

[133] Berlin District Court verdict, ibid., p. 131.
[134] Ibid., p. 154.
[135] Ibid., p. 132.
[136] Ibid., p. 155.
[137] Ibid.

more engaged in older memories–that is, to the extent that people thought about the past instead of just focusing on the demands of the present. When Germany united, the older generation of both Eastern and Western Germans shared in common not only their involvement with the Nazi regime but also the losses they and their families had suffered during and after the war. While the Wall trials were taking place, Germans were engaged in lengthy public debates about coming to terms with the Holocaust[138] and how and whether this could be captured in a national memorial.[139] There were also widespread discussions about what millions of Germans had endured during the Allied bombings[140] and with the expulsion of ethnic Germans from their homes in the east which will be discussed further in Chapter Four.[141] This all left relatively little space for those who felt it was important to remember, grapple with, and even commemorate the more recent past related to the Berlin Wall. Throughout these first years after the fall of the Wall, however, there were some who insisted that Germans must remember the history of the Wall, preserve some sections of it, and commemorate its victims. It is to these activists we turn in the next chapter.

---

[138] Daniel Jonah Goldhagen, *Hitler's Willing Executioners: Ordinary Germans and the Holocaust* (New York: Knopf, 1996); and Volker Ullrich, "Daniel J. Goldhagen in Deutschland: Die Buchtournee wurde zum Triumphzug," *Zeit*, September 13, 1996.

[139] Niven, *Facing the Nazi Past*, pp. 194–232.

[140] Jörg Friedrich, *Der Brand. Deutschland im Bombenkrieg, 1940–1945* (Berlin: Propyläen, 2002); and W. G. Sebald, *Luftkrieg und Literatur* (Munich: Carl Hanser, 1999).

[141] "German Government Approves Expellees Museum," *Spiegel*, March 19, 2008; Charles Hawley, "Germany and Its World War II Victims: Historians Condemn Commemoration Day Proposal," *Spiegel*, February 15, 2011; and Günter Grass, *Im Krebsgang* (Göttingen: Steidl, 2002).

2

The Fight over Memory at Bernauer Strasse

For many years after the fall of the Wall, a small minority of memory activists worked to counter the majority impulse to remove the Wall from the landscape and from memory. The combination of the physical dismantling of the Wall, the joyous performances of Beethoven, and the trials connected to deaths at the Wall were all meant to draw that period of German history to a close–or just remember the happy end of it–and allow people to move on, even as others were focused on the deeper, more problematic past connected to the Holocaust. Pastor Manfred Fischer, however, sought to keep attention on the Wall and was seized by the instinct to treat it as a crime scene: by protecting it from anyone who sought to remove a part of it.[1] He understood, as Michael Schmidt's father Horst did, that people had been killed at the Wall and that this should not be forgotten.

Fischer had his own painful experience with the Berlin Wall. Since 1975 he had been the pastor of West Berlin's Reconciliation parish. When the East Germans erected the Wall in 1961, it divided his parish and literally surrounded the massive red brick Church of Reconciliation, which had been built in 1892, prohibiting its use for anything other than as a post for border soldiers in the death strip. Since the parish house had been on the East Berlin side of the Wall, the church built a new parish house on the West Berlin side of Bernauer Strasse in 1965, including a room for worship on the second floor that had a view into the border zone across the street and of the lonely church within it.

Ten years after Fischer arrived at Bernauer Strasse, the GDR authorities blew up the Church of Reconciliation. In two violent steps in January 1985, they first demolished the nave (Figure 5), and then the church tower a week later. While the congregation had not been able to get to their church for decades, the vision of the church steeple reaching up above the Wall helped them hold out hope that they would someday be able to use it again. Now that hope was gone. Watching the seventy-five-meter-tall tower keeling over and crashing to the ground in a plume of smoke was devastating.

---

[1] Interview with Manfred Fischer, October 6, 2009; and Fischer, "Leben mit der Mauer: Reflexionen eines Betroffenen," in Peter Möbius and Helmut Trotnow, eds., *Mauern sind nicht für ewig gebaut: Zur Geschichte der Berliner Mauer* (Berlin: Propyläen, 1990), p. 78.

The pastor organized a three-day ceremony to bid farewell to the church, his first major public performance as a memory activist connected to the Berlin Wall and far from his last. Indeed, in the years after the fall of the Berlin Wall, Fischer would become perhaps the most important memory activist fighting to preserve some of the remains of the Wall and to transform the area around his parish center on Bernauer Strasse into an official Berlin Wall Memorial. He was one of the few who sympathized with the November 10, 1989 appeal of former chancellor and West Berlin mayor Willy Brandt, "to leave standing a piece of this abominable edifice" to help future generations understand what Germans had lived through.[2]

In the tumultuous weeks and months following the toppling of the Wall, Fischer and some other activists and officials were able to preserve a few remnants of the Wall at several locations, as described in Chapter One, none of which were guaranteed to last, since initially there was no widespread popular or official support to preserve parts of the Wall: a block-long section of the Wall at Bernauer Strasse; another of similar length at Niederkirchner Strasse, directly above the ruins of the Gestapo cellars and across the street from the Berlin parliament building; a long section at a historic Prussian cemetery, the Invalidenfriedhof; a section near the Reichstag; and a nearly mile-long expanse called the "East Side Gallery" where artists from around the world celebrated the fall of the Wall by painting it with more than 100 murals. Fischer's sustained efforts over many years at Bernauer Strasse, combined with those of an official at the German Historical Museum, Helmut Trotnow, are the main reason there is now a Berlin Wall Memorial that educates hundreds of thousands of people each year about the history of the Berlin Wall and Bernauer Strasse. As the mayor of Berlin, Klaus Wowereit, observed when awarding Fischer the Federal Order of Merit in 2013, "His example shows how a single person through his civic engagement in society can have an impact, can instigate and shape a central issue,"[3] namely the memory of the Berlin Wall.

Pastor Manfred Fischer

Fischer had long liked a challenge. In fact, this is what had attracted him to West Berlin and the Reconciliation parish to begin with: he wanted to be in West Berlin, near the Wall, in a community that needed him. After growing up in Frankfurt am Main, Fischer was inspired by the student movement of the 1960s, which was particularly strong at the universities in West Berlin. At the

---

[2] Willy Brandt's speech, Rathaus Schöneberg, Berlin, November 10, 1989, www.willy-brandt-biografie.de/quellen/bedeutende-reden/rede-vor-dem-rathaus-schoeneberg-zum-fall-der-berliner-mauer-10-november-1989/.

[3] Der Regierende Bürgermeister, Senatskanzlei, "Wowereit überreicht Pfarrer Manfred Fischer Bundesverdienstkreuz–Bildtermin," press release, March 11, 2013.

age of twenty-one, he began his studies at the Church University of West Berlin in 1969. Students there and throughout the country were questioning the whole postwar system in West Germany, including the universities, the government, and even their parents, about their roles during the Nazi period. In the students' eyes there were too many Nazi-era holdovers in universities, the law, the economy, and in other positions of responsibility. It was a time of protest and change, and Fischer soaked it all up. When he finished his interdisciplinary religious studies, he was offered several church positions and took the one with the Reconciliation community on Bernauer Strasse.[4]

The plan was for him to be trained for two years by a pastor there, but as it turned out there was no pastor and Fischer was left to figure things out as he went. Few members of the clergy wanted to come to the isolated city of West Berlin and even fewer wanted to be right up against the Berlin Wall "at the end of the world," as Fischer would call it.[5] This was definitely the challenge the twenty-seven-year-old clergyman was looking for, and it also offered him the chance to be innovative in formulating ways to serve the community in what had become a run-down area in the Wedding district of West Berlin. The first person Fischer met upon his arrival was a bailiff who asked him for the address of a debtor in his congregation.[6] Coming from a working-class neighborhood in northern Frankfurt, this kind of environment was quite familiar to him.[7]

In the aftermath of the erection of the Wall in 1961, the area could no longer play its former role as a key thoroughfare between northern and central Berlin. Businesses closed down as many of their former customers were trapped on the other side of the Wall, and people moved away from the front line. Like so many others, the Reconciliation congregation was divided by the Wall. From the second and third floors of the parish building and from the pastor's apartment there, Fischer could see the death strip and the border guards and hear the barking of the guard dogs. At night the beams of the floodlights in the death strip reached his apartment.[8]

The end of Bernauer Strasse, just two blocks from the parish center, was closed off by the Wall on two sides (as seen in Figure 1), making the area feel particularly isolated. In the first days after the border was sealed, some of the residents had jumped from their houses on the eastern side of the street to freedom on the western side. Residents on the western side would help build tunnels in the following years to assist others in escaping from the East. The

---

[4] Interview with Manfred Fischer, October 6, 2009.

[5] "Manfred Fischer, der Pfarrer an der Mauer," February 23, 2013, www.evangelisch.de/inhalte/79123/23-02-2013/manfred-fischer-der-pfarrer-der-mauer.

[6] Christina Fischer, "Ewige Suche nach Gemeinsamkeiten," *Berliner Zeitung*, October 2, 1999.

[7] Interview with Rainer Just, June 26, 2018.

[8] Christine Richter, "Der lange Streit um die Mauer ist zu Ende," *Berliner Zeitung*, August 13, 1998.

houses on the eastern side of the street were evacuated, walled up, and eventually demolished. Bernauer Strasse was not a happy place to live. With scant optimism about the future of the area, many people resorted to alcohol and drug use.

This was the situation when Manfred Fischer arrived in 1975. He wanted to help people who felt down-and-out, following in the footsteps of previous clergymen in the Reconciliation community who had served to alleviate social problems among the population since the church opened in 1894.[9] He was a passionate, creative, deeply religious man, and he threw himself into his new position, never dreaming that he would end up staying there for thirty-eight years under vastly changing circumstances.

Increasingly worried about the slum-like neighborhood, in the 1970s the city of West Berlin decided to carry out a wholesale redevelopment of the area. Since it was less expensive to tear down thousands of old houses and build new ones than to renovate the old ones, this is what the city did in the late 1970s and early 1980s, implementing the largest such redevelopment project in Europe at the time. Municipal officials also persuaded thousands of people to move to new housing in the Reinickendorf district in the northern part of West Berlin, since the redevelopment involved reducing the housing stock by 50 percent. The process was accompanied by angry protests as people felt their lives were being uprooted for the second time in little more than twenty years, the erection of the Berlin Wall being the first. Fischer and his parishioners were part of these protests against what he called the "cold redevelopment" of the neighborhood.[10]

In an effort to forestall the city's demolition of the neighboring Schrippen Church, Fischer and others from the parish had taken part in the occupation of the building in late 1979. The Reconciliation and Schippen churches had long had close ties. Due to bomb damage to the Church of Reconciliation during World War II, parishioners had worshipped in the Schrippen Church from 1943 until 1949 while some of the damage was repaired in their own church. They used the Schrippen Church again from 1961 to 1965 when the Church of Reconciliation was off-limits behind the Berlin Wall and until the new parish house was completed on the western side of Bernauer Strasse. The Schrippen Church had opened its doors in 1902 and got its name from the rolls of bread (called *Schrippen* in Berlin) given to the very poor parishioners, along with coffee, before church services. Over the decades of its existence, it helped people of all ages who were unemployed and homeless, including orphans, young pregnant women, drug addicts, the ill, the aged and infirm, and generally people in need. The Schrippen

---

[9] Helmut Trotnow, "Understanding the Present by Looking Back at the Past," in The Berlin Wall – Memorial Site and Exhibition Center Association, ed., *Berlin Wall: Memorial Site Exhibition Center and the Chapel of Reconciliation on Bernauer Strasse* (Berlin: Jaron, 1999), p. 9.

[10] "31: Sanierungsgebiet Wedding," *berlin: street. berlin für neugierige*, www.berlinstreet.de/ brunnenstrasse/brunnen31.

Church also gave people jobs: sorting through all the discarded clothes and other household items picked up around Berlin, which they then repaired and used or sold to make money to buy the rolls and coffee for the community. The church's altruistic mission was one shared by Fischer, and he became very involved in the Schrippen Church as did many of his parishioners.[11]

They were, therefore, quite angry when the city destroyed the Schrippen Church in March 1980. The experience likely contributed to Fischer's decision, together with the parish council, to hire a public relations expert, Rainer Just, in 1981, to help connect to the neighborhood and beyond on the redevelopment issue and many others. Fischer did his best to help the residents, opening his parish house to people protesting the plans to demolish houses and lobbying the West Berlin government to respond to their concerns.[12] When the redevelopment process was finally completed in 1983–84, the pastor planned a much-needed sabbatical for the following year in the United States.

The lost battles in the redevelopment process were not the only matters weighing heavily on Fischer before leaving for sabbatical. Dramatic and sometimes opaque developments had been brewing with regard to the future of the Church of Reconciliation standing in the Berlin Wall border zone. In the aftermath of the erection of the Wall and the closure of the church, the parish community in East Berlin had joined the neighboring Elisabeth Church, leaving no recognized authority to represent the interests of the former Reconciliation parish. Central church leaders in East Berlin had been pushing for the removal of the sacred and artistic objects from the closed-up church so as to either display them in another church or safeguard them for some future day when the church might be open again. The mayor of Mitte, the district of East Berlin where the church was located, declared that the objects could only be transferred if central church leaders gave permission to demolish the church. The church leaders refused.

In early 1982, Manfred Stolpe became the Consistorial President of the eastern part of the then-divided Protestant Church Council of Berlin and Brandenburg. The ambitious Stolpe developed a plan that he thought would gain support from both his political and church colleagues: a land swap. If

---

[11] After the fall of the Wall, Fischer would become the chairman not only of the Berlin Wall Association based at his Reconciliation parish, but also the chairman of the Schrippen Church Association. On the Schrippen Church and on its ties with the Church of Reconciliation, see Evangelische Versöhnungsgemeinde, *100 Jahre Versöhnungskirche – von der richtigen Seite betrachtet konnte man sie regelrecht schön finden, Schriftenreihe Wedding, Band 7* (Berlin: Mackensen, 1994); Gerrit Wegener, "Die Versöhnungskapelle in Berlin-Mitte" (Munich: GRIN, 2007); Cornelia Frey, "Countdown zum Überfall," *Zeit* 14 (March 28, 1980); and schrippenkirche.eu/. See also the documentary about the Schrippen Church, including an interview with Fischer: Helmut Zermin, "Geschichte der Schrippenkirche und des Verein Schrippenkirche e.V in Berlin Wedding" (April 30, 2017), www.youtube.com/watch?v=GMdtaaMMxnc.

[12] Interview with Manfred Fischer, October 6, 2009.

Fischer's Reconciliation parish in West Berlin would agree to give up the land and church, transferring them to the East Berlin central church leadership, the latter could then find another piece of land elsewhere in East Berlin for a new parish center. Since the Reconciliation congregation no longer existed in East Berlin, the parish center would be for other Protestants in East Berlin who had no place of worship for their community. Instead of holding on to a church that was unused and impossible to access, Fischer and his superiors serving on the West Berlin side of the Protestant Church Council would thus enable more East Berliners to have a place of worship.

In April 1983, the East Berlin representatives on the Church Council proposed the exchange to the West Berlin representatives, and in May the latter asked Fischer and his parish council to agree. As the historian Christian Halbrock has observed in his study of the matter, the thirty-five-year-old pastor no doubt "felt himself overwhelmed by the situation. Due to the democratic principles of the church synod, all responsibility rested on him and the parish council." In addition, "the engagement of the [church] consistories in the West and East as well as the [favorable] vote of the [church] superintendent in Wedding," the district of Berlin where Fischer's parish was located, all made it clear that the land swap issue was one that "had implications far beyond the bounds of just [Fischer's] parish" and that he was being pressed to agree. Rainer Just remembered years later how alone Fischer felt at the time.[13]

It was hard to imagine that the division of Berlin and Germany would end any time soon, enabling access to the Church of Reconciliation. Hence, relinquishing the church and the land seemed to be the realistic thing to do. Hidden behind this, however, was a sense of the possibility or even likelihood of the East Germans destroying the Church of Reconciliation if the deal went through.

In May 1983 Fischer met twice with his parish council and, on May 31, Fischer and the parish council agreed to give up the land and the church "putting aside their reservations." In April 1984, the land swap was implemented and the Church of Reconciliation and its land no longer belonged to Fischer's parish. Fischer himself had not felt a connection to the huge old church in the death strip, but he was still unsettled by it all and uncertain as to what would happen next.[14]

In the summer of 1984, Fischer was feeling the effects of these disquieting developments as well as the impact of nine years of hard work in his parish community in the face of the West Berlin demolition and renovation process. He developed asthma and at times required oxygen to help him breathe. The

---

[13] Interview with Rainer Just, June 26, 2018.

[14] Unless otherwise noted, this section on what led up to the demolition of the Church of Reconciliation in 1985 is drawn from the study by Christian Halbrock, "Weggesprengt: Die Versöhnungskirche im Todesstreifen der Berliner Mauer 1961–1985," *Horch und Guck* (special issue, 2008), pp. 61–68.

pastor needed a break and requested a year-long sabbatical in the USA to give him a chance to learn all he could about how American churches engaged in outreach with their communities. He hoped to learn how he could help develop new church communications strategies in Germany,[15] as he sought to reach more people and persuade them to come to church at a time when fewer and fewer people in Germany were regular churchgoers. Church leaders granted him permission to go. Fischer would rely on his close colleague and friend Rainer Just to manage things while he was away.[16]

While in the United States, the young pastor wanted a chance to think about the next step in his career, feeling that after nearly ten years with the Reconciliation parish it was time to move on. Fischer spent time in Manhattan and Los Angeles in 1984–85, visiting many churches and surveying the art scene. Years later Fischer would remember vividly his experience of being the only white person in a church in Harlem, moved by the passion and participation of African Americans in the service. He did all he could to experience the broad artistic and cultural scene and its connection to churches and return with new ideas, inspired by the wide-ranging ways American churches were connecting with the community.

Thus it was that Manfred Fischer was in the United States watching television when he saw the Church of Reconciliation being blown up by the East Germans in January 1985. In December 1984, sacred and artistic pieces had been removed from the church nave, and in early January 1985 preparations for demolition began. On January 18, the bells and clock were taken from the church tower, and the East Germans announced they would demolish the nave on January 22 and the tower on February 12. Signs had been put up on Bernauer Strasse the day before announcing the demolition.[17] The media picked this up and journalists from all over the world camped out with their cameras to capture the moments when the East Germans blew up first the nave of the church on January 22 (Figure 5) and then the church tower. Although they originally planned to destroy the tower in February, in view of the international condemnation of the destruction of the nave and calls to keep the tower, the SED regime decided to get rid of the tower as soon as possible, demolishing it on January 28.[18]

---

[15] Interviews with Manfred Fischer, October 6, 2009, and Rainer Just, June 26, 2018.

[16] Interview with Rainer Just, June 26, 2018.

[17] The Berlin Wall – Memorial Site and Exhibition Center Association, ed., *Berlin Wall: Memorial Site*, p. 43.

[18] "Abriß der Versöhnungskirche an der Bernauer Strasse," *Tagesspiegel*, January 16, 1985; and "Schiff der Versöhnungskirche an Bernauer Strasse gesprengt," *Tagesspiegel*, January 23, 1985. For video footage of the demolition of the nave and tower and an interview with Pastor Johannes Hildebrandt, whose father had been the minister of the Church of Reconciliation before the Wall was erected, see rbb, Die Berliner Mauer, Geschichte in Bildern, "22. Januar 1985: Versöhnungskirche gesprengt," www.berlin-mauer.de/videos/sprengung-der-versoehnungskirche-695/.

Figure 5 Demolition of nave of Church of Reconciliation as seen from the balcony of the Reconciliation parish center, Bernauer Strasse, January 22, 1985
Source: Archive, Versöhnungsgemeinde Berlin-Wedding, F-030506.

Always in need of hard currency, the East German regime had a television crew film it all and then sold the rights to ABC News.[19] This is presumably how Fischer saw it on television in the USA. Not even five years after he had witnessed the destruction of the Schrippen Church, it was quite a shock to see a second church so important to his parish be demolished: "I almost fell out of my chair, I never thought they would really blow up the church."[20]

Years later, Fischer recalled feeling that it was "impossible" not to agree to the wishes of the East Berlin church to create another space for Protestant worshippers and thus to surrender the church and its land in the death strip to enable this.[21] Fischer's agreement no doubt contributed to the East German leadership's move in 1985 to demolish the church and probably haunted Fischer long afterwards, going a long way to explaining his passionate and persistent activism in pushing to remember the Wall after 1989.[22] Knowing Fischer was out of the country may have made it easier for the East German

---

[19] Halbrock, "Weggesprengt."

[20] Uwe Aulich, "Stücke eines gesprengten Gotteshauses: Ausstellung zur Geschichte der Versöhnungsgemeinde," *Berliner Zeitung*, October 10, 1998.

[21] "Manfred Fischer, der Pfarrer an der Mauer," February 23, 2013.

[22] Thomas Rogalla, "Mauerpfarrer Manfred Fischer ist tot," *Berliner Zeitung*, December 9, 2013; and Halbrock, "Weggesprengt."

leaders, who probably believed that without him around his parishioners might not protest the destruction as vociferously.

In the wake of the demolition of the church, Fischer consulted by phone with Rainer Just back at Bernauer Strasse about whether to return to Berlin or complete his sabbatical year. Perhaps surprisingly, they decided he should stay in the USA until the end of his sabbatical in the summer.[23] The pastor now put aside any thoughts of finding another position. As he put it later, "there was *so little* on American television about Germany, so it was a huge thing that the destruction of the church was shown on television there. It felt like a clear answer to what I was supposed to do: go home and stay with the parish. Sort of like the voice of God."[24]

When he returned months later, Fischer saw how upset some of his parishioners were. He had never liked the massive neo-Gothic church from the days of the Kaiser, and he felt it would have been much too big for the small postwar, post-Wall parish. But now he understood that it had remained a psychological force in their lives: seeing it on the other side of the Wall was painful but also had given the parishioners a sense of hope that one day they would regain access to it. From the windows of his apartment and from the hall of worship in the Reconciliation parish building, Fischer looked out every day on the church and the Wall. Now the latter remained without the former. As Fischer put it later to a documentary journalist: "The question was: what now? Should the parish continue to exist? It was a low point for the congregation."[25] He realized it was important to mourn the loss and began planning a way to do this.[26]

In May 1986, the pastor oversaw a three-day ceremony of mourning featuring a speech, discussions, a dance performance, music, and an art exhibit.[27] A natural fighter himself, Fischer sought to strengthen people's willpower to resist not just the Wall but also other threats such as nuclear weapons, consumer culture, or even the high cost of meat. To address his parishioners and other guests at the ceremony, Fischer stood on the platform that had been used by politicians, tourists, and others to look over into the death strip. A loudspeaker broadcast his words to both sides of the Wall and border soldiers (*Grenzer*) watched from windows in the guard tower behind him. Fischer looked at the people gathered below him on Bernauer Strasse and enjoined them to "come together... We invite you to have the courage to leap over walls that divide us. We invite you to

[23] Interview with Rainer Just, June 26, 2018.

[24] Interview with Manfred Fischer, October 6, 2009.

[25] Manfred Fischer in video interview with Ralf Gründer, "Symbolishe Handlungen tragen die stille Kraft," September 10, 1999, archive of Versöhnungsgemeinde, Berlin-Wedding.

[26] Ibid.

[27] Interview with Manfred Fischer, October 6, 2009. See also the flyer from the three-day event, "Kunst & Kirche," May 23–25, 1986, archive of the Versöhnungsgemeinde, Berlin-Wedding.

gain courage from this ceremony. We *can* do something. And if we have trust in symbolic actions, we know that symbols have a quiet power to transform the 'impossible' into possibilities."[28] The dedicated clergyman would try to use the destruction of the Church of Reconciliation as a chance to bring people together and to urge them to be active citizens. The wide-ranging discussions with parish members and others combined with the art exhibit were all organized around the slogan "Leap Across the Wall" (*Mauersprung*). Fischer sought to foster the conviction that people could "make the leap" and take action in their daily lives instead of passively accepting losses, even as he no doubt struggled to accept the role his agreement to give up the Church of Reconciliation had played in the destruction of the church.

The pastor had returned from the USA full of ideas about creative ways to reach his parishioners and neighbors. One participant in the May 1986 commemoration told Fischer how inspired she was by the discussions in his parish that went beyond the old "conservative approach examining the meaning of the Bible in this and that passage" and instead talked about what it meant for them in their lives at the time.[29] Indeed, German public television station ZDF would do a story the following year about the kinds of innovative approaches Fischer took as a pastor. He reflected on camera that "the demolition of the church" in the border strip seemed to him to be "a symbol of the end of a certain kind of church," the old huge churches with great distance between the minister and the congregants. Fischer practiced a much less hierarchical approach. He believed that churches must be built from people, not from bricks and mortar. He invited congregants to sit with him around a table after the church services and made them feel that "criticisms and ideas were welcome." This oval table would become the inspiration decades later for the design of the Chapel of Reconciliation that would be erected where the church had been.

As young and old gathered with him, they spoke about issues in their daily lives and about faith. Not only did he welcome them inside the provisional church on the top floor of the parish building, but he went out into the neighborhood to meet people where they were. Fischer and Just had, in fact, started a series of walks around the community for people to learn about its history and get to know each other. It was Just who helped Fischer plan the three-day ceremony in 1986, videoed some of it, and would be at Fischer's

---

[28] The text of Fischer's *Mauerrede* or "Wall speech" was printed in the flyer, "Kunst & Kirche," and a video of him making the speech is available, "Pfarrer Manfred Fischer – Mauer Predigt," May 26, 1986, archive of the Versöhnungsgemeinde, Berlin-Wedding; and "81. Manuskriptseite der Predigt," in Möbius and Trotnow, eds., *Mauern sind nicht für ewig gebaut*. See also Manfred Fischer, "The History of the 'Chapel of Reconciliation'," in The Berlin Wall – Memorial Site and Exhibition Center Association, ed., *Berlin Wall: Memorial Site*, pp. 34–35.

[29] "Pfarrer Manfred Fischer – Mauer Predigt."

side for many more significant activities at the church over the next decades.[30]

Three years later, when widespread protests swept the GDR in the fall of 1989, Fischer followed the developments closely and with concern. Ironically, the man of faith had no faith that the citizens on the streets could prevail. He thought their marches, candles, songs, and chants of "No violence!" ("*Keine Gewalt!*"), would be met with a bloodbath. When the Wall opened on the night of November 9, Fischer was still worried. Some of his parishioners went over to the East. He feared they would be imprisoned, but his fears proved unfounded.[31] Fischer himself biked only as far as one of the border crossing points, Invalidenstrasse, to see the scene. He felt jubilation but also some uneasiness about what would happen next. He sensed that much would change on both sides of the Wall in the weeks and months to come.[32] And he was not happy with all the so-called Wall peckers who began to chip away at the Wall at Bernauer Strasse and elsewhere:

> I couldn't bring myself to hammer on the Wall and take a piece as a souvenir. It was a death machine, not a souvenir. It was dangerous. We must retain part of it so people will have *some* idea of what it was like. I had an instinct but not a plan. I just knew that we needed to secure the crime scene, preserve the clues. And to do that, we needed to get some of the Wall declared a historic landmark that could not be touched.[33]

Luckily for Fischer, he soon met someone with whom he could join forces to make this happen.

Initial Efforts to Create a Berlin Wall Memorial at Bernauer Strasse

Helmut Trotnow was a historian working at the Federal Republic's German Historical Museum (*Deutsches Historisches Museum*, DHM) as the head of the department for history and memorial sites. He had the same instinct Fischer did that some of the Wall must be saved as a memorial and was dismayed at all the people removing pieces of it. While Fischer had an emotional engagement with the history of the Berlin Wall that fueled his approach, Trotnow had a more intellectual basis for his conviction that the history of the Wall must be remembered. Trained as a historian in West Germany and England and having no relatives in the GDR, Trotnow had an outsider's approach. From his time studying in England, he had encountered people's fascination with the division of Berlin by a Wall. Living in West Berlin when the Wall fell, he witnessed the

---

[30] See the ZDF "Tagebuch" section of the video compilation, "Pfarrer Manfred Fischer – Mauer Predigt."

[31] Interview with Manfred Fischer, October 6, 2009.

[32] Christina Fischer, "Ewige Suche nach Gemeinsamkeiten," *Berliner Zeitung*, October 2, 1999.

[33] Interview with Manfred Fischer, October 6, 2009.

continuation of this fascination, albeit in a different way as people flocked to the city to take pieces of the fallen Wall. Trotnow's historian's instinct told him that the Wall was now a unique artifact that could offer future generations a glimpse of a whole period of German and world history. He was certain that future generations would have many questions about the Wall and the division; questions that preserving some of the Wall for a Berlin Wall Memorial could help answer.[34]

Trotnow initially had to fight an uphill battle among his West German colleagues to convince them that there should be a Berlin Wall Memorial. They were shocked at his proposal, which they thought was nonsensical. They assumed everyone would want the Wall to be completely torn down and left in the past.[35] Furthermore, coming from the West, most of them felt no connection to the Berlin Wall or to the East in general, a sentiment the interior minister, Wolfgang Schäuble, observed among colleagues as well.[36] They could not imagine that there was any need to save some part of what they saw as East German history. Trotnow kept explaining to them and to others, as did Fischer, that there should be a place to remember victims of the Wall, a place where family members could go to mourn their lost loved ones.

In the winter of 1989–90, Trotnow reached out to his counterpart Peter Möbius at the GDR Museum of German History to work together to gain support from their governments for preserving part of the Wall. They quickly agreed that Bernauer Strasse should be the focus of their efforts because of the dramatic history connected to the Wall there. Indeed, photographs and television footage from Bernauer Strasse had sent dramatic images around the world in the days and years after the border was sealed, with many of the images becoming iconic. The border between East and West Berlin divided the two sides of the street. Images of the aftermath of August 13, 1961 included a woman sliding down a rope from her apartment on the East Berlin side of the street to the West Berlin sidewalk just below. Other East Germans jumped out of their windows into nets held by firemen, some making it safely and others, such as Ida Siekmann, a fifty-nine-year-old nurse, dying in the process. There were even instances of East German border guards entering people's apartments to stop them from escaping and trying to pull them back in through the window as West Berliners below tried to help the would-be escapees down to the street.

---

[34] Interview with Helmut Trotnow, March 17, 2010.

[35] Ibid.; see also Trotnow's remarks at the roundtable discussion, "Gesprächsrunde: 'Gefunden und verloren: Metamorphose von der Sperranlage zum (fast verschwundenen) Denkmal'," in Deutsches Nationalkomitee für Denkmalschutz, *Tagung Mauer und Grenze – Denkmal und Gedenken, Schriftenreihe des Deutschen Nationalkomitees für Denkmalschutz* 76, no. 2 (October 2009), pp. 55 and 62.

[36] Interview with Wolfgang Schäuble, May 26, 2004.

Less dramatic, but very moving nonetheless, was the image of parents in their apartment on the East Berlin side of the street using a clothes line to lower down a bouquet of flowers to a bridal pair standing on the sidewalk in West Berlin below.[37] A photographer from Hamburg captured the moment when nineteen-year-old border soldier Conrad Schumann jumped over the barbed wire on August 15, throwing off his submachine gun while in the air above the wire. AP bought the picture of Schumann's leap to the West and it was featured on the front pages of newspapers around the globe.[38] As the months and years went by, people dug tunnels under the Wall at Bernauer Strasse, helped by the fact that the water table there was relatively low, making it less likely the tunnels would be flooded when it rained. In 1964, fifty-seven people were able to escape using one such tunnel before the East German authorities were alerted and closed it down.[39] Trotnow, Fischer, and others, including some government officials, would repeatedly refer to both the events themselves and their resonance throughout the world as justification for preserving some of the Berlin Wall on Bernauer Strasse and creating a memorial.

Since Bernauer Strasse was in a less central location than the Brandenburg Gate or Checkpoint Charlie, Trotnow and Möbius felt they had a far better chance of being able to preserve the Wall there than at the other world-famous sites that attracted Wall peckers coming to take their own pieces of the Wall. That was also the reason that multiple parts of the border installations, not just the external and internal Wall, remained largely intact at Bernauer Strasse. Around New Year's, Trotnow and Möbius met Fischer for the first time. He recounted to them many personal stories about how the Wall had affected people's lives at Bernauer Strasse, and they became even more convinced that this was the place for a Wall Memorial.[40] They sought to protect a block-long section of the outer and inner Wall and border strip there between Ackerstrasse and Bergstrasse, across the street from Fischer's parish building.

Fischer was deeply gratified by their support for his plans to remember the history of the Wall, arguing: "In order for a person to grasp something, he needs something to grasp on to," namely, a section of the Wall.[41] The pastor

---

[37] Gabriele Riedle, "Wo genau stand die Mauer?" *Zeit Online*, August 2, 1991. The CNN *Cold War* series documentary featured many of these dramatic scenes, particularly in Episode 9 about the Berlin Wall, "Mousetrap."

[38] "Conrad Schumann; Soldier Photographed Fleeing to West Berlin," *Los Angeles Times*, June 23, 1998; and Imre Karacs, "The Leap of Hope That Ended in Despair," *Independent*, June 24, 1998.

[39] Gregg Mitchell, *The Tunnels: Escapes under the Berlin Wall and the Historic Films the JFK White House Tried to Kill* (New York: Crown, 2016); and Thomas Henseler and Susanne Buddenberg, *Tunnel 57: A True Escape Story* (Berlin: Ch. Links, 2013).

[40] Interview with Helmut Trotnow, March 17, 2010.

[41] Thomas Rogalla, "Mauerpfarrer Manfred Fischer ist tot," *Berliner Zeitung*, December 9, 2013; and Florian Fuchs, "Wie Pastor Manfred Fischer erst unter dem Betonwall litt – und ein Stück davon nach 189 rettete," *Süddeutsche Zeitung*, August 13/14/15, 2011.

felt that he and Trotnow were "the perfect team" and that it was a "stroke of good luck" that they met. Fischer's participation in protests against government policies over the years had not endeared him to politicians, but Trotnow was a DHM official and thus had good connections to Chancellor Kohl's government. It had after all been Kohl's idea to create the DHM as a federal institution. With Trotnow working the government angle and Fischer working on the ground at Bernauer Strasse, they could hopefully get somewhere in bucking the mass euphoria for tearing down the Wall.[42] At the time and indeed for many years, most people told Fischer and Trotnow they were crazy to want to create a Berlin Wall Memorial. Many were even hostile toward their efforts as Trotnow discovered when he found the windshield wipers on his car were smashed after he left a meeting in Wedding.[43]

Fischer and Trotnow took to the media in an attempt to gain support. In January 1990, they were featured on East German radio and in March on a new East German television station, Elf 99 (1199). Fischer explained to television viewers that they wanted "future generations to see. . .what happened here, the human misery that occurred when from one night to the next people were separated from their families on the other side of the street." At a time when people were removing pieces of the Wall so quickly, he argued for the importance of keeping some of it to remind people that "the attempt made to separate people who belonged together. . .ultimately was doomed to fail." The pastor also understood that the hopeful message of the toppling of the Wall had resonance far beyond Bernauer Strasse and Germany, declaring,

> This isn't the only wall in the world. It is an extreme example of something that exists all over the world. And here you can see: it must fail. You cannot divide what belongs together. We will show people who come here: where there are walls, where there are divisions, in a world where there are more walls as the world gets smaller, these must fail. People can learn that here.[44]

Fischer felt the media coverage was absolutely essential to their cause.[45] He also knew he needed political support. Accordingly, he and the Reconciliation parish council wrote to West Berlin's Governing Mayor, Walter Momper, in June requesting his help in preserving the remaining section of the Wall on Bernauer Strasse and creating a documentation center with information about the history of the Wall.[46]

---

[42] Interview with Manfred Fischer, October 6, 2009.

[43] Helmut Trotnow, "Auch die Mauer an der Bernauer Strasse wäre fast abgerissen worden," *Tagesspiegel*, August 3, 2011.

[44] See the "DDR TV 1990" section of the video compilation, "Pfarrer Manfred Fischer – Mauer Predigt," Archive, Versöhnungsgemeinde Berlin-Wedding.

[45] Interview with Manfred Fischer, October 6, 2009.

[46] Carola S. Rudnick, *Die andere Hälfte der Erinnerung: Die DDR in der deutschen Geschichtspolitik nach 1989* (Bielefeld: transcript Verlag 2011), p. 548.

The campaign of Fischer, Trotnow, and Möbius to convince people of the significance of the Wall and its history at Bernauer Strasse ironically led to its selection as a site to begin the final, official demolition of the Wall on June 13, 1990. The city counselors for construction from East and West Berlin both climbed into the small cabin of the bulldozer for the occasion.[47] The Wall at Bernauer Strasse blocking off Ackerstrasse was removed to allow traffic to flow through Ackerstrasse for the first time in almost twenty-nine years. The section of the Wall planned for a memorial just south of this along Bernauer Strasse between Ackerstrasse and Bergstrasse, however, was not touched – except by Wall peckers, of course.

A few days later, however, Fischer made an urgent call to Trotnow to tell him that the East German military was at Bernauer Strasse about to remove these sections of the Wall. Trotnow grabbed his papers testifying to DHM's permission to preserve those pieces of the Wall and rushed via the Brandenburg Gate over to Bernauer Strasse. With a worried Fischer by his side, Trotnow found the person in charge of the East German units removing the Wall and showed him the papers about preserving that section of the Wall. The officer in charge stopped the work and directed the demolition team to move farther down the street to other sections of the Wall.[48]

Two months later, Fischer and Trotnow seized on the anniversary of the erection of the Berlin Wall on August 13 as a chance to redouble their efforts to create a Wall memorial and documentation center. Fischer hosted a press conference at his parish center, joined by Trotnow, Möbius, and the East German Special Commissioner for the Removal of the Wall, Hagen Koch, who, in spite of his job title, shared their views on the necessity of a memorial.[49] Together, they posted a notice signed by Fischer (Figure 6) asking Wall peckers, "please don't 'peck at' this piece of the Wall! . . .Help us to preserve an authentic and worthy memorial especially for the victims of this Wall."[50] Fischer had held countless discussions with Wall peckers, trying – sometimes successfully, sometimes not – to dissuade them from removing fragments.[51] He argued passionately that it was essential to honor the victims of the Berlin Wall with a memorial. After all, "the Wall was not just a bunch of nicely painted pieces as can now be seen in museums in Uzbekistan, Latvia, South Korea or the United States." It was part of a death strip, and in his view it was

---

[47] Gabriele Camphausen and Manfred Fischer, "Die bürgerschaftliche Durchsetzung der Gedenkstätte an der Bernauer Strasse," in Klaus-Dietmar Henke, ed., *Die Mauer* (Munich: Deutscher Taschenbuch Verlag, 2011), p. 358.

[48] Interview with Helmut Trotnow, August 9, 2011; and Trotnow, "Auch die Mauer an der Bernauer Strasse wäre fast abgerissen worden," *Tagesspiegel*, August 3, 2011.

[49] "Bezirk hält nichts von Mauer-Gedenkstätte," *Tagesspiegel*, August 14, 1990.

[50] Ibid.; and Camphausen and Fischer, "Die bürgerschaftliche Durchsetzung," p. 359.

[51] Manfred Fischer, "Leben mit der Mauer: Reflexionen eines Betroffenen," in Trotnow and Möbius, eds., *Mauern sind nicht für ewig gebaut*, p. 76.

Figure 6 Manfred Fischer (in suit) erecting notice to Wall peckers not to touch the Wall, August 13, 1990
Source: Archive, Versöhnungsgemeinde Berlin-Wedding, 114-50s.

essential to remember this.[52] The pastor had also been known to run across the street from his parish center to block bulldozers from removing pieces of the Wall for use by construction companies.[53] He clearly needed much more serious backing to handle this ongoing problem.

The four Wall memorial allies announced at the press conference that they were working to preserve a section of the Wall at Bernauer Strasse and were in

[52] "Bezirk hält nichts von Mauer-Gedenkstätte," *Tagesspiegel*, August 14, 1990.
[53] The first time Fischer stopped a construction company's bulldozer from taking pieces of the Wall from the site of the planned memorial was in July 1990. Camphausen and Fischer, "Die bürgerschaftliche Durchsetzung," p. 359.

the process of collecting photographs, documents, artifacts, and stories about the Wall to make accessible in a museum or documentation center. Trotnow and Möbius insisted that key questions about the Wall would need to be answered, including for future generations: "Why was there a border? Who built it? What happened at this border? How did people in the East and West live with the border?" Koch presented some of the documents from the East German military archives in Potsdam, such as the order to the border troops on August 12, 1961 to close the border at midnight. The initiators of the Wall museum sought to create "an exact documentation of the situation before and after the building of the Wall."[54] Some of these were featured in a book Trotnow and Möbius had published a few months earlier with an afterword by Fischer. The book contained historical pictures of dramatic moments at the Wall at Bernauer Strasse and was accompanied by a short introduction explaining the history and why it was important to remember it.[55]

Conflicts over Memory on Bernauer Strasse

Manfred Fischer and the Reconciliation parish were not the only residents of the section of Bernauer Strasse where they sought to preserve the remains of the Wall. As it happened, the other two main occupants of that part of the street were also religious institutions, and so it came to pass that three Protestant ministers were engaged for years in a bitter public battle over whether to preserve or remove the Wall there. Fischer was in the minority.

The leaders of the Sophien Church community (Sophien) from the former East Berlin and the Lazarus Parish, Hospital and Deaconess Nursing Home (Lazarus) from the former West Berlin were fundamentally and passionately opposed to Fischer and Trotnow's plans. They had been just as affected by the Berlin Wall as Fischer's Reconciliation Church and parish had been and had very different approaches to the question of memory. None of them was more justified than the others; each of their perspectives was fully understandable.[56] Different views on how to treat the past in the present played out all over Berlin, along the former inner-German border, and along the whole Iron Curtain border: the conflict between the urge to destroy the border and the desire to preserve at least some of it. Citizens' initiatives were formed on both sides of the issue and local, state, and national officials weighed in on both sides. No approach would satisfy everyone.[57]

---

[54] "Bezirk hält nichts von Mauer-Gedenkstätte," *Tagesspiegel*, August 14, 1990.

[55] Trotnow and Möbius, eds., *Mauern sind nicht für ewig gebaut.*

[56] Gabriele Riedle, "Wo genau stand die Mauer?" *Zeit*, August 2, 1991.

[57] Maren Ullrich, *Geteilte Ansichten: Erinnerungslandschaft Deutsch-Deutsche Grenze* (Berlin: Aufbau Verlag GmbH, 2006); and Rudnick, *Die andere Hälfte der Erinnerung*, esp. pp. 655–729.

The land with the remaining section of the Wall had been part of the Sophien parish's second cemetery since 1827.[58] The Sophien Church itself, along with its first cemetery, was located nearly a mile away. This second cemetery became necessary due to a population expansion in the early nineteenth century. At the time, the cemetery was just outside of the city boundaries, but as the population expanded, so did the city limits. By 1961, this cemetery was near the middle of the city on the edge of East Berlin's border with West Berlin. When the GDR sealed the border, parts of the cemetery grounds, including many graves, were then located in the border zone of the Berlin Wall, as the Church of Reconciliation itself had been. Initially, the border troops merely separated a roughly forty-yard area of the cemetery that was in the border zone with a fence. Then they stopped allowing any burials in that area and a special pass was required to visit graves anywhere in the cemetery. Soon they began exhuming graves.[59]

In the midst of this traumatic period, the Sophien Church hosted the Reverend Martin Luther King in September 1964. King did not waste the opportunity to make his views on the Wall felt. The subtext of the words he used in his sermon was crystal clear to the congregation: "Where people dismantle the walls of hostility which separate them from their brothers, Christ realizes his charge of reconciliation."[60] The congregation spontaneously sang, "Let my people go."[61] Yet freedom and reconciliation were far away. In 1966–67, the *Grenzer* exhumed and reburied more than 1,000 graves from the forty-yard area. Sophien got no compensation, to say nothing of any sort of apology, since in the SED regime's view, these measures were undertaken to defend the security of the GDR. In 1976, Sophien agreed to sell the forty-yard area to the GDR authorities, and in 1985 it sold another area of more than fifteen yards. The church used the money to renovate its baroque church tower

---

[58] This section on the history of the Sophien Church and cemetery is drawn from Axel Klausmeier and Gerhard Sälter, "Der Sophienfriedhof in Berlin-Mitte als Gegenstand der Erinnerungspolitik," in Christian Dirks, Axel Klausmeier and Gerhard Sälter, *"Verschüttet. "Leben, Bombentod und Erinnerung an die Berliner Familie Jaschkowitz," Jüdische Miniaturen, Band 110* (Berlin: Hentrich & Hentrich and Centrum Judaicum, 2011), pp. 51–78; and "Historischer Sophienfriedhof" and "Der Sophiengemeinde," in Deutsches Historisches Museum GmbH, ed., *Architektonisch-künstlerischer Ideenwettbewerb. Gedenkstätte Berliner Mauer in der Bernauer Strasse. Ausschreibung* (Berlin: Deutsches Historisches Museum, April 1994), pp. 34–38.

[59] For the story of one family who had to deal with this, see Maria Nooke, "'I would not want to go through something like that again.' A Contemporary Witness Reports on his Experiences on Bernauer Strasse," in The Berlin Wall – Memorial Site and Exhibition Center Association, ed., *Berlin Wall Memorial Site,* pp. 54–55.

[60] Lars-Broder Keil, "Wie Martin Luther King Ost-Berlin bewegte," *Welt,* September 13, 2014.

[61] Julia Haak, "Sophienkirche Berlin: Wo schon Martin Luther King predigte," *Berliner Zeitung,* June 14, 2013.

and other church property. Thus, both the Reconciliation parish in West Berlin and the Sophien parish in East Berlin gave in to pressure to vacate the border zone.

When the Wall fell, Johannes Hildebrandt was the pastor of the Sophien Church. In addition, he was one of the sons of Helmut Hildebrandt who had been the pastor of the Church of Reconciliation from 1946 to 1961. After 1989, Johannes Hildebrandt was vehemently against keeping any of the Wall on what had been – and he hoped would be again – the property of the Sophien cemetery. He would remain an opponent of Fischer's goals there for nearly two decades. After all, the Wall represented the East German regime that had not only taken some of the Sophien cemetery to make room for the death strip but also taken the Reconciliation Church away from his father. Images of the Wall and the guards blocking access to the Reconciliation Church when he was young and then the searing memory of the church being blown up in 1985, which he witnessed live, made Johannes Hildebrandt fiercely opposed to preserving any part of the former Berlin Wall. The fact that many of the graves in the Sophien cemetery had been moved by the SED authorities only increased his passionate feelings that the Wall must be completely eliminated. He certainly did not want to see the state again taking the land from the cemetery grounds, not even for a Wall memorial.[62]

Pastor Hildebrandt and his brother Jörg thought there should be a different kind of memorial at Bernauer Strasse. Jörg Hildebrandt proposed to Fischer in early 1990 that the bells that had been saved from the Church of Reconciliation should be displayed as a memorial on the site of the former church to remind people of the "injustice of the division and its consequences." At the time, apparently Fischer did not support this idea, although he later would.[63] In April 1990, Johannes Hildebrandt brought the issue of the bells as a memorial to the Berlin-Mitte Round Table talks being held among new civil society groups and the East German regime. He urged the members of the Round Table to support the proposal to "create a memorial to remember the victims of the erection of the Wall, the inner-German border and the border regulations. This includes those who died, were injured, imprisoned and families torn apart. A bell tower could be erected on the foundation walls of the Church of Reconciliation in which could be placed the three bells that were saved from the Church of Reconciliation." The Round Table agreed unanimously to support the proposal and forward it to Berlin's Central Round Table.[64]

---

[62] Moritz Müller-Wirth, "Erinnerung an einem Ort des Schreckes," *Tagesspiegel*, July 6, 1991.

[63] Halbrock, "Weggesprengt."

[64] Protokoll der Beratung des Runden Tisches am 19.04.1990, 17.00 Uhr im Rat des Stadtbezirkes Berlin-Mitte – Berolinasaal, Robert-Havemann-Gesellschaft Archives (RHG), SD 12, pp. 4–5.

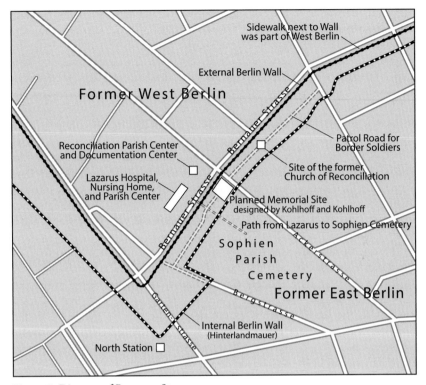

Figure 7 Diagram of Bernauer Strasse

In September, a month before German unification, the moderator of the Berlin-Mitte Round Table, Joachim Koppehl, joined by senior representatives of the SPD in East Berlin, urged the East Berlin mayor to back the creation of a "Memorial to the Church of Reconciliation." Koppehl and the SPD members argued that the site where the church had stood before being destroyed "was most suitable to document for mankind the perversion of thinking and behavior that surrounded the object of 'the Wall' and thus to serve as a memorial." They also suggested that this idea could be coupled with the developing plans for a Wall Museum on Bernauer Strasse.[65] Eventually that would in fact happen, but not before years of conflict between the Reconciliation and Sophien parishes and their leaders.

Fischer's other pastoral opponent to preserving the Wall on Bernauer Strasse was right next door to his parish building and apartment. Pastor

---

[65] Letter from Joachim Koppehl, moderator of the Berlin-Mitte Round Table, to the Mayor of East Berlin, Tono Schwierzina, regarding a memorial to the Church of Reconciliation, September 3, 1990, from the papers of Maria Nooke, email of November 1, 2011.

Hartmut Albruschat of the Lazarus Parish, Hospital and Deaconess Nursing Home also disagreed with Fischer's plan. Founded in 1865, Lazarus became the hospital for the congregation of the nearby St. Elisabeth Church, with the deaconesses serving as nurses and other caretakers. The deaconesses had their final resting place in the Sophien cemetery across the street. With the closing of the border, Lazarus was cut off from both the St. Elisabeth Church and the Sophien cemetery. In addition, at the time nearly fifty of its deaconesses were in service in the GDR. Lazarus was in West Berlin and its key connections in the East were now closed off behind the Wall. Lazarus's doctors and nurses would soon treat East Berliners who were injured when they escaped across the border. They would also treat West Berliners who tried to take their own lives by driving their cars at high speeds down Bernauer Strasse to crash into the Wall at the end of the street just one block from the hospital.[66] For the twenty-eight years the Wall stood, the Lazarus's residents and hospital patients had a view of the Wall and the death strip from their windows.

Pastor Albruschat based his opposition to preserving the Wall in front of his Lazarus campus on several grounds. First, the Lazarus inhabitants had looked at the Wall long enough. It would upset and depress them to have to look at it any longer. Second, the Wall stood blocking the path that led from Lazarus to the burial grounds of the deaconesses across the street in the Sophien cemetery. They should be able to access the cemetery easily again. Finally, Albruschat complained that "a memorial would bring additional disturbances and hustle and bustle due to the well-known strains of tourists." As of late September 1990, Albruschat had gathered the signatures of 650 supporters against a Wall memorial. They wanted the Wall completely removed. If there was to be some sort of memorial at Bernauer Strasse, Albruschat proposed, as Hildebrandt had, that the memorial be on the land one block up the street where the Reconciliation Church had been, not in front of his hospital and nursing home.[67] In light of the clear stances of Sophien and Lazarus, the district mayor of Wedding argued that the proposal to preserve the Wall at Bernauer Strasse was against "the clear will of the citizens" and that there was "no longer room in Berlin for walls."[68]

Removing the last pieces of the Wall at Bernauer Strasse would of course run counter to the pleas of Fischer, Trotnow, and others that only by preserving it could future generations gain a sense of what it had been like. At a time when the widely held view of the Wall had changed from that of a deadly border to a symbol of freedom that so many Wall peckers wanted a piece of,

---

[66] "Das Lazarus Kranken- und Diakonissenhaus," in Deutsches Historisches Museum GmbH, ed., *Architektonisch-künstlerischer Ideenwettbewerb*, pp. 41–42.

[67] Pfarrer Hartmut Albruschat, "Mauer Museum? Ja, aber nicht vor unserer Tür!" *Berliner Morgenpost*, September 30, 1990.

[68] "Bezirk hält nichts von Mauer-Gedenkstätte," *Tagesspiegel*, August 14, 1990.

Trotnow warned readers of the *Berliner Morgenpost* in September 1990 against a "Wall myth." He reminded them that the Wall represented one of the most "inhumane moments in German history" and asserted that Germans "owe it to the victims to preserve a worthy and authentic memorial" and to explain the history of the Berlin Wall in a new documentation center or museum. He announced that the DHM had drafted plans to do this at Bernauer Strasse.[69]

The DHM was a relatively new project of the West German government, overseen by the West German interior ministry. Two months before unification, Interior Minister Wolfgang Schäuble had urged East German Prime Minister Lothar de Maizière to preserve the Wall at Bernauer Strasse.[70] De Maizière agreed and instructed his Minister for Disarmament and Defense, Rainer Eppelmann, to prevent the remaining section of the Wall at Bernauer Strasse from being demolished.[71] Eppelmann was a Protestant pastor and part of the East German opposition movement. His parents and siblings lived in West Germany, where he was not allowed to visit them. He felt that Germans, himself included, had suffered from "Wall sickness" (*Mauerkrankheit*) for long enough. Eppelmann was the wrong person to ask to help preserve the Wall.[72] He shared the desire of Hildebrandt and Albruschat to be completely rid of the hated Wall and thus did not stop the ongoing demolition in spite of being directed by his boss to do so, leaving Trotnow and Fischer to continue fighting their rearguard action.[73]

Other officials in East Berlin did, however, endorse moves to make sure the Wall and its history were not forgotten, including the Berlin-Mitte Round Table, the East German Institute for Historic Preservation, the Volkskammer, and the East Berlin magistrate. A newly created "Bernauer Strasse Citizens' Initiative" also supported Trotnow and Fischer's plans. At various points in late 1989 and 1990, East Berlin policymakers took steps to place the section of the Wall on Bernauer Strasse between Ackerstrasse and Bergstrasse under historic landmark protection. This was not, however, enough to stop individual Wall peckers, other parts of the government, and construction companies from removing pieces of it.[74] In fact, the first and last freely elected East Berlin city parliament held a panicked discussion in mid-

[69] Helmut Trotnow, "Das Mauer-Museum muß mitten in der Stadt stehen," *Berliner Morgenpost*, August 23, 1990. See also Trotnow, "Understanding the Present by Looking Back at the Past," pp. 11–12; and Trotnow and Möbius, eds., *Mauern sind nicht für ewig gebaut*, pp. 9–12.

[70] Letter from West German Interior Minister Wolfgang Schäuble to East German Prime Minister Lothar de Maizière, August 10, 1990, Bundesarchiv (BArch), 20/6070a, p. 241. See also "Bezirk hält nichts von Mauer-Gedenkstätte," *Tagesspiegel*, August 14, 1990; and Camphausen and Fischer, "Die bürgeschaftliche Durchsetzung," p. 359.

[71] Letter from GDR Prime Minister Lothar de Maizière to Interior Minister Wolfgang Schäuble, August 16, 1990, BArch, 20/6540.

[72] Interview with Rainer Eppelmann, Berlin, April 20, 2010.

[73] Rudnick, *Die andere Hälfte der Erinnerung*, p. 554.

[74] Camphausen and Fischer, "Die bürgerschaftliche Durchsetzung," pp. 356–61.

June 1990 about the urgency of ensuring that some sections of the Wall were preserved.[75] On the day before German unification, the East German office for historical preservation granted historic landmark status to the Wall at Bernauer Strasse and several other sites, requiring that the Wall there must be preserved.

Remembering the Wall after Unification

With German unification on October 3, 1990, the issue of creating a Berlin Wall Memorial and preserving parts of the Wall was transferred, as was everything else, into the hands of the new German government and new Berlin municipal government. Trotnow and Fischer continued to press their case. Trotnow over-saw an elaboration of DHM's plans for the future of Bernauer Strasse. These consisted of three components: a memorial for victims of the Wall; a museum; and a reconstruction of a section of the former border strip. The working draft of the design in April 1991 showed that the reconstructed border strip would be located in front of the Reconciliation parish center, abutting the end of the remaining section of the Wall at Ackerstrasse (in the area that would later become the Kohlhoff & Kohlhoff memorial as depicted in Figure 7), and the museum and memorial would be located in front of the Lazarus complex.[76]

Thus, all three components would be located where the block-long sec-tion of Wall remained on Bernauer Strasse between Ackerstrasse and Bergstrasse, would be visible from both the Reconciliation and Lazarus buildings, and would include land that had been part of the Sophien ceme-tery, ignoring the wishes of the latter two communities. For the memorial, DHM intended to use objects saved from the Church of Reconciliation before it was demolished and planned to erect a commemorative panel with the names of all the known victims of the Wall. The museum would incorporate authentic written, photographic, and film sources as well as other artifacts to explain the history of the Wall.

The most controversial part of DHM's plans for Bernauer Strasse involved reconstructing parts of the border zone that had been removed, including the external and internal Walls (with authentic pieces brought back to add to what was still standing), anti-tank obstacles, floodlights, electronic signal lines, watchtowers, and a Trabant and motorcycle used by the border troops. Trotnow had moved quickly to secure some of these items from the border

---

[75] Stadtverordnetenversammlung von Berlin, 1. Wahlperiode, 4. Sitzung, Plenarprotokoll 1/4, Berlin, Mittwoch, 20, Juni 1990, p.125, Landesarchiv Berlin (LAB), C Rep. 100–1, Nr. 209.

[76] Senat von Berlin, Senatsverwaltung für Kulturelle Angelegenheiten, Senatsvorlage Nr. 503/91, Anhang, Projektbeschreibung des Deutschen Historischen Museum, "Gedenkstätte und Museum 'Berliner Mauer' in der Bernauer Strasse, Stand April 1991," pp. 1–2, LAB, D Rep. 002/831, p. 6.

zone (with help from former East German border soldiers, to the outrage of Pastor Hildebrandt) as they were removed. The border installations were stored in the basement of DHM's headquarters in the famous old Zeughaus building on Unter den Linden, ready to be brought back and put into place in a re-created border strip. Trotnow believed that it would be essential for future generations to see the border strip in its entirety (minus the armed guards with an order to shoot), to understand what the Berlin Wall had been.[77]

To preserve these elements of the former border once they were returned to their original location and to prevent any souvenir seekers from taking them, the area would not be accessible to visitors who would instead view it from an observation platform. This would recall the observation platform at Bernauer Strasse used for so many years by people to look over the Wall into the death strip, the platform where Fischer stood in May 1986 to speak at the ceremony of mourning for the demolished Church of Reconciliation. At one point in the summer of 1991, Trotnow had in mind that the reconstructed border strip would be covered with a glass roof to keep it secure. He later withdrew this component of the plans, although the final design would need to find some way to prevent visitors from direct access to these artifacts.[78]

While Trotnow had federal backing, municipal support was another question entirely. So soon after unification, the municipal government of Berlin was largely focused on rejoining and rebuilding the inner city where the Wall had been. In fact, in the early 1990s when the united party formed by the East German Alliance 90 (*Bündnis 90*) and the West German Greens (*Die Grüne*) called, in Berlin's House of Representatives, for "a master plan for dealing with the Wall, including stopping any destruction of the Wall,"[79] the Senate responded that such a "master plan was not desired by the Senate," which instead favored "rebuilding as much as possible in the former border zone...to bring both halves of the city back together."[80]

Grappling with how to handle the few remains of the Wall was certainly not a priority, particularly when there were vehement disagreements at Bernauer Strasse and elsewhere about this. Yet city officials tried to find some sort of compromise solution that would satisfy all parties on Bernauer Strasse. In April 1991, parliamentarians from Berlin's House of Representatives hosted the diverse inhabitants of Bernauer Strasse for a discussion. A month later the

---

[77] Ibid., pp. 2–3; and interview with Helmut Trotnow, March 17, 2010.

[78] Rudnick, *Die andere Hälfte der Erinnerung*, p. 570.

[79] Abgeordnetenhaus von Berlin, 12. Wahlperiode, Drucksache 12/1307, "Antrag der Fraktion Bündnis 90/Die Grüne (AL)/UFV über Umgang mit der Mauer," March 18, 1992.

[80] Report of the Berlin Senate to the House of Representatives, Abgeordnetenhaus von Berlin, 12. Wahlperiode, "Mitteilung – zur Kenntnisnahme – über Umgang mit der Mauer – Drsn Nr. 12/1307, Nr. 12/1601 und Nr. 12/1601-1 – Schlußbericht," Drucksache 12/255, March 3, 1993.

committee on cultural affairs of the Berlin parliament had such a contentious session on the issue with Fischer, Hildebrandt, Albruschat, and others from the neighborhood that the committee ran out of time to address the other matter that had been on the agenda for the session – the issue of renaming streets named for communists in the east.[81]

In his testimony, Fischer sought to rise above – or perhaps to trump – the local disagreements on Bernauer Strasse by appealing to a wider public interest in remembering the Berlin Wall. Fischer repeatedly stressed to parliamentarians both the Wall's impact on the residents of Bernauer Strasse *and* the global significance and memory of the Wall, reminding the parliamentarians that "Bernauer Strasse was known around the world as the Wall Street. Tragedies occurred here. The demolition [of the remaining sections of the Wall] would obliterate a piece of tragic German history, and that cannot be in any one's interest."[82] Fischer thus presented the politicians with two kinds of historical grounds for preserving the Wall.

At the May meeting of the cultural affairs department, Senator Ulrich Roloff-Momin was impressed by the domestic aspect of Fischer's argument, observing, "We must visibly show the constriction of the city. Perhaps it will be necessary to have a solution here against the desires of the people directly affected at the site."[83] Irana Rusta of the SPD picked up on Fischer's point about global memory, arguing that "the interests of local residents might have only limited weight in the decision about what to do with the remains of the Wall, since, "in 1961 the name Bernauer Strasse went around the entire world."[84] An association of tour guides from eastern and western Berlin also lobbied the Berlin Senate to preserve the Wall at Bernauer Strasse, where they had been taking German and foreign tourists since 1961. They now asserted that "no foreign guest will understand why there should be no more of this Wall which was unique in the world due to its barbarism and political short-sightedness. It would be just as short-sighted and. . .politically foolish now to behave as if the Wall never existed."[85] This would not be the last time that memory activists in Germany would reference global interest in the Wall to justify the preservation of the Wall and commemoration of important aspects

[81] Jochen Metzner, "Mauer-Reste: Debatte über Gedenkstätte im Kulturausschuß," *Tagesspiegel*, May 7, 1991.

[82] Helmut Caspar, "Bemalte Betonplatten als Mahnmal der Erinnerung: Kontroverse Diskussion über die Erhaltung von zweihundert Metern Mauer an der Bernauer Strasse," *Neue Zeit*, April 25, 1991.

[83] Jochen Metzner, "Mauer-Reste: Debatte über Gedenkstätte im Kulturausschuß," *Tagesspiegel*, May 7, 1991.

[84] Ibid.

[85] Letter from Andrea von Klobuczinsky, managing director of Berlin Guide, to Senator Volker Hassemer. "Gedenkpark 'Berliner Mauer' an der Bernauer Strasse," Stiftung DHM, Hausarchiv, DHM, Trotnow-WBM 10.

of its history. Although only a minority in the early 1990s argued this way, they essentially felt: *It was our Wall. People still want to know about it. We should be the ones to explain its history.*

Yet supporting the preservation of the Berlin Wall at the site did not mean supporting a re-creation of the border strip by bringing back the elements that had been there when the Wall fell. Several members of the committee on cultural affairs were concerned about any re-creation. They feared it would become "an adventure park" instead of a site for "quiet commemoration." Several years later a Bundestag commission of inquiry on the GDR would also argue that "reconstruction of an authentic site is problematic and only makes sense in exceptional cases."[86] Some in the Berlin Senate committee worried that a reconstruction would somehow minimize how terrible the border actually was, since the reconstruction could never fully mimic the reality but might be taken for the reality. Trotnow attempted to reassure the parliamentarians that DHM planned to make the memorial a site of "dignified remembrance" for the people who were killed at the once deadly border.[87]

Volker Hassemer, the senator for city planning and environmental protection whose portfolio included historic landmark preservation, was charged with trying to find a consensus among the three parishes feuding on Bernauer Strasse. Hassemer met with them in June and July 1991, but no consensus held for long.[88] Meanwhile, his colleague Cultural Senator Roloff-Momin was tasked with formulating a recommendation in advance of the fortieth anniversary of the erection of the Wall in mid-August about whether or not to support DHM's plans.[89] Roloff-Momin hosted a meeting in early July with pastors Fischer, Hildebrandt, and Albruschat at which each reiterated their strongly-held views. Yet Fischer bolstered his case in a different way this time. He read from a letter he had received from a former East German refugee, Klaus-Peter Eich, in support of plans to preserve the Wall as a memorial.

Eich had escaped across the border at Bernauer Strasse in October 1961. In the process, however, he had been shot by *Grenzer* and had been a paraplegic

---

[86] Deutscher Bundestag, ed., "Schlussbericht," in *Materialien der Enquete-Kommission "Überwindung der Folgen der SED-Diktatur im Prozeß der deutschen Einheit", Band 1* (Baden-Baden: Nomos Verlag, 1999), p. 617.

[87] Ibid.; and Moritz Müller-Wirth, "Erinnerung an einem Ort des Schreckens," *Tagesspiegel*, July 6, 1991.

[88] DHM, Anlage zur Senatsvorlage, "Gedenkstätte und Museum 'Berliner Mauer' in der Bernauer Strasse. Projektbeschreibung des Deutschen Historischen Museums," Nachtrag, Sachstand: 17. June 1991, p. 5, LAB, D Rep. 002/831. See also Camphausen and Fischer, "Die bürgerschaftliche Durchsetzung," pp. 361–62.

[89] Confidential memo from Hamann in the office of the governing mayor regarding "Errichtung einer Gedenkstätte und eines Museums 'Berliner Mauer' durch die Deutsches Historisches Musem-GmbH in der Bernauer Strasse. Senatsbeschluß Nr. 503/91 vom 2. Juli 1991," July 4, 1991, Senatsverwaltung für Wissenschaft, Forschung und Kultur (SWFKB), Gedenkstätte Berliner Mauer (GBM), Nr. 480.

Figure 8 Left to right: Helmut Trotnow, Manfred Fischer, Christoph Stölzl, press conference, Reconciliation parish center (with stained glass window), August 12, 1991 Source: Archive, Versöhnungsgemeinde Berlin-Wedding, F-005020.

ever since. After hearing Fischer speak on *Deutschlandfunk* about his plans for a memorial, Eich wrote to him saying that he wanted to "help with all means possible." He made his motivation clear: "As one of the first victims of the Wall..., I believe we have an obligation not to allow our fellow citizens who were killed by the despotic GDR regime to be forgotten."[90] A press conference led by DHM Director Christoph Stölzl himself at Fischer's parish center on August 12, 1991 (Figure 8) reiterated this appeal and their plans for the memorial site.[91]

Senator Roloff-Momin's committee on cultural affairs decided to recommend that the Senate support DHM's plans for a memorial, a museum, and an observation platform, as well as the reconstruction of a section of the former border zone. In the senator's view, the Wall at Bernauer Strasse was "the most historically significant of the remaining segments in Berlin." It was "unique" since it was the "only remaining piece [of the Wall] from a typical residential area of Berlin where daily life during the period of division is visible." He also noted its wider importance as "an important document of the European

[90] Letter from Dr. Phil. Klaus-Peter Eich to Pastor Manfred Fischer, September 14, 1990, Stiftung DHM, Hausarchiv, DHM, Trotnow-WBM 10. See also Müller-Wirth, "Erinnerung an einem Ort des Schreckens," *Tagesspiegel*, July 6, 1991.
[91] "Fragen an die Gedenkstätte Bernauer Strasse," *Neue Zeit*, August 13, 1991.

history of the Cold War." The Wall was a "testimony to a horrific past,"[92] and it was important to create "a dignified and authentic site of memory which can help future generations and visitors [German and non-German] to the city understand the inhumanity of the politics which erected this border."[93] Equally important, however, Roloff-Momin declared that with its fall, the Wall "also symbolized the power of and the desire for freedom...the fulfillment of the hope that oppression and paternalism anywhere in the world can be overcome. [Its] significance and effect go far beyond the level of a local memorial," which is made clear "above all by its resonance with foreign visitors."[94] In his view, the requirements of national and global memory both necessitated preserving and commemorating the Wall.

His colleague Senator Hassemer, however, had significant reservations about the DHM plans. In particular, he was against returning any of the former elements of the border strip that had been removed.[95] Roloff-Momin requested multiple times that Hassemer certify that the whole area at Bernauer Strasse where the Wall remains stood must be returned to its October 2, 1990 condition when the East German authorities declared it a national historic landmark.[96] This would have meant returning many elements of the border strip. Hassemer refused, declaring that returning the border strip to its former state was not a requirement of historic preservation. One of his colleagues, Gabi Dolf-Bonekämper, argued that returning anything to the site would not be "authentic" and would have problematic effects: "The horror of the place belongs to those who lived it, not to those who come to visit it now... .Reconstruction makes you think you lived the real thing, but you did *not*."[97] Moreover, she asserted that "the authentic terror" could not come from any reconstruction, since "it came not from the things but from the system,"[98] especially the orders from the leaders to shoot people trying to escape and *Grenzer* implementing that order.

Senator Hassemer also complained about the "abundantly high-handed behavior" of DHM officials – i.e., Trotnow – trying to "create faits accompli"

---

[92] Letter from Ulrich Roloff-Momin to Volker Hassemer, June 6, 1991, SWFKB, GBM, Nr. 480.

[93] Ulrich Roloff-Momin's draft Senate resolution, Senatsverwaltung für Kulturelle Angelegenheiten, Senatsvorlage Nr. 503/91, June 25, 1991, LAB, D Rep. 002/831.

[94] Letter from Ulrich Roloff-Momin to Volker Hassemer, June 6, 1991, SWFKB, GBM, Nr. 480.

[95] Interview with Volker Hassemer, July 17, 2007.

[96] Letter from Ulrich Roloff-Momin to Volker Hassemer, July 30, 1991, SWFKB, GBM, Nr. 480.

[97] Interview with Gabi Dolf-Bonekämper, April 12, 2010.

[98] Gabi Dolff-Bonekämper, "Die Berliner Mauer – ein verschwindendes Denkmal," speech to an international conference of art historians in Amsterdam, September 3, 1996, a copy of which was sent to Rainer Klemke in the Senate's cultural department on September 12, 1996, SWFKB, GBM, Nr. 24.

by pushing ahead to realize their plans at Bernauer Strasse.[99] Hassemer also felt that preserving and remembering the Wall was not a financial priority for Berlin when there was so much else that urgently needed to be done in the newly united city.[100] In addition, he was moved by the appeals of the Lazarus and Sophien communities against the DHM plans, as was Dolf-Bonekämper. The latter had first learned about the Lazarus hospital years earlier while living in Stuttgart, where she met a nurse who had cared for people who had been shot when escaping over the Berlin Wall.[101]

The day before the Senate session on the fortieth anniversary of the building of the Wall, a meeting of senators worked out a partial compromise whereby the size of the memorial site would be reduced significantly from 232 yards to 142 yards along Bernauer Strasse, with the rest of the area to be returned to the Sophien parish for use as a cemetery. On the other hand, calls by Sophien and Lazarus, backed by Hassemer, to transfer the site of the future museum and memorial to the grounds of the former Church of Reconciliation one block north of the site under discussion were rebuffed. Roloff-Momin successfully pushed back against this on the grounds that there were no remaining pieces of the Wall there. The whole point of the DHM plan was to make the authentic remnants of the Berlin Wall the focus of the future memorial site.[102] In addition, the Reconciliation community had its own plans for the grounds of the former Church of Reconciliation, assuming they got the land back. They would not agree to trade this land for the area where the Wall remains stood. They sought to erect a building there that would function as a commemorative site, a place for gatherings on the history of the Church of Reconciliation and the role of the Protestant Church in the GDR, and for meetings on broad contemporary cultural matters.[103] These plans would be changed several years later to focus on building a Chapel of Reconciliation.

---

[99] See Volker Hassemer's letter to Ulrich Roloff-Momin of July 31, 1991, ibid.; and the letter to Helmut Trotnow from Hassemer's deputy, state secretary Wolfgang Branoner, on July 8, 1991, ibid.

[100] Interview with Volker Hassemer, July 17, 2007.

[101] Interview with Gabi Dolf-Bonekämper, April 12, 2010.

[102] Meeting of Senator Hassemer, Transportation Senator Haase, and Roloff-Momin's deputy, State Secretary Hildebrandt, Senatsverwaltung für Kulturelle Angelegenheiten, Senatsvorlage ATO (Außertagesordnung), August 12, 1991, SWFKB, GMB, No. 480.

[103] Letter from Dahlheim of the Senate department for cultural affairs to Dr. Gabi Dolff-Bonekämper of the Senate department for city planning and environmental protection, regarding "Mitzeichnungsschreiben Sen Hassemer zur Kleinen Anfrage Nr. 279 der Abgeordneten Delau vom 14. März 1991 über Fortbestand der Berliner Mauer zwischen Nordbahnhof und Ackerstrasse," January 29, 1992, SWFKB, GBM, Nr. 464. See also the three-page description sent from Fischer to Dahlheim on January 28, 1992, "Projekt Bernauer 4," SWFKB, GMB, Nr. 468.

On August 13, 1991, the Senate backed the creation of a "site of memory and a memorial to the former Wall and its victims at Bernauer Strasse," to include a memorial, a museum, and the remaining pieces of the Wall and all the other elements to be returned to the former border. This is what Fischer and Trotnow had long wanted. Yet the Senate resolution had Hassemer's influence all over it, stating that, "the concerns of the residents there should be respected without putting in question the basic decisions on the issue. If possible, the site of memory and commemoration [the museum and memorial the DHM planned to put in the middle of the former death strip] should not involve the territory of the former Sophien cemetery."[104] In essence, this Senate resolution did not guarantee anything as far as Fischer and Trotnow were concerned.[105] Everything they had planned was to be located on the former territory of Sophien's cemetery. The Senate resolution also pointedly did not place the remaining sections of the Wall under historic landmark protection, although the Senate would do this the following year. The resolution even declared that some of the Wall still standing in front of Lazarus might be removed from consideration as a historic landmark or demolished.[106] The resolution did at least contain a provision against the expansion of the two-lane road at Bernauer Strasse into a highway, as the senator for transportation had proposed.

With ongoing disagreements about where exactly on Bernauer Strasse the memorial and border reconstruction should be located, none of DHM's plans could be carried out. The main impediment was Sophien's refusal to cooperate. DHM needed to commission a variety of professionals to realize their plans: preservation experts to secure the Wall, protect it from ongoing weather damage, and deal with the asbestos sealing of the top; other experts to lay water and electricity lines; and landscaping contractors. They also needed a museum professional to develop a design for the museum. Trotnow, the most obvious person for the job, had a full-time position with many responsibilities at the DHM, so he could not be the one to do this.[107] DHM also foresaw an artistic design competition to create the memorial for the victims of the Wall, but the museum could not announce such a competition without agreement from Hildebrandt and the Sophien community about the use of the land.

---

[104] Der Senate von Berlin, Senatsbeschluß Nr. 629/91 vom 13. August 1991, "Errichtung einer Erinnerungs- und Gedenkstätte an die ehemalige Mauer und ihre Opfer in der Bernauer Strasse," LAB, D Rep. 002/957.

[105] Interview with Manfred Fischer, October 6, 2009; and Camphausen and Fischer, "Die bürgerschaftliche Durchsetzung," pp. 362–63.

[106] Rudnick, Die andere Hälfte der Erinnerung, p. 573.

[107] Senat von Berlin, Senatsverwaltung für Kulturelle Angelegenheiten, Senatsvorlage Nr. 503/91, Anhang, Projektbeschreibung des Deutschen Historischen Museum, "Gedenkstätte und Museum 'Berliner Mauer' in der Bernauer Strasse, Stand April 1991," pp. 3–4, LAB, D Rep. 002/831.

The Senate engaged in multiple rounds of contentious negotiations with Hildebrandt. In the meantime, DHM surrounded the Wall remains and some of the adjacent area with a fence to preserve them and keep people out (both Wall peckers and Hildebrandt). Several times Sophien broke through the fence to plant trees (which the Senate removed) or put up signs against the use of the land by DHM. More than two years after the Senate resolution, the Senate and Sophien reached an agreement in October 1993, paving the way to move ahead with the competition to design the memorial. Yet like the Senate resolution of August 13, 1991, the agreement signed by Roloff-Momin, Hassemer, and Pastor Hildebrandt left room for differing interpretations.

Whereas the DHM plans had been for a "Berlin Wall Memorial Site," Hildebrandt emphasized that his cemetery contained mass graves of victims of World War II bombings. Hence, the agreement signed by the Senate with Sophien referred to a "Memorial Site for the Victims of the Second World War and German Division."[108] As it would turn out, however, there was no evidence that any graves remained in the border strip after the East German border troops had carried out so many reburials.[109] Yet in 1993, officials took Hildebrandt's claims as the truth and allowed this consideration to strongly affect their plans for the memorial and for the competition to design it.[110]

The signed agreement stated that the Senate and Sophien backed the memorial and also supported Sophien's use of the former area of its cemetery. They pledged that they would each "take into account the concerns of the other." This sounded like no agreement whatsoever, but actually it did form the basis of a path forward, at least initially. The agreement referenced the entire 232 yards between Ackerstrasse and Bergstrasse along the remaining section of the Wall that DHM planned to use for the site, but also specified that the actual memorial should comprise (as the Senate compromise of August 12, 1991 had said) a smaller 77-yard area. The agreement envisioned a rectangular shaped area (as in the DHM plans, although smaller) measuring 77 yards in length and 66 yards in width between the former outer and inner Walls as the core site. (This is the area marked as Planned Memorial Site in Figure 7.) Another key change to the original DHM plans, in line with the objections of

---

[108]   The Senate-Sophien five-page agreement was part of the April 1994 materials contained in the announcement of the design competition for constructing the Berlin Wall Memorial. "Vereinbarung zwischen dem Land Berlin vertreten durch den Senator für Kulturelle Angelegenheiten, Herrn Ulrich Roloff-Momin und den Senator für Stadtentwicklung und Umweltschutz, Herrn Volker Hassemer, und der Evangelischen Sophiengemeinde zu Berlin, Große Hamburger Straße 31, 10115 Berlin, vertreten durch ihren Gemeindekirchenrat," October 20, 1993, in Deutsches Historisches Museum GmbH, ed., *Architektonisch-künstlerischer Ideenwettbewerb.*

[109]   Jörn Hasselmann, "Keine Beweise für Massengräber unter der alten Grenzmauer," *Tagesspiegel,* April 24, 1997.

[110]   Rudnick, *Die andere Hälfte der Erinnerung,* p. 597.

Pastor Hildebrandt and Senator Hassemer, was that no reconstruction of the former border strip between the external and internal Walls would be allowed. The area, however, would be maintained as a zone separated from the cemetery so that people could at least see the depth of the former border zone even if it would not contain the anti-vehicle obstacles, guard tower, signal wires, motorcycle, and other components Trotnow had been saving.

If any mass graves were found on the site, as Hildebrandt had been claiming without proof, the agreement would have to be modified to comply with the German laws concerning gravesites. Sophien had the right to select the chairman of the jury for the competition and to be involved in writing the competition guidelines. Regarding ownership of the land, the Senate promised Hildebrandt it would try to get the federal government to return the land to the parish, and Hildebrandt promised that he would then transfer to the Berlin government the permanent right to use the land for the memorial.

Creating a Berlin Wall Memorial

Thus, nearly three years after the Berlin Senate had passed a resolution for a Berlin Wall Memorial, DHM was finally able to announce, in April 1994, an artistic design competition to create the memorial. The federal government would provide the funds, earmarking DM1.5 million. The sponsors of the competition represented all interested groups: DHM, three departments of the Senate, the Wedding and Mitte governments, and the Sophien, Lazarus, and Reconciliation communities. Architects, landscape architects, and artists were eligible to apply and were encouraged to cooperate with historians, curators, writers, and sculptors. Jury members were drawn from these groups as well as from the government and church. The competitors were charged to formulate a design that would integrate the whole border area (without any reconstruction), create an accessible memorial to victims, and show and explain the layers of history at Bernauer Strasse. The guidelines for "the Berlin Wall Memorial on Bernauer Strasse" were sent out in late April. Proposals were due in August and the jury met in early October 1994.[111]

In contrast to the initial DHM plans, this competition only included a memorial and the remains of the Wall, not a museum. The competitors were essentially expected to create an outdoor exhibit that would "expose and highlight" the "historical layers of the site," which were currently "fragmented and difficult to 'read'."[112] To this end, they were provided with historical background on the whole area at Bernauer Strasse, including the history of the Berlin Wall, the Sophien parish and cemetery, the Reconciliation parish and church, and Lazarus. The core task for the competitors, however, was to create a design that would encompass

---

[111] DHM, "Architektonisch-künstlerischer Ideenwettbewerb," April 1994.
[112] Ibid., pp. 3, 27.

two parts of the memorial and their surroundings, especially the Sophien cemetery. The two parts consisted of the 77-yard length of Wall along Bernauer Strasse
and the unreconstructed former death strip; and a 66-yard-wide area perpendicular to it along Ackerstrasse. The guidelines left open how the entrants would deal
with the additional remnants of the Wall beyond the specified 77 yards.

Multiple times in the guidelines, contestants were reminded that they
needed to include information on the history of the Sophien cemetery in
their future memorial.

The competition jury met for three days in early October to decide which of
the 259 entries should win the competition. The jury did not find any of the
proposals to be worthy of winning first place. Instead, they chose three entries to
win second place. One of these, designed by the architects Kohlhoff & Kohlhoff,
proposed adding two twenty-foot-tall stainless steel walls perpendicular to and
closing off the area between the former external and internal Walls of the border
strip, creating a rectangular area that would not be accessible. The Wall and
former border strip would be endlessly reflected in the interior side of the
stainless steel walls as a reminder of how seemingly infinite the border had
been. The external sides of the added walls would be rust colored to represent
the Iron Curtain. While the other two second-prize winners proposed encompassing much longer sections (142 and 232 yards) of the remaining Wall, this
entry called for using just the 77 yards specified in the guidelines. It also planned
an observation platform and the addition of a path behind the old
Hinterlandmauer for visitors to peer through the small slits in this Wall into
the closed-off former death strip.[113]

Since the jury did not pick a winner, it was left to the Berlin Senate to
decide. In December 1994, the Senate chose the minimalist Kohlhoff &
Kohlhoff proposal solely, as the deciding Senate committee said, because
Sophien "would not have accepted any other solution,"[114] since the other
two designs included more Wall than Sophien wanted. Thus, what DHM
had started in 1990 as a plan for a memorial to the victims of the Berlin Wall
to include as much as possible of the remaining section of the Wall at Bernauer
Strasse and to construct a museum to explain the history had been significantly
changed due to persistent intervention by the Sophien community.

In May 1995, the Sophien parish regained ownership of the land. In spite of
Sophien's agreement with the Senate that it would allow a memorial to be
constructed on this land, it hardened it approach instead. Ongoing resistance by
Sophien and others to the plans delayed the start of construction of the memorial
for another two years. In April 1997, just when the federal government released the
funding for the realization of the Kohlhoff & Kohlhoff design and before construction had begun, Sophien made its most aggressive move yet. It removed two

[113] Rudnick, *Die andere Hälfte der Erinnerung*, pp. 595–97.
[114] Ibid., p. 597.

Figure 9 Two gaps created in the Wall (center and far right) by the Sophien parish, spring 1997 (steel columns added in 2009)
Source: Hope M. Harrison.

large sections of the Wall. In two separate actions, Sophien officials commissioned the removal of thirty-two segments of Berlin Wall, first one section of seventeen yards and then a week later a second section of seventeen yards (Figure 9).

The new Senator for City Planning and Environmental Protection, Peter Strieder, directed police to step in after the first removal but, after they left, Hildebrandt followed up with the second removal upon getting the green light from a local official in spite of the Senate directives. Sophien blatantly disregarded the historic landmark status of the Wall. Pastor Hildebrandt claimed, still with no proof, that the Wall had stood over two mass graves of victims of Allied bombing in World War II. He had requested permission the previous year to remove the Wall sections based on this claim. When he received no answer from the Senate about any plans to mark the graves and in spite of being told by the office of historic preservation that nothing in the area could be changed, he went ahead with the unilateral action.[115]

Hildebrandt had pushed so far now that the pendulum of political support for his concerns swung the other way. Strieder was much more committed to preserving all possible remains of the Wall at Bernauer Strasse than his predecessor Volker Hassemer had been. Strieder called for a scientific study to determine whether there were in fact mass graves at the site. The study found that there were none. The Senate, strongly backed by the new cultural senator,

---

[115] Ua, "Sophien-Pfarrer ignoriert Mauer-Beschlüsse," *Berliner Zeitung*, April 30, 1997; Vera Gaserow, "Das Gerangel um ein Stückchen Mauer," *Zeit Online*, May 2, 1997; and Rudnick, *Die andere Hälfte der Erinnerung*, p. 603.

Peter Radunski, then decided that the memorial site should encompass not just the smaller area of the Kohlhoff & Kohlhoff memorial (the 77 yards) but also the full extent of the Wall remnants along Bernauer Strasse (232 yards), which now had two gaps in it due to Sophien's actions. Strieder actually wanted to cancel the Kohlhoff & Kohlhoff memorial, which he found too artificial next to the actual Wall remains, but Radunski feared that this would cause the federal government to withdraw its funding. Hence, Strieder appealed to the architects to find a way to integrate the longer section of the Wall between Bergstrasse and Ackerstrasse into their design, instead of just the 77 yards. Pastor Fischer and the district government of Wedding agreed with this approach.[116]

Fischer had long expressed skepticism about Hildebrandt's claims of the existence of mass graves at the site and been frustrated by the influence Hildebrandt exerted on the plans for the Berlin Wall Memorial.[117] Now that it was clear the Wall remains did not stand on former graves, it seemed that Hildebrandt's influence was finally diminishing. Fischer pointedly reiterated to the press: "The preservation of the last remains of the Wall has unique a historical dimension. It overrides local interests and the concerns of a single parish."[118]

The Voice of the Victims

One final conflict developed from another direction before the Kohlhoff & Kohlhoff memorial would be completed. This concerned the wording to be inscribed on the memorial as well as other aspects of the design.[119] In the view of the Group of Victims and Survivors of the Wall and Inner-German Border, the planned inscription – "in commemoration of the victims of the division" – sounded passive and vague. The group insisted that the inscription be changed to make it much clearer that they were victims of East Germany's communist regime.

In early 1998, Klaus-Peter Eich drafted a letter sent by the group to Chancellor Kohl, his interior minister, and others to voice their concerns. Michael Schmidt's parents Horst and Dorothea Schmidt were among those who signed the letter.[120] The signatories to the letter argued that the Wall trials clearly showed "that the political and legal responsibility for the deaths at the Wall and the barbed wire" lay at the feet of the East German military and political leaders. Instead of blaming "an imaginary apparatus like the Cold War

---

[116] Ibid., pp. 604–610.
[117] Ua, "Sophien-Pfarrer ignoriert Mauer-Beschlüsse," *Berliner Zeitung*, April 30, 1997.
[118] Gaserow, "Das Gerangel um ein Stückchen Mauer," *Zeit Online*, May 2, 1997.
[119] See also Rudnick, *Die andere Hälfte der Erinnerung*, pp. 615–18.
[120] Kreis der Opfer und der Hinterbliebenen der Opfer der Berliner Mauer und der innerdeutschen Grenze, "Memorandum. Mahn- und Gedenkstätte für die Opfer der SED-Diktatur an der Berliner Mauer und der innerdeutschen Grenze," January 26, 1998, SWFKB, GBM, Nr. K17.

or the division of Germany," they declared that just as "people in the Nazi concentration camps were not killed by some anonymous machinery," so the victims of the Wall were killed or injured by "a clear combination of decision makers, paper-pushers, order-givers and order-receivers." In sum, "Victims of the Wall and the border installations were kept quiet by the SED dictatorship. Are we to be victims again on the altar of communist lies in reunited Germany?" they pointedly asked.

Eich had become a staunch advocate for victims of the Wall since his initial approach to Fischer years earlier. Indeed, in 1996 at a Bundestag ceremony for the thirty-fifth anniversary of the erection of the Wall, he chastised the MPs, declaring that until then, "victims and the loved ones they left behind [were] only invited to speak on talk shows or in the tabloids." He described to the parliamentarians how he had been "shot in the back with no warning call or warning shots" when escaping over the barbed wire at Bernauer Strasse on October 12, 1961. This was followed by much time in hospital treating his resulting physical and emotional injuries. He was sharply critical of the government's approach to the Wall: the large number of suspended sentences in the Wall trials; the lack of a memorial to victims of the Wall as of 1996; and insufficient financial and social support for people who suffered because of the Wall. He wondered "what happened to the politicians who used to be so critical when people were killed at the border?"[121] Two years later in discussions about the Berlin Wall Memorial, Eich and others in the "group of victims and survivors" kept up the pressure on their elected representatives.

In addition to calling for changes in the wording of the dedication, the group castigated the Kohlhoff & Kohlhoff design as a completely inappropriate example of "art work with the Wall," maintaining that "the steel walls trivialize the Wall" and transform the former death strip into a "hall of mirrors." All of this added up in their view to an effort to downplay the East German regime generally and its border regime specifically. This of course was never the plan of Trotnow or Fischer, both of whom had emphasized from the start the need to preserve the Wall at Bernauer Strasse to show the tyranny of the GDR leadership that had caused so much pain. Yet the Senate had chosen the Kohlhoff & Kohlhoff design and its minimalistic approach. The victims' group demanded a voice in the (now advanced) process of creating the Berlin Wall Memorial, the kind of voice that they

[121] Remarks by Klaus-Peter Eich at the "Öffentliche Gedenkveranstaltung aus Anlaß des 35. Jahrestages des Baus der Berliner Mauer," in *Materialien der Enquete-Kommission "Überwindung der Folgen der SED-Diktatur in Prozess der deutschen Einheit,"* Band I, p. 945. Eich was in fact so critical of the government that he was not invited to speak or to distribute his speech. Another victim who was invited to speak, Ilse Leopold, turned over the podium to Eich. Ibid., pp. 942–43. See also Renate Oschlies, "Beifall für ungebetenen Redner: Eklat bei Gedenkfeier des Bundestages zu Ehren der Maueropfer," *Berliner Zeitung,* August 14, 1996.

felt the Sophien parish had unjustifiably been granted for far too long. They appealed for a reconstruction of all the elements of the old border and urged Kohl to veto the Kohlhoff & Kohlhoff memorial just as he had vetoed an early version of the Holocaust memorial.

Initially, the federal government and the Berlin Senate did not give in to the demand to change the wording of the dedication. Thus, the original text engraved in June 1998 on the Ackerstrasse side of the Kohlhoff & Kohlhoff memorial mentioned the "victims of the division." The Berlin Senate then had second thoughts and suggested to the federal interior ministry that they comply with the wishes of the victims and their survivors before the official unveiling of the memorial. The interior minister agreed. Accordingly, and after nearly four years of disputes, on August 13, 1998, the Berlin Wall Memorial designed by Kohlhoff & Kohlhoff was dedicated "in memory of the division of the city from August 13, 1961 to November 9, 1989, and in remembrance of the victims of communist tyranny."[122] The final, recently modified three words of the inscription were attached with a provisional piece of metal until they could be properly engraved.[123] The federal minister for environmental protection, Angela Merkel, Mayor Diepgen, and Protestant Church provost Heinrich Lüdtke each gave short addresses at the opening, as did Klaus-Peter Eich from his wheelchair.[124] While Eich was still not happy with the design, he was satisfied that the government had responded to the criticisms about the wording of the dedication.

When the rectangular Kohlhoff & Kohlhoff memorial (Figure 10) opened to the public with its two steel walls connecting the remains of the Berlin Wall and *Hinterlandmauer*, there was massive criticism of the design.[125] Visitors complained that it was cold and confusing and conveyed nearly nothing of what it was like to actually live with the Wall, to say nothing of being killed trying to cross it. A ninety-year-old woman who had lived at Bernauer Strasse since 1920 said, "It looked much different before, much more threatening." The shiny stainless steel wall on one side and the dedication on the other side with rusty steel bore no resemblance to the original Wall. Even worse, since the two added elements were much taller than the original pieces of the Wall standing at the site, they made the latter seem much smaller and rather

---

[122] Rudnick, *Die andere Hälfte der Erinnerung*, pp. 618–23. See also Trotnow, "Understanding the Present by Looking Back at the Past," p. 21.

[123] Kerstin Rottmann, "Steine, die Antwort geben auf Fragen zur deutschen Teilung," *Welt*, August 13, 1998.

[124] Landespressedienst aus dem Senat, Michael-Andreas Butz, press statement No. 152, "Veranstaltungen zum 13. August: Einweihung der Gedenkstätte Beriner Mauer und Kranzniederlegung am Fechter-Mahnmal," August 10, 1998.

[125] Rottmann, "Steine, die Antwort geben auf Fragen zur deutschen Teilung."

Figure 10 Steel wall of Kohlhoff & Kohlhoff memorial towering above the Berlin Wall
Source: Hope M. Harrison.

harmless, as the former victims and their survivors had argued.[126] In the absence of an observation platform for viewing the closed-off, largely empty rectangular area of the former border strip, visitors could only see into the area by peering through the little gaps in the original *Hinterlandmauer*. As one visitor lamented when looking through the gaps, "this lacks anything that makes it clear that people were shot here."[127] Indeed, in naming the Kohlhoff & Kohlhoff proposal one of the second-place winners, the jury itself had called the design one of "minimum consensus" in which "the significance of the site is lost."[128] The mirror effect of the stainless steel walls was also lost in the rain and with dirt and dust.[129] As Manfred Fischer described to a reporter from *Die Welt*, "Time and again I see people standing helplessly in front of

[126] "Gedenken an die Maueropfer," *Wiener Zeitung*, August 14, 1998; and Gabriele Camphausen, "The Monument on the Berlin Wall Memorial Site," in The Berlin Wall – Memorial Site and Exhibition Center Association, ed., *Berlin Wall Memorial Site*, p. 21.

[127] Thomas Eisenkrätzer, "Ich vermisse alles. Hier wird die Geschichte verschönt," *Berliner Zeitung*, August 8, 1998.

[128] "Spuren verwischen: Mauerdenkmal," *Focus Magazine* 17, April 24, 1995.

[129] "Gedenken an die Maueropfer," *Wiener Zeitung*, August 14, 1998; and Rottmann, "Steine, die Antwort geben auf Fragen zur deutschen Teilung," *Welt*, August 13, 1998.

the steel wall. Then they come to us across the street [at the Reconciliation parish center] with their questions."[130]

Nine years after the fall of the Berlin Wall and the start of efforts by Fischer and Trotnow to preserve some of the Wall and remember its history, there was finally a national Berlin Wall Memorial at Bernauer Strasse. Few were fully satisfied with this memorial, but it marked an important first step in broadening German memory culture to include victims of the Berlin Wall. The contentious process leading to the creation of the memorial reflected the variety of German attitudes both toward the past and its meaning for the present. Disagreements among the residents of Bernauer Strasse and municipal politicians about whether and how much to preserve of the Wall and what to say about its history delayed the erection of a memorial, as did the broader context of Berliners wanting to move on and leave the Wall behind.

As Fischer and Trotnow encountered challenges to their instinct that the history of the Wall must be remembered and described, they sought ways to exert more control over their capacity to do this. Fischer would become particularly adept at this in the years to come.

---

[130] Ibid.

3

Creating a Berlin Wall Memorial Ensemble
at Bernauer Strasse

While the conflicts with the Sophien parish played out over creating a Berlin Wall Memorial and a whole site for remembering the Berlin Wall in the former death strip, Manfred Fischer oversaw activities in his own parish to remember the Wall and its victims. Both inside the parish center and outside where the demolished church used to be, he hosted temporary exhibits on the history of the Wall and on the past, present, and future of Bernauer Strasse, including putting up signs to mark remnants of houses that had been demolished by the GDR border troops on the eastern side of the street. With a future documentation center in mind, he continued to gather documents, photographs, and testimonies from people who had experienced the Wall at Bernauer Strasse – many of whom came to find him and tell their stories. Through all of this, Fischer also served as the pastor to his community in church services and other religious and non-religious activities. He was essentially doing two jobs at once.

He was full of energy and creativity in finding ways to keep the history of the Berlin Wall alive. Instead of being worn down by the fight to preserve as much as possible of the Wall at Bernauer Strasse, he seemed to draw energy from it. Even as Trotnow was called away to found the new Allied Museum on the role of the American, British, and French forces in West Berlin and West Germany during the Cold War, Fischer stayed on and intensified his efforts to create structures – both physical and administrative – that would help preserve memory of the Wall and teach new generations about its history. His location right across the street from the Berlin Wall had long been the guiding factor in his engagement with the effects of the Wall. Now Fischer would develop new ways to turn that location to his advantage in his quest to highlight the history of the Wall, as he had when he ran across the street in 1990 to stop bulldozers from removing pieces of it.

Frustrated by only sporadic political support for remembering the Wall over the previous years, Fischer would also expand his political outreach, especially since political support was essential for financial support. He would find, however, that gaining political and economic support for his efforts at Bernauer Strasse would inject more politics into the process of remembering the Berlin Wall than he was often comfortable with. In the political landscape of united Berlin and Germany, some of the old divisions remained, joined by new ones. Attitudes toward the history of the Wall would increasingly become politicized, and Fischer's efforts to create a site of memory of the Wall at Bernauer Strasse would get caught up in broader political contestations over the history and legacy of the Wall. The more success Fischer and his colleagues at Bernauer Strasse achieved in putting the history of the Wall in a public spotlight, the more political and other groups would seek to use that history for their own contemporary purposes. Historical anniversaries would increasingly become moments reflecting divided views of history and its current relevance.

Fischer's Proposal for a Memorial Ensemble

While the federal government had funded and the Berlin Senate had negotiated the location and design for the Berlin Wall Memorial as created by Kohlhoff & Kohlhoff, Fischer sought a solution to the problem of conveying the history of the Berlin Wall as he and Trotnow had originally planned. The site needed the documentation center or museum that they had long discussed but had not come to fruition. Fischer and his parishioners had been treating their parish center as an exhibition space for years. Now they would make this official.

In the summer of 1997, in response to the actions of Sophien removing thirty-two segments of the Berlin Wall at Bernauer Strasse and in view of the insufficiencies of the Kohlhoff & Kohlhoff memorial design which had not yet been executed, Fischer and his parishioners put forward a four-part proposal to the Berlin Senate for a future Berlin Wall Memorial Ensemble to be added to the Kohlhoff & Kohlhoff design: 1) the donation of part of the Reconciliation parish building for a museum, or as they called it, the Documentation Center; 2) the addition of an observation deck to the parish building so that visitors could see into the area of the former death strip walled off by the Kohlhoff & Kohlhoff memorial and understand what it meant; 3) the guaranteed preservation of the remaining pieces of the Wall along Bernauer Strasse; and 4) the erection of a small Chapel of Reconciliation on part of the foundations of the former Church of Reconciliation.[1] Fischer would come to call this plan "Kohlhoff plus ensemble."[2]

This plan would mark the beginning of what, over the next twenty years, would develop into a much larger, publicly funded Berlin Wall Memorial

---

[1] Gabriele Camphausen and Manfred Fischer, "Die bürgerschaftliche Durchsetzung der Gedenkstätte an der Bernauer Strasse," in Klaus-Dietmar Henke, ed., *Die Mauer* (Munich: Deutscher Taschenbuch Verlag, 2011), pp. 367–69; and the report and recommended Senate resolution by the Senator for Science, Research and Culture, Peter Radunski, on creating a Berlin Wall ensemble at Bernauer Strasse, "Errichtung der Gedenkstätte Berliner Mauer an der Bernauer Straße nach dem Entwurf der Architekten Kohlhoff & Kohlhoff." Senatsverwaltung für Wissenschaft, Forschung und Kultur, "Senatsvorlage Nr. 983/97, zur Beschlußfassung, für die Sitzung am Dienstag, dem 5. August 1997," July 23, 1997, esp. pp. 3–4 on Fischer's plans and the need for funding for the Documentation Center and observation platform. LAB, D Rep. 002/8019.

[2] Interview with Manfred Fischer, October 15, 2009.

Site, which would eventually attract more than one million visitors a year. In the summer of 1997, however, Fischer himself likely could not have dreamed of such a prospect. The architect and urban planner Günther Schlusche later observed that the parish's ensemble proposal "elevated the planning to a standard that was on par with the commemoration of the Nazi past: it acknowledged that visitors today can only appreciate the authenticity of the site when it has been carefully interpreted and decoded through explanatory educational methods."[3] The site could not effectively stand on its own, but must be explained, particularly to future generations, as Trotnow had declared from the start.

While senators argued about what to do in the wake of Sophien's removal of the two large sections of the Wall, Fischer surprised them all like a *deus ex machina* with this plan. As point three mentioned, his proposal meant the Senate had to finally ensure that Sophien would not remove any more pieces of the Wall. The federal government supported Fischer's proposal. Given that the Berlin Senate was relying on the federal funds for the Kohlhoff & Kohlhoff memorial, the Senate had little choice but to go along as well, as it did on August 5, 1997.[4] A press statement that day by Peter Radunski, the Senator for Science, Research and Culture, also announced the plans to use the Reconciliation parish building "to show exemplary documentation portraying the history, effects and fall of the Wall. This area lies on the western side [of the street] and thus provides the necessary tranquility for the [Kohlhoff & Kohlhoff] memorial at the cemetery [on the other side of the street]. The [Reconciliation parish] building was the answer at the time to the erection of the Wall and is thus itself a document of that period."[5]

The following day Fischer, Hildebrandt, senior church leaders, and senators agreed that Fischer's parish house would house the Documentation Center and observation platform and that the Wall remains would be preserved along the entire 232-yard area on Bernauer Strasse. Hildebrandt made it clear, however,

---

[3] Günter Schlusche, "From the Fall of the Wall to the Berlin Wall Memorial: How an Urban Commemorative Space Was Created," in Axel Klausmeier, ed., *The Berlin Wall: Berlin Wall Memorial Exhibition Catalog*, trans. Miriamne Fields (Berlin: Ch. Links, 2015), p. 165.

[4] Der Senate von Berlin, Senatsbeschluß Nr. 983/97, "Errichtung der Gedenkstätte Berliner Mauer an der Bernauer Straße nach dem Entwurf der Architekten Kohlhoff & Kohlhoff," August 5, 1997, LAB, D Rep. 002/8019; and the report and recommended Senate resolution by the Senator for Science, Research and Culture, Peter Radunski, on creating a Berlin Wall ensemble at Bernauer Strasse, "Errichtung der Gedenkstätte Berliner Mauer an der Bernauer Straße nach dem Entwurf der Architekten Kohlhoff & Kohlhoff." Senatsverwaltung für Wissenschaft, Forschung und Kultur, "Senatsvorlage Nr. 983/97, zur Beschlußfassung, für die Sitzung am Dienstag, dem 5. August 1997," July 23, 1997, ibid., p. 2.

[5] Senatsverwaltung für Wissenschaft, Forschung und Kultur, Pressemitteilung für die Senatsvorlage Nr. "Errichtung der Gedenkstätte Berliner Mauer an der Berliner Mauer nach dem Entwurf von Kohlhoff & Kohlhoff" für die Sitzung am 5. August 1997, LAB, D Rep. 002/8019.

that he would not agree to return the thirty-two segments he had removed.[6] They were on display nearby in the former death strip and there they would stay.

Clearly tired of the long-running conflict between Fischer and Hildebrandt and wanting to make absolutely sure they would work cooperatively in the future and not stray from the compromise they had reached, Bishop Wolfgang Huber, together with Fischer and Hildebrandt, and joined by Albruschat from Lazarus, held a press conference in the former death strip on August 13, 1997. Huber stated in no uncertain terms that the future design of the memorial site must equally respect the memory of the Wall and the ongoing functioning of the Sophien cemetery. He emphasized that all of the historical layers of the site must be portrayed, from World War II through the Wall and afterwards. The bishop went out of his way to express gratitude to Hildebrandt for agreeing to allow the Berlin Wall Memorial to be located on the territory of his cemetery and commended Fischer for his initiatives to create a Documentation Center and a Chapel of Reconciliation.[7]

When it was Fischer's turn to speak, he asked rhetorically whether the compromise struck with Sophien had been a "bad compromise," clearly implying that he thought it was and that the sections of the Wall removed by Sophien should be returned to their original location. Yet instead he answered his own question by declaring, "No, the bishop speaks for the church," no doubt reminding himself of this as much as telling others. Fischer was forced to give up on his goal of having the whole length of the Wall along Bernauer Strasse remain intact. While he was grateful for Huber's words of support for his planned Documentation Center, he was concerned that the Senate had not yet committed to providing funds for it or for the observation platform. He needed about DM2 million and would have to fight for reliable funding for nearly ten more years. Fischer was never one to give up, however.

The Chapel of Reconciliation

Fischer had more control over the plans to construct a small Chapel of Reconciliation where the massive old church had stood at Bernauer Strasse 4 than he did over the Berlin Wall Memorial created by Kohlhoff & Kohlhoff or over funding for the Documentation Center. Since Fischer had arrived at his parish more than twenty years earlier, he had never had a separate building for worship. Just as Pastor Hildebrandt had petitioned the government for the return of land the GDR had taken from the Sophien cemetery, so Fischer had

---

[6] "Vermerk über das Gespräch 6. August 1997 zwischen Herrn Dr. Bischof Huber, Herrn Generalsuperintendent Passauer, Herrn Pfarrer Hildebrandt (Sophien-Gemeinde), Herrn Pfarrer Fischer (Versöhnungsgemeinde), Herrn Senator Strieder über die Gestaltung der Mauer an der Bernauer Straße," pp. 1–2, SWFKB, GBM, Nr. 24.

[7] Press conference, Bernauer Strasse, August 13, 1997. Video provided by Rainer Just, Stiftung Berliner Mauer.

petitioned for restitution of the property where the Church of Reconciliation had stood before being blown up. The Reconciliation community regained ownership of the land in November 1995.[8] After considering initial ideas for an open-air "city cloister" or "flower church," the parish decided this would be insufficient and would not offer the necessary protection from the elements for the sacred items from the Church of Reconciliation that were slowly being returned to the parish. Hence, they decided in favor of building a small Chapel of Reconciliation and began to raise private funds for it. Fischer looked forward to finally having the parish community building and the place for worship at two separate sites, albeit just half a block apart. He also hoped the chapel would attract some former members of the congregation to return.

The Chapel of Reconciliation would become the third piece of the developing memorial ensemble at Bernauer Strasse, with the original Wall and the Kohlhoff & Kohlhoff memorial being the first two. Fischer hoped that the chapel would be a place to foster healing. The Documentation Center would focus on disseminating knowledge about the history of the Wall, but the chapel would be a place to reach the spirit, to help heal the wounds from the Wall, wounds that Fischer himself felt. The chapel would also integrate more closely the two strands of Fischer's activities: running the parish and remembering the Wall. Fischer's dual roles as pastor and memory activist were mutually reinforcing and were increasingly expressed in his ways of performing memory of the Wall. His oratorical skills were equally prized in his work as a minister and as a memory activist. His intuitive sense of the power of marking occasions would move his parishioners as well as politicians and the wider public in the years to come, as they had with his May 1986 address mourning the demolition of the church.

Remembering the past and fostering reconciliation remained core missions of Fischer's ministry. Indeed, he hoped that once the chapel was open former victims of the Wall and their families as well as some of the "builders of the Wall" would come to find solace there. That would be a "great sign" of the chapel living up to its name Fischer believed. "I would hold out my hand to them." One of the officers of the border troops who had taken a bench from inside the church before it was destroyed now gave it back. That was a start.[9]

Since the fall of the Wall, important artifacts from inside the old church had been returned to the parish, including the three bells and the cross from the tower, the wooden altarpiece, the rose window from the entrance, the full-size Christ figure, the baptismal font, and the altar Bible that had been inscribed by Empress Augusta Victoria at the dedication of the church in

---

[8] Uta Grüttner, "Ein Ort der Stille und Begegnung," *Berliner Zeitung,* August 20, 1996; and Versöhnungsgemeinde, "Zahlen und Fakten zur *Evangelischen Versöhnungsgemeinde; Geschichtsdaten, ein kurzer Überblick,*" www.kirche-versoehnung.de/fakten.htm.

[9] Uwe Aulich, "Vor Elf Jahren fiel die Mauer – Die neue Versöhnungskapelle auf dem ehemaligen Todesstreifen erinnert an die Teilung der Stadt," *Berliner Zeitung,* November 10, 2000.

1894.[10] Fischer celebrated the return of these special parts of the parish's history in a service on Sunday November 22, 1995, the Protestant Day of Prayer and Penance (*Buß- und Bettag*). Now in possession of some key historical components of the church, the parish decided to locate the new chapel where the apse of the old church had been and to return the rescued bells and the altar of the old church to their original locations on the site.[11]

The parish solicited proposals for the chapel's design and by the time they chose the Berlin architects Rudolf Reitermann and Peter Sassenroth in 1996, they had already raised DM200,000. Many private sponsors, led by Günter and Waldtraut Braun, would ultimately contribute to the DM1.6 million structure.[12] Bishop Huber, a strong supporter of Fischer's efforts at Bernauer Strasse, knew the Brauns as well as the chair of the board of Berliner Volksbank, Rudolf Prast, and enlisted their help.[13] In the large gallery space of the bank's new headquarters at Potsdamer Platz, Prast hosted an exhibit about the history of the church and the plans for the chapel. He noted that the bank had "also experienced the drama and pain of the division" and thus "had much in common with the [Reconciliation] community."[14]

Fischer fostered connections with a wide and varied group of supporters. In the spring of 1998, he, Rainer Just, and others from the parish and important institutions in Berlin, including Prast and former cultural senator Hassemer, formed the Berlin Wall Memorial Supporters' Association (*Förderverein Gedenkstätte Berliner Mauer*).[15] Although the first task of the association was the construction of the Chapel of Reconciliation, the members had in mind the whole gamut of future work to expand and solidify the ensemble as the Berlin Wall Memorial Site.[16]

The new supporters' association and the parishioners were deeply involved in the process of creating the Chapel of Reconciliation, which they saw as an

---

[10] Manfred Richter, "Neubau einer Kapelle der Versöhnung im ehemaligen Mauerstreifen," *Kunst+Kirche* 63, no. 1 (2000), pp. 45–46, www.versoehnungskapelle.de/texte/seite.php?id=109180.

[11] Manfred Fischer, "The History of the 'Chapel of Reconciliation'," in The Berlin Wall – Memorial Site and Exhibition Center Association, ed., *Berlin Wall Memorial Site, Exhibition Center and the Chapel of Reconciliation on Bernauer Strasse* (Berlin: Jaron Verlag, 1999), p. 36. These were the same bells the Hildebrandt brothers had earlier hoped would stand as a memorial to the old church but which would now be joined by the new chapel.

[12] Interview with Rudolf Prast, October 31, 2018.

[13] Ibid.

[14] Uwe Aulich, "Bank sammelt Geld für Kapelle," *Berliner Zeitung*, October 29, 1998; and Uwe Aulich, "Stücke eines gesprengten Gotteshaus: Ausstellung zur Geschichte der Versöhnungsgemeinde," *Berliner Zeitung*, October 14, 1998.

[15] Die Versöhnungsgemeinde, "Zahlen und Fakten zur *Evangelischen Versöhnungsgemeinde*," www.kirche-versoehnung.de/fakten.htm; and author's correspondence with Rainer Just, September 7, 2018.

[16] Correspondence with Rainer Just, September 7, 2018.

essential element of a broader Berlin Wall Memorial Site. Their vision for the chapel included simple materials, an environmentally sustainable, minimalistic structure, and the preservation of historical traces of both the church and the border zone. In March 1998, the architects presented their plans to an assembly of parishioners. Reitermann and Sassenroth proposed an oval-shaped chapel made of concrete and steel and surrounded by glass. The parishioners liked the shape but not the materials. In spite of the fact that Fischer had made clear to the architects that concrete – the material used in the Berlin Wall – was "the last material that should be used" in the chapel, the architects stuck to their proposal. As a result, Fischer and the parishioners rejected it.[17]

The parish favored natural materials like clay and wood, not concrete. As Fischer later wrote, "Clay also meant for us the use of 'healing earth' on the wounds of the city. The application of clay packs on the skin for healing is well-known. Wasn't there also a wound to be healed here, a wound to the earth and to the spirit of the city?"[18] Since the parish planned to limit costs and damage to the environment by forgoing heating in the chapel, a material like clay would also keep the chapel warmer than other materials and would add some moisture to the dry air in the winter. Accordingly, the parish persuaded two experts at the Technical University of Berlin, Klaus Dierks and Christoph Ziegert, to work with the architects in using clay as the main material for the chapel. In April the architects submitted a modified proposal using clay, and the parish accepted it.

The material used would ultimately be loam, a combination of clay, sand, and silt, and the world-renowned loam architect Martin Rauch would supervise the construction.[19] Utilizing loam even allowed the builders to incorporate some parts of the old, destroyed church in the construction. The compressed loam to make the walls needed to be combined with a raw aggregating material. In excavating the foundation of the old church, workers discovered some broken bricks left from its demolition. These were then mixed with the loam for the walls. As Fischer observed, "The old church was destroyed with destructive energy, and this gave us the material to utilize in a new way – thanks to constructive energy."[20] A small window in the floor of the chapel would give visitors a sense of that destructive past as they looked into the basement of the old church and saw not just the foundations of the destroyed church but also some of the hollow blocks used in the first stage of constructing the Berlin Wall.[21]

---

[17] Interview with Manfred Fischer, October 15, 2009.

[18] Manfred Fischer, "Zwischen Glas und Stahl – Lehm," *Reformatio* 3 (2002), www.versoehnungskapelle.de/texte/seite.php?id=109224%20.

[19] Rudolf Stegers, "Chapel of Reconciliation," *Architektur Aktuell* 3 (2001), pp. 66–75, www.kapelle-versoehnung.de/bin/englisch/geschichtelamellen.php; and www.lehmtonerde.at/en/projects/project.php?pID=28.

[20] Fischer, "Zwischen Glas und Stahl – Lehm."

[21] Susanne Kippenberger, "Ein Wunder angucken," *Tagesspiegel*, August 7, 2001, www.versoehnungskapelle.de/texte/seite.php?id=109183.

The loam chapel would be surrounded by a covered louvered colonnade made of wood, with the latter offering an intermediate space between the outside world and the sacred space inside the chapel, as well as providing an area for exhibits related to the church and the Wall. The foundation of the old church would be demarcated for all to see, and since the church had been much bigger than the chapel, the latter would have significant free space around it, giving it some distance from streets and other buildings. The parish had already planted the surrounding area with wild flowers and would eventually plant it with rye to make the communion bread. Growing living, life-sustaining things in the former death strip would be another way of overcoming the past.

Pastor Fischer was skilled at creating moments that would make an impression. Even though the chapel was not yet complete, he was careful to celebrate each key step in the process. He hosted an outdoor Easter service in the spring of 1999 on the grounds where construction of the chapel would soon begin. The three bells from the Church of Reconciliation had been returned to their original site, and the Easter service began with Fischer and parishioners ringing the bells. A month later the bells rang again, after having been placed in a thirteen-foot-tall wooden truss on the site where the old bell tower had been. Fischer formally dedicated the bells at a ceremony for the laying of the chapel's cornerstone on Pentecost in late May.[22] Another ceremony would take place on November 9, the tenth anniversary of the fall of the Wall.

For the process of building the chapel, the pastor and his congregation came up with an inventive approach that would remember the division, carry out the mission of reconciliation, and keep down the costs. They cooperated with *Offene Häuser* (the Open Houses Association) to engage young volunteers from Eastern and Western European countries in the process of constructing the chapel. The parish noted that while "Berliners generally see the Berlin Wall as *their* Wall, . . .they lose sight of the fact that the inner-German border was a Europe-wide border between systems. The collective work on the Chapel of Reconciliation by young volunteers from France and Poland, Spain and Ukraine, Sweden and Romania symbolizes the overcoming of the division of Europe in a unique way."[23] In the summer and fall of 1999, the volunteers worked with professionals to build the chapel with its loam walls.

Fischer timed the topping out ceremony of the chapel for the tenth anniversary of the fall of the Wall. For Fischer, it was a profound moment to

---

[22] Uwe Aulich, "Baubeginn für Kapelle der Versöhnung," *Berliner Zeitung*, March 3,1999; and Uwe Aulich, "Die Glocken der Versöhnungskirche sind an die Bernauer Straße zurückgekehrt," *Berliner Zeitung*, May 21, 1999.

[23] Evangelische Versöhnungsgemeinde Berlin, "Die gebaute Kapelle," www.versoehnungska pelle.de/seite/109156/bauplanung.html; Die Versöhnungsgemeinde, "Zahlen und Fakten zur *Evangelischen Versöhnungsgemeinde*," www.kirche-versoehnung.de/fakten.htm; and Richter, "Neubau einer Kapelle der Versöhnung im ehemaligen Mauer-Streifen."

see the basic structure finally standing on the former death strip: Now "the wounds are starting to heal for me."[24] The original wooden altarpiece was reconstructed and mounted in a niche in the chapel on the spot where it had been located in the much bigger church. On November 9, 1999, the Reconciliation parish also became a member of the Community of the Cross of Nails connected with Coventry Cathedral. The famous cathedral had been destroyed by German bombs in World War II and embraced a mission of reconciliation after the war, giving each new member of the community a bronze sculpture called "Reconciliation." The sculpture depicts two kneeling figures reaching across a divide to embrace each other, each with their head on the other's shoulder. They are clearly exhausted from the conflict between them and are turning to reconciliation instead of enmity. In the version of the sculpture given to the Chapel of Reconciliation, a Bible and a piece of barbed wire are on the ground between the two figures as they reach over to each other. Fischer had the sculpture placed outside, to the left of the entrance to the chapel on the grounds of the former death strip. The original cross from atop the tower of the Church of Reconciliation, twisted from its flight to the ground during the demolition, was placed on the right side of the chapel.

Although Fischer began to hold services in the nearly completed chapel in December 1999, he timed the formal dedication of the completed Chapel of Reconciliation (Figure 11) for the anniversary of the fall of the Wall the following year, more than fifteen years after the Church of Reconciliation had been demolished and nearly forty years after the last service had been held in the former church. At the dedication service on November 9, 2000, Bishop Huber gave the sermon. Speaking from the new loam altar, Huber declared that the Chapel of Reconciliation was both "a unique sign of our thanks to God for overcoming the division and fostering reconciliation" and "a sign against resignation, a sign of hope." Remembering not just the fall of the Wall on November 9, 1989, but also *Kristallnacht* of November 9, 1938, Huber proclaimed that henceforth November 9 "must become a signal for tolerance and shared humanity for every part of our country" and "we will start here, here in the Chapel of Reconciliation."[25]

The superintendent of the Protestant Church in northern Germany, Martin-Michael Passauer, saw the Church of Reconciliation as "a symbol of the eventful history of Berlin." With the government beginning its move from Bonn to Berlin in 1999, Germans were grappling with "questions of political and cultural identity," and "the culture of memory has a decisive place in

---

[24] Uwe Aulich, "Vor Elf Jahren fiel die Mauer – Die neue Versöhnungskapelle auf dem ehemaligen Todesstreifen erinnert an die Teilung der Stadt," *Berliner Zeitung*, November 10, 2000.

[25] Bishop Wolfgang Huber, excerpts from sermon at the dedication of the Chapel of Reconciliation, November 9, 2000, www.versoehnungskapelle.de/texte/seite.php?id=108512.

Figure 11 Chapel of Reconciliation with loam walls
Source: Photographer: Philip Gunkel. Archive, Versöhnungsgemeinde Berlin-Wedding, MG_4006.

these." Fischer's ministry was a prime example of making these connections. As Passauer declared: "Religion is not a private matter, but part of public life."[26] The highly unusual near fusion Fischer was carrying out between his church and the Berlin Wall Memorial Ensemble would take this to a whole new level.

This had been particularly clear when Fischer made his "Kohlhoff plus ensemble" proposal to the Berlin Senate in June 1997. The year before, Fischer had donated space in his parish center to former East German civic activists and others who had formed a "citizens' office" (*Bürgerbüro*) to help people who had been persecuted in the GDR seek restitution and have former criminal convictions (such as being charged with attempting to escape) overturned. The office also directed people in need to counselors for post-traumatic stress disorder and other maladies from which they were suffering. In addition, the *Bürgerbüro* sought to make more people aware of the way dissidents had been victimized in the GDR.[27] A few years later in another key step in grappling with the past, Fischer would begin leading individual prayers in memory of people killed at the Wall once research had been done to identify these people. This would further

[26] Martin-Michael Passauer, excerpts from speech at the Berliner Volksbank at Potsdamer Platz for the exhibit "Berlin im Wandel – Versöhnung der Auftrag," January 28, 1999, www.versoehnungskapelle.de/seite/109156/bauplanung.html.
[27] www.buergerbuero-berlin.de/; and interview with Manfred Fischer, October 15, 2009.

consolidate the chapel as part of the Berlin Wall Memorial ensemble at Bernauer Strasse. Under Fischer's real and metaphorical roof, there was much activity devoted to confronting the East German past and looking to the future.

Creating a Berlin Wall Association and Documentation Center

Fischer, his allies, and his parishioners could not do all this work on their own, and it became clear that there needed to be a structure to oversee the expansion of activities connected to remembering the Berlin Wall. The process of forming the Documentation Center with an administrative body to oversee it took place in parallel with the creation of the Chapel of Reconciliation.

In November 1997, Senator for City Planning, Peter Strieder, and Berlin's State Secretary for Science, Research and Culture, Lutz von Pufendorf, appointed a working group to develop a conceptual plan for the Documentation Center. The historian and museum expert, Gabriele Camphausen, joined Fischer and Trotnow in this group. The group was chaired by von Pufendorf and presented its plan in March 1998 to build on Fischer and Trotnow's work in using photographs, documents, and personal testimonies to elucidate the history of the Berlin Wall. Eight months later, with backing from the Berlin Senate, the Berlin Wall Association – Memorial Site and Documentation Center (*Verein Berliner Mauer – Gedenkstätte and Dokumentationszentrum*) was constituted. As agreed, Fischer provided space for it in his parish building.[28] In essence, this was the first step in the Senate "outsourcing" control over (or stepping back again from control over) the whole ensemble area that would come to be known as the Berlin Wall Memorial Site (*Gedenkstätte Berliner Mauer*).[29] Ten years later the Berlin Wall Association would become the Berlin Wall Foundation (*Stiftung Berliner Mauer*), which continues to oversee the memorial site at Bernauer Strasse and beyond.

In addition to Fischer, Trotnow, and Camphausen, other founding members of the Berlin Wall Association included: Berliner Volksbank board chair Rudolf Prast, Bishop Huber, the *Spiegel* journalist Stefan Berg (who grew up close to the Wall in East Berlin and wrote frequently about GDR history),[30] the historian and political scientist Peter Steinbach (then a professor at the Free University of Berlin and the director of the German Resistance Memorial Site dedicated to the Nazi resistance), Ehrhart Neubert (a minister, theologian, and civic activist from the GDR who became the director of the research and education department at the Stasi Records Authority in 1997 and was a founding member of the *Bürgerbüro* in residence at Fischer's parish center),

---

[28] Gabriele Camphausen, "Berliner Mauer-Gedenkstätte und Dokumentationszentrum, e.V. Bilanz und Perspektiven der Vereinstätigkeit," August 2004, p. 3. Given to the author by Camphausen.

[29] Camphausen and Fischer, "Die bürgerschaftliche Durchsetzung," pp. 370, 372.

[30] Stefan Berg, "Einheit. Die wissen nichts," *Spiegel*, September 27, 2010.

as well as officials from the Berlin Senate's department on science, research and culture (von Pufendorf and Marie-Luise Waga), and others. The association also reached out to one of the most prominent journalists in Berlin at the time, Manfred Rexin, to be the first chair of the advisory council. At the time, media coverage of the Wall was dominated by the conservative Springer publishing house, and the Berlin Wall Association wanted to change that and reach a wider audience. The presence of Berg from *Der Spiegel* helped with this too.

Gabriele Camphausen was elected chair of the Berlin Wall Association. In the early 1990s, she had worked alongside Trotnow at the Berlin-Karlshorst museum and memorial site, where the Nazis had surrendered to the Soviets and which became a museum of the history of German-Soviet relations.[31] Camphausen then served as the director of the museum and memorial site at the former Stasi prison in Berlin-Hohenschönhausen from 1995 to 1998. In 1998, when she became the (volunteer) chair of the Berlin Wall Association, she moved from her full-time position at Hohenschönhausen to a new full-time position as manager of the Topography of Terror, the memorial site in the heart of Berlin connected to the Nazi leadership and particularly the Gestapo, their secret police. Just as Fischer and Trotnow had been trying to establish a Berlin Wall Memorial Site, these other important historical sites were being developed as memorials and museums in the wake of unification and renewed German grappling with history. Experts at one site connected to Germany's difficult history often moved to another after gaining experience.

In Camphausen's case, however, she was doing it all at once: working full-time at another site, first related to the Stasi and then related to the Nazi leadership, while also helping to get the Berlin Wall Memorial Ensemble and especially the Documentation Center established.[32] With Berlin under major financial duress due to the ending of decades-long Cold War subsidies from the federal government (which now had other more pressing tasks, especially financing the move of the government from Bonn to Berlin) and also the need to bring the eastern part of the city up to western standards, Berlin was strapped for funds. A further financial drain was the fact that the separate institutions built up in eastern and western Berlin during the years of division meant that the city was now faced with funding double and triple universities, hospitals, orchestras, opera houses, libraries, and other public institutions. One way politicians got around the tight financial situation was by relying on committed citizens to carry more than their fair share of the load. Camphausen was a prime example of this when officials in the Senate's cultural affairs department asked her to help with the Documentation Center.

---

[31] Email from Helmut Trotnow, November 7, 2011; interview with Gabriele Camphausen, November 6, 2018.

[32] Correspondence with Gabriele Camphausen, September 11, 2018, and interview November 6, 2018.

Figure 12 Manfred Fischer and Gabriele Camphausen, Documentation Center, Berlin
Wall Memorial
Source: Gabriele Camphausen.

Camphausen (Figure 12) essentially took on the role of historian and
organizer that Trotnow had long played at Bernauer Strasse, since Trotnow
was increasingly pulled away by his position at the Allied Museum. Trotnow
had been in charge of planning for the new Allied Museum in Berlin-Dahlem
since 1993 and became its founding director when it opened in 1996. He
remained involved at Bernauer Strasse through the late 1990s and the foundation of the Berlin Wall Association. Hence, while it had been Trotnow who
had drafted plans in the early 1990s for the site at Bernauer Strasse, it was
Camphausen who drafted the conceptual plans for the Documentation
Center in the late 1990s, together with Fischer, Trotnow, and other members
of the working group.

She would oversee the evolution of the Berlin Wall Memorial Ensemble
focusing on the Documentation Center for much of the next ten years; the
whole time, incredibly, in a volunteer capacity while working elsewhere in a
full-time position, and initially without much financial or staffing support at
Bernauer Strasse. Camphausen spent hours talking to Fischer and to others
who had personal histories with the Wall at Bernauer Strasse and were coming
in almost daily to the parish building-cum-Documentation Center to share
their stories. The Berlin Wall Association hired two part-time employees to
conduct interviews with these people, Maria Nooke and Doris Liebermann,

both of whom had been civic activists in the GDR.[33] All the publicity surrounding the Kohlhoff & Kohlhoff memorial, the pieces of Wall the Sophien
community had removed along Bernauer Strasse, and the plans for a new
Documentation Center brought people from far and wide to seek out Fischer
and Camphausen to tell them about their own experiences with the Wall.
Camphausen realized that having come from West Germany, she had taken
the Wall for granted, not thinking much about it. Now that she heard many
stories of both triumph and tragedy connected with the Wall, Camphausen
became deeply engaged with the site and expanded her knowledge with further
reading and research.[34]

The March 1998 working group plan for the Documentation Center sought to
provide information to visitors about how Bernauer Strasse and its residents were
affected by the Berlin Wall and about the broader global context of the Cold War
and the division of Germany. Instead of focusing on transmitting one message, as
victims' groups had insisted should be done with the Kohlhoff & Kohlhoff
memorial's dedication to "victims of communist tyranny," the founders of the
Documentation Center sought to present a wide range of historical information
and let visitors come to their own conclusions. While clearly condemning the
Wall and the East German regime that built it, the working group did not want to
hit visitors over the head with a political approach, favoring instead a more
professional, "neutral" approach to the history of the Berlin Wall.[35] They believed,
as Trotnow testified to the Bundestag, that dictating the meaning of a historical
site was not an effective approach, especially not with young people. Instead,
enabling a historical site, even one with authentic relics such as the Berlin Wall,
"to speak" and to attract young people took careful "pedagogical packaging."[36]

---

[33] Uwe Aulich, "Dokumentation zur Mauer öffnet am 9. November," *Berliner Zeitung*,
July 2 1999.

[34] Interview with Gabriele Camphausen, December 15, 2009.

[35] Verein Beriner Mauer – Gedenkstätte und Dokumentationszentrum e.V., "Das
Dokumentationszentrum 'Berliner Mauer' im Rahmen des Ensembles 'Gedenkstätte
und Dokumentationszentrum Berliner Mauer' in der Bernauer Strasse," March 1998,
cited in Rudnick, *Die andere Hälfte der Erinnerung*, p. 618.

[36] Trotnow's testimony at the Bundestag's public hearing, Protokoll über die 91. Sitzung des
Innenausschusses, "Beteiligung des Bundes an Mahn- und Gedenkstätten," March 7, 1994,
in Deutscher Bundestag, ed. *Materialien der Enquete-Kommission "Aufarbeitung von
Geschichte und Folgen der SED-Diktatur in Deutschland," Band IX, Formen und Ziele der
Auseinandersetzung mit den beiden Diktaturen in Deutschland* (Baden-Baden: Nomos
Verlag, 1995). The Bundestag's commission of inquiry on the SED would ultimately
share Trotnow's conclusion in its final report, arguing that not just victims but also
professional historians must be involved in the work of memorial sites and that care
must be taken to provide information to visitors so that the memorial site could "speak"
about the history that occurred there. See the final report of the second commission of
inquiry, Deutscher Bundestag, ed., "Schlussbericht," *Materialien der Enquete-Kommission
"Überwindung der Folgen der SED-Diktatur im Prozeß der deutschen Einheit,"* p. 617.

The group favored the use of pictures, films, and audio recordings, instead of lengthy text to portray individual biographical, national, and international perspectives on the Berlin Wall.[37] They planned to have multimedia platforms in the Documentation Center and information panels outside along the street to mark places where events related to the Wall occurred, such as the location of tunnels, escapes, and deaths at the Wall. The exhibition would also describe resistance to the Wall; the actual construction of the Wall and the death strip; how the Wall affected the Sophien and Reconciliation communities; and post-1989 debates about a Berlin Wall memorial. It would feature a built-to-scale model of Bernauer Strasse when the Wall stood, and a list of victims of the Wall would be displayed in a prominent place.[38]

On summer weekends in the late 1990s, up to 1,000 tourists were visiting the area surrounding the Wall remains and the Kohlhoff & Kohlhoff memorial. Members of the Berlin Wall Association and freelance, part-time workers offered informational tours.[39] They expected the number of visitors to increase once they had completed the exhibit, which they anticipated would be ready in 2001.[40] Nothing would be possible, however, without significantly enhanced funding, and this presented a major challenge. The Berlin Senate had provided DM46,000 in start-up funds for the Documentation Center in 1998 and then another DM300,000 the following year. Berlin officials believed the federal government should provide the rest of the estimated DM3 million to hire staff, redesign the building, and add an observation platform and elevator.[41] After all, the federal government had paid for the Kohlhoff & Kohlhoff memorial and the Berlin Wall represented national history, not just city history.[42] Some

---

[37] Gabriele Camphausen, "Gedenkstätte 'Berliner Mauer' in der Bernauer Straße. Konzeptionelle Vorschläge," March 2, 1998, SWFKB, GBM, Nr. K18, cited in Rudnick, *Die andere Hälfte der Erinnerung*, p. 617.

[38] Marie Luise Waga, Senate Department on Science, Research and Culture, "Gedenkstätte Berliner Mauer an der Bernauer Strasse," August 10, 1998, SWFKB, GMB, Nr. 24; and Uwe Aulich, "Der erste Lehm für die neue Kapelle wird im Mai gestampft. Bernauer Strasse: Dokumentation zur Mauer erst 2001 fertig," *Berliner Zeitung*, December 4, 1998.

[39] Uwe Aulich, "Dokumentation zur Mauer öffnet am 9. November," *Berliner Zeitung*, July 2, 1999; and correspondence with Camphausen, September 11, 2018.

[40] Uwe Aulich, "Der erste Lehm für die neue Kapelle wird im Mai gestampft," *Berliner Zeitung*, December 4, 1998.

[41] Marie Luise Waga, Senate Department on Science, Research and Culture, "Gedenkstätte Berliner Mauer an der Bernauer Strasse," August 10, 1998, SWFKB, GMB, Nr. 24.

[42] Letter from State Secretary for Finance, Peter Kurth, to State Secretary Lutz von Pufendorf, "Betr.: Mitzeichnung des Schreibens an den Hauptausschuß zu Kap. 17 01 – SenWissKult. Hier: Beschluß des Abgeordnetenhauses von Berlin zum Haushaltsplan 1998 vom 26.11.1997 über die qualifizierte Sperrung der Ausgaben bei Titel 688 11 – Zuschüsse für bezirksübergreifende kulturelle Aktivitäten – in Höhe von 300,000 DM (Tacheles)," September 18, 1998, SWFKB, GBM, Nr. 20.

Bundestag members agreed, but others were reluctant to allocate the funds and believed the municipal government should cover all the costs.

The Bundestag's Approach to the Berlin Wall

Inspired by a wish to move faster to confront the East German communist past than had occurred in either East or West Germany with the Nazi past, the Bundestag held two commissions of inquiry on East Germany between 1992 and 1998.[43] Together with the law on establishing the Federal Commission for the Records of the Former East German State Security Service (BStU, hereafter, Stasi Records Authority) and opening up the Stasi files to a wide range of individuals and groups, the leaders of united Germany sought to gain a greater understanding of how the whole East German regime and society had functioned, including at the fortified border. Chaired by Rainer Eppelmann, the Bundestag commissions were tasked with "contributing to political-historical analyses and a political-moral assessment" of what they called from the start "the SED dictatorship."[44] The distribution of party membership on the commissions reflected that of the federal government as a whole, with the conservative CDU having the strongest voice. Although Kohl's CDU had provided massive amounts of aid to the East German regime in its final years and Kohl himself had hosted Honecker on an official visit to Bonn in 1987, this history was now overlooked as the CDU and others directed a critical spotlight on the former SED regime.

The Berlin Wall and the broader East-West German border regime were among the subjects examined by the commissions. As we have seen, Eppelmann had been an East German civic activist who enthusiastically presided over the removal of the Berlin Wall in the months before unification.[45] In the mid-1990s, however, he cautioned his colleagues "not to forget August 13," the day the GDR regime began to build the Berlin Wall, and emphasized the importance of remembering the history of the Wall.[46] While the courts were holding trials of officials responsible at all levels for killing people at the border,

---

[43] On the commissions of inquiry, see Andrew Beattie, *Playing Politics with History: The Bundestag Inquiries into East Germany* (New York: Berghahn Books, 2008); and A. James McAdams, *Judging the Past in Unified Germany* (New York: Cambridge University Press, 2001), pp. 88–123.

[44] Deutscher Bundestag, ed., *Materialien der Enquete-Kommission "Aufarbeitung von Geschichte und Folgen der SED-Diktatur in Deutschland," Band I,* (Baden-Baden: Nomos Verlag, 1995), p. 155.

[45] Interview with Rainer Eppelmann, March 26, 2004.

[46] Rainer Eppelmann's remarks at the "Öffentliche Gedenkveranstaltung aus Anlaß des 35. Jahrestages des Baus der Berliner Mauer," August 13, 1996, in Deutscher Bundestag, ed., *Materialien der Enquete-Kommission "Überwindung der Folgen der SED-Diktatur in Prozess der deutschen Einheit" Band I,* p. 934.

the Bundestag commissions also investigated the development of the border regime and the impact it had on the population, ranging from a claustrophobic "Wall sickness" to death.[47]

The first commission of inquiry, operating from 1991 to 1994, was called "Working through the History and Consequences of the SED Dictatorship in Germany."[48] It focused on six periods, including the 1960–61 period surrounding the building of the Berlin Wall, and eight areas, one of which was human rights violations, including at the Berlin Wall. The second commission, operating from 1995 to 1998 and entitled, "Overcoming the Consequences of the SED Dictatorship in the Process of German Unity," looked for ways to alleviate the deleterious consequences of the SED regime such as by recognizing and remembering those who had suffered, including at the Berlin Wall.[49]

The second commission's final report explicitly called for supporting the Documentation Center at Bernauer Strasse. Noting that the federal government had already funded the Kohlhoff & Kohlhoff memorial, the commission recommended that the Bundestag should "supplement this with a scientifically-based documentation of the Berlin Wall and the division of Berlin."[50] The commission noted that "memorials in the Berlin area have a significance beyond the region, encompassing the whole country. The multiplicity of historical sites and of learning and documentation opportunities of memorials at authentic sites in the Berlin area create a unique teaching and learning platform for the history of both dictatorships in Germany," which the report noted would only become more important when the Bundestag and government moved from Bonn to Berlin in a few years time and when the city could expect increasing numbers of visitors.[51] The report also called for the creation of a Federal Foundation for Reappraising the SED Dictatorship (*Stiftung zur Aufarbeitung der SED-Diktatur*) which commission members intended would continue the wide-ranging investigation of the history of the East German

---

[47] Hans-Jürgen Fischbeck in Zusammenarbeit mit Ludwig Mehlhorn und Stephan Bickhardt, "Das Mauersyndrom – die Rückwirkung des Grenzregimes auf die Bevölkerung der DDR," in Deutscher Bundestag, ed., *Materialien der Enquete-Kommission "Aufarbeitung von Geschichte und Folgen der SED-Diktatur in Deutschland,"* Band IV/2, pp. 1188–1211; and Hans-Jürgen Grasemann, "Das DDR-Grenzregime und seine Folgen. Der Tod an der Grenze," in Deutscher Bundestag, ed., *Materialien der Enquete-Kommission "Überwindung der Folgen der SED-Diktatur,"* Band VIII/2, pp. 1209–55.

[48] Deutscher Bundestag, ed., *Materialien der Enquete-Kommission "Aufarbeitung von Geschichte und Folgen der SED-Diktatur in Deutschland."*

[49] Deutscher Bundestag, ed., *Materialien der Enquete-Kommission "Überwindung der Folgen der SED-Diktatur in Prozess der deutschen Einheit."*

[50] Deutscher Bundestag, ed., "Schlußbericht," Enquete-Kommission "Überwindung der Folgen der SED-Diktatur in Prozess der deutschen Einheit," *Materialien der Enquete-Kommission "Überwindung der Folgen der SED-Diktatur in Prozess der deutschen Einheit,"* Band I, p. 643. See also pp. 613, 622, and 640.

[51] Ibid., p. 623.

regime and disseminate information about the forty years of communism in Germany. This foundation has existed since 1998.

Not only did the final Bundestag commission report support Fischer and Camphausen's efforts to highlight the history of the Wall at Bernauer Strasse, it also called for the federal and Berlin municipal governments to formulate a master plan for commemorating the Berlin Wall. It would take years for this to happen, however.

The Federal Government and Commemoration at Authentic Historical Sites

In contrast to the pre-unification system in West Germany in which all issues of history, memorials, museums, and education were left to individual states to handle and not the federal government, unified Germany under Chancellor Helmut Kohl – who had earned a doctorate in history and political science – decided that on some nationally important questions relating to history, the federal government should be involved. This included supporting memorials to victims of the Nazi and East German regimes. Thus, the commission of inquiry's final report also tasked the government with devising a framework for federal involvement in supporting key memorial sites connected to both periods.

The report expressed very strong sentiments about confronting the past and the relevance of this process for contemporary German national identity, declaring: "the necessity of working through and remembering both [Nazi and communist] dictatorships is part of a democratic self-conception in united Germany today. The memory of both dictatorships...strengthens the awareness of the value of liberty, justice and democracy. This, together with the necessary investigation into the history of both dictatorships, is the core of the anti-totalitarian consensus [i.e., a commitment to democracy] and the democratic memory culture of the Germans."[52]

In sum, to be a real democracy, dark parts of the past must be openly and publicly grappled with, commemorated, and atoned for – "by the entire government and all of society."[53] This was important not only for the Germans themselves at the end of the twentieth century but also for future generations to make sure the terrible past would not be repeated. In addition, as the final report asserted, "Germany's European neighbors and the whole world will measure the credibility of united Germany particularly by" the degree to which it "keeps alive the memory of these dictatorships," such as at Bernauer Strasse.[54]

---

[52] Ibid., p. 587.
[53] Ibid., p. 613.
[54] Ibid., p. 589.

Two fundamental ways the parliament members urged to preserve memories of Nazi and communist crimes are at the core of this book: the maintenance of authentic historical sites and the commemoration of important historical dates, particularly on anniversaries. The commission maintained that "historical days of remembrance offer an occasion to have debates about the historical self-image of the nation."[55] Moreover, "symbolic and protocol ceremonies particularly on historically important anniversaries are. . .necessary in a democratic state," since "they offer the opportunity to make visible the democratic and national self-image of the Germans."[56] Given the crimes of the Nazis and the communists in Germany, that self-image involves guilt and responsibility, contrition, and a commitment to expose and learn from the past for the future. This practice of "democratic memory culture" is not meant to be expressed just on anniversaries but also "in daily political behavior."[57]

In the view of the Bundestag commissioners, authentic historical sites were the most appropriate place for this responsible remembrance of the past, noting that "the special significance of memorials lies in the authenticity of the historical site."[58] They gave much thought to this issue and consulted with members of victims' groups, directors of memorial sites, and historians, including on the question of authentic sites related to the division of Berlin and Germany and the border.[59] Trotnow was among those who advised the Bundestag. The commission concluded: "In democratic memory culture, the memorial sites in remembrance of the Nazi and communist dictatorships are of central importance. They give an irreplaceable testimony to the memory of terror, repression and resistance. They are signs of the acknowledgement and moral rehabilitation for the victims of the dictatorships by the democratic state."[60] In addition, "mourning, commemorating and learning are inextricably connected at these sites."[61]

While the commissioners insisted that they did not intend to dictate "a united or mandatory view of history" at commemorative sites, they did argue that "there should be a clear normative orientation, since there can be no neutrality vis-à-vis inhumanity and genocide. If you speak about political crimes or crimes against humanity and its victims, then you must address law and justice as well as human and civil rights,"[62] such as the right to life violated by the killing of people at the Berlin Wall. The final report declared that "all victims' groups have the right, individually at the site of their suffering,

[55] Ibid., p. 613.
[56] Ibid., p. 626.
[57] Ibid.
[58] Ibid., p. 613.
[59] Ibid.
[60] Ibid., p. 588.
[61] Ibid., p. 613.
[62] Ibid.

to be recognized by the naming of names and their fate" as to "sharpen the understanding of the historical dimension of the crime."[63] In addition to providing information about victims, the Bundestag members also recommended that historical sites should tell the stories of people who opposed and resisted the Nazi and communist regimes and survived. The stories of people who were perpetrators should be included as well.

By providing this information at authentic sites, not only would Germans learn about the history, but others would as well. The report pointed out that foreign delegations, including heads of state and representatives of memorial sites in other countries, often visit commemorative sites in Berlin. The German historical sites "are observed carefully, particularly by representatives from other post-dictatorial societies."[64] Thus, with these sites, Germany had the chance "to bolster ideas of understanding, tolerance and democracy worldwide."[65] Indeed, as Trotnow noted, even with the fall of the Wall, "the world has not become a more secure place. . . . The fundamental values of freedom and democracy are still threatened today. That is reason enough to keep the historical memory of the Berlin Wall alive."[66]

Following the recommendation of the Bundestag's commission of inquiry in 1998, the federal government adopted a "concept for future federal funding for memorial sites" in June 1999. The government indicated that institutions "located at sites of extraordinary historical importance" with "a specific unique profile based on the authenticity of the site" and with a "scholarly, museological and pedagogical plan for a memorial site" could receive some federal funding. The Documentation Center on Bernauer Strasse seemed to fit this profile perfectly. The concept declared that the federal government would provide support for the Berlin Wall Documentation Center from the new Capital Cultural Funds geared toward supporting cultural activities in Berlin as the government moved its seat from the old capital in Bonn to the new one.[67] Yet, words on paper did not turn into actual funding very quickly.

---

[63] Ibid., p. 617.

[64] Ibid., p. 624.

[65] Ibid., p. 622. For more on these kinds of aims at such sites, see Paul Williams, *Memorial Museums* (New York: Oxford University Press, 2007).

[66] Helmut Trotnow, "Understanding the Present by Looking Back at the Past," in The Berlin Wall – Memorial Site and Exhibition Center Association, ed., *Berlin Wall Memorial Site, Exhibition Center and the Chapel of Reconciliation on Bernauer Strasse*, p. 12.

[67] For the conceptualization of future federal funding for memorial sites, see Unterrichtung durch die Bundesregierung, "Konzeption der künftigen Gedenkstättenförderung des Bundes und Bericht der Bundesregierung über die Beteiligung des Bundes an Gedenkstätten in der Bundesrepublik Deutschland," July 27, 1999, Deutscher Bundestag, Drucksache 14/1569, pp. 3–6, esp. p. 5 where the federal government commits to providing some unspecified amount of funding from the Capital Cultural Funds for the Documentation Center.

Commemorating the Tenth Anniversary of the Fall of the Wall at Bernauer Strasse

The memory activists at Bernauer Strasse planned to open the Documentation Center when they had all the materials necessary for a thorough exhibit on the Wall, which they hoped would be in time for the tenth anniversary of the fall of the Wall. In the final days of 1998, using funds from Berlin since the federal government had not yet allocated any, Camphausen had hired Maria Nooke as the first staff member to work at the Documentation Center, albeit initially with only a three-month contract. Nooke, soon joined by Doris Liebermann, was tasked with interviewing people who had experienced the Wall so that some of their stories could be featured in the new exhibit. Most of the people she spoke to had lived or worked at Bernauer Strasse or had escaped through a tunnel there. A few border soldiers also came in to talk about their service at the Wall; not many, since for the most part they did not talk about their stories except with each other.[68] Even with help with interviews, Camphausen realized in the summer of 1999 that they only had enough materials ready to proceed with a relatively small opening exhibit on November 9. She hoped the Documentation Center received more funds beforehand.[69]

Camphausen, Fischer, and Trotnow worked together to develop the exhibit. A journalist visiting Fischer from the *Berliner Zeitung* in the fall of 1999 observed that the pastor "had little time and hardly any space in his own [parish] center. In his apartment and his work space at Bernauer Strasse 111, every free area is covered with material for the Documentation Center.... .[And t]he pastor's schedule is packed."[70] Fischer was also hosting an exhibit on the history of the Church of Reconciliation in the foyer as part of his efforts to raise funds for the chapel.

After much pressure exerted by Camphausen and others, the federal government finally came through with some support from the Capital Culture Funds two months before the planned opening in November. Thus, instead of opening an extensive exhibit, a redesigned space, and an observation tower, Camphausen, Fischer, and their small team settled for opening a small exhibit for only three months. Entitled *Grenzblicke* (Views of the Border), the exhibit presented photographs and film footage illustrating the effects of the Wall on the residents of Bernauer Strasse between 1961 and 1989.[71]

---

[68] Interview with Maria Nooke, April 15, 2010.
[69] Uwe Aulich, "Dokumentation zur Mauer öffnet am 9. November," *Berliner Zeitung*, July 2, 1999.
[70] Christina Fischer, "Ewige Suche nach Gemeinsamkeiten," *Berliner Zeitung*, October 2, 1999.
[71] "Grenzblicke. Werkshau des Dokumentationszentrums Berliner Mauer," in Verein Berliner Mauer – Gedenkstätte und Dokumentationszentrum (Gabriele Camphausen, Maria Nooke) ed., *Die Berliner Mauer*, trans. Mariamne Fields (Dresden: Michel Sandstein Verlag, 2002), pp. 4–59; Uwe Aulich, "Dokumentationszentrum öffnet an der 'Bernauer'," *Berliner Zeitung*, November 9, 1999; and Rudnick, *Die andere Hälfte der Erinnerung*, pp. 624–25.

The dramatic visual reminders of the history of Bernauer Strasse included the sealing of the border, the demolition of houses along the border, the exhuming of graves in the Sophien cemetery, and border guards' use of the tower of the Church of Reconciliation as an observation point.[72]

Marie-Luise Waga of the Berlin Senate's department on science, research and culture was quite critical of her superiors for not coming through with additional funds. She believed that since Fischer had donated significant space in his parish center, which had a market price at the time of DM5 million, the Berlin government should have responded with a significant financial contribution. Moreover, she argued that the Berlin Wall Association's plans were "the first coherent conceptualization for dealing with the Wall" in Berlin at a time when there were increasing calls for a "master plan" to guide the approach to the few areas with sections of the Wall remaining.[73] She felt the reduced opening of the Documentation Center with such a small exhibit was an embarrassment.

To accompany the opening of the *Grenzblicke* exhibit, the Berlin Wall Association published a small booklet. With texts by Camphausen, Trotnow, Fischer, and others, the booklet explained the history of the site before and after the fall of the Wall, what they planned to do in the Documentation Center and with the Chapel of Reconciliation, and why it all mattered. The texts were accompanied by pictures, documents, and a chronology of post-1989 developments regarding a Berlin Wall Memorial at Bernauer Strasse. Just as Trotnow and Möbius had published a small booklet with texts and pictures to make the case in 1990 for establishing a Berlin Wall Memorial, this booklet shared similar goals of historical education, publicity, and persuasion.[74] In his text in the 1999 booklet, Trotnow maintained that, "the history of this border cannot be conveyed to future generations by the [Kohlhoff & Kohlhoff] monument alone." To understand "what the Berlin Wall was, why it was built, how people lived with it and the causes and consequences of its removal," the Documentation Center was "absolutely necessary."[75]

Camphausen made a thinly disguised appeal in the booklet to politicians to show their support for this part of German history by providing funding. After noting that "important questions about financing still need to be resolved,"

Rudnick's account is misleading in saying that Mayor Diepgen did not participate in the opening at Bernauer Strasse. He attended the 1:30 p.m. topping off ceremony at the Chapel of Reconciliation but not the 2:30 p.m. opening of the Documentation Center exhibit, since he was hosting a commemorative session of the Senate at that time.

[72] Interview with Gabriele Campausen, December 15, 2009.
[73] Marie-Luise Waga, Senate Department on Science, Research and Culture, "Gedenkstätte Berliner Mauer an der Bernauer Strasse," August 10, 1998, SWFKB, GMB, Nr. 24.
[74] The Berlin Wall – Memorial Site and Exhibition Center Association, ed., *Berlin Wall Memorial Site, Exhibition Center and the Chapel of Reconciliation on Bernauer Strasse*.
[75] Trotnow, "Understanding the Present by Looking Back at the Past," p. 12.

Camphausen asserted the importance of "confronting the difficult questions of German history" and insisted that "this is a challenge which both Berlin, as an historical location and as the new capital city, and the Federal Republic of Germany must meet." She insisted: "The Wall must be accepted as a part of East-West German history and must be preserved in the public memory." She urged Germans to grapple with "our recent history" in order to "help maintain our social capacity to remember."[76]

In addition to the exhibit opening on the tenth anniversary of the fall of the Wall, Fischer had hosted the topping off ceremony at the Chapel of Reconciliation earlier in the day. Mayor Diepgen attended this ceremony and laid a wreath for victims at the Kohlhoff & Kohlhoff memorial. Speaking in the wooden frame of the chapel, Diepgen commemorated the victims of the Wall and asserted the importance of remembering the history of the Wall and drawing lessons from it, particularly "about where the spirit of tyranny can lead" but also "to offer hope for a future in which differences do not divide people." He referred to the importance of the "memorial, Documentation Center and Chapel of Reconciliation" in conveying this history but did not pledge any of the much-needed monies for the Berlin Wall Association to be able to do this. Instead, he called, as a recent Senate resolution had, for the return of the sections of the Wall removed by the Sophien community to where they had been, to extend the section of the Wall on Bernauer Strasse, and to reconstruct the whole former border strip within the Kohlhoff & Kohlhoff memorial.[77]

In spite of the insistence of the Sophien parish that it would not allow this, Diepgen and others had clearly not given up. After Diepgen, Fischer, and others had laid wreaths at the Kohlhoff & Kohlhoff memorial, the mayor went on to host a commemorative ceremony at the Berlin Senate. It was left to a senior official from the federal interior ministry to give some words of welcome at the opening of the Documentation Center.

Although Mayor Diepgen had come to Bernauer Strasse to mark the tenth anniversary, most other politicians instead continued the long-standing tradition of laying a wreath at the Peter Fechter memorial. Fechter had been eighteen years old on August 17, 1962 when he was shot trying to escape across the Wall not far from Checkpoint Charlie. Following the shots, Fechter collapsed to the ground and slowly bled to death, crying out for help as *Grenzer* hesitated and people watching from the West Berlin side screamed for help. People in the West also took pictures and films that could be used as evidence

---

[76] Camphausen, "The Berlin Wall Exhibition Center," p. 30.

[77] Eberhard Diepgen, remarks at the topping-off ceremony of the Chapel of Reconciliation, Landespressedienst, "Gedenkveranstaltung an der Gedenkstätte Berliner Mauer," November 9, 1999. See also Lutz Hager, "Richtfest auf ehemaligem Mauerstreifen," *Berliner Zeitung*, November 10, 1999.

against the soldiers and would make headlines around the world the next day.[78] Within hours, a wooden cross was erected for Peter Fechter on the West Berlin side of the Wall, and ever since then, on August 17, West Berlin politicians had gathered to lay a wreath there for Fechter and all the others killed at the Berlin Wall, a practice that political leaders continued in united Germany.[79] For the tenth anniversary of the fall of the Wall, a bronze pillar carrying the inscription, "He just wanted freedom," replaced the wooden cross.[80] Mayor Diepgen and other political leaders from Berlin were there for the ceremony on the morning of August 13, 1999.

Nooke and her colleagues at the Berlin Wall Association believed that the memorial at Bernauer Strasse should also be a gathering point for commemoration on key anniversaries related to the Wall and not just the Fechter memorial. She did not think it was right that more politicians went to the Fechter memorial on the tenth anniversary than to what was after all the national Berlin Wall Memorial at Bernauer Strasse. This inspired her to reach out to representatives from the legislative and executive branches of the government and to the political parties to attend commemorative events at Bernauer Strasse in future. While she felt it was strange to send out invitations to prominent politicians in the name of the Berlin Wall Association instead of coming from a political leader, she and her colleagues pushed ahead.

Nooke's husband Günter also helped draw more political attention to the Berlin Wall Memorial. As the deputy chair and spokesman of the CDU/CSU parliamentary group's committee on cultural and media affairs, he was in a good position to highlight the importance of commemorating the victims of the Berlin Wall and remembering the history of the Wall at Bernauer Strasse. Once the federal government moved to Berlin, Maria Nooke also reached out to the minister presidents of the German states to participate in the national commemoration of victims of the Wall at Bernauer Strasse.[81]

Remaining at the Berlin Wall Memorial for nearly twenty years and ultimately becoming deputy director, Maria Nooke played an essential role in establishing the site as an important source of information and discussion about the history of the Berlin Wall. Having grown up in the GDR, and joining the opposition along with her husband, Nooke had her own memories of the

---

[78] Christoph Hamann, "Schnapschuss und Ikone. Das Foto von Peter Fechters Fluchtversuch 1962," *Zeithistorische Forschungen/Studies in Contemporary History* 2 (2005), pp. 292–99. Hans-Hermann Hertle and Maria Nooke, eds., *The Victims at the Berlin Wall, 1961–1989* (Berlin: Ch. Links, 2011), pp. 102–5; and www.berliner-mauer-gedenkstaette.de/en/1962–300,353,2.html.

[79] "Gedenken an die Opfer der Mauer," *Neue Zeit*, August 14, 1990.

[80] "Ein neues Denkmal für den Flüchtling," *Berliner Zeitung*, August 16, 1997; Pertti Ahonen, *Death at the Berlin Wall* (New York: Oxford University Press, 2011), pp. 136, 278–80; and Anna Kaminsky, ed., *Orte des Erinnerns* (Berlin: Ch. Links, 2016), p. 64.

[81] Interviews with Maria Nooke, July 5, 2005 and April 15, 2010.

Figure 13 Maria Nooke with picture of boarded-up houses and Church of Reconciliation blocked by the Wall
Source: Photographer: Gesa Simons. Stiftung Berliner Mauer-1397.

Wall.[82] Particularly strong was her memory of visiting her aunt in West Berlin in 1986, at a time when the East German regime was softening restrictions on visiting the West in return for major financial assistance from the FRG. Nooke and her cousin visited the observation platform on the West Berlin side of the Wall at Potsdamer Platz. They climbed up the steps and looked across the border strip. "The moment when I stood up there was a rather terrible one. I suddenly realized how close together we [both parts of Berlin] were. It was incomprehensible to me that the Wall went right through the center of the city there."[83] Years later, she believed it was important for people to remember or learn about what it had been like when the Wall stood (Figure 13). The Documentation Center and Wall remains were fundamental methods to facilitate memory and learning.

Politics on the Tenth Anniversary of the Fall of the Wall

It was not just the group at Bernauer Strasse who felt that the years of division had ongoing relevance and should not be forgotten. Ten years after the fall of the Wall, people from the east were still suffering in some ways as we shall see,

---

[82] Interview with Maria Nooke, July 5, 2005; and her profile on revolution89.de.

[83] Interview with Maria Nooke conducted by Markus Köhler, August 29, 2012, www.tunnelfluchten.de/interview/nooke.html.

particularly economically, at least compared to those in the west, and this led to important changes in their voting behavior. Economically, socially, and in terms of voting habits, a border remained. This cast a definite shadow over the tenth anniversary commemorations at the Bundestag, the Senate, and the Brandenburg Gate.

Political leaders felt compelled in ceremonies on November 9 to address the ongoing legacy and challenges from both the division and the period since unification. Their speeches offer an opportunity to take stock of the sense of German national identity ten years after the fall of the Wall and also to see the ways politicians used the history of the Berlin Wall for their own ends. As noted in the introduction, historical anniversaries can serve to unite people in a certain view of the past, but they can also accentuate differences in perspectives on the past. The more that politicians and others directed attention to the Wall, the more room there was for differences in approach. Many of the themes raised in speeches for the tenth anniversary of the fall of the Wall would be raised in future years as well, but the relative weight given to these themes would change quite dramatically, especially over the following decade, as we shall see.

At a time when the unemployment rate was twice as high in the eastern part of the country (18 percent) as in the western parts (9 percent) and when east German workers were earning on average only 78 percent of what their western counterparts were paid, many in the east were disappointed or disillusioned. In eastern Germany, 37 percent of women were unemployed, leading significant numbers of them to move to the west.[84] Unification was a particularly rough transition for many people in the so-called new federal states (*neue Bundesländer*), since under socialism there had generally been full employment – even if not always with interesting jobs and good pay, it was better than being unemployed. Moreover, many east Germans felt that they had been colonized and were viewed as second-class citizens. The improved infrastructure and air quality in the east did not always compensate for these sentiments.[85] Rainer Eppelmann appealed to his fellow citizens from the east on November 9, 1999, "to remember gratefully that it was possible" to bring down the Wall and to let that memory "help us when current problems sometimes wear us down and make us grouchy." He declared, "We really

---

[84] For comparative unemployment in east and west Germany in 1999, see Bundesanstalt für Arbeit, "Arbeitsmarkt 1999 – Arbeitsmarktanalyse für die alten und die neuen Länder," *Amtliche Nachrichten der Bundesanstalt für Arbeit* 48, Sondernummer (June 28, 2000), p. 13, https://statistik.arbeitsagentur.de/Statistikdaten/Detail/199912/ama/heft-arbeits markt/arbeitsmarkt-d-0-pdf.pdf. On comparative average wages, see "Höhe des Bruttodurchschnittslohns je Beschäftigten in Ost- und Westdeutschland von 1996 bis 2017. 1999, de.statista.com/statistik/daten/studie/36305/umfrage/bruttodurchschnitt-slohn-in-ostdeutschland-und-westdeutschland/.

[85] "Togetherness: A Balance Sheet," *Economist*, September 30, 2000.

have many reasons to be quite happy and proud and full of hope! – If only we could just let ourselves feel this."[86]

Former eastern Germans were not the only ones frustrated with unification. Western Germans were unhappy that more than 5 percent of their tax monies (the so-called Solidarity tax, or *Soli*) continued to be directed toward building up the east. More than DM1.2 trillion ($540 billion) were transferred to the *neue Bundesländer* in the first ten years after unification.[87] In surveys about satisfaction with unification, 29 percent of west Germans admitted to feeling more concern than happiness with unification.[88] They did not always offer a warm welcome to the two million eastern Germans who moved to the west for better job opportunities in the first ten years.

The challenges that came with unification were most obvious in Berlin, the one federal state that was comprised of people from the former East and West. In his speech to the Berlin Senate on November 9, 1999, Mayor Diepgen advised that Berliners should "pause for a moment, take a breath, and look to the future," since "we will clearly need another ten years for the completion of German reunification internally."[89] In Berlin and beyond, there was much talk of *Besser-Wessis* ("better [a.k.a. arrogant] westerners") and *Jammern-Ossis* ("whining easterners").

In 1999, four million Germans, 10.5 percent of the population, were out of work. This was the main reason Chancellor Helmut Kohl and his CDU were ousted in the 1998 federal elections, with the CDU percentage of the vote plummeting from 43.7 percent in the 1994 elections to 35.1 percent in the 1998 elections. The SPD's Gerhard Schröder succeeded Kohl and declared that if he had not reduced the number of unemployed to 3.5 million by 2002, he should not be reelected. The East German SED successor party, the PDS (Party of Democratic Socialism) also gained in the 1998 elections, garnering 5.1 percent of the vote. Among Berliners who voted in the federal election, 13.4 percent voted for the PDS. The PDS's popularity differed dramatically between eastern and western Berlin: 30 percent of east Berliners compared to just 2.7 percent of west Berliners favored the PDS.[90] In the Berlin municipal elections in 1999, the PDS garnered nearly 18 percent of the vote.

---

[86] Rainer Eppelmann, "Ansprache bei der Feierstunde des Berliner Senats am 9. November 1999," author's collection of documents.

[87] "Togetherness: a balance sheet," *Economist*, September 30, 2000.

[88] Allensbacher Archiv, IfD-Umfragen, "Die Wiedervereinigung – ein Grund zur Freude II," Institut für Demoskopie Allensbach, in Thomas Petersen, "Das Ende der 'Mauer in den Köpfen.' Eine Dokumentation des Beitrags von Dr. Thomas Petersen in der *Frankfurter Allgemeinen Zeitung* Nr. 269 vom 19. November 2014."

[89] Speech by mayor Eberhard Diepgen, "Festakt des Berliner Senats zum 10. Jahrestag des Mauerfalls," State Press Office, Berlin, November 9, 1999.

[90] On Berlin voting in the 1998 federal elections, see Der Landeswahlleiter, ed., "Wahlen in Berlin am 21. Oktober 2001," *Berliner Statistik* (Berlin: Statistisches Landesamt Berlin,

Mayor Diepgen was fully aware that many east Berliners no longer supported him or the CDU. To fight back against expanding PDS popularity in Berlin, Diepgen criticized anyone who engaged in "the nostalgic romanticization of a tyrannical regime," namely the former SED regime, which many PDS members had been a part of.[91] Paying more attention to the brutal history of the Berlin Wall was a way to make the PDS look bad. This goes a long way to explaining both why Diepgen participated in the commemorations at the Fechter memorial and at Bernauer Strasse and why, in the latter case, he called for displaying as much of the former border as possible: returning the pieces of the Wall Sophien had removed, extending the remaining sections by adding more pieces that had once stood along Bernauer Strasse, and reconstructing the other elements of the former border there. While Diepgen had not consistently pushed over the past eight years of his leadership in Berlin for expanding the remnants of the former border at Bernauer Strasse, now that the PDS had scored such electoral gains, he changed his approach. The more people could see of what the deadly border had been, the worse he assumed the PDS would look as the successor to the party that built the Wall and made it so deadly. Not surprisingly, Diepgen used the opportunity on November 9, 1999 to hail the decision of the Federal Court of Justice the day before upholding the convictions of Krenz, Schabowski, and Kleiber for deaths at the Wall.[92]

In addition to using the anniversary to criticize the former East German regime and the current PDS as well as to remember the victims and recognize the ongoing complications of bringing east and west together since the fall of the Wall, the political leaders and former East German civic activists who gave public addresses in November 1999 had much to say about why the Wall fell. They spoke of the variety of groups who contributed to toppling the Wall, including: the East Germans who took to the streets in Berlin, Leipzig, and many other cities; the individual leaders of East German opposition groups; and the leaders and citizens in Poland, Hungary, and the Soviet Union. Different emphases came from different personal experiences and historical understandings as well as various beliefs of what would resonate best with specific groups of citizens. No one mentioned the role of the East German authorities, including those stationed at the crossing points in the Berlin Wall, who relinquished control and allowed East German citizens to pass through to the West.

2001), p. 17, www.wahlen-berlin.de/historie/Wahlen/Landeswahlleiterbericht_AH2001 .pdf.

[91] Eberhard Diepgen, "Gedenkveranstaltung an der Gedenkstätte Berliner Mauer," State Press Office, November 9, 1999.

[92] Ulrich Deupmann, "Schröder würdigt den Freiheitswillen der ostdeutschen: Bundestag erinnert mit Festakt an den Fall der Berliner Mauer," *Berliner Zeitung*, November 10, 1999; and Sigrid Averesch, "Gericht macht SED-Politbüro für die Mauertoten verantwortlich," *Berliner Zeitung*, November 9, 1999.

Chancellor Schröder declared in no uncertain terms – and most pointedly among politicians from the West – how important the people of East Germany had been in bringing down the Wall: "First and foremost, the Wall was not brought down in Washington, Bonn or Moscow. It was pushed over by courageous and intrepid people, namely from east to west. . . .The fact that we are able to celebrate November 9 today as a day of democracy and freedom. . .is above all due to the people of the former GDR."[93] While Schröder likely believed this, it may also be that in contrast to Diepgen's more hard-line approach of emphasizing how terrible the Wall and the former SED regime were in an effort to counter the rising popularity of the PDS, Schröder believed a carrot would be more effective than a stick in appealing to PDS supporters in the east.

Political leaders from east and west emphasized the fundamental impact on Germany's broad historical narrative of the behavior of the East German protestors. Joachim Gauck, the former pastor and civic activist who in 1999 was the head of the federal Stasi Records Authority, declared that the "East Germans made a historic gift not just to themselves but to all Germans. We all now belong to the family of nations that are characterized by revolutions for liberty." This achievement by the East Germans "shone all the brighter" because of their "56-year-long political powerlessness under National Socialism and communist tyranny."[94] This view would gain widespread political support a decade later, and Gauck as well as Chancellor Schröder were among the first to express it publicly. Schröder emphasized in his speech at the Bundestag: "With their civic courage the people in the former GDR enriched German history with a unique contribution: the experience that peaceful tenacity and democratic public spirit can bring down dictatorships." He declared that the celebration on the tenth anniversary should thus be one "of joy and also of pride," the latter being a word used quite infrequently by political leaders about German history.[95] At a time of ongoing economic and political differences between east and west, Schröder no doubt meant to inspire all Germans with this narrative, which was so different than the more traditional narrative about German history focusing on the dark days of the Nazi past.

The chancellor's remarks were also probably geared toward counteracting the conflation of the fall of the Wall and German unification by several speakers and in the planning for the ceremony in the Bundestag. The German, Soviet, and American leaders from 1989 to 1990 – Chancellor Helmut Kohl, President Mikhail Gorbachev, and President George H. W. Bush – were invited to give addresses for the occasion. This emphasis on

---

[93] Rede von Bundeskanzler Gerhard Schröder anlässlich der Sonderveranstaltung "10. Jahrestag des Mauerfalls" im Deutschen Bundestag, November 9, 1999.

[94] Rede von Joachim Gauck, Bundesbeauftrager für die Unterlagen des Staatssicherheitsdientes der ehemaligen DDR, Deutscher Bundestag, November 9, 1999.

[95] Rede von Bundeskanzler Gerhard Schröder anlässlich der Sonderveranstaltung "10. Jahrestag des Mauerfalls" im Deutschen Bundestag, November 9, 1999.

what came in the year *after* the fall of the Wall was resented by many east Germans. Only belatedly did the Bundestag planners realize that it might be a good idea to have a former East German as an invited speaker as well (in addition to the Bundestag President Wolfgang Thierse who was from the east). Hence, Gauck had been invited at rather the last minute.

Although Kohl, Bush, and Gorbachev spoke of the fall of the Wall and the important role of the East Germans on the streets and of reforms in other neighboring communist countries, their focus was on what they knew most personally, namely the developments after November 9 leading to unification and how cooperation among the three of them had been so important. Gauck, however, took care to list the names of key East German civic activists and of the cities and towns in the GDR where significant popular protests occurred. Thierse recognized the "self-liberation of the East Germans" and declared that "ten years ago the East German populace was the hero" who showed that "German history can turn out well for once."[96] The weight of the Holocaust obliquely referenced by Thierse was made clear by several other speakers who remembered the Nazi attacks on the Jews on November 9, 1938, *Kristallnacht*, even as they celebrated November 9, 1989.

The commemoration in the Berlin Senate offered a more significant focus on the East Germans of 1989 than the Bundestag did. Several members of the former opposition were invited to speak, including Stephan Hilsberg, Rainer Eppelmann, and Marianne Birthler.[97] Hilsberg spoke of the "student heroes" who escaped from East Berlin and then built tunnels under the Wall at Bernauer Strasse and elsewhere to help their girlfriends and other East Germans escape, particularly in the early years. He also lamented that so many people in both east and west had grown used to the Wall over time.[98] This was not an aspect of the history of the Wall that people spoke about much, especially politicians, since it implicated all political parties in the former East and West.

The late afternoon and evening celebration at the Brandenburg Gate featured popular musicians as well as speeches by the chancellor, the mayor, the federal minister for youth, and former East German civic activists. In spite of all the political speeches at the Senate and Bundestag about the essential role of the East Germans in bringing down the Wall, however, the biggest cheers from the crowd at the Gate were for Gorbachev and Kohl, not for any East

---

[96] Rede von Wolfgang Thierse, Präsident des Deutschen Bundestages anlässlich der Sonderveranstaltung "10. Jahrestag des Mauerfalls" im Deutschen Bundestag, November 9, 1999.

[97] Stephan Hilsberg, Rainer Eppelmann, Marianne Birthler, et. al., *Reden von Bürgerrechtlern aus Anlaß des Jahrestages der Maueröffnung. Berlin, 9. November 1999* (Berlin: Berliner Forum, 1999). For Mayor Diepgen's remarks, see Landespressedienst, "Festakt des Berliner Senats zum 10. Jahrestag des Mauerfalls," November 9, 1999.

[98] Stephan Hilsberg, "Maueröffnung und Demokratie," speech to the Berlin Senate, November 9, 1999, author's collection of documents.

Germans.[99] Gorbachev had been a hero to many in both East and West Germany due to his reforms in the late 1980s and his ultimate willingness to give up the GDR, and Kohl's active leadership after the fall of the Wall pushing toward unification seemed easier to identify and applaud than masses of mostly nameless East Germans.

Aside from the tenth anniversary commemorations, and in spite of the engagement by Fischer, Camphausen, and victims' groups calling to remember the Wall, to say nothing of the ongoing streams of foreign tourists who wanted to see more of the Wall, there was still not much abiding political or widespread German public interest in it. Indeed, when Christian Bormann, a hobby historian from eastern Berlin, discovered a large section of the original 1960s version of the Berlin Wall in an out-of-the-way area in 1999, he decided not to make it public. He thought "Berlin wasn't ready for this discovery when I came across it" and probably would have torn it down.[100] Only many years later, in January 2018, when weather and age threatened the integrity of the Wall remnants did Bormann announce his discovery.[101] Similarly, in the late 1990s, a workman who was implementing the Senate's decision to mark the Wall's former inner-city path with a double row of cobblestones noted, "It's primarily the tourists who are interested in this and who take many pictures. But most Berliners say it's crazy and that no one cares" where the Wall was.[102] In 1999, for the vast majority of Germans, the focus was on the construction of government offices as well as apartments, shopping malls, homes, hotels, and other buildings in the center of the city where the death strip of the Berlin Wall once stood. Less Wall, not more, was called for.

This general atmosphere did not help the cause of gaining support to complete the construction of the Documentation Center within Fischer's parish center and the bigger exhibit. As of 2000, the Berlin Wall Association had still not received the necessary funding, and in early April, Camphausen announced that the association could only pay its employees until the end of the month. The Documentation Center would have to close if the government did not help.[103] Camphausen had requested DM 500,000 for 2000 but had yet to be given any positive answer by Berlin or the federal government. As she and

[99] "Das Fest: 'Winds of Change' mit 166 Cellos," *Berliner Zeitung*, November 10, 1999; and "Gottesdienste und Rock-Musik: Termine am 9. November," *Berliner Zeitung*, November 9, 1999.

[100] Rick Noack, "As Germans Celebrate the Absence of the Berlin Wall, a New Piece of It Is Discovered," *Washington Post*, February 5, 2018.

[101] Mike Wilms, "Pankow: Heimatforscher entdeckt 80 Meter langes Stück der Berliner Mauer," *Berliner Zeitung*, January 23, 2018.

[102] Andreas Kopietz, "Pflastersteine erinnern an den Mauerverlauf," *Berliner Zeitung*, September 8, 1998.

[103] Uwe Aulich, "Dokumentationsstätte is von Schließung bedroht. Bund und Senat streiten um das Mauer-Zentrum," *Berliner Zeitung*, April 7, 2000.

Fischer later confessed, "in order to make progress in consolidating the historical site at Bernauer Strasse, it required nerves of steel and a willingness to work massive hours."[104] Indeed, the stress of it all was so much that Camphausen had to take a break for much of 2000, with Fischer assuming leadership in her stead and Maria Nooke being appointed project director. Trotnow, still a member of the board of the Berlin Wall Association, called for "a policy decision on the future financing of the Documentation Center." Without funding for staff, they could not go through the hundreds of historical files they had collected or carry out interviews with people who had direct experience with the Wall.

Although the 1999 coalition treaty of the CDU-SPD government in Berlin had pledged support for the Documentation Center[105] and Diepgen himself had observed: "I don't think a society can heal or the affected people can be helped if the historical truth remains under lock and key," the finance department had not allocated funds for it.[106] The Documentation Center was precisely the kind of place to expose the "historical truth" of the Wall in great depth, yet Diepgen continued to insist that the federal government must support the site due to its national – and not just municipal – significance. Eventually, Diepgen's Senate did provide DM200,000 in 2000 for the Documentation Center.[107] As it turned out, even the mayor could have benefited from learning more about the Wall. That might have prevented him from making the mistake of referring to mines at the Berlin Wall, as he did in his address to the Senate on the tenth anniversary of the fall of the Wall.[108] While there were mines along the inner-German border, they were not part of the Berlin Wall border fortifications.

In the spring of 2001, Diepgen's government provided a further DM618,000 for the larger exhibit set to open for the fortieth anniversary of the building of the Wall in August. The Berlin Wall Association needed a minimum of DM600,000 each year to develop the documentary collection and to lead tours of the whole site. Three thousand people were coming every week to the memorial ensemble.[109] In 2002, the Documentation Center would begin to receive regular funding from Wall Property Funds comprised

---

[104] Camphausen and Fischer, "Die bürgerschaftliche Durchsetzung," p. 373.

[105] CDU-SPD Koalitionsvereinberung, December 7, 1999, p. 67. See also p. 88 on preserving remnants of the Berlin Wall.

[106] Remarks by Mayor Eberhard Diepgen at the "Öffentliche Gedenkveranstaltung aus Anlaß des 35. Jahrestages des Baus der Berliner Mauer," August 13, 1996, in Deutscher Bundestag, ed., *Materialien der Enquete-Kommission "Überwindung der Folgen der SED-Diktatur in Prozess der deutschen Einheit,"* Band I, pp. 939–40.

[107] Rudnick, *Die andere Hälfte der Erinnerung,* pp. 627–30.

[108] Speech by Mayor Eberhard Diepgen, "Festakt des Berliner Senats zum 10. Jahrestag des Mauerfalls," State Press Office, Berlin, November 9 1999.

[109] Uwe Aulich, "Zweite Ausbaustufe im Dokumentationszentrum. Ausstellung zum 13. August wird vorbereitet," *Berliner Zeitung,* April 3, 2001.

of the profits made when the federal government sold the land along the former border strip (at a fraction of the market value) back to the original owners or at market value to others and gave the proceeds to the states, such as Berlin, to allocate. Maria Nooke's husband Günter helped make the case for funding the Documentation Center to officials in the Berlin Senate as did the new cultural senator, Christoph Stölzl, who had been the director of DHM with whom Trotnow had worked so closely.[110]

Politicization of Wall Memory on the Fortieth Anniversary of the Erection of the Wall

Timed to open on this anniversary, the new, larger exhibit at the Documentation Center focused on the building of the Wall and was entitled "August 13, 1961." Camphausen and Nooke oversaw the preparations for the exhibit, and the research for it was carried out by Nooke and two other part-time employees, Doris Liebermann and the historian Gerhard Sälter. The exhibit examined the construction of the Wall from municipal, national, and Allied perspectives. Visitors learned about the impact of the Wall on the city by listening to recordings of interviews with Berliners and radio broadcasts from the time. The national view of the Wall came from a display of archival documents telling the story of the process of sealing the border and the responses to this. The Allied view of the Wall came from Allied photographers who were still permitted to travel between East and West Berlin and took pictures and some videos of the construction of the border installations from both sides.

The exhibit contained historical documents, photographs, maps, and diagrams on sealing the border as well as graphs depicting the number of people who escaped each year. It featured East German propaganda songs about building the Wall, measures taken to strengthen the border in response to escapes, the order to shoot people trying to escape, the forced expulsion of those living along the border and then the boarding up and demolition of their houses. It also showed protests against the Wall, *Grenzer* who refused to shoot, and media coverage of victims at the Wall while highlighting several sites along the Wall, including Bernauer Strasse, Checkpoint Charlie, and the Brandenburg Gate.[111]

A few months before the opening of the exhibit, the Berlin government collapsed due to a corruption scandal regarding a CDU member and a bank owned by the city. Diepgen, who had been mayor for most of the previous

---

[110] Interview with Maria Nooke, April 15, 2010.
[111] Verein Berliner Mauer, "Berlin, 13. August 1961. Eine Ausstellung zum 40. Jahrestages des Mauerbaus," in Verein Berliner Mauer – Gedenkstätte und Dokumentationszentrum (Gabriele Camphausen, Maria Nooke) ed., *Die Berliner Mauer*, trans. Mariamne Fields (Dresden: Michel Sandstein Verlag, 2002), pp. 59–179.

twenty years, was pushed out by his SPD coalition partners. A new minority government was established on June 16, 2001 between the SPD and the Greens. SPD leader and Interim Mayor Klaus Wowereit made it clear he was considering forming a coalition with the PDS.[112] The fact that the SPD did not immediately rule out the possibility of having as a coalition partner the successor party to the one that had built and "perfected" the Wall was highly controversial. For the Berlin Wall Association, with a site dedicated to "victims of the German division and communist tyranny" and in need of funding from the city of Berlin, the prospect of an SPD-PDS coalition government complicated an already challenging situation. Fischer, Trotnow, Camphausen, and their team had long sought political recognition and financial support, but the political crisis in Berlin would soon lead to some very uncomfortable moments and would no doubt lead the small staff at the Documentation Center to think, "Be careful what you wish for."

The day after the interim minority government was formed under Wowereit happened to be June 17, the anniversary of the 1953 East German uprising that had been put down by Soviet tanks. At the public commemorations of the uprising, there were large and violent demonstrations against the PDS. As a result, the PDS representatives, although preparing for the chance to be part of the coalition government with the SPD, were concerned about attending the fortieth anniversary commemorations of the erection of Berlin Wall, including the opening of the Documentation Center in August.[113] The PDS was divided between older, less contrite members who had made their careers in the GDR and younger, more flexible members. Under pressure to distance themselves from the SED, the PDS had formed a historical commission, which issued a statement about the Wall in June. The statement reflected the influence of both stalwart and more flexible groups, which did little to reassure many in the general public, especially victims of the Wall.

The PDS statement spoke of "respect and regret" for the "victims of the border regime" whose deaths and injuries "could not be justified in any way." But it did not make an apology. Furthermore, it seemed to show as much concern for the "great moral pressure on the *Grenzer*" due to the "high level of military and political responsibility they had" as for the citizens who were shot by them, and it praised the border soldiers and their superiors for not interfering with the opening of the Wall in 1989. The statement also referred to the Wall as a result of Nazi policies, World War II, and the Cold War, including policies carried out by German politicians on both sides, and did not affix any primary culpability onto GDR leaders. The PDS historical commission declared that the Wall "fixed the status quo in Europe," which helped "stabilize the global political

---

[112] Tony Paterson, "Berlin Crippled in Crisis of Corruption and £23 Billion in Debt," *Telegraph*, April 8, 2001; and interview with Maria Nooke, July 5, 2005.

[113] Interview with Maria Nooke, July 5, 2005.

situation and preserve peace," and thus "enabled the détente" that followed, reminiscent of some of the arguments made by the defense in the Wall trials. The PDS commission seemed to lament that the Wall had been seen as a "mark of Cain which isolated the GDR internationally and discredited the SED."[114]

The die was cast for confrontations between political parties and between politicians and victims of the GDR regime on the occasion of the fortieth anniversary of the erection of the Wall. The efforts of the Berlin Wall Association to obtain political participation in marking the August 13 date at Bernauer Strasse finally paid off when Chancellor Schröder (SPD) agreed to attend, setting in motion some tense moments that would shortly follow. Interim Mayor Wowereit had not initially planned to attend the fortieth anniversary events at the Berlin Wall Memorial, no doubt due to the heated criticism of him for holding discussions with the PDS about forming a coalition government. Once the chancellor committed to attending the opening of the Documentation Center and the other commemorative activities at Bernauer Strasse, especially laying wreaths at the Kohlhoff & Kohlhoff memorial, however, Wowereit could not very well abstain from attendance.

The fortieth anniversary of the building of the Wall received broader political attention than previous anniversaries had, with multiple commemorative events at the Berlin Wall Memorial and elsewhere in Berlin and beyond. Flags were lowered to half-staff at official buildings throughout Berlin and most other states, and President Johannes Rau delivered a prime-time, nationwide television address.[115] A variety of factors contributed to this increased attention to the memory of the Wall.

The anniversary was one of the first major national events since the government's move to Berlin. Hence it offered a prime opportunity for what Daqing Yang and Mike Mochizuki have called anniversary politics.[116] Political leaders sought to use the anniversary of the Wall to disseminate their views of its history and contemporary relevance as well as to score points with voters and certain interest groups, particularly since Berlin elections were approaching in October and national elections the following year. In addition, in light of the ongoing challenges in united Germany for many people from the east, there was a sense that more should be done to acknowledge what many of them had endured with the Berlin Wall and other difficult aspects of life in the GDR. This was particularly necessary in Berlin if an SPD coalition with the PDS was going to have a chance of being accepted. Finally, there was a growing sense that maybe Germans had acted too quickly in trying to put the GDR past and

---

[114] PDS Historische Kommission, "Zum 40. Jahrestag des Baus der Berliner Mauer. Erklärung der Historischen Kommission beim Parteivorstand der PDS," June 26, 2001.
[115] Dpa, "Berlin und Bundesländer gedachten Maueropfer," *Handelsblatt*, August 13, 2001.
[116] Daqing Yang and Mike Mochizuki, eds., *Memory, Identity, and Commemorations of World War II: Anniversary Politics in Asia Pacific* (Lanham: Lexington, 2018), p. xix.

the Berlin Wall behind them without fully coming to terms with both. As Maria Nooke told the *New York Times*: with the passage of time after the initial "feeling of liberation" and desire to "tear the wall down as fast as possible, . . .there is now awareness that at least parts of the wall need to be preserved" and the history and victims remembered.[117] While some Berlin Wall trials were ongoing, many of the former victims and their survivors, such as Horst Schmidt, were quite dissatisfied with what they saw as very light sentences in most of the trials that had been completed. In addition, at a time when work on the Holocaust Memorial was progressing, people who felt victimized by the GDR regime and the Berlin Wall felt they were being forgotten.

Party politics and intense emotions on the part of some former East Germans collided on the anniversary. As a journalist for Reuters observed, "Instead of bringing Germans together to mark the tragic events that divided the country with gray concrete, barbed wire and armed guards, the Wall anniversary has become a divisive political background."[118] The CDU would try everything possible to regain power, including using the Wall's anniversary to attack not just the PDS but also the SPD. Conservative politicians knew they were losing ground in Berlin, especially in the eastern part, where the PDS was gaining support, having won nearly 40 percent of the vote there in 1999.[119] Thus, the CDU went on the offensive the day before the fortieth anniversary, holding an afternoon rally at Checkpoint Charlie, attended by more than 2,000 invitees. Federal CDU chair Angela Merkel, CSU chief Edmund Stoiber, former mayor Diepgen, and his anointed successor Frank Steffel all gave speeches urging people to vote for the CDU, not the SPD or PDS, and expressing outrage at a possible SPD-PDS coalition.

Merkel called the potential coalition "a betrayal of the ideals" of social democracy. She also remembered visiting her grandmother in West Germany with her parents two weeks before the border closure: "My parents had the sense that they would not be able to see her soon again and said a long goodbye," she told the crowd. She insisted that, "Everyone who fought for freedom has a right to be remembered" and reminded the crowd that this included the people killed or injured at the border as well as the tens of thousands of people imprisoned in the GDR for attempted or suspected plans for *Republikflucht*.[120] Stoiber declared that "a coalition with the PDS is

[117] Edmund L. Andrews, "The Wall Berlin Can't Quite Demolish," *New York Times*, August 13, 2001.

[118] Reuters, "Berlin Wall Becomes Battle Cry on Anniversary Eve," *New York Times*, August 12, 2001.

[119] Der Landeswahlleiter, ed., "Wahlen in Berlin am 21. Oktober 2001," *Berliner Statistik* (Berlin: Statistisches Landesamt Berlin, 2001), p. 50.

[120] Reuters, "Berlin Wall Becomes Battle Cry on Anniversary Eve," *New York Times*, August 12, 2001; and dpa, "Mauerbau: Union attackiert SPD und PDS," *Sächsische Zeitung*, August 13, 2001.

a pact with the socialism" of the former SED. He insisted that "we must name the enemies of democracy and oppose them." Steffel accused the PDS of engaging in "historical lies" instead of taking responsibility.[121] Diepgen took a leaf from the old Cold War handbook when he argued, "Our American friends would never understand why they defended freedom in Berlin for so long if the communists now become part of the government."[122]

The SPD and PDS were on the defensive about the Wall and eager to show the public that they took the past seriously and were ready to govern together for all Berliners. Chancellor Schröder tried to nip criticism in the bud when he released a statement on August 12 declaring, "The SED regime admitted its moral and political bankruptcy when it made the division of Germany concrete and walled in the German capital."[123] The PDS candidate for mayor, Gregor Gysi asserted, however, that "today's members don't bear the individual guilt of the officials who decided to build the wall and that an apology would be 'too cheap, too self-righteous and not credible'."[124] After all, Gysi said, "there is nothing that will bring justice for those killed at the wall or against the inhumane border regime."[125]

In an interview with Berlin's *Tagesspiegel* two days before the anniversary, Wowereit made it clear that he would prefer a coalition with the Greens and FDP. He had grown up in the southwest of West Berlin near the border. As an eight-year-old when the Berlin Wall was built, he "couldn't get far on his bike...before hitting the border." He remembered experiencing "confrontations at the Wall and along the transit routes" between West Berlin and West Germany and feeling "powerless and helpless." As the legal successor to the SED, he believed the PDS carried responsibility for the Wall and that it must distance itself from the former East German regime and apologize to the victims in a real, deep substantive way, not just with "lip service as part of an election campaign."[126]

Berlin's SPD leader and interim mayor drew a parallel with what the Germans had been through when taking responsibility for the Nazis' crimes,

---

[121] Christine Richter, "Zum Checkpoint Charlie nur mit Eintrittskarte. Mehr als 2,000 Menschen kamen zur CDU-Veranstaltung," *Berlin Online*, August 13, 2001; Associated Press, "Germany Marks Wall's Anniversary," *New York Times*, August 13, 2001; and Reuters, "Berlin Wall Becomes Battle Cry on Anniversary Eve," *New York Times*, August 12, 2001.

[122] dpa, "Mauerbau: Union attackiert SPD und PDS," *Sächsische Zeitung*, August 13, 2001.

[123] Reuters, "Berlin Wall Becomes Battle Cry on Anniversary Eve," *New York Times*, August 12, 2001.

[124] Associated Press, "Germany Marks Wall's Anniversary," *New York Times*, August 13, 2001.

[125] Ibid.; and "Wall Victims Demand Apologies for Barrier," *Birmingham Post*, August 14, 2001.

[126] "Der Mauerbau: Klaus Wowereit im Interview: 'Herr Gysi soll sich nicht zu früh seinen Anzug bügeln'," *Tagesspiegel*, August, 11, 2001.

asserting: "No one in the PDS can individually reject responsibility even if they personally had nothing to do with the violations of human rights in the GDR. Each German has responsibility to the victims of the Nazis. I can't say that I was born later and have no responsibility. We also have an obligation for future generations." Wowereit argued that "we must learn from our history, from the Nazi period as well as from the SED dictatorship." He declared that Gysi "would be well advised to apologize" for the Wall, and he advised the top PDS politician "not to iron his suit too soon" and assume that he would be part of the ruling coalition.[127] In light of all the focus on the PDS, the Associated Press observed that the Germans were "focused less on history and more on present concerns over whether the successor party" to the SED "has properly reconciled with its brutal past and the dreaded barrier."[128]

On August 13, 2001, commemorative ceremonies took place at Bernauer Strasse, Peter Fechter's memorial, Checkpoint Charlie, the Berlin Senate, and elsewhere, with most of the ceremonies shown live on the Phoenix television network, which devoted twenty-four hours to the anniversary. At the Berlin Wall Memorial Site, the morning began with the bells tolling and a church service in the Chapel of Reconciliation, the laying of wreaths at the Kohlhoff & Kohlhoff memorial, and the opening of the Documentation Center. This anniversary in fact marked the beginning of Bernauer Strasse's status as the main site for Wall commemorations with high-level political participation. It also marked the most divisive moment in commemorating the Wall since unification.

Merkel and Steffel of the CDU laid wreaths at the memorial on Bernauer Strasse early in the morning and separate from the SPD, as did the PDS. Multiple people who had suffered under the GDR regime also gathered at the Kohlhoff & Kohlhoff memorial to pay their respects to those who had lost their lives and to express their concerns about an SPD-PDS coalition. The police had to intervene in the morning when some of the former victims carried away two wreaths brought by the PDS: one man was detained while others voiced their outrage about the PDS. Gustav Rust, who had spent nine years in GDR prisons, arrived wearing a prison uniform and handcuffs. He called the possible coalition with the PDS "a disgrace."[129] Klaus-Peter Eich declared that a possible coalition with the PDS "before they have acknowledged their guilt...[would be] a mockery."[130]

As hundreds stood in the pouring rain, Chancellor Schröder arrived a short time later to lay a wreath of red roses at the Kohlhoff & Kohlhoff memorial. He

---

[127] Ibid.

[128] Associated Press, "Germany Marks Wall's Anniversary," *New York Times*, August 13, 2001.

[129] Reuters, "Emotions Flare as Germany Marks 40 Years of Wall," *New York Times*, August 13, 2001; and dpa, "40 Jahre Mauerbau: Proteste bei Schröders Kranzniederlegung," *Welt Online*, August 13, 2001.

[130] "Wall Victims Demand Apologies for Barrier," *Birmingham Post*, August 14, 2001.

Figure 14 Left to right: Manfred Fischer, Klaus Wowereit, Gabriele Camphausen, Gerhard Schröder (in center), Documentation Center, Berlin Wall Memorial, August 13, 2001
Source: Photographer: Christian Jungeblodt. Stiftung Berliner Mauer-3160.

was booed and jeered and called a "traitor."[131] Mayor Wowereit had the same experience earlier in the day when he laid a wreath at the Peter Fechter memorial. Demonstrators there called him a "traitor" and a "hypocrite."[132] The chancellor apparently had not planned to speak at Bernauer Strasse, but felt he had to in light of the protests.[133] Across the street from the memorial, at the opening of the redesigned Documentation Center (Figure 14) and its exhibit on "Berlin, August 13, 1961," Schröder declared that "only by remembering what has happened can we be in a position, together and independent from party-political directives, to make sure that such a thing can never happen again."[134] This kind of "never again" argument had long been at the root of German confrontation with and education about the Holocaust. Politicians and memory activists would increasingly apply it to the Berlin Wall and the SED regime as well.

[131] Reuters, "Emotions Flare as Germany Marks 40 Years of Wall," *New York Times*, August 13, 2001.
[132] "Mauerbau: SED-Opfer protestieren gegen PDS und SPD," *Frankfurter Allgemeine Zeitung*, August 13, 2001.
[133] Interview with Maria Nooke, July 5, 2005.
[134] dpa, "40 Jahre Mauerbau: Proteste bei Schröders Kranzniederlegung," *Welt Online*, August 13, 2001.

The presence of Chancellor Schröder together with Bundestag President Thierse and Interim Mayor Wowereit at the Documentation Center marked a milestone in the efforts of Fischer, Trotnow, Camphausen, and Nooke to gain official recognition of the importance of the Berlin Wall Memorial ensemble. Welcoming the political leaders to what had been Fischer's parish center and home for more than twenty-five years (although he had recently moved out of his living space there to make room for the staff of the Documentation Center) represented a whole new stage in his work. Wowereit's invitation to Pastor Fischer to give an address to the Berlin Senate at the noontime commemorative ceremony was another indication of growing official appreciation of his work – nearly twelve years after he first started his struggle to preserve some of the Berlin Wall. Yet the political attention also brought the site into the contemporary political maelstrom surrounding the Wall, an unwanted consequence of the efforts of the memory activists at Bernauer Strasse.

At the official ceremony at the Berlin Senate, with 300 invited guests, Wowereit repeated his call for the PDS to apologize to the victims and their families for the suffering they endured because of the Berlin Wall. He made it clear that in his view the PDS had not gone far enough in confronting, recognizing, and atoning for the SED past. Declaring that anyone who wanted to be part of the government "must energetically object when the Wall and barbed wire are justified as means for securing peace," Wowereit insisted that GDR state crimes should not be forgotten. In spite of his efforts and his words, members of GDR victims' groups interrupted the proceedings to point the finger at Wowereit and the SPD. They unfurled a banner calling the PDS the "party of Wall murderers" and declared, "Anyone who forms a coalition with the builders of the Wall mocks the victims."[135]

The interim mayor had been having intensive conversations since June with representatives of groups of victims of the GDR regime about their experiences and needs and finally persuaded one of them, the eighty-year-old Heinz Gerull, to speak on behalf of the victims at the Senate's commemorative ceremony for the fortieth anniversary. Yet Gerull was actually more of a victim of Stalin's terror than of the GDR regime, having been kidnapped off the street by Soviet agents in 1949, convicted by a Soviet court in Potsdam on bogus charges of being an American spy and sent in 1950 to a Soviet forced labor camp above the Arctic Circle. Presumably Wowereit had not been able to persuade anyone who had suffered more directly at the hands of the SED regime to speak at an occasion hosted by a mayor who refused to rule out a coalition with the

---

[135] Tobias Miller, "'Die Narbe im Stadtkörper darf nicht verschwinden'," *Berliner Zeitung*, August 14, 2001.

PDS. Gerull too was sharply critical in his speech of any plans to join forces with the PDS.[136]

Bundestag President Thierse gave the main speech at the Senate for the occasion. He had been seventeen years old when the Wall was erected and forty-six when it fell, thus spending the prime of his life walled in. He urged empathy for former East Germans and their problems, since "after all they were imprisoned for decades."[137] Thierse himself had been arrested when he rushed from East Berlin to see his sick mother at home on the border with the FRG, since he had not applied for the necessary permission to enter the GDR's border zone.[138] He spoke of the Wall as "a scar on the body of the city" and went into great detail about what it meant, how the border regime developed over twenty-eight years, and what it was like to live under these circumstances and how most people somehow "got used to it." He mourned "the more than one hundred people who died as a direct result of the use of force by GDR border soldiers" and – in what could have been seen as an advertisement for the research and educational work being undertaken at the Berlin Wall Memorial's Documentation Center – lamented that it was still not clear how many people had been killed at the Wall.

Thierse also referred to the ongoing difficulties of adjustment being endured by many from the former East who perhaps had "unrealistic expectations" after their "self-liberation" and the fall of the Wall. He was critical of the common Western elision of the East German regime (generally referred to as an *Unrechtsstaat*) and the people. Accordingly, he asserted, "It is necessary to differentiate between condemning the system which built the Wall and judging the people who lived, who had to live in this system. . . .Even if many don't want to hear it: It really was possible to live a correct life in the wrong system."[139]

Ending his speech emphasizing the importance of remembering the Wall and its victims, Thierse spoke approvingly of the Senate's decision to grant historic landmark status to the few remaining sections of the Wall that had not yet been designated as such, and he praised all of those who had engaged in "Sisyphean labors" of fighting the trend of tearing down the Wall and forgetting about it. The Bundestag president singled out the work of Manfred Fischer, saying, "What Pastor Fischer, his parish, [and] the staff of the 'Bernauer Strasse' memorial site have achieved in recent years deserves [our] undivided respect." Thierse argued that memorial sites "cannot reproduce the terror of the Wall in all of its dimensions," but "in more subtle ways. . .they can make people think" and ask questions,

---

[136] Christine Richter, "Vertreter der Opferverbände spricht im Roten Rathaus," *Berliner Zeitung*, August 13, 2001; and Brigitte Grunert, "Der Mauerbau: Sprecher der Verwundeten," *Tagesspiegel*, August 11, 2001.

[137] dpa, "40 Jahre Mauerbau: Proteste bei Schröders Kranzniederlegung," *Welt Online*, August 13, 2001.

[138] Interview with Wolfgang Thierse, February 3, 2010.

[139] Thierse, "Rede zum 40. Jahrestag des Mauerbaus," August 13, 2001.

such as children asking their parents, "Why did you behave this or that way?"[140] This was precisely what Trotnow and Fischer had been arguing since 1990.

As befitting a religious figure, Pastor Fischer's speech sought to rise above the conflicts between political parties, between victims and perpetrators, and even between himself and Pastor Johannes Hildebrandt of the Sophien Church, while also continuing his mission of highlighting the need to document more of the history of the Berlin Wall. Valuing the performative aspect of memory, Fischer often deployed a visual aspect to his sermons and speeches, something to help the listeners focus on his words and remember his message. Thus, he held up to the invited guests at the Rotes Rathaus part of a brick, asking: "Do we really know the tragedy" of the Wall?

As Fischer explained, the brick came from the 150-year-old wall of the Sophien cemetery that the border troops made into part of the Berlin Wall by adding barbed wire to the top of it. The brick had not moved an inch but suddenly became something very different, as did so much else in Berlin on August 13, 1961, said Fischer. He described how the border soldiers dug up the graves at the Sophien cemetery to expand the Berlin Wall's depth and then over time erected the concrete wall that ultimately came down in 1989. Just as "the Berlin Wall was not actually built [overnight] but instead began to be built on August 13, 1961," Fischer said, so "it did not fall [overnight] on November 9, 1989, but instead has had to be carefully dismantled since then." The process of fully uniting east and west and removing what the writer Peter Schneider called the "wall in the mind" was ongoing.[141]

As if answering Thierse's point about not knowing the exact number of people who died at the Wall, Fischer spoke of the importance of giving names and histories to the victims, such as Ernst Mundt who tried to escape over the Sophien cemetery Berlin Wall in September 1962. He made it all the way to the outer Wall at Bernauer Strasse and was one step away from freedom when he was hit by two bullets. He fell back onto a burial mound in the cemetery while his cap with a bullet hole in it flew over the Wall and landed on the sidewalk on Bernauer Strasse in West Berlin. As Fischer explained, one of the Wall trials revealed the would-be escapee's name and that of the soldier who shot him: Ernst Mundt was shot while trying to escape by Karl-Heinz Maul. "I believe it is important that victims have names and perpetrators also," Fischer told the Senate. The Wall was "not just barbed wire and cement; it was also the barrels of guns." This one story occurred at just one small spot along the Wall. There were another 100 miles along the border with stories to tell, said Fischer, "and God knows how many victims. The

[140] Ibid.
[141] "Rede von Pfarrer Manfred Fischer zum 40. Jahrestag des Mauerbaus am 13. August 2001 auf der Gedenkveranstaltung im Berliner Rathaus," Stiftung Berliner Mauer Archive. On the "wall in the mind," see the 1982 novel written by Peter Schneider when the Wall still stood, *The Wall Jumper: A Berlin Story*, trans. Leigh Hafrey (Chicago: University of Chicago Press, 1998), p. 119.

concrete truth about the Wall is far from being known. . . .[A]nd the search for the truth must be oriented toward the victims."

Pastor Fischer concluded his remarks by talking about reconciliation, which "cannot be decreed by the perpetrators, the victims or so-called neutral third parties. Reconciliation is actually a gift. . .a gift from God. . .which heals both victims and perpetrators." He shared his sense of the "inner necessity" of providing a Chapel of Reconciliation "for self-reflection" precisely at the site that also commemorates victims, offers counseling, and documents the history of the Wall. It all went together for Fischer, and after so long trying to create such a place and space, he had finally succeeded.

In a prime-time, national television address that evening, President Rau spoke of the impact of the Wall on past and present, clearly having in mind the ways the divide was still present in perception and reality. He declared that the Germans had a double obligation with regard to the Wall: not to forget the suffering and injustice done to so many in the past, but also to overcome the old East-West divide in people's attitudes so as to do justice to the "gift of unity by constructing it together and in the interests of all."[142] As befitting the role of the German president as one meant to be above party politics, Rau tried to appeal to all Germans to make the unification of the country more of a reality in everyday life and thought.

The day after the anniversary, Chancellor Schröder embarked on a two-week tour of eastern Germany. The fact that the voting allegiances of people in the "new states" had not yet been fixed and that Schröder faced national elections the following year was clearly an important impulse for the trip. No doubt he hoped to show the people in the east that he cared about the challenges they faced and sought a closer understanding of these challenges.

Wall Memory after the Fortieth Anniversary

For the first time since unification and in spite of criticism by the CDU and by east German victims' groups, in the Berlin elections of October 2001 the SPD garnered more of the vote (29.7 percent) than the CDU (23.8 percent), confirming the SPD's Klaus Wowereit as the mayor. After preliminary talks with the FDP and Greens on forming a ruling coalition were unsuccessful, in mid-December and against the explicit wishes of Chancellor Schröder (who feared it would hurt his own chances for reelection the following year and who was also outraged at the PDS opposition to his decision to help US forces in Afghanistan after the September 11 terrorist attacks in the United States), Wowereit and his colleagues chose to form a ruling coalition with the PDS.

[142] "Fernsehansprache von Bundespräsident Johannes Rau zum 40. Jahrestag des Baus der Berliner Mauer," www.bundespraesident.de/SharedDocs/Reden/DE/Johannes-Rau/Reden/2001/08/20010813_Rede.html.

In its greatest electoral success ever, the PDS received 22.6 percent of the vote. Eleven years after unification, more than one in five Berliners voted for the SED successor party. The strength of the PDS in the former East Berlin was particularly clear, where it garnered 47.6 percent of the vote.[143] Gregor Gysi, whom the *New York Times* called the "effervescent leader" of the PDS, became deputy mayor.[144] Reaching out to the PDS base of voters who felt their concerns were not heard by the government, the SPD and PDS would "recognize the great efforts exerted thus far in the unification process, especially by people from the former eastern part of the city," and aim for "the establishment of equal opportunities in east and west [and] greater mutual respect for the lived biographies of those in each part of Berlin."[145]

Working out the details of the SPD-PDS coalition in treaty form took until mid-January 2002. A key sticking point was the PDS approach to the Berlin Wall and the former SED regime, which was hardly surprising after the controversial PDS statement on the Berlin Wall a few months earlier.[146] The parties pledged to work together to foster "the interior unity of Berlin," which was only possible "by keeping alive the history of the city and living up to the city's historic responsibility."[147] The coalition partners agreed that, "The open approach to crimes against democracy and individual rights, the assumption of responsibility and respect toward the victims as well as the preservation of their memory are conditions for reconciliation and internal unity. They are also conditions for this coalition." The SPD and less doctrinaire members of the PDS had prevailed in forcing the PDS to face up to the past.

The two parties hedged a bit, as had the judges in the Wall trials, on the question of the degree of responsibility of the former East German regime in building the Wall. The SPD and PDS directed blame to "the GDR and the Soviet Union who erected the Wall" and whose leaders "bore exclusive responsibility for the trauma" it caused. They did though seem to at least indirectly single out the East German regime for blame: "The shots at the Berlin Wall brought deep suffering and death to many people. They were the manifestation of a regime [presumably the SED] which disregarded even the rights to life and to bodily integrity to secure its own power." Seen as "a world-wide symbol of totalitarianism and contempt for humanity," the Wall "tore apart families and friends" who still feel the wounds from this time.

---

[143] Der Landeswahlleiter, ed., "Wahlen in Berlin am 21. Oktober 2001," *Berliner Statistik* (Berlin: Statistisches Landesamt Berlin, 2001).

[144] Edmund L. Andrews, "Once Reviled, Ex-Communists Join Coalition to Rule Berlin," *New York Times*, December 21, 2001.

[145] SPD-PDS Koalitionsvereinbarung, January 16, 2002, archiv.spd-berlin.de/w/files/spd-positionen/koalitionsvertrag2002.pdf.

[146] "Koalitionsvereinbarungen praktisch perfekt," *Spiegel Online*, January 7, 2002.

[147] SPD-PDS Koalitionsvereinbarung, January 16, 2002, p. 4.

In addition to their culpability for the Wall, "the SED regime together with the Soviet leaders was responsible for the violent suppression of the June 17, 1953 popular uprising. . .and many human rights violations, including the lack of basic rights to democracy and freedom in the GDR." The two parties also condemned the SED for the "persecution. . ., the imprisonment under inhumane conditions culminating in death, and the execution of people who thought differently," such as "social democrats and other parts of the democratic opposition." The new leaders cautioned that "the past can't permanently rule the future," as no doubt the PDS insisted, but that a successful future was only possible if "things are not suppressed, blocked out and covered up" about the past, as the SPD likely insisted.

As part of grappling with the past and teaching future generations about it, the coalition partners asserted the importance of creating and preserving memorial sites related to both Nazi and SED history. Confronting the details and effects of the division of Germany and of Berlin, they argued, would represent an important contribution to uniting the city and country. Accordingly, the SPD and PDS called for permanent support for the Berlin Wall Memorial Documentation Center and more generally for the development and implementation of a master plan for handling all remains of the Wall and border installations. They also noted more pragmatically in a later section of the coalition treaty that at a time of great financial shortfall such as they were facing in 2002, "tourism is one of the most vigorous growth sectors of Berlin's economy." They left it unsaid that the thing tourists to Berlin most wanted to see was the Berlin Wall.[148]

Indeed, already in the fall of 2001, the Berlin Senate had commissioned a study to record all the extant Wall and border remnants along the twenty-seven miles of the former inner-city border, leaving it to the neighboring state of Brandenburg to do this with the other nearly eighty miles of the path of the Wall on the outskirts of the city. Over the course of 2002 and 2003, historic preservationist and Berlin Wall expert Leo Schmidt[149] and one of his students at the University of Cottbus, Axel Klausmeier (both of whom were from western Germany), walked, biked, and drove along the former path of the Wall taking notes and pictures of every piece of Wall, trip wire, road marking, street light, markings on the side of a building, and anything else that had been part of the border strip.[150] *Die Zeit* would call Schmidt the Indiana Jones of the

---

[148] Ibid., p. 74.

[149] Schmidt had been thinking in an in-depth way about the Berlin Wall for years. See, for example, Polly Feversham and Leo Schmidt, *Die Berliner Mauer heute/The Berlin Wall Today* (Berlin: Verlag Bauwesen, 1999).

[150] Ian Johnson, "Missing History: Berlin Now Hunts for Traces of Wall," *Wall Street Journal*, September 25, 2003; and Kai Michel, "Die Mauer ist noch lange nicht weg," *Die Zeit*, August 7, 2003. The published book version of their research is Axel Klausmeier and Leo Schmidt, *Wall Remnants – Wall Traces* (Berlin/Bonn: Westkreuz-Verlag, 2004).

Wall.[151] Schmidt and Klausmeier's completed study comprised more than 800 pages. In accepting it, the Senator for Culture and Historic Preservation, Jörg Haspel, declared that the Wall was "the most important historical monument of the twentieth century," and "people come to Berlin expecting to see it."[152] Haspel, like Fischer and others, felt it was important to respond to visitors' interest in seeing the Berlin Wall.

Schmidt argued that the unique nature of the Berlin Wall would qualify its remains as a UNESCO world heritage site, pointing out that other dark historical sites like Auschwitz and Hiroshima were already on the UNESCO list.[153] The preservationist understood that "our history isn't shaped by beautiful things alone. Physical evidence of history should remain to augment documents and memories. If you destroy the site, it makes it easier to control the telling of history. My job is to preserve the evidence, especially where it hurts,"[154] a sentiment Fischer had long shared. Schmidt also maintained that, contrary to the prevailing association in Germany of the Wall with the repression of the SED regime, the Wall was also a very positive symbol of the peaceful, democratic overcoming of the East German regime and of the division of Berlin and Germany.[155]

While the Senate study focused on the remains of the Wall, a proposal from one of the opposition parties, the Greens (die Grüne), took another approach. Michael Cramer, a member of Berlin's House of Representatives representing die Grüne, called for preserving the empty space where the death strip had been as a "Wall trail" (Mauerweg) or a "green belt" (Grünes Band) around Berlin for walking and biking. As the Wall and the other elements of the death strip were removed, people took to using the space for walking their dogs, biking, and other recreational activities. Cramer wanted to keep it that way. Setting foot in an area that once could have cost you your life, now could be used in much more healthy ways, which in fact could extend one's lifespan instead of shortening it. The Green MP felt it was very important to remember the history of the Wall and in an environmentally sustainable way: "My generation was one where our parents didn't tell us anything about the past. So we wanted to moralize with everyone. We felt as strong as bears. I fought for ten years to keep the Brandenburg Gate closed to traffic [to protect it from pollution]. And the Berlin government wanted

---

[151] Kai Michel, "Die Mauer ist noch lange nicht weg," *Zeit*, August 7, 2003.

[152] Haspel quote from *Das Erste*, November 9, 2003.

[153] Petra Ahne, "Der Mauerläufer. Leo Schmidt hat die Reste der Grenze gesucht – und findet, dass sie Weltkulturerbe werden müssen," *Berliner Zeitung*, August 19, 2003; and "Nicht nur das Schöne. VZ-Gespräch mit Leo Schmidt: Worum sollte die Berliner Mauer Weltkulturerbe werden?" *Badische Zeitung*, August 21, 2003.

[154] Interview with Leo Schmidt, November 12, 2013.

[155] Marc Neller, interview with Leo Schmidt, "Die Mauer ist ein positives Symbol," *Tagesspiegel*, July 28, 2005.

a city highway at Bernauer Strasse, but we stopped this."[156] His next goal was creating a *Mauerweg*.

An avid cyclist and long-time physical education teacher from West Germany, Cramer had ridden his bike along the western side of the Wall in the summer of 1989, followed by the eastern side in the spring of 1990. Ever since reading about the closure of the border as a twelve year old, he had been fascinated by the Berlin Wall. He first visited Berlin in 1963 and took many pictures of the Wall at Bernauer Strasse and elsewhere with a camera his aunt had given him, something he would continue to do over the years the Wall stood. Once the Wall fell, Cramer and other members of the Green Party in Berlin began to call for some way to mark this former path of the Wall. Cramer's enthusiasm for this increased when he visited Boston in 1998 and saw the Freedom Trail with its brick line leading visitors to sites connected with the American Revolution. He thought, "this is exactly what we need in Berlin."[157]

In 2000, for the tenth anniversary of German unification and with the fortieth anniversary of the erection of the Wall looming the following year, Cramer proposed that the Berlin parliament establish a *Mauerweg* for walking and biking (*Radweg*) along the former border, complete with signs highlighting the history of the Wall. He called for the creation of "an educational *Mauerweg*," since "it's not just many tourists in Berlin who have come to ask 'where exactly was the Wall?' Even people who have long lived here find it difficult to remember exactly where the Wall was."[158] He recommended having signs on the trail with historical descriptions and pictures at key points within Berlin and surrounding it, and he proposed creating a brochure with more detail for people to take with them on the trail. In Cramer's view, the *Radweg* would offer "an ideal combination of history workshop and bike tourism, of free time and culture" and "would be a highlight of the city's tourism program."

After Cramer went public with his recommendations in an article in the *Tagesspiegel*, the photographer who accompanied him on the trail donated the pictures he had taken. Cramer used these to create a small brochure and gave it out to the press in 2001. He was happily surprised by the storm of interest his brochure created. Berlin's tabloid *B.Z.* published a two-page spread on the *Mauerweg/Radweg* and many other newspapers and media then picked up the story. His phone rang nonstop with more requests for the brochure. In three days, he gave out 2,000. In fourteen days it was 15,000, then 23,000. Cramer published the first edition of the Berlin Wall Bike Trail as a book in June 2001.[159] Over the summer,

---

[156] Interview with Michael Cramer, July 20, 2007.
[157] Ibid.
[158] Michael Cramer, "Positionen: Geschichte endlich erfahrbar machen," *Tagesspiegel*, October 4, 2000.
[159] Interview with Michael Cramer, July 20, 2007.

he led hundreds of cyclists on a tour of the *Mauer Radweg*, followed by television cameras for the main late evening news program, *Tagesthemen*. On one tour, Karin Gueffroy whose son Chris had been the last person shot and killed trying to escape in February 1989 talked about her son at the site where he was killed.[160]

For Germans and tourists, young and old, who did not know or could not remember where the Wall was and what happened along the Wall, the Wall trail was Cramer's remedy. The Berlin parliament and Senate gave their backing to the *Mauerweg* in 2001.[161] Over the next five years, Berlin would invest more than 4.4 million euros to maintain the trail and provide historical information along it.[162] Fifteen years after the government agreed to the Wall trail, Cramer would publish his eighth expanded, revised edition of the *Mauer Radweg* book with waterproof pages and downloadable GPS directions to make it easier for cyclists. In 2019, the government would commit to renovating the entire 100 miles of the *Mauerweg* beginning in 2020 for at least 12.4 million euros.[163]

In June 2003, the last step of Fischer's 1997 proposal for a Berlin Wall Memorial Ensemble at Bernauer Strasse was completed with the addition of an observation deck adjacent to the Documentation Center, finally allowing visitors a broader view of the former death strip and into the Kohlhoff & Kohlhoff memorial. With an infusion from the federal Wall Property Funds, the Berlin Wall Association was able to reopen a partially reconstructed Documentation Center with a new seminar room, outdoor listening station for visitors coming by after hours, and an adjoining tower complete with stairs and an elevator to reach the observation deck. The funds also allowed the Documentation Center to provide staff to lead historical bike tours along the *Mauerweg*. Bundesrat President Wolfgang Böhmer, the minister-president of the eastern state of Saxony-Anhalt, was at Bernauer Strasse to celebrate the expansion of the Documentation Center.[164]

This final step came just in time to accommodate the growing number of visitors interested in the Berlin Wall in the wake of widespread commemorations of the fiftieth anniversary of the East German uprising of June 17, 1953.[165] Germans were fascinated to learn about the circumstances under

---

[160] Interviews with Michael Cramer, July 20, 2007 and November 28, 2009.

[161] Peter Neumann, "160 Kilometer deutsche Geschichte," *Berliner Zeitung*, August 13, 2011.

[162] www.berlin.de/mauer/mauerweg/projektinformationen-zum-berliner-mauerweg-149112.php.

[163] Robert Kiesel, "Neues Pflaster für den Mauerweg," *Tagesspiegel*, January 8, 2019.

[164] Anemi Wick, "Der Todesstreifen von Oben," *Welt*, June 21, 2003; Camphausen, "Berliner Mauer-Gedenkstätte und Dokumentationszentrum e.V., Bilanz und Perspektiven der Vereinstätigkeit," August 2004, pp. 11–12; and Camphausen and Fischer, "Die bürgerschaftliche Durchsetzung," pp. 361–74.

[165] Edgar Wolfrum, "Neue Erinnerungskultur? Die Massenmedialisierung des 17. Juni 1953," *Aus Politik und Zeitgeschichte* 40–41 (September 29, 2003), pp. 33–39.

which over one million East Germans took to the streets in protest against the communist regime starting in East Berlin and spreading to more than 230 towns throughout the country.[166] With television, radio, and the newspapers full of information about the uprising and interviews with people who experienced it, Germans were inspired by this example of a democratic uprising in (East) German history, and wanted to know more about it, including about the Berlin Wall.[167] Indeed, in light of the broad attention to the anniversary of the uprising, Trotnow observed that "it won't be surprising if sooner or later we have a similar experience with regard to the history of the Berlin Wall."[168]

* * *

In the nearly fifteen years since the fall of the Wall, Fischer and his colleagues had sought political support to anchor memory of the Berlin Wall in German memory culture. They found, as memory activists generally do, that political engagement brought unexpected and sometimes unwanted results as politicians used memory of the Wall for their own purposes. Just as Fischer himself had used anniversaries connected to the Wall to mark milestones in the development of the Chapel of Reconciliation and the Documentation Center and to attract public attention to remembering the Wall, so politicians used the same anniversaries to transmit messages about their own or their political opponent's connection to the past and its current relevance. This is not to say that the motives of politicians with regard to the Wall and those who suffered because of it were purely instrumental; most if not all of the political leaders felt real sorrow and regret for those who were killed at the Wall. These feelings were often supplemented, however, by a party politics aspect of remembering the Wall, especially on Wall anniversaries.

Another striking aspect of approaches to the Wall concerned not just local or national memory but global memory. In justifying their arguments for the importance of preserving the memory of the Wall, both the team at Bernauer Strasse and public officials referred to global interest. Due to its iconic status during the Cold War and with its peaceful fall, people around the world remembered the Wall. From Wall peckers in the months following the toppling of the Wall to governments and private individuals around the world

---

[166] Christian F. Ostermann, ed., *Uprising in East Germany, 1953* (New York: Central European University Press, 2001); and Hope M. Harrison, *Driving the Soviets up the Wall* (Princeton: Princeton University Press, 2003), pp. 12–48. For an analysis of the development of memorial sites to the uprising, see Anna Saunders, *Memorializing the GDR* (NY: Berghahn 2018), pp. 159–93.

[167] Interviews with Gabriele Camphausen, December 15, 2009 and Tom Sello, February 10, 2010.

[168] Trotnow, "Sag mir, wo die Spuren sind . . . Berlin und der Umgang mit der Geschichte der Berliner Mauer," in Bernd Faulenbach, Franz-Josef Jelich, eds., *"Asymmetrisch verflochtene Parallelgeschichte?" Die Geschichte der Bundesrepublik und der DDR in Ausstellungen, Museen und Gedenkstätten* (Essen: Klartext, 2005), p. 166.

seeking to buy sections of the Wall to tourists visiting Berlin in the years afterwards wanting to see the Wall, global interest in the Berlin Wall continued unabated. Fischer, Cultural Senator Haspel, and Green MP Cramer with his Wall Trail were among those who believed they must respond to this outside interest and provide people with information and authentic remnants of the former border.

Yet in spite of calls by some municipal and federal politicians for a "master plan" to encompass remnants of the Wall and its memory, no such plan had been developed or was even in the works as of 2003. Such a plan would presumably include funding. Thus, while the memory activists at Bernauer Strasse now oversaw a memorial ensemble consisting of the Documentation Center, sections of the Wall, a monument to victims, and the Chapel of Reconciliation, they still lacked long-term financial support for their work. They would have help from the Wall Property Funds for a few years, but it was unclear what would happen after that. The Documentation Center was open for only a limited number of hours each week, and plans to expand the exhibit inside and provide more historical information for visitors outside along the former border could only progress slowly without additional funding to hire more staff and to pay them for more hours.

By 2003, Trotnow was no longer really involved at Bernauer Strasse, focusing on directing the Allied Museum. Camphausen had scaled back her involvement as well in light of her position at the Stasi Records Authority. Fischer remained and would not give up in his ever-expanding mission of reminding and/or educating people about the history of the Wall. He had not given up in 1985 after the Church of Reconciliation was destroyed by the East German regime. He had not given up in the 1990s during the battles with the Sophien parish about the use of their property to preserve the remains of the Wall and create the Berlin Wall Memorial. And he certainly would not give up now. Fischer could not have imagined that help in keeping alive the history of the Berlin Wall and the need to commemorate its victims would come from a very unexpected quarter, albeit one that would challenge the anchoring of the memory of the Wall at Bernauer Strasse.

4

Remembering the Wall at Checkpoint Charlie

On October 31, 2004, two weeks in advance of the fifteenth anniversary of the toppling of the Wall, the director of the private Checkpoint Charlie Wall Museum, Alexandra Hildebrandt, unveiled 1,065 wooden crosses in memory of the people killed at the Berlin Wall and along the entire former East German border.[1] She had leased the land for this outdoor installation at the central location of Checkpoint Charlie, just steps from her museum. In addition to the crosses (Figure 15), which soon increased in number to 1,075, Hildebrandt had more than 200 yards of the Berlin Wall reinstalled at Checkpoint Charlie located two miles south of the Berlin Wall Memorial ensemble at Bernauer Strasse. Many of the crosses had a picture of a person killed at the border, their name, dates of birth and death, and the reason for their death, such as "shot while trying to escape" or "drowned after being shot." For decades the museum had announced each year on August 13 the total number of people they believed had been killed at the border, but they had never done anything like this. No one had. And that was the point.

As a commentator in *Der Spiegel* magazine noted, Hildebrandt's "timing in light of the fifteenth anniversary of the fall of the Wall...could not have been better. The old Hildebrandt [who had run the museum for decades and died a few months earlier] certainly would have applauded his wife."[2] Politicians were not the only ones who could engage in anniversary politics. Indeed, Hildebrandt's action drew significant official and popular attention to the memory of the Wall and to its victims and ignited a battle between the museum director and the government over who should direct this memory, especially since Hildebrandt used her new memorial to chide the Berlin SPD-PDS government for not having done enough to commemorate victims of the Wall. While public officials as well as journalists, historians, and other experts

---

[1] See particularly the sections entitled "All they wanted was freedom" and "Memorial Place Checkpoint Charlie – Save the historic ground at Checkpoint Charlie!" "Freedom Obliges: The Freedom Memorial on Checkpoint Charlie Square" in Alexandra Hildebrandt's booklet for the press, "Freiheitsmahnmal am Platz Checkpoint Charlie, 'Sie wollten nur die Freiheit,' Gespräche mit der Bank – Trotzdem soll geräumt werden!", distributed at the 143rd press conference of the Working Group of August 13, Inc., June 28, 2005. These sections were clearly written in 2004 for the opening of the Freedom Memorial.

[2] Carsten Volkery, "Mehr Disneyland Wagen," *Spiegel*, October 29, 2004.

Figure 15 Crosses to commemorate victims of the Wall, Checkpoint Charlie,
November 2004
Source: Hope M. Harrison.

asserted that no one person or group should dominate the way the Wall was
commemorated, many participants in the contentious public debate believed
that the government had not been doing its job in regard to remembering the
Wall. The reaction to Hildebrandt's crosses showed that in spite of increased
political engagement at the Berlin Wall Memorial in recent years, as of 2004 it
had not been firmly anchored in public consciousness. Many people, including
Hildebrandt, saw the memorial at Bernauer Strasse as a small, out-of-the-way,
insignificant site compared to the heavily-trafficked Checkpoint Charlie (see
Figure 1).

The Berlin authorities who got involved at an early stage in the debate over
Hildebrandt's crosses agreed that the government had a key role in fostering
memory of victims of the Wall and pointed out that there already was a
national memorial to these victims at Bernauer Strasse, even though
Hildebrandt insisted that the cold, confusing Kohlhoff & Kohlhoff memorial
was insufficient. Berlin's public representatives also defended themselves
against Hildebrandt's accusations that they had not done enough, by declaring
that if there was more to be done, it was other parts of the government that
needed to act, not the part they themselves represented. Lower-level officials,

such as Joachim Zeller, the mayor of the district of Mitte, insisted that higher-level officials, such as the senator for culture or the mayor himself, needed to develop a comprehensive plan for how to handle the memory of the Wall.[3] Some higher-level officials, such as Senator for City Planning Ingeborg Junge-Reyer, agreed.[4] The vast majority of officials at all levels felt Hildebrandt had essentially usurped their job of handling the memorialization of victims of the Wall.

Many politicians were outraged that a private citizen could make such a strong commemorative statement at such a central site in Berlin. They were caught flat-footed and reacted defensively and angrily, no doubt in part because of the generally positive popular response to the crosses. The PDS Senator for Culture, Thomas Flierl, called Hildebrandt's action an "intolerable privatization of commemoration which is really a matter for the public sphere."[5] Once policymakers as well as historical experts began to criticize Hildebrandt for various inaccuracies of her Wall memorial and called for its removal, she fiercely defended it.

That Alexandra Hildebrandt would come to play such an important role in the German approach to the Wall and commemoration of its victims was far from obvious. She had in fact been born and raised in the Soviet Union and had not even heard of the Berlin Wall until the late 1980s. Alexandra Weissmann grew up in Kiev, Ukraine. Her father was an engineer of ethnic German descent, and her mother was a pediatrician. One of Alexandra's uncles had been in the gulag for fifteen years, leading her to observe later that "every family had some bad experiences under communism."[6] Alexandra initially followed in the footsteps of her father, completing a degree in electronic engineering and working at an arms factory on missile guidance. In 1986, however, she made a drastic career change and left the factory to study art. She became a painter and started exhibiting her work.

In the late 1980s, Alexandra joined other artists and the Kiev chamber choir on a trip to Munich and then to West Berlin. It was her first time outside of the Soviet bloc. While in West Berlin, she met a gallery owner who offered to show some of her paintings. More importantly, as it turned out, Alexandra was introduced to Rainer Hildebrandt. He was interested in art (his mother had been a painter and his father an art historian) and directed a museum, albeit not an art museum but one dedicated to the Wall. Even though he was seventy-six and she was thirty-one years old, the two fell in love and remained in almost

---

[3] "Zeller will Mauer-Konzept für Berlin," *Berliner Zeitung*, October 7, 2004.

[4] Peter Kirschey, "Dauerärgnis Checkpoint Charlie," *Neues Deutschland*, October 10, 2004; and interview with Ingeborg Junge-Reyer, November 22, 2004.

[5] Thomas Rogalla and Tobias Miller, "Das Geschäft mit der Mauer: Senatoren kritisieren Kunstaktion," *Berliner Zeitung*, October 11, 2004.

[6] Interview with Alexandra Hildebrandt, July 24, 2014.

daily phone contact upon her return to Kiev. Soon after German unification, Rainer persuaded Alexandra to move to Berlin. They married in 1995.[7] In the years to come, they would become two of the most important memory activists with regard to the Berlin Wall.

Unlike Alexandra's, Rainer Hildebrandt's background made him seem almost predestined to draw attention to victims of the Berlin Wall and communism. In fact, he had been doing this for decades, starting with exhibits in a space he rented in 1962 at Bernauer Strasse several blocks from the walled in Church of Reconciliation and at the Wall Museum he founded at Checkpoint Charlie in 1963. Hildebrandt's anti-authoritarian credentials were firmly established with his resistance to the Nazi regime. As a student in Berlin in the early 1940s, and no doubt influenced by the fact that his mother was Jewish, Hildebrandt joined the opposition against Hitler. The Nazis had forbidden his mother from painting professionally after 1935 and had removed his father from his university chair as an art historian in 1937. Rainer joined a resistance circle around one of his professors in Berlin, Albrecht Haushofer. The two became close friends and both were persecuted by the Nazis for their opposition. Hildebrandt was imprisoned by the Gestapo in 1943 for seventeen months. Haushofer was arrested in December 1944 and shot by the SS in April 1945. Decades later, Hildebrandt would request to be buried next to his old friend.

After World War II, Hildebrandt's experiences under the Nazis and his wish that he had done even more to oppose their brutal regime fueled his campaign against communism and his defense of human rights.[8] He consistently and loudly drew attention to missing German POWs in camps in the USSR and to German prisoners in the Soviet zone of Germany. He also publicized the brutal conditions in those camps and prisons. In 1948, Hildebrandt formed the Action Group against Inhumanity (*Kampfgruppe gegen Unmenschlichkeit*, KgU) to search for German prisoners in Soviet custody. With the establishment of the GDR in 1949 and the building of the Wall in 1961, Hildebrandt kept a spotlight on the crimes of the SED regime and the plight of East German citizens who expressed their opposition. In addition, he found ways to help people who wanted to leave or who had already left the GDR, and he sought to help others do the same. Hildebrandt's apartment

---

[7] Ibid.; and Jochim Stoltenberg's interview with Alexandra Hildebrandt, "Ein Leben wider das Vergessen," *Berliner Morgenpost*, November 7, 2004. According to Hildebrandt, the latter contains some errors in dates.

[8] Stephen Kinzer, "Berlin Journal. Germany Warms up to a 'Fossil of the Cold War'," *New York Times*, August 24, 1993. Rainer Hildebrandt also connected the Nazi and communist regimes. "One display [in his museum] traced the Wall to Hitler and his war, the conflict that led to the partitioning of his Third Reich and the rise of the DDR and the Wall." Peter Wyden, *Wall: The Inside Story of Divided Berlin* (New York: Simon and Schuster, 1989), p. 562.

served as a central meeting point both for planning escapes and celebrating their success afterwards.

For the entire period of the German division, the never-tiring resistance fighter wrote regularly for the West Berlin daily *Tagesspiegel* to inform West Germans about political prisoners in the GDR, border guards who had shot people trying to escape, abusive East German prison wardens, and many of the other ugly sides of the GDR. He also used this media platform when necessary to criticize the timidity or acquiescence of the West in the face of human rights violations in the GDR. While a sense of powerlessness, guilt or lack of interest led many in the FRG to increasingly turn away from the truth of what was happening in the GDR and at its borders, Hildebrandt called for the opposite. He was often very specific in his articles, providing the names of political prisoners who needed help or of notoriously cruel prison guards or prisons, such as Bautzen and Höheneck. He told personal stories of people who had been tortured in prison. Through his speeches, media appearances, and exhibits, he sought to ensure that people could not justifiably say "I didn't know," as so many had during the Nazi period and afterwards.

In October 1962, Hildebrandt opened an exhibit, "It happened at the Wall," in a two-room apartment he rented for this purpose on Bernauer Strasse, not far from where Manfred Fischer would live and serve as pastor of the Reconciliation parish thirteen years later. Hildebrandt had gone to Bernauer Strasse in August 1961, days after the border was sealed, and witnessed people jumping from their windows on the East Berlin side of the street. He was sickened and outraged when some people missed the nets held by West Berlin policemen and firemen and plunged to their deaths or sustained serious injuries. As Hildebrandt's anger grew, so did his determination to do all he could to document and protest against the Berlin Wall. The exhibit he opened on Bernauer Strasse was one important method. He hoped that with a display of photographs and objects related to the Wall, others would feel the rage he did and be spurred into action.[9] What Fischer later did at his Documentation Center, Hildebrandt had done decades before, although as Helmut Trotnow later maintained, Hildebrandt's "goal [in his exhibits] was never historical accuracy. Rather, he wanted to document political protest against the GDR's unjust regime."[10]

At Hildebrandt's small exhibit, visitors could learn details about the early Berlin Wall, see pictures and materials collected about the construction and guarding of the whole border zone, meet people who had escaped, and use

[9] Ibid., pp. 563–64.

[10] Helmut Trotnow, "Sag mir, wo die Spuren sind…Berlin und der Umgang mit der Geschichte der Berliner Mauer," in Bernd Faulenbach and Franz-Josef Jelich, eds., *"Asymmetrisch verflochtene Parallelgeschichte?" Die Geschichte der Bundesrepublik und der DDR in Ausstellungen, Museen und Gedenkstätten* (Essen: Klartext, 2005), p. 162.

binoculars to look over the Wall into the death strip. The escapees included border soldiers (*Grenzer*) who shared information about the rules and regulations at the Berlin Wall and the practice of rewarding *Grenzer* with money, gifts, and promotions for preventing people from escaping across the Wall. They also spoke of the *Grenzer* who purposely misfired or shot people in the legs instead of aiming to kill. Over 200,000 people visited Hildebrandt's small exhibit in the first six months.

The following year he established and became chairman of the August 13 Association dedicated to helping East Germans escape and fostering a network of people who had escaped. Hildebrandt later described the "feeling of happiness when you can say to the refugee at the border: We did it. We are across." He and his friends helped many East Germans including a *Grenzer* get to the West. When Hildebrandt opened an expanded Wall Museum at Checkpoint Charlie in 1963, he mounted a huge poster on he facade of the building that perhaps counterintuitively called on people to greet the GDR *Grenzer* in a friendly way: "Look through the uniform. The number of victims would be ten times greater if they all fired their guns in a targeted way."[11] This was also Hildebrandt's way of enticing *Grenzer* to at least not aim their guns to kill people trying to escape and perhaps even to tempt the *Grenzer* themselves to escape. In addition to his work helping people escape, Hildebrandt also used his August 13 Association, in the words of the journalist Peter Wyden, as "a source of public information for every statistic, every change in construction and in enforcement practices [at the Wall], [and] every newsworthy defection" via press conferences, publications, and exhibits. "As long as there was a wall, he would be its press agent, relentless, letting its monstrosities speak for themselves."[12]

Hildebrandt's Wall Museum quickly became world famous. His future wife Alexandra would take over decades later when he passed away. Located in the last building before the Checkpoint Charlie crossing point in the Berlin Wall, it became known as the "House at Checkpoint Charlie" or the "Checkpoint Charlie Museum." Checkpoint Charlie was the crossing point between East and West Berlin for American, British, French, and Soviet military and political officials as well as for non-German diplomats and tourists. According to wartime agreements among the Four Allies, they each were guaranteed access to both East and West Berlin, and this was their crossing point between the two. American, British, and French soldiers manned the Western side of Checkpoint Charlie, and Soviet and East German forces manned the Eastern side.

---

[11] Werner Kolhoff, "Sie muss stehenbleiben, weil die Dinge Geschichte erzählen," *Berliner Zeitung*, August 12, 1996.

[12] Wyden, *Wall*, p. 564.

Two months after the East Germans began building the Berlin Wall, Checkpoint Charlie was the site of the only direct US-Soviet tank standoff during the Cold War. The East German authorities attempted to control the access of Western Allied officials to East Berlin instead of leaving Soviet border officials in charge, as guaranteed in the wartime agreements. In response, the USA brought in tanks to support their right to access East Berlin, reiterating the point that all of Berlin remained under Four Power control, not that of the GDR. The Soviets responded in kind to the US tanks. At the height of the crisis on October 27–28, the Americans and Soviets each had ten tanks poised with their gun barrels aimed at each other, barely 100 yards apart at the checkpoint. Only a back channel for communication between US and Soviet leaders led to a de-escalation of the crisis and the removal of the tanks from both sides, one by one, in a tit-for-tat method begun by the Soviets.[13]

The eyes of the world remained on the site after the so-called Checkpoint Charlie crisis, making it a perfect place for Hildebrandt to continue to direct attention to the brutality of East German policies at the Berlin Wall and escapes across it. Situated so close to the Wall and Checkpoint Charlie, the museum profited from the large numbers of international tourists fascinated by the Wall.[14] Equally important, he and other "escape helpers" (*Fluchthelfer*) could look out of a small window in the back of the museum to observe the goings-on at Checkpoint Charlie, monitoring guards' movements on the Eastern side and planning and observing escapes from East to West Berlin.[15] The East German authorities were not at all happy with this and reportedly made attempts to kidnap Hildebrandt and also sent Stasi agents to snoop around his museum.[16]

In a tribute to the importance of the Wall and the strength of Hildebrandt's PR skills, he was joined at the opening of his museum on June 17, 1963 by the federal official in charge of policies concerning the GDR, Ernst Lemmer. Federal subsidies from Lemmer's office and admission fees financed the museum.[17] By opening the museum on the tenth anniversary of the East

---

[13] Frederick Kempe, *Berlin 1961: Kennedy, Khrushchev, and the Most Dangerous Place on Earth* (New York: G. P. Putnam's Sons, 2011).

[14] Wyden, *Wall*, p. 564.

[15] Sybille Frank, *Der Mauer um die Wette Gedenken. Die Formation einer Heritage-Industrie am Berliner Checkpoint Charlie* (Frankfurt: Campus Verlag, 2008), pp. 155–56.

[16] Alexandra Hildebrandt, introduction and ed., *German Post-War History in Selected Articles by Rainer Hildebrandt, 1949–1993* (Berlin: House at Checkpoint Charlie Publisher, 2002), p. 14.

[17] Federal subsidies were DM100,000 per year from 1963 to 1971, DM50,000 in 1972, DM30,000 in 1973, and then stopped. West German lottery monies funded the expansion of the museum's exhibit in 1987 to the building next door at Friedrichstrasse 43. Bert Lindler, "Berlin Wall museum will close its doors on Dec. 31," *The Stars and Stripes*, December 22, 1973; and Anna Kaminsky, ed., *Orte des Erinnerns*, 2nd rev. and expanded ed. (Berlin: Ch. Links, 2007), p. 63.

German uprising, Hildebrandt sought to draw attention to popular discontent in the GDR and to the plight of those who dared oppose it and were killed, imprisoned, or otherwise persecuted as a result. The initial exhibits focused on people killed during the uprising and in escape attempts across the Berlin Wall. Hildebrandt criticized the West for having done nothing in 1953 or 1961 to help the East German people. The exhibit was his way of supporting the East German people in their struggle against the communist regime. *Der Spiegel* news magazine would later call him "the most prominent opponent of the Wall in West Berlin."[18]

In its first ten years, four million people visited the Checkpoint Charlie Museum. They were particularly drawn by the expanding collection of original objects refugees utilized to escape, such as specially constructed cars, boats, planes, submarines, and hot air balloons. Checkpoint Charlie itself was the site of numerous escapes in which East Germans were smuggled out in specially designed compartments in cars (until the East German guards got wise to this and put a stop to it) or dressed up in Soviet or American military uniforms allowing them to be simply waved through the border. There were also failed escape attempts nearby or at the checkpoint that ended in death, such as that of Peter Fechter in August 1962, as described in Chapter 3. In January 1974, twenty-three-year-old East German policeman Burkhard Niering tried to escape at Checkpoint Charlie itself. He took a *Grenzer* hostage at gunpoint hoping this would discourage the other guards from firing. As the two approached the barrier to West Berlin, however, the *Grenzer* suddenly dropped to the ground and, in that moment, two other *Grenzer* fired on Niering. He died of his wounds a short time later.[19] These real-life events, as well as the spy novels (such as John le Carré's international best seller *The Spy Who Came in from the Cold* published in 1963) and movies (such as the James Bond film *Octopussy* in 1983) they inspired, further drew people to the Checkpoint Charlie Museum. Throughout the Cold War and beyond, the museum would rank as one of the most popular tourist attractions in Berlin.

In addition to Hildebrandt's exhibits at Bernauer Strasse (which he finally closed and integrated into the bigger exhibit in 1971) and at Checkpoint Charlie, he created traveling exhibits about the Wall and gave lectures in Berlin and elsewhere with titles such as "Resistance in the Soviet-Occupied Zone – and Us" and "What can we do about the Wall? What do we have to do against the Wall?" He felt obligated to speak out as much as possible, including in regular press conferences at his museum, about the brutal Wall and East German regime and the price East German people were paying. Hildebrandt

---

[18] *Spiegel*, June 17, 2004.

[19] Hans-Hermann Hertle and Maria Nooke, eds., *The Victims at the Berlin Wall: A Biographical Handbook, 1961–1989* (Berlin: Christoph Links Verlag, 2011), pp. 102–105 and 344–46.

also began his own publishing house in the museum to provide more information about the Wall. Over roughly thirty years, his book about the history of the Wall, *It Happened at the Wall*, would sell over one million copies.[20] Hildebrandt was particularly adept at attracting attention to his own and the museum's activities.

During the détente years of the 1970s, when the FRG sought to expand ties with the GDR, West German authorities grew concerned about Hildebrandt's unrelenting efforts to highlight the inhumanity of the East German border regime. The federal government accordingly stopped subsidizing his museum. West German leaders hoped they could induce reforms in East Germany by shifting from a policy of non-recognition to one of direct engagement with the SED regime, a policy known initally as "change through rapprochement" (*Wandel durch Annäherung*). Ironically, this policy was introduced by the same senior official who had initially helped Hildebrandt secure federal funding for his museum, Egon Bahr, the right-hand man of Willy Brandt when he was mayor of West Berlin when the Wall went up and when he became the West German chancellor who initiated détente, or *Ostpolitik*, with the East.[21] When Brandt's government stopped its support for Hildebrandt's museum, the West Berlin government stepped in to provide some funds to supplement the museum's income from entrance fees and publications.[22]

West German officials were particularly critical of Hildebrandt in 1978 when he planned to exhibit an East German SM-70 automatic-firing, splinter mine device. The SM-70 had been obtained by someone rather miraculously entering the death strip between West and East Germany from the western side, deactivating the device, and bringing it out. When FRG authorities detained Hildebrandt and demanded he hand over the device, he refused. A senior American military officer intervened and ultimately Hildebrandt was allowed to display the SM-70 in his museum.[23] While his focus remained on the inhumanity of the Wall, in the 1980s he broadened the museum's exhibits to include global examples of "the non-violent struggle for human rights," including sections on Gandhi, Walesa, and Sakharov.

The fame of the Checkpoint Charlie Museum and the Cold War crossing point lasted beyond the fall of the Wall. At the request of groups in the United States, Hildebrandt together with Trotnow of the *Deutsches Historisches Museum* (DHM) sponsored a traveling exhibit in the USA about the Wall.

---

[20] Dirk Verheyen, *United City, Divided Memories? Cold War Legacies in Contemporary Berlin* (Lanham: Lexington Books, 2008).

[21] Wyden, *Wall*, p. 564.

[22] Verheyen, *United City, Divided Memories?*, pp. 234–35.

[23] Kinzer, "Berlin Journal. Germany Warms up to a 'Fossil of the Cold War'," *New York Times*, August 24, 1993; and Wyden, *Wall*, pp. 434–37. Sadly, the person who took the SM-70 from the border, Michael Gartenschläger, made one trip too many to obtain such devices and was killed by East German border soldiers in his last attempt on May 1, 1976.

The exhibit, "Breakthrough: The Fight for Freedom at the Berlin Wall," made stops in Washington, DC, Atlanta, Boston, and Los Angeles in 1991–92. Meant to show the close friendship that developed during the Cold War between the United States on the one hand, and West Germany and West Berlin on the other, Hildebrandt and Trotnow also saw the exhibit as a good chance to express gratitude to the USA for supporting the freedom of West Berlin during the Cold War, preventing the communists from taking it over.[24]

The exhibit was originally meant to last six weeks but lasted far longer due to its popularity with Americans, so many of whom felt closely connected to the story of the fall of the Wall and the triumph of freedom.[25] The exhibit included one segment of the Wall, pictures of historical developments at the Wall, and original objects used by East Germans in their successful and unsuccessful escape attempts (drawn from the collection at Hildebrandt's museum), such as a homemade submarine and a BMW retrofitted to smuggle people across the border. The curators also made a short film that combined footage from speeches by famous Americans visiting West Berlin (including presidents, Martin Luther King, and others) with footage of East German escape attempts.

Checkpoint Charlie after the Fall of the Wall

In united Berlin, little remained of the old checkpoint. The Berlin Senate sold the land on either side of the street where the checkpoint itself used to be, hoping to benefit from investors who sought property at a central location in the reunited city. Yet the contract of sale obligated the buyer "to make available free of charge an appropriate area for an open-air Wall Memorial."[26] The details were to be worked out between the investor and the city of Berlin. The small, white guard booth where American soldiers had inspected documents at Checkpoint Charlie was no longer there. It had been removed with great fanfare on June 22, 1990 as one of the steps toward the unification of Berlin and Germany. The ceremony featured the foreign ministers of the Four Allies and of East and West Germany.

The same month, Hildebrandt, like Trotnow, wrote to Prime Minister de Maizière about the importance of saving various parts of the border.[27] Similar to Fischer and Trotnow at Bernauer Strasse, Hildebrandt was also a memory

---

[24] Helmut Trotnow, "Mr. Gorbatschow, reißen Sie die Mauer ein," *Welt*, October 31, 1991.

[25] Interview with Helmut Trotnow, March 17, 2010.

[26] Dr. Thomas Flierl, ed., "Gesamtkonzept zur Erinnerung an die Berliner Mauer: Dokumentation, Information und Gedenken," June 12, 2006, p. 8.

[27] Alexandra Hildebrandt, "Die Freiheit verpflichtet. Das Freiheitsmahnmal am Platz Checkpoint Charlie," in Ingeborg Siggelkow, ed., *Gedächtnis, Kultur und Politik* (Berlin: Frank & Timme, 2006), p. 109.

activist now and sought to display some remnants of the Wall and the border zone for people to see, although unlike at Bernauer Strasse there was no Wall left at Checkpoint Charlie. Instead, Hildebrandt collected other items to display, such as a guard tower and toll bars.

Taking a leaf from DHM's plans for Bernauer Strasse, Hildebrandt wrote to the Senate's department for cultural affairs in April 1991 requesting support for an outdoor display he had begun of elements of the former border using land he had leased from the new owners while they considered what they would build on the site. He asserted that he did not plan the display as a "reconstruction," which had been so criticized at Bernauer Strasse, but as a "topography of the German-German border as a monument" that would be designed by the winner of an artistic competition.[28] While Hildebrandt declared his backing for DHM's plans to preserve the Wall, reconstruct the border, and establish a Documentation Center at Bernauer Strasse, he not so subtly maintained that his "Topography" was "particularly [i.e., more] important" due to Checkpoint Charlie's central location, unlike that of Bernauer Strasse. He requested funding for a free brochure, two tour guides, and a guard to make sure no one took any of the items on display. He had even lined up as tour guides two former East German guards who served at Checkpoint Charlie.

Hildebrandt argued, as Fischer and Trotnow did, that "world interest in the Wall is great and will remain," noting that visitors to his still developing exhibit were taking many pictures and asking questions about the history of the Wall, for example about the people killed there and about the peaceful fall of the Wall (hence the need for the tour guides and the brochure). The museum director himself led the Swedish king and queen around the exhibit in 1991. Elements of the exhibit included a guard tower, some individual segments of the Wall, two toll bars, an anti-tank obstacle, light installations, and a couple of the posts painted with black, red, and gold that had marked the approach to the border in some places. The Topography exhibit was on display from the autumn of 1991 until the start of 1994 and contained three information panels: one about the technical aspects of the border; another about the Checkpoint Charlie tank crisis; and a third telling the story of the policeman-turned-attempted-escapee, Burkhard Niering. Foreshadowing the exhibit of crosses his wife would unveil in 2004, this earlier exhibit included a wooden cross with a picture of Niering.[29] Hildebrandt published an eight-page booklet to accompany the

---

[28] Letter from Rainer Hildebrandt, Hauke Jessen, and Günter Irrgang to Mr. Schreiber, an assistant in the Senate's committee for cultural affairs, with an attached five-page proposal, "Topographie der deutsch-deutschen Grenze als Mahnmal," April 29, 1991, LAB, D Rep. 001, Nr. 4695.

[29] For a picture of the cross for Niering at the 1991 exhibit, see, Alexandra Hildebrandt, *Rainer Hildebrandt. Ein Mensch. Begegnungen* (Berlin: Verlag Haus am Checkpoint Charlie), p. 71. Alexandra Hildebrandt used the same picture of Niering in the 2004 installation.

Topography exhibit.[30] Since the "Topography of Terror" site at the former Nazi headquarters was only two blocks away, Hildebrandt pointed out that "visitors would not have far to walk to understand historical connections."[31] He presumably had in mind the connection he felt between the Nazis' crimes and post-World War II Germany, whereby the Nazis' crimes led to the defeat and occupation of Germany and ultimately to its division.

In addition to emphasizing the importance of preserving elements of the former border at Checkpoint Charlie, Hildebrandt also frequently spoke out in favor of safeguarding the Wall in places where it still stood, such as at the East Side Gallery and Niederkirchnerstrasse. He was extremely upset that the Senate was not doing more in the 1990s to preserve all remaining sections of the Wall. In 1996, he publicly complained about the poor condition of the paintings at the East Side Gallery, given the graffiti painted on top of them and weather damage. He supported those who wanted to commission the artists to repaint their original murals. The Wall at Niederkirchnerstrasse was also the victim of graffiti artists, Wall peckers, and the effects of weather. In response, the Senate erected a fence around it to prevent people from getting to the Wall and to make sure it would not fall over and injure people. Hildebrandt thought the fence was of poor quality and looked like the kind of fence that would guard a dump. He proposed replacing it with a better one that he would supply. Hildebrandt enjoined the government: "Go to work! Save the Wall!"[32]

He also spoke passionately about the victims of the Wall and the importance of commemorating them. In his view, one key way to do this was to preserve sections of the Wall: "For the victims and all East Europeans the Wall is the trophy of a successful revolution. They all want to keep the Wall. It is as if the French would say, we don't want to see the Bastille anymore." As a journalist from the *Berliner Zeitung* pointed out, "But he isn't a victim or an East European. What makes him tick?" He found the answer in discussions with Hildebrandt about his past: his participation in the anti-Hitler resistance; his time in a Gestapo prison; and the fact his friend Albrecht Haushofer was killed by the Nazis. "I carry some guilt for his death in a certain way since I couldn't save him."[33] Remembering the deaths of East Germans due to another violent German regime was perhaps a way of helping Hildebrandt cope with his survivor's guilt.

In 1996, two years after he had closed down his Topography exhibit, Hildebrandt presented a model of his next attempt to display elements of the

[30] Alexandra Hildebrandt, "Die Freiheit verpflichtet," p.109.
[31] Rainer Hildebrandt, draft plan for his "Topographie der deutsch-deutschen Grenze als Mahnmal," April 29, 1991, LAB, D Rep. 001, Nr. 4695, pp. 1–3.
[32] Sabine Deckweth, "Hildebrandt ruft zur Rettung der Mauerrest auf," *Berliner Zeitung*, August 10, 1996.
[33] Kolhoff, "Sie muss stehenbleiben, weil die Dinge Geschichte erzählen," *Berliner Zeitung*, August 12, 1996.

former border area at Checkpoint Charlie. In the meantime, a group backing an American Business Center had bought the land where the checkpoint had been, and Hildebrandt was working on a deal with the investors to display the border installations in the rotunda of the yet-to-be-constructed building. The Kiev-based artist Albert Krizapolky had designed the new "Topography" model, which would include a guard tower and parts of the electronic contact fence, a dog run, bunker, anti-tank barrier, metal-tipped sheets, and wire mesh fence as well as nearly forty feet of the interior *Hinterlandmauer*. One of the most prominent members of the former GDR opposition, Bärbel Bohley, supported Hildebrandt's plans. The Berlin department for cultural affairs, however, did not. The spokesman for the office, Rainer Klemke, observed critically that Hildebrandt's proposed guard tower in the rotunda "was never here."[34] Indeed, there had not been a guard tower at Checkpoint Charlie when the Wall stood. This did not stop Hildebrandt from continuing to display the guard tower outside, and in the summer of 1996 it was topped by the installation of a golden "Lady Liberty" statue designed by the American artist John Powers.[35]

To hold the public's attention on victims of the Wall, each year on August 13, Hildebrandt continued the practice he had begun after the erection of the Wall of holding a press conference and announcing the number of people who had been killed trying to escape in Berlin and at the inner-German border. In 1997, this number was "at least 916 people." He also used the occasion to emphasize the importance of safeguarding remnants of the Wall ("This is history to touch!") and called to reinstall the sign in English, German, French, and Russian that stood on the American side of Checkpoint Charlie for decades, announcing: "You are leaving the American sector." (The sign was reinstalled the following year.) Another new addition to his proposal for an outdoor museum showing the border strip was to use natural stones to write the word *Mauer* (Wall) in several languages.[36]

While Hildebrandt's focus was always on the victims of the Wall, he also believed, as did Manfred Fischer, that a full understanding of the history of the Wall and of the SED regime, as well as true unification, could only come through a dialogue between former victims and perpetrators. Both victims and representatives of the GDR regime needed to contribute their experiences. Thus, he brought together for discussions at his museum people who were persecuted in the GDR, such as for trying to escape, with former members of the Stasi and Stasi informants. "How was it [all] possible? How were

---

[34] Marlies Emmerich, "Erstes Modell vorgestellt: Rotunde soll an ehemalige Grenzanlagen erinnern," *Berliner Zeitung*, April 20, 1996.
[35] "Neue Zeiten für Lady Liberty," *Tagesspiegel*, September 23, 1996.
[36] Thorkit Treichel, "916 Menschen starben bei Fluchtversuchen," *Berliner Zeitung*, August 12, 1997.

individuals misused or given support? Responsibility for this is mutual."[37] Hildebrandt even hosted Günter Schabowski at his museum in 1997 just as the Politburo trial was drawing to a close.

Hildebrandt disagreed with the decision to include Schabowski in the same trial with Egon Krenz and Günther Kleiber, arguing that "this was a blow against working the past" in a productive way. Hildebrandt did not believe that Schabowski bore the same blame as his two colleagues, especially since it was Schabowski who (albeit erroneously) announced the opening of the border on November 9. The museum director was critical of the general exclusion of people who had been part of the SED regime in united Germany's efforts to come to terms with the East German past. Hildebrandt asked, "Why should people who knew how the system functioned not also be involved [in dialogues about confronting the past]?" A contributing factor to Hildebrandt's support of Schabowski may have been the fact that Hildebrandt's wife Alexandra was close friends with Schabowski's wife, and the two couples enjoyed many garden parties at the Hildebrandts' house in Berlin's Grunewald district.[38]

By the early 2000s, the Checkpoint Charlie Museum was second in popularity among Berlin tourists only to the Pergamon Museum housing the Pergamon altar from ancient Greece. Whereas the relatively new Berlin Wall Documentation Center at Bernauer Strasse had 150,000 visitors per year, the long-established Checkpoint Charlie Museum had 700,000, with particularly busy days drawing 3,500 people.[39] In an effort to re-create more of a sense of the Cold War border at Checkpoint Charlie and to capitalize on the site's popularity with tourists, Rainer and Alexandra Hildebrandt installed, in the middle of Friedrichstrasse, a replica of the former Allied guard booth on August 13, 2000. This was meant to be the beginning of implementing their design for a "Checkpoint Charlie Showplace" in the rotunda of the still-not-constructed building nearby.

In spite of the fact that neither the investors nor the Berlin Senate sup- ported them, the Hildebrandts kept developing their plans and even expanded their proposed design to include a statue of Gorbachev and a replica of the Statue of Liberty.[40] In December, however, the property owners suddenly

---

[37] Rainer Hildebrandt, "Appeal to All Who Are Considered to be 'Burdened'," June 1992, cited in Alexandra Hildebrandt, introduction and ed., *German Post-War History in Selected Articles by Rainer Hildebrandt*, p. 15. See also Verheyen, *United City, Divided Memories?*, p. 235; Kinzer, "Berlin Journal. Germany Warms up to a 'Fossil of the Cold War'," *New York Times*, August 24, 1993; and Kolhoff, "Sie muss stehenbleiben," *Berliner Zeitung*, August 12, 1996.

[38] "Beistand für den 'Mauer-Öffner'," *Berliner Zeitung*, August 20, 1997.

[39] Frank, *Die Mauer um die Wette Gedenken*, p. 214; and Sascha Lehnartz, "Das Kreuz mit der Mauer," *Frankfurter Allgemeine Zeitung*, November 8, 2004.

[40] Iris Brennberger and Andreas Kopietz, "Der Checkpoint Charlie kommt wieder, 13. August – Jahrestag des Mauerbaus," *Berliner Zeitung*, August 12, 2000; and Alexander Knoke, "Am Checkpoint Charlie darf kein Jahrmarkt entstehen," *Berliner Zeitung*, February 22, 2003.

removed the tower. When Hildebrandt asked Thomas Flierl, the Berlin senator for culture, for permission to return other border installations to the site, he received a negative response.[41]

City officials had not entirely abdicated the site to private actors, however. The Berlin Senate sponsored an art competition in the late 1990s to mark former border crossings. In 1998 this resulted in the installation of a large, illuminated, two-sided frame atop a sixteen-foot pole displaying photographs of an American soldier on one side and a Russian soldier on the other.[42] The following year the Senate added an information post on the tank standoff as part of the new "Berlin Wall History Mile."[43] In 1997, the Senate had chosen Checkpoint Charlie as the start of a project marking the path of the former Wall with a double row of cobblestones. Contrary to Hildebrandt's urgings, however, the Senate was not prepared at the time to do more to evoke the history of Checkpoint Charlie.

As Manfred Fischer was celebrating the opening of the Documentation Center with Chancellor Schröder, Bundestag President Thierse, and Mayor Wowereit on the fortieth anniversary of the erection of the Wall on August 13, 2001, Hildebrandt organized his own event at Checkpoint Charlie. He hosted the grandson of General Lucius D. Clay, father of the Berlin Airlift of 1948–49, at a commemorative ceremony that took place outside of the replica of the former Allied guard post. Hildebrandt remained incensed that there was still "not one single place in Berlin where you can see all of the components of the wall at one time – the *Hinterlandmauer*, the electric fences, the observation tower, the guard houses. It's a sin," he told a reporter from the *New York Times*.[44] Others before and after Hildebrandt would share his conviction of the importance of showing the former Berlin Wall border strip in as complete a reconstruction as possible (minus the living parts of it with the soldiers and dogs) to provide a more authentic feeling for the threat it had posed to those trying to escape across it. Yet without those living elements, and the order to shoot refugees, it would have been only a shadow of its former self. Nonetheless, it surely would have made a strong impression on people who had not personally experienced the Wall.

Hildebrandt increasingly turned over the reins of the museum to Alexandra as he grew older. After marrying Rainer in 1995, Alexandra had started out as his assistant and a member of the board of the August 13 Association. She became a member of the executive board of trustees in

---

[41] Alexandra Hildebrandt, "Die Freiheit verpflichtet," p. 113.

[42] Sybille Frank, "Competing for the Best Wall Memorial," in Konrad H. Jarausch, Christian F. Ostermann, and Andreas Etges, eds., *The Cold War: Historiography, Memory, Representation* (Berlin/Boston: Walter de Gruyter 2017), p. 271.

[43] Frank, *Die Mauer um die Wette Gedenken*, pp. 169–70.

[44] Edmund L. Andrews, "The Wall Berlin Can't Quite Demolish," *New York Times*, August 13, 2001.

1999, and finally the director of the board and the museum in December 2003. In the late 1990s and early 2000s, there were increasing accusations and even lawsuits by former employees about financial improprieties and claims that the Hildebrandts' profit motive dominated their approach and resulted in low pay and difficult working conditions for employees. Resignations by employees and members of the August 13 Association followed. In light of this, the director of the Federal Agency for Political Education (*Bundeszentrale*), Thomas Krüger, who had been contributing some funds to the museum, had his accountant go through the books. The accountant found some inconsistencies and Krüger stopped supporting the museum in 2002.[45] Two years later, Alexandra Hildebrandt dissolved the August 13 Association, created a new Rainer Hildebrandt Foundation based in Switzerland, and made herself the president. Criticism of her profit motives grew stronger.[46]

With investors in the empty land at Checkpoint Charlie going bankrupt without building anything and the Senate unwilling to buy back the land, the Hildebrandts were not the only ones seeking to benefit from the tourists who flocked to Checkpoint Charlie. More and more individual entrepreneurs set up stands on both sides of the street in the empty block along Friedrichstrasse where the old checkpoint had been, selling "authentic" pieces of the Wall as well as hats, flags, pins, shirts, and other souvenirs with East German and Soviet insignia on them. As the increasingly old and frail Rainer turned over greater responsibility for the museum to the much younger and energetic Alexandra, her complaints about the free-for-all atmosphere of temporary stands selling souvenirs, food, and drinks on the street at Checkpoint Charlie grew louder.

In the early 2000s, Alexandra remonstrated about the "kitschy" vendors "trivializing the historic site" and declared her intention to find sponsors to back a plan to convert the empty space at Friedrichstrasse into what she and her husband now called "Checkpoint Charlie Platz" with a reconstructed section of the border. She argued that this was necessary to "more appropriately" remember the division of Berlin and make "Checkpoint Charlie recognizable again" as the "sacred" site it once was.[47] To this end, Rainer secured a contract in August 2003 to lease the empty land on both sides of Friedrichstrasse from the Berliner Volksbank, the latest owner of the site. Rainer and Alexandra then secretly began designing the installation of crosses

---

[45] M. Engel and D. Konnerth, "Wir arbeiteten in Angst und Schrecken," *Berliner Zeitung*, November 21, 1998; Marijke Engel, "Hildebrandt will bleiben," *Berliner Zeitung*, January 19, 1999; and Peter Wensierski and Sandra Wiest, "Goldener Lebensabend," *Spiegel*, February 9, 2002.

[46] Frank, *Die Mauer um die Wette Gedenken*, p. 310.

[47] Brennberger and Kopietz, "Der Checkpoint Charlie kommt wieder," *Berliner Zeitung*, August 12, 2000; Knoke, "Am Checkpoint Charlie darf kein Jahrmarkt entstehen," *Berliner Zeitung*, February 22, 2003; and Jutta Schütz, "Checkpoint Charlie: Wo Weltgeschichte geschrieben wurde," *Stern*, September 9, 2003.

and Wall that Alexandra would unveil dramatically the following year.[48] At a press conference on August 12, 2003, Alexandra announced that the August 13 Association had learned that 1,008 people had been killed at the GDR border in Berlin and beyond. She called for a monument with the names and birthdates of the people killed.[49] The following month she reiterated her calls for a "Checkpoint Charlie Platz."[50]

In January 2004, Rainer died at the age of 89. In the wake of his death, the forty-five-year-old widow undertook a series of controversial actions in the summer and fall of 2004 designed to bring attention to the history and victims of divided Berlin and Germany. These would climax in the fall with Alexandra's unveiling of the crosses in what she called the "Freedom Memorial" (Freiheitsmahnmal) for victims of the Wall, but began in June when she wrapped in blue plastic the replica of the former Allied guardhouse standing outside near the museum. Hildebrandt did this to protest against the young student actors who for months had been dressing up as GDR border guards and charging tourists one euro to have their picture taken with them in front of the guardhouse. One of the young men dressing up as an East German soldier (ahistorically, since they were never stationed on this side of the checkpoint) was a stripper at night and "defended his actions at Checkpoint Charlie variously by speaking of the right of tourists to have nice pictures, historical requirements or needing money as a student."[51]

Hildebrandt found the students' behavior an "undignified spectacle" at a site of such historic significance.[52] She expressed criticism of this "commercialization" of the site[53] and declared: "I cannot tolerate that history is falsified by these students."[54] Having tourists pay an entrance fee to her museum where they could learn about the history of the Wall was one thing; having them pay for a sort of reenactment was another. Flowers left around the guardhouse in memory of Rainer–inspired by the picture of him his widow placed at a window inside– by people wanting to honor him gave Alexandra further grounds to denounce the actions of the uniformed student actors as "tasteless."[55]

---

[48] Alexandra Hildebrandt, "Memorial Place Checkpoint Charlie – Save the Historic Ground at Checkpoint Charlie!", part of the materials given out at the 143rd press conference of the August 13 Working Group, Inc., June 28, 2005.

[49] Matthias Lohre, "Mehr Mauertote als bisher bekannt," Spiegel Online, August 12, 2003; and Anke Springer, "Mehr als 1000 Tote an der Grenze," Berliner Zeitung, August 13, 2003.

[50] Schütz, "Checkpoint Charlie: Wo Weltgeschichte geschrieben wurde," Stern, September 19, 2003.

[51] Veronika Nickel, "Neue Folge in der Checkpoint-Charlie-Posse," taz, June 15, 2004.

[52] Ulrich Paul, "Kalter Krieg am Checkpoint Charlie," Berliner Zeitung, June 4, 2004.

[53] Karin Schmidl, "Touristen können wieder Fotos machen," Berliner Zeitung, June 16, 2004.

[54] Uwe Rada, "Wem gehört Checkpoint Charlie?" taz, June 5, 2004.

[55] Ulrich Paul, "Kalter Krieg am Checkpoint Charlie," Berliner Zeitung, June 4, 2004.

After eleven days, the district authorities ordered Hildebrandt to remove the plastic and forbade the students from charging the tourists for pictures.[56] Unlike her response in two other controversies to come, Hildebrandt complied and removed the blue plastic as required on June 15. The widespread public discussions about the goings-on at Checkpoint Charlie in June led to the first calls for a district or citywide plan "to regulate what is allowed at Checkpoint Charlie"[57] and further fueled earlier proposals "to integrate the Wall Museum there into a master plan for all similar memorials."[58] However, it would take the firestorm of debate surrounding the crosses four months later to get Berlin officials to actually begin to formulate such a plan, by which point they would have weathered yet another highly publicized conflict with Alexandra Hildebrandt.

No sooner did she remove the plastic sheeting around the guardhouse than Hildebrandt was called upon to remove from the facade of the federal finance ministry the massive pictures of the June 17, 1953 East German popular uprising she had installed there. The Hildebrandts had received permission to install the photographs there for two weeks in June 2003. Rainer had aimed to draw attention to the courage and sacrifices of the East German protestors of June 1953 and had gotten permission back in 1994–95 to hang the pictures. In East German times, the current finance ministry building had been the government's headquarters, and it was there that thousands of workers had gathered on June 16, 1953 demanding reforms and calling for a strike the next day if their demands were not met. When the two-week period the Hildebrandts had been allotted to hang the pictures for the fiftieth anniversary of the uprising expired in June 2003, they refused to remove them. The photographs were still hanging there in the summer of 2004.

Alexandra argued that the history of the uprising should be remembered beyond anniversaries and that the artistic memorial that had been dedicated in 2000 to the uprising was insufficient. The memorial was hard to see, since it was located flat on the ground in front of the building and looked, as she said, like "a bathtub" or a "fish pond."[59] The case went to court, which ruled against Hildebrandt in September 2004, instructing her to remove the

---

[56] Karin Schmidl, "Mit dem 'Mummenschanz' ist Schluss am Checkpoint Charlie," *Berliner Zeitung*, June 12, 2004; and Schmidl, "Touristen können wieder Fotos machen," *Berliner Zeitung*, June 16, 2004.

[57] Quote from Franz Schulz, the city construction counselor for the district of Friedrichshain-Kreuzberg, cited in Karin Schmidl, "Unruhe am Checkpoint Charlie," *Berliner Zeitung*, June 5, 2004.

[58] Schmidl, "Touristen können wieder Fotos machen," *Berliner Zeitung*, June 16, 2004, citing an official from the Berlin Senate's Office of Cultural Affairs.

[59] Michael Sontheimer, "Gerangel um Fotofateln an Eichels Wand," *Spiegel Online*, June 17, 2004; and Thomas Rogalla, "Zu viel Erinnerung an den Aufstand des 17. Juni," *Berliner Zeitung*, June 17, 2004. For more on the memorial to the June 1953 Uprising, see Saunders, *Memorializing the GDR*, pp. 165–72.

pictures. She appealed, but then rescinded her appeal in February 2005 and had the pictures removed four months later after the anniversary of the uprising in June 2005. Although she lost in the short run, in the long run her pressure helped persuade the Berlin authorities to name the area in front of the finance ministry "1953 Popular Uprising Square" in 2013. Developments with Hildebrandt's crosses at Checkpoint Charlie would follow a somewhat similar path.

The Fifteenth Anniversary of the Fall of the Wall

For much of the same 2004–5 period that Hildebrandt was fighting her battle to keep the photos of the 1953 uprising hanging on the facade of the finance ministry building, she was simultaneously waging an even bigger and more controversial battle over remembering the Berlin Wall at Checkpoint Charlie.[60] In August 2004, at her press conference for the anniversary of the erection of the Wall, she announced that the August 13 Association had identified 1,065 deaths at the GDR border, fifty-seven more cases than the previous year. She declined to reveal all the sources for the research, saying that doing so "could endanger future research."[61] She was also quite secretive about her plans for the fifteenth anniversary of the fall of the Wall in November.

Over the next couple of months, information and rumors circulated. In late September, there were reports that Hildebrandt would erect a block or two of Wall featuring 120 Wall segments at Checkpoint Charlie and that she would have artists paint on them and then display them in countries that were still divided.[62] In early October, she confirmed that she planned to invite artists from North and South Korea, Cyprus, Israel, and Palestine to paint the pieces of the Wall, a decision she reversed in November. She promised she would remove the Wall by January 1, 2005 and donate some of the Wall pieces to those divided countries.[63]

As details trickled out about her plans and the press asked her more questions, Hildebrandt declared that her aim was "to stop the contamination of this place, to banish the ugly stalls [selling souvenirs, food, and drinks], and restore the dignity of this historic place."[64] She told reporters that she wanted to show "that something is not right here" and castigated politicians for watching passively for fifteen years as Checkpoint Charlie became "a garbage

---

[60] For an in-depth and supportive analysis of Hildebrandt's "Freedom Monument" and the response to it, see Frank, *Der Mauer um die Wette Gedenken.*

[61] "Mehr Tote an der DDR-Mauer als bisher bekannt," *Berliner Zeitung*, August 13, 2004.

[62] Thomas Fülling and Rainer L. Hein, "Die Mauer kommt wieder," *Welt*, September 29, 2004.

[63] Uwe Aulich, "Mauerkunst und Disneyland," *Berliner Zeitung*, October 5, 2004.

[64] "Museums-Chefin Alexandra Hildebrandt: Darum baue ich die Mauer wieder auf!" *B.Z.*, October 9, 2004.

dump like in Cairo."[65] The first reports that wooden crosses for victims of the Wall were part of her plans surfaced in mid-October,[66] and by October 20 journalists were writing that she would open her outdoor "art installation" of crosses and the Wall on Sunday October 31.[67]

On October 25, the tall, wooden crosses were visible and Hildebrandt told the *Berliner Morgenpost* that she was creating a "site of commemoration" to "remember victims of the German division and the Wall," as she asserted had long been necessary.[68] Indeed at her press conference the year before on August 13, 2003, she had called for "a memorial with all names and birthdates of the people killed at the border."[69] At the time, her husband had been designing the *Freiheitsmahnmal* and had already signed the lease with the Volksbank for the land outside at Checkpoint Charlie where it would stand.[70] Now in the fall of 2004, each cross had the name, age, and a photograph (where possible) of someone killed at the Wall, similar to the cross for Burkhard Niering included in Rainer's Topography exhibit of 1991–94. Alexandra said she would try to buy the land from the Volksbank so that the crosses and Wall could remain at Checkpoint Charlie beyond the end of her lease on December 31.[71]

When a *Morgenpost* journalist observed that the many crosses standing so closely together were reminiscent of the stelae of the Holocaust Memorial being built a few blocks away, Hildebrandt responded: "That is also [my] intention. One memorial is for the victims of the first and ours is for the victims of the second German dictatorship."[72] She declared that her memorial would "bring a counterpart to the Holocaust memorial."[73] These comments elicited much criticism from politicians, members of the Jewish community, journalists, and others. Although Hildebrandt later backpedaled,[74] many never forgave her for what they felt was a slight to the victims of the Holocaust. It was also the case that her memorial for the victims was comprised entirely of

---

[65] Andrea Puppe and Stefan Schulz, "Die Mauer muss weg," *Berliner Morgenpost*, October 11, 2004; and Rogalla and Miller, "Das Geschäft mit der Mauer: Senatoren kritisieren Kunstaktion," *Berliner Zeitung*, October 11, 2004.

[66] Rogalla and Miller, ibid.

[67] "Eingemauert," *Berliner Zeitung*, October 20, 2004.

[68] Stefan Schulz, "1065 Holzkreuze für die Opfer der Teilung und des Mauerbaus," *Berliner Morgenpost*, October 26, 2004.

[69] Anke Springer, "Mehr als 1,000 Tote an der Grenze," *Berliner Zeitung*, August 13, 2003.

[70] See the text inscribed on a plaque as part of the installation of crosses in October 2004, Alexandra Hildebrandt, "Memorial Place Checkpoint Charlie – Save the Historic Ground at Checkpoint Charlie!"

[71] Stefan Schulz, "1,065 Holzkreuze für die Opfer der Teilung und des Mauerbaus," *Berliner Morgenpost*, October 26, 2004.

[72] Ibid.

[73] Jana Sittnick, "Die Frau meint es ernst," *taz*, October 30, 2004.

[74] Jochim Stoltenberg, interview with Alexandra Hildebrandt, "Ein Leben wider das Vergessen," *Berliner Morgenpost*, November 7, 2004.

crosses, which might not have been the best way to commemorate any of the (albeit minority of) non-Christian victims of the Wall, such as the Turkish children Cengaver Katranci and Cetin Mert.[75]

Most discussions in Berlin about historical memory and victims had been focused on the Holocaust and particularly on the plans to build the Holocaust Memorial.[76] Writing in Berlin's *Tagesspiegel* about Hildebrandt's crosses for victims of the Berlin Wall in the context of German memory culture, Bernhard Schulz noted that since unification, Holocaust memory dominated all others, so that "the memory of catastrophes" before the Holocaust, such as World War I, and after, such as the Berlin Wall, were forgotten.[77] He maintained that "remembering the Berlin Wall with its 1,065 deaths is a necessary, constituent part of German collective memory" and should replace the "collective amnesia" about the victims. Debates about the relative weight to accord communist and Nazi victims in German memory policy would continue and become particularly emotional in the years to come, as will be discussed in Chapter 6. Just as it took decades in West Germany to develop a consensus over how to deal with the Nazi past, so Schulz observed that there was no consensus, as of 2004, on how to remember the injustice of the GDR system. In particular, he argued that Germans must "find a form which can reflect the monstrosity of the 28-year SED border regime: politically, aesthetically and – emotionally." Hildebrandt's crosses and the Berlin Wall Memorial at Bernauer Strasse were two quite different approaches. Schulz found the former much more likely to inspire widespread consideration of the place of victims of the SED regime in the context of broader German history.

While Hildebrandt and Fischer were focused on commemorating the Wall and its victims, the early 2000s saw many Germans absorbed in remembering their experience as victims of the Allied bombings in World War II and as expellees when they were forced out of lands to the east. W. G. Sebald's (1999) *A Natural History of Destruction* (*Luftkrieg und Literatur*) and particularly Jörg Friedrich's 2002 book *The Fire: Germany in the Bombing War, 1940–1945* (*Der Brand: Deutschland im Bombenkrieg, 1940–1945*) garnered much attention for their descriptions of the bombings. Friedrich's book went into great detail on the mass deaths of Germans by fire and suffocation as a result of the bombings. His work was serialized in the German tabloid *Bild* and became

---

[75] Pertti Ahonen, *Death at the Berlin Wall* (New York: Oxford University Press, 2011), pp. 196–201; and Hertle and Nooke, eds., *The Victims at the Berlin Wall*, pp. 325 and 358.

[76] Bill Niven, "The Holocaust Memorial," in *Facing the Nazi Past: United Germany and the Legacy of the Third Reich* (New York: Routledge, 2002), pp. 194–232; and Gerd Knischewski and Ulla Spittler, "Remembering in the Berlin Republic: The Debate about the Central *Holocaust* Memorial in Berlin," *Debatte* 13, no. 1 (April 2005), pp. 25–42.

[77] Bernhard Schulz, "Das Kreuz mit der Erinnerung: Kitsch oder historische Notwendigkeit? Zum Versuch, am Berliner Checkpoint Charlie der Maueropfer zu gedenken," *Tagesspiegel*, November 9, 2004.

a best seller. It inspired television documentaries and newspaper series.[78] Widespread discussions of the World War II Allied bombings also fed into arguments against the US invasion of Iraq in 2003, with German television and other commentators expressing sympathy for Iraqis, since, "we know what it is like to be bombed."[79] Similarly, Bernd Eichinger's film *Downfall* (*Der Untergang*), depicted Hitler's last ten days in his bunker in Berlin as the city was being bombed. Many of the scenes showed the terrifying experience of people in the streets during the bombing, and the Führer as completely uninterested in their suffering. The film attracted 480,000 viewers for its opening weekend in September 2004, one month before Hildebrandt unveiled her crosses. Millions went on to see the film.[80]

In addition to widespread engagement in recalling the bombings of World War II, German society in the early 2000s was also reliving the experience of the approximately thirteen million Germans who were expelled from the east in the wake of Germany's loss in the war, the so-called expellees (*Vertriebene*). Nobel Prize winning author Günter Grass's 2002 novel *Crabwalk* (*Im Krebsgang*) told the story of the sinking of the *Wilhelm Gustloff* in January 1945 after it left port in Danzig. The ship was overflowing with more than 9,000 mostly German refugees fleeing the advancing Red Army and was sunk by a Russian torpedo. The book quickly became a best seller and led to a series of articles on the experiences of the expellees in the news magazine *Der Spiegel* and a five-part documentary on public television.[81] In 2000, the German Union of Expellees (*Bund der Vertriebenen*) established a foundation to enlist backing for the creation of a Center against Expulsions (*Zentrum gegen Vertreibungen*), in Berlin. Over the next few years, the proposal gained support in the Bundestag even as controversy swirled around its focus on Germans as victims of World War II, especially in the face of objections raised by the Czechs and Poles.[82]

---

[78] Robert G. Moeller, "Germans as Victims?" *History and Memory* 17, nos. 1–2 (Fall 2005), pp. 147–94.

[79] German evening news, "Tagesschau," ZDF, March 21, 2003; and Andreas Huyssen, "Air War Legacies: From Dresden to Baghdad," in Bill Niven, ed., *Germans as Victims* (New York: Palgrave Macmillan, 2006), pp. 181–93.

[80] "German Film on Hitler's Demise a Box Office Hit," *Irish Times*, September 20, 2004; and Bill Niven, "Introduction: German Victimhood at the Turn of the Millennium," in Niven, ed., *Germans as Victims*, p. 16.

[81] Moeller, "Germans as Victims?", p. 149. In 2002, the author Christoph Hein also published a novel about expellees, in this case portraying the difficult reception they received in East Germany, *Landnahme* (*Settlement*). On discussions about the expellees being inspired in the 1990s by refugees from the wars in Yugoslavia, see Karoline von Oppen and Stefan Wolff, "From the Margins to the Centre? The Discourse on Expellees and Victimhood in Germany," in Niven, ed., *Germans as Victims*, pp. 194–209.

[82] Wolfgang Benz, "Zur Debatte: Flucht, Vertreibung, Versöhnung," *Bundeszentrale für politische Bildung*, online dossier, November 12, 2008; and the online compilation of articles and speeches between 2002 and 2006 about creating the Center against Expulsions, *Zeitgeschichte Online* (January 2006).

Against this backdrop of Germans focusing on their own suffering during and as a result of World War II, Hildebrandt's *Freiheitsmahnmal* was unveiled on October 31. She effectively added another group of German victims to those who had been the subject of so much media attention and public memory, something the developments at Bernauer Strasse with the Berlin Wall Memorial had not quite achieved on such a public scale. In addition to the crosses and pieces of the Wall, Hildebrandt's memorial featured plaques in German, English, French, and Russian about the need to commemorate those who had been killed at the East German border. One plaque noted: "In 1990, the senate of Berlin sold this **most important plot in the free world** to private investors. The investors were told to erect a monument in a central place, which was supposed to keep the spirit and historical importance of this location alive."[83] (Emphasis in original.) This, however, had not yet occurred, since no investor stayed at the site long enough to actually build anything. Yet Hildebrandt's plaque put the onus on the government: "Until today, the people in charge have done nothing to meet this demand. We, the citizens, do not want to accept this reality 15 years after the fall of the Wall." Hildebrandt thus claimed to speak for "the citizens." The plaque further announced that "the citizens' action committee 'August 13 Working Group, Inc.' works 80 meters away from Checkpoint Charlie" at the Wall Museum and was the sponsor of the memorial. This no doubt helped lure visitors to the museum after viewing the memorial.

Five hundred people were in attendance for the opening of the memorial. Joining Hildebrandt to speak at the ceremony were Sergei Khrushchev, the son of the Soviet leader who finally had backed the building of the Wall in 1961, and Ursula Jünemann, the mother of Burkhard Niering.[84] Jünemann told the crowd: "I stand here as a representative for all mothers and fathers whose children perished at the Wall."[85] She remembered how she felt in 1974: "I cried so much then, was so outraged at the state. This memorial is important. Also for my son."[86] Not all the relatives of victims were happy with Hildebrandt's crosses. Karin Gueffroy, for example, whose son Chris had been killed trying to escape across the Wall felt that the memorial was Hildebrandt's latest method for obtaining publicity for her museum. Hildebrandt was using the fate and memory of victims for her own purposes, and Gueffroy went out of her way to avoid the installation at Checkpoint Charlie. Gueffroy and other family members

---

[83] See the text inscribed on a plaque as part of the installation of crosses in October 2004, Alexandra Hildebrandt, "Memorial Place Checkpoint Charlie – Save the historic ground at Checkpoint Charlie!"

[84] Anna Reimann, "Mauer-Mahnmal im Touristenrummel," *Spiegel Online*, October 31, 2004.

[85] Ibid.

[86] "Wieder Tränen an der Mauer," *B.Z.*, October 31, 2004.

were also critical that Hildebrandt had not asked permission from the survivors of the victims to include them in her memorial.[87]

Yet many survivors and members of victims' associations from the former GDR were grateful to Hildebrandt. Tourists and journalists from Germany and all over the world came in droves to see the memorial to victims of the Wall.[88] The *Tagesspiegel* commented that Hildebrandt "had more feel for the historic gravity of this place than the entire Senate."[89] The *taz* newspaper observed that Hildebrandt "has filled a void with her 'art action'," a void left by public officials.[90] Many found it a very powerful and moving site, more so than the Kohlhoff & Kohlhoff memorial at Bernauer Strasse, which illustrated in the view of one journalist, the "bloodless, spasmodic and cerebral official approach to commemoration."[91] Even Hans Ottomeyer, the new director of the DHM, which had overseen the Bernauer Strasse memorial design competition before his arrival, jumped into the discussion, calling the Kohlhoff & Kohlhoff memorial "sterile."[92] Hildebrandt maintained that her husband had been critical of the memorial at Bernauer Strasse, which he felt was "just art and not at all clear what it means," a sentiment shared by many others since it opened in 1998.[93]

Nonetheless, Alexandra observed years later that it was "important to have various initiatives all grappling with past. The more initiatives, the narrower the chance of forgetting. The memorial at Checkpoint Charlie got people interested, wanting to know more. Then they could read more. And they could learn about the key role of the GDR regime in building the Wall." Believing that people "can only really figure things out reading at home quietly," the museum director expressed the wish that "people will read more about Wall...and develop an instinct for history. The lack of it is dangerous."[94]

In spite of these noble thoughts, several aspects of the *Freiheitsmahnmal* and Hildebrandt's statements about it were controversial, including her comparison of it to the Holocaust Memorial. No part of her memorial was based on

---

[87] Ibid.; and interview with Maria Nooke, July 5, 2005.

[88] Thomas Loy, "Botschaft mit Kreuzen. Wie gedenkt man der Mauer – lieber authentisch oder mit Gemüt?" *Tagesspiegel*, November 2, 2004; Jan Feddersen, "Irritierend unkompliziert. Das Mauermuseum ist Berlins grösste Touristenattraktion. Das rot-rote Establishment reagiert auf den Erfolg verstört," *taz*, November 2, 2004; Guntram Doelfs, "Checkpoint: Besucher wollen dauerhafte Kunstaktion," *Berliner Morgenpost*, November 8, 2004.

[89] Werner van Bebber, "Zwischen Ramsch und Russenmützen," *Tagesspiegel*, November 2, 2004.

[90] Philipp Gessler, "Gegen das glatte Gedenken," *taz*, November 6, 2004.

[91] For a thoughtful article comparing Hildebrandt's commemoration of the Wall at Checkpoint Charlie positively in relation to the memorial at Bernauer Strasse, see ibid.

[92] Michael Sontheimer, "Zweiter Tod," *Spiegel*, July 4, 2005.

[93] Interview with Alexandra Hildebrandt, November 10, 2004.

[94] Interview with Alexandra Hildebrandt, July 24, 2014.

historically grounded research. Hildebrandt would not answer questions about how she formulated the number of victims of the Wall; and she had no board of advisers of historians and scholars who had done research on victims of the Wall. In addition, the pieces of the Wall she resurrected were not situated in their original location nor were they painted the correct color. For all of these reasons, most historians and experts, including Maria Nooke and Gabriele Camphausen at Bernauer Strasse, were disparaging of Hildebrandt's "Wall monument." They urged that professional research be devoted to ascertaining the real number of people killed at the Wall and their personal backgrounds and also called for a broader plan for dealing with the memory of the Berlin Wall.[95] Nooke labelled Hildebrandt's installation "Disneyland" and found it "unsuitable for portraying the problematic nature of the Wall."[96] Camphausen observed that the elements at Checkpoint Charlie looked like "stage props."[97]

What many viewed as Hildebrandt's unilateral, self-righteous style also played a role in the widespread professional and official critique of her latest initiative. Anna Kaminsky, the managing director of the Federal Foundation for Reappraising the SED Dictatorship, called Hildebrandt's crosses "guerrilla memorials."[98] Berlin's weekly magazine *tip* put Hildebrandt at the top of their list of the 100 "most embarrassing Berliners," declaring that she was "Berlin's greatest affliction." With a "mixture of a fanatical sense of mission and cold greed," *tip* observed, Hildebrandt covers the city with her "memorial weapons" of Walls, crosses, and devotional objects of refugees. She is the "historical revisionist heiress of Checkpoint Charlie."[99]

Experts on the history of the Wall and on historical preservation pointed out that in fact no one had died at Checkpoint Charlie (which was, however, also true of the Holocaust Memorial) unlike, for example, at Bernauer Strasse. Camphausen observed that "Checkpoint Charlie is primarily connected with the history of the Allies and is not...associated as a site of victims of the Wall."[100] Hildebrandt countered that "it would be erroneous to claim that a monument can only be erected on the original site of the event. The decisive thing is that it is accessible and understandable to many people. Checkpoint Charlie is known around the world. . . .Millions of people come to Checkpoint Charlie where world history is manifested. A monument to freedom must exist

---

[95] "Das Geschäft mit der Mauer: Senatoren kritisieren Kunstaktion," *Berliner Zeitung*, October 11, 2004.

[96] Puppe and Schulz, "Die Mauer muss weg," *Berliner Morgenpost*, October 11, 2004.

[97] Aulich, "Mauerkunst und Disneyland," *Berliner Zeitung*, October 5, 2004.

[98] Anna Kaminsky, "Remembering the Wall," in Kaminsky, ed., *Where in the World Is the Berlin Wall?*, p. 33.

[99] Elmar Schütze, "Und am peinlichsten ist," *Berliner Zeitung*, December 29, 2004.

[100] Volkery, "Mehr Disneyland wagen," *Spiegel*, October 29, 2004.

Figure 16 Alexandra Hildebrandt (right) with Winston Churchill's granddaughter Edwina Sandys and her husband Richard Kaplan, November 2004
Source: Photographer: Yves Sucksdorff. Mauer Museum, Haus am Checkpoint Charlie.

here."[101] Thus, in her view, "the government must understand that monuments are for the people and must be understood by them. They must be centrally located, obvious and easy to get to even spontaneously."[102]

Using the accessibility of a memorial site's location as a measure of its success is rather an unusual argument. The accessibility of a memorial's message, however, has more logic. People certainly need to be able to understand a memorial in order to learn something from it. Fischer's observation of the many visitors to Bernauer Strasse who regarded the Kohlhoff & Kohlhoff memorial with confusion and then came across the street to the Documentation Center to get answers spoke to this issue. Yet Hildebrandt went too far in insisting that popular acceptance of a monument "should be the decisive criterion for policy."[103] An accurate view of history is not always a popular thing.

With her memorial crosses (Figure 16), Hildebrandt declared that she wanted "to provide a place where relatives of victims of the Wall could come to leave flowers." Ignoring Bernauer Strasse, she pointed out: "For many the monument [at Checkpoint Charlie] is the only place where they can commemorate those

---

[101] Alexandra Hildebrandt, "Die Freiheit verpflichtet," p. 115.
[102] Interview with Alexandra Hildebrandt, November 10, 2004.
[103] Alexandra Hildebrandt, "Die Freiheit verpflichtet," p. 117.

they have lost."[104] In addition, she felt a strong obligation to honor her deceased husband.[105] Thinking of him, she pointed to the continuity of the memorial with what Rainer had done while the Wall stood, "registering victims of the Wall and erecting wooden crosses along the Wall to bring it all to the public's attention."[106] It was he, after all, who had taught her so much about the history of the Wall. Regarding her own motivations, Hildebrandt would later observe that "after seeing the Wall, the exhibit in the [Checkpoint Charlie Museum], hearing the personal stories, reading Rainer's private archives, all of that – it gets to you. You can't believe what really happened. You can't be indifferent once you learn all of that."[107]

The passionate memory activist and PR expert in Alexandra Hildebrandt believed that the killing of people at the Berlin Wall was a very emotional matter and that this should be made clear. Indeed, her crosses had a strong emotional impact on people, including families of victims, others who had suffered in the GDR and many in the general public. Instead of aiming for an obvious emotional effect, many German politicians, historians, and memorial experts, including at Bernauer Strasse, had long favored a more restrained approach to memorials.[108] In response to Hildebrandt's crosses, a number of critics implied that the only appropriate way to remember people killed at the Wall was in a quiet way and not at a place full of tourists on most days. As the heritage historian Sybille Frank has described, many historical experts "seemed to think that memorial sites and tourist sites must be two very different things."[109] Hildebrandt clearly thought differently. She also believed that, "Politicians should not be afraid of having monuments laden with feeling, since precisely because they make people feel affected and even provoke tears, they create an easing of tension" and "can effect a certain closure on working through grief."[110]

While experts debated the relative importance of authenticity, emotion, location, and sponsorship of memorials in general and specifically in the case of her *Freiheitsmahnmal*, Hildebrandt, together with Sergei Khrushchev and others sent a public letter to Mayor Wowereit on November 4, declaring that the Senate had thus far not appropriately commemorated those who died at the border and calling for the *Freiheitsmahnmal* to be permitted to remain longer at Checkpoint Charlie with an extension of her lease to the land there.[111] Public

[104] Ibid., pp. 115–16.
[105] Interview with Alexandra Hildebrandt, July 24, 2014.
[106] Alexandra Hildebrandt, "Die Freiheit verpflichtet," p. 115.
[107] Interview with Alexandra Hildebrandt, July 24, 2014.
[108] Hope M. Harrison, "Mit Gefühl," *Tagesspiegel*, November 9, 2014.
[109] Frank, *Die Mauer um die Wette Gedenken*, p. 254.
[110] Alexandra Hildebrandt, "Die Freiheit verpflichtet," pp. 118–20.
[111] Dpa, "Neue Initiative unterstützt Kreuz-Denkmal," *Berliner Zeitung*, November 4, 2004; and Klaus Joachim Herrmann, "Offener Brief in Russisch für die Kreuze," *Neues Deutschland*, November 4, 2004.

discussion was dominated by the ongoing popular success of the crosses. This exerted pressure on the government to respond, since the majority of visitors to the monument felt that Hildebrandt's initiative had filled a void even with the existence of the Kohlhoff & Kohlhoff memorial at Bernauer Strasse. Harald Strunz of the Union of Victims' Associations of Communist Tyranny (UOKG), told the Berlin Senate:

> Rarely since 1989 has a political chess move been so unanimously welcomed by different parts of the population as in the case of Alexandra Hildebrand; the dead have finally received a place where they can be named and mourned as a group of victims. Removing [the memorial]... would be a gross offense against the thoughts and feelings of the largest group of opponents of communist terror. After a more careful verification of the biographical data, the Wall crosses should be integrated into discussions regarding a master plan for commemorating the Berlin Wall....[And t]he current official Bernauer Strasse Memorial, the masterwork of star architects [Kohlhoff & Kohlhoff], must disappear.[112]

Spurred on by Hildebrandt's attention to the Wall, journalists also published articles with titles such as "Man, where exactly was the Wall anyway?"[113] There was widespread public agreement now, fifteen years after the fall of the Wall, that the history of the Wall was harder and harder to sense in the city and that this needed to change, something Fischer and his colleagues had long been arguing. Fischer's efforts were now given a big boost by the debates stirred up by the crosses at Checkpoint Charlie. The pastor himself did not approve of Hildebrandt's approach, but he would come to recognize the important role she played in drawing attention to the history and victims of the Berlin Wall.[114]

The journalist Sven Felix Kellerhoff fittingly summed up the debate over Hildebrandt and her crosses:

> Some say she's a PR expert, but she doesn't actually plan in advance what the effect of many of her statements may be. Her interests include the victims of the Wall, the success of her museum and the memory of her husband – and all three are indivisible for her. She is right when she says, "For fifteen years no one has listened to our calls for an appropriate design for the world historical site at Checkpoint Charlie. Now we have made a mark." Whether the crosses remain or not, she will continue to scandalize, provoke and therefore make it so the victims of the Wall will not be completely forgotten.[115]

---

[112] Harald Strunz, Union der Opferverbände Kommunistischer Gewaltherrschaft e.V. (UOKG), comments for Cultural Senator Thomas Flierl's April 18, 2005 hearing on a plan for commemorating the Berlin Wall, "Überlegungen zum Gedenkkonzept der Berliner Mauer," p. 2.

[113] Thomas Rogalla, "Mensch, wo stand denn die Mauer?" *Berliner Zeitung*, November 5, 2004.

[114] Interview with Manfred Fischer, October 6, 2009.

[115] Sven Felix Kellerhoff, "1,065 Holzkreuze, 2,700 Betonstelen," *Welt*, November 2, 2004.

The crosses would in fact remain not just through December, as prescribed in the lease agreement Hildebrandt signed, but until the summer of the following year, continuing to attract many visitors and much media attention.

In the meantime, a new bank conglomerate, BAG, acquired the property at Checkpoint Charlie and lost patience with Hildebrandt occupying the land long after her lease had concluded. BAG appealed to the police to remove the crosses and pieces of Wall. Initially, the Berlin authorities set July 4, 2005 as the date to do this. Given that Hildebrandt had been appealing for help to US President George W. Bush, other prominent Republicans, and members of the military, some of whom urged the Berlin government to preserve the memorial, setting the demolition date for American Independence Day put the Berlin government in a rather embarrassing position. The U.S. "Republicans in Germany" had even created a "Freedom Memorial Project" to work with Hildebrandt's museum to raise funds so she could buy the land. The authorities postponed the demolition by twenty-four hours.[116]

When the police dismantled and carried away the crosses and Wall in the early morning hours of July 5, 2005, Hildebrandt declared this to be a "second death" for the victims of the Wall.[117] She watched the police remove the memorial "in the pouring rain as if the heavens were crying," as she lamented.[118] Yet she refused offers from Superintendent Passauer of the Protestant Church in Berlin and Brandenburg to move the crosses to the Sophien cemetery at Bernauer Strasse.[119] Her desire to commemorate the victims had its limits: the Checkpoint Charlie location near her museum was essential to her. Similarly, when asked whether she would display one of the cross inside her museum, Hildebrandt answered: "It is not the time yet. The time will come."[120]

Although Hildebrandt's memorial was removed, its impact was long-lasting. Within weeks of Hildebrandt's unveiling of the crosses in the fall of 2004, the Berlin Senate began an extensive process to formulate a citywide approach for remembering the Berlin Wall and its victims, the subject of the next chapter.

---

[116] Tom Goeller, "Berlin Wall Memorial to Be Razed," *Washington Times*, June 27, 2005. This article and other relevant documents were distributed by Hildebrandt at the 143rd press conference of the August 13 Working Group Inc., June 28, 2005.

[117] Michael Sontheimer, "Zweiter Tod," *Spiegel*, July 4, 2005.

[118] Alexandra Hildebrandt, "Die Freiheit verpflichtet," p. 117.

[119] Interviews with Maria Nooke, July 5, 2005 and Rainer Eppelman, April 20, 2010; and comments by Manfred Wilke, Deutscher Bundestag, Ausschuss für Kultur und Medien, Protokoll 15/60, June 15, 2005, p. 22.

[120] Interview with Alexandra Hildebrandt, July 24, 2014. Hildebrandt did display 50 of the crosses again on August 13, 2011, in the middle of the street in front of her museum for the fiftieth anniversary of the construction of the Wall. "Das ist sehr berührend," *Tagesspiegel*, August 14, 2011.

5

The Berlin Senate's "Master Plan for Remembering the Berlin Wall"

Alexandra Hildebrandt had thrown down the gauntlet to the German government and public to do more to remember victims of the Berlin Wall. In Germany, as in many countries, only high-level official support ensures the widespread attention to and funding for commemorative initiatives. Manfred Fischer and his colleagues at Bernauer Strasse, as well as some members of the Bundestag such as Rainer Eppelmann, had succeeded at certain moments in directing attention to the Wall and its victims, but in many ways they were still fighting to be heard. Hildebrandt's "Freedom Memorial" at Checkpoint Charlie helped shift some of German memory policy, *Erinnerungspolitik*, toward the Wall.

After decades of developing a deep sense of historical responsibility for the Holocaust, few German politicians wanted to be seen as ignoring the needs of victims, including, in the wake of Hildebrandt's crosses, victims of the Berlin Wall. Intensive public debates unleashed by the crosses at Checkpoint Charlie served as the impetus for a major official commitment to the historical commemoration of the Berlin Wall. This commitment would be codified by the Berlin Senate in 2006 with a *Gesamtkonzept zur Erinnerung an die Berliner Mauer* ("Master Plan for Remembering the Berlin Wall," hereafter *Gesamtkonzept*), the subject of this chapter. Two years later the federal government would back this with a broad plan for the federal funding of memorials, the subject of the next chapter.[1] Once officials embraced the call to address the history of the Wall, they would ultimately go about implementing it in the same thorough way German officials had employed in coming to terms with the Nazi past, albeit not without experiencing continued conflicts about how to do so.

---

[1] Dr. Thomas Flierl, ed., "Gesamtkonzept zur Erinnerung an die Berliner Mauer: Dokumentation, Information und Gedenken," June 12, 2006 (hereafter referred to as *Gesamtkonzept*); and Unterrichtung durch den Beauftragten der Bundesregierung für Kultur und Medien, "Fortschreibung der Gedenkstättenkonzeption des Bundes. Verantwortung wahrnehmen, Aufarbeitung verstärken, Gedenken vertiefen," Deutscher Bundestag, Drucksache 16/9875, June 19, 2008.

The Origins of Berlin's *Gesamtkonzept*

Since the 1990s politicians and others had been calling for a coherent, comprehensive approach to the various sites connected to the Berlin Wall. In 1992, the parliamentary group of *Bündnis 90/ Die Grüne* (Alliance 90/the Greens) in Berlin's House of Representatives had put forward a motion for "a *Gesamtkonzeption* on dealing with the Wall, including halting any removal of the Wall" and prohibiting construction in the former border zone. They proposed the creation of a commission to formulate a *Gesamtkonzeption* for the consideration of multiple issues: (1) what to do with Wall remains at Bernauer Strasse, the Invaliden cemetery, Niederkirchner Strasse, the East Side Gallery, and elsewhere; (2) how to mark places where people were killed at the Wall; (3) how to mark the actual path of the Wall; (4) the ecological and climate effects of the flora and fauna filling the area where the border had been; (5) the popularity of using the former patrol path for walking and biking and that they hoped could become a Wall trail (*Mauerweg*); and (6) methods of commemorating the Wall in exhibits and museums. They expected a plan to be formulated by the end of October 1992 and were critical that the Senate "got lost in conflicts about details regarding the former border strip, such as with the Sophien parish," instead of thinking more comprehensively about an approach.[2]

As we have seen, several of the *Bündnis 90/ Die Grüne* proposals had been implemented by 2004, but there was still no *Gesamtkonzept* to guide the first two items and the last. Although the Senate created a working group for this purpose in its office for cultural affairs, at the time Hildebrandt unveiled her crosses the working group had not actually formulated a plan. In 2004, the group was operating on the assumption that "the existing memorial sites are sufficient," as Cultural Senator Thomas Flierl declared in late October, and that it was only necessary to "better connect the existing sites." To do this, they were working on an audio tour that would explain the various sites connected to the Wall. Visitors could listen to the audio tour on a Walkman or Palm Pilot, the latest technological devices at the time.[3]

---

[2] See, for example, the motion in the Berlin House of Representatives from Bündnis 90/Die Grüne for a "master plan on dealing with the Wall," "Antrag der Fraktion Bündnis 90/Die Grüne (AL)/UFV über Umgang mit der Mauer," Abgeordnetenhaus von Berlin, Drucksache 12/1307, March 18, 1992; the letter from Cultural Senator Peter Radunski to Environmental Senator Peter Strieder on August 16, 1996, "Betr.: Umgang mit der Mauer in Berlin," SWFKB, GBM, Nr. 24; and Helmut Trotnow, "Sag mir, wo die Spuren sind...Berlin und der Umgang mit der Geschichte der Berliner Mauer," in Bernd Faulenbach and Franz-Josef Jelich, eds., *"Asymmetrisch verflochtene Parallelgeschichte?" Die Geschichte der Bundesrepublik und der DDR in Ausstellungen, Museen und Gedenkstätten* (Essen: Klartext, 2005), pp. 157–66.

[3] Thomas Rogalla and Tobias Miller, "Das Geschäft mit der Mauer: Senatoren kritisieren Kunstaktion," *Berliner Zeitung*, October 11, 2004; and Carsten Volkery, "Mehr Disneyland wagen," *Spiegel*, October 29, 2004.

At the same time, and independent of Hildebrandt's Wall crosses, a handful of members of the Bundestag also called for more attention to be given to the history of the Berlin Wall. They, however, wanted the focus of attention on the Wall and its victims to be at the Brandenburg Gate, not at Checkpoint Charlie or at Bernauer Strasse. No doubt part of the reason for this was the location of the Gate right next to the seat of parliament in the Reichstag.

On November 4, 2004, four parliament members proposed that a "Central Site of Memory for the Berlin Wall," an *Ort des Erinnerns*, be created at the Brandenburg Gate.[4] The parliamentarians represented the former East and West and four political parties – the Free Democratic Party (FDP), the Social Democratic Party (SPD), Bündnis 90/Die Grüne, and the Christian Democratic Union (CDU). They argued that the pictures broadcast around the world on November 9, 1989 of people celebrating on the Wall at the Brandenburg Gate made it the site most associated with the Berlin Wall. They called for a site at the Gate to provide information about the Wall, including both the opening of the Wall in 1989 and the twenty-eight years during which the Brandenburg Gate was surrounded by the death strip, preventing any movement through it.[5] They thus added an important new component of Wall memory to Hildebrandt's focus on victims of the Wall: the Wall as a joyful site of memory due to its peaceful fall.

The MPs urged that an artistic monument be created near the Gate that would both commemorate victims of the Wall and celebrate the toppling of the Wall, a complicated task for any artist. They called on the federal government and the Berlin authorities to work together to develop a "conceptual frame-work and proposed procedure" for "documenting and remembering the Berlin Wall in its local and national contexts and considering its individual and social impact."[6] This should be completed by August 13, 2005, the following year's anniversary of the border closure in Berlin.

A week after the proposal by Bundestag members, there was also pressure from within the Berlin parliament for action on remembering the Wall. On

---

[4] Antrag der Abgeordneten Carl-Ludwig Thiele (FDP), Stephan Hilsberg (SPD), Franziska Eichstädt-Bohlig (Bündnis 90/Die Grünen), Werner Kuhn (CDU) und anderer, Gelände um das Brandenburger Tor als zentraler Ort des Erinnerns an die Berliner Mauer, des Gedenkens an ihre Opfer und der Freude über die Überwindung der deutschen Teilung" (hereafter, "Ort des Erinnerns"), Deutscher Bundestag, November 4, 2004. See also Thomas Fülling, "Zentrales Gedenken an die Mauer. Parteiübergreifende Initiative von Bundestagsabgeordneten fordert Erinnerungsort nahe dem Brandenburger Tor," *Berliner Morgenpost*, November 6, 2004.

[5] Interviews with Carl-Ludwig Thiele and Werner Kuhn on November 11, 2004, Franziska Eichstädt-Bohlig on November 19, 2004, and Stephan Hilsberg on November 22, 2004.

[6] "Ort des Erinnerns," November 4, 2004.

November 11, 2004, the opposition parties seized on the criticism of Mayor Klaus Wowereit's SPD-PDS government that had been leveled by Hildebrandt and broad sections of the public for not doing more on the Wall. Not content with Cultural Senator Flierl's statement that a new audio guide to connect Berlin Wall sites was all that was needed, the CDU and *Bündnis 90/Die Grüne* pushed the Berlin Senate to develop a master plan. The CDU's proposal was the more ambitious of the two, calling on the Senate to formulate an approach for the public presentation of and reckoning with the Nazi and communist dictatorships in Germany.[7] The Greens' proposal was centered on the Wall and the need for a plan that would "keep the division of Berlin and the remembrance of its victims alive in the cityscape." It pushed for the Senate to work with the federal government and the relevant districts of Berlin to come up with a *Gesamtkonzept* for "documenting the Berlin Wall as evidence of the division of Berlin, including preserving the remaining pieces and making them more visible and understandable."[8]

The Berlin House of Representatives met on November 11 to commemorate the fifteenth anniversary of the fall of the Berlin Wall. Party politics and the legacy of the division made for a raucous, emotional, often hostile discussion about how to deal with the history of the Wall and the commemoration of its victims. The parliament members themselves had lived through the division, experiencing the Wall when it stood as a deadly border. Hence, these were not theoretical discussions about how to handle a distant past; they were emotional outpourings mixed with politics, a potent combination.[9]

The opposition parties, particularly the CDU and FDP, sharply criticized the role of the PDS in deciding how to treat the Berlin Wall, since Cultural Senator Flierl of the PDS was overseeing the development of a *Gesamtkonzept*. Opposition to Flierl and his role was heightened by the revelation just days before the parliament session that one of the candidates he was considering for an important city position had worked for the Stasi. PDS parliamentarians were repeatedly shouted down and interrupted when speaking. Some representatives called loudly for Flierl's resignation or for the mayor to fire

[7] Dringlicher Antrag der Fraktion der CDU, "Gesamtkonzept zur öffentlichen Darstellung und Aufarbeitung der jüngsten Deutschen Zeitgeschichte in der Hauptstadt Berlin," Abgeordnetenhaus von Berlin, Drucksache 15/3378, November 11, 2004.

[8] Dringlicher Antrag der Fraktion Bündnis 90/Die Grünen, "Die Teilung Berlins und die Erinnerung an ihre Opfer im Stadtbild wach halten," Abgeordnetenhaus von Berlin, Drucksache 15/3377, November 11, 2004.

[9] Aktuelle Stunde, "Bilanz 15 Jahre nach dem Mauerfall – die Einheit gestalten und der Opfer gedenken," Abgeordnetenhaus von Berlin, Plenarprotokoll 15/59, November 11, 2004, pp. 4922–41. The author was also present at the session. Hope M. Harrison, "Berlin's *Gesamtkonzept* for Remembering the Berlin Wall," in Konrad H. Jarausch, Christian F. Ostermann, and Andreas Etges, eds., *The Cold War* (Berlin/Boston: Walter de Gruyter, 2017) pp. 239–66.

him.[10] MPs stormed out of the room, and the chair had to repeatedly pound the gavel, calling for order in the midst of many raised and angry voices.

This all put Wowereit on the defensive, as did the repeated demands of the district mayor of Mitte, Joachim Zeller, in whose district Checkpoint Charlie was located, for a comprehensive Berlin plan to deal with the memory of the Berlin Wall instead of just developing an audio guide.[11] While as discussed in Chapter 3 the SPD and PDS had committed in their 2002 coalition treaty to commemorating victims of the Wall, developing a master plan for remembering the Wall, and supporting the Documentation Center at Bernauer Strasse, they had not done much on this in more than two years.[12] The leaders had been rather quiet on the subject of the Berlin Wall, clearly hoping to avoid a repeat of the heckling Wowereit, Chancellor Schröder, and others in the SPD and PDS had endured on the fortieth anniversary of the erection of the Wall in 2001.

In the parliamentary session of November 11, 2004, Wowereit adopted a position somewhere in the center of the debate about what was necessary to commemorate the Wall. On the one hand, he argued that the existing Berlin Wall Memorial site at Bernauer Strasse was sufficient and attracted many visitors and that therefore nothing new needed to be created, including by Hildebrandt at Checkpoint Charlie. He referred to the many existing sites connected with the Wall in Berlin, concluding: "Berlin really has no lack of memorials and sites of memory." On the other hand, he agreed that, "we must connect [the sites] better and integrate them into a common plan so they attract more attention." The fact that 40 percent of Berliners under the age of thirty did not know what happened on November 9, 1989, the mayor lamented, demonstrated that something more needed to be done. Accordingly, he announced that the Senate had begun work on a citywide plan, directed by Flierl, for remembering the Berlin Wall.[13]

Flierl directed an interagency task force to take stock of the remains of the Berlin Wall and the whole border zone (much of which had been catalogued by Leo Schmidt and Axel Klausmeier in 2001–3) and to formulate a plan for dealing with them in the future.[14] The Working Group on Commemorating

---

[10] Martin Lindner (FDP) called for the mayor to remove Flierl from his post, ibid., p. 4930.

[11] Uwe Aulich, "Zeller will Mauer-Konzept für Berlin. Mittes Bürgermeister missfallen die Privatprojeke am Checkpoint Charlie," *Berliner Zeitung*, October 7, 2004.

[12] SPD-PDS Koalitionsvereinbarung, January 16, 2002, p. 4, archiv.spd-berlin.de/w/files/spd-positionen/koalitionsvertrag2002.pdf.

[13] Aktuelle Stunde, "Bilanz 15 Jahre nach dem Mauerfall – die Einheit gestalten und der Opfer gedenken," Abgeordnetenhaus von Berlin, Plenarprotokoll 15/59, November 11, 2004, pp. 4933–34.

[14] Flierl had also convened an interagency task force on Checkpoint Charlie and historical commemoration in the summer of 2004 in the wake of the controversy between Hildebrandt and the student actors there. The task force had only met once and without high-ranking officials in attendance. "Senatorin will Mauer nur bis Silvester dulden,"

the Wall (*Arbeitsgruppe Mauergedenken*) met two weeks after the parliamentary debate and was coordinated by Rainer Klemke, whose portfolio within the cultural department encompassed memorial sites and museums connected with contemporary history. Klemke recognized the significant impact of Hildebrandt's crosses even if he did not agree with her approach.[15] Observing that some critics believed Berlin had too many sites connected with commemorating the Wall and others believed there were not enough, Klemke announced: "We want to take a middle path."[16]

Klemke's task force was comprised of representatives of the Senate chancellery, including its departments for culture and city planning, the federal minister for culture, the Berlin Forum for History and the Present, the Berlin Wall Association at Bernauer Strasse, the Federal Foundation for Reappraising the SED Dictatorship, and the central Berlin districts that had been separated by the Wall – Mitte and Friedrichshain-Kreuzberg. The task force would also meet with members of victims' groups, historians, and other experts to exchange ideas and report on progress regarding a *Gesamtkonzept*.

Motivations for Remembering the Wall with a *Gesamtkonzept*

Policymakers and others involved in the debate were fueled by a combination of motivations in calling for more attention to the history of the Berlin Wall. These included political aims, personal connections to the Wall, supporting tourism, a commitment to drawing lessons from history, and a sense of moral and historical responsibility. Wowereit and Flierl were clearly under pressure to show they took the history and legacy of the Wall seriously. They had been on the defensive in 2001 for the fortieth anniversary of the erection of the Wall, and they were again three years later with all the attention on the fifteenth anniversary of the toppling of the Wall. Just as Wowereit had called on the PDS in 2001 as the successor party to the SPD to confront the history of the Wall and apologize to victims in more than just "lip service as part of an election campaign,"[17] so Wowereit now had to show that his government as a whole was facing this history in a forthright and sensitive way. He and Flierl also made it abundantly clear that they did not want to cede to Alexandra Hildebrandt the

---

Berliner Morgenpost, October 8, 2004; and author's interview with Rainer Klemke, November 24, 2004.

[15] Rainer Klemke, "Between disappearance and remembrance: remembering the Berlin Wall today," in Anna Kaminsky, ed., *Where in the World Is the Berlin Wall?* (Berlin: Berlin Story Verlag, 2014), p. 252.

[16] Andreas Puppe and Stefan Schulz, "Die Mauer muss weg," *Berliner Morgenpost*, October 11, 2004.

[17] "Der Mauerbau: Klaus Wowereit im Interview: 'Herr Gysi soll sich nicht zu früh seinen Anzug bügeln'," *Tagesspiegel*, August, 11, 2001.

primary influence over Wall memory. They were thus highly motivated to construct a convincing plan to remember the Wall and commemorate the victims.

Policymakers at the municipal and federal levels also had quite personal reasons for supporting the memory of the Wall. For many, remembering the Berlin Wall was a part of their own life history. They had lived through the years in which the Wall stood, whether on the eastern or the western side, and they felt this history was receding with fewer and fewer relics and reminders of it. In their proposal of November 4, the Bundestag members lamented that "the memory of the division of Berlin, Germany and the world threatens to disappear." Noting that "an entire generation was influenced by the division of Germany and the world," they argued, "there is a great need to remember."[18] It felt strange and somehow wrong to them that it was nearly impossible for their children or grandchildren to understand or feel what it had been like.[19] As Green MP Franziska Eichstädt-Bohlig observed, "Pariser Platz is so nice now and nothing there serves as a reminder of the division and that it was part of the death strip" on the eastern side of the Brandenburg Gate.[20] Her colleague Carl-Ludwig Thiele of the FDP spoke of how hard it was to explain to his seventeen-year-old son what the death strip at the Wall had been like: "Young people who see remains of the Wall in Berlin today often wonder: People couldn't get over *that*? The world was divided by *this* wall?"[21] The remains of the Wall required more explanation for young people and others who had not experienced it.

Another reason for devoting increased attention to the history of the Berlin Wall was the desire to extract from it certain lessons of history, particularly for young Germans who did not live through it. Policymakers and others emphasized the need to preserve pieces of the Wall as part of the "political education" (*politische Bildung*) of young people. Accordingly, they saw pieces of the Wall as "elements for the living memory of a dictatorship which part of Germany had to put up with for 40 years."[22] "In the interest of democracy," young people should know about the communist system in the GDR that created the deadly

---

[18] "Ort des Erinnerns," November 4, 2004.

[19] See in particular the comments of the primary initiator of the proposal, Carl-Ludwig Thiele: Deutscher Bundestag, Plenarprotokoll 15/163, March 10, 2005, p. 15, 309; Deutscher Bundestag Ausschuss für Kultur und Medien, Protokoll 15/60, June 15, 2005, p. 14; and Deutscher Bundestag, Plenarprotokoll 15/184, June 30, 2005, pp. 17, 447–48.

[20] Franziska Eichstädt-Bohlig, Deutscher Bundestag, Plenarprotokoll 15/163, March 10, 2005, pp. 15, 310–11.

[21] Carl-Ludwig Thiele, Deutscher Bundestag, Plenarprotokoll 15/184, June 30, 2005, p. 17447.

[22] Uwe Lehmann-Brauns, Abgeordnetenhaus von Berlin, Ausschuss für Kulturelle Angelegenheiten, Wortprotokoll 15/58, April 25, 2005, p. 2.

Berlin Wall.[23] Young people should understand that the freedoms they have and take for granted, including the freedom to travel all over the country and beyond, have not always existed and were in fact severely limited while Germany was divided.

Tourists' interest in the Berlin Wall played an important role in the deliberations about developing a plan for remembering the Wall. Part of the impetus for the Berlin Senate to develop an approach to the history and remains of the Wall came from tourists asking, "Where is the Wall?" Heinz Buri, cultural commissioner of Berlin's tourism office, had known Klemke for many years and took part in Klemke's working group. He knew first-hand from his conversations with tourists and journalists that the Wall was a great way to sell Berlin. It attracted visitors to the city; visitors who stayed in hotels, dined at restaurants, bought souvenirs, and generally contributed to Berlin's economy. For him, "the more Wall, the better."[24] Indeed, a survey of tourists in 2004 demonstrated their great interest in contemporary history, listing the desire to see the Berlin Wall as their top goal and the Brandenburg Gate as their second goal.[25] Berlin's director of tourism, Hanns Peter Nerger, concluded that with her installation of crosses and sections of the Wall at Checkpoint Charlie, "Frau Hildebrandt had stepped into a vacuum that politicians have not occupied."[26] Buri and Nerger repeatedly pressed the Senate to do more to highlight the Wall.[27] Tourists were interested in both the brutal past of the Wall and its peaceful fall, the former an example of "dark tourism," stemming from the "human fascination with danger, mortality and loss."[28]

Again and again in the debates in the fall of 2004 and afterwards, public officials, historians, journalists, and others spoke of tourists' desire to see and learn about the Wall, tourists' frustration that this was harder to do than they expected, and the importance of satisfying the tourists' interest in the Wall. Some argued in particular that tourists should be able to see and learn about the Wall at the main tourist destinations, such as the Brandenburg Gate (as Bundestag members maintained) and Checkpoint Charlie (as Hildebrandt asserted). Certainly part of the interest in providing tourists with more of what they wanted was connected with Berlin's ever-present shortage of

---

[23] Brigitte Lange, Abgeordnetenhaus von Berlin, ibid., p. 5.

[24] Interview with Heinz Buri, July 25, 2007.

[25] Sybille Frank, *Die Mauer um die Wette Gedenken* (New York: Campus Verlag, 2009), p. 175.

[26] "Wowi ist Mauermahnmal zu kompliziert," *taz*, November 2, 2004.

[27] Interview with Thomas Flierl, November 26, 2009.

[28] Paul William, *Memorial Museums: The Global Rush to Commemorate Atrocities* (New York: Berg, 2007), p. 142. On Berlin as a site of dark tourism, see Hanno Hochmuth, "Die Attraktion der Schattenorte," *Tagesspiegel*, February 13, 2015. See also www.dark-tour ism.com.

funds.[29] Anything that was such a draw for tourists and their wallets should be made more accessible. Economic need, however, was not the whole story.

For some policymakers and historical experts, there seemed to be a kind of historical obligation involved in giving national and international tourists the information and experience they were looking for related to the Berlin Wall, as Fischer and Trotnow had long emphasized and Hildebrandt had recently highlighted. Bundestag member Eichstädt-Bohlig argued in March 2005: "Berliners, Germans and people from all over the world come to the Gate to see the history of the German division, the iron curtain and the cold war."[30] She maintained that, "Tourists...search for memory at [the Brandenburg Gate.]...I think all people – wherever they come from – have the right to search for memory at this place. I think it's very important that this requirement is satisfied."[31] Similarly, the CDU members in Berlin's House of Representatives asserted that the city must respond to the "desire of Berliners and national and international visitors for more information on the dimensions and course of the Berlin Wall in the heart of Berlin."[32] Scholarly backing for this argument came from the historians Konrad Jarausch, Martin Sabrow, and Hans-Hermann Hertle in a March 2005 public memorandum: "At a time of booming *public history*, we should take account of the tourists from within Germany and beyond who look in vain for remnants of the Wall precisely in the central memory area around the Brandenburg Gate and the Reichstag."[33] An analogous argument was given by Alexandra Hildebrandt: "People look for the Wall at Checkpoint

[29] Hubertus Knabe and Manfred Wilke, "Die Wunden der Teilung sichtbar machen. Vorschläge für ein Konzept der Erinnerung an die untergegangene SED-Diktatur," *Horch und Guck* 49 (2004), November 23, 2004. See also the written statement by Harald Strunz, deputy chairman of UOKG, "Überlegungen zum Gedenkkonzept der Berliner Mauer," for the April 18, 2005 presentation of Flierl's draft commemorative plan for the Wall in the Berlin parliament, www.uokg.de/Text/akt039flirlkonzept.htm. The date on this version of the document is April 22, 2005, but it is identical to what was presented to the hearing on April 18.

[30] Deutscher Bundestag, Plenarprotokoll 15/163, March 10, 2005, p. 15331.

[31] Deutscher Bundestag, Plenarprotokoll 15/184, June 30, 2005, p. 17446.

[32] Dringlicher Antrag der Fraktion der CDU, "Gesamtkonzept zur öffentlichen Darstellung und Aufarbeitung der jüngsten Deutschen Zeitgeschichte in der Hauptstadt Berlin," Abgeordnetenhaus von Berlin, Drucksache 15/3378, November 11, 2004.

[33] Konrad H. Jarausch, Martin Sabrow, and Hans-Hermann Hertle, "Die Berliner Mauer – Erinnerung ohne Ort? Memorandum zur Bewahrung der Berliner Mauer als Erinnerungsort" (hereafter, ZZF memo), March 9, 2005, p. 4. For scholarly analysis of the interaction between tourism and national identity, see Duncan Light, "Gazing on Communism: Heritage Tourism and post-Communist Identities in Germany, Hungary and Romania," *Tourism Geographies* 2, no. 2 (2002), pp. 157–76; and G. H. Ashworth and P. J. Larkham, eds., *Building a New Heritage: Tourism, Culture and Identity in the New Europe* (New York: Routledge, 1994).

Charlie,"[34] a site that she emphasized had been visited by prominent people from all over the world both when the Wall stood and since its fall, people such as Winston Churchill's granddaughter Edwina Sandys (see Figure 16 in Chapter 4).[35]

Beyond the importance of highlighting the history of the Wall for young Germans and tourists at these key locations, others argued more generally about what could be called a moral responsibility to the world to remember the Berlin Wall. The historian Klaus-Dietmar Henke testified to the Berlin parliament: "The Berlin Wall belongs to world cultural heritage as a historical-political symbol. The city of Berlin and the Federal Republic of Germany must fulfill their responsibility for this heritage at [a] high level...So far the state and federal governments have fulfilled their responsibility shamefully."[36] Likewise, Harald Strunz, deputy chair of the Union of Victims' Associations of Communist Tyranny (UOKG), declared: "The rise and fall of the Berlin Wall belong – also in the view of the entire cultural world – to the historical heritage of this city and one should not squander such a heritage."[37]

The responsibility many Germans felt about confronting and remembering the history of the Wall was not just to the world, but also to themselves. With the legacy of "two German dictatorships in the 20th century," policymakers and others often spoke of the importance of fostering a post-unification "democratic memory culture" in Germany, which in their view necessitated dealing with the dark past of the Berlin Wall and showing the next generation how to do so as well. More specifically, Hubertus Knabe, director of the memorial at the former central Stasi remand prison in Berlin-Hohenschönhausen, and the historian Manfred Wilke declared in November 2004 that remembering the Wall and the SED regime that created it "is part of democratic self-consciousness. This memory contributes to strengthening consciousness about freedom, justice and democracy."[38] Thus, preserving remains of the Wall and the death strip

---

[34] Alexandra Hildebrandt quoted by Volkery, "Mehr Disneyland wagen. Checkpoint Charlie," *Spiegel*, October 29, 2004.

[35] Alexandra Hildebrandt, "Freedom Obliges: The Freedom Memorial on Checkpoint Charlie Square," in her booklet for the press, "Freiheitsmahnmal am Platz Checkpoint Charlie, 'Sie wollten nur die Freiheit,' Gespräche mit der Bank – Trotzdem soll geräumt werden!", distributed at the 143rd press conference of the Working Group of August 13, Inc., June 28, 2005.

[36] Klaus-Dietmar Henke, "Gedenkkonzept Berliner Mauer," statement to Berlin parliament on Flierl's Gedenkkonzept on the Berlin Wall, April 18, 2005, www.bundesstiftung-aufarbeitung.de/uploads/pdf/va180405henke.pdf.

[37] Strunz, statement to Berlin parliament, on Flierl's Gedenkkonzept on the Berlin Wall, April 18, 2005, www.uokg.de/Text/akt039flirlkonzept.htm.

[38] Dringlicher Antrag der Fraktion der CDU, "Gesamtkonzept zur öffentlichen Darstellung und Aufarbeitung der jüngsten Deutschen Zeitgeschichte in der Hauptstadt Berlin," Abgeordnetenhaus von Berlin, Drucksache 15/3378, November 11, 2004. On the capacity of memorial sites and memorial museums to instill civic activism in their visitors to prevent

and providing information about them were essential parts of this democratic memory culture. The SPD-PDS coalition treaty of 2001 had also observed that "democratic engagement needs historical orientation."[39] Just as German politicians had long argued that the Holocaust must be examined, discussed, taught about, and learned from, so they were beginning to argue that the East German regime and its Wall should come under similar scrutiny. A consensus on the lessons of the Berlin Wall and its relationship to "freedom, justice and democracy," however, would be elusive.

Memory Activists in the Berlin Senate

While Thomas Flierl and Rainer Klemke may not have conceived of themselves at the time as memory activists for the Berlin Wall, in retrospect that is what they became in the process of formulating the *Gesamtkonzept*. The two men had very different backgrounds, with Flierl coming from East Germany and Klemke from West Germany, but their work to preserve Wall memory and commemorate its victims beyond what Manfred Fischer and Alexandra Hildebrandt had done was essential to the long-term institutionalization of the memory of the Wall and is now visible at many sites in Berlin. Unlike Fischer and Hildebrandt, who were private citizens with their own motives for fostering memory of the Wall at specific locations, Flierl and Klemke were government officials. Yet they also had their own reasons for devoting great energy to highlighting the history of the Wall.

Flierl was born in 1957 in East Berlin. His father was an architect and convinced communist who moved from the FRG to the GDR in 1950 to take part in building the East German state. Since Flierl's mother died in childbirth, he was raised by his father and grandmother. Relatives of both of his parents still lived in the West and came to visit East Berlin whenever possible. As a teenager he was relieved that he did not have to serve at the border. Flierl's grandfather in the West was a big fan of West German Chancellor Willy Brandt's *Ostpolitik*, making Flierl more predisposed to cooperation with the SPD than some others in the SED and later PDS. In the late 1970s and early 1980s when Flierl was studying philosophy at Humboldt University in East Berlin, he was grateful when one of his cousins from West Berlin brought him books on philosophy, books deemed insufficiently in line with Marxism-Leninism for the library at Humboldt.[40] Hence, the cultural senator's

---

a repeat of past atrocities, see Williams, *Memorial Museums*, pp. 146–50. See also the work of the International Coalition of Historic Site Museums of Conscience, www.sitesof conscience.org; and Anna Saunders, *Memorializing the GDR* (NY: Berghahn, 2018).

[39] SPD-PDS Koalitionsvereinbarung, January 7, 2002, p. 126.

[40] Interview with Thomas Flierl, November 29, 2009.

background was not as simplistically pro-SED as some of his opponents tried to make out.

Studying philosophy and cultural studies in the GDR, Flierl developed strong views about the role of culture, including historic landmarks, in East Berlin. When the GDR decided to demolish a historic landmark – three gasometers that were no longer in use – in the Prenzlauer Berg district of central Berlin in 1984, Flierl was openly critical.[41] The three gasometers were the only remaining examples in Europe of late nineteenth century gas holders constructed from brick, and they were located at the center of the industrial and working-class area in this district of Berlin. Flierl argued that the gasometers represented an important part of Berlin's history and should be preserved. The SED leaders, however, decided to remove them to ensure an unobstructed view of a new monument memorializing the communist leader Ernst Thälmann.

For Flierl's public objection to the plans to destroy the gasometers, he was forced to leave his position as a research assistant in the aesthetics and art department at Humboldt in 1985.[42] He was, however, allowed to finish his doctorate in aesthetics and was employed from 1987 to 1990 in the GDR cultural ministry working on a committee that focused on cultural sites in East Berlin. Instead of a career as an academic studying and commenting on cultural issues as he had planned, Flierl was pushed – rather ironically in light of his opposition to the authorities on the gasometers – to the policymaking side of culture. It is not clear why the party leaders thought it would be safer to have a critic involved in implementing policy than in commenting on policy, but there were many aspects of the East German communist system that defied logic.

In the late 1980s, Flierl and other more open thinkers in the GDR cultural ministry found inspiration in Gorbachev's efforts to create a "Common European Home" to lessen the division in Europe. An opening up of cultural policies within Europe also meant that Flierl was allowed to travel to West Berlin to use the libraries there, starting in 1987 – something he greatly valued and something that–in spite of his earlier outspokenness–was generally a privilege only granted to people trusted by the regime. He hoped that Gorbachev's initiatives would make it possible for the GDR to enact serious reforms to bring about socialist democracy. He was shocked by the opening of the Berlin Wall, which he felt should have been opened by reformist East German leaders instead of by pressure from people on the streets. He knew

---

[41] See Flierl's speech to the SED party section meeting of the aesthetics and art history department at Humboldt University on "Gegen den Abriss der Gasometer in Berlin-Prenzlauer Berg. Eine Rede vor der Sektionsparteiversammlung. 1984," July 9, 1984, in Ute Tischler and Arlett Mattescheck, eds., *Berlin: Perspektiven durch Kultur. Texte und Projekte* (Berlin: Theater der Zeit, Recherchen 45, 2007), pp. 16–21.

[42] Uwe Rada, "Intellektueller Parteisoldat," *taz.de*, January 11, 2002.

instinctively that his dream of a reformed socialist regime in the GDR would now be impossible.[43]

In the period leading up to unification, Flierl served on a joint East-West committee that dealt with cultural matters in Berlin and Brandenburg, including the question of whether to preserve sections of the rapidly disappearing Berlin Wall as historic landmarks. He was involved in the decision to grant this status to a block-long section of the Wall across the street from the Berlin parliament building on Niederkirchnerstrasse. He could not have imagined then that fifteen years later, he would be tasked with creating and implementing a master plan for preserving and remembering the Wall.

When Germany united and the SED transformed itself into the PDS, Flierl felt that the party had not reformed enough. He left the party in 1991 and only rejoined it in 1999 in the wake of NATO's air strikes on Serbia following the latter's attack on Kosovo.[44] In the 1990s, Flierl held positions as head of the cultural department in Prenzlauer Berg, a member of the Berlin parliament (representing the PDS, although he ran as an independent), and city councillor for urban development in the Mitte district of Berlin. He gained a reputation for refusing to allow companies to display large advertisements in central Berlin, arguing that the money they would bring was not worth ruining the historic atmosphere or at least what little there was left of it.

In the 1990s, Flierl was deeply involved in the emotional debates about how to handle aspects of the GDR past still visible in the cityscape, such as monuments and street names dedicated to communist heroes. He argued against rapidly tearing down monuments and changing street names without a broad public debate first.[45] In his view, this approach would just repeat the non-democratic way they had been introduced in the GDR. He favored projects that added to or commented on the memorials (such as covering them with rapidly growing plants or barbed wire) in ways that would provoke a discussion about why they had been erected and why they should be removed. Coming from a long-standing intellectual approach to the role of monuments in cultural life, Flierl may very well have believed what he said, but his critics assumed he was just looking for a way to preserve communist monuments and street names in united Germany. In either case, his experience with these issues in his various roles in the 1990s gave him some preparation for what he would face in the following decade as cultural senator.

---

[43] Interview with Thomas Flierl, November 29, 2009.

[44] Holger Kulick, "Interview mit Thomas Flierl (PDS). 'Respekt ist eine besondere Kultur'," *Spiegel Online*, January 10, 2002; and Marina Achenbach, "Plötzlich ist er da," *Freitag.de*, January 18, 2002.

[45] Thomas Flierl, "Kultur Jetzt! Eine Bilanz der Kulturpolitik 2002 bis 2006," in Tischler and Müller, eds., *Berlin: Perspektiven durch Kultur*, pp. 22–36, drawn from a speech Flierl gave in March 1992. On these debates, see Saunders, *Memorializing the GDR*, pp. 55–109.

In 2001, when the PDS joined the ruling coalition of Berlin for the first time since the collapse of East Germany, Flierl as we have seen in Chapter 3 was deeply involved in formulating the language for the important section of the coalition treaty devoted to the East German past and the Wall.[46] When interviewed in January 2002 about dealing with the Wall in his new position as cultural senator, Flierl pledged to help provide support for memorials connected to the division of Berlin and Germany and to repression in the GDR. He noted in particular: "I think it is a scandal that the Berlin Wall Memorial is not secure and is only partially financed. Historical work will have a very high priority for me in the future."[47] It would take Hildebrandt's crosses at Checkpoint Charlie two and a half years later, however, to bring Flierl back to a focus on the memory of the Wall and formulating a master plan for it.[48] By that point, he would be highly motivated to show that, contrary to the assertions of his political critics, he could develop an appropriate and convincing *Gesamtkonzept* for remembering the Wall and its victims, in spite of his current and former party affiliation.

Flierl worked closely with Rainer Klemke, nine years his senior, who threw himself into his job as coordinator of the interagency task force on the *Gesamtkonzept*. A tall man with a ready smile and an aptitude for networking, Klemke had been in the Senate's department for cultural affairs for thirteen years already in 2004. He started out as the press spokesman for the department in 1991 and rose to be deputy department head in 1996 and the overseer of all museums, memorials, and archives in Berlin related to contemporary history. In a city whose history has played such a fundamental, often brutal, role in German, European, and world affairs, this is an extremely important and sensitive position. Klemke had been dealing extensively with the memory of the Nazi past in museums, monuments, and memorials, with the national Memorial to the Murdered Jews of Europe set to be completed and dedicated in 2005. He was about to get as deeply involved with East German history as he had been with Nazi history.

Born in 1948 in western Berlin, Klemke was thirteen years old when the Wall was built and forty-one when it came down. Raised in West Berlin, Klemke nonetheless had many relatives and friends in East Berlin and East Germany. In the years after the Wall was erected, the young Rainer and his parents visited relatives and friends in the East regularly. He was a strong supporter of Brandt's *Ostpolitik* as Flierl's grandfather had been. Indeed,

---

[46] Holger Kulick, "Berliner Senat. Gysi nimmt Wirtschaft, Thomas Flierl statt Bisky Kultur," *Spiegel Online*, January 9, 2002.

[47] Kulick, "Interview mit Thomas Flierl," *Spiegel Online*, January 10, 2002; and Kulick, "Berliner Kultursenat. Flierl statt Bisky – Der neue Mann," *Spiegel Online*, January 10, 2002.

[48] Interviews with Thomas Flierl, November 26, 2009, and Rainer Klemke, November 24, 2004.

Klemke had helped to bolster domestic support for Brandt's détente policy by working on many election campaigns for proponents of his *Ostpolitik*.[49]

Once East and West Germany established diplomatic relations in 1972, Rainer and his parents went east every month. Each time, they packed their Toyota van full of items either not available or of very poor quality in the GDR: coffee, chocolate, pineapples, peaches, nylon stockings, toys, diapers, Mickey Mouse books, rock music tapes, car radios, replacement car parts, silverware, new and used clothing, and even gold wedding rings for relatives getting married. Klemke hid some of these things in various specially constructed parts of the van to make sure the border guards would not confiscate them. His family once even used their van to move some relatives from one part of the GDR to another, an endeavor that attracted much attention and led the new neighbors to wonder whether a family from the West was moving into their village. Among the more than fifty members of Klemke's family in the GDR, one of them was a captain in the defense ministry and was prohibited from speaking to relatives visiting from the West.

The fall of the Wall was a huge relief for Klemke's family, as was unification. He and his wife bought a house near relatives in the Brandenburg countryside northeast of Berlin in what had been the GDR, while also maintaining an apartment in central, western Berlin. What had been impossible for twenty-eight years was now normal: moving back and forth between residences in the east and west. Yet Klemke and his family would never take this for granted. At every birthday gathering of their family and friends since the fall of the Wall, someone still inevitably referred to the Wall and all they had been forced to cope with, feeling deep gratitude that the division was now in the past.

Klemke's first serious encounters with the political memory of the Wall occurred when he became the press spokesman for the Berlin Senate in 1991 and then five years later when he became deputy head of the department of cultural affairs. Manfred Fischer and Helmut Trotnow as well as Gabi Dolf-Bonekämper of the historic preservation office in Berlin repeatedly expressed to him throughout the 1990s the urgency of Senate action to preserve the remains of the Wall, particularly at Bernauer Strasse, before it was too late. His second, much deeper encounter with commemorating the Wall would be overseeing Flierl's Working Group on Remembering the Berlin Wall. Indeed, Klemke would come to see the *Gesamtkonzept* as the crowning achievement of his career. With tireless dedication, famously long hours, and great energy, he would oversee the formulation of the *Gesamtkonzept* over the

---

[49] The information on Rainer Klemke's background comes from many interviews the author conducted with him: November 24, 2004; July 5, 2005; July 19, 2005; July 27, 2007; December 18, 2009; January 25, 2010; August 2, 2011; and November 15, 2013; and by email on January 6 and 9, 2014.

next two years and its implementation over the subsequent six years until his retirement in 2012 and even afterwards. Another person in his position might not have taken quite the activist approach that he did. With a sparkle in his eyes and a big smile, he would later observe: "This is the most interesting thing I have done in my life."[50]

Aside from his Protestant work ethic, Klemke's memories of the twenty-eight years his family was divided by the Wall no doubt fueled his fire to keep the history of the Wall alive for others to learn from. In his many trips back and forth across the border, he had developed increasingly critical views about the GDR regime, the *Grenzer*, and others who supported the infamous border. Klemke's experiences with the GDR regime and the Berlin Wall deepened his appreciation of democracy, which he developed as a member of the 1968 generation in West Berlin, as did Manfred Fischer. At that time, the city (and especially the Free University where Klemke was a student) was a center of student protests against former Nazis who still had not been removed from power and against traditional, conservative ways in the university, government, and other parts of society. Klemke held leadership positions on commissions devoted to reforming the education system in the wake of these protests. From that time, he became passionate about democracy and the democratic process, believing it to be essential that Germany's capital city shine a light on the dark aspects of its past (both the Nazi and SED regimes) so as to learn from them and not repeat them in the future.

It was especially important for Klemke (Figure 17) that the *Gesamtkonzept* facilitate opportunities for young people to learn about what life was like in Berlin and Germany during the years of the Wall and division and the East German communist regime. In this way, he hoped to pass on an appreciation of the importance of democracy and a commitment to it. With a combination of openness and determination, he guided the formulation of the *Gesamtkonzept* for Remembering the Berlin Wall.

A natural bridge-builder, Klemke reached out to all sorts of individuals and groups to participate in the brainstorming sessions of the task force. He drew on the views and advice of a variety of individuals, groups, and institutions who had a stake in remembering the Wall and who had knowledge about and/ or experience with the history of the Wall, including historical experts, the heads of museums, monuments and memorials connected with the Wall and GDR repression, historic preservation specialists, and victims of the GDR regime. Alexandra Hildebrandt was the only museum head who ignored invitations to attend the task force meetings.[51]

One key group that had been intimately connected with the history of the Wall was not invited to the task force deliberations: former members of the

---

[50] Interview with Rainer Klemke, November 15, 2013.
[51] Interview with Thomas Flierl, November 26, 2009.

Figure 17 Rainer Klemke (second from left) with (left to right) Klaus-Dietmar Henke, Axel Klausmeier, Manfred Fischer; November 9, 2009
Source: Hope M. Harrison.

East German military, secret police, and government who had supported the Wall. Particularly in a Berlin coalition government with the PDS as one of the two ruling parties, anything in the *Gesamtkonzept* process that smacked of being apologetic toward the SED would be and was shot down quickly by criticism from many sides. Thus, even if Klemke or Flierl had any inclination (which they seemingly did not) to involve individuals or groups with more positive views of the East German regime or who wanted to talk about their experience of standing guard at the Wall, these plans would have been quickly torpedoed. In general, former power-holders in the GDR were not involved in the Senate's task force, in spite of the reality, as Rainer Hildebrandt had argued, that it was necessary to have contributions from both former victims and perpetrators for a thorough understanding of the history of the Wall.

 Flierl gave Klemke much leeway in guiding the process of developing the *Gesamtkonzept*, including in deciding how to run the task force and drafting some of the text of the plan. The two made an interesting team, and each felt the other was essential, working synergistically as Fischer and Trotnow had. Flierl knew that he was a lightning rod and that Klemke was not. Even without the baggage of representing the PDS in the government, the position of cultural senator in Berlin has been described by *Die Welt* as "one of the hottest seats in Germany."[52] Similarly, *Die Zeit* has observed that "more than anywhere else culture in Berlin is a symbolic battleground on which other bigger things are fought over. The person in charge of culture in Berlin lives with scars and burns that are difficult to heal."[53] This was certainly the case for Flierl. Indeed, one key group refused to meet with Flierl about the *Gesamtkonzept* but was instead hosted by Mayor Wowereit himself: victims of political persecution in the GDR.[54] After being harshly treated by the GDR authorities, many of them having been imprisoned, they could not accept members of the PDS in the Berlin government and certainly not a PDS cultural minister dealing with the GDR past.

The Working Group on Remembering the Wall included private consultations, public hearings, a bus tour by task force members to view sites connected with the Wall, and a lively public debate with participation from journalists and experts on the Wall, on German history, and on commemoration. Drawing on the meetings and debates, Flierl developed a plan in multiple stages over the next eighteen months. He submitted a draft Berlin Wall Commemorative Plan (*Gedenkkonzept*) to the Berlin parliament on April 18, 2005 at a session with expert commentators.[55] At a discussion on the draft plan in the parliament's committee on cultural affairs in late April, Flierl continued to come under fire for his background and membership in the PDS, with some from the CDU still calling for him to resign.[56] There was much more support for his draft plan than for the senator himself. Thus, one month later, the parliament voted to commission the Senate to proceed with the development of "a *Gesamtkonzept* for the documentation of the Berlin Wall." The parliamentarians mandated that the master plan must lay out a path to accomplish three goals: the long-term preservation of the authentic material remains of the Wall and their increased visibility in the cityscape; the public commemoration of those killed at the Wall in an appropriate and dignified way; and a clear delineation of the finances necessary to accomplish this.[57] The Bundestag's committee on culture and media gave its backing to this mandate in June 2005. Over the following year, the task force continued its work and met with a wide

---

[52] Matthias Heine, "Thomas Flierl taktiert sich ins Aus. Porträt des Berliner Kultursenators (PDS)," *Welt*, December 11, 2013.

[53] Thomas E. Schmidt, "Kulturpolitik: Der neue Berliner Kulturkampf," *Zeit Online*, November 11, 2004.

[54] Interviews with Rainer Klemke, July 19, 2005 and Thomas Flierl, November 26, 2009.

[55] Flierl, "Gedenkkonzept Berliner Mauer. Bestandsaufnahme und Handlungsempfehlungen vorgestellt bei der Veranstaltung der Stiftung zur Aufarbeitung der SED-Diktatur am 18. April 2005 im Abgeordnetenhaus von Berlin" (hereafter, Flierl's *Gedenkkonzept*).

[56] Uwe Lehmann-Brauns, Abgeordnetenhaus von Berlin, Wortprotokoll 15/58, Ausschuss für Kulturelle Angelegenheiten, April 25, 2005, p. 4.

[57] As described in, *Gesamtkonzept*, p. 14.

range of interested parties. In June 2006, Flierl presented the finalized "*Gesamtkonzept* for Remembering the Berlin Wall."

What Should Be the Focus of Narratives about the Wall?

Once the Berlin authorities, led by Flierl and backed by the Bundestag, decided in 2004 to act to make the history of the Wall more visible in Berlin, the subsequent process involved multiple debates: How and where should the Wall be remembered? What description or narrative should be attached to sites connected with the Wall? Were all remains of the Wall of equal importance for commemoration? Should any part of the Wall and former border strip be reconstructed?

Particularly in the wake of Hildebrandt's crosses, the focus for most was on remembering and commemorating the victims of the Wall, especially people who were killed trying to escape from the GDR. But some observers did not feel this was sufficient. Calling for a broader focus on different groups of people involved in and affected by the Berlin Wall, the Federal Commissioner for the Stasi Files, Marianne Birthler, told the Bundestag in June 2005:

> There is no question that Wall commemorations always mean first commemorating the victims. But not only because I'm a Berliner, also because I am an East German, . . .it irritates me sometimes that Wall commemorations are reduced to people killed at the Wall. Of course we should commemorate them. But too often in the debates, it is mentioned too quickly that there were millions of victims of the Wall, a whole people in prison, including infringements on civil society which existed in isolation for 40 years, the personal tragedies, also the families that were ripped apart. The sealing off of a people. We must [also] name those who were politically responsible [for all of this].[58]

Other participants in the debate over the *Gesamtkonzept* on remembering the Wall agreed that attention must also be directed to the perpetrators.

Several experts, including the historians Manfred Wilke and Klaus-Dietmar Henke, called to testify at the Berlin parliament about Flierl's draft plan in April 2005, had been very critical that the plan left out a focus on the SED perpetrators at various levels who were responsible for the deaths of people at the Wall. Due to Flierl's own background, these experts thought it was no coincidence that his draft *Gedenkkonzept* did not specifically blame the SED for the deaths at the Wall.[59] The final *Gesamtkonzept* would take a much

---

[58] Marianne Birthler, statement at hearing, Deutscher Bundestag, Ausschuss für Kultur und Medien, Protokoll 15/60, June 15, 2005, p. 5. Maria Nooke agreed with Birthler on the importance of examining a broader category of victims; interview with Maria Nooke, July 5, 2005.

[59] This was clear in written statements by Manfred Wilke, Klaus-Dietmar Henke, and Thomas Rogalla for the April 18, 2005 Berlin parliament hearing on Flierl's *Gedenkkonzept*, author's collection of documents.

stronger line against the East German leaders, describing in depth "the monstrous border regime where the state had its own citizens shot"[60] to prevent them from "escaping to the West and thus at the same time to secure SED rule in the entire GDR." The *Gesamtkonzept* declared that the Wall "was and remains the symbol of the denial of basic human rights in the GDR, the symbol of political repression and the structural weaknesses of the state socialist system in general."[61] The final master plan followed Birthler's advice on including perpetrators and considering a broader group of victims.

Beyond victims and perpetrators, a third topic that experts believed should be featured at sites connected with the Berlin Wall was the peaceful fall of the Wall in November 1989 and the role of the East German civic opposition movement in bringing this about. There had been discussion of this during the commemoration of the tenth anniversary of the fall of the Wall, particularly in speeches by Chancellor Schröder and Joachim Gauck, but this aspect of history had not been highlighted much further. In November 2004, some politicians and experts expressed their surprise and frustration that there was still no place in Berlin that commemorated and celebrated this "peaceful revolution." As far as they were concerned, any *Gesamtkonzept* on the Wall needed to include information about and celebration of the peaceful toppling of the Wall and the role of the East German civic opposition, as had been supported by some members of the Bundestag in November 2004 in their proposal to create a site of memory (*Ort des Erinnerns*) about the Wall at the Brandenburg Gate.

One of the initiators of the Bundestag motion, Stephan Hilsberg, observed, "People overcame the Wall with their own power. This can and should make one proud."[62] He wanted this history to be visible in Berlin. Similarly, Knabe and Wilke deplored the fact that: "Nowhere in the city do we honor the fantastic peaceful movement for freedom which in autumn 1989 led to the fall of the Wall and the SED dictatorship." They argued that Berlin now had "the chance to show the positive side of GDR history and to honor those who fought for freedom and democracy under great personal risk."[63] Some CDU members of the Bundestag led by Günter Nooke felt the same way and had been lobbying for several years in vain for the creation of a Freedom and Unity Monument to celebrate the events of 1989–90, including the achievements of the East German peaceful revolution, as will be discussed further in Chapter 8.[64] The joy of the fall of the Wall many felt

---

[60] *Gesamtkonzept*, p. 5.

[61] Ibid., p. 4.

[62] Stephan Hilsberg, Deutscher Bundestag, Plenarprotokoll 15/184, June 30, 2005.

[63] Hubertus Knabe and Manfred Wilke, "Die Wunden der Teilung sichtbar machen. Vorschläge für ein Konzept der Erinnerung an die untergegangene SED-Diktatur," *Horch und Guck* 49 (2004), November 23, 2004.

[64] Günter Nooke, statement at hearing, Deutscher Bundestag, Ausschuss für Kultur und Medien, Protokoll 15/60, June 15, 2005, p. 8. See also the first proposal sponsored by Nooke and others in the Bundestag, Antrag, "Errichtung eines Einheits- und

was reflected in Leonard Bernstein's performances of Beethoven's Ninth Symphony in December 1989 had no physical representation in the capital city.

A fourth focus of discussions about a master plan for dealing with the Wall concerned the meaning and lessons of the Wall. As had long been the case with German examination of the Nazi past, so in the case of grappling with the SED past and the Wall, the main goal was to make sure they could never happen again. The Bundestag proposal of November 2004 calling for a site of memory of the Wall at the Brandenburg Gate had made this clear, insisting that the history of the Wall must be made visible so that "history will not be repeated and so that never again will despotism and ideology be placed above human rights and human dignity."[65] Key to not repeating this history was making sure German citizens, especially younger generations, understood it. Policymakers and historians in sessions at the Berlin House of Representatives, the Bundestag, and elsewhere repeatedly argued that the history of the Wall was best seen as a struggle between democracy and tyranny, between freedom and despotism.[66] Comprehending the ways in which the Wall represented the SED's curtailment of the freedom of East German citizens could give German citizens a sense of the importance of freedom and democracy. While much of this was true, it was also the case that deploying this logic avoided discussing the widespread acceptance of the Berlin Wall for so long by many Germans in East and West, whether more actively or passively.

For Bundestag member Thiele (FDP), the struggle for and victory of freedom was at the core of the meaning of the Berlin Wall and was an essential part of German "national identity which must be visible," as he hoped it would be at the Brandenburg Gate.[67] At the Bundestag plenary session of June 30, 2005, which ended with a unanimous vote in favor of working with Berlin on the *Gesamtkonzept* and creating a site of memory of the Wall at the Brandenburg Gate, Stephan Hilsberg (SPD) passionately described the educational task involved in remembering the Wall:

> We can't just forget about [the Wall] as if we have a bad conscience. . . .We must show it all, and not just dryly, correctly in details and with scholarly methods but also emotionally and engagingly. We must give emotional

---

Freiheitsdenkmals auf der Berliner Schlossfreiheit," Deutscher Bundestag, Drucksache 14/3126, April 6, 2000. Nooke and others initiated the idea in May 1998, as p. 5 of the Bundestag motion describes.

[65] Proposal for "Ort des Erinnerns am Brandenburger Tor," November 4, 2004.

[66] See, for example, the statements by the historians Klaus-Dietmar Henke and Manfred Wilke in advance of the April 18, 2005 Berlin parliament's public hearing with Flierl on his *Gedenkkonzept*: Wilke, "Gedenkkonzept Berliner Mauer" and Henke, "Gedenkkonzept Berliner Mauer," author's collection of documents. See also the comments by Marianne Birthler at the hearing, Deutscher Bundestag, Ausschuss für Kultur und Medien, Protokoll 15/60, June 15, 2005; and the remarks of Karl-Ludwig Thiele, Deutscher Bundestag, Plenarprotokoll 15/163, March 10, 2005.

[67] Karl-Ludwig Thiele, Deutscher Bundestag, Plenarprotokoll 15/184, June 30, 2005, p. 17448.

answers – the opposition to dictatorship, the surge for freedom and democracy. We must show the importance of democracy as a guarantor for freedom, independence, self-reliance and emancipation. Democracy solves problems much better than dictatorship.[68]

Alexandra Hildebrandt would surely have agreed with Hilsberg's comments on the emotional aspect of remembering the Wall. On the capacity of the Bundestag to legislate lessons of history, Günter Nooke (CDU) cautioned the Bundestag: "The state has some responsibility for commemoration but it is not the owner of commemoration. History will always be debated among historians and in society."[69] The battles over memory at Bernauer Strasse in the 1990s were a prime example of this.

In the end the *Gesamtkonzept* declared that the history of the Wall showed that, "Over the long run, democracy and human rights cannot be withheld from people."[70] It argued that in the educational work carried out at Bernauer Strasse's Documentation Center, for example, "Fundamental issues of dictatorship and democracy can be presented and discussed...by connecting [them] with concrete life experiences" of individuals there.[71] The meaning of the Wall was found not only in its brutal impact on people's lives as long as it stood but, as the *Gesamtkonzept* pointed out, also with the fall of the Wall, it "became a symbol of a successful movement for democracy and freedom unique in German history."[72] This latter point, however, would not really gain significant traction among politicians and the general public until several years later with the celebration of the twentieth anniversary of the fall of the Wall, as we shall see.

These first four approaches to the history of the Wall were focused on Germany: the victims, the perpetrators, the civic opposition that toppled the Wall in 1989, and the meaning and lessons to be drawn from the history of the Wall. A fifth approach stepped back from this German focus and looked at the Wall in the broader context of European and global history during the Cold War. The historian Konrad Jarausch, Dieter Vorsteher of the DHM, and Bundestag member Markus Meckel (SPD) all argued that a crucial component of the Senate's plan to commemorate the Wall needed to be international. For people who lived through the Cold War, the Wall's "rupture through Berlin expressed the struggle between two worlds"[73] that raged

---

[68] Stephan Hilsberg, Deutscher Bundestag, Plenarprotokoll 15/184, June 30, 2005, p. 17443.

[69] Günter Nooke, ibid., p. 17446.

[70] *Gesamtkonzept*, p. 5.

[71] Ibid., p. 35.

[72] Ibid., p. 5.

[73] ZZF memo, "Die Berliner Mauer – Erinnerung ohne Ort?" March 9, 2005, p. 5. See also Flierl's *Gedenkkonzept*, April 18, 2005, which quotes extensively from the ZZF memo, pp. 16–18.

during the Cold War, the conflict between communism and democracy. They insisted that this broader context was crucial for understanding the rise and fall of the Berlin Wall.

Thus, Jarausch, Vorsteher, and Meckel called for the creation of a new museum depicting the European and global context of the Wall. The location they had in mind for the museum was at Checkpoint Charlie, on the site where Hildebrandt's crosses had been.[74] This would, in their view and that of the Senate, offer a more "professional approach" to history at Checkpoint Charlie than that offered by Hildebrandt. Suggested names for the new museum were "Museum of European Division" or "Cold War Museum." Two draft plans for such a museum were drawn up by Vorsteher and by Jarausch and were included as appendices to the finalized *Gesamtkonzept* in June 2006, which backed the general idea of a museum devoted to the international context of the Wall.[75] Thus, the *Gesamtkonzept* not only responded generally to the challenge laid down by Hildebrandt that the government had not done enough to remember the Wall but also specifically contained a strategy to take over educating the public on the site where her crosses had been.

While most politicians and experts involved in the debate about how to deal with the history of the Berlin Wall favored a combination of these five approaches, another perspective was held by some former members of the East German leadership, army, and border soldiers, as discussed in Chapter 1 with the Wall trials. As we have seen, this group objected to a critical view of the Wall, arguing instead that it was necessary and that they had been fulfilling their duty to protect the GDR by defending and maintaining it.[76] A new line of argument came from former East German leader Hans Modrow in 2004 during the Iraq War: "Each week in Iraq many more people die than died at the Wall."[77] By relativizing the deaths at the Berlin Wall in this way, Modrow meant both to downplay the nature of the regime at the Wall and also to criticize the West. It is important to understand that outside of the mainstream narrative, which was very critical of the Wall as a violation of human rights, a

---

[74] Markus Meckel, Deutscher Bundestag, Plenarprotokoll 15/163, March 10, 2005, p. 15310, and Deutscher Bundestag, Ausschuss für Kultur und Medien, Protokoll 15/60, June 15, 2005, p. 19; Flierl's *Gedenkkonzept*, April 18, 2005, p. 18; and Konrad Jarausch, written statement for hearing, Deutscher Bundestag, Ausschuss für Kultur und Medien, June 15, 2005, Ausschussdrucksache, Nr. 15 (21) 178.

[75] The Vorsteher and Jarausch draft plans for a Cold War Museum were included as appendices, "Skizzen für ein Museum des kalten Krieges," to the *Gesamtkonzept: Anhang, Gesamtkonzept Berliner Mauer – Texte und Materialien*. There were two: Dieter Vorsteher, "Checkpoint Charlie – Museum des kalten Krieges in Europa," pp. 14–17, and Konrad Jarausch, "Die Teilung Europas und ihre Überwindung. Ein neues Museum des kalten Krieges?" pp. 17–20.

[76] See for example the book by Heinz Kessler and Fritz Streletz, *Ohne die Mauer hätte es Krieg gewesen. Zeitzeugen und Dokumente geben Auskunft* (Berlin: Edition Ost, 2011).

[77] Interview with Hans Modrow, March 29, 2004.

view shared by the main officials and experts involved in developing the *Gesamtkonzept* as well as most of the media, there was another perspective lurking in the background.

Reconstructing Parts of the Wall or Not?

Just as there were debates over what to focus on in narrating the history of the Wall, there were also controversies about the aesthetics and the physical approach to remembering the Wall. In particular, there was a tense divide between people who continued the argument that only the reconstruction of a section of the layers of the former border strip at the Berlin Wall could convincingly convey what it had been like, and others who vehemently and often condescendingly responded that this would create a kind of "Disneyland" (the greatest criticism possible in Berlin) instead of an "authentic site" that visitors could take seriously.[78] Proposals by Helmut Trotnow and Rainer Hildebrandt in the 1990s for a reconstruction of the former death strip, supported by some in the Berlin Senate, were repeated by others in the 2000s, during both the formulation and implementation of the *Gesamtkonzept*.

The deep emotions and hostility expressed in this "authenticity vs. Disneyland" debate indicated that something deeper was going on than just a difference in aesthetic approach. Advocates of reconstruction (including members of victims' groups and conservative politicians and newspapers), as we have seen, were suspicious that anything short of reconstruction was an attempt to downplay the brutality of the Wall and the repressive nature of the SED regime. Former victims were particularly eager for a partial reconstruction.[79] Some prominent historians and experts also maintained that the best way to give people a sense of the former Berlin Wall was to reconstruct some of it. Indeed, the first of several recommendations made in the March 2005 memorandum by Jarausch, Sabrow, and Hertle urged the combination of authentic remains with some reconstruction of the former death strip at Bernauer Strasse.[80]

---

[78] Sybille Frank, "Competing for the Best Wall Memorial," in Konrad H. Jarausch, Christian F. Ostermann, Andreas Etges, eds., *The Cold War*, pp. 276–77.

[79] Harald Strunz, UOKG, written statement to the hearing on Flierl's *Gedenkkonzept*, Berlin parliament, April 18, 2005, author's collection of documents; and open letter of May 29, 2006 signed by the leaders of the UOKG, the Vereinigung der Opfer des Stalinismus (VOS), et al., reprinted in Martin Sabrow, Rainer Eckert, Monika Flacke, et al., eds., *Wohin treibt die DDR-Erinnerung? Dokumentation einer Debatte* (Göttingen: Vandenhoeck & Ruprecht, 2007), p. 293.

[80] ZZF memo, "Die Berliner Mauer – Erinnerung ohne Ort?" March 9, 2005. See also Jarausch's observations about this at Abgeordnetenhaus von Berlin, Ausschuss für Kulturelle Angelegenheiten, Wortprotokoll 15/58, April 25, 2005, p. 11.

Arguing against reconstruction and insisting on what Sybille Frank has called an "essentialist concept of authenticity," experts in historic preservation joined by Mayor Wowereit, Senator Flierl, Klemke, and others countered that there was in fact no way to recreate the fear and deadly force behind the Berlin Wall, which had after all included aggressive dogs and armed soldiers with an order to shoot people trying to escape.[81] Moreover, the critics of reconstruction asserted, following the reigning principles of historic preservation, that only authentic remains (ones still standing – not, for example Wall segments that had been removed, were in storage, and could be put back in their original locations) were appropriate to commemorate the Wall.[82] Reconstructions belonged in museums, or "Disneyland" or "Hollywood," not at memorials.[83] The site must be left "as found" to be authentic. Anything else, they argued, would not be convincing as a historic site, including Hildebrandt's crosses.

Behind the debate over reconstruction of the Wall was also a lack of consensus on what the Wall remains or reconstruction should convey to visitors. Those favoring reconstruction generally wanted to focus on a simple, basic narrative: the Wall and the SED regime behind it were evil, violated human rights, and killed people. They wanted a clear, emotional message that would be easily grasped when looking at the layers of obstacles to prevent people from leaving East Germany.[84] Those advocating authenticity, including the founders of the Berlin Wall Memorial, favored a more restrained, as they called it, professional approach – one that did not appeal to "cheap emotions" or look like a Wall "theme park" – that would more dispassionately educate people about the victims, the perpetrators, and the whole context surrounding the Berlin Wall, allowing visitors to come to their own conclusions.

---

[81] Thomas Flierl ("we cannot reconstruct the fear," p. 14) and Michael Braun ("we can't really portray the brutality of the Wall as it was," p. 16), Abgeordnetenhaus von Berlin, Ausschuss für Kulturelle Angelegentheiten, Wortprotokoll 15/58, April 25, 2005.

[82] The Burra Charter, signed in 1979 in Australia by the International Council on Monuments and Sites (ICOMOS) and updated several times since, prioritizes authentic relics of the past that remain *in situ* and advocates as little modification of the original site as found as possible. See also Gabi Dolf-Bonekämper, "Denkmalschutz für die Mauer," *Die Denkmalpflege* 58 (1/2000), pp. 33–40, esp. pp. 35, 37.

[83] Leo Schmidt, Gabriele Camphausen, and Rainer Klemke expressed this view at a meeting with experts on commemorating the Berlin Wall convened by the Berlin Senate's department on science, research and culture, February 2–3, 2005. Monica Geyler-von Bernus and Birgit Kahl of the Berliner Forum für Geschichte und Gegenwart e.V., "Protokoll der Experten-Anhörung," February 11, 2005. Flierl also shared this view on not reconstructing the former death strip, Abgeordnetenhaus von Berlin, Ausschuss für Kulturelle Angelegenheiten, Inhaltsprotokoll Kult 15/79, June 26, 2006, p. 13.

[84] See the comments by Hubertus Knabe at a meeting of the task force hosted by the Berlin State Commissioner for Stasi Records, Martin Gutzeit, "Treffen des Arbeitskreises II (AK II), Ergebnis-Protokoll," March 11, 2005, protocol by Elena Demke, April 15, 2005, p. 4.

Arguing in favor of the latter at a task force meeting in March 2005 was Günter Morsch of the Brandenburg Foundation on Memorials. He noted that similar debates about whether to reconstruct or not had occurred regarding Nazi-era sites. In contrast to those who argued in 2005 that young people could only understand what the Berlin Wall death strip had really been like if as much as possible of it were reconstructed, Morsch maintained the opposite. He reported that in cases where former Nazi sites were reconstructed, young people were alienated by the reconstruction and often saw the reconstruction as laughable. They preferred the challenge of looking for traces of the past instead of being faced with something that seemed artificial and thus did not evoke the emotions experienced by people who had experienced the real thing.[85]

The challenge for the Berlin Wall task force was to develop a solution that would contain elements of both approaches: something authentic that also left an emotional impression of what the Wall was like. A possible solution was offered by Anna Kaminsky, the director of the Federal Foundation for Reappraising the SED Dictatorship. She was not persuaded by what she termed the "purity requirement" touted by historic preservationists. She referred to the popular success of Hildebrandt's crosses with visitors, which she noted were not "based on academically graceful historical or authentic points of view." Rather, she observed:

> People are going where they think they will find and be able to see something that gives them a sense or a picture of the division of the city and the Wall. In this connection, I would request that the museological or historical preservation "purity requirement" that forbids any sort of reconstruction of anything that once disappeared or was demolished be creatively examined and particularly at the large...site at Bernauer Strasse...to consider how the Wall as an edifice in its depth of layers and in its various stages of construction and form can be again made comprehensible and visible.[86]

In the final *Gesamtkonzept*, "authenticity" would triumph over reconstruction but in such a way as to satisfy Kaminsky and others who wanted the history of the Wall to be more "comprehensible and visible."

Which Wall Sites Should Be the Focus of Memory?

In discussions about a *Gesamtkonzept*, a major question was where the focus of memory of the Berlin Wall should be: at the Brandenburg Gate, Checkpoint Charlie, Bernauer Strasse, or elsewhere. As the importance of authenticity

---

[85] Günter Morsch, ibid., pp. 6–7.
[86] Anna Kaminsky, Abgeordnetenhaus von Berlin, Ausschuss für Kulturelle Angelegenheiten, Wortprotokoll 15/58, April 25, 2005, p. 6.

gained support in the task force discussions, a focus on Bernauer Strasse developed quickly among both politicians and experts due to the forward and rear segments of the Berlin Wall that remained there and not at the other sites. Flierl and Klemke were both convinced that Bernauer Strasse should be the key site. A bus tour in February 2005 by members of Klemke's task force to Bernauer Strasse and other sites connected with the Wall helped solidify this growing consensus. Manfred Fischer and Gabriele Camphausen were part of Klemke's task force and also had their own "Bernauer Strasse task force" meeting simultaneously to plan for the future development of the site.[87] The latter would be a key source of information for the former and ultimately for the *Gesamtkonzept*.

By April 2005, when Flierl presented a draft *Gedenkkonzept* and hosted a hearing of the department of cultural affairs with experts on the plan, Bernauer Strasse was already viewed as the primary site in a decentralized plan that would involve other sites as well. As Thomas Rogalla, a journalist for the *Berliner Zeitung* who frequently wrote on grappling with the East German past and the Wall, told Flierl and his colleagues, "It is the greatest deed of this plan that finally, finally, the value of the area at Bernauer Strasse with Wall remains has been re-discovered as an authentic site of memory." He observed that "with all the recent media coverage of Frau Hildebrandt's crosses, the impression has arisen that Checkpoint Charlie was the focus of Wall history. Bernauer Strasse is the much more relevant place. . .[since] the brutality of the erection of the Wall, the severity of the division into two parts is still traceable in the cityscape" there.[88]

Rogalla implored the Senate that it "must act quickly" and secure the land along Bernauer Strasse to ensure that no new construction projects would be allowed in that area of the former border. Otherwise, he said, "While those in mourning are laying a wreath for victims of the Wall (Figure 18), cheerful people drinking beer on a balcony and with a television droning in the background will be looking out of an apartment building that will be built right next to the memorial site." There were also plans for a supermarket, and mourners would see advertisements announcing, "Bargain buys! Special offers! A backyard grill for only 19.99!" Rogalla declared that "it was high time" for the Senate to act and reminded them that, "The story of commemorating the Wall is a story of many missed opportunities."[89] Others joined Rogalla in making this

---

[87] Gabriele Camphausen, final editor, "Konzept zum Ausbau der Gedenklandschaft Bernauer Strasse," September 14, 2005. This drew on Camphausen's December 2004 draft and was presented to the Bernauer Strasse task force in the fall of 2005. Author's collection of documents.

[88] Thomas Rogalla, written statement in advance of Senate hearing on Flierl's *Gedenkkonzept* on April 18, 2005, "Stellungnahme zum 'Gedenkkonzept Berliner Mauer' des Senators für Kultur," p. 2. Author's collection of documents.

[89] Ibid., pp. 1, 3, 4.

Figure 18 German leaders laying wreaths at the Kohlhoff & Kohlhoff Berlin Wall Memorial, August 13, 2011
Source: Photographer: Jürgen Hochmuth. Stiftung Berliner Mauer-2373.

argument, and in September 2005 the Berlin Senate granted Bernauer Strasse historic landmark status, protecting a seven-block area from any sort of construction due to its "extraordinary political significance for the city" and preserving it for use in an expanded Berlin Wall Memorial.[90]

The first guideline laid out in the final 2006 *Gesamtkonzept* for remembering the Berlin Wall was to preserve "authentic relics" to show both the length and the depth of the former border so that people who had never seen it could gain a sense of what it had been like. The *Gesamtkonzept* noted that Bernauer Strasse was the only site that met this criterion.[91] Hence the largest section (eighteen pages), of the sixty-seven-page *Gesamtkonzept* was devoted to a

[90] "Feststellung einer Flache an der Bernauer Strasse im Bezirk Mitte als Gebiet von aussergewöhnlicher stadtpolitischer Bedeutung," Senatsbeschluss Nr. 2947/05, September 27, 2005, SWFKB, KC 2. Senat. Vorlagen. Beschlüsse."
[91] *Gesamtkonzept*, p. 17. Yet, as Sybille Frank and others have pointed out, the remnants of the Wall at Bernauer Strasse are not completely authentic in the "purist," "essentialist" sense. The Wall has been treated with chemicals since 1990 to help preserve it from the effects of weather and time, graffiti has been removed, and a guard tower has been added to the site since the original one had been removed. Thus, Frank has argued that the Berlin authorities modified their original "essentialist concept of authenticity" to one where "authenticity meant being located at an original site." Frank, "Competing for the Best Wall Memorial," p. 277.

detailed description of steps to be taken at Bernauer Strasse to present a much more thorough, convincing, and even emotional way of remembering the Wall. While the master plan adopted a decentralized approach that featured multiple sites, Bernauer Strasse was prioritized as the "central site for commemorating victims of the Berlin Wall" in the capital city and the site where the history of the Wall – its rise and fall – would be explained and made visible by using surviving relics of the border zone in combination with pictures, models, video and audio stations.[92]

The *Gesamtkonzept* insisted that "competing sites of central commemoration must be avoided,"[93] clearly having in mind Hildebrandt's actions at Checkpoint Charlie. It did, however, allow that individuals killed at the Wall should also be commemorated at the location where they were killed and "respected the desire of the Bundestag" to highlight the history of the Wall at the Brandenburg Gate.[94] In another clear response to Hildebrandt and others who maintained that Bernauer Strasse was not sufficiently centrally located to be a major site connected to the Wall, the *Gesamtkonzept* noted that with the expansion of the city's metro system, Bernauer Strasse "would in the future be a 10-minute ride" from the city's main train station, the *Hauptbahnhof.*

With backing from the Senate's *Gesamtkonzept*, the existing one-block site at Bernauer Strasse would expand to encompass seven blocks of an outdoor exhibit on the land where the former border had been. This exhibit would be open twenty-four hours a day, seven days a week, and would be anchored at one end by the train station at North Station (*Nordbahnhof*) and at the other by the Wall Park (*Mauerpark*). It would trace the former path of the Wall over 0.8 miles. This outdoor area would include remains and markings of the layers of the border zone, information about where people were killed or escaped, the location of escape tunnels, foundations of buildings destroyed by East German border troops, the history of the Sophien cemetery and the Lazarus community, and other such detailed, specific information to make the history of the area come alive with the help of photos, videos, and recordings (particularly interviews with people who experienced the Wall at Bernauer Strasse) placed around the site.

As for the narrative that would be presented at the expanded, improved site, the *Gesamtkonzept* observed that the history of Bernauer Strasse before and after the fall of the Wall together with the Documentation Center made it a very appropriate place to show "the responsibility of the SED for the Wall regime and for the style and method of securing the border area," on the one hand, and to demonstrate "the overcoming of the Wall and the regime based on it," on the other. In addition, due to the post-1990 conflicts at Bernauer Strasse about how to treat the Wall, the site "showcased a venue for the

[92] *Gesamtkonzept*, p. 17.
[93] Ibid., pp. 17, 38.
[94] Ibid., p. 17.

pluralistic and often tense appropriation of history in a democratically constituted society."[95]

Special attention both outside in the former death strip and inside at the Documentation Center would be given to individual and collective commemoration of people killed at the Wall in such a way as to "provoke empathy."[96] This would include a photo gallery of these people with their names and biographical information. On the question of how to handle the commemoration of *Grenzer* who were killed "by refugees, refugee helpers or their own 'comrades'," the *Gesamtkonzept* left this to be decided by the leaders of the Documentation Center.[97] In addition, the plan provided for three new things: a visitor's center; an exhibit inside Nordbahnhof on the so-called ghost train stations, which had been closed, as that station had been, while the city was divided by the Wall; and a permanent exhibit in the Documentation Center covering the local, national, and global contexts necessary to understand the Berlin Wall and its history. The entire area would be called the Berlin Wall Memorial Site.

As part of the consensus on the importance of Bernauer Strasse that quickly developed already in December 2004 and January 2005, Bundestag members had pulled back from their proposal that the Brandenburg Gate should be "the central site" for commemorating the Wall. Instead they called for a "site of information" at the Gate and for the "upgrading" of the Documentation Center at Bernauer Strasse.[98] The *Gesamtkonzept* provided for a "site of information" about the Berlin Wall and the Gate to be housed inside the Brandenburg Gate metro station, which was then under construction. The Senate sought to use this important, central location to direct visitors to other places in Berlin connected with the Wall and to give them basic historical information via the use of large historical pictures, maps,

---

[95] Ibid., pp., 18–19.

[96] Ibid., p. 19.

[97] Ibid., p. 4.

[98] See the revised Bundestag proposal, "Gelände um das Brandenburger Tor als Ort des Erinnerns an die Berliner Mauer, des Gedenkens an ihre Opfer und der Freude über die Überwindung der deutschen Teilung," Deutscher Bundestag, Drucksache 15/4795, January 28, 2005; and the final motion, Beschlussempfehlung und Bericht des Ausschusses für Kultur und Medien (21. Ausschuss), Deutscher Bundestag, Drucksache 15/5854, June 29, 2005, which was unanimously passed by the Bundestag on June 30, 2005 (Plenarprotokoll 15/184, p. 17448). The initial proposal for an artistic monument at the Gate for the dual purpose of commemorating the victims of the Wall and celebrating the fall of the Wall was never realized. Bundestag members decided that it was too complicated to do both of these things, and they decided to separate the two. Victims of the Wall would be commemorated at Bernauer Strasse, and the joy of the fall of the Wall would be expressed through an artistic Freedom and Unity Monument which will be discussed in Chapter 8.

multimedia installations, and computer terminals. The site opened in August 2009.

The most specific impetus for the *Gesamtkonzept* had been Hildebrandt's crosses at Checkpoint Charlie, and the Berlin Senate was eager to make, as it said, "more appropriate"[99] use of this central, historic site and also to put a stop to the "latent competition with the Documentation Center at Bernauer Strasse."[100] While the plan noted that Hildebrandt's crosses, combined with "tourists and tourist agencies" had revealed "the deficits in memory policy" in Berlin,[101] it also argued that her memorial "could not remain permanently."[102] When the owner of the property where Hildebrandt's crosses had been installed declared bankruptcy, the Senate hoped that the next buyer (a group of Irish investors) would be willing to cooperate by providing space to house an exhibit related to the history of the site. In the meantime, the *Gesamtkonzept* supported an interim solution on the empty land, agreed upon by the investors.

This interim solution, which opened in August 2006, consisted of a block-long fence of billboards at street level, called Checkpoint Gallery. It described the history of Checkpoint Charlie and the Berlin Wall and directed visitors to other sites in Berlin connected with the Berlin Wall, East Germany, and the Cold War. The longer-term vision of the *Gesamtkonzept*, however, was to create a Cold War museum there. The major museums, memorials, and universities in Berlin dealing with the Cold War, together with the Cold War International History Project based in Washington, DC and a group of experts on the history of the Cold War, agreed to collaborate in the planning.[103]

In addition to the core sites at Bernauer Strasse, the Brandenburg Gate, and Checkpoint Charlie, the *Gesamtkonzept* supported the preservation of a multiplicity of other sites. Some of these contained remnants of the Wall: Niederkirchnerstrasse; Potsdamer Platz; the East Side Gallery; the artist Ben Wagin's "Parliament of Trees," which used parts of the former border combined with art to create a memorial to victims of the Wall; and the Bundestag Library, which incorporated parts of the Wall located at the site. Others featured parts of the broader former border area, such as Checkpoint Bravo at Dreilinden-Drewitz, which had been the southwestern entrance to

---

[99] *Gesamtkonzept*, pp. 8, 41.
[100] Ibid., p. 8.
[101] Ibid., p. 12.
[102] Ibid.
[103] Struggles between investors and the Berlin Senate, financial problems of investors, and public disputes about the future of Checkpoint Charlie have kept the process stalled beyond the opening of a one-room, provisional exhibit, "BlackBox Cold War," at the site.

West Berlin from the transit routes across the GDR from the FRG, and guard towers at Kiele Eck and Schlesische Busch. Another key site featured in the *Gesamtkonzept* was the *Tränenpalast* (Palace of Tears) at the central Friedrichstrasse train station where East and West Berliners and Germans had waited under the harsh eyes of the border police to cross the border or to meet or bid farewell to their visiting friends or relatives. Small memorials that had been erected for people killed at the Wall were also included. Given that the Wall had snaked its way over twenty-seven miles through the inner city of Berlin and a further seventy miles around the outskirts of what had been West Berlin, it made sense to highlight as many places along that path as possible.

The *Gesamtkonzept* also incorporated three existing methods of marking the course of the former border. Since 1996, the Berlin Wall History Mile featured a series of large panels on the street at key historic locations with descriptions in German, English, French, and Russian of major events related to the Wall that took place at those locations. Second, at some former locations of the Wall, there was a double row of cobblestones laid in the street marking the outer part of the Berlin Wall, the so-called forward wall that stood on the border to West Berlin. At intervals along the double row of cobblestones, inlaid cast iron plates read "*Berliner Mauer, 1961–1989.*" Finally, the Berlin Wall trail (*Mauerweg*), which had been established in 2001 as a walking and biking path along the former border strip, was also included in the *Gesamtkonzept*.

Approval of the *Gesamtkonzept*

Although initially upstaged by a private individual, namely Alexandra Hildebrandt, German public officials ultimately seized hold of the commemoration of the Wall and of the narrative to be told about the history of the Wall with the *Gesamtkonzept*. Learning from the reaction to Hildebrandt's crosses and from Marianne Birthler's plea to commemorate not just the people who were killed trying to escape, the cover page of the *Gesamtkonzept* noted that it was

> dedicated to all of those who against their wishes were prevented from going from one district of Berlin to another, from Germany to Germany, from a dictatorial system to the democratically constituted part of their nation, who lost their health or their life [trying to cross the border], who because of their failed or compromised attempt to do this ended up being robbed of their human rights in the central Stasi prison at Hohenschönhausen or other prisons, to those whose life plans and futures were destroyed because of the division of Berlin, Germany and the world.[104]

---

[104] *Gesamtkonzept*, p. 1.

As a form of recompense for the suffering endured by these groups of victims, the *Gesamtkonzept* pledged to highlight the history of that suffering and make it visible for future generations. Furthermore, the plan asserted that "without the Wall, the GDR could not have existed," as several of the GDR's top leaders had declared in the Wall trials.[105] The *Gesamtkonzept* declared that confronting the history of the Berlin Wall was a necessary step toward "coming to terms with the consequences of the SED dictatorship and constructing internal German unity,"[106] language that was reminiscent of the preamble to the SPD-PDS coalition treaty of 2002.[107]

On June 12, 2006, Flierl presented the plan to Berlin's House of Representatives and on June 20, the Senate met at the Berlin Wall Memorial's Documentation Center to back the *Gesamtkonzept*, with Fischer and Camphausen happily in attendance. A television report from June 20 shows Fischer, Wowereit, and Flierl on the observation platform on top of the building looking over at the former death strip and discussing plans for the future of the site.[108] Parliamentary approval for the master plan followed.

The final *Gesamtkonzept* described the history of the Wall and efforts to remember it and its victims since 1989, inventoried all remains of the Berlin Wall border strip and memorial sites, laid out a series of guidelines for future steps, focused on the development of key sites, outlined ways to highlight and connect all sites related to the Wall, and provided a budget. The deadline for the implementation of the master plan was set for the fiftieth anniversary of the building of the Wall in 2011, although full implementation would extend to 2014 and in some small ways even beyond. With the passage of the *Gesamtkonzept* and after enduring much criticism of his role in the process, Flierl would feel "doubly confirmed" as the senator responsible for the master plan when the CDU opposition in the Berlin parliament praised the plan as "smart and correct" and the Bundestag also gave it broad support.[109]

The Berlin Senate estimated that the implementation of the plan over the subsequent six years would cost forty million euros. In outlining the budget for the following five years, the Senate "assume[d] that the federal government will participate in paying at least half of the costs for implementing [this] plan, since the documentation and the remembrance of the Berlin Wall as well as the commemoration of the victims are national obligations." The office of the federal commissioner on culture had been involved throughout the planning process,

---

[105] Ibid., p. 5.

[106] Ibid., p. 3.

[107] SPD-PDS Koalitionsvereinbarung, January 16, 2002.

[108] rbb, *Abendschau*, June 20, 2006. This footage is visible in the 2014 permanent exhibit, *The Berlin Wall*, in the Documentation Center at the Berlin Wall Memorial.

[109] Flierl, "Kultur Jetzt! Eine Bilanz der Kulturpolitik 2002 bis 2006," in Tischler and Müller, eds., *Berlin: Perspektiven durch Kultur*, pp. 247–48. This section of the text was written for Flierl's election campaign for the September 2006 elections to the Berlin parliament.

both before and after the elections of 2005, which brought Angela Merkel to power as Gerhard Schröder's successor. The Senate particularly expected federal help in buying property and expanding the Berlin Wall Memorial at Bernauer Strasse as well as developing the sites at the Brandenburg Gate and Checkpoint Charlie. Cooperation between the Berlin authorities and the federal government would be essential for implementing the *Gesamtkonzept*.

With a detailed blueprint for preserving and explaining the Wall and its history, the *Gesamtkonzept* set out to remedy the prevailing situation in which "the existing Wall sites and commemoration sites are not grouped together, and there are no directions to the museum establishments in which one can learn about the origins and effects of the Wall in an appropriate way."[110] Accordingly, officials would create more explanatory plaques and information boards at Wall sites (in German and English) and directions to the sites would be much more prominent on the street, on maps, in brochures, via the internet, audioguides with handheld GPS systems, smartphone apps on the Wall for use at Bernauer Strasse and elsewhere, multimedia cell phone messaging, a special "Wall ticket" for use on public transportation, and via tourist agencies with multiple Wall tours (by foot, boat, bicycle, bus, and Segway) on offer. The Berlin Senate developed a "communication plan" to use all media possible to get out the word about sites connected with the history of the Berlin Wall, including a uniform logo and a website: www.berlin.de/mauer. The website started in German and later expanded to English, French, Spanish, Italian, and Russian.

The *Gesamtkonzept* institutionalized and expanded existing historical sites and commemorative rituals connected with the Wall, especially on the anniversaries of its rise and fall as we shall see, and added some new ones. The wide-ranging public discussion about remembering the Wall surrounding the formulation of the *Gesamtkonzept* had a multiplier effect on Wall-related activities and even the establishment of other Wall-related sites. Support for the *Gesamtkonzept* has also meant that political leaders have devoted much more attention to the Wall and its history in their speeches and activities. The media has similarly maintained a steady focus on the Wall.

While the implementation of the *Gesamtkonzept* has made it much easier to find remnants of the Wall and to learn about the history of the Wall, there is still no consensus on the place of it and the SED regime in German history, as was clear in the Wall trials and as will be discussed in subsequent chapters.[111] Groups of former East German military, Stasi, and party officials still gather regularly, sometimes in their uniforms, to remember the "good

---

[110] *Gesamtkonzept*, p. 12.

[111] Thomas Grossbölting, "Die DDR im vereinten Deutschland," *Aus Politik und Zeitgeschichte* 25–26 (2010); Grossbölting, "Geschichtskonstruktion zwischen Wissenschaft und Populärkultur," *Aus Politik und Zeitgeschichte*, October 8, 2013; and Klaus Christoph, "'Aufarbeitung der SED-Diktatur' – heute so wie gestern?" *Aus Politik und Zeitgeschichte*, October 8, 2013.

old days."[112] Their views are not the dominant ones in the public sphere and their numbers are declining with each passing year, but they represent a sometimes vocal minority. Some Germans wonder whether divided opinion on the post-World War II history of Germany will remain as long as it has in the United States with regard to the Civil War.[113] Partly because a small minority of former East Germans continue to defend the Berlin Wall and the East German regime, the majority of the political and cultural elite of united Germany believe that it is all the more important that young Germans and foreign tourists who visit Berlin have ample opportunity to learn about the Wall and its victims. The *Gesamtkonzept* makes this possible.

In recognition of the importance of the Berlin Wall Memorial Site and of Manfred Fischer's role in developing it, the year after the adoption of the *Gesamtkonzept* Mayor Wowereit awarded him Berlin's Order of Merit in 2007. Gabriele Camphausen would receive the award two years later. Presumably Alexandra Hildebrandt was not considered for this honor, since her motives and methods seemed to many people to be less about the public good of providing reliable information on the history of the Berlin Wall than was the case at the Berlin Wall Memorial. Yet with their *Gesamtkonzept*, Flierl and Klemke built not only on the work of Fischer, Camphausen and others, but also of Hildebrandt. The *Gesamtkonzept* brought public commemoration of the history of the Wall to the next level by institutionalizing it within the Berlin government. The process of doing this in the federal government would take longer, however, and involve even more fundamental conflicts than had been the case in the Berlin government.

---

[112] Rainer Erices and Jan Schönfelder, "Auftritt vor DDR-Altkadern," Mitteldeutscher Rundfunk, July 30, 2013; and "DDR-Gespenster: Stasi-Offiziere wollen wieder marschieren," *B.Z.*, December 10, 2013. For information on one such group, the Joint Initiative to Protect the Social Rights of Former Members of the GDR Armed Forces and Customs Administration (ISOR), see www.isor-sozialverein.de/.

[113] Former Bundestag member (SPD) Hans-Ulrich Klose, for example, has made reference to this. Conversation with author, August 1, 2011.

6

The Federal Government and Memory of the
Berlin Wall

While the Berlin government was taking major steps in the mid-2000s to remember the Wall and commemorate its victims with the *Gesamtkonzept*, several memory wars played out in the process of institutionalizing federal policy regarding the Berlin Wall. Most fundamental among them was the divisive debate over calibrating the balance between memories of the Nazi and communist regimes in German "democratic memory culture." Although two Bundestag commissions of inquiry in the 1990s on the SED regime and a federal plan passed in 1999 for funding memorials had called for more attention to the communist period, including at memorial sites to victims of the regime such as at Bernauer Strasse, this had not occurred as of the fall of 2004 with the unveiling of Hildebrandt's crosses. Other ongoing disputes at the federal level concerned the respective roles of the federal vs. state governments and the place of public officials vs. private individuals (including historians) in memory policy.

A Federal Balancing Act between Nazi and Communist History and Commemoration

Obtaining significant federal support for projects and memorials concerned with the East German past and the Berlin Wall continued to be an uphill battle while the Nazi past remained the clear priority of the government. The Bundestag's commissions of inquiry on the "SED dictatorship" in the 1990s brought the government deeply into debates concerned with the Nazi and communists pasts, arguing that doing so was an essential part of "democratic memory culture." Yet serious disagreements developed and were never quite resolved about how much to focus on Nazi vs. East German communist history, in spite of the commitment in the final report to examining both and commemorating the victims of both in a non-hierarchical way. The final report in 1998 tried to at least cover over differences by agreeing on language to use when discussing the Nazi and communist regimes: "The Nazi crimes should not be relativized when confronting the crimes of Stalinism. The Stalinist crimes should not be downplayed by references to Nazi crimes."[1] The supposed consensus on facing up to both, however, turned out to be illusory. In spite of commission chair Rainer Eppelmann's insistence that it was important to "avoid a hierarchy of victims' groups" between those who suffered at the hands of the Nazis and communists,[2] many people, particularly among West Germans, felt that attention to GDR victims and crimes effectively downplayed the Holocaust, the last thing public officials wanted in the new "Berlin Republic."

This became clear over the next decade as Bundestag members and many others became engulfed in impassioned debates about the relative importance of the Nazi and communist pasts. These emotional discussions were also taking place in the "bloodlands" across Eastern and Central Europe and in Eurasia in the wake of the end of the Cold War and the downfall of communist regimes, as new regimes sought to establish themselves and place themselves in a national historical context. Many believed the communists were just as guilty as the Nazis had been and generally saw their own nations as victims of these regimes and their occupying forces, not as collaborators, to say nothing of key Nazi or communist actors. New institutions were formed to tell the story of victims of communism and bodies were ceremoniously reburied to give them the respect they had not received from the communists, even as economic difficulties in the transition from planned to capitalist economies made some nostalgic for aspects of the old regimes.[3] While Western Europeans had focused their memory policies on Holocaust crimes, countries behind the former Iron Curtain were now focused on the crimes of communism and were increasingly concentrating their memory policies on these and even enacting laws on historical memory, starting with Poland's 1998 law criminalizing the denial of Nazi *and* communist crimes.[4] Concerns with communist

---

[1] Deutscher Bundestag, ed., "Schlußbericht," in *Materialien der Enquete-Kommission "Überwindung der Folgen der SED-Diktatur im Prozeß der deutschen Einheit," Band 1* (Baden-Baden: Nomos Verlag, 1999), p. 614.

[2] Ibid., p. 617.

[3] Nikolay Koposov, *Memory Laws, Memory Wars: The Politics of the Past in Europe and Russia* (New York: Cambridge University Press, 2018); Katherine Verdery, *The Political Lives of Dead Bodies: Reburial and Postsocialist Change* (New York: Columbia University Press, 1999); Svetlana Boym, *The Future of Nostalgia* (New York: Perseus, 2001); and Tina Rosenberg, *The Haunted Land: Facing Europe's Ghosts after Communism* (New York: Vintage Books, 1995). The "bloodlands" reference comes from Timothy Snyder, *Bloodlands: Europe between Hitler and Stalin* (New York: Basic Books, 2010).

[4] Nikolay Koposov, *Memory Laws, Memory Wars*, pp. 160–61. In Germany, there is still no central memorial to all of the victims of the East German regime. Victims and their supporters have long called for such a memorial, particularly since the 2005 dedication of the Holocaust Memorial. In 2012, the Union of Victims' Associations of Communist Tyranny (UOKG) formally launched a petition for "a monument to commemorate all the victims of communist tyranny" at a "central location in Berlin," noting that such memorials had long ago been unveiled in other countries of the former Soviet bloc. UOKG, "Aufruf zur Errichtung eines Mahnmals zum Gedenken an die Opfer der

crimes reached the broader European level in the 2000s when the Parliamentary Assembly of the Council of Europe condemned "the crimes of totalitarian communist regimes" with their "massive human rights violations" in 2006.[5] Three years later the European Parliament declared August 23 the "European Day of Remembrance for Victims of Stalinism and Nazism," noting that while the Holocaust was unique, the countries of Central and Eastern Europe suffered under both Nazism and communism "and from the perspective of the victims it is immaterial which regime deprived them of their liberty or tortured or murdered them for whatever reason."[6]

Germany itself occupied a fault line in debates over memory policy, or *Erinnerungspolitik*, with the West German focus on Holocaust memory being challenged by a new East German focus on communist memory. Since Germany had been home to Hitler's Nazi regime, it was much more complicated for Germans than their neighbors to the east to engage in a comparison of Nazi and communist crimes or victims, since this invited charges that the Germans sought to downplay their role as Nazi perpetrators. Yet victims of the former East German regime, including people who had been wounded while trying to escape across the Berlin Wall, demanded that they be heard and that their experiences be commemorated.

A key point of contention in German *Erinnerungspolitik* in the 2000s centered on how to calibrate official support for communist-era sites as compared to Nazi-era sites. Monuments and memorials became a central battleground in the German memory wars.[7] The memorial sites at issue were primarily in locations

---

kommunistischen Gewaltherrschaft." UOKG activism led to Bundestag support for the idea on the twenty-fifth anniversary of German unification in 2015, although the government has not provided funding for such a memorial. AFP, "Bundestag will Mahnmal für Opfer des Kommunismus," October 2, 2015. On the efforts to the UOKG to achieve this, see Sven Felix Kellerhoff, "Opfer des SED-Regimes fordern endlich ein Mahnmal," *Die Welt*, October 1, 2015.

[5] Parliamentary Assembly, Council of Europe, "Need for international condemnation of crimes of totalitarian communist regimes," Resolution 1481, January 25, 2006.

[6] European Parliament resolution on European conscience and totalitarianism, April 2, 2009. For works examining the question of a common European memory culture vs. separate national memory cultures, see Malgorzata Pakier and Bo Strath, eds., *A European Memory? Contested Histories and Policies of Remembrance* (New York: Berghahn Books, 2010); and Etienne François, Kornelia Kończal, Robert Traba, and Stefan Troebst, *Geschichtspolitik in Europa seit 1989: Deutschland, Frankreich und Polen im internationalen Vergleich* (Göttingen: Wallstein Verlag, 2013). See also the EU-backed museum in Brussels, the House of European History, which opened in 2017 and endeavors to "explore how history has shaped a sense of European memory," historia-europa.ep.eu/en/permanent-exhibition.

[7] The main political parties brought motions in spring 1999 to urge the government to act as soon as possible on the recommendations of the Bundestag commission of inquiry on "Overcoming the Effects of the SED Dictatorship in the Process of German Unity." The CDU/CSU emphasized the necessity of supporting memorials to both German dictatorships and their victims, and the SPD with Bündnis 90/Die Grüne emphasized the

where crimes against victims were perpetrated, such as concentration camps, prisons, or the Berlin Wall death strip, but also included symbolic, artistic memorials erected in central locations, as was the case with the Holocaust Memorial.

When Chancellor Kohl's CDU lost to Gerhard Schröder's SPD in elections in the fall of 1998, it was up to the new government to respond to the Bundestag's call for guidelines on federal support for national memorial sites. Schröder's government did this in July 1999 with a "*Konzept* for Future Federal Support for Memorial Sites."[8] This *Konzept* reiterated the long-standing policy that the establishment and support of memorial sites was primarily a matter for the German states but it also now provided for some federal funding of authentic sites with national and/or international significance. The *Konzept* pledged to double federal funding over the following four years from DM10 million to DM20 million and expanded the number of sites it would support with "double-burdened" Nazi and communist pasts. The *Konzept* also mandated that the states had to contribute "an appropriate amount" of the costs of the memorials in their jurisdiction. A committee of experts would advise the government about which funding applications to support. Memorials located in Berlin would be eligible for further funding from special monies devoted to Capital Cultural Funds, some of which as we have seen had gone to the Documentation Center at Bernauer Strasse.

Although when the Christian Democrats had been in power at the national and Berlin levels in the 1990s, they had not expanded support for communist-era sites, now that they were in opposition they declared that the *Konzept* placed insufficient emphasis on the communist past in comparison to the Nazi past, especially compared to what the final report of the Bundestag's second commission of inquiry on the SED had recommended in 1998. As rapporteur of the CDU/CSU parliamentary group on memory culture, Günter Nooke, the husband of Maria Nooke at the Berlin Wall Memorial, led the way in 2000 with a motion calling on the federal government and the city of Berlin to formulate "A Comprehensive *Konzeption* for Memorial Sites in Berlin for Victims of the SED Dictatorship" by May 2001.[9] Like his colleagues throughout Central and

---

importance of supporting and strengthening "democratic memory culture" in Germany. See Antrag Fraktion der CDU/CSU, "Beteiligung des Bundes an Gedenkstätten und Mahmalen zur Erinnerung an die beiden deutschen Diktaturen und ihre Opfer," Deutscher Bundestag, Drucksache 14/656, March 23, 1999; and Antrag der Fraktion Bündnis 90/Die Grüne "Konzeption zur Förderung und Festigung der demokratischen Erinnerungskultur," Deutscher Bundestag, Drucksache 14/796, April 20, 1999.

8 Unterrichtung durch die Bundesregierung, "Konzeption der künftigen Gedenkstättenförderung des Bundes und Bericht der Bundesregierung über die Beteiligung des Bundes an Gedenkstätten in der Bundesrepublik Deutschland," Deutscher Bundestag, Drucksache 14/1569, July 27, 1999.

9 Antrag der Abgeordneten Günter Nooke, Dr. Norbert Lammert, Ulrich Adam, et. al., "Gesamtkonzeption für Berliner Gedenkstätten für die Opfer der SED-Diktatur notwendig," Deutscher Bundestag, Drucksache 14/4641, November 14, 2000.

Eastern Europe who had opposed communist regimes, Günter Nooke wanted more attention to both the victims and the perpetrators of communism.

Nooke was deeply personally committed to shining a spotlight on the transgressions of the SED regime and remembering its victims. Together with his wife, Nooke had been a civic activist connected with the Protestant Church. He grew up in a small town ninety minutes southeast of Berlin on the Polish border and remembered being awoken in the early morning hours in August 1968 as a column of Soviet tanks rumbled by the house on their way south to Czechoslovakia to crush the Prague Spring. His critical view of the SED regime deepened as a result of his service in the army in the late 1970s where he experienced "the worst side of the SED system."[10] After studying physics at the University of Leipzig while Maria worked with children in church groups in the region, the two returned to the area where they had grown up and became increasingly engaged in church-sponsored opposition groups for peace and environmental security in the GDR.

When their third child was born in 1988, Nooke felt he had reached a turning point in his life. He did not want his children to endure thirty years of communism as he would have in 1989. He also felt that one day he and Maria would have to justify to their children their decision to stay in the GDR instead of trying to leave. There would be only two options for what they could tell their children: they did not realize how bad things were in the GDR or they did realize and endeavored to change things. He and Maria opted for the latter. Hence, they co-founded their church's opposition newspaper "Awakening" (*Aufbruch*) in 1988 and participated in the Protestant Church's nationwide Ecumenical Assembly for Justice, Peace, and the Preservation of Creation in 1988–89. Many future leaders of the opposition movement first met at this assembly. In early October 1989, Nooke was one of the co-founders of a new political movement, Democratic Awakening (*Demokratische Aufbruch*), which soon became a political party.

The Nookes knew their opposition activities were risky. They could end up imprisoned and their children taken by the state and placed in an orphanage. Hence, in September 1989, Günter and Maria had their church pastor sign and stamp their statement declaring that in the event of their imprisonment, their children would be cared for by their grandparents. A few weeks later, on October 9, they were deeply relieved when they heard that the mass demonstration in Leipzig had not been shut down by security forces. The Nookes were emboldened by this as were hundreds of thousands of others in the GDR and they began to help organize Monday evening demonstrations in their

---

[10] Günter Nooke, "Wir trauten uns nicht, die auf der Strasse liegende Macht aufzuheben," in Eckhard Jesse, ed., *Eine Revolution und ihre Folgen: 15 Bürgerrechtler ziehen Bilanz* (Berlin: LinksDruck GmbH, 2001), p. 95.

town.[11] On November 4, Günter Nooke joined the crowd of 500,000 people at Berlin's Alexanderplatz with tears in his eyes. After the fall of the Wall, he went on to become one of the participants in the church-moderated Central Round Table talks between the government and opposition, and in the March 1990 elections, he was elected to the last East German parliament.[12]

Several years after unification, Nooke joined the CDU and was elected to the Bundestag in 1998. He was particularly engaged in *Erinnerungspolitik* related to the GDR and was among those who first argued that Germans should remember the victims of the communist regime and not just the Nazi regime. Privately he felt that "the East Germans had paid the price for the Holocaust,"[13] since with the occupation and division of Germany after the defeat of the Nazi regime, East Germans suffered far more than the West Germans did. The May 2001 CDU/CSU motion he put forward argued that the three main sites in Berlin associated with the crimes of the East German regime – the Berlin Wall Memorial, the former Stasi prison at Hohenschönhausen, and the former Stasi headquarters at Normannenstrasse – required funding both for urgently needed basic maintenance work and more long-term support.

In the Bundestag's plenary debate on the motion in January 2001, Nooke argued aggressively, probably too aggressively, for equal treatment of the Nazi and communist crimes and victims. He emphasized that the federal government's support for sites connected to the communist past was "peanuts" compared to its support for Nazi-related memorials. Even more offensive to Nazi victims and their supporters, Nooke was critical that Chancellor Schröder and Bundestag President Thierse had laid wreaths at Berlin's main synagogue on Oranienburger Strasse on November 9, 2000 in honor of the Nazi victims of *Kristallnacht* but did nothing to mark the anniversary of the fall of the Berlin Wall on the same day. Nooke had written to the federal government on the most recent anniversary of the erection of the Wall (August 13, 2000), to ask whether they planned to commemorate victims of the Wall and was dismayed to learn that nothing was planned. He used the plenary debate in January 2001 and the presence of the federal minister for culture to issue a reminder that the fortieth anniversary of the erection of the Wall was approaching in August and that it would be a good time for the federal government to show "national engagement" and "live up to its responsibility."[14] His wife, as we have seen, was

---

[11] Radio interview with Maria Nooke, "Stasi ließ Mauertote verscharren," *NWZ (Nordwest Zeitung) Online*, November 7, 2011.

[12] Günter Nooke, "Wir trauten uns nicht, die auf der Strasse liegende Macht aufzuheben," pp. 93–107; and www.bundesstiftung-aufarbeitung.de/wer-war-wer-in-der-ddr-%2363% 3B-1424.html?ID=2530.

[13] Interview with Günter Nooke, November 25, 2004.

[14] Günter Nooke's comments, Deutscher Bundestag, Plenarprotokoll 14/143, January 18, 2001, p. 14059.

also calling on government officials to attend the commemoration at Bernauer Strasse,[15] and indeed Chancellor Schröder and Mayor Wowereit attended the fortieth anniversary commemorations at Bernauer Strasse where they came under much criticism from victims of the former East German regime.

The Bundestag rejected the CDU/CSU motion, arguing that the federal government was in fact involved in supporting the three Berlin sites Nooke mentioned, albeit not as extensively as the motion called for.[16] The ruling SPD was also critical that the motion "tries to play off victims of each dictatorship against each other." Nooke countered that opposition to his motion was based on a sense of "first and second class victims," with the communist victims clearly meant to be second class: "I think it is. . .inappropriate that on the one hand sites of commemoration of the national socialist dictatorship are financially and bureaucratically well supported – which I want to expressively welcome – but we have very little left for victims of the SED regime. We don't want to give the impression that the memorial sites for the second dictatorship are not as important to us."[17] Yet that was clearly what the majority of Bundestag members believed was justified.

Two years later, having learned from this loss, Nooke and his colleagues tried again, but with a different approach. On November 4, 2003, they changed the proposal from one that focused solely on a plan for communist-related sites to one that called for "Support for Memorial Sites on the History of Dictatorship in Germany – A Comprehensive *Konzept* for a Worthy Commemoration of All Victims of Both German Dictatorships."[18] Omitting memorials on the Nazi past from the first motion had not worked, so they were included in a second motion. This motion encompassed four categories of sites to be part of a "Memorial Concept": sites related to the Nazi past; a double Nazi and communist past (in many cases the Soviet occupiers and then East German rulers used Nazi prisons and camps for their own purposes); East German repression and resistance (including Hohenschönhausen and

---

[15] Interviews with Maria Nooke, July 5, 2005 and April 15, 2010.

[16] Beschlussempfehlung und Bericht des Ausschusses für Kultur und Medien (23. Ausschuss) zu dem Antrag der Abgeordneten Günter Nooke, Dr. Norbert Lammert, Ulrich Adam, weiterer Abgeordneter und der Fraktion der CDU/CSU (Drucksache 14/ 4641), Deutscher Bundestag, Drucksache 14/7014, October 2, 2001; and Deutscher Bundestag, Plenarprotokoll 14/242, June 13, 2002, p. 24344.

[17] Angelika Krüger-Leißner (SPD), speech inserted into the protocol of the plenary session, Anlage 19, "Zu Protokoll gegebene Reden," ibid., p. 24385; and Günter Nooke, ibid., p. 24387–24388.

[18] Antrag der Abgeordneten Günter Nooke, Bernd Neumann (Bremen), Renate Blank, et al of the CDU/CSU, "Förderung von Gedenkstätten zur Diktaturgeschichte in Deutschland – Gesamtkonzept für ein würdiges Gedenken aller Opfer der beiden deutschen Diktaturen," Deutscher Bundestag, Drucksache 15/1874, November 4, 2003.

Normannenstrasse from the previous motion); and the division of Germany (including the Berlin Wall Memorial from the previous motion). But the CDU/CSU committed another faux pas with this motion.

The new motion referred to the recently passed "Law on Creating the Foundation for Memorial Sites in Saxony Remembering Victims of Political Tyranny" as a model to be emulated.[19] This foundation had existed in the state of Saxony since 1994, but a new law went into effect in April 2003 to guide the foundation, and it had been controversial even before the CDU/CSU Bundestag motion of November drew more attention to it.[20] The foundation encompassed five memorial sites connected to Nazi and communist crimes and to opposition against those regimes, uniting large groups of victims together in one body in a way that particularly worried and angered the victims of the Nazi period.

The advisory board of the foundation included representatives from two pre-1945 and two post-1945 groups of victims. The groups representing Nazi victims (especially those who were Jewish, but also others) tried to work from within the foundation to make sure that the importance and singularity of the Nazi crimes were not diminished. Yet when Nooke's new motion identified the law on memorials in the state of Saxony as a useful model, this was the final straw and these groups resigned from the foundation, with the Central Council of Jews in Germany leading the way. The Council argued that "Nazi crimes were being analogized and relativized in comparison to the crimes of Stalinism and the GDR's secret police" and that forcing all the victims' groups to work together risked equalizing the fundamental difference between the crimes of the Nazis...and the arbitrary rule of communism in East Germany."[21]

The Central Council of Jews in Germany was joined by the Central Council of German Sinti and Roma, the Federal Association of Victims of Military Justice, and the Association of those Persecuted by the Nazi Regime in leaving the memorial foundation in Saxony. Volkhard Knigge, speaker of the Consortium of Concentration Camp Memorial Sites in Germany and director of the Buchenwald Memorial, declared that the "warnings of the Central Council of Jews in Germany of a paradigm change in Erinnerungspolitik were justified." To them, increased attention given to the communist past

---

[19] Ibid., p. 1.
[20] Gesetz zur Errichtung der Stiftung Sächsische Gedenkstätten zur Erinnerung an die Opfer politischer Gewaltherrschaft (Sächsisches Gedenkstättenstiftungsgesetz – SächsGedenkStG), April 22, 2003, in Sächsisches Gesetz- und Verordnungsblatt, Nr. 6, May 14, 2003, pp. 107–9.
[21] Zentralrat der Juden in Deutschland, "Zentralrat legt Mitarbeit in der 'Stiftung Sächsische Gedenkstätten' nieder," January, 21 2004; and "Zentralrat der Juden verlässt Sachsen-Stiftung," Sächsische Zeitung, January 22, 2004.

meant a turning away from the importance of the Nazi past. Knigge criticized the CDU/CSU motion for "party-political instrumentalization of memory" and feared that "the equation of both dictatorships downplays and relativizes Nazi crimes and opens the door to false comparisons, competitive counting of victims, and distorted representations of history."[22] A stronger indictment could not be made.

Jewish and other groups representing Nazi victims were not the only ones who felt offended by the tone of the public discussions about coming to terms with the past. Amidst this criticism on behalf of Nazi victims, the victims of communism, including people who had suffered because of the Wall, and former GDR opposition activists, also felt that their roles were being marginalized in united German history.[23] No one was happy.

Due to the significant public backlash, Nooke and his colleagues retracted their motion to wait for a better time. At a panel discussion hosted by the Konrad Adenauer Foundation in Berlin in January 2004, Nooke summed up his views on both the history being debated and commemoration of it: "Without doubt: Bautzen [viewed by many as the most notorious prison in the GDR] is not Auschwitz. But still Bautzen is a part of our national consciousness as a synonym for the crimes of SED rule.... Just as the peaceful revolution of fall [19]89 is of essential significance for all of Germany as the only successful revolution for liberty in German history, ...commemoration of the injustice of the SED regime also belongs to federal German memory culture."[24] No doubt influenced by his own participation in the East German opposition, Nooke had strong views about remembering East German history and was not going to give up.

In May 2004, the CDU/CSU submitted the motion again, but this time with two key changes: the reference to the foundation on memorials in Saxony was deleted; and the following sentence was added: "With its murder of millions of European Jews, the National Socialist regime committed a unique crime which will always require special commemoration."[25] The backers of the proposal hoped that the combination of this language and the decision made the

---

[22] Prof. Dr. Volkhard Knigge, "Erinnerungspolitischer Paradigmenwechsel," Presseerklärung, Arbeitsgemeinschaft der KZ-Gedenkstätten in der Bundesrepublik Deutschland, January 26, 2004.

[23] Günter Buchstab, "Einführung," in Buchstab, ed., *Zur Gedenkstättenproblematik. Dokumentation der Veranstaltung vom 30. Januar 2004* (Sankt Augustin: Konrad-Adenauer-Stiftung, 2004), pp. 6–7; and Matthias Rößler, "Zur Stiftung Sächsische Gedenkstätten," ibid., pp. 32–33.

[24] Günter Nooke, "Förderung von Gedenkstätten zur Diktaturgeschichte in Deutschland," ibid., pp. 10–11.

[25] Antrag der Abgeordneten Günter Nooke, Bernd Neumann (Bremen), Renate Blank, et. al., "Förderung von Gedenkstätten zur Diktaturgeschichte in Deutschland – Gesamtkonzept für ein würdiges Gedenken aller Opfer der beiden deutschen Diktaturen," Deutscher Bundestag, Drucksache 15/3048, May 4, 2004.

previous November to include both Nazi and communist sites in the motion would overcome opposition. Instead, the new motion initially brought on far more public opposition. The wide-ranging debate among politicians, the media, victims' groups, historians, and others in Saxony, Berlin, and beyond about how to compare the regimes, crimes, and victims of the Nazis and the Soviet and East German communists reminded many of West Germany's *Historikerstreit* in the late 1980s about whether the Holocaust was unique or whether mass killings by communist regimes such as Stalin's were equivalent.

Before and after the Bundestag's plenary debate about the motion in June 2004, the public debate intensified, going beyond German borders with the directors of Yad Vashem in Israel and the concentration camp memorial Theresienstadt/Terezin in the Czech Republic writing to German federal authorities in outrage and taking the side of the Nazi victims in the controversy.[26] A senior Israeli official warned that "passing this law would lead to a radical change in the relations which have been developed to this point between the Jewish people and Germany."[27]

During the plenary session, the federal Commissioner for Culture and Media, Christina Weiss (SPD), observed that although Nooke had taken out the "incriminating references" to the foundation on memorials in Saxony, he clearly "still seeks a paradigm change in the treatment of history and thus also in history policy." She insisted that the motion "relativizes the crimes of national socialism against European Jews, which can only harm the reputation of Germany abroad."[28] She and others referred to the vehement national and international criticism of the motion and urged the CDU/CSU to rescind the motion and "return to the consensus that had been found" (although that consensus seemed to have been lost) or risk "destroying the credibility of the democratic memory culture in our country."[29]

Contrary to the final report of the Bundestag commission of inquiry in 1998 that democratic memory culture required confronting both the Nazi and communist pasts in Germany, Weiss was essentially arguing that it required primary attention to the Nazi past. At the June 2004 Bundestag plenary debate on the CDU/CSU motion, Nooke repeatedly implored his colleagues to look more carefully at the motion to see that it did not equalize the Nazi and communist crimes and in fact highlighted the Holocaust as a "unique crime." He even had the motion translated into English so that

---

[26] Letter from Jan Nunk, Director of the Theresienstadt Memorial, to CDU/CSU faction chair Angela Merkel, June 2, 2004 (copy shared with the author by Günter Nooke); and Ulrike Plewnia, "Klotzen statt kleckern. Der CDU-Politiker Günter Nooke will die SED-Gedenkstätten aufwerten und provoziert Streit," *Focus* 26 (2004), p. 80.

[27] As described by Angelika Krüger-Leißner during the plenary debate, Deutscher Bundestag, Plenarprotokoll 15/114, June 17, 2004, p. 10464.

[28] Dr. Christina Weiss, ibid., pp. 10459–60.

[29] Angelika Krüger-Leißner, ibid., pp. 10463–65.

English-speaking international critics could read the motion for themselves. Nearly fifteen years after the fall of the Wall, it was still difficult to find support for granting significant attention and financial support to victims of the communist regime and their commemoration.

In spite of the raw wounds the motion touched for many, the Bundestag referred the motion forward to several parliamentary committees, setting a minimal goal of at least taking stock of what had been done regarding Nazi and communist memorials since the 1999 federal *Konzept* on funding memorial sites. The widespread attention to Alexandra Hildebrandt's crosses for victims of the Wall several months later effectively bolstered Nooke's case. The completion of the national Holocaust Memorial the following year also helped assuage the concerns of Jews and others that a "paradigm change" was underway in Germany against the longstanding focus on the Nazi period in *Erinnerungspolitik*. Hence, debates continued in the Bundestag about a new federal plan on memorials connected with both Nazi *and* communist history.

Modifying the Federal Plan on Memorials, *Gedenkstättenkonzeption*

The Bundestag's Committee on Culture and the Media held public hearings with experts on Nazi and communist history in 2005 and 2007 to solicit their advice on the CDU/CSU motion and on revising the 1999 federal memorial *Konzept*. In addition, Cultural Commissioner Weiss established an expert commission led by Martin Sabrow of the Center for Contemporary History to study East German history and make recommendations about ways to grapple with and disseminate knowledge about that history. The commission's recommendations a year later included creating an umbrella organization over the various museums, memorials, and research institutions dealing with East German history, a "History Network [*Geschichtsverbund*] for Working through the SED Dictatorship." The proposal that this *Geschichtsverbund* would, among other things, study "everyday life" (*Alltagsleben*) in the GDR and not just the state instruments of repression such as the Berlin Wall and the Stasi sparked great controversy, in part because by then the government was dominated by the CDU.[30] The conservatives generally favored an approach that highlighted the brutality of the SED regime instead of a softer examination of "everyday life." The *Geschichtsverbund* was never created.

Sabrow was also among the experts who were consulted by the Bundestag Committee on Culture and the Media about modifying the federal plan on memorials. The experts included professional historians as well as directors of museums, memorial sites, and associations dealing with history. At the 2005 hearing, only Thomas Lutz, the director of the Consortium of Concentration

---

[30] Martin Sabrow, Rainer Eckert, Monika Flacke, et. al., eds., *Wohin treibt die DDR-Erinnerung? Dokumentation einer Debatte* (Göttingen: Vandenhoeck & Ruprecht, 2007).

Camp Memorial Sites at the Topography of Terror in Berlin, offered a strong critique of the proposal to treat Nazi and communist sites similarly and thus to increase support for communist sites. The majority of the experts, on the other hand, agreed that the *Konzept* should be modified and that Nazi and communist memorial sites connected with both regimes should be part of a common *Konzept* and treated similarly.[31]

In fact, both the former Commissioner for Stasi Records Joachim Gauck and the historian Bernd Faulenbach pointed out that this approach had been agreed on seven years earlier and reminded Bundestag members that the 1998 final report of the second Bundestag commission of inquiry on the SED had "found a formula that provided a basis for the necessary grappling with both dictatorships of the last century in Germany."[32] Faulenbach had developed the wording that was used in that report: "The Nazi crimes should not be relativized when confronting the crimes of Stalinism. The Stalinist crimes should not be downplayed by the reference to Nazi crimes."[33] Gauck and Faulenbach argued that this language should also be used in a revised memorial *Konzept*.

The experts' consensus was that the federal government should become more involved in funding memorial sites instead of placing primary emphasis on the states, localities, and civil society to do this as had long been the tradition and was expressed in the constitution, the *Grundgesetz*.[34] Since the eastern states and Berlin were financially strapped, it was difficult for them to do much to preserve and further develop key memorial sites connected to the SED past, such as the Berlin Wall Memorial and the Stasi prison in Hohenschönhausen, or the Nazi past. And as it happened, the main historical sites connected to the Nazi and communist pasts were located in the eastern states and Berlin.[35]

---

[31] Deutscher Bundestag, Ausschuss für Kultur und Medien, Protokoll 15/50, February 16, 2005.

[32] Dr. h.c. Joachim Gauck, "Stellungnahme," Deutscher Bundestag, Ausschuss für Kultur und Medien, Ausschussdrucksache Nr. 15 (21) 157, pp. 3–4. See also Prof. Dr. Bernd Faulenbach, "Schriftliche Stellungnahme zur Anhörung im Ausschuss für Kultur und Medien des Deutschen Bundestages am 16.2.2005," Ausschuss für Kultur und Medien, Ausschussdrucksache Nr. 15 (21) 158, p. 8.

[33] Deutscher Bundestag, ed., "Schlußbericht," in *Materialien der Enquete-Kommission "Überwindung der Folgen der SED-Diktatur im Prozeß der deutschen Einheit,"* Band 1, p. 614.

[34] The experts were asked to submit written answers to a list of questions in advance so as to help guide the discussion at the hearing. The statements are found at Deutscher Bundestag, Ausschuss für Kultur und Medien 15. Wahlperiode, Ausschussdrucksache Nr. 15 (21) 153, 154, 155, 156, 157, and 158. For the protocol of the hearing itself, see Deutscher Bundestag, Ausschuss für Kultur und Medien, Protokoll 15/50, February 16, 2005.

[35] Rainer Eckert and Hubertus Knabe emphasized this for communist-era sites and Thomas Lutz did for Nazi-era sites. Some of the Bundestag members made this point at the June 2004 plenary session as well: Hans-Joachim Otto (FDP), Deutscher Bundestag,

When Angela Merkel's CDU/CSU coalition took over the government in the fall of 2005 and negotiated a coalition treaty with the SPD, the parties committed to "updating the federal *Konzept* for funding memorial sites with the goal of an appropriate consideration of both dictatorships in Germany," thus adopting the wording of Nooke's CDU-CSU motion.[36] Just as it was more often members of the CDU than the SPD who backed the reconstruction of the Berlin Wall border zone so as to portray the brutality of the SED regime, so it was also generally CDU members who were more comfortable comparing the Nazi and communist regimes, since this too emphasized the brutality of the SED state.

For nearly two years the new CDU Commissioner for Culture and Media, Bernd Neumann, developed a revised *Konzept* for memorials in consultation with directors of memorial sites, historians, and other experts in a similar process to that of Flierl and Klemke's task force on remembering the Berlin Wall. In July 2007, Neumann presented a draft plan with the unwieldy title, "Recognize responsibility, strengthen confrontation with the past, and deepen remembrance," to the Bundestag Committee on Culture and Media.[37] The committee invited ten experts to comment on the draft plan in a public hearing in November. The Bundestag members gave the experts four pages of detailed questions on the draft of an "Updated Memorial Concept," including the questions of whether there had been a sufficiently differentiated discussion of the Nazi and SED dictatorships and whether sites dealing with the communist past needed "considerable strengthening."[38]

Most of the invited experts agreed the draft was a good basis for updating and expanding federal support for memorial sites connected to both the Nazi and communist pasts. They specifically discussed the sentence about "not relativizing Nazi crimes or downplaying SED injustices" and whether that wording was satisfactory. This time it was Salomon Korn, Vice President of

Plenarprotokoll 15/114, June 17, 2004, p. 10460 as well as Angelika Krüger-Leißner (SPD), ibid., p. 10464.

[36] "Gemeinsam für Deutschland. Mit Mut und Menschlichkeit," Koalitionsvertrag von CDU, CSU und SPD, November 11, 2005, p. 132.

[37] Der Bundesbeauftrage der Bundesregierung für Kultur und Medien, "Verantwortung wahrnehmen, Aufarbeitung verstärken, Gedenken vertiefen," (Fortschreibung der Gedenkstättenkonzeption gemäß Koalitionsvertrag vom 11.11.2005 zur Vorlage an den Ausschuss für Kultur und Medien des Deutschen Bundestages), Entwurf (Stand: June 22, 2007), Deutscher Bundestag Ausschuss f. Kultur u. Medien, Ausschussdrucksache Nr. 16 (22) 127, July 4, 2007.

[38] "Fragenkatalog zur Anhörung des Ausschusses für Kultur und Medien am 7. November zu den Vorschlägen des BKM zur Weiterentwicklung des Gedenkstättenkonzepts vom 22. Juni 2007 (im folgenden BKM-Entwurf)," Deutscher Bundestag, 16. Wahlperiode, Ausschuss für Kultur und Medien, "Mitteilung, Öffentliche Anhörung, Fortschreibung der Gedenkstättenkonzeption," October 31, 2007, pp. 4–7.

the Central Council of Jews in Germany, who was most skeptical of that wording and of tackling these two parts of German history with one *Konzept*. He felt that the *Konzept* did not make a clear enough distinction between the Nazi and SED regimes and warned against speaking of "two dictatorships" or a "double past." Instead he favored the language "two dictatorships on German soil." Korn reiterated that the GDR was not just a German dictatorship, that it had been imposed from outside by the Soviets, whereas the Nazi rule was a German one. In addition, the Germans did not liberate themselves from Nazi rule and needed help from the outside, whereas the liberation of 1989 came from inside Germany. Thus, he expressed deep concern about any unitary approach to a comparison of the Nazi and communist regimes in Germany.[39]

The other experts, however, argued that facing both of these pasts and even comparing them did not imply viewing them as equal.[40] In fact, both the 2007 draft and the final updated federal *Gedenkstättenkonzeption* in 2008 emphasized the "historically unique dimensions of the National Socialist regime of terror" and the "singularity of the Holocaust." They also made clear that "it is absolutely essential to take account of the differences between the Nazi rule and the SED dictatorship. National Socialist Germany caused suffering to millions through its policies of persecution and execution." The final memorial plan reiterated that "the genocide of six million Jews was a crime against humanity of previously unseen dimensions and has singular significance in German, European and worldwide memory culture." Yet, as the *Gedenkstättenkonzeption* argued, "it is also the task of state and society to remember the injustice of the SED dictatorship."[41]

---

[39] Deutscher Bundestag, Ausschuss für Kultur und Medien, "Öffentliche Anhörung, Fortschreibung der Gedenkstättenkonzeption," Protokoll Nr. 16/42, November 7, 2007, pp. 19–22.

[40] Ibid. All Bundestag factions supported the *Gedenkstättenkonzeption* except the SED/PDS successor party, the Left (*die Linke*). Lukrezia Jochimsen led the charge in the plenary debate arguing that the memorial plan ignored the "silence and lies of the postwar Federal Republic, the Nazis in high positions, the late concentration camp trials, the work at memorial sites that was almost only done by those who had suffered and the decades-long protracted issue of restitution." She was also critical that the new plan devoted much more attention to the communist past than to the Nazi past. Deutscher Bundestag, Plenarprotokoll 16/187, November 13, 2008, pp. 20091–92. On the debate about "two German dictatorships," see also Aleida Assmann, *Das neue Unbehagen an der Erinnerungskultur* (Munich: C. H. Beck, 2013), pp. 112–13.

[41] Unterrichtung durch den Beauftragten der Bundesregierung für Kultur und Medien, "Fortschreibung der Gedenkstättenkonzeption des Bundes," Deutscher Bundestag, Drucksache 16/9875, June 19, 2008, p. 2.

Korn's preferred language about "two dictatorships on German soil" was reflected in the final version of the *Gedenkstättenkonzeption* in wording about "remembrance of the dictatorial past in Germany" as opposed to the language that had been used in the commissions of inquiry in the 1990s on "two German dictatorships of the twentieth century."[42] Faulenbach's comparative wording used in the 1998 Bundestag report about "not relativizing Nazi crimes or downplaying SED injustices," however, was now reprised a decade later in the *Gedenkstättenkonzeption*, as he and Gauck had urged.[43] The revised *Gedenkstättenkonzeption* largely ended what had been a long, emotional debate and opened up the opportunity for change in federal *Erinnerungspolitik*.[44]

The main significance of the 2008 updated memorial plan for the present study was increased federal attention to and support for sites connected with the East German regime: "The federal government seeks to intensify the process of working through the dictatorship in the SBZ [the Soviet Occupation Zone of 1945–49] and in the GDR as well as the commemoration of their victims."[45] The *Gedenkstättenkonzeption* specified four topics to be highlighted at memorials, museums, and other sites of memory related to the communist past: the division and the border; surveillance and persecution; society and everyday life (clearly building on the work of the Sabrow commission); and resistance and opposition. The Berlin Wall Memorial was among the sites that would henceforth receive 50 percent of its annual operational funding from the federal government, a practice that had begun the year before. Several SED-era sites would also receive this annual institutional support and a large group of sites, including Bernauer Strasse, would receive federal support for specific programs and projects. It should be noted, however, that overall federal funding for Nazi-era sites continued to surpass that of communist-era sites.

---

[42] Ibid.

[43] Ibid., p. 2. Bernd Faulenbach introduced the key verbs "relativized" and "minimized" in 1991 in the context of describing the Nazi wartime and communist postwar crimes carried out at Sachsenhausen. See his testimony to a public hearing of the Bundestag's Committee on Culture and Media in 2005, "Schriftliche Stellungnahme zur Anhörung im Ausschuss für Kultur und Medien des Deutschen Bundestages," February 15, 2005, Ausschussdrucksache Nr. 15 (21) 158, pp. 8–9; and author's interview with Bernd Faulenbach, Washington, DC, September 12, 2013.

[44] Philipp Oehmk, "Erinnerungskultur: Zwickmühle der Vergangenheit," *Spiegel* 21 (May 19, 2008), pp. 166–68; and Thomas Lackmann, "An der Grenze. Ein Fall für den Moderator: Kulturstaatsminister Neumann und das neue Gedenkstättenkonzept," *Tagesspiegel*, June 19, 2008.

[45] Unterrichtung durch den Beauftragten der Bundesregierung für Kultur und Medien, "Fortschreibung der Gedenkstättenkonzeption des Bundes," June 19, 2008 p. 2.

Politics, Education, and Memory

The *Gedenkstättenkonzeption* and Commissioner Neumann's description of it placed great emphasis on education and specifically on the *Bundeszentrale für politische Bildung* (*Bundeszentrale*) and on schools dealing with the Nazi and communist pasts. In introducing his memorial plan to the Bundestag in 2008, Minister Neumann noted: "The understanding of one's own history contributes to identity formation in every state." He declared that the *Gedenkstättenkonzeption* was a "milestone for German memory culture" and demonstrated that the federal government "takes account of Germany's historical and moral obligation" to view its past, including the dark sides, openly. The new Memorial Plan stated: "History must be worked through rigorously. The lessons of these chapters in our history must be imparted anew to each generation."[46] Politicians as well as leaders of the expanded Berlin Wall Memorial and other such sites would increasingly refer to them as places for learning (*Lernorte*).[47]

Disseminating history policy (*Geschichtspolitik*) – whether it be about the crimes of the Nazis or communists or the glories of the peaceful revolution – involves many public institutions, including the federal government surrounding the chancellor, the president, the Bundestag, the commissioner for culture, various federally-sponsored institutions such as the *Stiftung Aufarbeitung der SED-Diktatur*, the *Bundeszentrale*, the Stasi Records Authority, and the state-level branches of some of these. Large amounts of state funding go into all of this. The 2008 federal *Gedenkstättenkonzeption* involved a total of 35 million euros in 2008 and 2009, and the 2006 Berlin *Gesamtkonzept*, as we have seen, had a price tag of 40 million euros. These two plans are among the many instruments Germans have for implementing *Geschichtspolitik*.

German leaders have become increasingly involved in intervening in *Geschichtspolitik* in spite of the fact that the *Grundgesetz* of 1949 stipulated that the constituent states and not the federal government had primary authority on most domestic issues, including cultural policy and education, such as how to approach German history. Chancellor Helmut Kohl began this process when he founded the *Deutsches Historisches Museum* in 1987.[48] In 1998, Chancellor Gerhard Schröder went a step further when he created

---

[46] Unterrichtung durch den Beauftragten der Bundesregierung für Kultur und Medien, "Fortschreibung der Gedenkstättenkonzeption des Bundes," p. 1.

[47] See for example the speech by Berlin Wall Foundation director Axel Klausmeier on the fiftieth anniversary of the erection of the Wall, "Begrüßung zur zentralen Gedenkveranstaltung des Landes und des Bundes am 13.08.2011 in der Gedenkstätte Berliner Mauer," August 13, 2011.

[48] See Kohl's speech at the ceremony marking the creation of the German Historical Museum, Reichstag, Berlin, October 28, 1987, in Christoph Stölzl, ed., *Deutsches*

a ministerial-level federal commissioner for culture and media (*Bundesbeauftragter für Kultur und Medien*, BKM).[49] At the same time, a Bundestag committee for culture and media (*Ausschuss für Kultur und Medien*) was also created. Blocked by the opposition from creating a fully-fledged ministry of culture (which has not existed in Germany since Goebbels' Nazi propaganda ministry),[50] the leader of BKM nonetheless would eventually manage a staff of nearly 250 people by 2015. The Cultural Commissioner reports directly to the chancellor, participates in cabinet meetings, and has an office in the chancellery. BKM's mission is to oversee cultural institutions and projects of national significance, such as DHM and – in cooperation with the Berlin Senate – the Berlin Wall Memorial.

Under both Schröder and his successor, Angela Merkel, BKM has played an increasingly important role in grappling with and commemorating the past, including the Berlin Wall. The Cultural Commissioner gives speeches and releases statements on important historical anniversaries, such as the rise and fall of the Berlin Wall and on dates related to the Nazi past. As we have seen with its 2008 *Gedenkstättenkonzeption*, BKM also provides financial support for authentic sites, museums, monuments, and memorials related to the Nazi and East German pasts, such as the Berlin Wall Memorial. BKM devotes about one hundred million euros each year to remembering the East German past, and since 2013 provides annual reports on its activities related to this.[51]

The intensive governmental involvement in *Geschichtspolitik* has raised some red flags. German scholars have commented critically on the purse strings that come with state involvement in memorials, monuments, and museums. Markus Goldbeck has pointed to "the ambivalence of state funding," which on the one hand offers "a chance for working through the GDR past," but on the other hand allows a "dangerous dependence" on state funds that can affect how institutions connected to history policy depict the past.[52]

Historisches Museum. Ideen – Kontroversen – Perspektiven (Frankfurt am Main: Propyläen, 1988), pp. 651–54.

[49] Gerhard Schröder, "Regierungserklärung des Bundeskanzlers," Deutscher Bundestag, Plenarprotokoll 14/3, Bonn, November 10, 1998, p. 62. On the background to creating this new position, see the *Spiegel* interview with candidate Schröder's advisors on cultural policy, Jürgen Flimm, Arnulf Conradi and Dieter Gorny, "Ein geistiger Aufbruch," *Spiegel* 13 (1998), pp. 154–57.

[50] Hugh Eakin, "Schröder's Kulturkampf," *The Nation*, October 24, 2002.

[51] Bernd Neumann, "Rede vom Staatsminister Bernd Neumann zum Bericht der Bundesregierung zum Stand der Aufarbeitung der SED-Diktatur," Deutscher Bundestag, Plenarprotokoll 17/232, March 22, 2013, p. 29005.

[52] Markus Goldbeck, "Die Ambivalenz staatlicher Förderung: Eine Chance für die DDR-Aufarbeitung oder 'gefährliche Abhängigkeit'?" *Jahrbuch für Historische Kommunismusforschung* (Berlin: Metropol Verlag, 2014), pp. 1–16.

Erik Mayer has specifically called the "*Gedenkstättenkonzeption* an instrument for controlling history policy."[53] More broadly, Thomas Großbölting and Klaus Christoph maintain that state-sponsored history policy results in a biased, undifferentiated black-and-white approach to examining GDR history.[54] Certainly the widespread use of the terms "dictatorship" (*Diktatur*) and "unjust state" (*Unrechtsstaat*) to describe the GDR, often including references to the Berlin Wall as a prime example of these, was a large part of what they had in mind.

Historians have also raised other concerns about governmental involvement in *Geschichtspolitik*. Professor Martin Sabrow of the Center for Contemporary History in Potsdam and Berlin's Humboldt University expressed his concern when he was invited by the Bundestag in 2007 to speak at the public hearing about the draft of the updated *Gedenkstättenkonzeption*, as did Joachim Scholtyseck of the Institute of History at the University of Bonn. At the hearing, both historians warned that the government seemed to be trying to construct a historical consensus and argued that historical research belongs in the university, not in the policy arena.[55] Sabrow was critical that the government was trying to pull history out of the universities and bring it into the government and to memorials and museums."[56]

When Bundestag President Thierse asked Sabrow how they could avoid what Sabrow referred to as "the danger of a state or public determination of a historical consensus," Sabrow responded that "it is rather difficult to discuss this in the political realm. After all, we are making political decisions here and already the fact that university historians are appearing as history-policy actors is a problem, Herr Dr. Thierse. I don't think it is resolvable. But I think it is important that we are aware of this."[57] Similarly, when Helmut Trotnow testified at a Bundestag hearing on memorials in the early 1990s, he had argued

---

[53] Erik Meyer, "Die Gedenkstättenkonzeption des Bundes als Instrument zur geschichtspolitischen Steuerung," in Bernd Wagner, ed., *Jahrbuch für Kulturpolitik 2009. Band 9. Thema: Erinnerungskulturen und Geschichtspolitik* (Essen: Klartext, 2009), pp. 101–8.

[54] Thomas Großbölting, "Die DDR im vereinten Deutschland," *Aus Politik und Zeitgeschichte*, Issue on *Zukunft der Erinnerung* 25–26/2010 (June 21, 2010); and Klaus Christoph, "'Aufarbeitung der SED-Diktatur' – heute so wie gestern? Essay," *Aus Politik und Zeitgeschichte*, Issue on *Geschichte als Instrument* 42–43/2013 (October 8, 2013).

[55] Deutscher Bundestag, Öffentliche Anhörung, Fortschreibung der Gedenkstättenkonzeption, Ausschuss für Kultur und Medien, Protokoll Nr. 16/42, November 7, 2007, pp. 42–43.

[56] Ibid. Some of Sabrow's criticism may have stemmed from the fact that he was likely unhappy that the recommendations of his expert commission from 2006 were not all adopted and were publicly criticized as expressing *Ostalgie* in wanting to look more at everyday life in GDR and not just at instruments of repression.

[57] Ibid., pp. 14–15.

that deciding "which central site or sites, which historical events or victims should be remembered" is a "value judgement" to be made by the people's elected representatives.[58]

Policymakers in Germany seek input on *Geschichtspolitik* from historians and other experts, but only the policymakers have the power to decide which projects get funded. Yet it is generally the historians and other experts who have the detailed information to make a case for federal support, and their input can and often does sway policymakers. Hence there tends to be a rather circular relationship between policymakers and historical experts on making history policy. German historians even serve on historical commissions affiliated with political parties, as has been the case, for example, with Bernd Faulenbach and Martin Sabrow with the SPD and Manfred Wilke with the CDU.

In addition to BKM, another central instrument in the government's commitment to *Geschichtspolitik* and its dissemination is the Federal Agency for Political Education, or *Bundeszentrale*. To non-German ears, the name of this agency sounds Orwellian and all too close to the Nazi propaganda ministry, but for Germans it is meant to be the opposite. Although the West German *Grundgesetz* of 1949 favored the devolution of power from the center on most issues, an initial belief that a hands-off policy was the most democratic approach has been transformed over the decades into a principled stand that a laissez-faire policy is not enough. Officials have feared that German citizens cannot be trusted to be active democrats on their own and that instead the best guarantee for a healthy "democratic political culture" is strong state support for democratic values in education, including specifically the provision of information about and the drawing of lessons from the dark chapters of the German past.

After being established in the early 1950s (or reestablished to succeed a similar state-run agency from the imperial and Weimar periods), the *Bundeszentrale* became a core conduit for this type of education by the 1970s and remains so. Since the West German push to confront history came from below in 1968, officials decided that from thenceforth the state needed to take the lead to ensure that Germans confronted the dark parts of the country's past and had the historical information to do so. After all, the Germans themselves had not brought about an end to Hitler's despicable regime; the Allies had. The

---

[58] Trotnow's testimony at the Bundestag's public hearing, Protokoll über die 91. Sitzung des Innenausschusses, "Beteiligung des Bundes an Mahn- und Gedenkstätten," March 7, 1994 in Deutscher Bundestag, ed. *Materialien der Enquete-Kommission "Aufarbeitung von Geschichte und Folgen der SED-Diktatur in Deutschland," Band IX, Formen und Ziele der Auseinandersetzung mit den beiden Diktaturen in Deutschland* (Baden-Baden: Nomos Verlag/Frankfurt: Suhrkamp Verlag, 1995), p. 304.

fundamental mission of the *Bundeszentrale* is to help inculcate in German citizens the values of liberty, democracy, the rule of law, and human rights and to inspire them to be active in protecting these.[59] Officials believe that educating citizens about periods in German history when this did not happen, particularly during the Nazi and communist periods, will make Germans more inclined to make sure these experiences will not be repeated. The *Bundeszentrale* also aims to help teachers, students, and regular citizens be skeptical of dominant historical narratives, training them to think critically and question assumptions.[60]

Federal support for the *Bundeszentrale* provides for free or very inexpensive publications, conferences, and seminars about the Nazi and East German pasts geared toward teachers, students, and the general public. One key educational resource on the Berlin Wall funded by the *Bundeszentrale* is the multimedia website *chronik-der-mauer.de* (Chronicle of the Wall). More than 2.5 million visitors have accessed the website since 2008. The historian Hans-Hermann Hertle has been responsible for much of the content of the website, which was inspired by his book, *Chronik des Mauerfalls* (*Chronicle of the Fall of the Wall*), now in its twelfth printing.[61] In terms of the number and type of books published in German and English on the history of the Berlin Wall, ranging from scholarly books to works more oriented to the general public (including tourists) with short descriptions and pictures, Hertle is probably the most prolific memory activist from the ranks of historians. His pocket-sized book, *The Berlin Wall Story*, is a best seller in English and German and is available at most tourist shops throughout Berlin and at the Berlin Wall Memorial with which he has long been deeply engaged, at times as a member of the scientific advisory board. Hertle's prize-winning documentary film, *When the Wall Came Tumbling Down: Fifty Hours that Changed the World*, has also achieved a cult following.

The *Bundesstiftung zur Aufarbeitung der SED-Diktatur* (The Federal Foundation for Reappraising the SED Dictatorship or *Stiftung Aufarbeitung*) has significantly expanded its educational function since its founding by the Bundestag in 1998. A full-time staff member coordinates a variety of educational programs for students and teachers. The *Stiftung*

---

[59] Interviews with *Bundeszentrale* director Thomas Krüger, November 4, 2013; and with Holger Kulick, *Bundeszentrale* editor for online content concerning East German history, November 6, 2018.

[60] Interviews with Thomas Krüger, November 4, 2013, and with Bernd Faulenbach (in Washington, DC), September 12, 2013. See also Wolfgang Sander and Peter Steinbach, eds., *Politische Bildung in Deutschland* (Bonn: Bundeszentrale für Politische Bildung, 2014).

[61] Correspondence with Hans-Hermann Hertle, January 9, 2019.

Aufarbeitung regularly holds competitions for high school students to design posters about various aspects of East German history, including for anniversaries related to the Wall, and holds conferences for students and teachers. The website of the foundation also provides materials for lesson plans and information on speakers available to visit schools to share their experiences of living in the GDR.[62]

Expanding the Berlin Wall Memorial Site at Bernauer Strasse

Berlin's *Gesamtkonzept* and the federal government's *Gedenkstättenkonzeption* committed them to supporting the permanence, stability, and wide-ranging nature of the information offered to visitors at the Berlin Wall Memorial so as to strengthen its capacity to educate people about the history of the Wall. In addition to the municipal and federal governments each providing half of the costs of the maintenance of the memorial site, they would also fund specific projects such as the massive expansion of the site called for in the *Gesamtkonzept*. The site would be extended to cover seven blocks and nearly one mile of the former death strip with an outdoor exhibit. It would also include a new exhibit in the Documentation Center and the opening of a separate visitors' center. The amount of funding required for the expansion at Bernauer Strasse totaled over thirty-three million euros.

The federal government paid nearly eighteen million euros to purchase and lease property along Bernauer Strasse so that it could be used as part of the memorial. The outdoor exhibit along seven blocks of the former death strip was paid for with 4 million euros from federal and municipal funds for improving the regional economy and with 5.6 million euros from EU funding for regional development. The 2.45 million euros required to construct the visitors' center was provided by federal and municipal funds. The remodeling of the Documentation Center for a new, enlarged, permanent exhibit was funded with 2.3 million euros from the Berlin government. The exhibit itself was financed with 750,000 euros from BKM's funds for memorial sites.[63]

The Berlin Wall Memorial also received support to preserve the sections of outer and inner Wall. Some of the funds came from assets of the former GDR leadership, the so-called PMO funds from the "party and mass organizations of the GDR."[64] These monies (some of which have been found in Bank Austria in Switzerland and some of which are still being sought[65]) from the former East

---

[62] www.bundesstiftung-aufarbeitung.de/bildungsarbeit-1130.html.

[63] Günther Schlusche, "From the Fall of the Wall to the Berlin Wall Memorial," in Axel Klausmeier, ed., *The Berlin Wall: Berlin Wall Memorial Exhibition Catalog*, trans. Miriamne Fields (Berlin: Ch. Links, 2015), p. 174, n. 30.

[64] Ibid.

[65] Kko/dpa, "Deutsche Behörde gewinnt Rechtsstreit um verschollene DDR-Millionen," *Spiegel Online*, February 6, 2019. The subject of the missing East German funds was

German leadership are distributed each year by the federal government to the states, which then designate the recipients. Devoting a portion of the money amassed and kept in secret accounts by the leaders responsible for the Berlin Wall to now preserve and elucidate the history of the Wall was a particularly fitting use of the funds.

In July 2007, the Berlin Senate's office for city planning launched an international design competition for expanding the Berlin Wall Memorial site.[66] Contestants were tasked with finding convincing ways to make the history of the site before and after the fall of the Wall come alive by using all available remnants of that history and highlighting parts of the history that were not visible, such as places where people were killed or escaped and the location of tunnels. The guidelines made clear that the competition sponsors did not want "an easily consumable 'ready-made dish' or a confusing 'Wall-Disneyland'," arguing instead that the presentation of "traces" of the past would draw on the "visitors' imagination" and would result in "more long-lasting and emotionally moving impressions."[67] The competition announcement noted that "the public debate about Hildebrandt's crosses had encouraged the Senate to focus its *Gesamtkonzept* on Bernauer Strasse as the central site for commemorating victims of the Wall and "to significantly expand the size and strengthen the quality" of the site.[68]

Competition entrants were to be comprised of a team of architects (for the new visitors' center), landscape architects (for the area along the former border strip), and exhibit designers (for the outdoor and indoor exhibits). The landscape architect Donata Valentin chaired the jury composed of six architecture and design experts and five experts on the site and its history (including Manfred Fischer and Rainer Klemke). A broader group of experts was involved in the process of narrowing the entrants down to a list of thirteen from the initial forty-seven. This broader group included representatives from victims' groups, the church (including the Sophien and Reconciliation parishes and more senior levels of the Protestant Church), the Berlin Wall Memorial, and the federal and municipal governments.[69]

When the jury met in December to decide on the winner from the final group of thirteen, they established a set of criteria for approaches they favored and did not favor, some of which had been previously laid out in the *Gesamtkonzept*. Design approaches to be avoided included: anything that

---

also dealt with in the fourth and final season of Friedemann Fromm's popular ARD television series, *Weissensee*, in 2018.

[66] Berlin Senatverwaltung für Stadtentwicklung, "Erweiterung der Gedenkstätte Berliner Mauer, Berlin Mitte, offener Realisierungswettbewerb für Hochbau, Freiraum und Ausstellung," Auslobung, July 2007.

[67] Ibid., p. 95.

[68] Ibid., p. 31.

[69] Berlin Senatverwaltung für Stadtentwicklung, "Erweiterung der Gedenkstätte Berliner Mauer," Ergebnisprotokoll, December 17, 2017.

intervened too much with the site and thus overshadowed it; and the use of the brass-plated, so-called stumbling blocks (*Stolpersteine*) that were installed in sidewalks throughout Berlin to draw attention to houses that had been inhabited by Jews and other groups targeted by the Nazis for deportation and murder. The jury sought to avoid any "blending or equivalence of the Nazi and SED dictatorships." The design elements the jury favored included: individual commemoration of victims of the Wall; vertical markings to show the path of the Wall in places where no segments remained; marking the former eastern view of the Wall instead of just the more commonly known western view of the Wall; highlighting the obvious difference between anything added and the original Wall; the use of rust-colored Corten steel, which would match the two outside walls of the Kohlhoff & Kohlhoff memorial; and three-dimensional renderings of former guard towers. Finally, they favored designs that would be accessible both to people who had lived with the Wall and those who had no experience of it.[70]

The jury decided unanimously to award the first prize to a group comprised of the firms Mola Winkelmüller Architects and the landscape architects Sinai-Faust.Schroll.Schwarz of ON Architecture based in Berlin.[71] They were particularly impressed with their design for a "Window of Remembrance," a structure in the middle of the former death strip that would display individual pictures of people killed at the Wall. The jury also liked their use of tall, narrow columns to extend the path of the external, western Wall, columns that looked similar to the steel reinforcements used in the actual Wall, some of which had been exposed over time as the cement covering them fell off; flat markings in the ground to denote the internal, eastern Wall; thicker round columns to display visual and audio information about historical occurrences at locations along Bernauer Strasse and in the former death strip; and the way they left much of the former death strip as a grassy area. The primary material the designers proposed for most aspects of the outside area and for the external walls of the new visitors' center was Corten steel, making the design in the eyes of the jury "an extraordinarily coherent work."[72]

Now that they had decided on the architects, the scientific advisory board of the Berlin Wall Association formed a working group in January 2008 to develop detailed plans for the content of the indoor and outdoor exhibits. This working group included members of the board and others: board chair Klaus-Dietmar Henke (pictured in Figure 17 in Chapter 5), deputy chair Petra Morawe, Manfred Fischer, Maria Nooke, Gerhard Sälter, Gabriele

---

[70] Ibid., p. 7.

[71] For the winning proposal, see Berlin Senatverwaltung für Stadtentwicklung, "Erweiterung der Gedenkstätte Berliner Mauer," Bericht der Vorprüfung zur 2. Preisgerichtssitzung, December 12, 2007, pp. 24–25.

[72] Berlin Senatverwaltung für Stadtentwicklung, "Erweiterung der Gedenkstätte Berliner Mauer," Ergebnisprotokoll, December 12, 2017, p. 9.

Camphausen, Manfred Wilke, Leo Schmidt, Axel Klausmeier, Rainer Klemke (representing the Berlin Senate), Christian Freiesleben (representing BKM), and Günther Schlusche who was in charge of the logistical details such as the property and construction contracts, having done the same for Berlin's Holocaust Memorial. Sälter would ultimately play the lead role in formulating the content of exhibits. The historian had been at the Berlin Wall Memorial since 2000, and as a university student had worked during the dramatic year of 1989–90 at the Marienfelde Refugee Camp in West Berlin, which took in tens of thousands of East Germans that year.[73]

As the Berlin Wall Memorial was becoming a bigger, more complicated and important institution, it was given a new administrative form in September 2008 when Berlin's House of Representatives enacted a law creating the Berlin Wall Foundation (*Stiftung Berliner Mauer*).[74] This replaced the Berlin Wall Association (*Verein Berliner Mauer*), which had operated for ten years. The new foundation encompassed both the expanding Berlin Wall Memorial at Bernauer Strasse and the Marienfelde Refugee Camp memorial site in southern Berlin. The latter had welcomed over one million East German refugees to West Berlin between its opening in 1953 and German unification in 1990. The Berlin Wall Foundation had multiple missions: "to document and convey the history of the Berlin Wall and the refugee movements from the German Democratic Republic[,]...to preserve the historic sites and authentic remnants and to enable a dignified commemoration of the victims of commu- nist tyranny." To fulfill its missions, the foundation was expected to produce "exhibits, events, publications and other forms of historical-political educa- tion" and to do to this "in cooperation with other relevant institutions such as the Protestant Reconciliation parish and the Sophien Church community."

Once the Berlin Wall Foundation was formed, a six-person foundation council was created with representatives of the municipal and federal govern- ments, the Protestant Church, and from the Berlin Wall and Marienfelde memorials to oversee the work at the two sites. Berlin's cultural senator, André Schmitz, was the first chair of the foundation council and Ingeborg Berggreen-Merkel of BKM was the deputy chair. With government represen- tatives now officially a part of the leadership of the Berlin Wall Memorial Foundation, politics had a greater chance of influencing the activities at Bernauer Strasse, although the scientific advisory council, tasked with over- seeing daily operations, and other expert advisers sought to limit that influence as much as possible.

---

[73] Interview with Gerhard Sälter, November 5, 2018; and Julia Haak, "Gerhard Sälter: Der Forscher von der Bernauer Strasse," *Berliner Zeitung*, May 10, 2019.

[74] Gesetz über die Errichtung der Stiftung Berliner Mauer (Mauerstiftungsgesetz, MAUStG), September 17, 2008, in *Gesetz und Verordnungsblatt für Berlin* 64, no. 24 (September 27, 2008), pp. 250–52.

The final step in restructuring the operations of the Berlin Wall Memorial Site was to decide on a foundation director. After debates about whether to appoint an internal candidate or launch an open search, the council, pushed by the expert advisory board, decided on the latter. The search yielded a top external candidate, Axel Klausmeier, who had worked with Leo Schmidt in the department of architectural conservation at the Brandenburg University of Technology in Cottbus. Together they had carried out the Berlin Senate-sponsored project of locating and cataloguing all remains of the former Berlin Wall border strip in 2001–3, and since 2007 they had been engaged in a major research project sponsored by the prestigious German Research Association examining the Berlin Wall as a symbol of the Cold War.[75] Klausmeier was also a member of the working group to design the content of the expanded exhibit at the Berlin Wall Memorial.

While Klausmeier had begun his professional life focusing on landscape architecture in the gardens of English country estates and on the British architect Thomas Ripley, the subject of his dissertation, he had long been fascinated by the Wall. He first visited Berlin as a fourteen-year-old in 1981, traveling with classmates from his home in West Germany's Ruhr area. He made multiple trips to Berlin afterwards to see both the East and the West as long as the Wall stood. A few months after the fall of the Wall, he even visited Bernauer Strasse. In 2001, when Klausmeier joined Schmidt in Cottbus, his professional focus turned from English country gardens to his fascination with the Berlin Wall and with "uncomfortable monuments." By 2008 when he applied to be the director of the new Berlin Wall Foundation, the Wall had become the focus of his career.[76]

Some on the foundation council, however, had concerns about Klausmeier's background, particularly with the fact that he was from the West, not the East. The Berlin Wall Memorial had always been dominated by people from the West: Fischer, Trotnow, and Camphausen. Some thought it was time for that to change. Many German institutions devoted to examining the East German past (the Stasi Records Authority and the *Stiftung Aufarbeitung*, for example) were (and as of this writing still are) led by former East Germans who were part of the opposition. Maria Nooke, who had been at the Berlin Wall Memorial for ten years, had precisely this background. She also had backing from the CDU.[77] Yet although she was officially the managing

---

[75] Katrin Juntke, "Das 'Gesicht der Berliner Mauer' kommt aus Cottbus," press release, Informationsdienst Wissenschaft, Brandenburgische Technische Universität Cottbus, November 10, 2008.

[76] "Der Spurensicherer," *Tagesspiegel*, November 11, 2008; and author's correspondence with Klausmeier, September 11, 2018.

[77] For a sense of the arguments the CDU probably brought to bear in favor of Nooke over Klausmeier, see the op-ed by Sven Felix Kellerhoff in the conservative newspaper, *Welt*, "Axel Klausmeier, der neue Hüter der Mauer," *Welt*, November 7, 2008.

director of the site, Manfred Fischer was effectively in charge and the two had increasing differences of opinion about how to constitute the site. Camphausen, whom many in the Senate hoped would in fact become the director of the new foundation, had taken a medical leave of absence and was not inclined to become the director.

In the end, it came down to a competition between Klausmeier and Nooke for the position in the fall of 2008. Since any decision by the memorial board would have to be approved by the foundation council, on which the political parties were represented, party politics came into the deliberations. The board of the Berlin Wall Memorial strongly favored Klausmeier and recommended him to the federation council. After some backstage political maneuvering followed by intensive deliberations at the council meeting on November 7, 2008, the foundation council voted to offer the directorship to Klausmeier. Nooke became the deputy director. The two took up their new positions in January 2009.

No sooner had Klausmeier (pictured in Figure 17 in Chapter 5) taken up his post as director of the Berlin Wall Foundation, then he found himself embroiled in an issue that threatened the future development of the site and also seemed to highlight different perspectives between people from the East and West twenty years after the fall of the Wall. While the jury that picked the winning design for the expansion of the Berlin Wall Memorial had supported the proposal to install tall, thin columns of rust-colored Corten steel to mark the path of the Wall along Bernauer Strasse where no Wall segments remained, now that this plan was on the verge of being implemented there was a firestorm of opposition from victims' groups, the CDU, and even members of the board of the memorial. The board was supposed to vote on the matter in early February. News of this was leaked to the press and an emotional debate followed, postponing the board's decision.

Opponents argued that filling in the gaps in the Wall (including the two created in 1997 when the Sophien community had removed thirty-two segments) with the Corten steel rods instead of using original pieces of the Wall itself (which were still on display in the middle of the former death strip where the Sophien community had installed them after moving them) made the Berlin Wall and the border regime seem much less oppressive and deadly than they had been. Moreover, the guidelines for the expansion competition had explicitly stated that proposed designs could include returning the pieces of the Wall removed in 1997 to their original locations and even declared that this was "desirable."[78] Since the winning design refrained from doing this, critics accused the Berlin Wall Foundation of trying to downplay the brutal nature of the East German regime.

---

[78] Berlin Senatverwaltung für Stadtentwicklung, "Erweiterung der Gedenkstätte Berliner Mauer," Auslobung, July 2017, pp. 94 and 96, quote from p. 96.

They sought to stop the implementation of the design and called not only for the return of the thirty-two pieces of the Wall but also for reconstructing, at the site, sections of the first three generations of the Wall that preceded the fourth generation currently seen in what remained on Bernauer Strasse.[79] Politicians from the CDU and the Greens supported these critics, as did officials at Berlin's tourist office, calling for more reconstruction at the site instead of settling just for the narrow Corten steel columns.[80] Sven Felix Kellerhoff argued in *Die Welt* that other sites along the former East-West German border contained a convincing combination of authentic and reconstructed elements and that there was no good reason why the Berlin Wall Memorial could not do this as well.[81] As we have seen, arguments that as much reconstruction as possible would help aid the understanding of people who had not experienced the Wall went as far back as Helmut Trotnow and Rainer Hildebrandt in 1990 and 1991. Maria Nooke was among those who continued this argument in February 2009.[82]

Further complicating matters, in a reprise of the conflicts of the 1990s, since the land where the Wall and its gaps stood was owned by the Sophien Church and had contained parts of its cemetery, church representatives announced in February 2009 that they would block the use of their land by the Berlin Wall Memorial if the pieces of the Wall were returned to their original locations.[83] The church community argued that the gaps in the Wall showed developments at the site since 1990 and thus also represented the general overcoming of the Wall, a key aspect of the history of the site. Holger Kulick, who was the head of the Sophien community's cemetery committee, invited politicians to tour the site in early February as part of his efforts to convince them of this point of view.[84] The conflict threatened to stop any further progress on the expansion of the Berlin Wall Memorial.

The scientific board of the memorial was divided about what to do and some members from the former East, including Joachim Gauck, even resigned over the issue, although Nooke did not. Gauck maintained that the history of the Sophien cemetery was "of much less importance than the history of the brutality of the Wall. The big political history, the history of power and

---

[79] Sven Felix Kellerhoff, "'Alles Burra, oder was?' Das falsche Gedenken der Stiftung Berliner Mauer: Eine Polemik," *Deutschland Archiv* 42 (4/2009), pp. 589–93.

[80] Kellerhoff, "Todesstreifen soll wieder aufgebaut werden," *Welt Online*, February 4, 2009; and Hildburg Bruns, "Krach um diese Mauerlücke," *Bild*, February 4, 2009.

[81] Kellerhoff, "Todesstreifen soll wieder aufgebaut werden," *Welt Online*, February 4, 2009.

[82] Thomas Rogalla, "Wie viel Mauer braucht man zum Gedenken?" *Berliner Zeitung*, February 13, 2009.

[83] Werner van Bebber, "Berliner Mauer: Lückenhafte Erinnerung," *Tagesspiegel*, March 1, 2009.

[84] Interview with Holger Kulick of the Sophien parish and the scientific board of the Berlin Wall Foundation, November 6, 2018; and Rogalla, "Wie viel Mauer braucht man zum Gedenken?" *Berliner Zeitung*, February 13, 2009.

powerlessness, should be portrayed in this national memorial. But not the feelings of a group that have special, particular interests there, because they have their cemetery there." Gauck said he might feel differently if the thirty-two pieces of removed Wall were not right nearby and thus easily movable back to where they had been. Since the Wall segments were there, however, the plan to utilize the Corten steel columns instead was a "second best solution. And if we are taking such a big step as to construct a memorial site here [that will last] for generations, then we should adopt the best [solution] and not the second best."[85] Gauck was also clearly not persuaded by the Sophien argument made by Kulick that it was important to mark the history of the site after 1990, including Sophien's removal of the pieces of Wall. For him, the "brutality of the Wall" was the key thing that should be portrayed, not post-1990 disagreements about how to treat the remains of the Wall. Although divisions over how the expanded Berlin Wall Memorial should look were not just based on the previous East-West division, there was certainly a vocal contingent from the East among the members of the scientific advisory board who were against the Corten steel compared to a contingent from the West, including director Klausmeier, who supported the winning design.

At the end of February 2009, the remaining majority of the board decided to support the winning design with the Corten steel rods and not insist on filling in the gaps with pieces of the original Wall (see Figure 9 in Chapter 2). They did not want to risk losing the use of the key land owned by the Sophien Church in the memorial. In addition, since Klausmeier had a background in historic preservation, he argued for the importance of adhering to the guidelines for historic preservation contained in the 1979 "Burra Charter" of the International Council on Monuments and Sites (ICOMOS), the main body on such issues. These guidelines were strictly against any reconstruction of a site and favored presenting it "as found" at the time, just as historic landmark experts had argued in the 1990s against plans for reconstruction. Klausmeier viewed the critics' desire for reconstruction as a recipe for "Disneyland at Bernauer Strasse." He also emphasized that nothing – no amount of reconstruction – could possibly bring back the fear connected with the former Berlin Wall, since there were no longer armed guards with an order to shoot would-be escapees at the site. Hence, the task was to provide enough information with authentic remains, personal stories, photographs, and films so that people could imagine how it had been.[86] Of course, one could argue that the Corten

---

[85] rbb, Klartext, "20 Jahre Mauerfall – Streit um Gedenkstätte Bernauer Strasse," February 11, 2009.

[86] Axel Klausmeier, "Ein Memorialort neuer Prägung: Die Erweiterung der 'Gedenkstätte Berliner Mauer' an der Bernauer Strasse," *Deutschland Archiv* 42 (5/2009), pp. 892–900; and "Ein unbequemes Denkmal mitten in der Stadt. Interview mit Prof. Dr. Axel Klausmeier, Direktor der Stiftung Berliner Mauer," *Deutschland Archiv*, August 9, 2013.

steel columns to mark the path of the Wall did, in fact, represent a certain kind of reconstruction, albeit a subtle one.

In early March the foundation council agreed with the board's recommendation to proceed as planned with the Corten steel columns.[87] The later addition of other more powerful, evocative elements to the memorial, particularly the Window of Commemoration (*Fenster des Gedenkens*) for the victims of the Wall, would help mute the criticism of the narrow Corten steel rods which people could easily walk between. The path of the Wall was thus far more porous than it had been with all the concrete segments, but that reflected the fact that the Wall was no longer closed or a border. A week after the Berlin Wall Memorial Foundation agreed not to fill in the gaps with the pieces of Wall and instead to mark the Wall's path with the steel columns, the Sophien church community agreed (again) to allow its cemetery property to be used as part of the memorial.[88]

While this issue was resolved at Bernauer Strasse, even if not to everyone's satisfaction, another problem lingered – that of property owners who did not want to sacrifice some or all of their front or backyards to the expanded Berlin Wall Memorial Site. Part of the expansion plan was to show the former patrol route for the border soldiers' vehicles within the border strip. The *Gesamtkonzept* sought to highlight the patrol route not just in the first block of Bernauer Strasse between Gartenstrasse and Ackerstrasse on the land owned by the Sophien parish but also along the other six blocks north, starting with the block where the Chapel of Reconciliation stood and stretching to Schwedter Strasse. There were many other property owners in the other six blocks. Hence, a significant portion of federal funding (about twenty-eight million euros) for the *Gesamtkonzept* was to buy land from property owners along these six blocks.

Most property owners settled with the state of Berlin, allowing part of their front or backyards to be used by the memorial for the patrol route and other markings concerning historical events connected with the Wall (such as escapes or arrests) that took place there; but a few banded together to limit the further expansion of the outdoor exhibit area of the Berlin Wall Memorial, not wanting to give up their yards.[89] After starting a mediation process in 2011,

---

[87] Stiftung Berliner Mauer press release, "Stiftungsrat einig: Planungen für Gedenkstätte Berliner Mauer bestätigt," March 3, 2009.

[88] Many new, younger members of the Sophien parish were more supportive of the plans for the Berlin Wall Memorial than its older leaders had been. Interview with Horst Kulick, November 6, 2018; and see Günter Schlusche, "From the Fall of the Wall to the Berlin Wall Memorial: How an Urban Commemorative Space Was Created," in Axel Klausmeier, ed, *The Berlin Wall: Berlin Wall Memorial Exhibition Catalog*, trans. Miriamne Fields (Berlin: Ch. Links, 2015), p. 170.

[89] Barbara Junge (a journalist and co-owner of one of the properties), "50 Jahre Mauer. Von Gassen und Sackgassen," *Tagesspiegel*, August 8, 2011.

three property owners were still holding out as of 2019, preventing an uninterrupted path of the former patrol route along part of one block.[90] The block is
not in the central area of the memorial but is located between Brunnenstrasse
and Ruppiner Strasse. The houses there front onto Schönholzer Strasse, which
runs parallel to Bernauer Strasse, and their backyards are located partially in
the former death strip, including where the patrol route was.

In the case of one of those houses, Ulrich Stark had bought the property in
1994. Stark had moved from East to West Berlin before the border was closed
and afterwards he helped people escape, as did his father. Ulrich Stark became
a property developer in West Berlin and when the Wall fell he looked for
a house to buy. He did not intend to buy something on the former border, but
the house on Schönholzer Strasse had all that he and his wife were looking for,
so they bought it. The backyard, however, was very small, since it backed onto
the former border strip. In 1996, the federal government passed a law on
property at the former Wall (*Mauergrundstücksgesetz*), which gave the Starks
the opportunity to buy more land to extend their backyard as long as there was
no public need for the land. Knowing the significance of the site, Stark asked
repeatedly whether the government would want the land in the former border
strip for a memorial. As we have seen, however, in the 1990s, most people
wanted to leave the Wall in the past and Manfred Fischer and Helmut Trotnow
were fighting to keep just one block of the Wall further south on Bernauer
Strasse. Assured that the government did not want to construct a memorial
along the former border strip where the Starks' house was, they bought the
land to extend their backyard.[91]

In 2006 with the *Gesamtkonzept* this all changed, as the Berlin Senate and
the federal government decided that they did in fact want to expand the site of
the Berlin Wall Memorial. In the meantime, however, Stark's son Holger and
Holger's wife Barbara Junge, both journalists, were living in the house with
their children and did not want to give up part of their backyard. In fact, they
had removed the patrol route, planted grass, bushes, and fruit trees, installed
a swing set, and put up a fence. Thus, the Berlin Wall Memorial had to create
a detour from the patrol route around their yard and the other two nearby.[92]
As we have seen in the case of the Sophien community, finding common

---

[90] Holger Stark (a journalist and co-owner of one of the properties), speech to the final
mediation session of February 11, 2012. Thomas Knorr-Siedow, Urban Plus,
"Vermittlungsverfahren Bebauungsplan 1-40b Erweiterter Bereich Gedenkstätte
Berliner Mauer, Abschlussmediation, February 11, 2012, Handlungsvorschläge des
Vermittlers." Documents shared with the author by Holger Stark.

[91] Interviews with Ulrich Stark, July 24 and 30, 2014, and with his son, Holger Stark, and
daughter-in-law Barbara Junge, July 4, 2014.

[92] The foundation is still involved in talks with the property owners and at times requests
that their backyards be open to the public on key dates such as November 9.
Correspondence with Holger Stark, February 22, 2019.

ground between the interests of the Berlin Wall Memorial and those of other property owners has not always been easy.

By the late 2000s, federal officials had weathered a series of contentious debates on the relative weight to devote to Nazi and communist history in their *Erinnerungpolitik* and ended up making a new commitment to examine and highlight the history of East Germany and the Berlin Wall. This was reflected in backing for the expansion of the Berlin Wall Memorial Site from one block to nearly one mile so as to present a more thorough picture of what the Wall had meant to individuals, the city, the country, and the world. Exactly how to talk about the history of the Wall, which narrative or narratives to emphasize, would remain, however, a source of contention at the memorial and beyond.

7

Victims and Perpetrators

Since the fall of the Wall, memory activists have long centered the memory of the Wall on victims, particularly those killed trying to escape. Manfred Fischer's efforts to preserve the Wall as a "crime scene," the erection of the Kohlhoff & Kohlhoff memorial at Bernauer Strasse, Alexandra Hildebrandt's cemetery of crosses at Checkpoint Charlie, Berlin's master plan (*Gesamtkonzept*) for remembering the Wall, and the federal government's plan for memorials (*Gedenkstättenkonzeption*) were all illustrative of this focus. This would remain the case with the expansion of the Berlin Wall Memorial Site at Bernauer Strasse. Simultaneously, however, a contentious process of examining and remembering the perpetrators also took place, yet this time outside of the courtroom.

The Berlin Wall Memorial and Victims

Inspired by Hildebrandt's crosses, both the Gesamtkonzept of 2006 and the 2007 guidelines for the design competition to expand the outdoor exhibit in the former death strip at Bernauer Strasse stated that, "the task of the memorial site is to name the dead by their names, show their faces and their biographies to the public, anchor them in public memory, and create a site for individual mourning as well as collective public commemoration."[1] The staff of the Berlin Wall Memorial had previously been focusing on how the Wall affected the lives of people living and working along Bernauer Strasse and not specifically on people who had been killed at the Wall.[2] To accomplish the new mandate, researchers needed to ascertain the identities of the people killed at the Wall.[3]

---

[1] Senatsverwaltung für Stadtentwicklung, "Erweiterung der Gedenkstätte Berliner Mauer, Berlin Mitte, offener Realisierungswettbewerb für Hochbau, Freiraum und Ausstellung, Auslobung," Berlin, July 2007, p. 94, www.stadtentwicklung.berlin.de/aktuell/wettbe werbe/ergebnisse/2007/bernauer_strasse/bernauer_strasse_auslobung.pdf.

[2] Interview with Gabriele Camphausen, November 6, 2018.

[3] Konrad Jarausch repeatedly emphasized the importance of this. See his testimony to the Berlin parliament's Committee for Cultural Affairs during an expert hearing on dealing with GDR history and the Wall, Abgeordnetenhaus von Berlin, Ausschuss für Kulturelle Angelegenheiten, Wortprotokoll Kult 15/58, April 25, 2005, p. 9; and his testimony to the Bundestag's Committee on Culture and Media during an expert hearing about

The historian and head of the national Memorial on German Resistance (to the Nazis), Peter Steinbach, had urged the staff of the Berlin Wall Memorial in the early 2000s to do the necessary research, and each year on August 13 when Rainer and/or Alexandra Hildebrandt hosted a press conference at the Checkpoint Charlie Museum and declared the number of the supposed victims of the East German border, journalists asked the staff of the Berlin Wall Memorial how many people they believed were killed at the border. They had no answer. The board discussed the importance of investigating how many people were killed at the Wall but did not have the funding or personnel to carry out this research.[4] The fact that no one had done this in the years since 1989 was an indication of the low priority that had been placed on dealing with this part of German history and of concern about competing with victims of the Holocaust. Hildebrandt's crosses changed this.

In December 2004, Maria Nooke as project director at the Berlin Wall Memorial decided to start the process of determining the actual number of people killed at the Wall, beginning with the inner-city border. She soon learned that Hans-Hermann Hertle of the Center for Contemporary History was compiling information about people killed on the outer border between Brandenburg and West Berlin. They decided to join forces. Nooke and Hertle were deep into the research by the summer of 2005 when a senior official from the federal commission for culture (BKM), Knut Nevermann, visited Nooke at the Berlin Wall Memorial shortly after the removal of Hildebrandt's crosses. Given the public response to the crosses, BKM understood that more needed to be done to commemorate the victims. Nevermann favored a more professional approach than the one taken by Hildebrandt, who had provided no information on how she arrived at the number of 1,075 people killed at the Wall and the inner-German border. Nooke described her work with Hertle to Nevermann and, by the end of the summer, BKM had agreed to fund a two-year project to investigate the biographies of individuals who were killed at the Wall.[5]

Nooke and Hertle were already scouring multiple archives and conducting interviews to find out as much as they could about people who had been killed at the Wall. With some initial information yielding biographical details about individuals killed at the Wall, on August 13, 2005 Pastor Fischer began to hold memorial prayer services for them at the Chapel of Reconciliation. The results of Hertle and Nooke's research were presented in press conferences and public ceremonies starting in 2007 and finally in a book, *The Victims at the Berlin Wall, 1961–1989: A Biographical Handbook*, published in German in 2009 and

---

commemorating the Wall at the Brandenburg Gate and about cooperating with Flierl's *Gedenkkonzept*, Deutscher Bundestag, Ausschuss für Kultur und Medien, Protokoll 15/60, June 15, 2005, p. 7.

[4] Interview with Maria Nooke, April 15, 2010.

[5] Ibid.; and interview with Knut Nevermann, March 29, 2010.

in English in 2011. At the time of publication, Nooke and Hertle had found conclusive information about 136 people killed at the Wall.[6]

Meanwhile, the scientific advisory board (*Beirat*) of the Berlin Wall Memorial considered how to make the victims visible at the site. Petra Morawe had been in the East German opposition and was a board member. She visited Hildebrandt's crosses and saw a woman placing flowers by one of them. Morawe spoke to the woman and learned that the cross was for her niece who had been killed at the border. The woman told Morawe how much it meant to her to have a place to mourn and clearly did not consider the Kohlhoff & Kohlhoff memorial such a place. Morawe and the other board members deliberated about how to create a more appropriate place for relatives to mourn at Bernauer Strasse, "a place that would give the victims their names back."

In a September 2005 proposal entitled, "Concept on the Issue of Commemoration," Morawe suggested creating an outdoor photo gallery with pictures of the victims taken "in everyday situations" with their names and dates of birth and death presented in what she called "a death book that one could walk up to." She proposed putting this photo gallery on the steel wall of the Kohlhoff & Kohlhoff memorial, which faced the Sophien cemetery. Morawe found inspiration for this proposal from visiting a memorial to Nazi victims that took this approach with pictures and names. It also left spaces to add more victims as they became known.[7]

Initially Morawe's proposal was controversial with some other *Beirat* members who felt that such a picture gallery "would be emotionally overwhelming for visitors." Just as the broader public debate about commemorating the Wall and its victims featured disagreements about how "professional" and "restrained" vs. how "emotional" commemoration should be, so did debates among board members of the Berlin Wall Memorial. On the board, it was often people from the east who favored approaches that involved showing how brutal the border regime was, bringing back a guard tower to the site, and reconstructing more of the former border, while people from the west were more inclined toward restraint in depicting the Wall. There were of course exceptions to this, as in the case of *Beirat* chair Klaus-Dietmar Henke who was from the west and initially favored reconstruction but then changed his mind.[8]

---

[6] In 2013, two more victims were identified: "Museum ermittelt 137. Berliner Todes-Opfer," *Bild*, August 13, 2013; and "138. Berliner Mauer-Opfer ermittelt," *Tagesspiegel*, November 15, 2013. As of 2019, 140 victims have been identified, www.chronik-der-mauer.de/todesopfer/.

[7] Petra Morawe, "Enwurf zum Thema Gedenken," for the task force meeting at Bernauer Strasse on September 25, 2005; and interview with Morawe, July 7, 2014.

[8] Interviews with Klaus-Dietmar Henke, December 22, 2009; Petra Morawe, July 7, 2014; Marianne Birthler, July 7, 2014; and Manfred Fischer, October 6 and 15, 2009.

Figure 19 *Fenster des Gedenkens*, Berlin Wall Memorial
Source: Hope M. Harrison.

Morawe's vision of a photo gallery of victims was essentially sanctioned by both the *Gesamtkonzept* and the 2007 guidelines for the architectural competition for the expansion of Bernauer Strasse to "give the victims names and faces." Moreover, the guidelines for the expansion made clear that the outdoor exhibit in the former death strip must appeal to people emotionally[9] and provide them with a real sense of what the Berlin Wall meant.

In May 2010, nearly six years after Hildebrandt had unveiled her crosses, the Berlin Wall Foundation and Mayor Wowereit completed the first stage of the expansion of the site and dedicated a Window of Commemoration (*Fenster des Gedenkens*), to those killed at the Wall (Figure 19). This permanent structure features rows of "windows" with pictures of the individual victims, including Michael Schmidt whose lethal attempt to escape was described in Chapter 1 (see Figure 4). The *Fenster* provides their names and the dates of their birth and death. Families and friends of the victims were invited to the ceremony, which included a moment when they all placed white roses in their loved one's "*Fenster*." They, the media, and the general public found the *Fenster* to be a much more appropriate and moving way to commemorate those killed at the Wall than the Kohlhoff & Kohlhoff memorial. The *Fenster des Gedenkens* became the emotional heart of the Berlin Wall Memorial. Information on those killed at the Wall is also presented in the indoor exhibit at Bernauer Strasse as well as in the Bundestag's library and online at the chronik-der-mauer.de website.

---

[9] Senatsverwaltung für Stadtentwicklung, "Erweiterung der Gedenkstätte Berliner Mauer, Auslobung," Berlin, July 2007, p. 9.

The *Gesamtkonzept* had called for people killed at the border to be commemorated not only in a central location at Bernauer Strasse but also at the site where they were actually killed. In 2009, Berlin and Brandenburg began joint commemoration of those who were killed on the outer border between Berlin and Brandenburg. People who had been killed in the center of Berlin had been memorialized already in the former West Berlin and since unification with crosses and other signs of respect at specific sites near where they had been killed.[10] This had been much less the case for people killed outside of the city center. Starting in 2009, individual steel columns were installed to mark the sites where people were killed trying to escape all along the former outer ring of the Wall. These stelae included a picture of the person and biographical information in German and English. In 2013, Hertle and Nooke published a joint German/English handbook, *The Victims at the Berlin-Brandenburg Border, 1961–1989*.[11] The forty-six victims at this border had previously been included among the victims whose biographies Hertle and Nooke had made public in 2009.

Another group of Wall victims to be commemorated were people who were forced out of their houses as their homes were either integrated into the border zone or razed to make room for the fortified border. The expanded outdoor exhibit at Bernauer Strasse included "archeological windows" displaying the foundations of buildings razed by the East German regime at the border. The commemoration of victims has also included people who were imprisoned for trying to escape from the GDR or on suspicion of planning to escape or helping others escape. Tens of thousands of these people ended up in Stasi prisons, such as at Berlin-Hohenschönhausen, now a memorial museum. Research to ascertain the biographies of several hundred people killed at the East-West German border is still ongoing.[12] Current estimates are that a further 200 people were killed trying to escape across the Baltic Sea and up to 300 were killed attempting to get to the West from other Soviet bloc countries.[13]

---

[10] Pertti Ahonen, *Death at the Berlin Wall* (New York: Oxford University Press, 2011); and Anna Saunders, *Memorializing the GDR* (NY: Berghahn, 2018), pp. 214–24.

[11] Maria Nooke and Hans-Hermann Hertle, eds., *Die Todesopfer am Aussenring der Berliner Mauer 1961–1989. The Victims at the Berlin-Brandenburg Border, 1961–1989* (Berlin/Potsdam: Center for Civic Education of the Federal State of Brandenburg, 2013).

[12] For a contested study of the 327 victims documented at the inner-German border, see Klaus Schroeder and Jochen Staadt, eds., *Die Todesopfer des DDR-Grenzregimes an der innerdeutschen Grenze 1949–1989: Ein biografisches Handbuch* (Frankfurt am Main: Peter Lang, 2017); Gabi Probst, "Zahl der Toten an inner-deutscher Grenze vermütlich falsch," rbb, November 6, 2018; and Alexander Fröhlich, "Umstrittene Studie zu Mauertoten 'nicht verfügbar'," *Tagesspiegel*, November 8, 2018.

[13] Andreas Conrad, "327 Tote an innerdeutscher Grenze," *Tagesspiegel*, June 7, 2017.

The Fiftieth Anniversary of the Erection of the Berlin Wall, August 2011

The broadest public commemoration to date of victims of the Wall and the border took place on the fiftieth anniversary of the erection of the Wall in 2011. It included an official ceremony at the Berlin Wall Memorial, widespread media coverage, the publication of many books on the Wall,[14] scholarly debates and conferences, photography and art exhibits, an interactive 3-D virtual installation of the Wall,[15] and a new musical on the Wall. Newspapers were filled with detailed maps of the path of the Wall and with documents related to the process of erecting the Wall. The ongoing international interest in the Berlin Wall was clear in 2011 with the European Union's designation of the Berlin Wall Memorial as a site of European cultural heritage and UNESCO's registration of a selection of photographs and documents related to the rise and fall of the Wall in its "Memory of the World" collection. A website in German, English, French, and Russian provided information on the many events planned to commemorate the history of the Wall, 50JahreMauerbau.de (50 Years since the Construction of the Wall).

For months, German and especially Berlin newspapers, television, and radio were filled with accounts by East Germans who suffered because of the Wall and border, stories of classmates, family, friends, and lovers divided by the Wall. Some newspapers such as the *Berliner Morgenpost, Berliner Zeitung*, and *Bild* profiled such individuals every day in what seemed to be a cathartic telling and retelling of stories. On the weekend of the anniversary, the *Berliner Zeitung* featured an East Berlin high school class that graduated just before the Wall was erected. The paper profiled ten classmates and teachers and the separate lives they lived in East and West Berlin after the border was closed. On the fiftieth anniversary, eighteen of the classmates reunited at the school.[16]

---

[14] Highly publicized books that appeared in Germany in 2011 about the Wall include Klaus-Dietmar Henke, ed., *Die Mauer* (Munich: Deutscher Taschenbuch Verlag, 2011); Hope M. Harrison, *Ulbrichts Mauer* (Berlin: Propyläen, 2011); Manfred Wilke, *Der Weg zur Mauer* (Berlin: Ch. Links, 2011); Frederick Kempe, *Berlin 1961* (Munich: Siedler, 2011); Jens Schöne, *Ende einer Utopie* (Berlin: Berlin Story Verlag, 2011); and Heinz Keßler and Fritz Streletz, *Ohne die Mauer hätte es Krieg gegeben: Zwei Zeitzeugen erinnern sich* (Berlin: edition ost, 2011). There were also many books published with photographs of the Wall such as Karl-Ludwig Lange, *Die Berliner Mauer, Fotografien 1973 bis heute* (Erfurt: Sutton, 2011); Jost-A. Bösenberg and J.-F. Huffmann, *Mauerjahre: Leben in geteilten Berlin* (Hamburg: Edel-Verlag, 2011); and Annett Gröschner and Arwed Messmer, eds., *Aus anderer Sicht: Die frühe Berliner Mauer/The Other View: The Early Berlin Wall* (Berlin: Hatje Cantz, 2011).

[15] www.virtuelle-mauer-berlin.de/assets/download/VM_goes_school_2012_Infomappe.pdf.

[16] Thomas Leinkauf, "Klassentreffen," *Berliner Zeitung*, August 13–14, 2011. Similarly, in 2006, Dietrich Garstka told the story of his class at an East German high school that took a stand in 1956 in support of the Hungarian Revolution, leading to great pressure on them by the East German authorities and the decision of many of the classmates, including Garstka, to flee to the West. In 1996, the classmates who stayed in the East and those who fled to the West gathered again at their old high school in Storkow, Brandenburg for a reunion. Garstka, *Das schweigende Klassenzimmer* (Berlin: Ullstein, 2006). The story got

Documentaries and historically inspired made-for-television films added to an immersion in the history of 1961 and the years of Berlin's division afterwards.[17] As Peter Schneider observed, "many in the West had not known these stories, had not really known how East Germans responded to the Wall."[18] So often in united Germany it seemed that people from the West spoke, and people from the East listened. Now that was reversed.

While political leaders and the families and friends of victims had been gathering at Bernauer Strasse for years on August 13 and November 9 to commemorate victims of the Wall, the fiftieth anniversary on August 13, 2011 was the most important such moment. Manfred Fischer had prepared for the occasion for months. Since midnight the night before and all morning until the beginning of the official ceremony at 10 a.m., people had gathered in the Chapel of Reconciliation to read the names and biographies of people killed at the Wall. In many cases a family member or friend read the biography of their loved one, beginning with the last person shot at the Wall, Chris Gueffroy in 1989, and ending with the first person who died there, Ida Siekmann, twelve days after the border was closed. *Deutschlandradio* broadcast the readings live.

Following the readings in the chapel, Federal President Christian Wulff, Chancellor Angela Merkel, Mayor Wowereit and other German leaders, relatives of victims, and other invited guests gathered for a ceremony outside. The two-hour ceremony was televised live nationally by ARD and by *Deutsche Welle* internationally. The commemoration included speeches, a prayer service, a laying of wreaths at the memorial, and a citywide moment of silence. Thousands gathered along Bernauer Strasse to watch the big screens showing the ceremony for those without official invitations for seats in front of the stage. Throughout the day, an estimated 20,000 people came to the Berlin Wall Memorial.[19]

The speeches by politicians reflected the prevailing political view that the Wall and the whole East German regime behind it were unjust (*Unrecht*) and violated human rights. Political leaders condemned any other view as *Ostalgie* and a "belittling" (*Verharmlosung*) of the true brutality of the regime. Mayor Wowereit expressed this particularly vehemently: "Those who nostalgically idealize the division and the Wall deserve no understanding. The Wall was part of a dictatorial system, an unjust regime [*Unrechtsstaat*]. And it is horrifying

---

much more attention when it was made into a movie in 2018. The English version is entitled, *The Silent Revolution.*

[17] Documentaries broadcast on the history of the Wall in August 2011 included: *Die Vergessenen – Tod, wo andere Urlaub machen* on RTL, August 7; *Goodbye DDR-Spektakuläre Mauerfluchten* on ZDF, August 7; *Geheimakte Mauerbau – Die Nacht der Entscheidung,* ZDF, August 9; and the four-hour Spiegel TV documentary, *50 Jahre Mauerbau* on VOX, August 13, 2011. Kurt Sagatz, "Mauer Fantasien," *Tagesspiegel,* August 7, 2011.

[18] Conversation with Peter Schneider, August 12, 2011.

[19] Nina Apin, "Open-Air-Geschichtsstunde," *taz,* August 14, 2011.

that there are still some people today who think that the SED had good reasons for sealing off the border. No! There are no good reasons and no justification for injustice, for the violation of human rights, for death at the Wall and the barbed wire."[20] The fact that Wowereit was up for reelection the following month and was considering all coalition options, including with the Greens and the CDU, and seemingly would not continue his coalition with the PDS likely contributed to the aggressive tone of his remarks. They were echoed by Cultural Commissioner Bernd Neumann.

In his remarks, President Wulff told the story of the first person killed at the Wall, Ida Siekmann, on August 22, 1961: "Here on Bernauer Strasse, she wanted to jump from [her apartment on] the third floor to freedom. In her desperation, she first threw down bedding, hoping to cushion the jump. It didn't help. She died one day before her 59th birthday." He also spoke about twenty-four-year-old Günter Litfin who tried to swim across a canal in the center of Berlin between East and West and was shot and killed in the water two days after Ida Siekmann had died of her injuries. "We bow our heads before all those who were killed at the Wall and the...inner-German border, the borders to third states, and in the Baltic Sea."[21] By focusing on individual stories, the federal president made the brutal nature of East Germany's border regime clear to all.

Yet the president also sought to reassure eastern Germans that his criticism of the SED regime was "not meant to devalue lives lived in the GDR. Due to the injustice that was perpetrated in the name of all Germans before 1945, the east Germans particularly suffered." He expressed his admiration for how "fellow citizens in the GDR were able to cope with their lives under authoritarian circumstances" and how "millions remained role models with great moral effort." While East Germans were facing such challenges, the president criticized the "shameful apathy" among West Germans about the Wall, many of whom felt themselves "barely affected by the fate of millions of Germans on the other side of the barbed wire." Remembering 1989, Wulff praised and thanked those in the GDR who, with "heroic courage," took to the streets demanding change and thus helped bring down the Wall and unite Germany.

Freya Klier represented those on "the other side of the barbed wire" at the anniversary ceremony. At the age of eighteen, Klier had been imprisoned at Hohenschönhausen for attempting to escape via the Baltic Sea. A sailor saw her and reported her. She was captured and endured brutal treatment in prison. Klier spoke with great empathy of her prison cellmate Susanne, a young

---

[20] Mayor Wowereit, speech at the Berlin Wall Memorial, August 13, 2011, www.berlin.de/rbmskzl/aktuelles/pressemitteilungen/2011/pressemitteilung.53377.php.

[21] German President Christian Wulff, speech at the Berlin Wall Memorial, "Schätzen und schützen wir die Freiheit," August 13, 2011, www.bundespraesident.de/SharedDocs/Reden/DE/Christian-Wulff/Reden/2011/08/110813-Gedenkveranstaltung-Mauerbau.html.

architecture student, who had tried to escape across the East-West German border from Thuringia but was reported by two separate people who lived near the border and saw her. As Klier recalled, "I tried to imagine how eager comrades sprang out of bed, first went to the window in the dark, then rushed to the telephone to plunge into misfortune people whose entire criminality consisted of wanting to leave the GDR."[22] Klier urged the audience to remember not just those who were killed or injured trying to escape, but all of their family members left behind, including children who were put in orphanages when their parents were killed or imprisoned.

Giving victims of the Wall a chance to speak and tell their stories has been an important part of implementing the *Gesamtkonzept*, and the Berlin Wall Memorial has been particularly active in offering victims this chance. Other victims would speak later in the afternoon at public sessions at the memorial site about their attempts to escape, their imprisonment, and their lives along Bernauer Strasse. They would be joined by former West Berlin policemen and others who helped people escape across, under, or over the Wall.

Part of the morning's official ceremony included a moment Fischer had choreographed carefully. A former resident of Bernauer Strasse 4 had once given Fischer a key to their house, which had been torn down by the East Germans to create the Berlin Wall. Fischer wanted Klausmeier to have the key for the exhibit in the Documentation Center, but he decided that it would be a more powerful moment if the German president was involved, helping to anchor the Berlin Wall Memorial as a major national commemorative site. It would also make good theater for those watching at the site and on national television. Accordingly, standing outside in the former death strip, just steps from where the house at Bernauer Strasse 4 had been, Fischer handed the key to President Wulff (Figure 20), saying, "Let this be a sign that the Berlin Wall Memorial site unlocks the memory of the division of the city to its visitors: a key to the history of the Wall." Wulff accepted the key and handed it on to Klausmeier.[23]

The key was also quite fitting, because the day marked the completion of the second stage of the expansion of the memorial site, now to include the block surrounding the Chapel of Reconciliation, a block that featured archaeological sites displaying the foundations of houses like the one at Bernauer Strasse 4 that had been destroyed to build the border. In this block of the expansion, by the use of big round pillars containing photographs, recordings and live film excerpts, as well as other markers in the ground at locations where

[22] Freya Klier, speech at the Berlin Wall Memorial, August 13, 2011, www.berliner-mauer-gedenkstaette.de/de/uploads/50jahrestag_dokumente/rede_klier_13_08_2011.pdf.

[23] Interview with Manfred Fischer, August 17, 2011; and "Liturgie: Pfarrer Manfred Fischer, Predigt: Bischof Dr. Markus Dröge am 13. August 2011, 50. Jahrestag des Mauerbaus bei der Ökumenischen Andacht in der Kapelle der Versöhnung."

Figure 20 Manfred Fischer handing key to President Christian Wulff, Berlin Wall
Memorial, August 13, 2011
Source: Photographer: Jürgen Hochmuth, Stiftung Berliner Mauer-2401.

dramatic events connected to the erection of the Wall occurred, visitors
learned about people who jumped out of their windows to escape to the
West when the border was closed, the four tunnels built under the border in
this one block, and stories of some who made it to the West and some who died
trying. Inside the Chapel of Reconciliation with its loam walls (Figure 11 in
Chapter 3), visitors could also read about the history of the Church of
Reconciliation and its 1985 demolition, see relics from the church, and take
part in daily prayers for people killed at the Wall.[24]

Leading up to the August 2011 anniversary, Manfred Fischer had worked
with key institutions in Berlin, including the *Tagesspiegel* newspaper and the
public transportation system, to implement a moment of silence in the city at
noon in honor of the victims of the Wall.[25] The man who in 1989 wanted to
preserve part of the Wall as a crime scene, was finally going to make sure that
those who were killed there received widespread acknowledgment. Three days

---

[24] Rolf Lautenschläger, "Spuren der gelöschten Stadt," *taz*, August 12, 2011. The Berlin Wall
Memorial now has brochures in English and German for each section of the expanded
site, including this block, which is called "Area B: The Destruction of the City." The
brochures give information on each of the "incident markers" in the area, telling many
personal stories.

[25] Interviews with Manfred Fischer, August 17, 2011, and Gerd Nowakowski of the
Tagesspiegel, July 28, 2014.

before the anniversary, Mayor Wowereit and federal Cultural Commissioner Neumann backed Fischer's plan by appealing to Berliners to observe a moment of silence on August 13 in honor of all those who were killed trying to escape, all the families that were divided, and in commemoration of the division of Berlin and Germany. The Berlin Transportation Authority announced that wherever possible trains and buses would also come to a halt. Just before the moment of silence at the Berlin Wall Memorial, seven of the most senior German leaders lined up with the director of the Berlin Wall Foundation to lay wreaths for victims at the memorial as Fischer looked on (see Figure 18, Chapter 5). At noon, the leaders stood solemnly with their heads bowed as church bells rang at the Chapel of Reconciliation and throughout the city.[26] The moment was a powerful statement about both the place of commemorating victims of the Wall and the importance of the memorial site itself in German *Geschichtspolitik*. As Bishop Markus Dröge said during the ceremony in the chapel, "The memory of the Wall...belongs to the soul of Berlin and to the collective memory of our country."[27]

After the moment of silence, followed by the national anthem, Fischer concluded the ceremony by leading everyone in the song, *Die Gedanken sind frei* ("Thoughts are Free"). The song dates back to the early nineteenth century and was sung by many people who resisted the Nazi and GDR regimes. One stanza particularly makes it clear why the song resonated with people imprisoned in the GDR for trying to escape: "And if I am confined to a dark dungeon, this is all wasted work. Because my thoughts break the bars and walls asunder, thoughts are free!" As Fischer sang confidently and clearly, Chancellor Merkel stood next to him smiling shyly and singing along as did the president, mayor, and other leading politicians (Figure 21). Things had changed dramatically in the more than twenty years since Fischer started his fight for a memorial for victims of the Wall at Bernauer Strasse.

In addition to a ceremony at the Berlin Wall Memorial, a few days earlier the mayors of Berlin and Brandenburg had unveiled memorials to two people who had been killed on the external border of Berlin.[28] To draw attention to these and other victims, Alexandra Hildebrandt took out a two-page, centerfold ad in the *Berliner Morgenpost* on the weekend of the fiftieth anniversary with a list of people killed not just at the Wall and elsewhere along the entire East German border but under a variety of circumstances between 1945 and 1990, such as people killed during the Berlin blockade and airlift, Soviet Red Army deserters, East German soldiers who were killed, and people who took

---

[26] Thomas Rogalla, "Berlin soll am 13. August eine Minute lang schweigen," *Berliner Zeitung*, August 10, 2011.

[27] Bishop Dröge's sermon, "Liturgie: Pfarrer Manfred Fischer, Predigt: Bischof Dr. Markus Dröge am 13. August 2011, 50. Jahrestag des Mauerbaus bei der Ökumenischen Andacht in der Kapelle der Versöhnung."

[28] Jürgen Stich, "Platzeck und Wowereit kommen am 8. August nach Teltow," *Märkische Allgemeine*, August 3, 2011.

Figure 21 Manfred Fischer (middle) leading top German officials in song (left to right): Constitutional Court Justice Susanne Baer, Bundesrat President Hannelore Kraft, Chancellor Angela Merkel, Bundestag President Norbert Lammert, President Christian Wulff, Mayor Klaus Wowereit, Berlin Wall Memorial, August 13, 2011
Source: Hope M. Harrison.

their own lives in Stasi prisons.[29] She also brought back for one day fifty of the crosses she had installed at Checkpoint Charlie in 2004. In view of the great attention on the Berlin Wall Memorial, with the state ceremony there, Hildebrandt no doubt also sought to make sure that her Checkpoint Charlie Museum was not overlooked.

The fiftieth anniversary saw a reprise of debates featured during the Wall trials about who was more to blame for the existence of the Wall and its deadly character – the East German or Soviet leaders. Former East German defense minister Heinz Kessler and his deputy Fritz Streletz, both of whom had been tried in the 1990s, published a book together that maintained, as its title declared, *Without the Wall, There Would Have Been War*.[30] Cynically citing President Kennedy's private comment (which was later publicized) to an aide in the wake of the erection of the

[29] "Wir trauern um die Todesopfer des Grenzregimes der Sowjetische Besatzungszone/DDR/der Sozialistischen Einheitspartei Deutschlands," *Berliner Morgenpost*, pp. 6–7.

[30] Heinz Keßler and Fritz Streletz, *Ohne die Mauer hätte es Krieg gegeben: Zwei Zeitzeugen erinnern sich* (Berlin: edition ost, 2011).

Wall that, "a wall is a hell of a lot better than a war,"[31] the two former military leaders insisted that the Wall had kept the peace at the center of the Cold War.[32] They also continued the argument they made on trial that Moscow bore the brunt of the responsibility. It was not just former East German leaders with axes to grind who were involved in the debate; there was a vigorous debate among scholars in books and articles published for the anniversary as well.

The present author argued, as noted in the introduction, that the East German leadership under Walter Ulbricht bore primary responsibility for the idea to build a wall and for the implementation of the lethal border regime. Thus, the Berlin Wall was fundamentally a German matter that could not be pushed onto others' shoulders.[33] The German historians Manfred Wilke and Gerhard Wettig agreed that Ulbricht's role was very important, but generally placed more emphasis on the role of Soviet leader Nikita Khrushchev.[34] Taking a different view of the history, Frederick Kempe asserted that President Kennedy had essentially given Khrushchev and Ulbricht the green light to seal off the border in Berlin as long as it did not interrupt Western access to West Berlin.[35] Whole issues of journals were devoted to the history of the closure of the border and debates about that history.[36] Bookstores had prominent displays of books about the Wall. The media, public lectures, and conferences all took up the question of

[31] For Kennedy's quote, see Kenneth P. O'Donnell, David F. Powers, and Joe McCarthy, *"Johnny we hardly knew ye:" Memoirs of John Fitzgerald Kennedy* (Boston: Little Brown, 1972), p. 303. For a critical discussion of Kennedy's role in the crisis leading to the Berlin Wall, see Fabian Ruegers, "Kennedy, Adenauer, and the Making of the Berlin Wall, 1958–1961," Stanford University doctoral dissertation (May 2011), p. 241.

[32] Matthias Meisner, "Mauerbau – das beste, was Deutschland passieren konnte," *Tagesspiegel*, May 21, 2011.

[33] Hope M. Harrison, *Ulbrichts Mauer* (Berlin: Propyläen, 2011); Harrison, "Walter Ulbricht und der Bau der Mauer," *Deutschland Archiv* 44 (2011), pp. 15–22; Harrison, "Walter Ulbrichts 'dringender Wunsch,'" *Aus Politik und Zeigeschichte* 61, nos. 31–34 (August 1, 2011), pp. 8–15; and interview by Sven Felix Kellerhoff with Harrison, "Eine deutsche Angelegenheit," *Welt*, August 11, 2011.

[34] Manfred Wilke, *Der Weg zur Mauer*. Wilke's argument also emphasized Ulbricht's role and he was often quoted as agreeing that Ulbricht was essential in understanding the decision to seal the border; Hannes Schwenger, "Herzen aus Stein," *Der Tagesspiegel*, August 8, 2011. Gerhard Wettig, "Die UdSSR und die Berliner Mauer," *Deutschland Archiv* 44 (2011), p. 14; and Wettig, "Chruschtschow, Ulbricht und die Berliner Mauer," *Aus Politik und Zeigeschichte* 61, nos. 31–34 (August 1, 2011), pp. 16–21.

[35] Kempe, *Berlin 1961*. Much of Kempe's argument was also made by Fabian Ruegers, "Kennedy, Adenauer, and the Making of the Berlin Wall, 1958–1961."

[36] See for example, "Sonderheft 50 Jahre Mauerbau," *Deutschland Archiv"* 44 (2011); "50 Jahre Mauerbau," *Aus Politik und Zeitgeschichte* 61, nos. 31–34 (August 1, 2011); and "Special Issue: The Berlin Wall after Fifty Years: 1961–2011," *German Politics and Society* 29, no. 2 (Summer 2011).

the original responsibility for the Wall.[37] Party politics played a role in the debates as well.

Gesine Lötzsch, co-chair of the SED-PDS successor party, the Left (*die Linke*), insisted a few days before August 13 that the Wall was the result of World War II and the division of Germany that followed. She maintained that the building of the Wall could only be understood in the context of the Nazi attack on the Soviet Union, which took place twenty years beforehand. In her very passive rendition of history, she said nothing about the role of the SED or about victims of the Wall.[38] In one fell swoop, she seemed to demolish the progress others in her party had made over the previous ten years in facing up to SED responsibility for the Wall. CDU politicians and others fired back that her aversion to the truth was "irresponsible and caused immense harm to achieving internal unity" in Germany. Moreover, they pointed out that her statement ignored the latest results of historical research and amounted to "the distortion of history."[39] The general secretary of the CSU, Alexander Dobrindt, went so far as to call for a monitoring of *die Linke* by the German domestic intelligence service, which among other tasks monitors people who deny the Holocaust, the latter being a crime in Germany.[40] Thus, Dobrindt was putting the denial of East German responsibility for the Wall on a level with denial of the Holocaust.

In the midst of an election campaign in Mecklenburg-Pommerania, a group on the far left, the Anti-Capitalist Left (AKL), published a position paper in late July justifying the Wall as "an urgent necessity," arguing that "there was no reasonable alternative" due to all the people fleeing the GDR for the more prosperous FRG and that the Wall "prevented war," which presumably they thought would have come if the refugee exodus was not stopped. The same group refused to stand during a moment of silence for victims of the Wall on August 13 in the state parliament in Rostock.[41] The vice chair of *die Linke* in the Bundestag, Dietmar Bartsch, was present in Rostock and reprimanded the group, "There are no ifs, ands, or buts about the need to stand [out of respect] for the dead." He also declared that,

---

[37] Winfried Sträter, "Wie kam es zum Bau der Berliner Mauer?" *Deutschlandradio*, July 13, 2011, 7:30 p.m.; and Sven Felix Kellerhoff, "Ulbrichts, Chruschtschows – oder etwa doch Kennedys Mauer?" *Welt Online*, July 29, 2011. The historians Manfred Wilke, Gerhard Wettig, the present author, and others also held several public debates on the issue at the Berlin Wall Memorial, the Allied Museum, and on *Deutschlandradio*.

[38] Matthias Meisner, "Lötzsch erklärt den Mauerbau," *Tagesspiegel*, August 10, 2011.

[39] CDU/CSU Bundestag caucus press release citing CDU Bundestag member Klaus Brähmig's criticism of Lötzsch, "Brähmig: 50 Jahre Mauerbau – Linke klittert Geschichte," August 11, 2011.

[40] "Niemand hat vor, eine Debatte zu führen," *Süddeutsche Zeitung*, August 31, 2011.

[41] "Linke-Gruppe boykottiert Schweigeminute für Maueropfer," *Spiegel Online*, August 13, 2011.

"Socialism, democracy and freedom cannot be achieved with walls." Other senior leaders of *die Linke* and its historical commission joined in the criticism of the AKL and of Lötzsch.[42]

Yet in a survey in Berlin just before the anniversary, more than one-third of Berliners and nearly three-quarters of those in *die Linke* believed that the erection of the Wall "to stop the exodus of skilled workers from the GDR and stabilize the political situation in the GDR and thus also in all of Germany" was "completely or somewhat justified."[43] Among those from West Berlin or who had moved to Berlin after unification, nearly three-quarters disagreed. Thomas Flierl, who by this point was the city planning spokesman for *die Linke* in Berlin's parliament, and no longer the cultural senator, argued that "from today's vantage point, nothing can justify the erection of the Wall."[44]

The survey question, however, had asked whether the erection of the Wall was "necessary and justified from the perspective of the time" in 1961. Many from the former East clearly thought, as the leaders in 1961 had maintained, that it was. At a moment when German political leaders in 2011 aimed to express their empathy for victims of the Berlin Wall, especially those killed trying to escape, and primarily viewed the Wall as something to be criticized as a manifestation of the "unjust SED dictatorship," as Mayor Wowereit, President Wulff, and Cultural Commissioner Neumann emphasized on August 13 at Bernauer Strasse, not all Germans saw the Wall in this way.

For those who sought a lighter approach to the Wall and the history of the GDR, complete with a story of lovers divided by the Wall, a new musical, *Hinterm Horizont* (*Beyond the Horizon*) had been playing all year to sold-out audiences at Potsdamer Platz.[45] Before the fun started with song and dance, however, the first five minutes featured an astonishingly succinct history lesson with black and white footage of the Wall and a narrator highlighting key moments from the construction of the Wall to its toppling. Based partly on the real life of the West German rock star Udo Lindenberg and using his music, the musical proved so popular that it played for five years and added English subtitles for all the non-German speakers who were interested in the history of the Berlin Wall. More than two million people saw the show, one-third of whom were Berliners, another third came from northern and eastern

---

[42] Ibid.; and Matthias Meisner, "Lötzsch erklärt den Mauerbau," *Tagesspiegel*, August 10, 2011.

[43] Regine Zylka, "Mauerbau war damals richtig," *Berliner Zeitung*, August 3, 2011; and Nina Apin, "Mauerbau hat immer noch Fans," *taz*, August 3, 2011.

[44] Ibid.

[45] Ulrich Waller (producer) and Thomas Brussig (screenplay), *Hinterm Horizont. Das Berlin-Musical über das Mädchen aus Ostberlin mit den Hits von Udo Lindenberg* (Berlin: Stage Management, 2011).

Germany, and the rest were international tourists.[46] The musical moved to Hamburg for another year after its Berlin run.

The Berlin Wall Memorial and *Grenzer*

While most of the focus on those in the death strip of the Berlin Wall has been on people who tried to escape, especially those who were killed in the process, the other group of East Germans who were at the Berlin Wall were of course the border soldiers (*Grenzsoldaten* or *Grenzer*). They have been a much less prominent feature of public memory of the Wall and when they have been featured, it has been controversial. Yet as times passes and young people know less about the Wall, there is more need to explain the whole system that led to the killing of people trying to escape.[47] With increased distance from the years when the Wall stood, more people also feel less of an emotional aversion to investigating the experiences of the *Grenzer*, to including their stories in the overall history of the Wall along with those of people who tried to escape.

After the Wall trials of the 1990s, *Grenzer* largely disappeared from public discussions. Portrayals of individuals at the Wall were primarily of people killed there, not of those who pulled the trigger. Former border soldiers had no desire to come forward and risk being publicly vilified, and few of the memory activists who were engaged in resurrecting the memory of the Berlin Wall wanted to give any sort of "voice" to the *Grenzer*, in part probably fearing that they would be criticized for portraying those who killed or injured people trying to escape in any sort of human way. Just as it took longer to integrate Nazi perpetrators into public memory and *Erinnerungspolitik* of the Holocaust than it did to commemorate the victims, so it is proving to be similar regarding the historical memory of the Berlin Wall and the GDR regime.[48] In many ways it is easier to apologize and mourn for victims than to recognize perpetrators in our midst. Morally speaking, one would usually rather be the victim than the perpetrator. It feels easier and is certainly much more inspirational for most people to imagine fellow citizens dying in their quest for liberty than pulling the trigger to prevent it.

---

[46] Andreas Conrad, "Musicaltheater am Potsdamer Platz wird geschlossen," *Tagesspiegel*, January 20, 2016.

[47] Similarly, the main exhibit at Auschwitz, which opened in 1967, was redesigned from 2011 to 2013 to devote more attention to the perpetrators than was possible and necessary initially. As the Holocaust has become more distant history, young people know less about it and need be taught more about the Nazi regime and its "Final Solution." Michael Kimmelman, "Auschwitz Shifts from Memorializing to Teaching," *New York Times*, February 18, 2011.

[48] Gerhard Paul, "Von Psychopathen, Technokraten des Terrors und 'ganz gewöhnliche' Deutschen: Die Täter der Shoah im Spiegel der Forschung," in Gerhard Paul, ed., *Die Täter der Shoah: Fanatische Nationalsozialisten oder ganz normale Deutsche?* (Göttingen: Wallstein Verlag, 2002), pp. 13–90.

The guidelines for the expansion of the Berlin Wall Memorial made clear the political views of the crafters: "At the center of the design plan must be the sensory experience of the violent character of the border area, which served the SED as an instrument to secure its dictatorship which had no democratic legitimacy and which was the condition for the existence of the GDR."[49] The 2008 *Gedenkstättenkonzeption* also specified that the expansion of the Berlin Wall Memorial at Bernauer Strasse must make clear "the horror of the border regime."[50] There was no mention, however, of whether and how much "the horror of the border regime" would include the *Grenzer* themselves.

The Berlin Wall Memorial staff had been slowly and quietly including *Grenzer* in their historical work and in interviews.[51] Recognizing that more research had been done on the victims of the Wall than on the East German people and institutions who propped up the Wall, the Berlin Wall Memorial sponsored a two-day conference in 2007 on the border regime. The conference included presentations on the roles played by the *Grenzer*, the Stasi, the police, and volunteer informers in maintaining the border. It also featured presentations about individuals who were killed at the border in Berlin and elsewhere.[52] The memorial staff hoped the conference would foster more scholarly research and more interaction between universities and memorial sites at the former border on the functioning of East Germany's border regime. Not surprisingly, the discussions about the border among the scholars and representatives of memorial sites were far less emotional than the dramatic confrontations that would occur six months later at the Berlin Wall Memorial between former victims and perpetrators.

In July 2007, the Berlin Wall Memorial hosted an advance screening of a documentary film by Florian Huber about three people killed at the Wall. Family members of these people as well as representatives of the border troops and the Stasi were in the audience. The documentary, *Wenn Tote stören: Vom Sterben an der Mauer (When Fatalities Are Bothersome: On Dying at the*

---

[49] Senatsverwaltung für Stadtentwicklung, "Erweiterung der Gedenkstätte Berliner Mauer, Auslobung," Berlin, July 2007, pp. 93–94.

[50] Unterrichtung durch den Beauftragten der Bundesregierung für Kultur und Medien, "Forschreibung der Gedenkstättenkonzeption des Bundes. Verantwortung wahrnehmen, Aufarbeitung verstärken, Gedenken vertiefen," Deutscher Bundestag, Drucksache 16/ 9875, June 19, 2008, p. 8.

[51] Interview with Maria Nooke, April 15, 2010.

[52] Udo Baron, "Die Todesopfer an der Berliner Mauer – Ergebnisse und Probleme eines Forschungsprojekts," presentation at workshop, "Das Grenzregime der DDR," Gedenkstätte Berliner Mauer," January 19, 2007. Another presenter at the conference spoke about people who died at the inner-German border and the challenges of deciding which categories of people to include in historical research: Detlef Schmiechen-Ackermann, "Die Grenztoten an der innerdeutschen Grenze – Umrisse eins Forschungsprojekts." See also the review of the conference by Jörg Morre, "Das Grenzregime der DDR," *H-Soz-u-Kult, H-Net Reviews* (May 2007).

Border), featured reenactments, historical evidence, and interviews with family members of those who were killed and with some of those who had been part of the border regime either as a *Grenzer* or as a member of the Stasi.[53] Researchers led by Nooke and Hertle were in the midst of intensive investigations for their forthcoming book about individual victims of the Wall, including the three profiled in the film. Nooke and Hertle were also the historical consultants for the documentary, which aired a week later on ARD, one of the two main German public television stations.

At the screening, it turned out that neither the victims nor the former perpetrators were happy with the film. From the victims' perspective, as one critical reviewer observed, Huber's film allowed "the Stasi and border troops officers to airily spread their lies about the murderous regime at the border," even if in each case, Huber then "refuted them by correctly citing the facts."[54] But giving them the chance to say, for example, as Colonel Günter Leo of the Border Command in central Berlin did, that there was no order to shoot people trying to escape (*Schiessbefehl*), was extremely upsetting to some. This was only slightly offset by the subsequent interview with a former *Grenzer* of the same Central Border Command, Roland Egersdörfer, who contradicted Colonel Leo: "We were always told verbally. . .before every shift. . .to detain or destroy border violators."

From the perspective of the *Grenzer*, the fact that the film did not discuss any of the border soldiers killed at the border and only looked at civilians was unsatisfactory. Günter Ganßauge, an officer in the border troops who was interviewed in the documentary and also present at the screening, was quite angry that none of his comments to the film director about *Grenzer* killed at the border were included in the film. This provoked outrage among others in the room, believing that Ganßauge was trying to "offset the refugees who were killed with the dead *Grenzer*."[55]

The tense mood during the discussion of the film continued at the reception afterwards. A former Stasi officer who had been in charge of one of the main checkpoints in the Berlin Wall, Hans-Dieter Behrendt, had appeared in the film and was in attendance that evening. He was accosted by an angry attendee who screamed at him, "You are one of *them!*" When Behrendt's wife asked this person to leave her husband alone, their response was to grab Frau Behrendt and knock her over. She fell to the ground and was in such pain due to a recent hip replacement that she could not walk. Frau Behrendt was rushed to hospital.[56] It

---

[53] The film was sponsored by NDR and first aired on ARD at 10:45 p.m. on August 1, 2007.

[54] Sven Felix Kellerhoff, "Als der Freiheitsdrang das Leben kostete," *Welt*, August 1, 2007.

[55] In the wake of this event, an attendee who had helped people escape from the GDR, Burkhart Veigel, wrote up a commentary, which it should be noted contains some errors: "Mauertote," Fluchthilfe.de. www.fluchthilfe.de/files/pdfs/Mauertote.pdf

[56] Interview with Hans-Dieter Behrendt, Potsdam, July 8, 2014; and email correspondence with Maria Nooke, April 28, 2018. See also "Falsche Einschätzung," *taz*, July 31, 2007.

was one thing to have representatives of former victims and perpetrators appear in the same film, but it was quite another having them in the same room together.

The adversarial atmosphere and some of the discussions at this film screening foreshadowed what would become a major controversy two years later about whether former *Grenzer* who died at the Wall should be included in the commemoration of victims at the Berlin Wall Memorial in what was initially called a *Fenster der Erinnerung* (Window of Memory) but was ultimately named a *Fenster des Gedenkens* (Window of Commemoration). Hertle and Nooke had found eight cases of *Grenzer* who were killed on duty at the border.[57] In the final stages of planning the *Fenster* there was an intense, acrimonious discussion among board members and also the public about whether these eight *Grenzer* – who had been killed either by another border soldier, by someone trying to escape, or by a ricochet bullet fired from the West – should be included in the *Fenster* or not.[58] Nooke was among those who thought *Grenzer* should be included.[59] Family members of people who had been killed at the Wall trying to escape and people who had been imprisoned in the GDR for trying to escape were strongly against including the border soldiers in the *Fenster*.

The idea of including *Grenzer* was so incendiary that even the editorial board of Rundfunk Berlin-Brandenburg (rbb) had a long debate about it and whether to air a story about it. Ultimately rbb decided to present both sides of the debate in a feature that aired in June 2009, a few weeks before the board of the Berlin Wall Memorial would vote about how to treat the eight *Grenzer*. A reporter accompanied the new Berlin Wall Memorial Foundation Director, Axel Klausmeier, to a meeting in Lower Saxony with representatives of multiple associations of victims of the former East German regime to solicit their views. Klausmeier shared with them plans of how the *Fenster* would look, showing them that each "window" would have a picture of a victim and that below each window there would be a niche where people could place flowers or candles.

Klausmeier did not have an easy time of it. Edith Fiedler, who had been imprisoned at the brutal Stasi prison for women at Hoheneck for trying to escape, made her opposition to including the border soldiers very clear: "I could never go to this *Fenster* if *Grenzer* were also there." Another victim, Helmut Ebel, told Klausmeier, "They can be remembered...but not at the same memorial."[60] Klausmeier also knew that one of his board members who

[57] Hertle and Nooke, eds., *The Victims at the Berlin Wall, 1961–1989*, p. 499. See also their section on "border soldier suicides and fatal accidents," pp. 472–75.

[58] Jaspis, "Grenzverletzer sind zu stellen oder zu vernichten," www.suedwatch.de/blog/?p=1526.

[59] Interview with Maria Nooke, April 15, 2010. See also T. Denkler's interview with her, "Auch Grenzsoldaten können Opfer sein," *Süddeutsche Zeitung*, May 17, 2010; and Markus Köhler's interview with her for Tunnelfluchten.de, August 29, 2012.

[60] Katrin Aue, "Neuer Streit um Mauergedenkstätte – Wer ist Opfer, wer ist Täter?" rbb, June 17, 2009.

represented the Union of Victims' Associations of Communist Tyranny (UOKG), Rainer Wagner, was against including the eight *Grenzer*.[61]

But not all were completely against the idea of including *Grenzer* in the memorial. Supporters gave a variety of justifications for including them. Karl Hafen of the International Society for Human Rights, felt that "hate should not continue beyond death. Thus, I believe that if the dead will be listed there, all should be listed."[62] Karin Gueffroy, whose son Chris was killed by *Grenzer* when he tried to escape, was initially "very torn" about the question of including border soldiers in the memorial, "but the more I thought about it, that they also all had families, parents, siblings, maybe even children, [the more I thought] that they [should] also have a place somewhere [at the Berlin Wall Memorial Site] where family can perhaps put a candle or leave flowers."[63] But if the people who died at the Wall were placed in alphabetical order in the memorial *Fenster*, one of the eight *Grenzer* in question, Peter Göring (who had shot at a fourteen-year-old trying to escape and had then himself been killed by the ricochet effect of a bullet shot by a West Berlin policeman), would be placed next to her son, Chris Gueffroy. This was more than she could stomach, leading her to speak of the *Grenzer* having "a place *somewhere* here" (emphasis added) instead of directly in the *Fenster*.[64]

The debate among former victims, their families, and others was not about *Grenzer* who were killed when they themselves tried to escape (they would definitely be included in the *Fenster*), just about those who were killed for other reasons while on duty. Yet there was disagreement about whether it was possible to see some of the latter group, the eight at issue, in a more differentiated light. The case of Ulrich Steinhauer in 1980 stands out. Border soldiers always served in pairs, and the pairs were rotated frequently so that they would not grow to trust each other and plan an escape together. Steinhauer was killed while on duty by his partner who shot him five times and escaped.[65] Many felt Steinhauer should be included in the *Fenster*.

With all of these considerations and more in mind, the board (*Beirat*) of the Berlin Wall Memorial Foundation met on July 3, 2009 to discuss and vote on whether to include the eight Grenzer in the *Fenster*. The *Beirat* included historians, museum and memorial experts, former victims of the GDR, and official observers from the Berlin and federal agencies dealing with memorial sites. Due to great public interest in what was a very contentious issue, the *Beirat* decided to post excerpts of their meeting online. No names of *Beirat*

[61] Interviews with Rainer Wagner (by phone) April 30, 2010, and Maria Nooke, April 15, 2010.
[62] Katrin Aue, "Neuer Streit um Mauergedenkstätte," rbb, June 17, 2009.
[63] Ibid.
[64] Ibid.
[65] Ibid.; and T. Denkler's interview with Maria Nooke, "Auch Grenzsoldaten können Opfer sein," *Süddeutsche Zeitung*, May 17, 2010.

members were provided in the excerpts, although several comments were attributed to the (nameless) board chair, whose identity could be easily found on the website of the Berlin Wall Memorial Foundation: the historian Klaus-Dietmar Henke.[66] The debate ranged from specific discussions about *Grenzer* to more general observations about German memory culture.

Henke opened the discussion stating that the decision facing the *Beirat* was about "much more than 'just' a memorial" and was really about "a core issue of our culture of remembrance." Thus, the issue had "considerable human, historical, moral and political dimensions." He pointed to the broad context of the established German memory culture regarding the GDR, which placed priority on honoring victims of the SED dictatorship, such as people killed or imprisoned for trying to escape across the Berlin Wall. The clear implication was that Henke did not feel the *Grenzer* should be included in the *Fenster*.

Another board member argued similarly and more pointedly, maintaining that the primary post-1989 "narrative of the [Berlin Wall] Memorial Site" highlighted "people who fought for freedom, suffered (and sometimes died) because of their desire for freedom and ultimately obtained this freedom. The '*Fenster*'...would be the culmination of this narrative and would be a digni-fied...venerating commemoration for those victims who died at the [Wall] erected by the dictatorship."

Thus, in the view of this *Beirat* member, to suddenly include in public commemoration some of those who were part of maintaining the SED regime by standing armed at the border, willing to shoot people trying to escape "would be a 180-degree change" that would be "hard to accept and communicate" – especially "at a prominent site" such as the Berlin Wall Memorial. The *Beirat* member insisted that "including the *Grenzer* who died on duty would blow up this narrative...and devalue the whole memorial site." *Grenzer*, even those killed on duty, in this view were not welcome in Germany's established memory culture. Others at the meeting argued that six of the eight border soldiers being considered had in fact volunteered to join the riot police and then were transferred to the border troops. Since they had volunteered instead of being drafted, these *Beirat* members felt they should be considered perpetrators, not victims. In addition, some argued that "the Wall was not possible without the *Grenzer*," making them by definition perpetrators.

Other members of the *Beirat*, however, believed that the eight *Grenzer*, or at least most of them, should in fact be included in the *Fenster*. They supported

---

[66] The excerpts from the meeting were published on the website of the Berlin Wall Memorial (the link is no longer accessible) and on a blogsite in southern Germany that is still accessible as of May 13, 2019: Jaspis, "Grenzverletzer sind zu stellen oder zu vernichten," www.suedwatch.de/blog/?p=1526. See also T. Denkler's interview with Maria Nooke, "Auch Grenzsoldaten können Opfer sein," *Süddeutsche Zeitung*, May 17, 2010.

this on multiple grounds. One maintained that "a democratic society should not presume to make moral judgments" or create a "hierarchy of those people who were killed."[67] This board member urged that the *Beirat* not come to a decision immediately, but allow more time for broader public discussions about the issue. Another board member claimed that effectively there was a "state-of-emergency" and "martial law" in the border zone, which resulted in the "suspension of human norms." Thus, everyone killed there "whether by accidents, misfortunes or gunshots" should be mourned.

A third board member insisted that, "Serving at the border did not automatically mean accepting the order to shoot, especially for the not insignificant number of [*Grenzer*] who themselves entertained plans to escape." He believed that with the exception of Peter Göring, the other seven *Grenzer* "were not perpetrators who shot or killed; they were – like all others – victims of the terroristic border system." The idea that some perpetrators in authoritarian regimes are also victims is a subject that many scholars have studied in different countries and circumstances around the world, especially among members of the military.[68] Yet scholarly study of the multiple ways in which some perpetrators can also be victims is very different from putting them side-by-side in a state-sponsored monument.

One *Beirat* member argued for a "window of contemplation" to be different from the "window of memory," thus separating the *Grenzer* from the other victims. The main *Fenster*, in his view, "should only include people who showed moral courage," i.e., the East German citizens who fled to freedom in the West. But given that "*Grenzer* were able to evade the use of firearms," not always shooting people who tried to escape and given that "some of them went to the border to flee themselves," there should also be a separate "window of contemplation" for them. To bolster his proposal, this board member referred to Karin Gueffroy and how she changed her mind from "categorically rejecting the inclusion of border soldiers in the *Fenster*" to then "adopting the position that a functioning democracy needs to tolerate the inclusion of the border soldiers." He proposed that the eight *Grenzer* should be allowed, with accompanying explanation, to be remembered in the "window of contemplation."

Another member of the *Beirat* agreed, citing a 2007 book by Hans-Hermann Hertle that distinguished three categories of victims killed at the

[67] Deputy chair of the board, Petra Morawe, felt that "everyone is the same in death" and did not feel it was right to have a division between people who "should be mourned and those who should not be mourned." She argued that the *Grenzer* should be included in the *Fenster*, but in such a way as to delineate them, such as by using another color. Interview with Petra Morawe, July 7, 2014.

[68] Michael Rothberg, "Trauma Theory, Implicated Subjects, and the Question of Israel/Palestine," address at the 2014 convention of the Modern Language Association in Chicago, May 2, 2014, profession.mla.org/trauma-theory-implicated-subjects-and-the-question-of-israel-palestine/.

Figure 22 Commemorative pillar for border soldiers near *Fenster des Gedenkens*
Source: Hope M. Harrison.

Berlin Wall: East German citizens who were shot, had a fatal accident or killed
themselves while trying to escape; people from East and West who were not
intending to escape but were shot or had fatal accidents at the border; and the
eight border soldiers killed on duty.[69] This board member argued that victims
in the first two categories should be included in the *Fenster*, and the *Grenzer*
should be remembered separately. The same *Beirat* member, however, urged
that all of the victims should be included in the documentation provided for
visitors at the Berlin Wall Memorial's Documentation Center and in the
noontime prayers for victims of the Wall in the Chapel of Reconciliation.

After this intensive debate of the *Beirat*, a sizable majority voted in favor of not
including the border soldiers in the *Fenster* but providing a "separate information
point" nearby to remember them (Figure 22). The governing council of the Berlin
Wall Foundation, the *Stiftungsrat*, comprised of state and federal government
officials and representatives of the Berlin Wall Memorial Foundation met on
July 28 and unanimously agreed on this approach to what became the Window
of Commemoration (*Fenster des Gedenkens*).

When the *Fenster* was officially unveiled on May 21, 2010, the ceremony
focused on the civilian victims of the Wall and did not mention the *Grenzer*
directly.[70] Holger Kulick of the Sophien Church parish did, however, use the

[69] Hans-Hermann Hertle, *The Berlin Wall – Monument of the Cold War* (Berlin: Ch. Links,
2007), pp. 103–9.
[70] A review in the *Süddeutsche Zeitung* was critical that the border soldiers were not
included in the *Fenster*, arguing that "each person is worthy of remembrance" and that
the GDR's "inhumane system made not only its opponents but also its supporters into

Figure 23 Holger Kulick giving Klaus Wowereit a target practice figure, Berlin Wall Memorial, May 21, 2010
Source: Hope M. Harrison.

ceremony to donate to the memorial a stunning artifact from a *Grenzer* training area near Berlin: a human torso-sized sheet of metal painted green with a white circle near the top and indentations from bullets hitting it (Figure 23). Some of the white paint representing the area of the chest had come off from all the shots that had struck the target.[71] After the ceremony during which loved ones placed a white rose at the space for their family member in the *Fenster*, a reporter noticed that a white rose had also been placed by the information pillar about the *Grenzer*.[72]

Many of the victims' families and board members had been concerned that providing any area dedicated to former *Grenzer* on the grounds of the Berlin Wall Memorial might be used not just by their family members to mourn, but also by former members of the border troops and the GDR regime for other

victims." Thorsen Denkler, "Des Erinnerns ist jeder würdig," *Süddeutsche Zeitung*, May 17, 2010.

[71] Holger Kulick, speech at unveiling of the *Fenster des Gedenkens*, May 21, 2010; and interview with Kulick, November 6, 2018.

[72] Thomas Rogalla, "Angehörige von Maueropfern kamen in die Gedenkstätte Bernauer Straße zur Ausstellungseröffnung: 'Die Tote bekommen ihre Würde zurück'," *Berliner Zeitung*, May 22, 2010.

purposes. These concerns were proven justified the following year. On December 1, 2011, the sixty-fifth anniversary of the founding of the GDR's border troops, members of the Association of Former GDR Border Soldiers and its closely related Society for Legal and Humanitarian Support laid a wreath at the column for the *Grenzer*. In the GDR this was standard practice on December 1, the official "Day of the Border Troops," when *Grenzer* who died at the border were treated as heroes for "protecting the sovereignty of the GDR from border violators." Attached to the wreath in 2011 was a ribbon reading: "Honorable Commemoration for the comrades who were killed while on border duty for the GDR. You are not forgotten."

Authorities at the Berlin Wall Memorial removed the wreath, declaring that "the territory of the memorial cannot be used for political demonstrations in this tradition." The Berlin Wall Memorial Foundation was critical of what it saw as "political instrumentalization [of the site] by nostalgic people who were whitewashing history and by anti-democratic forces."[73] While the foundation was willing to provide space at the memorial site for information about the eight *Grenzer*, it was not willing to "honor" them "for their service to the GDR," which had built the Wall and instituted an order to shoot people trying to escape.

The *Beirat* did, however, agree on the importance of presenting the *Grenzer* as part of the history of the Wall. Hence, the new permanent exhibit that opened in 2014 in the Documentation Center contained a section called, "To shoot or not to shoot." It presented a range of views held by border soldiers and the context of their service, characterized by both intense pressure to prevent any escapes and long periods of boredom. The exhibit allowed the *Grenzer* to speak for themselves, with one declaring, "I acted on behalf of the GDR and the law was on my side," and another lamenting, "We shot an innocent person." The exhibit also used documents to convey the attitude of *Grenzer*, such as the case of a border soldier involved in transporting a fatally wounded refugee, "It's the dead man's own fault... .It really angers me personally, since I now have to clean up the really filthy car." A chart showing the number of desertions each year from the border troops and the army told another story about *Grenzer* attitudes toward their positions.

The incidents at the Berlin Wall Memorial in 2007 and 2011, with former *Grenzer* defending their service at the GDR's border, make clear why many individuals and institutions have been very careful with or shied away from

---

[73] Stiftung Berliner Mauer, Pressemitteilung, "Absage an geschichtsverklärende Nostalgiker und antidemokratische Kräfte," December 1, 2011. For the angry response of former members of the border troops to the removal of their wreath, see Günter Ganßauge, compilation and commentary, "Zur Geschichte der Grenztruppen der DDR gehören unsere Opfer und ihre Ehrung," Sonderdruck der Arbeitsgruppe Grenze, Gesellschaft zur Rechlichen und Humanitären Unterstützung e.V. (Berlin: October 2012), www.okv-ev.de/Dokumente/GRH/GRH_Sonderdruck_Grenze.pdf.

including former *Grenzer* in Germany's *Erinnerungskultur*. Yet historians, filmmakers, writers, photographers, and others have slowly demonstrated increased willingness to examine the border soldiers as individuals and as a group – feeling, however, that they face a fine line between investigating and understanding the backgrounds, behavior, and *milieu* of the *Grenzer*, on the one hand, and normalizing or excusing their behavior, on the other.

Historians and *Grenzer*

Particularly since 2009, historians such as Gerhard Sälter of the Berlin Wall Memorial and Jochen Maurer, a lieutenant-colonel in the Bundeswehr and a historian at the Bundeswehr's Center for Military and Social Sciences in Potsdam, have published works examining the everyday life of *Grenzer*: who they were, what motivated them, and how they fit into the broader tasks and goals of the East German military, political, and Stasi structures.[74]

Approximately 50,000 border soldiers served in any given year between 1961 and 1989, with 13,000 of them deployed at the Berlin Wall and most of the rest at the inner-German border.[75] Over time, a total of roughly 600,000 East Germans served at the border.[76] After the GDR introduced the draft in 1962 requiring men between the ages of eighteen and fifty to serve in the army for eighteen months, most of the men serving at the border were young conscripts, often between the ages of eighteen and twenty-one.

These young *Grenzer* had to be trained ideologically, socially, and militarily so that they would in fact stop people trying to escape, including with the use of their Kalashnikov assault rifle. Housed together in barracks with limited contact with the outside world and subject to ideological training about being at the front line against "the imperialist adversary" and about how people seeking to flee were "helping the enemy," the border troops were constantly pressured about the need to obey orders if they did not want to be sent to the military prison at Schwedt or suffer other punishments.

---

[74] Gerhard Sälter, *Grenzpolizisten: Konformität, Verweigerung und Repression in der Grenzpolizei und den Grenztruppen der DDR 1952 bis 1965* (Berlin: Ch. Links, 2009); Jochen Maurer, *Dienst an der Mauer: Der Alltag der Grenztruppen rund um Berlin* (Berlin: Ch. Links, 2011); Maurer, *Halt – Staatsgrenze! Alltag, Dienst und Innenansichten der Grenztruppen der DDR* (Berlin: Ch. Links, 2015); and Maurer and Sälter, "The Double Task of the East German Border Guards: Policing the Border and Military Functions," *German Politics and Society* 29, no. 2 (Summer 2011), pp. 23–39. Peter Joachim Lapp has also written multiple books on the border soldiers and the border as a whole, including *Grenzregime der DDR* (Berlin: Helios, 2013).

[75] Maurer, *Dienst an der Mauer*, pp. 41, 217. See also Dietmar Schultke, *"Keiner kommt durch." Die Geschichte der innerdeutschen Grenze und der Berliner Mauer* (Berlin: Aufbau Taschenbuch Verlag, 2008), p. 121.

[76] Evelyn Finger, "Wie man einen *Schiessbefehl* verweigert," *Zeit*, October 30, 2007.

Skeptical as to how reliable they really were, the Stasi infiltrated all ranks of the *Grenzer* with the result that they were permeated by the Stasi more than any other organization in the GDR. In 1987, for example, for every thirteen soldiers in *Grenzkommando Mitte* (the border command in Berlin encompassing the Wall), one of them was working for the Stasi. At the officer level, it was one in every five.[77] In addition, locals living near the border who were voluntary informants for the Stasi were also on the lookout for *Grenzer* – or anyone else – acting suspiciously. Stasi infiltration created an uneasy atmosphere in which a border soldier never knew how much he could trust his colleagues. The two-person shift work also contributed to this, since the *Grenzer* were never allowed to guard any part of the border on their own; rather, the work was done in ever-rotating pairs so that one soldier would always be watching the other.[78] Each *Grenzer* was rated for estimated reliability on a scale with three designations: extremely reliable, circumscribed reliability, and unreliable.[79] In the more specific language of the Stasi and border troops' superiors, these groups were called: "core (positive part of the collective), reserve (variable and uncertain), and the rest (hesitant and negative)."[80]

In the light of these assessments, Sälter and Maurer argue against the main image of border guards as being fiercely loyal to the regime and to its order to shoot people trying to escape. Maurer emphasizes the disillusionment among many of the *Grenzer* when they realized, at the latest after a few weeks of service, that the militarized border, and their own role armed with guns, was not primarily to stop an attack from the "Western adversary," but to prevent East Germans (including border soldiers seeking to desert) from escaping. This was particularly obvious to *Grenzer* in Berlin. As one of them described, "Sometimes on duty you would see a person in West Berlin looking over at us from an observation platform and then see the same person later strolling around Alexanderplatz" in East Berlin.[81] Clearly, people from the West were allowed to visit the East, so how much of an enemy could they represent? Taking this all in while on border duty provoked some uncomfortable thoughts among the *Grenzer*.

Maurer surmises that, "The majority of the draftees served their time in the border troops with more of an inner resistance than with a feeling of conviction."[82] Yet he also notes that he has seen "no concrete records of how

[77] Maurer, *Dienst an der Mauer*, p. 128; and Maurer and Sälter, "The Double Task of the East German Border Guards," p. 31.

[78] Schultke, "*Keiner kommt durch*," p. 147; and Maurer, *Dienst an der Mauer*, pp. 91–94, 164. This is where Uwe Hapke and Udo Walther were stationed when they shot Michael Schmidt in 1984 as described in Chapter 1.

[79] Maurer and Sälter, "The Double Task of the East German Border Guards," p. 34.

[80] Review of Maurer's 2011 book: Klaus Pokatzky, "Die Mauer aus einer anderen Sicht," *Deutschlandfunk Kultur – Buchkritik*, August 11, 2011.

[81] Interview with Roland Egersdörfer, July 22, 2014.

[82] Maurer, *Dienst an der Mauer*, p. 165.

high the proportion of the draftees was who carried out their compulsory service in the border troops with conviction and how high the number was of those who just did it to comply with the law on the draft."[83] Both Sälter and Maurer have found evidence of men who were not punished for refusing to join the border troops (and thus were deployed elsewhere in the army) as well as evidence that those who did agree to be in the border troops and who successfully stopped people from fleeing, including by shooting them, were given money, promotions, a nice watch, and extra vacation time as rewards, as we saw in Chapter 1 in the trial of the *Grenzer* who killed Michael Schmidt.

There were also cases of soldiers who were disciplined in a variety of ways for not shooting at would-be escapees or purposely shooting to the side of them. These ranged from forfeiting vacation days, being demoted, being detained for several days, or (in only one documented case) being sent to a military prison. Some soldiers were so alienated by their border service and their life in the GDR that they deserted to the West. Maurer notes that of the 45,000 border troops serving each year between 1977 and 1986, 107 *Grenzer* deserted, averaging about eleven per year.[84] Others were "weeded out" of the border troops for being unreliable, as was the case, for example, for 280 conscripts who served at the Berlin Wall between January 1971 and June 1972.[85]

Filmmakers and *Grenzer*

Historical research as well as the trials of the 1990s have demonstrated that *Grenzer* did not all approach their military service at the border in the same way. Filmmakers have also sought to portray this more differentiated image of border soldiers and have pushed the boundaries of Germany's memory culture by putting *Grenzer* at the center of their films. While the 2007 documentary that premiered at the Berlin Wall Memorial, *Wenn Tote stören*, included interviews with former border soldiers, they were not the focus of the film, which remained clearly on civilians killed at the Berlin Wall by *Grenzer*. Two films sponsored by ZDF, Germany's most prominent public television station for historical subjects, however, put the focus on the experiences and feelings of the border soldiers themselves.

The first was a feature film that premiered on September 7, 2007 late in the evening on ARTE, a European cultural channel co-funded by Germany, and a month later on ZDF at prime-time. The second film broke through all taboos: it was a documentary that premiered on ZDF at prime-time on September 15, 2015 and included interviews with six former border soldiers. Bringing *Grenzer* into people's living rooms on prime-time public television directly after the evening news was groundbreaking.

---

[83] Ibid., p. 162.
[84] Ibid., p. 200.
[85] Maurer and Sälter, "The Double Task of the East German Border Guards," p. 32.

Both films tackled the perspective of the border soldiers and dealt with escapes or attempted escapes. The 2007 film, *An die Grenze* (*At the Border*), was written by Stefan Kolditz who had served at the inner-German border in the mid-1970s, near where he set the film. It was rebroadcast for the fiftieth anniversary of the erection of the Wall in 2011.[86] The 2015 documentary, *Tödliche Grenze – Der Schütze und sein Opfer* (*Deadly Border – the Shooter and His Victim*), was written by Thomas Gaevert (who grew up in the GDR and served in the army for two years) and Volker Schmidt-Sondermann (who grew up in the FRG). Millions of Germans and others have seen these films since the premieres due to multiple rebroadcasts and online access.

The films differ in some significant ways with regard to the border soldiers. In *An die Grenze*, the soldiers do not kill anyone; instead two of them are killed by a soldier deserting from an army unit. In *Tödliche Grenze*, on the other hand, a border soldier kills a boy trying to escape, and some of the *Grenzer* involved appear in the documentary. Yet each film takes the viewer inside the world and the minds of young border soldiers, showing what they felt, how they acted when faced with someone escaping, and how they interacted with their colleagues and superiors.

Both films depict the surprise and shock when the *Grenzer* realize the brutal border regime is actually primarily directed inwards against East Germans trying to leave instead of against West Germans, and both emphasize the pressure from the company leader to continue their perfect record of allowing no escapes. Countering the view of *Grenzer* as being loyal killers for the regime, the films give a close-up, personal look at the nervousness many soldiers felt about being on duty at the border, wondering: Will someone try to escape and kill or wound me in the process? Will I have to shoot someone trying to escape? Will I actually be able to pull the trigger when/if it comes down to it? The movies are both set at the inner-German border in a quiet, forested area, not in Berlin.

An die Grenze draws on the experiences of Kolditz and his colleagues serving at the border to tell a fictitious story. Its protagonist, Alexander Karow, is a nineteen-year-old East Berliner, who is drafted into the army in 1974. Alex is happy to get away from his overbearing father who is a famous East German chemistry professor and wants his son follow in his footsteps. Alex, however, wants to become a photographer. When the draft board asks him whether he would be willing to serve at the border and use his gun to shoot people if

---

[86] Another rather melodramatic film that focused on the perspective of a fictional border soldier who was plagued for twenty years by guilt for killing someone trying to escape, *Der Mauerschütze*, premiered with Arte and NDR in 2010 and was rebroadcast by Arte (July 29, 2011) and ARD (August 3, 2011) for the fiftieth anniversary of the erection of the Wall in 2011. Kurt Sagatz, "Mauer Fantasien," *Tagesspiegel*, August 7, 2011.

necessary, Alex responds in the affirmative. After training, he is stationed at the inner-German border between Thuringia and Bavaria on the edge of a tiny village.

Alex is very anxious and clearly reluctant to be at the border and to use his rifle. He makes friends in his unit, including with a Private Gappa with whom Alex is sometimes paired for duty. Gappa defends Alex from some of the hazing he is subjected to, particularly from a hostile Private Kerner. More importantly, when Alex and Gappa are on duty together in a guard tower early on, Gappa shows Alex the breadth of the border and the evidence that it is really directed inward, particularly with the self-firing splinter mine devices, SM-70s, mounted on the final border fence and facing inwards. Gappa also points out a cross just on the other side of the border, erected in the West for someone killed trying to escape.

Alex falls in love with a local girl, Christine, sometimes sneaking out of the barracks to meet her. She gives him her grandfather's old camera, which he uses to develop his skills as a photographer. He takes pictures of Christine and also, secretly, of the border, including the SM-70s. They develop the pictures in a darkroom in the basement of her house, where she lives with her grandmother and brother, Knut. It turns out that Knut is an opponent of the East German regime. He finds the pictures and sends one of them to the West German permanent representative (ambassador) in East Berlin. This part of the story alludes to the reality of the 1970s when SED leaders had been denying the existence of the SM-70s in spite of much evidence, which was why Rainer Hildebrandt's display of one at his Checkpoint Charlie Wall Museum had been so important.

There are two climactic points in the film. The first concerns another event based on real life: the desertion and escape of a conscript from a tank regiment of the National People's Army (*Nationale Volksarmee*, NVA) who killed two *Grenzer* in the process. In December 1975, Werner Weinhold took a machine gun, ammunition, and a stolen car and headed to the border. When he got there, he shot and killed Private Klaus-Peter Seidel and serviceman Jürgen Lange and escaped to the West.[87] In the film, the event is moved up to 1974, and Alex's friend Gappa is one of the two *Grenzer* killed by the deserter.

Gappa and a partner on duty are shown crouching in the bushes as they nervously listen for signs of the deserter. Two other *Grenzer* on duty nearby duck out of sight when the deserter runs by them toward the border, vowing to tell their superiors, "We didn't see anything." Meanwhile, tired of crouching down, Gappa's partner stands up to shake a cramp out of his leg. Gappa gets up to pull him down and at that moment both are shot in the back by the deserter. Hearing the shots, Alex and his partner rush to Gappa's post. They find both

---

[87] "Republikflucht mit blutigem Ende: Werner Weinholds Weg in den Westen," *Spiegel*, no date; and "Gefreiter Klaus-Peter Seidel," *Forschungsverbund SED-Staat*, FU-Berlin, www.fu-berlin.de/sites/fsed/Das-DDR-Grenzregime/Todesfaelle-im-Grenzdien/Seidel_Klaus-Peter/index.html.

soldiers dead. Alex is shocked and distraught at losing his friend. He vomits and then fires multiple rounds toward the border screaming and crying, angry and full of sorrow. The incident leaves him – and the others serving with him – even more upset about being at the border than before. The two *Grenzer* who let the deserter pass them without shooting are found out and sent away, apparently to prison.

In the second climactic moment, which takes place at the end of the film, Christine tells Alex that her brother Knut cannot endure living in the GDR anymore and wants to escape. She asks Alex if there are weak spots in the border. Once Alex is assured that Christine is not planning on going with her brother, he tells her about a spot where there are no landmines or SM-70s. On the fateful night, however, both Knut and Christine come running through the forest to where Karow is on duty with a partner whom he has drugged with a sedative in his tea and is consequently asleep. Karow is then faced with a decision about whether to help his girlfriend and her brother escape or stop them. He lets them go and nearly follows them, but in the end he decides not to.

An die Grenze is clearly sympathetic to the border soldiers and particularly to Karow, its hero, an approach that called forth both praise and criticism. The film won the prestigious Grimme prize for its "path-breaking" portrayal of the border from the perspective of the *Grenzer*. The jury hailed the film for "avoiding common clichés and judgments" and for its "differentiated," not "black and white view" of history.[88] In advance of the premiere, ZDF editor Günther van Endert called it a "radically honest film" and made an unusual exception to the programming schedule, allowing the film to be ten minutes longer than the norm.[89] The ZDF advance press release about the film summarized what the editors saw as the message of the film: At the border, Alex "experiences through the half-official, brutal ruling mechanisms within the military" a reflection of "the society from which it comes. He finds and loses a true friend. And he meets and enjoys his first great love. At the end he hates the border regime. But he has grown up." The film "portrays him and his 'comrades' as normal young men, with passions, worries, hopes and desires for their lives, beyond the usual stereotypes."[90]

---

[88] "Begründung der Jury," 44. Adolf-Grimme-Preis 2008. This is not the only film where Kolditz has highlighted stories about people in complicated historical circumstances – in both the GDR and Nazi periods. He wrote the screenplays for two ZDF mini-series covering the Nazi period and World War II: *Dresden* (2006) about the bombing of the city at end of World War II and *Unsere Mütter, unsere Väter* (2013), about the fates of five young people in Nazi Germany. The latter film in particular dealt with the complicated lines between perpetrators and victims, guilty and not guilty, as he did in *An die Grenze*.

[89] Torsten Wahl, "Autor Stefan Kolditz gilt in der TV-Branche als Experte für Zeitgeschichte: 'Jetzt gibt's was auf die Fresse'," *Berliner Zeitung*, October 29, 2007.

[90] Ibid.

The screenplay writer, Kolditz, was born and raised in the GDR just outside of the southwestern corner of West Berlin. When the GDR began to erect the Berlin Wall in 1961, border soldiers installed a barbed wire fence through his family's suddenly much smaller backyard at their house on a lake, Griebnitzsee. They were no longer allowed to access the lake, and since their house was in the restricted border area, others could only visit with the permission of the East German authorities.[91] This experience may have inspired the line both Alex's girlfriend Christine and later Alex, under very different circumstances, use in the film: "If you have no choice, how can you know which side is the right one?" When Christine first says it to Alex, she means it to question his allegiance to the GDR. When Alex later (and wiser) says it to his father, he is criticizing his father's support for the East German system.

ZDF rebroadcast *An die Grenze* as "the film of the week" in August 2011 for the fiftieth anniversary of the building of the Berlin Wall. For the occasion, ZDF interviewed the actor Jürgen Heinrich, who played the political officer Captain Dobbs in the film. Heinrich was from the GDR and carried out his compulsory military service in the mid-1960s.[92] He described the character he played: Dobbs "was a broken figure – a fully disillusioned man, who was torn between his political ideals and the sobering reality." Realizing his wife was also betraying him, he ultimately killed himself in the film. He had lost faith in his wife and perhaps in the whole East German system.

The journalist Evelyn Finger, reviewing the film for *Die Zeit*, called it "an extraordinary television movie," which showed a very different image of the border soldier than the common view: "He crouches in bushes on the edge of the socialist world not as its courageous guard, but its bad conscience."[93] Finger lauded the filmmakers for not dividing the GDR before the fall of the Wall into terrible *Grenzer* and wonderful border violators, "perpetrators in uniform and victims in regular clothes." Instead, in her view the film "portrays the conflict about totalitarianism as an internal conflict in the border zone." Finger found that the film's focus on *Grenzer* as "just people too" was the "revisionist-seeming point of a resolutely antirevisionist film." The overall indictment of the system by the filmmakers was clear to Finger: "At the end of the film, Alex's best friend is dead, his leader has committed suicide, his first love has fled to West, and he himself remains halfheartedly in the GDR."

The writer and journalist Roman Grafe had a diametrically opposed view. He was very critical of the film and its "lying fairy tale of a good border soldier." Grafe condemned the film as "the continuation of GDR propaganda by other means" and a "way for conformists to feel good." He was outraged that none of

[91] Regine Sylvester, "Stefan Kolditz: Der Kopf, aus dem die Bilder kommen," *Berliner Zeitung*, March 13, 2013.

[92] Gitta Deutz-Záboji, interview with Jürgen Heinrich, ZDF, August 8, 2011.

[93] Evelyn Finger, "Wie man einen *Schiessbefehl* verweigert," *Zeit*, October 30, 2007.

the thousands of arrests of civilian refugees was included in the film, which instead showed an army deserter killing two *Grenzer*. Grafe, who also grew up in the GDR, had a very different experience than Kolditz did. Grafe opposed the regime and kept applying for permission to leave, with the result that, unlike Kolditz, he was not allowed to go to university. Grafe was finally granted permission to leave for the FRG in 1989. Kolditz, on the other hand, served his time in the border troops and then attended East Berlin's prestigious Humboldt University. His father was a famous East German film director, and Kolditz was able to follow in his father's footsteps in the GDR. Grafe was critical of Kolditz's view that "the Wall was 'the result of the Cold War' – like an SED-functionary," as Grafe opined. This explaining away of any East German agency, in Grafe's view, was also apparent in the film.[94]

The other film to be examined for its depiction of the perspective of border soldiers, *Tödliche Grenze – Der Schütze und sein Opfer* (*Deadly Border – the Shooter and His Victim*) was even more pathbreaking, since it was a documentary film and featured six real former *Grenzer* and also because the escape and killing at the center of the film was that of a civilian, not a member of the military.[95] ZDF timed the film's release for the twenty-fifth anniversary of German unification in the fall of 2015.

The documentary depicts the real story of two fifteen-year-old boys in December 1979 who tried to escape across the inner-German border in the Harz mountains and of the *Grenzer* who stopped them using fifty-one shots. Heiko Runge was killed by one of the shots. His friend, Uwe Fleischhauer, survived. Although the documentary includes multiple interviews with Fleischhauer, most of the attention is on the border soldiers and how anxious they were serving at the border, simultaneously worrying about having to shoot someone trying to escape and being punished if they refrained from shooting. This is made clear with the first interview in the documentary in which a former *Grenzer* speaks about how the machine gun's "magazine rattled because we were shaking. [It was] all extremely tense."

In advance of the film's airing, the director of ZDF's programming on contemporary history, Stefan Brauburger, said that twenty-five years after unification it was important "to remember the common but also the divided history, which is particularly palpably expressed in individual stories," such as those told by people who tried to escape and those who tried to stop them.[96]

---

[94] Roman Grafe, "Wohlfühldichtung für Mitläufer: Das Lügenmärchen vom guten Stasi-Mann," in Grafe, ed., *Die Schuld der Mitläufer: Anpassen oder Widerstehen in der DDR* (Munich: Pantheon, 2010), pp. 175–87.

[95] Volker Schmidt-Sondermann and Thomas Gaevert, "Tödliche Grenze – Der Schütze und sein Opfer," ZDF, September 15, 2015, www.youtube.com/watch?v=PkM3zchztr8. The historian Jochen Maurer was a consultant for the film.

[96] "Heute um 20,15 Uhr (15.09.2015) im ZDR: ZDFzeit: Tödliche Grenze – Der Schütze und sein Opfer – Dokumentation," lokalkompass.de, Bochum, September 15, 2015.

The film does this through a combination of interviews, reenactments, and a narrator's explanations. Brauburger noted that a story of two young men trying to escape was particularly relevant at a time when refugees from Syria, Iraq, and elsewhere were flooding into Germany in the fall of 2015.[97] But it was not the story of people trying to escape that made the film unique and controversial; it was the sympathetic approach to the *Grenzer* and the interviews with them on camera.

As the ZDF press release stated, the film's authors, Thomas Gaevert and Volker Schmidt-Sondermann, sought to understand: "How was it possible to make deadly shooters out of young respectable [*unbescholtenen*] GDR citizens who had to carry out their military service at the border?"[98] Those familiar with literature on the Holocaust will find this question reminiscent of those posed by the American historian Christopher Browning about the middle-aged men from Hamburg in a police battalion that murdered tens of thousands of Polish Jews. In his 1992 book *Ordinary Men: Reserve Police Battalion 101 and the Final Solution in Poland*, Browning asked: "How did these men first become mass murderers? ... What choices, if any, did they have, and how did they respond?"[99] While the Holocaust and the crimes committed by the East German regime have vast differences, not least in scale, the desire to understand more about the individual perpetrators involved is similar and has provoked similar controversies.

The killing of Heiko Junge depicted in *Tödliche Grenze* took place along the part of the inner-German border guarded by Company 7, which was led by Major Piotr Piotrowski, a real person, unlike Dobbs in *An die Grenze*. Several former *Grenzer* who appear in the documentary talk about the extreme stress of serving under Piotrowski due to his high demands and harsh treatment of them. In their telling, Piotrowski was obsessed with maintaining his unblemished legacy of allowing no one to escape along his section of the border. The narrator of the film tells us that Piotrowski was trained soon after World War II by former Nazi military officers. The young *Grenzer* seemed equally afraid of shooting someone trying to escape and Piotrowski's wrath if they did not. Older now, the former *Grenzer* on camera also make it clear that in Piotrowski's view, there should be no warning shots, no firing around the person to scare them and make them stop; nothing but an immediate shot to the body would suffice to ensure that the person could not escape.

The film's narrator tells us that some border soldiers were "tormented by thoughts about how to escape from this system." Andreas Schlick, a *Grenzer* from Company 7, talks about wondering "how long can you endure the stress in this

[97] ZDF Pressemitteilung, "ZDF-Dokumentation: 'Tödliche Grenze – Der Schütze und sein Opfer'/DDR Grenzsoldaten und ihr Opfer äußern sich erstmals in einem Film," September 11, 2015.

[98] Ibid.

[99] Christopher R. Browning, *Ordinary Men: Reserve Police Battalion 101 and the Final Solution in Poland, revised edition* (New York: Harper Perennial, 2017), p. 37.

company? How long can you submit to this? You have a firearm, a border right nearby. You could walk twenty meters further and begin a free life." In addition to the fear of being faced with someone trying to escape and with Piotrowski's aggressive approach, Schlick tells the viewers, "sometimes we barely slept in the fall or early winter when deer set off the signal wires at the border fourteen or fifteen times per night." Fear and fatigue was not a good combination. The reenactment portrays the nervousness of both the would-be escapees, Runge and Fleischhauer, and of the two *Grenzer* who would find and fire on them, Claus Meyer (aged twenty-three) and Jürgen Albrecht (aged twenty). Meyer, who is "the shooter" of the film's title, did not agree to appear in the film and is given the alias Karsten Wolf in the reenactment, although the court case in the 1990s publicized his name. Albrecht has passed away and his real name is used in the film.

In their escape attempt, Runge and Fleischhauer made it past the first fence and signal wire, unknowingly setting off an alarm in the barracks of the border troops and also unaware that there was another fence somewhere ahead before they would reach the West German border. In the reenactment Meyer/Wolf is shown as being very nervous when ordered to go find the people who set off the alarm signal in the border zone. There was no way to know how many fugitives set off the signal wire and whether they were armed or not. Wolf and Albrecht were paired up as a team in the search and fifty-five yards away Eberhardt Otto and Harald Quart, both of whom appear in the documentary, were posted as a team. Wolf and Albrecht saw the "border violators" first and fired on them, with Otto, Quart, and others watching from their own posts.

In the film, after shooting and seeing one boy drop to the ground, Wolf and Albrecht have looks of horror on their faces at what they have done and start running toward the boy. Knowing he fired the shot that felled the boy, Wolf is deeply distressed and throws off his machine gun. When a senior officer arrives and declares that the boy, Heiko Runge, is dead, Wolf keeps crying out desperately, "Why didn't he just stop and stand still [instead of running when told to stop]?" Back in the barracks, Wolf is beside himself in shock at what he has just done. Wolf and Albrecht are told to compose a written report of what happened. In the reenactment, Wolf is extremely upset, asking: "What should I write? What should I write?" Albrecht tells him: "We had no other choice!" Wolf: "But the bastard is dead! He is dead!"

The *Grenzer* who had been posted next to them, Otto and Quart, try to calm them down in the barracks, without much success. Otto tells the documentary viewers, Wolf "totally fell apart. His whole body was shaking. The two shooters couldn't stop talking about it. They needed to vent, even though they were told not to talk about it." Wolf and Albrecht were given some money and a bonus vacation, partly as a reward for stopping would-be escapees, but also to get them out of the barracks as soon as possible to try to keep it all secret especially because Heiko Runge was a minor. Minors were not supposed to be fired on, since, in the eyes of the GDR leaders, this would make the regime look brutal. Shooting others trying to escape, however, was seen as part of their sovereign right to maintain control of their borders.

The film goes on to show how much was covered up so that no one would know a minor had been shot. Piotrowski was removed and replaced by the much less brutal, twenty-three-year-old Frank Lorenz who is interviewed in the film. Lorenz speaks with a smug pride about the changes he implemented, relying more on technology to make it much less likely that would-be escapees would ever get to the deadly border zone: more signal wires were attached to the first fence to catch people at the beginning so they would not need to be killed by *Grenzer* or by the landmines or the SM-70s mounted on the second, outer fence on the inner-German border, although not at the Berlin Wall. Lorenz declared that he tried to secure the border "with reasonable, I would say, human methods."[100] Adding more dogs at the border and expanding the web of informants who lived nearby and watched the border also helped catch fugitives without killing them.

While most of the documentary after the shooting focuses on the border soldiers and on the Stasi's efforts to cover up Runge's death and its cause, the film also depicts the marathon interrogations the captured survivor, fifteen-year-old Fleischhauer, had to endure at the hands of the Stasi. After ten hours of interrogations, he was taken to the Stasi prison Rote Ochse in Halle where he was imprisoned for eight months. Fleischhauer is given the last word in the film. He accompanies the film crew back to the forest in the Harz mountains where his friend was killed during the escape attempt, his first time back there since that terrible day in December 1979. He is haunted by his memories of that day. He has tried to forget but can't. He muses about how "senseless" the border and the regime behind it were: "And for what? To shoot kids? People who wanted to get out? Why?" Unlike some other aspects of the film, this ending easily fits in with the main strand of German memory culture related to the Berlin Wall and the inner-German border.

The former *Grenzer* Harald Quart, on the other hand, uttered the most controversial lines of the 2015 film: "That they drafted nineteen-year-old little rascals, pressed a gun in their hand and said: Here, if someone comes. . .do something. This was a major crime in my view. As nineteen-year-olds, we had no life experience. To some extent, we didn't know what we were doing. It's the truth. This was the biggest crime in my view – what *they* [their superiors/the system] did to *us*." This was precisely the kind of statement that Florian Huber, the author and director of the 2007 documentary shown in a pre-release screening at the Berlin Wall Memorial, *Wenn Tote stören*, avoided including from his interviews with members of the former GDR border troops, which consequently angered some of them.

---

[100] On changes over time to the border installations in Berlin and along the inner-German border, see Axel Klausmeier and Leo Schmidt, *Wall Remnants – Wall Traces*, pp. 14–17; Hertle, *The Berlin Wall*, pp. 90–100; and Schultke, *"Keiner kommt durch,"* esp. pp. 84–87.

Maintaining that what was done to the *Grenzer* was the "biggest crime" and thus a bigger crime than killing people trying to escape would certainly be greeted with outrage not just by family members of those killed at the border.[101] The director of the documentary, Schmidt-Sondermann, however, decided to include this self-exculpating statement. Somewhat less objectionable were the comments by another border soldier in the film, Eberhardt Otto, who summarized his current view of the GDR's border regime: "The whole system was to keep East Germans in, not to protect the GDR from the FRG as they said it was. It was fanaticism by generals and officers. In my view, [it was] totally sick." He thus also blames his former superiors, but his rather regretful demeanor on camera comes across in a more palatable way than Quart's more aggressive rant.

The film and interviews with the two writers indicated that many of the former *Grenzer* remained haunted by their service at the border. The director and co-author, Schmidt-Sondermann, spoke of how it is still "a traumatic issue" for both sides and recounted that the former border soldiers he spoke to, some of whom appeared in the film and some of whom did not, "still really have anxiety about" it all. One soldier whom he tried to persuade to speak on camera "ended up drinking too much alcohol the night before, because it was all too difficult for him, and he had to be brought to the hospital."[102] As for "the shooter" himself, the other co-author of the film, Gaevert, told the Berlin *Tagesspiegel* that he "is still very traumatized" and fears that the film "will negatively influence his life again." In Gaevert's view, the shooter had the "right to forget" since the expiration of his one-year suspended sentence in 1997[103] and thus the right to not appear in the film.[104] Schmidt-Sondermann told the *Neue Osnabrücker Zeitung* that the shooter "absolutely wanted to be left out" of the film.[105]

---

[101] In his review, the journalist Hendrik Steinkuhl argues that in using this interview, the director "is too generous to the border soldiers," "Flucht aus der DDR: Doku zum Tod eines 15-Jährigen," *Neue Osnabrücker Zeitung*, September 15, 2015.

[102] "Ein DDR_Fluchtversuch und seine Folgen," interview with Volker Schmidt-Sondermann by Korbinian Frenzel, *Deutschlandfunk Kultur*, September 15, 2015.

[103] Claus Meyer and Jürgen Albrecht were brought to trial by the Magdeburg public prosecutor's office in 1995–96 and were convicted and sentenced in May 1996. As the guard leader who gave the order to shoot, Albrecht was sentenced to fourteen months in prison, a sentence that was then suspended. As the one who shot the deadly bullet, Meyer was sentenced to a year in prison, also suspended. During the trial, Albrecht testified that he knew the shoot-to-kill order was a violation of human rights and that you "couldn't just bump off a person who wanted to go to the other side." But he got "agitated" and didn't want "that they would get through [the border] and then I would be punished." Roman Grafe, *Deutsche Gerechtigkeit: Prozesse gegen DDR-Grenzschützen und ihre Befehlsgeber* (Munich: Siedler, 2004), p. 270. See also "Mauermorde: 'Einfach umgemäht," *Spiegel* 37 (1995), pp. 90–91.

[104] Thomas Gehringer, "Zwei Junge, ein Schuss," *Tagesspiegel*, September 15, 2015.

[105] Hendrik Steinkuhl, "Flucht aus der DDR: Doku zum Tod eines 15-Jährigen," *Neue Osnabrücker Zeitung*, September 15, 2015. Stefan Weinert's 2014 documentary film, *Die Familie*, profiled the families of five people who were killed trying to escape across the Berlin

The journalist Hendrik Steinkuhl defended the very human portrayal of the border soldiers in *Tödliche Grenze*, writing,

> It has nothing to do with revisionism or an erroneous understanding that [the film] also illuminates what a miserable situation many of the Wall soldiers found themselves in. Forced into service with a weapon, deployed to the border against the supposed class enemy, indoctrinated and, in the case of the seventh border company, provoked to hate people who tried to escape, whose border crossing must be stopped by any means. Who wants to put themselves there and place full moral blame on these young men for those people killed at the border?[106]

Steinkuhl argued that "25 years after [unification], it must be possible to show the *Grenzer* as what at least many of them also were: namely, victims."[107] This view, however, has not gained widespread support in German *Geschichtspolitik*.

Photography Exhibits and *Grenzer*

Another way of injecting border soldiers into the public memory of the Berlin Wall has been through photography exhibits. The East German writer Annett Gröschner and West German photographer Arwed Messmer, both born in 1964, created two photography exhibits of the Berlin Wall, the first timed to open just before the fiftieth anniversary of the erection of the Wall in 2011 and the second five years later. What made the exhibits so unusual and arresting was that the photographs were taken by *Grenzer* and depicted the early stages of the Berlin Wall border zone in the mid-1960s as seen from the East, as opposed to the usual (and generally much later) view of the Wall from the West. Gröschner and Messmer combined the images of the border with pictures of the *Grenzer* and with records about them, including reprimands and commendations by their superiors as well as notes from the *Grenzer* about things they witnessed and heard at the border.

The exhibits were accompanied by catalogues in German and English and were funded by the German Federal Cultural Foundation and the *Stiftung*

Wall and included a scene with a former shooter who felt the same way. At the end of the film, which screened in movie theaters, a brother of one of the victims accompanied Weinert and his film crew to meet the *Grenzer* who killed his brother. The former soldier was quite upset and did not want to talk to Weinert. The brother stayed back in the distance behind a tree while Weinert went to the door of the house. The former soldier lamented that Weinert's letter asking him to speak with the victim's brother about what he did "ruined the pre-Christmas period" for him, bringing it all back. "I was a victim too," he said. Stefan Weinert (director, screenplay, producer), *Die Familie*, the Core Films, 2014.

[106] Hendrik Steinkuhl, "Flucht aus der DDR: Doku zum Tod eines 15-Jährigen," *Neue Osnabrücker Zeitung*, September 15, 2015.

[107] Ibid.

Aufarbeitung.[108] Showing the first exhibit in 2011, at a time when most of the focus in German *Erinnerungspolitik* was on those killed at the Wall and not on the *Grenzer* themselves, made it stand out from the many other events connected with the anniversary. Indeed, as Messmer said in the introduction to the catalogue, "We see our exhibition as an artistic alternative to official commemoration of the anniversary." Writing in an essay in the 2016 catalogue, Matthias Flügge observed more pointedly that the exhibits "spare us the hackneyed indignation which is released on cue at each anniversary." Gröschner clarified, lest anyone think they did not see the Wall in a critical way, that their exhibits portrayed "the other view, but not in a political, rather in an artistic sense." She believed that, "You do not need any great expressions of indignation, the material just explains itself," since it makes clear that the East German regime "used any means available to make sure [the] population did not run away."[109]

Gröschner grew up in the GDR and moved from Magdeburg to East Berlin in 1983. As she told a reporter from the *Tagesspiegel*, she suppressed thinking about the Wall and never dreamed that it would disappear. She recalled that there were very few places where you could actually get close to the Wall and remembered her shock and confusion one day when she stood on Wollankstrasse and noticed that the tram tracks went under the Wall and clearly had once connected East and West Berlin. She also was stunned that beyond the Wall she could see West Berliners waiting for a train up on the elevated platform at the Wollankstrasse station: "It was like in a movie."[110]

When the Wall fell, Gröschner became a writer, historian, and journalist and found herself increasingly drawn to projects with some connection to the East German past whether with museum exhibits for which she provided primary source materials or in novels she wrote. She and Messmer started collaborating in 1992, soon after he moved from West Germany to Berlin. He examined the topography of modern cities and especially Berlin, photographing its transformation. He also created some panoramic photographs of eastern German landscapes. Both Messmer and Gröschner were interested in everyday life in the GDR.

---

[108] The first exhibit was held in Berlin from August 5 to October 3, 2011 and had an accompanying bilingual catalogue, Annett Gröschner and Arwed Messmer, eds., *Aus anderer Sicht: Die frühe Berliner Mauer/The Other View: The Early Berlin Wall* (Berlin: Hatje Cantz, 2011). The second exhibit was held in Berlin from May 27 to August 21, 2016 and was also accompanied by a bilingual catalogue, Gröschner and Messmer, eds., *Inventarisierung der Macht: Die Berliner Mauer aus anderer Sicht /Taking Stock of Power: An Other View of the Berlin Wall* (Berlin: Hatje Cantz, 2016).

[109] Interview with Gröschner in the 2011 catalogue.

[110] Christina Tilmann, "Mauerpanoramen: Die volle Breitseite," *Tagesspiegel*, August 3, 2011. This was the area where Michael Schmidt had tried unsuccessfully to escape in 1984.

In the mid-1990s they worked together on an exhibit about Gleimstrasse, a street that had been cut off by the Wall and was not far from Bernauer Strasse. For the project, Gröschner consulted files in the former East German military archives and came across the 35-mm negatives of the border, which Messmer would ultimately turn into panoramic photographs for their exhibits on the Berlin Wall in 2011 and 2016. Gröschner was quite surprised that almost no historians had consulted the files she was reading about the *Grenzer* nor had they found the pictures. Instead, most of the people in the reading room with her at the military archives had served in the East German military.[111]

In preparing the initial catalogue and exhibit, Gröschner looked for some of the *Grenzer* who took the pictures. Most of those she found, however, did not want to talk about their time at the border. Gröschner was also reluctant to put them in a position where they felt they had to justify themselves, since, as she expressed it, "I grew up with people telling me what to believe and that there was only one truth, the truth that belonged to those in power. In condemning one ideology I do not want to produce another. I always favor turning black and white into colors, showing the differences and contradictions. And in our case the greatest contradiction is a border soldier who becomes an escapee."[112] Instead, she and Messmer decided to let the photos and quotes from documents speak for themselves. For Gröschner, "the collage, the fragmentary, is the kind of aesthetics I find most appropriate for describing the recent German past, without moral or ideological ascription."[113] Messmer agreed, "We want to create a rich 'image' of the wall made up of many parts of a puzzle, and avoid agitation in any direction."[114]

At the centerpiece of the exhibits and catalogues were black and white photographs the *Grenzer* took of the Berlin Wall in 1965–66, as part of the military leaders' efforts to find and eliminate weak spots in the border. Messmer and Gröschner's first exhibit in 2011 featured the twenty-seven-mile border through the center of Berlin, and the second exhibit (after subsequently discovering additional pictures in the archives) five years later covered the entire ninety-six miles of the border surrounding West Berlin. From the negatives, Messmer digitally created massive panoramas for the exhibits, with some taking up an entire wall.

The panoramas of the border in Berlin are stunning in their bleakness, almost taking the viewer's breath away at their portrayal of the barren landscape and the multiple layers of blunt efforts to prevent East Germans from escaping by the use of barbed wire, debris, a low brick wall in some places, rickety guard towers, anti-tank obstacles, dog runs, cemetery walls, the facades of bricked up buildings, and

---

[111] Interview with Gröschner, 2016 exhibit catalogue.
[112] Interview with Gröschner, 2011 exhibit catalogue.
[113] Ibid.
[114] Interview with Messmer, 2011 exhibit catalogue.

of course the *Grenzer* themselves. The viewer can't help but wonder whether the soldiers were initially just as shocked at the view and at their role in creating the border strip. In addition, in those days before the Wall became the taller, prefabricated concrete edifice of the late 1970s and 1980s, one could easily see and hear people on the other side, so the border soldiers could see buildings and people in West Berlin and hear the insults and threats yelled at them from angry West Berliners, which the *Grenzer* then noted in reports given to their superiors.

With the photographic panoramas, the 2011 exhibit put the viewer in the shoes, or the boots, of some of the 13,000 *Grenzer* who served at the Berlin Wall in 1966, looking through their cameras at a vista largely unknown to contemporary viewers. Since it was forbidden in the East to get close to the Wall and photograph it, the images most people have of the Berlin Wall are from the Western side. The Wall is covered in colorful graffiti, and it is the tall, smooth Wall of November 1989 when it was pushed open. That later opaque, external Wall to the West did not exist in these pictures; instead one sees how it all began. This sense of the beginning packs a strong emotional punch, knowing, as the contemporary viewer does, that the Wall became less and less porous.

As Gröschner described, the photographs caused her to be stunned anew at how people could have become so used to the Berlin Wall, wondering, "How did we endure this?"[115] Yet looking at the pictures of the rather provisional elements along the border in 1965–66, one feels how easy it would have been to remove them all instead of ordering the *Grenzer* to make them more robust and permanent. Since this is not what happened, the viewer is left with a stronger sense of the agency of the border soldiers. They were the ones who were actually at the border and acted – yes, in carrying out orders – to solidify the Berlin Wall as an impregnable barrier preventing escapes, which Gröschner and so many others would become used to.

Official close-up portraits of the border soldiers' faces (with a black rectangular block across their eyes and some whitening of their faces to make them less identifiable) also make clear their role as agents. A few of these appeared in the 2011 exhibit in pairs as they were deployed at the border and almost seemed to be following the exhibit visitor around. The 2016 exhibit featured an entire wall with portraits of 120 of them. A massive panorama of the border hanging above these portraits included a soldier in the lower far right corner photographing the scene.

As displayed by Messmer and Gröschner, the border soldiers did not just appear as subjects, as agents of the border; the uniformity of their official portraits made it obvious they were part of a bureaucracy, occupying a layer of the military structure of the GDR. Moving from pictures of the border to portraits of the *Grenzer*, the viewer moved from the soldiers' view to their superiors' view of them, from the soldiers as subjects taking pictures to objects

---

[115] C. Tilmann, "Mauerpanoramen," *Tagesspiegel*, August 3, 2011.

having their pictures taken and their actions and words watched. This was particularly clear in one room of the 2016 exhibit called *Lob und Tadel* (Praise and Censure). On two opposite walls, Gröschner and Messmer provided quotations from evaluations of the border soldiers by their superiors.[116]

Individual soldiers were commended for "shooting well," displaying "exemplary order and discipline," showing "personal courage and vigilance in stopping a border violator," "always keeping his motorcycle in good condition and ready to use," and "enthusiasm" for service as a "guard dog handler." On the other hand, *Grenzer* were reprimanded for "falling asleep in the guard tower," being "nervous while on duty," "drawing figures in the snow out of boredom while on duty," "strongly disputing orders," "not displaying sufficient vigilance to stop an escape," "shooting with a single shot instead of short bursts of fire," "playing soccer while on duty," being in possession of pornography, and "meeting with girls from West Berlin" while off duty. A reviewer for the Berlin *taz* newspaper noted that "every cited, protocolled sentence...is not only a quote from those who were involved, but also testimony of a system of constant observation, adaptation, and normalization."[117]

Some of the reprimands clearly came from Stasi informers among the *Grenzer*. The border soldiers were not just watched and evaluated by their superiors, as Gröschner and Messmer slyly hint at by displaying in the first room of the 2016 exhibit the picture one *Grenzer* had photographed of another who was also photographing the vast border area; *Grenzer* were watching each other. They snitched to their superiors that another soldier listened to "enemy" radio stations, was "ashamed to have to wear his uniform on the way to his vacation," talked about "wanting to visit the West just for a day," expressed "the desire to leave the [SED] party," or even that a soldier was in possession of "a Mercedes toy car" (objectionable since it was manufactured by the West German enemy). *Grenzer* were also investigated for soliciting "luxury foods, dirty literature, pants with studs, nylon stockings and spark plugs" from people across the border, information that was most likely reported by border guards observing their colleagues.[118] Old ladies regularly threw over to the soldiers goods that were generally unavailable in the East such as cigarettes, schnapps, chocolate, oranges, and men's magazines. The *Grenzer* (at least some of them) dutifully noted everything down to create a record that they then delivered, along with the goods, to their superiors.

Another room of the 2016 exhibit contained two walls covered with pictures of 225 different guard towers, long before they were standardized

---

[116] Frank Junghänel, "Ausstellung: Die Berliner Mauer aus Sicht der DDR-Grenzer," *Berliner Zeitung*, May 27, 2016.

[117] Katrin Bettina Müller, "Stadt. Land. Schluss," *taz*, May 28, 2016.

[118] Wilfried Mommet, "Fotos von DDR-Grenzsoldaten: Berliner Mauer aus anderer Sicht," *Mitteldeutsche Zeitung*, August 2, 2016.

and made much sturdier, and a third wall with information on the guard dogs. Both the guard towers and dogs helped the soldiers carry out their orders to stop people from escaping. Around 800 dogs were stationed at the Berlin Wall with three designations: guard dogs deployed within the border strip – running free or attached to long dog runs – to stop anyone trying to escape; tracking dogs who led soldiers to a would-be escapee's location or to the site through which they had escaped; and dogs who protected the guards.

One wall of the exhibit and twenty-two pages of the exhibit catalogue displayed identical rectangular mini CVs of the dogs, providing their name, date of birth, breed, health, and designated duty.[119] With names like Lord, Sheik, Diana of the Border Court, Prinz, Quinte of the Devil's Face, or Rex, the dogs were an important part of the border. In the exhibit and in an essay in the catalogue where Gröschner describes how the dogs were handled and what happened to them afterwards, it is clear that the dogs were not treated very well. They were kept in the border strip no matter how hot or cold the weather was until they "became crazy or apathetic."[120] They received food and water sometimes only once a day, leaving many of them dehydrated, hungry, and exhausted.[121] They were shot when they tried to escape. As Regina Mönch wrote in the *Frankfurter Allgemeine Zeitung*, the exhibit "is like a memorial to massive dog abuse."[122]

The presence of dogs at the border, however, again makes clear that the main targets of the Berlin Wall were East Germans trying to escape. A reviewer for the *Mitteldeutsche Zeitung* shrewdly observed: "The dogs made the propaganda lie of the 'anti-fascist defensive barrier' especially obvious. The four-legged ones couldn't stop NATO troops or distinguish fascists from anti-fascists. They were supposed to either bite the Easterners immediately with their teeth or chase them into the shooting zone, deep into [what was] actually the anti-East German [i.e., not anti-fascist] defensive barrier."[123] Yet the work by Gröschner and Messmer illustrated that not all dogs did what they were supposed to. One dog stopped the soldiers from shooting instead of going after an escaping mother and child. Another attacked his two supervisors. He was killed with ten shots.[124]

---

[119] Christian Eger, "Berliner Mauer aus Ost-Sicht: So weit das Auge reicht," *Mitteldeutsche Zeitung*, August 9, 2016.

[120] "'Archetyp der Menschensperre.' Die Mauer aus anderer Sicht," n-tv book review, August 14, 2016.

[121] Jürgen Ritter and Peter Joachim Lapp, *Die Grenze: ein deutsches Bauwerk* (Berlin: Ch. Links, 2009), p. 116; and Dietmar Schultke, *"Keiner kommt durch"* (Berlin: Aufbau, 2008), pp. 87–89.

[122] Regina Mönch, "Provisorisch, aber mit brutalem Willen," *Frankfurter Allgemeine Zeitung*, July 6, 2016.

[123] Christian Eger, "Berliner Mauer aus Ost-Sicht," *Mitteldeutsche Zeitung*, August 9, 2016.

[124] Ibid.

Since the main task of border soldiers was to stop escape attempts, part of the 2011 exhibit and an entire room of the 2016 exhibit (and many pages of the catalogue) highlighted excerpts from their statements about arresting people trying to escape: "He was seized in the border area. He claimed he wanted to go get his hair cut." Or, "He said: 'Arrest me or shoot. One way or another I will try to get over there'."[125] Another refugee threatened: "I will keep in mind who you are, we will settle accounts."[126] The exhibits and catalogues also contained pictures, diagrams, and details of successful and unsuccessful escape attempts at specific sites along the Berlin Wall, sites that would have to be "perfected" along the border in the future. A series of pictures of escape tunnels and ladders in the catalogues, all carefully taken and described by the border soldiers, also told stories of escape, as did pictures of things left behind – a sock, a shoe, a ladder.

The work of Messmer and Gröschner showed the interactions of border guards not only with their superiors, with each other, with refugees, and with their dogs on the eastern side of the Berlin Wall, but also with people on the other side of the Wall. These interactions range from western expressions of anger ("Murderers, criminals! He is alive, has minor injuries and is in the hospital." Or "Scum Ulbricht slaves!") to girls taking off their shirts and sometimes more, at windows or in cars by the border and issuing invitations ("Come on over: we have nicer parties!"), to young boys calling over, "Please throw the ball back!" or a West Berlin policeman wryly asking, "Is it as cold there as it is here?"

Excerpts from these records provoked a broad range of emotions in those viewing the exhibits and catalogues. In the midst of helping demolish a building at the border on Bernauer Strasse, a *Grenzer* looks across to West Berlin and cries out, "Mama!" When the captain tells him to leave the building immediately, the soldier says through tears, "Can't you see that's my mother?" At another moment, the viewer reads the following record of what a border soldier heard: "Voices in water: 'I can't any more, let's turn around.' 'Come on, it's just a little farther'."[127]

The in-depth examination of border soldiers based on documents and pictures led a reviewer in the *Frankfurter Allgemeine Zeitung* to call Gröschner and Messmer's work "the counterproposal of two artists to the official didactics of commemoration."[128] Speaking at the opening of the 2011 exhibit, Hortensia

---

[125] Alexander Gumz, "Was nur DDR-Grenzer fotografieren durften," *Berliner Morgenpost*, June 1, 2016.

[126] Wilfried Mommet, "Fotos von DDR-Grenzsoldaten: Berliner Mauer aus anderer Sicht," *Mitteldeutsche Zeitung*, August 2, 2016.

[127] See both exhibit catalogues; Carsten Probst, "Von der anderen Seite der Mauer," *Deutschlandfunk*, August 13, 2011; and Jens Bisky, "'Werfen Sie bitte den Ball zurück!' Ungewohnte Perspecktiven auf die Mauer der 1960er," *Süddeutsche Zeitung*, August 30, 2016.

[128] Regina Mönch, "Provisorisch, aber mit brutalem Willen," *Frankfurter Allgemeine Zeitung*, July 6, 2016.

Völkers, chair and artistic director of the Federal German Cultural Foundation, observed: "Fifty years after the building and more than twenty years after the fall of the Wall, it is hard to leave behind the cliché pictures and commemoration routines regarding the division of Germany and to experience something new and surprising about the Berlin Wall."[129] She praised the exhibit for offering exactly this. A reviewer of the 2016 exhibit in the *Berliner Zeitung* observed similarly, "Regarding the Wall, the oft-cited collective memory is definitely not collective. People who grew up in Berlin's East saw the Wall at most from afar, for the interested person in the West it was a kind of all-round comic. One Wall, two views; a thousand Berliners, a thousand views."[130] A reviewer in the *Süddeutsche Zeitung* called it "a fantastic exhibit."[131]

Since the exhibits did not adopt the usual focus on people killed at the Wall, but instead looked more closely at those who killed them, there were also critics. A *Tagesspiegel* review of the 2011 exhibit argued that since Gröschner and Messmer "largely provide anecdotal episodes regarding stories of escape," this "downplays" the brutality of what was going on.[132] *Deutsche Welle* commentary on the 2016 exhibit argued that it left out "the victims, some who died trying to cross the border" and that accordingly the exhibit "leaves a somewhat bitter taste in the mouth."[133] But in a sign of a growing sense that examining the *Grenzer* was also important for the memory culture of the Berlin Wall, most reviews praised Gröschner and Messmer for their approach, which after all did also devote significant attention to people who escaped or died trying.

As time has passed since the demise of the Wall and the deadly border regime, a growing number of historians, filmmakers, and artists have delved into the experience of those who manned the border. This perspective is necessary to achieve a fuller historical image of the Wall. Thus, as we have seen, the Berlin Wall Memorial added information about *Grenzer* to both the indoor and outdoor exhibits there. Yet in official *Geschichtspolitik* and particularly in political speeches on anniversaries of the rise and fall of the Wall, it remains highly unusual to mention the border soldiers in anything but a very critical way.

Debates about how to view the Wall's victims and perpetrators have been joined by other disputes about the broader history of the Berlin Wall, including the factors leading to its rise and fall and the overall significance of the Wall in German history. It is to various perspectives on grappling with this broader history that we now turn.

---

[129] Hortensia Völkers, "Rede zur Eröffnung der Ausstellung," www.aus-anderer-sicht.de/ausstellung_eroeffnung050811.html.

[130] Frank Junghänel, "Ausstellung: Die Berliner Mauer aus Sicht der DDR-Grenzer," *Berliner Zeitung*, May 27, 2016.

[131] Stephanie Drees, "Der Rohbau des Monströsen," *Süddeutsche Zeitung*, August 11, 2011.

[132] C. Tilmann, "Mauerpanoramen," *Tagesspiegel*, August 3, 2011.

[133] Gero Schliess, "A New Exhibit Presents a Different View of the Berlin Wall – From the East," *Deutsche Welle*, May 31, 2016.

8

Conflicting Narratives about the Wall

Just as there is a spectrum of views on the role of border soldiers in the system surrounding the Berlin Wall, so Germans have differing perspectives on the attitudes and policies of both East and West Germans regarding the Wall when it stood, on the reasons for its fall, and on its legacy. Approaching the twentieth anniversary of the fall of the Wall in November 2009, one particular narrative about the fall of the Wall and the place of that moment in German history gained prominence, but it was not unchallenged.

Making Space in German *Geschichtspolitik* for "Positive" Memories

After the fall of the Wall and increasingly in the 2000s, some policymakers, historians, and other experts argued that in addition to remembering the victims of the Wall, especially those killed trying to escape, another aspect of the history of the Berlin Wall, its peaceful toppling, was something that should be remembered as well. Bundestag members had made this point in proposing a "site of memory" at the Brandenburg Gate in 2004, as had others during the discussions leading to the Berlin Senate's master plan (*Gesamtkonzept*) for remembering the Berlin Wall in 2006 and the federal government's memorial plan (*Gedenkstättenkonzeption*) in 2008. Politicians such as Bundestag member Günter Nooke of the CDU,[1] historians such as Manfred Wilke,[2] and other experts such as Leo Schmidt[3] had insisted that not only must the brutal part of the Berlin Wall's history be more visible in Berlin, but more should be done to

---

[1] Günter Nooke, statement, Deutscher Bundestag, Ausschuss für Kultur und Medien, Protokoll 15/60, June 15, 2005. See also the first proposal sponsored by Nooke and others in the Bundestag, Antrag, "Errichtung eines Einheits- und Freiheitsdenkmals auf der Berliner Schlossfreiheit," Deutscher Bundestag, Drucksache 14/3126, April 6, 2000. The initiative began in May 1998 by Nooke and others, as p. 5 of the Bundestag motion describes.

[2] Hubertus Knabe and Manfred Wilke, "Die Wunden der Teilung sichtbar machen. Vorschläge für ein Konzept der Erinnerung an die untergegangene SED-Diktatur," *Horch und Guck* 49 (2004), November 23, 2004.

[3] Leo Schmidt had been arguing since at least 2005 that Germans "should learn eventually to see the Wall also as a partially positive symbol" and not just as a "symbol for suffering, division and repression." Leo Schmidt, "Die Mauer ist ein positives Symbol," *Tagesspiegel*, July 28, 2005.

Figure 24 The Holocaust Memorial, Berlin
Source: Hope M. Harrison.

celebrate the fall of the Wall and the role played by East German citizens in bringing this about. As Bundestag member Stephan Hilsberg of the SPD declared, "People overcame the Wall with their own power. This can and should make one proud."[4] Although Joachim Gauck and Chancellor Gerhard Schröder had expressed this sentiment in 1999 on the tenth anniversary of the fall of the Wall, this perspective had not been dominant in Wall memory.

In all countries, national approaches to history exert important influences on the collective memory and sense of identity of any nation. While *Geschichtspolitik*, especially in Germany, may present examples of historical behavior that should be avoided, it generally also provides more heroic examples of history for emulation. The 2005 dedication of the massive Holocaust Memorial (Figure 24) in the center of Berlin "to the murdered Jews of Europe" was an important milestone in German memory policy. With its 2,711 concrete blocks reminiscent of gravestones, the government of united Germany sought to demonstrate that it was continuing the West German policy of recognizing German culpability in and contrition for the Holocaust. As we

---

[4] Stephan Hilsberg, Deutscher Bundestag, Plenarprotokoll 15/184, June 30, 2005, p. 17443.

have seen, for many, a fundamental reckoning with the Nazi past had to come before a significant focus on the communist past. Only after the government dedicated this memorial was it really possible for significant attention to be devoted to another part of German history, namely the Berlin Wall and its victims and memory. The intensive Bundestag debates in 2004–8 on a new federal memorial plan to remember both Nazi and communist history, to commemorate the victims and heroes and examine the perpetrators of both were also an important factor in expanding German *Geschichtspolitik.*

The intense focus on commemorating victims of the Wall that developed in the wake of Hildebrandt's crosses at Checkpoint Charlie was added to the heavy weight of things from the past for which many Germans were ashamed. German commemoration of victims of the Nazi regime with memorials to Jews, Sinti and Roma, homosexuals, and handicapped people who were euthanized as well as German remembrance of victims of the SED regime with memorials and museums to victims of the Wall and the Stasi, opened up some space in German *Erinnerungspolitik* for a very different kind of memory and historical narrative regarding the fall of the Wall.

A rather chance circumstance in 2006 pushed the Germans further along the path toward allowing themselves to celebrate something in their history instead of only looking back with regret. Germany hosted the World Cup soccer championships in the summer of 2006, and much of the country was swept up in a wave of enthusiastic support for their team. For the first time in decades, many Germans voluntarily waved their flag and dressed in the German national colors of black, red, and gold while cheering on the German soccer team. After the Nazis gave nationalism a bad name, most Germans had been loath to display the flag or even draw attention to themselves as Germans, favoring the term "European" to "German." This had continued in the wake of unification. Germans remained wary of worrying their neighbors with demonstrations of nationalism and focused on fitting in instead of standing out. Thus, the images during the soccer games of Germans carrying flags, painting their faces black, red, and gold, attaching small flags to their cars, and loudly cheering on their team, "Deutschland! Deutschland!" were quite arresting and were the subjects of many media commentaries in Germany and around the world.[5]

The Germans did not win the World Cup (they came in third place behind Italy and France), but the festive atmosphere in Germany while hosting the World Cup and rooting for their team through the semi-finals both reflected and affected how the Germans felt about themselves. Germans got into the spirit just like all the other "normal" countries did of waving their flag and celebrating their team and its victories. Yet yelling and screaming, "Hurrah Deutschland!" was not at all normal for Germans, and they clearly enjoyed the

---

[5] See, for example, Richard Bernstein, "In World Cup Surprise, Flags Fly with German Pride," *New York Times*, June 18, 2006.

chance. Many people felt great relief in forgetting, at least for a few weeks, the heavy weight of history and all the reasons to be ashamed of being German and just had fun supporting their team.

Interviewed a few years after this, German politicians and memory activists spoke about the importance of the World Cup for making Germans feel more comfortable in their own skins.[6] It made them more open to the possibility of being proud to be German and being proud of what (East) Germans did to bring about the peaceful fall of the Wall and then unification. In fact, Bundestag President Norbert Lammert (CDU) drew a connection between the two when he said that the "infectiously happy form of enlightened patriotism expressed during the soccer World Cup" could also "be fed by the proud memory of a successful peaceful revolution."[7] Lammert was speaking just days before the Bundestag vote in November 2007 in favor of the creation of a Freedom and Unity Monument (*Freiheits- und Einheitsdenkmal*) in Berlin.

Previous German leaders had encouraged being proud of German history and looking at more positive aspects of it. In 1974, West German President Gustav W. Heinemann (SPD) founded the Site of Remembrance of Movements for Freedom in German History (*Erinnerungsstätte für die Freiheitsbewegungen in der deutschen Geschichte*) in a baroque palace in Rastatt, not far from the border with the GDR. Heinemann's great grandfather had been among the revolutionaries of 1848 who fought for a parliamentary democracy and constitutional rights to replace the autocratic regime in German lands, a revolution that had some important short-term successes but was ultimately defeated.[8] Heinemann wanted to show West Germans that their democracy had deep historical roots going back to 1848. He believed that German "history including in school books should be [written] differently" than had been the case to that point; namely, that there should be more attention to liberal, democratic movements in German history.[9]

Chancellor Kohl created the *Deutsches Historisches Museum* in 1987 in part to give Germans a more positive sense of their history and identity. He and others around him felt that a sense of German historical identity had been replaced since World War II and the Holocaust by a fear of looking back at

---

[6] Interviews with Gabriele Camphausen, December 15, 2009; Joachim Gauck, January 7, 2010; and Wolfgang Thierse, February 3, 2010.

[7] Norbert Lammert, "Rede zum Tag der Deutschen Einheit," Schwerin, October 3, 2007. Joachim Gauck also emphasized that the World Cup had been crucial in developing a "normal" feeling of nationalism in Germany. Interview with Joachim Gauck, January 7, 2010.

[8] For a discussion of democracy in German history, see Manfred Görtemaker, *Orte der Demokratie* (Berlin: Bebra Verlag, 2005).

[9] Quote from President Gustav Heinemann's speech in Bremen, February 13, 1970, cited in, "Entstehungsgeschichte," Dauerausstellung, Erinnerungsstätte für die Freiheitsbewegungen in der deutschen Geschichte, Bundesarchiv Rastatt, www.bundesarchiv.de/erinnerungssta ette/dauerausstellung/geschichte/.

German history, leaving West Germans "homeless and thus rootless" and "without support."[10] Kohl and others believed that the West Germans needed a positive image of their identity and that the federal government should provide this in a *Deutsches Historisches Museum*.

Kohl's successor as chancellor, Gerhard Schröder of the SPD, also had a more affirmative view of German national identity and history. In his first address to the Bundestag upon his election in 1998, Schröder spoke of "democratic normality" and "a growing democratic self-confidence" in Germany.[11] He emphasized that his election represented "a generational change in the life of our nation" since he had been born after World War II. Schröder promised that this did not mean he would ignore "our historical responsibility," but that he was "proud of this country, its regions, its culture."

Chancellor Schröder used the word "proud" (*stolz*) probably more than any German leader had since World War II: "We are proud of the older people who built up this country after the war and created a place for it in a peaceful Europe. We are proud of the people in the East of our country who cast off the coercive system of the SED dictatorship and brought down the Wall." Schröder sought to draw on a positive, democratic past, which he claimed his new government represented and would bring Germany into the future: "What I am formulating here is the self-confidence of a grown nation which should not feel superior or inferior to anyone else, which stands by its history and its responsibility, but, even with all readiness to grapple with it, still looks ahead."[12] In this spirit, Schröder expanded the federal role in cultural matters by, as we have seen, creating a commissioner for culture to oversee a large commission for culture, BKM. This institution would then help support historical museums and memorials that highlighted not only difficult parts of the German past but also moments to be proud of.

The Freedom and Unity Monument

Increasing federal involvement in *Geschichtspolitik* generally as well as committing to highlight not just the dark parts of German history but also positive moments contributed to the Bundestag decision in 2007 to create a national Freedom and Unity Monument. Bundestag members believed it was

---

[10] Kohl's speech at the ceremony marking the creation of the German Historical Museum, the Reichstag, Berlin, October 28, 1987, in Christoph Stölzl, ed., *Deutsches Historisches Museum. Ideen – Kontroversen – Perspektiven* (Frankfurt am Main: Propyläen, 1988), p. 652.

[11] Gerhard Schröder, "Regierungserklärung des Bundeskanzlers," Deutscher Bundestag, Plenarprotokoll 14/3, Bonn, November 10, 1998, p. 47. See also Jan-Werner Müller, *Another Country: German Intellectuals, Unification, and National Identity* (New Haven: Yale University Press, 2000).

[12] Gerhard Schröder, "Regierungserklärung des Bundeskanzlers," November 10, 1998, p. 49.

important to celebrate the East German opposition movement, the fall of the Wall, and unification by building a monument. With the Holocaust Memorial of 2005 and other monuments and memorial sites in Berlin dedicated to the Nazi and East German periods and their victims, policymakers argued that it was high time for a positive monument to celebrate the fateful developments of 1989–90.

Parliamentary backing for a Freedom and Unity Monument was nearly twenty years in the making. It began in 1998, when four prominent public figures, two each from the former East (Günter Nooke and Lothar de Maizière) and the West (Jürgen Engert and Florian Mausbach), with strong CDU backing, called for a German Unification Monument in a central location in Berlin.[13] They wanted the monument to be constructed to mark the tenth anniversary of the fall of the Wall in 1999 and to "express the liberating joy unleashed by the fall of the Wall – a monument of historical happiness and tears of joy." Clearly having in mind the then-current focus on building a Holocaust memorial, the initiators emphasized that, "Monuments of shame and grief, [and] of pride and joy are necessary foundations of the new Germany and the new federal capital" of Berlin. The new monument they had in mind would offer the "pride and joy" in a country and capital city that had so many monuments and memorials to "shame and grief" from the German past. The initiators favored a "citizens' monument" instead of a more formal "state monument." They called for the monument to be located in front of the former imperial palace (which was in the process of being rebuilt to house public institutions such as museums and a library) on a site called the *Schlossfreiheit*.[14]

Significant support for this monument grew after the initial proposal, and in 2000, four Bundestag members from the former East (one each from CDU, SPD, Greens and FDP), joined by over 170 other parliamentarians, brought a motion for what was initially called a Unity and Freedom Monument (*Einheits- und Freiheitsdenkmal*), putting unity first and freedom second.[15] Although the motion did not gain a majority of support when brought to a vote in 2001, it did gain more adherents.[16] In addition, the party caucuses in the

---

[13] Günter Nooke, Lothar de Maizière, Jürgen Engert, Florian Mausbach, Initiative Deutsche Einheit, open letter, May 13, 1998.

[14] Interview with Andreas Apelt, July 19, 2007.

[15] G. Nooke, M. Meckel, W. Schulz, C. Pieper, et al., "Errichtung eines Einheits- und Freiheitsdenkmals auf der Berliner Schlossfreiheit," Deutscher Bundestag, Drucksache 14/3126, April 6, 2000.

[16] There was a short plenary discussion of the motion, Deutscher Bundestag, Plenarprotokoll 14/99, April 13, 2000. This was followed over a year later by a larger plenary discussion and vote, Deutscher Bundestag, Plenarprotokoll 14/199, Beratung der Beschlussempfehlung und des Berichts des Ausschusses für Kultur und Medien (23. Ausschuss) zu dem Antrag der Abgeordneten Günter Nooke, Markus Meckel, Werner

Bundestag agreed that any such monument should actually be called a "Freedom and Unity Monument" – not a "Unity and Freedom Monument" – since the freedom of the East Germans was achieved first via a popular revolution and the fall of the Wall in November 1989 and then via free elections in March 1990, before unification occurred in October.[17] Sentiment in favor of a monument celebrating 1989–90 contributed to the 2005 Bundestag resolution to create a "site of memory" at the Brandenburg Gate to mark not just the trauma of victims of the Berlin Wall but also "joy over the fall of the Wall and German unification."[18] In November 2007, there were finally enough votes in the Bundestag in support of the Freedom and Unity Monument.

The arguments made in support of the monument between 1998 and its Bundestag approval in 2007 were essential pieces in the creation of a positive narrative about the 1989–90 developments in German history that would come to dominate elite discourse in 2009 with the twentieth anniversary of the fall of the Wall, the subject of Chapter 9. Supporters of a Freedom and Unity Monument very consciously declared that Germany deserved "a positive national symbol" to honor the transformative developments of 1989–90.[19] The successful motion by the CDU/CSU in November 2007 stated that such a "monument is long overdue. Thus far no monument is dedicated to the happiest moment of German history and also to the whole history of freedom in our country."[20] This "happy history" should not be forgotten. Indeed, as one Bundestag member, Wolfgang Börnsen (CDU), asserted: "Memory needs form. Monuments are necessary. Without them, memory is lost," a sentiment long shared by Manfred Fischer. Bundestag Vice President Wolfgang Thierse declared that "the GDR population set in motion the first and only successful

Schulz (Leipzig) sowie weiteren Abgeordneten, "Errichtung eines Einheits- und Freiheitsdenkmals auf der Berliner Schlossfreiheit," November 9, 2001.

[17] Markus Meckel made the case persuasively in the plenary debate on April 13, 2000, Deutscher Bundestag, Plenarprotokoll 14/99, p. 9328, as did Stephan Hilsberg in the plenary debate on November 9, 2001, Deutscher Bundestag, Plenarprotokoll 14/199, pp. 19504–19505.

[18] Carl-Ludwig Thiele, Stephan Hilsberg, Franziska Eichstädt-Bohlig, Werner Kuhn, et al., "Gelände um das Brandenburger Tor als Ort des Erinnerns an die Berliner Mauer, des Gedenkens an ihre Opfer und der Freude über die Überwindung der deutschen Teilung," Deutscher Bundestag, Beschlussempfehlung und Bericht des Ausschusses für Kultur und Medien (21. Ausschuss), Drucksache 15/5854, June 29, 2005. The Bundestag unanimously approved the proposal on June 30, 2005, Plenarprotokoll 15/184, p. 17448. With the Berlin Senate's Gesamtkonzept, however, as we have seen the Bundestag decided to settle on a "site of information" at the Brandenburg Gate metro station instead of an artistic monument outside.

[19] Günter Nooke, Deutscher Bundestag, Plenarprotokoll 14/99, April 13, 2000, p. 9326.

[20] The CDU/CSU contribution to the discussion in the Bundestag's Committee on Culture and Media as summarized in the final report of the session on November 7, 2007. Deutscher Bundestag, Drucksache 16/6974, "Beschlussempfehlung und Bericht des Ausschusses für Kultur und Medien (22. Ausschuss)," November 7, 2007, p. 5.

peaceful revolution that Germany has experienced" and argued that this history should be visible in the capital city.[21]

While remembering this positive moment in German history was one key argument for the monument, policymakers referred to three additional arguments that flowed from this. First, by recognizing and honoring the fundamental East German role in the fall of the Wall and unification, the monument would hopefully make eastern Germans who were disaffected by some of the challenges of unification feel more a part of the united Germany, thus "accelerating the process of so-called internal unity," as Nooke posited in 2001.[22] At a public hearing at the Bundestag two days before the final vote on the monument in November 2007, Professor Klaus Schröder of the Free University of Berlin told lawmakers that "the achievement of the East Germans who peacefully overcame the dictatorship has not yet been sufficiently acknowledged. And this monument could do this."[23]

Second, by giving memory shape as a monument, this could help teach young Germans who did not live through 1989–90 about the dramatic history of the fall of the Wall and unification and also inspire the next generation to value democracy and freedom. Stephan Hilsberg (SPD) put it to his Bundestag colleagues that: "A society must be aware of its central values. It needs a place where its central values like freedom can be physically visible, a monument. . . . Freedom was a magic word for me as for many millions of citizens of the GDR."[24] Liberty and democracy were the two core values referred to by many

---

[21] Deutscher Bundestag, Plenarprotokoll 16/124, November 9, 2007. Multiple construction problems and debates about the best location and even whether there really should be such a monument have thus far prevented the winning design, "Citizens in Movement" (Bürger in Bewegung by Johannes Milla and Sasha Waltz), from being implemented. Stefan Berg, "Fledermäuse im Bauch," *Spiegel*, March 1, 2014; and Claudia van Laak, "Die Wippe wippt nicht: Erinnerung an Mauerfall," *Deutschlandfunk*, July 20, 2018.

[22] Günter Nooke, plenary discussion on the proposed monument, Deutscher Bundestag, Plenarprotokoll 14/199, Beratung der Beschlussempfehlung und des Berichts des Ausschusses für Kultur und Medien (23. Ausschuss) zu dem Antrag der Abgeordneten Günter Nooke, Markus Meckel, Werner Schulz (Leipzig) sowie weitern Abgeordneten, "Errichtung eines Einheits- und Freiheitsdenkmals auf der Berliner Schlossfreiheit," November 9, 2001, p. 19507. See also Eckart von Klaeden (CDU) in the same debate, p. 19511; and Wolfgang Thierse in the plenary debate six years later, Deutscher Bundestag, Plenarprotokoll 16/124, November 9, 2007, p. 12965.

[23] Klaus Schroeder, public hearing on the Updated Federal Memorial Plan with experts, Deutscher Bundestag, "Öffentliche Anhörung Fortschreibung der Gedenkstättenkonzeption," Ausschuss für Kultur und Medien, Protokoll Nr. 16/42, November 7, 2007, p. 44.

[24] Deutscher Bundestag, Beratung der Beschlussempfehlung und des Berichts des Ausschusses für Kultur und Medien (23. Ausschuss) zu dem Antrag der Abgeordneten Günter Nooke, Markus Meckel, Werner Schulz (Leipzig) sowie weitern Abgeordneten, "Errichtung eines Einheits- und Freiheitsdenkmals auf der Berliner Schlossfreiheit," Plenarprotokoll 14/199, November 9, 2001, p.19504. For a discussion of similar motivations for the post-unification development of monuments to the June 1953 Uprising, see Anna Saunders, *Memorializing the GDR* (NY: Berghahn, 2018), pp. 159–93.

politicians in the discussions. They maintained that it was the desire for freedom and democracy that had brought so many East Germans to march in the streets in the fall of 1989 and that this civic activism was what brought down the Berlin Wall and the SED regime.

FDP members in the Bundestag committee on culture and the media spoke of the Freedom and Unity Monument as "an important contribution to anchoring the existential significance of liberty more strongly in public consciousness."[25] Cornelia Pieper (FDP) asserted that the monument would be "a monument of living democracy. It is a monument for the civic courage of people in this country. It contains the message that only through a strong democracy, through the participation of the citizens, can the foundations for a liberal state with the rule-of-law be secured."[26] Bundestag members widely agreed that this monument would be important both to highlight how important the goals of freedom and democracy were in 1989–90 and also to reiterate the ongoing importance of maintaining and defending them whenever necessary.

Similarly, in the discussions of policymakers with experts about the updated federal *Gedenkstättenkonzeption* in 2005, Bernd Faulenbach had argued that "there should also be stronger support for institutions of remembrance...which foster the memory of the traditions of liberty and resistance in German and European history."[27] Several of the historical experts at the 2005 Bundestag hearing called for a new substantive emphasis at memorial sites beyond crimes and victims: they recommended that the sites do more to highlight the opposition and resistance against the Nazi and communist regimes.

Hubertus Knabe, the director of the Hohenschönhausen Stasi prison memorial, was critical that whereas there was a federal Memorial for German Resistance (*Gedenkstätte Deutscher Widerstand*) for the Nazi period, there was no such central site to honor opposition and resistance to the Soviet and East German regimes. He called for more attention to the June 1953 uprising and the 1989 peaceful revolution "to serve as inspiring examples to future generations."[28] He maintained that giving more attention to the opposition to the SED regime "can

---

[25] FDP statement at committee session, Deutscher Bundestag, Drucksache 16/6974, "Beschlussempfehlung und Bericht des Ausschusses für Kultur und Medien (22. Ausschuss)," November 7, 2007, p. 5.

[26] Cornelia Pieper, Deutscher Bundestag, Plenarprotokoll 14/99, April 13, 2000, p. 9330.

[27] Bernd Faulenbach, "Schriftliche Stellungnahme zur Anhörung im Ausschuss für Kultur und Medien des Deutschen Bundestages," Ausschussdrucksache Nr. 15 (21) 158, February 16, 2005, p. 5; and interview with Faulenbach, Washington, DC, September 12, 2013.

[28] Hubertus Knabe, statement in advance of hearing, "Anhörung im Kulturausschuss des Deutschen Bundestages zum Gedenkstättenkonzept des Bundes," Deutscher Bundestag, Ausschuss für Kultur und Medien 15. Wahlperiode, Ausschussdrucksache Nr. 15 (21) 155, February 16, 2005, pp. 3–4.

offer models for the young generation that one can carry out opposition in certain situations and that civic courage is important."[29] Rainer Eckert, director of a Leipzig museum on East German history and culture, *Zeitgeschichtliches Forum*, urged that the new federal memorial plan "should focus on resistance and opposition against the German dictatorships as the foundation of a democratic tradition" in united Germany.[30] These sentiments mirror a global trend since the end of the Cold War to use memorial sites to spur visitors toward political action connected to defending human rights and democracy, missions championed by the International Coalition of Historic Site Museums of Conscience founded in 1999.[31]

The third and final main theme of Bundestag members' advocacy for a Freedom and Unity Monument was the view that the peacefully transformative events of 1989–90 made it possible for Germans to use "the words 'the German people' and 'the German nation' no longer with shame but with a certain patriotic pride,'" as Cornelia Pieper of the FDP put it.[32] This shift from "shame" to "pride" was a core part of both the discussions about the proposed Freedom and Unity Monument and the twentieth anniversary celebrations of the fall of the Wall two years later. During the November 9, 2007 parliamentary debate about the monument, Bundestag Vice President Wolfgang Thierse (SPD) urged his fellow citizens to overcome their habitual focus only on the negative parts of their history and become more "normal" in remembering both the good and the bad in their history:

> We Germans should summon up all our courage and with a monument remember that German history could also go well for once and did go well. We should remember the *annus mirabilis*, the 1989/90 year of miracles.... Yes, we Germans are and remain obligated to remember our shameful deeds, especially the crimes of the Nazi regime and its victims. It was necessary and correct that the Bundestag decided...to locate the Holocaust Memorial in the center of the German capital. This thorn in our national flesh is painfully necessary. We must always remember the victims.
>
> But a nation undoubtedly cannot find direction from its failures alone. We Germans can also take some encouragement, for example, by remembering the friendly sides of our history, the strivings for liberty and unity, the revolutions and beginnings, the successes, without blocking out [or]

---

[29] Hubertus Knabe, comments at public hearing with experts considering the CDU/CSU motion on "Förderung von Gedenkstätten zur Diktaturgeschichte in Deutschland," Ausschuss für Kultur und Medien, Deutscher Bundestag, Protokoll 15/50, February 16, 2005, p. 10.

[30] Rainer Eckert, "Anhörung Kulturausschuss Deutscher Bundestag Gedenkstättenkonzept des Bundes," Deutscher Bundestag, Ausschuss für Kultur und Medien, Ausschussdrucksache Nr. 15 (21) 153, February 17, 2005, p. 1.

[31] Paul Williams, *Memorial Museums* (New York: Oxford University Press, 2007), esp. pp. 149–51.

[32] Cornelia Pieper, Deutscher Bundestag, Plenarprotokoll 14/99, April 13, 2000, p. 9330.

forgetting the contradictions, the failures, the shameful acts. . . .Let us finally be a normal, average, ordinary European nation that can do this.[33]

Whereas Thierse only called for Germans to become "normal" in remembering the good and bad in their history, others spoke more openly of the pride and self-confidence that Germans should feel after 1989–90. Cornelia Pieper declared that the monument "would be a sign of a newly won confidence of mature, self-assured citizens, a symbol for patriotism. It would be a symbol of a new, modern national self-confidence."[34] Bundestag President Norbert Lammert (CDU) also argued that the monument would be "important for the self-image and self-confidence of our country."[35] Eckart von Klaeden (CDU) asserted that the monument "can make a contribution to an enlightened patriotism based on the values of our constitution." He also voiced a view alluded to by many others but none as pointedly as he: "The East Germans with their Peaceful Revolution freed our nation from the stigma of never having won our own liberty."[36] After all, it was the Allies who rid Germany and Europe of fascism, not the Germans themselves. That was indeed a stigma felt by many Germans for decades.

In 2008, the year after the Bundestag voted to finance a Freedom and Unity Monument, the initiators were awarded the German National Prize. In his speech bestowing the prize, the chair of the board of the German National Foundation, Richard Schröder, declared: "Next to the monuments for heroes and victories of the empire and the memorials for victims of violence and the delusions of German dictators, a third type is now possible: a monument for a joyous event."[37] This sentiment, together with Berlin's *Gesamtkonzept* for the Berlin Wall, and the federal government's commitment to highlighting and commemorating both the Nazi and East German periods in its *Gedenkstättenkonzeption*, would lead to a sea change in German *Geschichtspolitik* on the occasion of the twentieth anniversary of the fall of the Wall in 2009.

---

[33] Wolfgang Thierse, Deutscher Bundestag, Plenarprotokoll 16/124, November 9, 2007, p. 12965.

[34] Cornelia Pieper, Deutscher Bundestag, Plenarprotokoll 14/199, Beratung der Beschlussempfehlung und des Berichts des Ausschusses für Kultur und Medien (23. Ausschuss) zu dem Antrag der Abgeordneten Günter Nooke, Markus Meckel, Werner Schulz (Leipzig) sowie weiteren Abgeordneten, "Errichtung eines Einheits- und Freiheitsdenkmals auf der Berliner Schlossfreiheit," November 9, 2001, p. 19507.

[35] Norbert Lammert, speech in Schwerin on the Day of German Unity, October 3, 2007.

[36] Eckart von Klaeden, Deutscher Bundestag, Plenarprotokoll 14/199, November 9, 2001, p. 19511.

[37] Richard Schröder, speech, Deutscher Nationalpreis 2008, Deutsche Nationalstiftung, June 17, 2008, p. 3.

Tom Sello and an Exhibit on the East German Peaceful Revolution

In the years that some politicians in the Bundestag were building support for a Freedom and Unity Monument, a very different kind of memory activist was hard at work gathering information to tell the story of the East Germans who called for change before and after the fall of the Wall, the East Germans who, in the words of (the West German MP) Eckard von Klaeden, "freed our nation from the stigma of never having won our own liberty." Tom Sello had been part of the East German opposition and, like many others with similar backgrounds, he believed that the story of these East Germans was insufficiently understood and respected in united Germany.[38] He set out to change that, not with a monument but with a website and then an exhibit.

Sello had been active in the East German opposition since 1980, focusing his concerns on the GDR's disregard for the environment and the resulting smog, acid rain, and dying forests. He was a central figure in the founding of the Environmental Library group in 1987, which became a focal point of opposition to the SED regime about environmental and other issues. Sello worked with groups investigating human rights violations in the GDR, and he supported the peace movement against the further deployment of atomic weapons in Germany and the attendant increased militarization of life in the GDR. Risking imprisonment, he passed out opposition leaflets and played a key role in investigating and publicizing to the West the falsified local election results in the GDR in May 1989. Sello also helped organize oppositional activities, such as keeping records of political prisoners, at the two key churches in East Berlin that provided support for such activities, the Zion and Gethsemane churches.

When the Wall opened, Sello initially stayed through the night at the Environmental Library printing an underground newspaper. The following morning, he and his family headed to West Berlin to see his mother, "since he wanted his children to see where their grandmother lived."[39] He continued his oppositional work for change in the months to follow, and after unification, the Environmental Library and Sello joined the Robert Havemann Society, an organization devoted to preserving the papers of East German civil rights activists. While SED and Stasi files were preserved in state sponsored archives, Sello and others wanted the papers of the opposition, "the other side," to be preserved and accessible as well so that the "voice of power" would not be the only one that survived in united Germany.[40]

In 2003, Sello was inspired by the widespread discussion surrounding the fiftieth anniversary of the June 1953 East German uprising, complete with ceremonies, films, books, and conferences. For the first time since unification,

---

[38] Interview with Tom Sello, February 10, 2010.
[39] Mary Elise Sarotte, *The Collapse* (New York: Basic Books, 2014), p. 166.
[40] See the explanation for the founding on their website, havemann-gesellschaft.de.

politicians and the media devoted great attention to the East Germans who had opposed the SED regime.[41] Sello sought to direct the same sort of attention and respect to the East German opposition in 1989. He realized that the twentieth anniversary of the fall of the Wall could be the perfect opportunity. But what would be the best way to portray that history in an engaging way to reach a large audience?

He found the answer to that question by chance when he was an invited speaker at a training program for schoolteachers in the summer of 2003. The teachers told Sello that their history classes generally got as far as 1945 and then rarely had time left to cover the history of divided Germany. Sello asked whether they portrayed any heroes who tried to resist the Nazis. Yes, they taught students about resistance groups such as the White Rose student group, but, they told Sello: "There were no such heroes in the GDR." "Not true," thought Sello, and he set out to provide information that would be of interest to schoolchildren by highlighting the biographies of young dissidents in the GDR.

By 2005, Sello had gathered enough information and interviews with people who like himself had taken action when they were young to resist the SED regime. He and the Robert Havemann Society partnered with the *Bundeszentrale* to create a multimedia website particularly geared toward young people, www.jugendopposition.de (Youth Opposition in the GDR). The site profiled sixteen young dissidents, the ways they resisted the regime and tried to change things, and how the regime responded, such as by imprisoning, expatriating, or otherwise trying to suppress their criticism. By relying on photos, videos, audio recordings, copies of original documents, and compact text explaining historical events, it gave young students (and anyone else interested in the history) a good sense of the various kinds of opposition activities in the GDR, including holding private meetings, demonstrating on the streets, illegally printing and circulating forbidden materials and information, monitoring the arrests of opposition members, and informing the West about their activities and how the regime was treating them. One could add to this list that creating a stage set looking like the Berlin Wall for Beethoven's opera *Fidelio* in October 1989 was a form of protest too.

The history portrayed on Sello's website began with the widespread youth protests against the GDR's decision in 1976 to expatriate the forty-year-old singer-songwriter and dissident Wolf Biermann while he was on tour in West Germany and ended in late 1989 after the fall of the Wall. Sello called the events of 1989 a real revolution, not a "failed revolution" or "half revolution," as some

---

[41] For articles discussing the widespread coverage of the fiftieth anniversary of 1953, see Edgar Wolfrum, "Die Massenmedialisierung des 17. Juni 1953," *Aus Politik und Zeitgeschichte* 40–41 (October 1, 2003); and Christoph Klessmann, "Gedenken und Erinnern," *Deutschland Archiv*, June 13, 2013.

civil rights activists felt when the GDR ceased to exist (instead of being reformed and remaining a separate state) and was absorbed into the FRG. The website on young dissidents in the GDR won the Grimme Online Award in 2005 in the category of "knowledge and education."[42] Another indication of the website's success was that the sixteen people it profiled were soon inundated with requests to speak at schools and elsewhere. The story of the East German opposition behind the Berlin Wall was gaining attention and ultimately would influence the narrative adopted by German leaders about 1989–90.

Sello sought a bigger platform and audience for his efforts to highlight the history of what he and others called "the peaceful revolution." He spoke with colleagues from the East German opposition milieu who agreed that 2009 would be a great opportunity to do something more. He wanted to find a method of conveying the history of the peaceful revolution to the broader public and not just to specialists or schoolchildren. To counter some lingering sentiments of *Ostalgie* for the East German past by people who were not as happy or well-off in united Germany as they had hoped and expected, Sello also wanted to remind his former fellow citizens what it "had really been like in 1989" and in the GDR in general; how rundown the buildings had been, how polluted the air, how scarce basic goods and rights had been.

Sello's views about East Germany were not shared by everyone from the former East. A 2009 survey showed that on the question of whether the GDR had been an *Unrechtsstaat* or not, opinion was quite divided in the east, with 51 percent answering in the affirmative and 40 percent disagreeing. Moreover, the majority of former East Germans surveyed (62 percent vs. 24 percent) felt that society had become more unjust not less since unification.[43] Sello wanted to tip the scales against this *Ostalgie* by "giving them their own memories back," reminding people in the east why they had been crying and screaming with joy on the night of November 9, 1989 with the opening of the Wall.[44]

In addition, Sello felt that the *Gesamtkonzept* for the Wall did not provide sufficient information on what led to the fall of the Wall and what he saw as the important role of the East German opposition. He wanted to make clear that the fall of the Wall was part of "the peaceful revolution" and not vice versa. There were information sites and plaques around the city about the history of the Berlin Wall, but there was nothing in the public space about the peaceful revolution. Sello came up with two ways to change this: a series of

---

[42] www.grimme-institut.de/html/index.php?id=163.

[43] Jörg Schönenborn, "Die Angst um die Arbeitsplatz wächst: ARD-DeutschlandTrend, November 2009," *Tagesschau*, November 5, 2009 www.tagesschau.de/inland/deutschland trend/deutschlandtrend942.html.

[44] Interview with Tom Sello, February 10, 2010.

informational pillars at key sites of the peaceful revolution (including the Zion and Gethsemane churches)[45] and an exhibit about the peaceful revolution in a major public space where people had congregated in the GDR – Alexanderplatz. This large square had been the site of a mass demonstration of 500,000 people in East Berlin on November 4, 1989 and was still a major, centrally located transportation hub in Berlin just steps from city hall, with 300,000 people passing through the square each day.

By the end of 2007, Sello had put together a plan for the exhibit and began to seek support to mount it. He found a strong ally in Rainer Klemke in the Senate's office of cultural affairs, and in 2008, Sello received funding from Berlin's lottery and from the federal government via BKM for his exhibit. The exhibit design was inspired by the huge banners carried by the crowd at the 1989 demonstration at Alexanderplatz. It featured an installation of banner-like photographs. There were captions in German and English detailing the exhibit's three sections on the dramatic developments leading to the fall of the Wall and then to German unification: "Awakening" (the early 1980s–summer 1989); "Revolution" (fall 1989–winter 1989/90); and "Unity" (the March 1990 East German elections through the unification of October 3, 1990).[46]

The exhibit provided both details and the broad context for key actions by the East German people in 1989–90, such as: the citizens who reported on the fraudulent results of the May 1989 GDR elections; the demonstrations in Leipzig, Berlin, and elsewhere in the fall and winter of 1989; the stream of East German refugees crossing the borders via Hungary, West German embassies in Central Europe, and then the Berlin Wall; the March 1990 elections that set the path for unification; and the September 1990 occupation of Stasi headquarters by citizens to protest the initial reluctance of the West German government to honor the Volkskammer's decision to open up the Stasi files. Sello's exhibit also illustrated the interaction between developments in East Germany and beyond its borders (in Poland, Hungary, the USSR, the USA, and West Germany) and how those affected the opening of the Wall and unification and the various steps in between.[47] Yet the exhibit's message was that the East Germans on the streets and working in opposition groups behind closed doors were the main historical actors, even if they were helped at various moments by others.

The historian Holger Starke, director of the City Museum of Dresden, shared Sello's instinct of creating an exhibit on the peaceful revolution and

---

[45] These pillars are featured on the www.revolution89.de website and described in Martin Jander, *Orte der Friedliche Revolution* (Berlin: Stadtwandel, 2009).

[46] For the exhibit catalogue, see Kulturprojekte Berlin GmbH, ed., *"Wir sind das Volk!" Magazin zur Ausstellung friedliche Revolution 1989/90* (Berlin: Kulturprojekte Berlin GmbH, 2009).

[47] There were apparently profound disagreements among former East German dissidents about what the exhibit should include. Interview with Tom Sello, July 9, 2014.

Figure 25 Opening of Peaceful Revolution exhibit, Alexanderplatz (left to right): Tom Sello, Moritz van Dülmen (behind Sello's left shoulder), Frank Walter Steinmeier, Klaus Wowereit, (next to Sello) May 2009
Source: Photographer: Dirk Vogel. Robert-Havemann-Gesellschaft.

putting it in context. Starke's exhibit examined the entire decade leading to the autumn of 1989, focusing on the people getting stronger and the government becoming weaker. It also examined post-1989 developments in Dresden by displaying, for example, a box of keys from closed up factories. The exhibit included historical films showing popular protests, the pollution of the air and the Elbe River, and the dilapidated state of the buildings in Dresden. Also featured in the exhibit was information about the performance of Beethoven's *Fidelio* at the Semperoper and the creation of the *Gruppe der 20*.[48]

In May 2009, Mayor Wowereit, Foreign Minister Frank Walter Steinmeier and federal Commissioner for Culture Bernd Neumann opened Sello's exhibit in Berlin (Figure 25), "'We are the People!' The Peaceful Revolution, 1989/90."[49] They all fully backed Sello's perspective and helped to make it the core of

---

[48] *"Keine Gewalt!" Revolution in Dresden 1989*, exhibit, Stadtmuseum Dresden, 2009–2010; interview with Holger Starke, Dresden, November 5, 2009. A book of essays and photographs accompanied the exhibit. Holger Starke, ed., *"Keine Gewalt!" Revolution in Dresden 1989* (Dresden: Sandstein Verlag, 2009). On the dilapidated state of the buildings in Dresden, see the book with photographs and essays, Andreas Krase, ed., *Transitions: The Dresden Project. Photographs by Fredrik Marsh* (Dresden: Technische Sammlungen Dresden, 2009).

[49] The exhibit's opening day was set for the anniversary of the May 7, 1989 East German local elections and the civic protests against the fraudulent results.

a new German *Geschichtspolitik* which would be heralded by Germany's leaders in a grand celebration on November 9, 2009, as will be illustrated in the next chapter. Wowereit observed that, "Twenty years since the peaceful revolution and twenty years since the fall of the Wall are occasions to commemorate, to remember, and to be proud of what has been achieved."[50] All three politicians praised the courageous East German citizens, "who risked life and limb" to protest against the SED's *Unrechtsstaat* and to call for freedom. Neumann spoke of the peaceful revolution as "the only lasting, successful revolution in German history." Germans should be "proud, because neither freedom in Eastern Germany nor German unity would have been possible without the resistance and opposition of people in the GDR."[51] Neumann, Wowereit, and Steinmeier (all from the West) expressed deep gratitude to these East Germans, some of whom were invited to the opening ceremony as honored guests.[52]

A few months later, Neumann gave an address in Rastatt at the opening of an exhibit there on "movements for freedom in the GDR." He reminded the audience that the "movements for liberty and unity of the nineteenth and twentieth centuries belong to the positive chapters of German history." Calling the peaceful revolution, "the most successful and happiest chapter in the history of German democracy," Neumann enthused: "What a finale of the twentieth century which had two world wars, Nazi terroristic rule, the Holocaust and the SED dictatorship."[53]

Interrogating the Peaceful Revolution Narrative on the Fall of the Wall

Not everyone looked back at 1989 in this way. Just a few years after the fall of the Wall, the writer Thomas Brussig, himself from East Germany, poked fun at the heroization of those who brought down the Wall and the competition to claim the mantle of destroyer of the Wall. The delusional, insecure hero of Brussig's satirical novel, *Helden wie Wir* (*Heroes like Us*), Klaus Uhltzsch, describes how he was responsible for the opening of the Wall at Bornholmer Strasse on November 9, 1989. The story is told through a lengthy interview

---

[50] "Rede des Regierenden Bürgermeisters von Berlin Klaus Wowereit zur Eröffnung der Ausstellung 'Friedliche Revolution 1989/90' am 7. Mai 2009 auf dem Alexanderplatz."

[51] "Rede des Kulturstaatsministers Bernd Neumann zur Eröffnung der Ausstellung 'Friedliche Revolution 1989/90' am 7. Mai 2009 auf dem Berliner Alexanderplatz."

[52] In addition to Wowereit's speech, see also "Rede des Bundesaußenministers und Vizekanzlers Frank-Walter Steinmeier zur Eröffnung der Ausstellung 'Friedliche Revolution 1989' am 7. Mai 2009 auf dem Berliner Alexanderplatz" and "Rede des Kulturstaatsministers Bernd Neumann zur Eröffnung der Ausstellung 'Friedliche Revolution 1989'."

[53] Bernd Neumann, "Rede vom Kulturstaatsminister Bernd Neumann anlässlich der Eröffnung der Ausstellung 'Wir sind das Volk: Freiheitsbewegungen in der DDR 1949-1989'," November 4, 2009, Ahnensaal des Rastatter Schlosses, Rastatt.

Klaus gives to a *New York Times* reporter, clearly representing the international interest in the fall of the Wall and the desire to meet (and congratulate) the hero or heroes of the epochal event.

Klaus explains to the reporter that a botched operation on his genitalia (injured when he fell while trying to storm the stage at the November 4, 1989 demonstration at Alexanderplatz) resulted in its swelling to far greater than its usual small size. While the doctors considered what to do to reduce the swelling, Klaus decided he wanted to keep his enlarged genitalia as it was and escaped from the hospital on the night of November 9. On the way to find a former lover who once made fun of his small willy, he got caught up in the crowd at Bornholmer Strasse wanting to cross over to West Berlin. Seeing the guards resisting the calls to open the border, Klaus suddenly thought of a way to change this. He decided to drop his pants to stun the guards into opening the border. The strategy worked! As he told the reporter at the end of the novel, "I am the *missing link* in recent German history!"[54] (Emphasis in original.)

Brussig is not the only one who is reluctant to lionize the role of the East German opposition in the fall of the Wall. There are a variety of challenges to the narrative favored by Sello and ultimately most of Germany's leading politicians in 2009, a narrative which will be elaborated upon in the next chapter. Some of these challenges stem from the belief that a focus on the East German opposition is insufficient to understand why the Wall was opened in November 1989, and others stem from a distrust of any official narrative about history as in the case of Annett Gröschner and the exhibit on the Berlin Wall she created with the photographer Arwed Messmer.

While there is no question that a defining feature of the dramatic developments in East Germany in the fall of 1989 was nonviolence – such as in Dresden on October 8 and especially during the October 9 demonstration of 70,000 people in Leipzig and the November 9 opening of the Wall in Berlin – there were some moments of violence.[55] The violence was mainly perpetrated by the East German security forces using clubs, water cannons, and tear gas against demonstrators on the streets and in vans on the way to prison or within prison grounds. Blood did flow.[56] There were also instances where protesters

---

[54] Thomas Brussig, *Helden wie Wir* (Frankfurt am Main: Fischer Taschenbuch Verlag, 1998), p. 323. The book was originally published in 1995.

[55] Martin Sabrow, ed., *1989 und die Rolle der Gewalt* (Göttingen: Wallstein Verlag, 2012). On the developments in Leipzig leading up to and during October 9, 1989, see Sarotte, *The Collapse*, pp. 30–82.

[56] Katharina Walkling-Spieker, interview with Kathy Kempen who was arrested and imprisoned with many others in East Berlin in October 1989, "25 Jahre Mauerfall. Brutale Prügel im Stasi-Knast," *Kölner Stadt-Anzeiger*, November 2, 2014; and Peter Steinbach, comments during a roundtable discussion, "Erinnerungsort DDR. Zwischen Aufarbeitung und Nostalgie. Die DDR in der Erinnerungskultur," Bundesstiftung zur Aufarbeitung der SED-Diktatur, April 8, 2014.

attacked security forces with their fists or threw stones, albeit generally to defend themselves or, as in the case of Dresden at the main train station on October 4, in an effort to get past security forces and jump aboard trains carrying East Germans who were being taken to West Germany from the latter's embassy in Prague.[57] The evening of October 7, the fortieth anniversary of the founding of the GDR, also saw significant violence in East Berlin, Leipzig, Dresden, Plauen, and elsewhere.[58]

The main narrative about nonviolence in the fall of 1989 focuses on the ordinary East German citizens on the streets and their widespread slogan of resistance, "*Keine Gewalt!*" ("No Violence!"). But of course the fact that the revolution of 1989 was largely peaceful was due not just to the behavior of the demonstrators. The reluctance to use force by many (but certainly not all) of the political and military officials (including Hans Modrow and Lothar de Maizière) from the top to the bottom of the hierarchy was also essential.[59] Much less public attention has been paid to this aspect of what in fact has become known as "the Peaceful Revolution." For example, the orders of Leipzig's second party secretary, Helmut Hackenberg, who was in charge on the pivotal evening of October 9, stand out. Hackenberg estimated the number of protesters on the ring road in central Leipzig to be 100,000 and that stopping them would be a very bloody affair. Instead, he gave the orders that "all deployed forces" should "begin the switch to self-defense" and only use force if the protestors attacked them or the surrounding buildings.[60] Another second secretary in Leipzig, Roland Wötzel, had been one of the signatories earlier in the day of an appeal to nonviolence coordinated by the conductor of Leipzig's famed Gewandhaus Orchestra, Kurt Masur.[61] Both Wötzel and Hackenberg, especially the latter, made significant contributions to the unexpectedly peaceful nature of what turned out to be a pivotal point in Leipzig and for the entire GDR on October 9.

Officials in East Berlin a month later, on November 9, were also key actors in keeping things peaceful at the Berlin Wall. The actions of Harald Jäger, the senior officer on duty at the Bornholmer Strasse crossing point that night resulted in the first opening of the Berlin Wall. A member of both the border police and the Stasi, Lieutenant Colonel Jäger had served for twenty-five years at Bornholmer Strasse. As more and more East German citizens gathered at his crossing point after Berlin party chief Günter Schabowski announced (erroneously) at a live press conference around 7 p.m. that the borders were open,

---

[57] "Gewalteskalation am Dresdener Hauptbahnhof," BStU, www.bstu.bund.de/DE/InDerRegion/Dresden/Notizen/2011_10_01_dresden-hauptbahnhof.html. See also Sarotte, *The Collapse*, pp. 30–31.

[58] "Samstag, der 7. Oktober 1989," www.chronikderwende.de.

[59] See the chapters by Martin Sabrow, Rüdiger Bergien, Jens Gieseke, and Heiner Bröckermann in Sabrow, ed., *1989 und die Rolle der Gewalt*.

[60] Sarotte, *The Collapse*, pp. 70–74.

[61] Ibid., pp. 69–71.

Jäger kept trying to reach his superiors in the Stasi for guidance on how to handle the growing crowds. He was told he could release the loudest, most troublesome people to cross into West Berlin, but this only made all the others waiting more angry and impatient. Hundreds then thousands of peaceful citizens kept arriving at the checkpoint. Jäger still received no guidance about what to do and eventually learned that the superiors he reached by phone did not believe his description of the powder keg situation at his checkpoint.

There were tens of thousands of impassioned East Germans crowding in against his sixty officers on duty. Jäger's colleagues were armed but had orders not to use their weapons. He was afraid that if the pressure grew and things somehow got out of control, some of the soldiers on duty might in fact use their weapons. Eventually around 11:30 p.m., Jäger decided to open the checkpoint for free passage and instructed two of his subordinates to pull open the final barrier leading to West Berlin. The crowds pushed through, Angela Merkel among them, cheering and crying tears of joy as they entered West Berlin. The Wall was opened with no bloodshed. Some of the East Germans crossing the border gave Jäger and the other officials bottles of sparkling wine as thanks.[62] Officials at other checkpoints followed Jäger's lead.

Jäger is not part of the dominant narrative of the fall of the Wall, and he was not invited to the twentieth anniversary celebrations in 2009 (although officials considered inviting Schabowski, but former East German civic activists argued forcefully against this). Jäger's personal history was too closely tied to the East German regime to fit comfortably into the main narrative of the brave East German dissidents demanding change. Jäger has been much more popular with journalists than with politicians commemorating the fall of the Wall.[63] His story was turned into a TV movie, *Bornholmer Strasse* (loosely based on history), for the twenty-fifth anniversary of the fall of the Wall in 2014. Its premiere on the main German public television station, ARD, in November 2014 was seen by nearly seven million viewers. The film won the most prestigious German media awards: the Bambi for the "TV hit event of the year" in 2014; and the Grimme prize for fiction in 2015. Jäger himself was even on hand to present the Bambi award to the filmmakers. Commentators and the juries for the awards noted the groundbreaking nature of the film, which told the story of the fall of the Wall not from the usual perspective of East German citizens on the street, but from the perspective of GDR border officials.

---

[62] Ibid., pp. 134–39, 145–47. See also Gerhard Haase-Hindenberg, *Der Mann, der die Mauer öffnete* (Munich: Wilhelm Heyne Verlag, 2007), pp. 165–99; and Antje Hildebrandt, "Der Spitzel mach die Mauer auf," *Zeit Online*, November 8, 2011.

[63] Haase-Hindenberg, *Der Mann, der die Mauer öffnete*; and interviews with Jäger conducted by Cordt Schnibben for *Spiegel* magazine, "The Soldier Who Opened the Berlin Wall. 'I Gave My People the Order – Raise the Barrier,'" *Spiegel Online*, November 9, 2009; and by Anne Haeming, "Der Grenzer, der die Mauer öffnete. 'Ich habe nur das Menschliche getan'," *taz.de*, November 5, 2014.

One interesting exception to the political silence surrounding Jäger's role in the opening of the Wall came in 2011 when Thomas de Maizière, then minister of defense, gave an address in Dresden on the occasion of the dedication of the Military History Museum of the Federal Armed Forces. De Maizière ruminated aloud about which traditions in German military history were worthy of emulation and asked: "Was Stasi Lieutenant Colonel Harald Jäger's disobedience...at Bornholmer Strasse on the night of November 9, 1989 an exemplary isolated act? Left alone by his superiors, listening to his own conscience, he decided on his own to end the [border] controls and open the crossing point."[64] De Maizière did not answer his own question, but raising it was the first and perhaps only example of a German official recognizing Jäger's important role in opening the Berlin Wall.

The defense minister's seeming praise of Jäger opened up a short-lived debate in 2011 about whether Jäger was a hero or not. Some said he did the only thing he really could have under the circumstances and doing the obvious thing does not make one heroic.[65] Thomas Brussig called Jäger a "hero of retreat." Former prime minister of Saxony, Kurt Biedenkopf, argued that Jäger was a hero because at Bornholmer Strasse that night, "he risked everything that had made up his life until that point." Former defense minister Franz Josef Jung observed that Jäger's opening of the border was exemplary, although he did it under great pressure from the crowds. He conceded that Jäger "made a considerable contribution to the indescribable stroke of historical luck that the fall of the Wall occurred without military incidents." Most commentators seemed to feel more comfortable speaking of the respect due to Jäger for his actions on November 9, 1989 than in calling him a hero.[66]

In his speech in Dresden, defense minister de Maizière also addressed the role of the East German army more generally in the peaceful revolution. He asked rhetorically, "Can we call it exemplary how some soldiers of the East German NVA [National People's Army] who, seeing [the army's] impending dissolution before their eyes – reliably and with discipline protected their stocks of weapons and munitions from misuse?" Their holding fire was essential in keeping the peaceful revolution peaceful. This, however, is generally only mentioned by those who continue to identify with and defend the former East German regime and often write in the socialist newspaper *Neues Deutschland*. As one author in *Neues Deutschland* noted, peaceful change is only possible when those in power allow it. The writer was critical that Chancellor Angela Merkel generally thanked "foreign communists" for their

---

[64] "Rede des Bundesministers der Verteidigung, Dr. Thomas de Maizière, anlässlich der Neueröffnung des Militärhistorischen Museums der Bundeswehr am 14. Oktober 2011 in Dresden," press and information office of the Federal Ministry of Defense.

[65] Antje Hildebrandt, "Der Spitzel macht die Mauer auf," *Zeit Online*, November 8, 2011.

[66] For contributions to the debate about whether Harald Jäger was a hero or not, see "Ist dieser man ein Held?" *Zeit*, November 9, 2011.

role in 1989, particularly Gorbachev, but expressed no such gratitude for how the East German power holders allowed things to unfold in 1989.[67]

Several contributors to a debate published in *Die Zeit* about whether or not Jäger was a hero also highlighted the importance of how those in power in the GDR peacefully gave up their power. Matthias Rogg, the director of the Military History Museum in Dresden, called for historians "to more clearly recognize those who loyally served the democratically elected final East German government and supported the dissolution of its armed forces." Markus Ulbig, interior minister of Saxony in 2011, was a member of the NVA in 1989 and "experienced its dissolution. This last chapter of the history of the NVA is for me one of the small miracles of reunification. The troops which were bristling with weapons and had been drilled in anti-imperialism, whose enemy had disappeared, dissolved themselves silently and with discipline. We who were drafted were simply sent home; into another country."[68]

There was no armed resistance against opening the Wall, ousting the SED regime, or fusing East Germany into West Germany. Some former NVA members ultimately joined the Federal Armed Forces (*Bundeswehr*), although they have not all always felt they were treated with the same respect as their colleagues from West Germany.[69] De Maizière's questions about Jäger and the NVA may have been geared toward reaching out to people in the German military who came from the former GDR, trying to make them feel they had something admirable in their history to draw on too.

The focus in the German narrative on the role of the East Germans on the streets in opening the Wall also overlooks both the impact of the thousands of people who fled the GDR via Hungary into Austria or via FRG embassies in Prague and elsewhere as well as what was going on within the SED leadership at the time.[70] SED chief Erich Honecker had been ousted in mid-October and the entire Politburo resigned on November 8, 1989, the day before the Wall fell. This leadership crisis affected society in general and people at all levels of the government, the Stasi, and the military, including people in positions at the border such as Harald Jäger, wondering each day what the next day would hold. Many of those in power in the GDR had less and less confidence that the old system worked any more. This important background is part of the reason that neither border officials like Jäger nor more senior political or military officials acted more aggressively to maintain control on the night of November 9 and afterwards.

[67] Jürgen Reents, "Der nötige Schlussstrich," *Neues Deutschland*, November 11, 2009.

[68] "Ist dieser man ein Held?" *Zeit*, November 9, 2011.

[69] Andrew Bickford, *Fallen Elites: The Military Other in Post-Unification Germany* (Stanford: Stanford University Press, 2011).

[70] Lothar de Maizière argues that the refugees at the Prague embassy exerted more pressure on the SED leadership than the people demonstrating on the streets. Interview with Lothar de Maizière, April 22, 2010.

The leaders had also been taking steps to liberalize the border regime, which was after all the point of Schabowski's remarks at the press conference on November 9. These steps were of course not the same as completely opening the Wall for freedom of movement back and forth, but they demonstrated that the leaders were not as committed to a sealed border as they had been.

Part of this was because the GDR was in dire financial straits, massively indebted to West Germany, the IMF, and others, and hoping to get infusions of deutsch marks from the FRG in return for slackening the border regime, as the top SED economist proposed in internal deliberations on October 31.[71] At the end of October, 1,000 people a day were applying for permission to leave the GDR. Meanwhile, popular demonstrations continued to grow.

East Germany's economic planning chief Gerhard Schürer argued in the Politburo that "if the demands are made first from the streets or even the factories, it would once again prevent us from taking the initiative" in trading the openness of the border for hard currency from West Germany.[72] Some of the East German leaders also assumed that if they made it easier for their citizens to travel to the West, they would certainly return home after their visits and would be more content with the GDR regime.[73] The SED under Honecker's successor, Krenz, was in the midst of negotiations with West Germany about economic aid in return for reforms when Schabowski's misunderstanding of the latest East German travel law led him to announce that the border was open on the evening of November 9.

Just as the peaceful revolution narrative of 1989–90 downplays the role of the East German authorities, it also tends to overlook the fact that not all of the East Germans calling for change wanted a Western-style system of democracy and capitalism or sought unification. In fact, some of the leaders of the opposition movement, including Bärbel Bohley and others in *Neues Forum*, were eager to create a new socialist democratic regime in the GDR. They felt that just when they finally gained the freedom to organize as they wanted and started to plan for a new system, most of their fellow citizens instead voted with their feet or at the ballot box for leaving the GDR behind and joining the FRG.[74] Friedrich Schorlemmer wondered at the time whether the fall of the Wall was "in fact the last revenge of the SED, designed to rob the civil rights movement of its revolution."[75]

---

[71] Hans-Hermann Hertle, "The Fall of the Wall: The Unintended Self-Dissolution of East Germany's Ruling Regime," *Cold War International History Project Bulletin* 12/13 (Fall/Winter 2001), pp. 134–35.

[72] Ibid., p. 135.

[73] Interview with Günter Schabowski, April 19, 2004.

[74] Charles Maier, *Dissolution: The Crisis of Communism and the End of East Germany* (Princeton: Princeton University Press, 1997), pp. 192–200.

[75] Hertle, "The Fall of the Wall," p. 131, citing Friedrich Schorlemmer, "Frieden vor Einheit sagen," in Peter Neumann, ed., *Träumen verboten. Aktuelle Stellungnahmen aus der DDR* (Göttingen: Lamuv, 1990), p. 54.

Finally, some who opposed the SED regime and had fled or been allowed to emigrate to the West were actually worried instead of happy when the Wall came down. They feared, as in the case of Mario Röllig, that their former Stasi interrogators or prison guards could now also come to the West and that they would have to face them again, no longer separated by the Berlin Wall.[76]

The West and the Wall

There are also issues with how West Germany is portrayed, whether directly or indirectly, in narratives of the fall of the Wall and the unification of Germany. First, the "happy" narrative about the peaceful revolution and the fall of the Wall has little resonance with some in the West. Many in West Germany, such as Bavarians, do not feel much of a connection to the fall of the Wall and unification of Germany, since those events for many years afterwards barely changed their lives. They often do not see the changes of 1989–90 as part of their own history. To the extent that they think about 1989–90, they tend to believe that the strength and attractiveness of the West and its system as well as the role of Chancellor Kohl were more important than anything East Germans did.

Second, the narrative's focus on the heroes of the peaceful revolution and the villains of the East German *Unrechtsstaat* generally ignores the extent to which West Germans and West Berliners, including their leaders, were bystanders. At a discussion in 2009 between high school students and former West Berlin mayor Eberhard Diepgen, one student asked him, "Did you do anything against the Wall? Did you protest?" Diepgen dodged the question by answering generally that "everyone" in West Berlin protested against the Wall.[77] Several years later, the writer Claudia Rusch enjoined, "Why doesn't anyone talk about the West German role in the Wall? Why didn't tens of thousands of West Germans approach the Wall and try to bring it down? This issue still bothers me. We talk about people standing by while atrocities are carried out in Rwanda, etc., but no one raises this about West Germany and the Wall."[78] East Germans are directly or indirectly asked why they did not stand up more and earlier against the system and the Wall, but that question is not directed toward West Germans.

The artist and architect Yadegar Asisi captured the passivity of the West vis-à-vis the Berlin Wall in his Wall panorama, *Die Mauer* (The Wall), erected at Checkpoint Charlie in 2012 just steps from Hildebrandt's Wall Museum. He created the 270-degree panorama to remind people how accustomed West Berliners became to the Wall instead of fighting against it. In retrospect, he felt

[76] Interview with Mario Röllig, July 30, 2014.

[77] Commemorative ceremony and dialogue sponsored by the Robert-Havemann-Gesellschaft, Gethsemane Church, Berlin, October 7, 2009.

[78] Claudia Rusch, comments at panel discussion, "Zwischen Aufarbeitung und Nostalgie. Die DDR in der Erinnerungskultur," sponsored by Stiftung Aufarbeitung, Berlin Landeszentrale für Stasi Unterlagen, and the Deutsche Gesellschaft, April 8, 2014.

shocked by this Western attitude.[79] Asisi himself lived in West Berlin with a view of the Wall in the 1980s. Years after the Wall was toppled, Asisi felt how strange it was that people who lived along the Wall in West Berlin got used to it and stopped seeing it for what it was: a deadly border. Instead it just became a backdrop to their daily life. His massive panorama reaching nearly fifteen feet to the ceiling depicted the section of Kreuzberg, West Berlin where Asisi lived. Based on historical reality, it showed houses right up against the Wall, an observation platform with people looking into the border area and across to the buildings of East Berlin on the other side, people strolling along the street, children playing, and West Berliners going about their normal lives without any regard for the Wall while the death strip was just on the other side of it.

When the panorama first opened, visitors who had experienced the Wall were surprised and moved at how much it evoked the feeling of the Wall. Standing on a platform in the middle of the panorama and being surrounded by it while the light changed to simulate day and night at the Wall gave people the first chance since 1989 to be reminded in a sensory way of what it had been like – or for others to get a first feeling of life at the border in the heart of Berlin. As the light in the panorama darkened, the lights in the death strip came on, lending an eerie feeling to what one knew was a reconstruction but produced tension nonetheless. An audiotrack accompanied the panorama, including sounds of people walking and talking on the streets, children playing, guard dogs barking in the death strip, and excerpts of key speeches by Berlin, German, and international politicians about the Wall, including Ulbricht and Honecker as well as Presidents Kennedy and Reagan. The panorama was not meant to be a permanent installation and initially Asisi had a contract for one year. The panorama was so popular, however, that the contract was extended through 2014 and again afterwards to 2019. As long as nothing is built by the investors who own the land where Asisi's Mauer Panorama is and where Hildebrandt's crosses once were, the panorama seems set to remain on display.

Florian Huber's 2007 documentary film discussed in the previous chapter, *Wenn Tote stören*, was also very critical of Western passivity vis-à-vis the Wall. The film's title, *When Deaths are Bothersome*, was clearly meant to apply equally to the West and the East. Huber interviewed multiple former West German politicians and former West Berliners who explained that they and the Western Allies had in fact gotten used to the situation with the Wall. In the film, Egon Bahr, who at the time was the top aid to West Berlin Mayor Willy Brandt, recounted the terrible incident of the shooting of Peter Fechter in 1962 as he tried to escape and the response of an American soldier nearby. Upset West Berliners watching Fechter lying on the ground bleeding implored the soldier: "Go get him and bring him over!" The American soldier told them: "That's beyond my competence. I'm not allowed to."

---

[79] Yadegar Asisi, *Die Mauer. Das Asisi Panorama zum geteilten Berlin* (Berlin: asisi Edition, 2012); and interview with Asisi, February 9, 2010.

The often triumphalist Western account of bad East Germany being absorbed into good West Germany leaves out the fact that most West Germans accepted and tolerated the regime on the other side of the Wall. Indeed, Helmut Kohl, hailed as "the chancellor of unity" after 1990, had in fact hosted SED chief Honecker in the capital city of Bonn in 1987. At official ceremonies on the occasion, both German flags flew while a West German military band played both national anthems. Kohl and Honecker reviewed the West German troops together and later toasted each other with champagne, as photographs from the time show. Starting with the establishment of official relations with the GDR in 1972 under the SPD's Chancellor Willy Brandt and continuing through the million-deutsch-mark credits granted to the GDR under Kohl's CDU government, both the main political parties in the West had in fact accepted the *Unrechtsstaat* while it existed. It could be argued that expecting most East German citizens to have fought against it was rather *Unrecht* in and of itself.

The official condemnation of the Berlin Wall in united Germany also skirts the question of the extent to which the closure of the border in 1961 helped de-escalate the burgeoning refugee crisis and kept the Cold War cold instead of hot in Central Europe. As increasing numbers of East Germans fled the country, with a veritable exodus occurring in the summer of 1961, there were serious concerns about whether the Soviets would intervene militarily to stop this or seize the "escape hatch" of West Berlin from the US, British, and French forces.[80] This might then have provoked a NATO response and escalated into nuclear war. Indeed, as we have seen, former East German defense minister Heinz Kessler, and his deputy, Fritz Streletz, have made the case that "without the Wall, there would have been war."[81] For them as well as for Krenz and some other former East German officials, the official narrative condemning the Wall and celebrating its fall are neither appealing nor convincing. Furthermore, as we have seen former East German prime minister Hans Modrow has criticized the use of the deaths at the Wall as a way to emphasize the brutality of the communist system by pointing out that US bombs in Iraq in 2003 and 2004 killed more people in one day than in the whole twenty-eight years the Wall stood.[82] He could have said the same things about the US war in Vietnam.

External Approaches to Remembering the Wall

While there have been differences of opinion within Germany on various aspects of the history of the Berlin Wall, controversies about the meaning of

---

[80] On developments leading to the erection of the Berlin Wall, see Hope M. Harrison, *Driving the Soviets up the Wall: Soviet-East German Relations, 1953–1961* (Princeton: Princeton University Press, 2003).

[81] Heinz Keßler and Fritz Streletz, *Ohne die Mauer hätte es Krieg gegeben. Zwei Zeitzeugen erinnern sich* (Berlin: edition ost, 2011).

[82] Interview with Hans Modrow, March 29, 2004.

the Wall have not been confined within German borders. Critical views of the main German narrative about the fall of the Wall, why it occurred, and its significance have engaged Poles, Hungarians, and Russians. Some of them have been quite disparaging of the focus of German and world attention on the fall of the Berlin Wall as the defining moment in the downfall of communism in Eastern and Central Europe, a focus that would be apparent on the twentieth anniversary as we shall see in the next chapter. Months before the fall of the Wall, the Poles, for example, began roundtable talks between the government and the opposition trade union Solidarity and then held partially free elections, which Solidarity won. Similarly, the Hungarians had reformed their government and opened the barbed wire border with Austria before the Wall fell. Russians argue that the process that led to the fall of the Wall actually began with Gorbachev's reforms and that he then lost control and relinquished the Soviet empire in Eastern and Central Europe, including the GDR.

The Poles are particularly resentful that the visually more dramatic fall of the Wall on November 9 is what people remember as the climactic moment of 1989 instead of the Polish elections on June 4. While the role of Poland's Solidarity was highlighted throughout the twentieth anniversary celebrations of the fall of the Berlin Wall, as will be demonstrated in the next chapter, especially with Solidarity leader Lech Walesa as a guest of honor at the festivities in Berlin, the Poles had long been frustrated that the world's attention was so fixated on the November 9 opening of the Wall as the symbol of the end of communism and not on Poland's elections of June 4, 1989, which really began the toppling of communist rule in Central and Eastern Europe. No doubt, global memory has focused on the opening of the Wall because it provided far more dramatic, emotional pictures than the comparatively staid voting in Poland did. "Photographs of 'wall peckers' and large sections of the wall being torn down are certainly a more vivid representation of the triumph of freedom than photographs of the June 4 elections, even if they did occur five months earlier," as a Polish journalist lamented.[83] People around the world felt and still feel more emotionally drawn to the fall of the Wall than to the elections in Poland. At a time of increasing reliance on visual media, the visual drama of watching footage of Berliners celebrating on the night of November 9 together with the ongoing availability of "real" pieces of the Berlin Wall to be purchased as keepsakes no doubt contribute to this. And, sadly, the dramatic, emotional pictures of June 4, 1989 were those of the Chinese crackdown on democracy activists in Tiananmen Square, not the elections in Poland.[84]

---

[83] Jacek Stawaski, "Berlin Wall: Lest We Forget Poland ...," *Polska Times*, Warsaw, 9 November 9, 2009.

[84] Pearce, "Who Owns a Movement's Memory?" pp. 173–74. See, for example, the banner headline, Nicholas D. Kristof, "Crackdown in Beijing; Troops Attack and Crush Beijing Protest; Thousands Fight Back, Scores are Killed," *New York Times*, June 4, 1989.

The sociologist Susan Pearce has written about Polish "revolution envy" toward Germany, a "concern that the 2009 attention to Berlin Wall commemorations would leave the important contributions of Poles in the shadows."[85] Indeed, speaking in the European Parliament in 2005, the former Solidarity activist turned politician, Bronislaw Geremek, observed that in 1980, nine years before the Wall was toppled: "The Polish Solidarity movement removed the first stone from the Berlin Wall, and our German colleagues ought not to forget this. [And in 1989,] the Round Table talks in Poland showed that it is possible to make the transition from a totalitarian system into freedom without any disruption of international peace."[86] The Poles have been trying to remind the world how important Solidarity was long before the fall of the Wall: "If we don't tell our story, the world will think it all began with the Berlin Wall."[87]

Thus, the Poles launched a public campaign in Germany in 2009 with large posters showing a picture of a roundtable meeting in 1989 with the caption: "It started with a Round Table." One of them was hung across several stories of the Polish embassy on Berlin's Unter den Linden surrounded by government offices and frequented by tourists. It was a real attention grabber, precisely as the Poles intended. For those who already knew about the Polish roundtable talks, it was a big reminder. For those who did not, it was an extraordinarily concise history lesson. As the Polish journalist Jacek Stawiksi asserted in 2009: "Safeguarding this [Polish] narrative is a moral obligation for our governments and presidents, and for future generations."[88]

The Poles were incensed when the European Commission produced a short film, "20th Anniversary of Democratic Change in Central and Eastern Europe," which completely left out Solidarity. Over less than three minutes, the film started with the Soviet intervention in Hungary in 1956, jumped to the protest movements of 1989, continued with the expansion of the European Union in 2004, and ended in 2009. The film showed a woman apparently giving birth to a baby boy on November 9, 1989 and then watching television coverage of the fall of the Wall from her hospital bed. The baby boy clearly represented freedom brought about by the fall of the Wall and is seen growing up until he turns twenty in 2009. In response to the Polish protests, the European Commission amended the film to include some footage of Solidarity.[89] Perhaps the Polish objections led to the text summarizing the film: "The Berlin Wall – to the rest of the world – is the symbol of the division of Europe. Its [sic] not what ended

---

[85] Pearce, "1989 as Collective Memory 'Refolution'," p. 229.

[86] Bronislaw Geremek, remarks during the debate over a Constitution Treaty for the European Parliament, Strasbourg, January 11, 2005.

[87] This assertion was made by a Pole to Susan Pearce. Pearce, "Who Owns a Movement's Memory?" p. 229.

[88] Stawaski, "Berlin Wall: Lest We Forget Poland . . .," *Polska Times*, Warsaw, 9 November 2009.

[89] Pearce, "Who Owns a Movement's Memory?" pp. 172–73.

communism. Its [sic] not what started the collapse of communism. It is purely the symbol of divided Europe!"[90]

Not satisfied with allowing the European Commission to have the last word or the last image, the Polish Ministry of Culture and Heritage produced its own short film, "It all began in Poland: The impossible became possible." At thirty-five seconds, the Polish film was even more succinct than the Commission's film and kept the focus all on Poland until the end. It highlighted "the Pope that inspired nations," "the first independent trade union Solidarity," "people who dared defy communism," and "the June 4, 1989 first free elections." After these important developments in Poland, the film tells us: "The Wall finally came down." The emphasis is clearly on "finally." The last clip reiterated once again: "1989. It all began in Poland. 20 years of freedom in Central Europe."[91]

In June 2009, Poland celebrated the twentieth anniversary of the pathbreaking elections of 1989 with ceremonies on June 3 in the Sejm in Warsaw, on June 4 at the Wawel Castle in Cracow and in Gdansk with European leaders attending, including Angela Merkel and the president of the European Parliament who happened to be German, Hans-Gert Pöttering. In Gdansk, where Solidarity had been born, there was a rock concert called "It all began in Gdansk" featuring the German band Scorpions who sang their famous song from 1989, "Wind of Change." As part of the concert, Walesa pushed the first of a series of twenty large red foam dominoes to symbolize the fall of communism in the Soviet bloc. A picture of Walesa toppling the first domino then became the first photo in a traveling exhibit entitled, "10 years, 10 months, 10 weeks, 10 days" about the revolutionary developments first in Poland (where it took ten years), then in Hungary (ten months), and the GDR (ten weeks), and Czechoslovakia (ten days), with communism toppling like dominoes. The exhibit was sponsored by the European Solidarity Center in Gdansk and emphasized that "it all began in Poland."[92]

The Russians, on the other hand, pointed out that in fact the first free elections in the Soviet bloc were not in Poland on June 4 but in Moscow on March 26, 1989 for the newly formed parliament, the Congress of People's Deputies.[93] This argument did not gain much support in Poland. Interviewed on Polish TV in 2009, Walesa was very critical of the outpouring of German gratitude to

---

[90] European Commission film, *20th Anniversary of Democratic Change in Central and Eastern Europe.* Germans could have protested that the film starts with the Soviet intervention in Hungary in 1956, completely ignoring the 1953 Soviet intervention in East Germany, www.youtube.com/watch?v=nhS55x8J7pw.

[91] Polish Ministry of Culture and Heritage, "It All Began in Poland: The Impossible Became Possible," www.youtube.com/watch?v=6DJenKPjsWw.

[92] coldwarsites.net/network/exhibitions/10-years-10-months-10-weeks-10-days-a-chronicle-of-violence. On the range of twentieth anniversary events in Poland, see Pearce, "Who Owns Movement's Memory?" pp. 174–78.

[93] Vladislav Zubok, comments made at public panel discussion, "The Polish Roundtable Talks and the End of the Cold War," London School of Economics, June 4, 2014.

Gorbachev and argued that: "Gorbachev wanted to bring down neither commun-ism nor the Wall." Walesa maintained that all the praise for Gorbachev meant that "we are building a Europe and a new reality based on lies." Instead, Walesa insisted that above all Pope John Paul II and Solidarity contributed to the over-coming of the Wall.[94] The former Polish leader was certainly right that Gorbachev did not seek the end of communism or the Berlin Wall; both were unintended consequences of his reforms and his misguided optimism, as it turned out, regarding the capacity of communism to reform and to satisfy people.[95]

The Hungarian approach has been to highlight their own role in the events of 1989 under the reformist Prime Minister Miklos Nemeth. In May 1989, Hungary and Austria held a joint ceremony at the border with the foreign ministers using clippers to dismantle the barbed wire – the first literal opening of the Iron Curtain. In early September, Hungary announced it would open its border to Austria for GDR citizens wanting to pass through to West Germany. This ended Hungary's solidarity with the leaders of its Soviet bloc ally East Germany, siding instead with the people leaving the GDR. Roughly 20,000 East Germans had been camped out in tents near the border wanting to go to West Germany and now they were given the green light to make their way there via Austria. This was a significant blow to the Iron Curtain, the Berlin Wall, and the SED regime. Gyula Horn was the Hungarian foreign minister at the time and the subtitle of his memoirs is, *Memoirs of the Hungarian Foreign Minister who opened the Iron Curtain.*[96] Even more pointedly arguing that Hungary caused the first breach in the Berlin Wall is the title of the historian Andreas Oplatka's book, *The First Crack in the Wall: September 1989 – Hungary Opens the Border*, published in German in 2009.[97]

For countries farther away from Germany and not involved in the revolu-tions of 1989, however, the fall of the Wall was viewed in a much more German-centric way. On television sets around the world in 1989, people had watched as East Germans came through the opening in the Wall into West Berlin crying, dancing, screaming with joy, kissing the ground and each other, drinking champagne, and repeatedly yelling out, "*Waaaahnsinn!*" ("Craaaazy!") The all-night party on top of the Wall at the Brandenburg Gate on November 9–10, 1989 was viewed or read about by millions of people

---

[94] As cited in "Berlin feiert den Jahrestag des Mauerfalls," *Zeit Online, Zeitgeschehen*, November 10, 2009.

[95] On the role of Gorbachev in the fall of the Wall, see Vladislav M. Zubok, "With His Back against the Wall: Gorbachev, Soviet Demise, and German Reunification," *Cold War History* 14, no. 4 (October 1, 2014), pp. 619–45; and Zubok, *A Failed Empire: The Soviet Union in the Cold War from Stalin to Gorbachev* (Chapel Hill: University of North Carolina Press, 2007).

[96] Gyula Horn, *Freiheit, die ich meine: Erinnerungen des ungarischen Aussenministers, der den eisernen Vorhang öffnete* (Hamburg: Hoffmann and Campe Verlag, 1991).

[97] Andreas Oplatka, *Der erste Riss in der Mauer: September 1989 – Ungarn öffnet die Grenze* (Vienna: Paul Zsolnay Verlag, 2009).

in every corner of the globe. What many had seen as the iconic symbol of the global Cold War and of communist rule was suddenly and astonishingly toppled peacefully overnight. The fall of the Wall was the subject of discussion around water coolers, on streets, in schools, and bars all over the world. "Did you see what happened in Berlin?" "Yes, it's amazing, isn't it?" Overnight, the image of the Wall as something brutal and permanent was transformed into something symbolizing joy, hope, and freedom.

People who had never been to Germany found themselves choked up with emotion at this display of such unfettered joy and gratitude on the Germans' faces. The moment seemed to get to someplace deep within us as human beings – a desire to be happy, to be free, to be whole. It transcended borders, making millions of people feel the joy the Germans felt. This wonderful feeling was like a magnet; people wanted to be a part of it – in 1989 and for the twentieth anniversary celebrations in 2009. As the Nobel Peace Prize laureate Muhammad Yunus declared in 2009, "The fall of the Wall was important for all of humanity."[98]

German memory activists such as Manfred Fischer, Alexandra Hildebrandt, and politicians in the Bundestag and Berlin Senate had long emphasized international interest in the Berlin Wall as part of the justification for why the Wall and its history should be more visible in the cityscape of Berlin.[99] And twenty years later, global memory of the opening of the Wall in 1989 was still strong. Reenactments of the fall of the Wall were staged in multiple countries for the anniversary.

Many Americans particularly were drawn to the fall of the Wall. They believed it demonstrated that their side had won the Cold War. Americans generally love a story about freedom and democracy triumphing over tyranny; and the reality in Berlin was better than any Hollywood film.[100] That the anchor of NBC Nightly News, Tom Brokaw, happened to be in Berlin on November 9, 1989 and could thus report live at the Brandenburg Gate only added to the deep sense of many Americans that they were part of the dramatic

---

[98] G. Asmuth and P. Gessler, "Die Geschichte weitergeben: 20. Jahrestag der Maueröffnung," *taz*, November 10, 2009.

[99] See, for example, the remarks by Bundestag member Franziska Eichstädt-Bohlig, Deutscher Bundestag Plenarprotokoll 15/163, March 10, 2005, p. 15331; and Plenarprotokoll 15/184, June 30, 2005, p. 17446; and by Alexandra Hildebrandt as quoted by Carsten Volkery, "Checkpoint Charlie. Mehr Disneyland wagen," *Spiegel*, October 20, 2004.

[100] On the USA and the end of the Cold War, see Melvyn P Leffler, *For the Soul of Mankind: The United States, the Soviet Union and the Cold War* (New York: Hill and Wang, 2008); James Graham Wilson, *The Triumph of Improvisation: Gorbachev's Adaptability, Reagan's Engagement and the End of the Cold War* (Ithaca: Cornell University Press, 2014) and Romesh Ratnazar, *Tear Down this Wall: A City, a President, and a Speech that Ended the Cold War* (New York: Simon and Schuster, 2010).

developments in Berlin.[101] In 2009, NBC and the other main US media outlets devoted great attention to the twentieth anniversary festivities in Berlin.[102]

In Los Angeles, the Wende Museum, which is dedicated to preserving cultural artifacts and personal histories of life from the communist side of the Iron Curtain and particularly from the GDR, bought ten original segments of the Wall to be the centerpiece of the museum's anniversary celebrations.[103] The Wall pieces, totaling forty feet in length, were placed on Wilshire Boulevard, a key East-West thoroughfare in the city, in mid-October. German and American artists were invited to paint on some sections of what the museum called "Wall Along Wilshire – Eastside Gallery West." On Sunday November 8, they added a manufactured extension of the real Wall segments, also with artists' paintings, and closed down the street at 11 p.m. Thousands came for a party that featured the German chanteuse Ute Lemper singing "Ghosts of Berlin" and a video message from Berlin's Mayor Wowereit. At midnight on November 9, the artists toppled the fake wall they had constructed across Wilshire Boulevard, with German television airing it live.[104] The ten original sections of the Wall remained at 5900 Wilshire Boulevard, and an additional piece of the Wall is located at the entrance to the Wende Museum itself.

Other cities around the world celebrated the twentieth anniversary of the fall of the Wall as well. In London, artists from the United Kingdom and Germany built an 11.5-foot wall made out of brick-like blocks of ice and then let people watch the "Work in Progress" melt outside of the German embassy. In Rome, the mayor hosted "A Wall Perceived" (*un muro percepito*) on the Spanish Steps, featuring replicas of pieces of the Wall and a multimedia event to celebrate the fall of the Wall. In Warsaw, students painted a replica of the Berlin Wall and then toppled it. At the Place de la Concorde in Paris, inspired by the cellist Mstislav Rostropovich's impromptu playing of Bach's cello suites at the Berlin Wall on November 11, 1989,[105] an outdoor concert featured twenty-seven cellists, one from each of the countries of the European Union. While they played, images of

---

[101] On Brokaw's presence in Berlin in 1989, see Sarotte, *The Collapse*, pp. xvii-xviii, 116–18, 130–31, 150–52.

[102] J.S. Marcus, "Celebrating the Fall of the Wall," *Wall Street Journal*, April 25–26, 2009. See also, "How Readers Acquired Bits of the Berlin Wall," NBCNews.com, November 6, 2009.

[103] www.wendemuseum.org/programs/wall-project.

[104] Yvonne Villarreal, "When the Two Halves of Berlin Became Whole Again. The 1989 Fall of the Cold War Barrier Will Be Marked in L.A. with 'A Wall across Wilshire,'" *Los Angeles Times*, November 6, 2009. See also, www.wendemuseum.org/support/special-events and www.wallproject.org/.

[105] Eric Dahan's interview with Mstislav Rostropovich, "Six French Interviews with Mstislav Rostropovich November 2005 to November 2006," translated by David Abrams with the assistance of French cellist Caroline Vincent, *Cello.org Newsletter*, www.cello.org/news letter/articles/rostrofrench/rostrofrench.htm.

the history of the Berlin Wall and the fall of communism were projected onto the facades of buildings lining the square. The French Minister of European Affairs explained that the concert was an opportunity "to show our German friends that [the fall of the Wall] is from now on part of our common European history."[106] In this vein, under the slogan "Europe Whole and Free," the European Commission held multiple events to celebrate the fall of the Wall and the unification of Europe. In Brussels, they erected a replica of Checkpoint Charlie and installed pieces of the Berlin Wall outside of the European Parliament where they held a commemorative session on November 11. Goethe Institutes and German embassies around the world also helped organize events, including many at American universities.[107]

In Spain, the Prince of Asturias Foundation used the anniversary as an occasion to confer on the city of Berlin the "Award for Concord." The award came with 50,000 euros and was to honor,

> [T]hose who, with the loss of their life or their freedom, fought in a direct way to surmount [the Berlin Wall], as well as. . .the millions of citizens who, after its fall, have been capable of building an open, welcoming and creative society over the scars of division, a nexus of concord in the heart of Germany and of Europe which contributes to understanding, coexistence, justice, peace and freedom in the world.[108]

Mayor Wowereit, together with his two predecessors Walter Momper and Eberhard Diepgen, travelled to Oviedo, Spain to accept the award. Wowereit noted that the award was "another expression of international recognition of the peaceful revolution of 1989, which had such a positive impact on the world." He also felt that the award gave "our city an obligation to do even more in the future."[109] With this in mind, the mayor announced that he would

---

[106] Katrin Bennhold, "France to Mark Fall of Berlin Wall with Musical Tribute," *New York Times*, November 3, 2009.

[107] The Goethe Institute in its 2009 "Wall Journey" (*Mauerreise*) invited artists from Germany, Korea, China, Mexico, Cyprus, Yemen, Israel, and Palestine to contribute their own large painted "domino" pieces to a reenactment of the toppling of the Wall at the main ceremony on November 9, 2009 in Berlin, www.goethe.de/ges/prj/mar/prj/enindex.htm. For more on the projects the Goethe Institute sponsored for the twentieth anniversary, see *Goethe-Institut 3.09, Geteilte Welten*, www.goethe.de/resources/files/pdf19/gi_03–09_web.pdf.

  In the USA, the German Information Center of the German Embassy, sponsored "Campus Weeks" with speaking and art competitions and other events at thirty universities to celebrate "Freedom without Walls," jhuwithoutwalls.files.wordpress.com/2009/09/freedomwithoutwalls_overviewforprojectmanagerswallartcompetition.pdf.

[108] "The Prince of Asturias Award for Concord, 2009. The City of Berlin, on the 20th Anniversary of the Fall of the Wall," Fundación Príncipe de Asturias, Oviedo, Spain, September 10, 2009. The foundation and prize name changed from "prince" to "princess" in 2015, www.fpa.es/en/tratarAplicacionPremiado.do.

[109] Ibid., Mayor Klaus Wowereit, statement upon learning of the award, September 10, 2009.

donate the prize money to the Berlin Wall Foundation to support its work, which "makes an important contribution to understanding, coexistence, justice, peace and freedom exactly in the spirit of the jury of the Prince of Asturias Foundation."[110]

The twentieth anniversary of the fall of the Wall also seemed to be on the mind of the Swedish Academy in Stockholm. It awarded the Nobel Prize in Literature in October to the Romanian-born German writer Herta Müller whose writing, the Academy noted, "depicts the landscape of the dispossessed," the lives of people like herself who had suffered under dictatorship. After enduring years of persecution due to her opposition to the brutal Ceaucescu regime in Romania and due to being part of a German-speaking minority, Müller immigrated to West Germany in 1987.[111] By the time of her award, she had been living in exile in (West) Berlin for thirty years, and this experience had only "serve[d] to sharpen [her] confrontation with dictatorship," as the Nobel committee noted.[112] In presenting Müller with the prize in 2009, the Academy told her: "You have shown great courage in uncompromisingly repudiating provincial repression and political terror. It is for the artistic value in that opposition that you merit this prize." Müller had endured persecution as so many of the East German opposition civic activists had and was made out of the same cloth. Honoring her was perhaps an indirect way of honoring them too.

Inspired by the fall of the Wall, the tenth annual World Summit of Nobel Peace Laureates chose November 2009 to meet in Berlin to "consider how the ideological, economic, strategic and religious walls that continue to divide humanity might best be dismantled and replaced with bridges of communication and understanding." Six individual peace prize laureates, including Gorbachev and Walesa (who argued about their mutual roles in contributing to the fall of the Wall[113]), as well as representatives of ten international groups that had won the prize were among those who attended on November 10–11 as was Mayor Wowereit. The summit's final statement called for removing walls preventing a nuclear-weapons-free world, walls between rich and poor and between cultural, religious, and ethnic communities, walls that stand in the way of combating climate change, and walls in the way of inter-generational justice.[114]

---

[110] "Prinz-von-Asturien-Preis: Wowereit unterstützt mit Preisgeld Stiftung Berliner Mauer," press statement from the mayor's office, October 23, 2009.

[111] Motoko Rich and Nicholas Kulish, "Herta Müller Wins Nobel Prize in Literature," *New York Times*, October 8, 2009.

[112] "The Nobel Prize in Literature 2009 – Presentation Speech." *Nobelprize.org.* Nobel Media AB 2014, www.nobelprize.org/nobel_prizes/literature/laureates/2009/presenta tion-speech.html.

[113] "Annie Lennox Honored by Berlin Summit of Nobel Peace Prize Laureates," *Deutsche Welle*, November 11, 2009.

[114] The event was hosted by the Rome-based Permanent Secretariat of the World Summit of Nobel Peace Laureates, a non-governmental, non-profit group, which is not affiliated

On the subject of walls still dividing, both the Palestinians and South Koreans held demonstrations on the occasion of the twentieth anniversary of the fall of the Wall, calling for change at their borders. Palestinians and others in the People's Campaign to Fight the Wall protested against the security barrier built by Israel to surround the West Bank. As people were celebrating in Berlin on November 9, 2009, in the West Bank town of Kalandia near the barrier's checkpoint to enter East Jerusalem, masked protestors used a truck to pull down a section of the concrete wall Israel had built. They then passed through the hole they had created, hoisted a Palestinian flag and set fire to some tires. Israeli forces responded with tear gas and stopped the incursion through the wall.[115] Half way around the globe, South Koreans demonstrated near the demilitarized zone with North Korea, calling for an end to the North Korean dictatorship and its policy of political imprisonment and releasing a balloon stocked with flyers critical of the regime.[116]

While Americans were celebrating the fall of the Wall in Los Angeles and many other cities, Mexicans and Central Americans south of the border continued to die in their efforts to reach and cross the border barriers into the United States, drowning in the Rio Grande, being killed by the smugglers they paid to get them to the USA, dying of thirst or hunger, or being killed while riding on top of the "death train" (el tren de la muerte) or "the Beast" (La Bestia), as it was also called. Those who made it across the border were not guaranteed acceptance or safety. In 2009, the US government was paying $1,300 to fix the double-layered border fence each time someone broke through. US Customs and Border Protection reported 416 deaths on the USA side of the border in the first ten months of 2009, a number that did not include the far greater number of deaths on the Mexican side of the border.[117] The trauma surrounding the Mexican-American border was expressed in the contributions by Mexican artists to the twentieth anniversary celebrations in Berlin.[118]

with the Norwegian Nobel Peace Prize committee, www.nobelpeacesummit.com/the-world-summit-of-nobel-peace-laureates/berlin-2009/.

[115] "Palestinians Break Israel's Wall," AlJazeera.com, November 9, 2009; Popular Struggle Coordination Committee, "Protesters Reenacted Fall of the Berlin Wall to Mark Its 20th Anniversary: 8 Meter Tall Concrete Wall Dividing Ramallah and Jerusalem Tipped-Over," International Solidarity Movement, press release, November 9, 2009, palsolidarity.org/2009/11/protesters-reenacted-the-fall-of-the-berlin-wall-to-mark-its-20th-anniversary-8-meter-tall-concrete-wall-dividing-ramallah-and-jerusalem-tipped-over/. For German coverage of this, see "Mauer-fall-Feiern: Dominosteine und Politprominenz," DiePresse.com, November 9, 2009.

[116] "Berlin Wall Celebrations Move South Koreans to Protest," Deutsche Welle, November 9, 2009.

[117] Robin Emmott, "A Costly U.S.-Mexico Border Wall, in Both Dollars and Deaths," Reuters, October 2, 2009.

[118] Mexican artists sent three large painted "dominoes" to be part of the November 9, 2009 celebrations in Berlin. Anna-Katrin Mellmann, "Mexiko – ein Land der Mauern,"

Participation in Berlin's twentieth anniversary celebrations took a sinister turn in China. The Berlin authorities hosted a Twitter site, www.berlintwitter wall.com, which was open from October 20 to November 15, with the hashtag #fotw (fall of the Wall). People were invited to "share your thoughts on the fall of the Berlin Wall or let us know which walls still have to come down to make our world a better place." Chinese citizens responded in droves with many of them calling for an end to internet censorship, or what they called "the Great Firewall of China."[119] Of the nearly 8,000 tweets on the site, almost 2,000 were from China. Within days, the Chinese government shut down access to the Twitter site from within China.

While some groups within Germany and outside of Germany viewed the fall of the Wall differently from the way Tom Sello, Bundestag supporters of the Freedom and Unity Monument, and others did, his emphasis on the East German peaceful revolution became the dominant narrative of the fall of the Wall in German public commemorations in 2009, and the celebratory instinct on display in so many world capitals would be mirrored in Berlin. The twentieth anniversary of the fall of the Wall marked a turning point in German *Erinnerungspolitik*, as we will see in the next chapter.

---

tagesschau Archiv, August 13, 2009, tsarchive.wordpress.com/2009/08/13/mauer106/. For pictures of the paintings, see "Piedras del Muro," a joint project of the Goethe Institut and the Border Cultural Center, Mexico City, www.border.com.mx/piedras-del-muro-goethe-institut-colectivoregistro-de-proyecto-5/. See also Kulturprojekte Berlin GmbH, ed., *Dominobuch: Geschichte(n) mit Dominoeffekt* (Berlin: Kulturprojekte Berlin GmbH, 2009), pp. 32, 35, 108.

[119] Reporters without Borders for Freedom of Information, "Berlin Twitter Wall Website Blocked Just Days after Its Launch," November 3 and 5, 2009, en.rsf.org/china-berlin-twitter-wall-website-03–11-2009,34897.html. See also Free Speech Debate, Dahrendorf Programme for the Study of Freedom, St. Antony's College, University of Oxford, "The Berlin Twitter Wall v the Great Firewall of China" (undated), freespeechdebate.com/en/case/the-berlin-twitter-wall-v-the-great-firewall-of-china/; and "China Blocks State-Funded Berlin Twitter Wall," *China Digital Times*, October 29, 2009, chinadigital-times.net/2009/10/china-blocks-state-funded-memorial-website-for-berlin-wall/.

9

Celebrating Heroes and a New Founding Myth

Until 2007 with the Bundestag's support for a Freedom and Unity Monument and then Tom Sello's Peaceful Revolution exhibit in 2009, the main focus of public discussions and commemoration of the Berlin Wall in Germany had been on the victims and particularly those who had been killed at the Wall by East German border soldiers. The Wall represented "a difficult past" that people either shied away from or addressed by commemorating the victims. Both the German experience in dealing with the Holocaust as well as the spark provided by Alexandra Hildebrandt's "Wall crosses" contributed to this situation. As the previous chapter demonstrated, however, a variety of factors led to a change of focus toward a celebration of the fall of the Wall and even a sense of pride that courageous East Germans had brought down the Wall and the East German communist regime in a "peaceful revolution." The "positive" side of the Wall – its end – was at the center of attention in 2009 instead of the "negative" side of the Wall – the brutality of the border regime and the people who were killed as a result.

In spite of the existence of counter-narratives inside Germany and beyond its borders, the events surrounding the twentieth anniversary of the fall of the Wall in Germany emphasized that there were heroes to laud and a much more positive way of looking at recent German history. Over the course of the year, it became increasingly common for German politicians to use the word "proud" in describing their sentiments about the fall of the Wall. Beginning with Sello's exhibit in May and then in discussions, news articles, and events especially in October and November 2009, the essential role of the East German people in bringing down the Wall and the communist regime behind it received widespread official sanction. In essence, 2009 saw the creation of a new official narrative, a new founding myth about the fall of the Wall and the birth of the new united German nation out of the first successful, democratic, Peaceful Revolution, capital P, capital R, in German history.

Surveys in the summer of 2009, however, indicated that Germans did not see the events of 1989 in this way. Instead, they viewed the reforms in the Soviet Union, Poland, and Hungary and the economic weakness of the GDR system as more important in leading to the fall of the Wall and of the SED regime than the East German demonstrations in the fall of

1989.[1] Angela Merkel herself had observed in a 1999 interview that East Germany had collapsed for economic reasons.[2] As chancellor in 2009, however, she emphasized the role of the East German peaceful revolutionaries who joined the reformers in other countries to the east in bringing down the Berlin Wall and communism.

Planning for the Twentieth Anniversary

Berlin's Mayor Klaus Wowereit started planning for 2009 almost two years in advance and allocated 4.3 million euros in lottery funds for the celebration.[3] Wowereit had grown up in Tempelhof, West Berlin, near the border with East Germany in the south of the city. He remembered the loss his mother and older sister felt after the building of the Wall when they could no longer see their friends who lived just across the border.[4] When the Wall came down in 1989, Wowereit was the Counselor for Education and Culture in Tempelhof and organized reunions with the neighboring East German community. Now, twenty years later, in the wake of the *Gesamtkonzept* for remembering the Berlin Wall which he and his cultural senator Thomas Flierl had overseen, the mayor was ready to celebrate. His interest was no doubt also engaged by the opportunity to bring German and foreign tourists – and their wallets – to Berlin for the festivities. Hotels, stores, the media, and other businesses sought to profit from the anniversary celebrations, which were the subject of a mass marketing campaign.[5] The mayor knew that a significant part of Berlin's attraction was its connection with the fall of the Wall.

Wowereit declared Berlin's "theme of the year" to be: "Twenty years since the fall of the Wall," and he commissioned a non-profit partner of the Berlin government, Kulturprojekte Berlin, to plan and coordinate the commemoration. In a press release on November 7, 2009 to launch the twentieth anniversary festivities, the mayor asserted that Berlin's "history with the dream of freedom" was the reason "it has become the first address for all of those who want to live this dream in a creative, tolerant,

---

[1] Statista, "Welcher der folgenden Faktoren war Ihrer Meinung nach für das Ende der SED-Herrschaft ausschlaggebend?" June 2009, https://de.statista.com/statistik/daten/studie/ 13022/umfrage/wichtigste-faktoren-fuer-ende-der-sed-herrschaft/.

[2] Angela Merkel, *Mein Weg: Angela Merkel im Gespräch mit Hugo Müller-Vogg* (Hamburg: Hoffmann und Campe, 2004), pp. 64, 70.

[3] Eva Dorothée Schmid, "Zum 20. Jahrestag des Mauerfalls plant der Senat Ausstellungen und ein Fest am Brandenburger Tor. Eine Grenze aus Dominosteinen," *Berliner Zeitung*, June 10, 2008.

[4] Klaus Wowereit with Hajo Schumacher, . . . *und das ist auch gut so: Mein Leben für die Politik* (Munich: Heyne Verlag, 2009), p. 20.

[5] On the increasing mass marketing of historical anniversaries in Germany, see Achim Landwehr, "Mein Jahr mit Luther. Thesen zur Geschichtskultur," meinjahrmitluther. wordpress.com/category/thesen-zur-geschichtskultur/.

cosmopolitan metropolis."[6] Kulturprojekte Berlin developed three main parts of the commemoration. The celebratory year began with small displays at a variety of key locations in Berlin such as Potsdamer Platz, the Berlin Wall Memorial, and the new central train station – so-called *Schauplätze* (Showplaces) – to demonstrate how the city had developed since the fall of the Wall and to project its future development.[7] In May, Sello's exhibit on the Peaceful Revolution opened at Alexanderplatz and the anniversary year culminated in a grand celebration at the Brandenburg Gate on November 9.

Sello's exhibit was accompanied by over ninety events, including lectures, guided tours, workshops, discussions, films, readings, and concerts, all featured on the www.revolution89.de website in six languages. The exhibit attracted millions of visitors. It was extended from its original end date in the fall of 2009 to October 2010 and was later given a permanent home in the courtyard of the museum-memorial at the former Stasi headquarters in Berlin-Lichtenberg, making a significant contribution to the dissemination of the narrative emphasizing the role of East Germans in the fall of the Wall. Mayor Wowereit awarded Sello the Order of Merit in the fall of 2009. At the ceremony, Wowereit spoke of 1989–90 as "the happiest hours in the recent history of this city and country." He honored "those who made it all possible," such as Sello for "his biography and his work, which show the courage individuals mustered to defy the SED dictatorship."[8]

President Horst Köhler,[9] the *Bundeszentrale*, and the Point Alpha Foundation at the former East-West German border between Thuringia and Hesse each similarly bestowed prizes on people and activities connected with the Peaceful Revolution and remembering it. The *Stiftung Aufarbeitung*

---

[6] "Wowereit zu 20 Jahre Friedliche Revolution und Mauerfall am 9. November 2009," press release from the office of the Governing Mayor of Berlin, November 6, 2009.

[7] Between January and October, a large floating red arrow and a red "info box" on the ground rotated to nearly twenty different spots in the city to show how specific buildings, structures, or neighborhoods had developed since the fall of the Wall, "20 Years of a Changing Berlin." Multimedia installations in the "info box" showed what had changed in the past twenty years and what was planned for the future. For catalogues of the rotating "info box" exhibits, see Kulturprojekte Berlin, ed., *Berliner Zukünfte. Darstellung und Bilanz – Perspektiven und Visionen* (Berlin: Kulturprojekte Berlin GmbH, 2009) and *20 Jahre Mauerfall. Documentation des Themenjahres 2009* (Berlin: Kulturprojekte Berlin GmbH, 2009). "Infobox '20 Jahre Mauerfall' eröffnet," *Tagesspiegel*, January 28, 2009.

[8] Speech of Klaus Wowereit, "Verleihung des Berliner Landesordens," October 1, 2009. Sello also received the federal Order of Merit from President Joachim Gauck in October 2013.

[9] Horst Köhler, "'Mut und Zivilcourage in Diktatur und Unfreiheit,' Grußwort von Bundespräsident Horst Köhler bei der Verleihung des Verdienstordens der Bundesrepublik Deutschland an Gegner des SED-Unrechts am 16. November 2009 in Schloss Bellevue, Bundespräsidialamt." See also Richard Herzinger, "Köhler ehrt demonstrative Gegner des DDR-Regimes," *Welt*, November 16, 2009; and "Bundesverdienstkreuze für ehemalige Häftlinge des Speziallagers Bautzen," Gedenkstätte Bautzen, Stiftung Sächsische Gedenkstätten, Pressemitteilung, November 13, 2009.

created a year-long series of activities connected to the 2009–10 celebration of "Twenty Years of the Peaceful Revolution and German Unity" and launched a web portal (www.zeitzeugenbuero.de/) with biographies and contact information of former East Germans who experienced the dramatic changes of 1989–90 and were willing to speak at schools. Unlike many others who adopted the term only in 2009, the *Stiftung Aufarbeitung* had been referring to the "Peaceful Revolution" since at least 2004.

Wowereit charged the thirty-eight-year-old Moritz van Dülmen, director of Kulturprojekte Berlin (see Figure 25), with overseeing the twentieth anniversary celebrations in Berlin. Van Dülmen had been eighteen years old when the Wall fell. He watched the dramatic events in Berlin on television from his home near the French border in West Germany's Saarland. In 2009, he was acutely aware of the risks for a West German supervising the anniversary of a momentous East German event: "The story of the fall of the Wall is so emotional and personal that one can only make mistakes – especially a young West German."[10] In an effort to guard against wrong moves, he consulted closely with Tom Sello on the history of 1989 and how to represent it.

The one thing van Dülmen was certain he wanted for the anniversary was a big celebration, a street festival with mass participation. His young age when the Wall came down no doubt contributed to his celebratory instinct. An older West German accustomed to *Erinnerungspolitik* focused on the Holocaust might have been wary of kicking up his heels on November 9 due to the shared anniversary with *Kristallnacht*; and an older East German might have been frustrated by unfulfilled dreams since unification. But what should be the central event? How could van Dülmen ensure mass participation? And how could he get the large numbers of young people who would be essential to creating a celebratory atmosphere? A 2007 survey showed that young Germans knew little about the history of the Wall. Only one-third of high school students knew the GDR had built the Wall, and some even believed the West had erected it. The survey also demonstrated that the more students learned about the GDR in school, the less likely they were to have a positive view of the GDR.[11] Van Dülmen thought the twentieth anniversary could be an occasion for students to learn more about the history of the Wall.

He also knew that people in Germany and around the world would expect the celebration to occur at the Brandenburg Gate as it had with people dancing

---

[10] Interview with Moritz van Dülmen, January 28, 2010.

[11] Björn Hengst and Peter Wensierski, "Bundeskanzler Honecker, SED-Chef Adenauer: Große Schülerbefragung," *Spiegel Online*, November 9, 2007. For the full results of the survey of more than 5,000 high school students in four German states, see Monika Deutz-Schroeder and Klaus Schroeder, *Soziales Paradies oder Stasi-Staat? Das DDR-Bild von Schülern – ein Ost-West-Vergleich* (Stamsried: Ernst Vögel, 2008). For a critique of the conclusions drawn by the Schroeders, see Martin Sabrow, "Wie, der Schüler kennt den Dicken mit der Zigarre nicht?" *Frankfurter Allgemeine Zeitung*, February 4, 2009.

on the Wall on that amazing night twenty years before. But what should he do? Rebuild the Wall somehow? Have Pink Floyd sing "Another Brick in the Wall"? Create a human chain? Mayor Wowereit wanted an event that would both look back to 1989 and also look forward by drawing lessons from the fall of the Wall. Van Dülmen brainstormed with his colleague Wolf Kühnelt and others.[12]

Kühnelt had grown up in East Berlin, and at the age of twenty-eight, he and his wife escaped from East Berlin in the trunk of a diplomat's Mercedes. Bundled up in several layers of clothing on a cold day in January 1971, they passed through Checkpoint Charlie undetected. After the GDR declared an amnesty in 1972 for people who had fled, Kühnelt returned to visit friends at a party in East Berlin. He was caught by the Stasi (who erroneously believed he was trying to help others escape) and imprisoned at Hohenschönhausen for three months before being released to West Berlin. Kühnelt went on to study museum pedagogy and ultimately became the director of event planning at Kulturprojekte Berlin.[13] Like van Dülmen, he looked forward to celebrating the fall of the Wall.

As van Dülmen and Kühnelt brainstormed in 2008 about what to do for the twentieth anniversary, they thought about the history of 1989. They talked about how so many factors led to the fall of the Wall, and the fall of the Wall in turn led to more dramatic developments. It was all a domino reaction. That was it! They would have school students paint rectangular blocks with stories portraying some aspect of Berlin and German history connected to the Wall, and the blocks would then be toppled like dominoes on November 9. They decided to contact schools in Berlin, invite their students to the exhibit on the Peaceful Revolution at Alexanderplatz and to design their own Wall dominoes (*Dominosteine*). This would make sure students learned some history and would also bring these young people to the celebration at the Brandenburg Gate. Depicting other walls that still should fall in the world would be another option for designing a *Dominostein*. This would satisfy the mayor's desire to look toward the future and the possibility of other walls being toppled.[14]

Van Dülmen and Kühnelt presented this idea to the mayor in the spring of 2008, and once Wowereit approved, they announced the plans in June 2008. The culmination of the "*Dominoaktion*" would be a display of the *Dominosteine* over three days, November 7–9, in a *Fest der Freiheit* (Festival of Freedom) centered around the Brandenburg Gate. After initially envisaging rather small, easily movable dominoes, experts on large-scale events advised

[12] Interview with Moritz van Dülmen, January 28, 2010.
[13] Correspondence with Wolf Kühnelt, March 26 and April 8, 2014; interview with Kühnelt, July 13, 2014.
[14] Interviews with Moritz van Dülmen, January 28, 2010, and Wolf Kühnelt, January 25, 2010.

the Kulturprojekte group to use bigger dominoes that would be more visible both on TV and over the shoulders of people in the large crowds expected on November 9. Van Dülmen worried that the *Dominosteine* might be seen as too childish and simplistic, particularly large ones. He consulted regularly with Sello and Manfred Fischer, both of whom expressed their support regarding his plan and their optimism that it would be successful.

The more than 1,000 *Dominosteine* to be painted by schoolchildren and others were made of Styrofoam and measured more than eight feet tall and three feet wide. They would be installed along one mile of the former path of the Wall between the Reichstag, the Brandenburg Gate, and Potsdamer Platz in central Berlin (see Figure 1). Kulturprojekte, Berlin's tourism office, the Goethe Institute, and the foreign ministry ultimately reached out to more than 15,000 schoolchildren and others in Berlin and beyond, to various cities and countries (including countries or groups divided in some way), companies, and particular individuals to give them the chance to contribute a *Dominostein*. Anyone interested in making a domino could fill out an application online by September 2009. Mayor Wowereit launched the *Dominoaktion* in March 2009 with students and artists painting dominoes outside at the Brandenburg Gate. The Mayor declared that "with this domino action, young people should occupy themselves with what the fall of the Wall meant."[15]

While the main target audience was German schoolchildren, Kulturprojekte also invited particular individuals with biographies in some way relevant to the fall of the Wall or more generally inspirational to design a domino. These included Lech Walesa, Vaclav Havel, Mikhail Gorbachev, and Nelson Mandela (whose message said, "It is always worth it to fight for freedom"). Van Dülmen wanted to show both that non-Germans had played crucial roles in the process leading to the fall of the Wall and also that "November 9, 1989 belongs not just to Berlin, East Germany or West Germany but to the whole world." He expected global attention to be directed to the festivities at the Brandenburg Gate on November 9, 2009 and to the final toppling of the *Dominosteine*. Van Dülmen negotiated with the German public television station ZDF to broadcast the celebration live throughout the country and to pay for large screens at the Brandenburg Gate so the expected tens of thousands of people in attendance could have good views throughout the evening.

Leipzig, October 9, 2009

Although for many in Germany and around the world (if not for the Poles or Hungarians), the fall of the Wall on November 9 was the most significant date in 1989, for those most engaged in the civic opposition to the SED, it was

---

[15] Anne Lena Mösken, "Jugendliche dürfen fürs Wende-Gedenken malen," *Berliner Zeitung*, March 19, 2009.

October 9 that marked the turning point, since that was the date when many East Germans lost their fear of opposing the regime due to the success of protestors in Leipzig. Churches in Leipzig had begun hosting regular peace prayers on Monday evenings in 1982. These attracted people opposed to the regime as well as many members of the Stasi to monitor them. The Monday night prayer meetings became particularly important in the fall of 1989 when they began to be regularly followed by demonstrations. They grew to become the most significant demonstrations in the GDR, and the demonstration in downtown Leipzig on October 9 became a turning point known as "the miracle of Leipzig."

In spite of rumors that there would be a Tiananmen Square type crackdown against the demonstrators, masses of brave citizens marched that evening with candles past the Stasi headquarters and along the central ring road chanting "We are the people!" (*"Wir sind das Volk!"*) and "No violence!" (*"Keine Gewalt!"*). While parents and children, brothers and sisters advised each other, "don't go out tonight; it's too risky," 70,000 people decided to go anyway.[16] Two dissidents managed to surreptitiously film some of the demonstration from the steeple of Leipzig's Reform Church and get the videotape to the exiled dissident Roland Jahn who had become a journalist in West Berlin. As East Germans watched the footage on West German television the next day and word spread of the success of the demonstration in Leipzig, tens of thousands and then hundreds of thousands of other East Germans were inspired to take to the streets in cities and towns across the GDR demanding change, including the freedom to travel.[17] East German officials later commented, "We were prepared for everything but candles and prayers."[18]

Leipzig's twentieth anniversary commemoration included an official state ceremony with speeches by German leaders, a peace prayer and ceremonial concert in the Nikolai Church, as well as a massive outdoor *Lichtfest* (Festival of Light), in a reference to the candles carried by the protestors in 1989. Chancellor Merkel, other German and foreign dignitaries, former East German civic activists and victims' groups participated in the state ceremony held in the concert hall of Leipzig's Gewandhaus orchestra located on the largest square in the city, the Augustusplatz. Both the Gewandhaus and the square had been key sites in 1989.

---

[16] Author's interviews with multiple people on the streets of Leipzig, October 8–9, 2009.

[17] Rainer Eckert, "Der 9. Oktober: Tag der Entscheidung in Leipzig," in Klaus-Dietmar Henke, ed., *Revolution und Vereinigung 1989/90. Als in Deutschland die Realität die Phantasie überholte* (Munich: Deutscher Taschenbuch Verlag, 2009), p. 222. See also Mary Elise Sarotte, *The Collapse: The Accident Fall of the Berlin Wall* (New York: Basic Books, 2014), especially chapters 2 and 3.

[18] Horst Sindermann of the SED Central Committee is credited with saying this. Jens Bauszus, "Das Wunder von Leipzig," *Focus Online*, October 9, 2009.

Indeed, the conductor of the Gewandhaus orchestra, Kurt Masur, had played an important role in mediating talks between protesters and the Leipzig government in October 1989 to keep things peaceful. After the fall of the Wall and unification, with the world now open to him, Masur became the director of the New York Philharmonic and the Orchestre National de France while also remaining the head of the Gewandhaus. At the age of eighty-two and visibly moved by recollections of the events twenty years before, Maestro Masur led the Gewandhaus orchestra for the invite-only commemoration, beginning with the national anthem and ending with Beethoven. In the evening, Masur would conduct a celebratory concert for the public in the Nikolai Church with the Gewandhaus orchestra joined by the famed Bach choir of Leipzig's Thomas Church.

The midday ceremony at the Gewandhaus featured speeches by President Horst Köhler, Leipzig Mayor Burkhard Jung, Minister-President of Saxony Stanislaw Tillich, and President of the Parliament of Saxony Matthias Rössler. The speakers all remembered Leipzig's October 9, 1989 with pride. President Köhler, himself originally from West Germany, described it as the day "the 'Peaceful Revolution' was born" and expressed his gratitude to the assembled guests: "Dear compatriots, many of you were there then – thank you. You can always and forever be proud of that."[19]

The former East German dissident, Werner Schulz, who had gone on to become a member of the Bundestag and then the European Parliament, gave a dramatic speech that earned much applause and provoked not a few tears. Schulz spoke to the capacity crowd in the Gewandhaus of the "unexpected superpower of 70,000" against which "the state was incapable of acting."[20] Schulz declared: "Without October 9 in Leipzig, there would have been no November 9 in Berlin. . . .Without the increasing readiness to go onto the streets, there wouldn't have been the crush of people at the Bornholmer Bridge" on the night of November 9 forcing the guards to make the unprecedented opening in the Berlin Wall at that crossing point.[21] Thus, it was the Peaceful Revolution that started the dramatic changes of 1989–90, not the fall of the Berlin Wall, which was essentially an effect (or a victim) of the Peaceful Revolution. Former East German civic activists and scholars, particularly from Leipzig, had already been using the term "Peaceful Revolution" for years, but it only came to frame the dominant narrative in 2009.[22]

---

[19] "Leipzig feiert Herbst '89 mit Grosskundgebung," *Focus Online*, October 9, 2009.

[20] Werner Schulz, "Was lange gärt wird Mut," Festakt "20 Jahre Friedliche Revolution," Gewandhaus Leipzig, October 9, 2009.

[21] This point was also made in the "Leipziger Thesen," Initiative "Tag der Friedlichen Revolution – Leipzig 9. Oktober 1989," September 4, 2009, www.herbst89.de/startseite/leipziger-thesen.html.

[22] Tobias Hollitzer, "15 Jahre Friedliche Revolution," *Aus Politik und Zeitgeschichte*, September 29, 2004; and Rainer Eckert, "Das historische Jahr 1990," *Aus Politik*

Competition between Leipzig and Berlin for the mantle of leader of the Peaceful Revolution was palpable on the twentieth anniversary. In both cities, one heard from residents: "*This* was the most important site of the Peaceful Revolution." Leipzigers spoke of the turning point of October 9 in Leipzig, while Berliners spoke of the key demonstrations in East Berlin on the fortieth anniversary of the GDR on October 7 and at Alexanderplatz on November 4 and of course the toppling of the Wall on November 9.[23] This rivalry between the cities had been evident when the Bundestag first decided in 2007 to support the building of a Freedom and Unity Monument in Berlin but not in Leipzig. In response to criticism for leaving out Leipzig, the Bundestag amended its stance and agreed in late 2008 to help support a monument in Leipzig that would "appropriately acknowledge the contribution of the citizens of Leipzig to the Peaceful Revolution."[24] The presence of both the federal chancellor and president at the ceremony in Leipzig bolstered the importance of that city in historical memory.[25]

In order to understand why some East Germans on the streets in Leipzig and elsewhere in 1989 were willing to risk so much to compel changes in the

---

und Zeitgeschichte, September 28, 2005. For a (West) German scholarly analysis of the two terms, see Martin Sabrow, "Wende oder Revolution? Keinesfalls nur eine scholastische Frage. Der Herbstumbruch vor 20 Jahren in deutschen Geschichtsbewusstsein," *Neues Deutschland*, November 21, 2009. An exhibit in Leipzig at the *Zeitgeschichtliches Forum* highlighted the Peaceful Revolution. Stiftung Haus der Geschichte und Zeitgeschichtliches Forum, eds., *Demokratie jetzt oder nie! Diktatur, Widerstand, Alltag* (Leipzig: Edition Leipzig, 2008). The new permanent exhibit that opened in 2018 at the *Zeitgeschichtliches Forum*, in contrast, devotes more attention to developments in the east since unification, *Unsere Geschichte. Diktatur und Demokratie nach 1945.*

[23] As Christoph Dieckmann wrote in 2009, "November 4, 1989 was the street party of the Peaceful Revolution. . . .But in united Germany, in what you could call official commemorations of 'the turn,' November 4 hardly plays a role." Dieckmann, "Welche Wandlung!" *Zeit, Geschichte* 2 (May 27, 2009).

[24] See the motion, "Freiheits- und Einheitsdenkmal gestalten," Drucksache 16/11200, December 3, 2008 and the vote agreeing to the motion, Deutscher Bundestag, Plenarprotokoll 16/193, December 4, 2008, pp. 20900–20901. On January 29, 2009, the federal government, the state of Saxony and the city of Leipzig agreed that the federal government would redirect five million euros to Leipzig of the original fifteen million euros planned for the Freedom and Unity Monument, and Saxony would contribute 1.5 million euros. As in Berlin, multiple controversies have prevented Leipzig's Freedom and Unity Monument from being built as of this writing.

[25] In an expanding acknowledgment of the breadth of the popular unrest in the fall of 1989, the speakers in Leipzig also remembered the demonstrations (some of which had been violently suppressed) in other East German cities – in Plauen, Halle, Dresden, Rostock, Schwerin, and of course Berlin. On monuments to the Peaceful Revolution erected in various German localities since 1989, see Anna Saunders, *Memorializing the GDR* (NY: Berghahn, 2018), pp. 215–313.

government, President Köhler made sure to remind people just what the East German state behind the Berlin Wall had been like, as Sello had sought to do with his exhibit. In doing so, Köhler used the memory of the Peaceful Revolution to bolster the dominant narrative of the SED as an *Unrechtsstaat* ("unjust state") and to undermine individuals and groups who looked back fondly on the GDR. The narratives of the heroic East Germans in the Peaceful Revolution and that of the SED *Unrechtsstaat* were intimately connected. As Köhler put it:

> Would the 70,000 people in Leipzig and the hundreds of thousands in Plauen, Dresden and Berlin and other cities in the GDR have gone onto the streets if the GDR had more good than bad sides? Would millions of people have left the GDR since 1949 if they had seen in it the possibility of voting freely and behaving independently, the possibility to travel, to choose their profession freely, if they had the opportunity to send their children to secondary schools and universities if they weren't a member of the worker or peasant class, if they were allowed to assemble freely and come together in associations, if they had the right to a fair trial?
>
> No, no, the Peaceful Revolution was no mistake. The citizens of the GDR knew that the situation could not continue any longer so unfree, so suffocating and so sad and they didn't want it to go on.[26]

With great public and media attention on the twentieth anniversary, Köhler seized the opportunity to highlight the reasons brave East Germans had taken to the streets and emphasized the "importance of keeping alive the memory of the SED dictatorship and resistance to it." Only this could "guard against idealizing" the nature of the East German communist regime. Mayor Jung of Leipzig struck a similar note.[27] At a time when some east Germans looked back nostalgically at the full employment, cheap, ubiquitous childcare, and the lack of capitalist competition in the GDR, German leaders reminded them of the downsides of life in the GDR.

President Köhler was aware, however, that many east Germans felt alienated by the general denunciation of the SED regime as an *Unrechtsstaat*. The term *Unrechtsstaat* has been used to describe East Germany since the early 1990s, with the Wall as a central piece of evidence, but the term came into widespread use during campaigns for the September 2009 federal elections when the terms *Unrechtsstaat* and GDR seemed to be almost fused together. This strategy backfired on the CDU and SPD. Although Merkel's CDU won the elections, a record number of people

---

[26] Horst Köhler, "70,000 Herzen," Festakt "20 Jahre Friedliche Revolution," Gewandhaus Leipzig, October 9, 2009.

[27] Burkhard Jung, "Rede des Oberbürgermeisters der Stadt Leipzig," Gewandhaus Leipzig, October 9, 2009.

voted for *die Linke* which earned nearly 12 percent of the overall vote and 28.5 percent of the vote in the east.

While the term *Unrechtsstaat* was widely used starting in 2009, it also unleashed a storm of controversy that made headlines that year and afterwards.[28] Many east Germans felt that this condemnation of the GDR as an unjust state also implied a damning of the lives they lived there, making them feel alienated from the united German state. This began a discussion about whether it was possible "to have lived a life of good within the bad state." It also revived a focus on studies of "everyday life" (*Alltagsleben*) in East Germany as opposed to focusing solely on the repressive machinery of the state. For some, however, changing the focus to *Alltagsleben* brought another contentious debate about whether this vantage point meant a deliberate downplaying of the unjust nature of the East German regime.

Unrechtsstaat and *Alltagsleben* both became polarizing terms at supposedly opposite ends of the spectrum of assessing the GDR. Efforts to find a middle ground had a hard time gaining traction.[29] In his address in Leipzig on October 9, 2009, Köhler tried to reassure German citizens from the east that he was not judging them when he criticized the GDR *Unrechtsstaat* and reached out to them as citizens of united Germany:

> The *Grundgesetz* [the German constitution] recognizes no second-class citizens. And the first class revolutionaries like those here in Leipzig should not let themselves be labeled this way. On the contrary: The East Germans in particular have earned much respect not only due to the wonderful autumn of 1989. Almost everything changed in the eastern states after 1990, while for West Germans much afterwards remained for years as it was before. The vast majority of East Germans have successfully mastered this fundamental change in their living conditions, this rupture in their own biographies. This is an achievement that is still recognized much too little and from which people should draw lessons.[30]

---

[28] "Luc Jochimsen: Die DDR war kein 'Unrechtsstaat'," *Frankfurter Allgemine Zeitung*, June 17, 2010. See also "Lothar de Maizière: 'DDR war kein Unrechtsstaat'," *Tagesspiegel*, August 23, 2010.

[29] "Linken-Politiker erklärt seine DDR-Interpretation," *Welt*, February 27, 2009; Jacob Comenetz, "Was Communist East Germany Unjust or Just Corrupt?" *Global News Journal*, May 22, 2009; and "Lothar de Maizière: 'DDR war kein Unrechtsstaat'," *Tagesspiegel*, August 23, 2010.

[30] Horst Köhler, "70,000 Herzen," Festakt "20 Jahre Friedliche Revolution," Gewandhaus Leipzig, October 9, 2009. German leaders, including Berlin Mayor Michael Müller and Bundestag President Wolfgang Schäuble would say nearly the same thing nine years later on Unity Day in 2018.

This statement of understanding by the German president was an important acknowledgment of the ongoing complications of uniting East and West. Köhler's reference to the "rupture" the fall of the Wall and unification caused in the lives of East Germans was uncommon at the time but would become much more common ten years later.

While most people could only watch the midday speeches by Köhler and the others on television, more than 100,000 people participated that evening in the *Lichtfest*, the re-creation of the candlelight march around the city center of October 9, 1989. People gathered first at the Augustusplatz to light 25,000 candles spelling "Leipzig '89" and then to march around the inner-city ring road.[31] The mass marketing of the event had succeeded in drawing people to Leipzig as it would a month later in Berlin. Using the slogans, "Leipzig Freedom," "The City with no Limits," and "Autumn '89," tourism offices from the city of Leipzig, the state of Saxony, and the federal government did their best to attract visitors to the celebration.[32] Many hotels were sold out in early October, and visitors from Leipzig's partner cities in Europe and elsewhere joined in the commemoration, including mayors from all over the world.

The city leaders in Leipzig who organized the events on October 9 and penned what they called the "Leipzig Theses" sought to use the anniversary to draw some lessons from the dramatic events of 1989. They expressed their concern that the civic engagement practiced by East Germans in 1989 was lacking in Germany in 2009 where so many were merely "spectators of democracy." They called for active civic participation to be revitalized in the future. They also argued that the knowledge gained from researching and confronting the crimes of the German past is essential to "an enlightened political consciousness" and that, "[h]istorical memory is a mandate for action in the present and future."[33] In this view, the history of the Nazi and communist crimes as well as of the Peaceful Revolution and the fall of the Wall all pointed to the importance of citizens standing up for democracy, freedom, and other human rights.

By the fall of 2009, examination of the Peaceful Revolution and the fall of the Wall was ubiquitous among the media, politicians and cultural institutions. Over 1,000 events took place in Berlin alone in the months

---

[31] Smaller versions of celebrating October 9, 1989 had occurred in 2007 and 2008. Leipzig had premiered the concept of "Night of Candles" in 2007 when thousands of people came to the courtyard outside the Nikolai Church to light candles that formed the shape "89." In 2008, this was expanded to include light installations and documentary and musical contributions. The 2009 celebration was much more elaborate than these had been.

[32] As of June 15, 2019, the Leipzig website was still accessible: www.leipziger-freiheit.de/lichtfest/lichtfest-2009/, whereas the Berlin website was not. On Leipzig's tourism office directing increased attention to October 9 starting in 2007, interview with Rainer Eckert, Leipzig, September 23, 2009.

[33] "Leipziger Thesen," Initiative "Tag der Friedlichen Revolution – Leipzig 9. Oktober 1989," September 4, 2009.

surrounding the twentieth anniversary of the fall of the Wall. The mayor's office sponsored a special website, www.berlin.de/mauerfall09, with information on activities related to the anniversary, including exhibits, conferences, guided tours, films, speeches, concerts, and ceremonies: 170,000 people per month accessed the website, and the two million hits on the day before the November 9 anniversary nearly shut it down. Germany's celebration of the fall of the Wall garnered widespread interest among both Germans and non-Germans.

Van Dülmen was right about the worldwide resonance of the fall of the Wall. Global memory of the Berlin Wall was active and enduring as the previous chapter demonstrated with worldwide celebrations and reenactments for the twentieth anniversary. For many, however, it was not enough to stay home in their own countries participating in festivities to mark the anniversary; they wanted to be in Berlin. Foreign leaders, not having been in Berlin in November 1989, wanted to be there this time around and participate in the twentieth anniversary celebrations. International media representatives wanted to report on it. In addition, a whole new generation of young people was eager to visit Berlin to see the Wall and to join in the party to celebrate its fall.

Merkel and the Twentieth Anniversary

Initially Chancellor Merkel and her staff demonstrated little interest in being part of the celebrations of the fall of the Wall, leaving them to Berlin's Mayor Wowereit. In spite of the fact that Merkel herself grew up in the GDR, she had generally shied away from identifying herself as East German and until the fall of 2009 rarely spoke about her East German background unless pressed by journalists or others. Part of this was no doubt due to a desire to be seen as an all-German politician, not an East German politician in united Germany, and part was due to the fact that she is a very private person. In addition, as a woman in a political world dominated by men, she probably felt in a sense that she had two strikes against her – her gender and her East German background – and thus focused on her political goals in the present and future, not on her past.

But there may be another reason for her long-time reluctance to speak in a personal way about life in the GDR: she was not one of the "heroes" of the East German opposition and the Peaceful Revolution. Instead, she was one of the far larger group of millions of East Germans who were somewhere in the middle: not members of the ruling elite but also not active opponents of the regime. Merkel had been quite open about this, saying: "I was no hero; I adapted [to the system]."[34] The gray area between the black-and-white extremes of the bad regime and the good opposition was hard to

---

[34] Martina Fietz, "Ich war keine Heldin. Ich habe mich angepasst," *Focus Online*, May 12, 2013.

find in public discourse.[35] Merkel might have helped changed this if she had been more willing to discuss her personal past and how she accommodated herself to life in the GDR.[36]

Merkel's "first political memory" was the building of the Berlin Wall.[37] Angela Kasner grew up as the daughter of a Protestant minister. Just weeks after she was born in 1954, her family moved from West Germany to East Germany for her father to take up a post at a church in the region where he had grown up about an hour northeast of Berlin. Other relatives stayed in the West. Days before the border in Berlin was closed on August 13, 1961, the Kasner family had been vacationing in Bavaria, West Germany, with Angela's maternal grandmother from Hamburg. On their way back home to Templin, her father noticed "barbed wire all over the place in the forests" and "felt that something was going to happen."[38]

The family was at home when they learned of the border closure. "Seeing the grownups around me, even my parents, so upset that they actually broke into tears, was something that shook me to the core."[39] The seven-year-old was "overcome with a sense of powerlessness."[40] Merkel remembers the "terrible atmosphere in the church" that Sunday, August 13, and how "stunned everyone was."[41] Like so many others, she was now part of a family whose lives were directly affected by – divided by – the building of the Berlin Wall. Merkel would not visit the FRG again for the next twenty-five years, although her grandmother and aunt from Hamburg would be allowed to visit the family in the GDR.

In school, Merkel studied mathematics and Russian, winning national awards in both. She practiced her Russian with the soldiers stationed at a large Soviet military base near her hometown and on visits to the Soviet Union. At the University of Leipzig, she studied physics, partly because a career in the hard sciences made it easier to avoid the influence of the state and party on her

---

[35] Roland Jahn tried to break through this in his book, *Wir angepassten: Überleben in der DDR* (Munich: Piper, 2015). See also Antje Sirleschtov, "Angela Merkel und ihre Vergangenheit: Woher wir kommen," *Tagesspiegel*, May 17, 2013. Sirleschtov lamented that without examining how the majority in the middle thought we cannot understand "how a handful of old men could lock up 16 million people for over 40 years behind an iron fence." Robert Ide also urged more attention to the question: "Why were so many people in the GDR followers for so long?" "Angela Merkels beredtes Schweigen," *Tagesspiegel*, May 27, 2013.

[36] Ibid.; and Antje Sirleschtov, "Angela Merkel und ihre Vergangenheit."

[37] Merkel, *Mein Weg*, p. 44.

[38] Ibid., p. 43.

[39] Merkel's toast at the State Dinner where President Obama awarded her the Presidential Medal of Freedom, "Remarks by President Obama and Chancellor Merkel in an Exchange of Toasts," The White House, Office of the Press Secretary, June 7, 2011.

[40] Stefan Kornelius, *Angela Merkel: The Chancellor and Her World* (London: Alma Books, 2013), p. 19.

[41] Merkel, *Mein Weg*, p. 44.

work. She then completed her doctorate and worked as a theoretical physicist in the Central Institute for Physical Chemistry of the East German Academy of Sciences in East Berlin, a privileged position.

While Merkel never joined East Germany's ruling party, the Socialist Unity Party (SED), she did join the communist youth organizations, the Young Pioneers and the Free German Youth (*Freie Deutsche Jugend*, FDJ). She joined the Young Pioneers, because, as she told an interviewer, without that membership, her good grades in school would not have led her teachers to give her a special "badge" of excellence, and she "absolutely wanted that badge."[42] Many young people joined the Young Pioneers and the FDJ so as not to be excluded from a myriad of activities with their friends and also to avoid being deprived of the opportunity to study at university. Merkel too has said that she joined for "community reasons,"[43] since she wanted "to belong,"[44] and that her membership was "seventy percent opportunism."[45]

Merkel's Stasi file apparently shows that the regime had questions about her loyalty, worrying that she displayed "political-ideological diversion." In the late 1970s, she had rebuffed a Stasi request that she become an informer, saying, as her parents had prepared her, "that's not for me, because I can't keep my mouth shut and always tell my friends things."[46] Rejecting the Stasi meant that she did not get the teaching position she wanted at a university, but instead was allowed to work at the Academy of Sciences where she would not have any students to infect with her views.[47]

Inspired by Poland's Solidarity, Merkel traveled to Poland three times in the early 1980s.[48] Upon crossing the border back into the GDR in August 1981, just months before martial law was declared in Poland to halt the protest movement begun by Solidarity, she was stopped by East German authorities at the border because she had a Solidarity newspaper, two pictures of a memorial to a Solidarity martyr in Gdynia, and a badge from Solidarity. None of these were allowed in the GDR and were confiscated.[49]

When Merkel was campaigning to become chancellor in 2005 and was faced with a variety of questions about her life in the GDR, many with the implicit criticism that she had not been a civic activist or fled the country, she said, "I

[42] Ibid., p. 52.
[43] "Merkel: Nichts verheimlicht, aber auch nicht alles erzählt," *Focus Online*, May 13, 2013.
[44] Gregor Mayntz, "Die DDR-Vergangenheit der Kanzlerin," *Rheinische Post, RP Online*, May 11, 2013.
[45] Quoted by George Packer in, "The Quiet German: The Astonishing Rise of Angela Merkel, the Most Powerful Woman in the World," *New Yorker*, December 1, 2014.
[46] Mayntz, "Die DDR-Vergangenheit der Kanzlerin"; and Evelyn Roll, *Die Kanzlerin. Angela Merkels Weg zur Macht* (Berlin: Ullstein, 2009), p. 28.
[47] Merkel, *Mein Weg*, pp. 58–59.
[48] Mayntz, "Die DDR-Vergangenheit der Kanzlerin."
[49] Ralf Georg Reuth and Günther Lachmann, *Das erste Leben der Angela M.* (Munich: Piper Verlag, Gmbh, 2013). Excerpted in *Focus Online*, May 13, 2013.

decided that if the system became too terrible, I would have to try to escape. But if it wasn't too bad then I wouldn't lead my life in opposition to the system, because I was scared of the damage it would do to me."[50] She knew about the advantages of the West from her visits before the Wall went up and from the gifts of clothes (especially her favorite Western jeans), food, and money from her relatives in Hamburg and from the Protestant Church in the FRG after 1961.[51] Her first trip to the West after the sealing of the border was not until 1986 when she was allowed to go to Hamburg for her cousin's wedding. The thirty-two-year-old Merkel was deeply impressed with the West on this visit. She later recounted: "It was at that wedding I realized that the socialist system wasn't going to last."[52] Not only could she see the vast differences between East and West Germany on this visit, but her train trip also gave her "a clear view of the watch towers and the death strip with armed guards, from the western side."[53]

Even at home in East Berlin, on her commute between her apartment and her office at the Academy of Sciences, "For several stretches, her train ran parallel to the Wall, the rooftops of West Berlin almost in reach."[54] In an interview in 2003, Merkel explained that she had "lived near the Wall, and it was depressing for me to pass along it every day. That was a real adjustment after...[her time at the University of] Leipzig," which was far from the border.[55] Merkel was fully aware of the lengths to which the SED regime resorted to prevent people from leaving. She looked forward to the day she would turn sixty (in 2014), the official retirement age for women in the GDR, when officials no longer cared whether people visiting the West came back. She planned to travel to the West regularly and was particularly set on visiting the United States.[56] Before then, if necessary, "the possibility of applying to emigrate was always a kind of mental emergency exit for me."[57]

---

[50] Packer, "The Quiet German."

[51] Antje Sirleschtov, "Wenn ein Mensch lebt," *Tagesspiegel*, May 13, 2013; Merkel, *Mein Weg*, pp. 48, 69; and Kornelius, *Angela Merkel*, p. 31.

[52] Kornelius, *Angela Merkel*, p. 30. See also Packer, "The Quiet German."

[53] Kornelius, *Angela Merkel*, pp. 30–31.

[54] Packer, "The Quiet German." See also Merkel's description to Queen Elizabeth II visiting Berlin in 2015 of how close she had lived to the Berlin Wall. "Merkel gibt der Queen eine Geschichtsstunde," *Berliner Morgenpost*, June 24, 2015.

[55] Merkel, *Mein Weg*, p. 59.

[56] As she told the audience of the Atlantik-Brücke in Washington in June 2009, she had long planned that when she turned sixty she would "travel to the FRG, exchange my GDR passport for a proper [i.e., West German] passport and then immediately set off on a trip to America." She was prepared to wait until she turned sixty. Instead, after the Wall opened, in January 1990, she and her husband traveled to California. Angela Merkel's address to the Atlantik-Brücke, Library of Congress, Washington, DC, June 25, 2009. See also, Angela Merkel, speech to a joint session of the U.S. Congress, "We Have No Time to Lose," *Spiegel Online*, November 3, 2009, and her toast at a White House State Dinner, "Remarks by President Obama and Chancellor Merkel in an Exchange of Toasts," The White House, Office of the Press Secretary, June 7, 2011. See also Angela Merkel, *Mein Weg*, p. 68.

[57] Merkel, *Mein Weg*, p. 65.

When Mikhail Gorbachev came to power in Moscow in 1985 and instituted reforms, Merkel hoped they would spread to the GDR. In the fall of 1989 when opposition groups and parties began to be established more formally in the GDR, she joined a group started by several Protestant ministers, Democratic Awakening (*Demokratische Aufbruch*). In the weeks and months after the fall of the Wall, Merkel became more involved with *Demokratische Aufbruch* when it became a political party, and in early 1990, she became the press secretary. After the first (and also last) free elections in the GDR in March 1990, *Demokratische Aufbruch* was taken over by the CDU, which was the clear winner of the elections, under Lothar de Maizière, setting the country on a fast track toward unification with West Germany.

In April 1990, Merkel became the deputy spokesperson for de Maizière's government.[58] Merkel then accompanied the new prime minister to domestic and foreign meetings and was present for fundamental moments in the process of German unification, including the negotiations on the Unification Treaty between the GDR and FRG and the Two Plus Four talks and treaty signed in Moscow by the two Germanys with the Four Powers whereby the latter gave up their rights in the country in return for certain obligations of the new united Germany.[59] In December 1990, Merkel was elected to the Bundestag, and in January 1991, she became the Minister for Youth and Family in Chancellor Helmut Kohl's cabinet. For years, Merkel would regularly commute across the freshly removed border between Berlin and Bonn for work and could finally visit her family in Hamburg whenever she wanted.

Nearly twenty years later, Merkel's government initially intended to focus on the May 2009 commemorations in Frankfurt of the sixtieth anniversary of the West German *Grundgesetz* and the twentieth anniversary celebration of German unification in October 2010 in Bremen. There was no plan for Chancellor Merkel to be involved in the November 9, 2009 celebrations of the toppling of the Wall. Van Dülmen and Kühnelt of Kulturprojekte Berlin consulted with an official at the Interior Ministry who told them that commemoration of the fall of the Wall was a matter for the Berlin government, not the federal government.[60] High-level international interest in participating in the November 9 festivities in Berlin, however, would change the chancellor's approach to the occasion.

Planning for 2009–10 began in the federal government in 2007. The Ministry of Justice was concentrating on the sixtieth anniversary of the *Grundgesetz* in 2009 to mark the importance of post-Nazi West Germany

---

[58] Kornelius, *Angela Merkel*, pp. 32–35.

[59] Alexander Osang, "Die Schläferin," *Spiegel*, November 9, 2009; and Gerd Langguth, *Angela Merkel* (Munich: Deutscher Taschenbuch Verlag, 2005), pp. 137–41.

[60] Interviews with Wolf Kühnert, January 25, 2010, and Moritz van Dülmen, January 28, 2010.

adopting a democratic constitution. Yet senior officials in the Interior Ministry warned that many eastern Germans still did not see the *Grundgesetz* as their own after nearly twenty years of unification. For eastern Germans, far more important would be the twentieth anniversary of the Peaceful Revolution and the fall of the Wall. Accordingly, the Interior Ministry officials argued that a double anniversary celebration would be necessary in 2009 to resonate with both western and eastern Germans. In May 2007, the federal government agreed on this approach.[61]

Funds from the Federal Commission for Culture and Media (BKM) provided substantial support for Sello's exhibit on the Peaceful Revolution, yet it remained to be seen what the federal government would do on November 9. Planning by the municipal government in Berlin in 2008 and through the spring and summer of 2009 grew more and more specific about a party with the *Dominosteine* on November 9 at the Brandenburg Gate. Berlin officials repeatedly asked federal officials what their contribution to the occasion would be, yet for months they got no answer.[62]

Meanwhile, calls kept coming in to the chancellor's office from foreign leaders and to the mayor's office from ambassadors seeking invitations to the celebrations, and from the world media. Some were subtle, wondering, "What are you planning? Should we come?" Others were less so.[63] Most of the staff members of the chancellor's press office, which would ultimately take the lead in organizing the chancellor's participation, were from the west and may not have felt the importance of November 9. The continued requests for information about and invitations to the November 9 celebrations, however, finally made it clear that the chancellor could not remain unengaged.[64] The twentieth anniversary commemoration of the fall of the Berlin Wall needed to have national and international dimensions instead of just being a municipal Berlin affair. Wall memory was beyond Germany's control. Merkel would participate.

The chancellor's office deliberated over the summer about how best to be involved on November 9. They sought both a site separate from the Brandenburg Gate for the chancellor to make a distinct contribution, and they also brainstormed about the best way to join Berlin officials at the Gate in the evening. In July they settled on Bornholmer Strasse as the place for a separate appearance by the chancellor on the afternoon of November 9 and began planning the details in

---

[61] Interview with Eberhard Kuhrt, July 24, 2014.

[62] Interviews with Moritz van Dülmen (January 28, 2010), Wolf Kühnelt (January 25, 2010), Klaus Wowereit (February 10, 2010), Tom Sello (February 10, 2010), Simone Leimbach (July 3, 2014), and Eberhard Kuhrt (July 24, 2014).

[63] Interviews with Jörg Hackeschmidt (July 7, 2014), Tilman Seeger (July 29, 2014), and Rainer Klemke (December 18, 2009).

[64] Ulrich Zawatka-Gerlach, "Gedenken an Mauerfall vor 25 Jahren. Wowereit erwartet mehr vom Bund," *Tagesspiegel*, January 8, 2014.

August.[65] Not only was this the first crossing in the Berlin Wall that opened on the night of November 9, 1989, but it was also where Angela Merkel herself had crossed into West Berlin that night along with 20,000 others.[66]

In spite of van Dülmen's elaborate plans, some in the CDU-dominated chancellery felt, no doubt affected by the summer 2009 federal election campaign, that the *Dominosteine* planned by the SPD-Linke Berlin government were too simplistic. Perhaps this is why Merkel herself never contributed a domino, even as Nobel Peace Prize laureates and others from Germany and all over the world did. Some CDU officials feared that Berlin's Red-Red coalition (in spite of its backing of Sello's exhibit) wanted to make it seem as if everything suddenly collapsed on November 9 after Schabowski's famous press conference instead of paying attention to what led up to it, the *Unrecht* nature of the SED regime, and why the opposition wanted changes.

Since the former civic activists were not very well known in united Germany, the chancellery wanted to give them a platform, similar in fact to Sello's motivations with the Peaceful Revolution exhibit. In addition, the chancellery wanted to support East German victims' groups whose members felt they were being left out of the twentieth anniversary commemorations, which focused on the fall of the Wall and not what people had suffered because of it and the regime that backed it. Thus, the chancellor decided to invite some members of these groups to mark the occasion with her at a gathering on the Böse bridge at Bornholmer Strasse.[67]

In reenacting her walk across the bridge from east to west, the chancellor would be joined by five groups of specially invited guests: members of the East German civil rights movement; representatives of East German churches; members of victims' groups; Polish, Hungarian, Czech, and Russian reformist leaders from 1989 (all of whom had already been invited by Berlin to participate in the *Dominoaktion*); and also regular people who had crossed the bridge on the night of November 9. Of the final group, chancellery officials had studied photographs of people who crossed the bridge that night, found some of them, and invited them to join the commemoration.[68]

Chancellor Merkel herself sent personal notes to each of the invited former East German civic activists in which she referred to their specific opposition activities and praised them for their courage.[69] It was particularly important to

---

[65] Interviews with Eberhard Kuhrt (July 24, 2014), Gunthart Gerke (BPA, July 31, 2014), Tilman Seeger (July 29, 2014), Jörg Hackeschmidt (July 7, 2014), and Uwe Spindeldreier (by phone, August 7, 2014).

[66] Merkel, *Mein Weg*, pp. 72–73.

[67] Interviews with Jörg Hackeschmidt (July 7, 2014), Eberhard Kuhrt (July 24, 2014), and Uwe Spindeldreier (by phone, August 7, 2014).

[68] Interview with Tilman Seeger, July 29, 2014.

[69] Damir Fras, Sabine Rennefanz, Sabine Deckwerth, Olivia Schoeller, "Spur der Steine," *Berliner Zeitung*, blog of the twentieth anniversary events in Berlin, November 8–9, 2009.

the chancellor to honor the former dissidents with the symbolic walk across the bridge.[70] While by her own admission, she had not joined their ranks in the GDR, Merkel now had great respect for the role they had played and sought to recognize them. Some of her staff also were very committed to highlighting the role of the civic activists. At the Federal Press Office, which was in charge of planning the logistics for the event on the bridge, Uwe Spindeldreier, for example, had the lead on reaching out to this group due to his long-standing connections to them. Although he had grown up in West Germany, after the fall of the Wall he relocated eastwards to Thuringia to help create Mitteldeutsche Rundfunk (MDR) and was deeply engaged in the eastern process of grappling with the GDR past and in this way had come into contact with former opposition members.

One of Merkel's speechwriters, Jörg Hackeschmidt, had many relatives in the GDR, since his parents had fled from Dresden to the FRG in 1957, four years before he was born. He had visited East Germany multiple times with his parents and thus had a personal connection to the fall of the Wall that had separated his family. He was also Merkel's lead speechwriter for historically-related events.[71] In Merkel's weekly podcast on November 7 about her plans for November 9, the chancellor highlighted the "civic activists who through their courageous action for freedom and democracy contributed very significantly to making the opening of the Wall possible" and also the churches, which "offered protection for freedom of thought in the former GDR, and [which] were courageous accompanists in the phase of the Monday demonstrations and peace prayers."[72]

Having settled on a plan for the chancellor at Bornholmer Strasse, the chancellery next needed to decide how to handle the evening celebration at the Brandenburg Gate and particularly whether to invite other sitting heads of state. The chancellery wanted to include the heads of state of the neighboring countries that had also experienced revolutions in 1989 and contributed to the events in Germany in 1989. But this did not seem enough. Merkel spoke with EU leaders over the summer and quickly realized that inviting only some of them would not do. They all wanted to come.[73] Thus, the chancellor invited all twenty-six EU leaders at the EU summit in Brussels on September 17, less than two months before the celebration.[74] The EU leaders of course included Britain and France, two of the Four Powers who had retained occupation rights in Berlin until the end of the Cold War. The USA and Russia were invited as well.

[70] Email correspondence with Jörg Hackeschmidt, July 8, 2014.
[71] Interview with Jörg Hackeschmidt, July 7, 2014.
[72] Video-Podcast der Bundeskanzlerin 36/09, www.bundeskanzlerin.de/Content/DE/Podcast/ 2009/2009–11-07-Video-Podcast/links/2009–11-07-text.pdf?__blob=publicationFile.
[73] Interviews with Jörg Hackeschmidt, July 7, 2014, and Eberhard Kuhrt, July 24,2014.
[74] Mohit Joshi, "Merkel Invites EU Leaders to Attend Berlin Celebrations," topnews.in, September 18, 2009, www.topnews.in/people/angela-merkel?page=3.

Although countries as far away as Australia expressed an interest in joining the celebrations, the chancellery drew the line at the Four Powers and the EU leaders. So great was high-level international interest in marking the twentieth anniversary of the fall of the Wall that chancellery officials felt that they "could have invited the whole world," which "expected to be able to participate."[75] After initially believing that there was no need for the chancellor to be involved on November 9, intense and high-level international interest in being part of the celebration compelled a dramatic change in thinking in Merkel's office between July and September 2009, bringing the chancellor deep into the plans for the festivities in November. Between September and November, federal and municipal officials collaborated closely to prepare for what would now be a major gathering of German and world leaders.

Conflating the Fall of the Wall with German Unification

At some moments in the lead-up to November 9, 2009, the gratitude German leaders and others expressed for the fall of the Wall became confused and fused with gratitude for the important role the leaders of the Four Powers had played in the process leading to German unification in the eleven months *after* the fall of the Wall. Some East Germans, however, wanted serious reforms in 1989 to create a more just, socialist GDR and did not seek unification with West Germany. They were happy to remember the dramatic changes made in 1989, including the opening of the Wall but not prepared to celebrate unification in quite the same way. Yet the twentieth anniversary festivities included a significant focus on unification. This was apparent at three events. The first took place in early October with the public performance on the streets of Berlin of a fairytale about unification, the second in late October to honor Kohl, Bush, and Gorbachev, and the third at the Brandenburg Gate on the night of November 9.

On October 1–3, the French street theater group, Royal de Luxe, presented its "Berlin Reunion" (*Le rendezvous de Berlin* or *Das Wiedersehen von Berlin*), a rather far-fetched fairy tale featuring two huge puppets moving around the city. The company's artistic director, Jean Luc Courcoult, had been commissioned by the Berlin *Festspiel* to create one of his mobile outdoor theater productions for the anniversary of the fall of the Wall, using prominent sites in the city as backdrops to his story. His story would include *both* the fall of the Wall and German unification. BKM, the German lottery, and Mercedes-Benz were among the sponsors of the work, which attracted almost two million spectators in early October.

Known for constructing massive puppets moved by small armies of carefully coordinated experts, Courcoult created two figures for the occasion: a

---

[75] Interview with Jörg Hackeschmidt, July 7, 2014.

giant "uncle" (50 feet tall and weighing 25 tons) and a smaller giantess "niece" (25 feet tall and weighing over 13 tons), who lived in Berlin long ago when it was swampland, according to his fairytale. One day "monsters from the land and sea" divided the city leaving part of it surrounded by a Wall. The uncle, the Giant, was left in the West, and the niece, the Little Giantess, was trapped in the East.[76] They searched for each other for many years. Eventually the uncle awoke a sleeping geyser at the bottom of the sea under Berlin and the geyser erupted, causing an earthquake and the Wall to fall!

This is the point at which the spectacle began in Berlin, with the uncle, a deep-sea diver, and his niece, each making their way eventually to a reunion at the Brandenburg Gate. They passed major Berlin landmarks along their journey and were thronged by tens of thousands of people at each turn. Outside city hall (located in what used to be East Berlin), the mayor welcomed the Little Giantess and saw her off on her way as she carried a large mailbag filled with copies of 90,000 letters the Stasi had intercepted, censored, or archived in the GDR. When she reached the Brandenburg Gate on October 3, the anniversary of unification, she began weeping, wondering how she could pass through the Gate to her uncle on the other side. She finally leapt over the Brandenburg Gate (with the help of cranes on either side) to fall into her uncle's arms. The next day, the two "walked" down the wide boulevard of June 17 Street together, strolled around the government quarter, boarded a boat on the Spree River and headed West as thousands of people waved farewell from the riverbanks and bridges.

The symbolism of the bigger, stronger man from the West attracting the smaller, weaker girl from the East was perhaps not quite what the organizers had been aiming for, but it was apt. West Germany had been two and half times the size of East Germany in landmass and almost four times the size in population, and even many years after unification, young women continued to move from the east to the west in search of better career opportunities. Almost two-thirds of the nearly two million Germans who moved from east to west in the twenty years since unification were women.[77] The general desire of both women and men in the East to have the freedoms and consumer goods of

---

[76] "Die Riesen in Berlin. Ein grossartiger Event begeisterte 2009 Berlin," October 10, 2009, accessible under "Veranstaltungen," on Berlin-av, www.berlin-audiovisuell.de/veranstaltun gen/die-riesen-in-berlin/; Karin Winkelsesser, "Theater im öffentlichen Raum. Ein 'Riesen'-Traum wird wahr," *Kultiversum, Die Kulturplatform* 6 (2009), p. 4, www.kultiver sum.de/All-Dossier/Open-Air-Maerchen-Royal-de-Luxe-Berlin-Ein-Riesen-Traum-wird-wahr.html; and "The Berlin Reunion," at boston.com, October 7, 2009, www.boston.com/ bigpicture/2009/10/the_berlin_reunion.html.

[77] Kirsten Grieshaber, "East German Women Flee for Western jobs," *Washington Post*, September 23, 2007; and Steffen Kroehnert and Sebastian Vollmer, "Where Have All Young Women Gone? Gender-Specific Migration from East to West Germany," back-ground paper for the World Bank's "World Development Report: Reshaping Economic Geography," June 2008, hdl.handle.net/10986/9253.

the West played a crucial role in the 1989–90 developments leading to the fall of the Wall and particularly to German unification less than a year later. These sorts of sober reflections, however, did not seem to mar the jubilant reception given to the story of the Giant and the Little Giantess in Berlin.

The second moment conflating the fall of the Wall and unification, albeit with far more gravitas, came at the end of October with a celebration hosted by the Konrad Adenauer Stiftung and the Springer publishing house (also closely affiliated with the CDU) to honor "unification chancellor" Helmut Kohl as well as Mikhail Gorbachev, and George H. W. Bush. With Kohl in failing health, members of the CDU, the party of both Kohl and Merkel, wanted to seize the opportunity – while he was still alive and able to travel to Berlin – to thank Kohl, Bush, and Gorbachev for the fact that "unification came 329 days after the fall of the Wall." On Saturday October 31, in the Friedrichstadtpalast theater in the heart of Berlin, the Adenauer Stiftung's chairman, Bernhard Vogel, opened the ceremony on "The Fall of the Wall and Reunification: The Victory of Freedom."

Vogel announced to the 1,800 invited guests, including all the top German leaders, members of the European Parliament, and more than seventy ambassadors, that in 1989–90, "freedom won, because the GDR citizens fought for it and because Gorbachev, Bush and Kohl helped it to break through." This was a significant modification of the main narrative of the Peaceful Revolution. The event was effectively a state ceremony and was broadcast live on cable television. President Köhler gave the keynote address, "Three Men, One Great Moment," followed by remarks from the three former statesmen. While all speakers made references to the brave East Germans and the Peaceful Revolution, the main focus was not on the fall of 1989 or the East Germans on the streets; it was on the contributions of Kohl, Bush, and Gorbachev to the unification of Germany.[78] In this narrative, Kohl seized the moment in the fall of 1989 and pushed ahead toward unification, Bush supported him, and Gorbachev acquiesced.[79]

A focus on unification and the "great men of history" was evident at many moments during the November 9 celebrations, to the consternation of many former East German civic activists, clergy, and others.[80] Many felt that by remembering 1989 and 1990 together, the role of the East German people in

---

[78] For the transcript of the event, see "Mauerfall und Wiedervereinigung – Der Sieg der Freiheit," Konrad Adenauer Stiftung, October 31, 2009, www.kas.de/wf/doc/kas_20488–544-1-30.pdf?101102141841. See also Daniela Vates, "Stolze alte Männer," *Berliner Zeitung*, November 2, 2009.

[79] On the central roles of Kohl, Bush, and Gorbachev, see Mary Elise Sarotte, *1989: The Struggle to Create Post-Cold War Europe* (Princeton: Princeton University Press, 2009); and Nicholas Kulish and Judy Dempsey, "Leaders in Berlin Retrace the Walk West," *New York Times*, November 10, 2009.

[80] See, for example, Tom Heneghan, "Some east German Protestants Feel Overlooked as Wall Recalled," FaithWorld blog, *Reuters*, November 6, 2009.

calling for change was overshadowed by the image of Kohl working with Bush and Gorbachev to make unification happen. It seemed that the declining health of Kohl was not the only reason for not waiting: a West German narrative of 1989–90 was pushing against an East German narrative.

This was also in evidence when the leaders of the Four Powers were each invited to make speeches along with Merkel and Wowereit on the night of November 9, 2009 at the Brandenburg Gate, consigning three former East German dissidents to just one joint cameo role in the evening's festivities. Many wondered why the Four Powers' leaders were invited to speak on this night instead of waiting for the following year's twentieth anniversary of unification. As one federal official would later observe, however, "the international guests definitely wanted to come on November 9, 2009, not on some other date."[81]

November 9, 2009

By the time November 9 arrived, any view that the anniversary of the fall of the Wall was relevant only to the city of Berlin had been overtaken by current and former local, national, and international officials – and many others – clamoring for seats at a variety of political, cultural, and religious ceremonies marking the twentieth anniversary. Suddenly it was *de rigueur* to be there, and no one wanted to be left out. Most hotels were fully booked. Seeking to capitalize on the moment, one hotel near the Brandenburg Gate, the Westin Grand, offered a unique "tear down the Wall" package: "a night at the hotel, along with a safety helmet, goggles and hammer and chisel" for use in chipping off pieces from an authentic section of the Berlin Wall in the hotel's lobby.[82] Tens of thousands of people thronged the area around the Wall dominoes. The spokesman for Berlin's tourism office gushed, "We are experiencing the best November weekend of all time in Berlin!"[83]

Moritz van Dülmen's instinct that Germany and the world would converge on Berlin for the celebration had proven correct. Of course, he, the city's tourism officials, and others had worked hard to make sure that people would come. Berlin's tourism office had a new "Be Berlin!" campaign and sent people around with *Dominosteine* to other cities in Germany where school students painted them with their own designs. The foreign ministry sent officials with *Dominosteine* to states in Central and Eastern Europe to facilitate their involvement. The Goethe Institute took *Dominosteine* on a *Mauerreise* ("Wall trip") to seven countries in which division and/or border experiences

---

[81] Interview with Eberhard Kuhrt, July 24, 2014.
[82] Scott Carmichael, "Berlin Hotel Offers Bed, Breakfast and a Piece of the Wall," Gadling. com, March 1, 2009.
[83] Jens Anker and Birgit Haas, "Die Welt feiert Deutschlands Einheit in Berlin," *Berliner Morgenpost*, November 7, 2009.

still affected people's daily lives: South Korea, the Turkish and Greek parts of Cyprus in divided Nicosia, Mexico, Israel, the Palestinian territories, and China. Yemen, which had been divided into north and south until unification in 1990, was also included. The British airline EasyJet had its own European *Dominosteine* competition and flew people to Berlin to participate in the festivities.[84]

Official and unofficial events marking the occasion varied from the whimsical to the profound. Stores all over Berlin had curtain sales to commemorate the fall of the Iron Curtain. Artists who painted murals on the Wall at East Side Gallery in 1990 were commissioned to renovate their paintings, and the site was unveiled anew on November 6. A theatrical installation, entitled *Engel über Berlin* ("Angels above Berlin"), featured eight actors dressed as angels with large white wings perched on balconies and rooftops along the former path of the Wall looking down at the passersby as the main character in Wim Wenders' 1987 film *Himmel über Berlin* (released in English as *Wings of Desire*) had done. Each of the eight angels represented a person whose life was connected with the Berlin Wall (such as a man who helped build an escape tunnel or a bride whose parents were on the other side of the Wall) but was no longer alive to experience the fall of the Wall.[85] At the popular *Mauerpark* (Wallpark), 170 guitarists (mostly from the Netherlands) joined together to create a "Berlin Wall of Sound."

An academic conference on "Falling Walls" convened scientists from Germany and all over the world to discuss breakthroughs in scientific research. Chancellor Merkel gave the keynote address. She called the ninth of November in German history a day of "*Traum and Trauma*" ("fantasy and agony"), before speaking on "Breaking the Walls of the 21st Century."[86] A concert in Berlin's cathedral brought together orchestras and choirs from eastern and western Berlin in an all-German program that included a movement from Beethoven's Ninth Symphony. The concert was broadcast live on German public radio as well as in multiple other countries in Europe, South Korea, the United States, and Canada.[87]

---

[84] Interviews with Moritz van Dülmen, January 28, 2010, and Wolf Kühnelt, January 25, 2010; Kulturprojekte Berlin, ed., *Dominobuch. Geschichte(n) mit Dominoeffekt* (Berlin: Kulturprojekte Berlin, 2009); and *Goethe-Institut 3.09, Geteilte Welten*, www.goethe.de/resources/files/pdf19/gi_03–09_web.pdf.

[85] On East Side Gallery, interview with the artist Kani Alavi, January 14, 2010. On "Angels above Berlin," Theater Anu in cooperation with Bartel Meyer, "Engelland – ein Erinnerungsprojekt," theater-anu.de; and "Engel über Berlin erinnern an Mauerfall," *B. Z.*, November 9, 2009.

[86] "Falling Walls Conference der Einstein Stiftung Berlin," forum Nachhaltig Wirtschaften, November 11, 2009; and "Rede von Bundeskanzlerin Merkel auf der Konferenz 'Falling Walls'," November 9, 2009. See also her speech from the evening before at Schloss Schöningen, "Rede von Bundeskanzlerin Dr. Angela Merkel zur Eröffnung des Freiheitsmuseums, 'Villa Schöningen,' am 8. November 2009 in Potsdam."

[87] Annabelle Seubert, "Live weltweit: Gedenkkonzert zum Mauerfall," *Tagesspiegel*, October 27, 2009.

The official events to mark the twentieth anniversary of the fall of the Wall on November 9 included an ecumenical church service at the Gethsemane Church, a ceremony at the Chapel of Reconciliation and opening of the new visitors' center at the Berlin Wall Memorial, Merkel's gathering at the Bornholmer Strasse bridge, a reception at the presidential palace, and the evening festivities with the *Dominosteine* at the Brandenburg Gate. In the rituals and speeches throughout the day, there were six focal points, sometimes in uneasy relation to each other, four of them looking to the past and two of them connected with the present and future. While the main focus of the day was on remembering the fall of the Wall and celebrating that momentous event, the emphasis on exactly whom to thank for the fall of the Wall oscillated between the East German civic activists and other citizens of the GDR, on the one hand, and other Central and East Europeans or world leaders, on the other.

First, throughout the day and in the weeks and months leading up to the anniversary, there was a competition, sometimes latent, sometimes palpable, among various individuals and groups over the question of who had played the most significant role in paving the way for the fall of the Wall. Was it the East German civic activists? Was it more generally the East German people, including both those who stayed in the GDR and protested en masse and those who left for the West? Was it the East Germans in Leipzig or in Berlin? Was it Solidarity in Poland for starting the move away from communism already in 1980 and then prevailing in the first semi-free elections in the Soviet bloc in June 1989? Was it Hungary for opening the barbed wire border with Austria and allowing East Germans to use this as their escape route to West Germany? Was it Gorbachev for initiating reforms and, in contrast to his predecessors, refusing to intervene to stop their effects in Poland, the GDR, and elsewhere? All of these questions were lurking around the twentieth anniversary festivities. Second, there was some conflation of the fall of the Wall and German unification as just discussed.

A third aspect of the twentieth anniversary commemorations was paying tribute to those who lost their lives at the Berlin Wall, those such as Michael Schmidt for whom the fall of the Wall in 1989 came too late, making it difficult for his father Horst Schmidt and all the others who had lost a loved one to celebrate. Just two days before the anniversary, leaders of Berlin and Brandenburg and the Berlin Wall Foundation unveiled the first individual memorials at sites where East Germans had been killed attempting to flee across the border on the outskirts of Berlin.[88]

---

[88] Memorial columns were unveiled on November 7, 2009 for Horst Kullack (1972), Herbert Kiebler (1975), and Eduard Wroblewski (1966) who had been killed when trying to escape, and to Christoph-Manuel Bramböck who was killed in an accident at the Wall in August 1990. The fourteen-year-old Bramböck was trying to get souvenir pieces of the Wall, and when he removed a piece of the Wall near the top, the attached concrete slab above it fell on him and killed him. Hans-Hermann Hertle and Maria Nooke, eds., *The*

The fourth focus of historical reflection on November 9, 2009 had nothing to do with the Berlin Wall, but everything to do with November 9. Some questioned whether it was right to focus public memory on the joyous November 9, 1989 when that day in 1938 had seen Nazi attacks on Jews during *Kristallnacht*. Thus, even this "happiest day in contemporary German history," as Chancellor Merkel and so many others called it,[89] was tempered by the remembrance – or was made even sweeter because of the remembrance[90] – of the thirteen brutal years of the Nazis as well as by the forty years of the communist regime and its Wall. In a reference to the competition for memory between November 9, 1938 and 1989, Mayor Wowereit declared in a speech at the Berlin Wall Memorial that there is "no hierarchy of commemoration. All victims are important to remember and must continue to be remembered."[91] He clearly felt the need to defend the day's focus on the Berlin Wall.

Two other key themes addressed on November 9, 2009 were directed more toward the present and the future than the past. The first recognized that while it had been twenty years since the fall of the Wall and nineteen years since unification, the process of uniting the two parts of the country was still ongoing. Although the majority of East Germans had greeted the fall of the Wall with joy and afterwards wanted unification with West Germany, a good number of them had endured a difficult transition to life in a democratic, capitalist system. Some former East Germans also were alienated by the prevailing Western judgment of the GDR as an *Unrechtsstaat* implied a disparagement of the lives they had lived in the GDR and of their own worth as individuals. During the course of the day, several German leaders tried to offer healing words about this, as President Köhler had in Leipzig. The final theme of the day was the drawing of lessons from the fall of the Wall for the present and the future. This was a striking commonality among the speakers throughout the day and evening on November 9, 2009.

The morning of November 9, 2009 began with a service at the Gethsemane Church with President Köhler, Chancellor Merkel, Bundestag leaders, and

---

Victims of the Berlin Wall, 1961–1989 (Berlin: Christoph Links, 2011). The initiative for the memorial columns had come from Harald Fiss, the honorary chair of the board of the Marienfelde Refugee Camp Memorial who had served as the head of the camp from 1985–90. Author's notes from the ceremony, November 7, 2009; and "Übergabe der ersten Stelen für die Mauertoten. Die Erinnerung an die Mauertoten wird Teil des Berliner Mauerwegs," Pressinformation, Erinnerungsstätte Notaufnahmelager Marienfelde, Stiftung Berliner Mauer, November 7, 2009. See also "Mein 9. November: Harald Fiss," Deutschlandradio Kultur – Die Mauer ist Weg, October 18, 2009.

[89] "Merkels emotionaler Kommentar zum Mauerfall," *Financial Times Deutschland*, November 7, 2009. See also "Rede von Bundeskanzlerin Merkel auf der Konferenz 'Falling Walls'," Einstein Stiftung Berlin, November 9, 2009.

[90] Ibid.

[91] Author's notes from Mayor Wowereit's speech, visitors' center, Berlin Wall Memorial, November 9, 2009.

many other senior officials and former civic activists in attendance. This Protestant church, as so many others,[92] had been a central gathering place of the East German opposition in 1989 and had also been Merkel's own parish community, although she had only infrequently attended services. Starting in early October 1989, the church had been open twenty-four hours a day to offer support to demonstrators and to monitor a phone that people from all over the GDR used to report on arrests and other moves by the authorities to suppress dissent.[93] A preliminary exhibit of some of the *Dominosteine* had opened in this church in October 2009 to highlight its important role in the Peaceful Revolution.

At the service, the Chairman of the Conference of German Bishops, Catholic Archbishop Robert Zollitsch, gave the sermon and focused on a passage from Psalm 18, "with my God, I can leap over a wall." This psalm was "much loved by Christians in the former GDR" and gave them hope. Zollitsch observed that it takes time to build up the strength to leap over a wall, and for many people in the GDR, that strength came from the prayer meetings in the churches: "each prayer broke a block off the Wall." But his remarks were not just directed at the events of 1989; they also were meant to address the ongoing challenges of uniting Germany in the wake of the fall of the Wall. Zollitsch, who grew up in West Germany, pointed out that "the Germans in the East did not choose their life behind the Wall and barbed wire." He reached out to East Germans with empathy: "Behind the Wall and barbed wire, people had to make accommodations and see how they could lead their lives in prescribed oppression but with decency and dignity."[94]

Zollitsch addressed the ongoing process of unification in a way that made clear that those in the west also needed to do their part: "The will toward understanding and deepening unity is not a one-way street. We are called upon together in east and west, to build more bridges to each other with patience and persistence." As so many others would that day, Zollitsch drew lessons from the fall of the Wall and from twentieth-century German history. "The memory of November 9, 1989 and no less the memory of the terrible events of...November 9, 1938 teach us unmistakably: Walls – whether real or in the

---

[92] On role of the churches in 1989, see Arnd Brummer, ed., *Vom Gebet zur Demo. 1989 – Die friedliche Revolution began in den Kirchen* (Frankfurt: Hansisches Druck-und Verlagshaus, 2009); and Christian Führer, *Und wir sind dabei gewesen: Die Revolution, die aus der Kirche kam* (Munich: Taschenbuchverlag, 2010).

[93] Marianne Birthler, *Halbes Land. Ganzes Land. Ganzes Leben* (Munich: Hanser Verlag, 2014), pp. 147–56.

[94] "'Mit meinem Gott überspringe ich Mauern' Predigt des Vorsitzenden der Deutschen Bischofskonferenz, Erzbischof Dr. Robert Zollitsch, beim ökumenischen Gottesdienst anlässlich der Gedenkveranstaltung '20 Jahre Mauerfall' am 9. November 2009 in Berlin." Pressemitteilungen der Deutschen Bischofskonferenz, www.ekd.de/download/091109_pm296_predigt_zollitsch.pdf.

hearts and minds of men – resolve no problems. On the contrary: they create problems. They spoil the future." He entreated the politicians and others at the service to make the most of the free, democratic state Germany had become: "Freedom requires responsibility, not a free ride. . . .There are potential wall builders everywhere, also today. They should not have power in society or in the church. . . .It is our duty now to help others who live in tyranny."

The Berlin Wall Memorial, Bernauer Strasse

While Merkel and Köhler attended the 9:30 a.m. service at Gethsemane Church, Mayor Wowereit and federal Cultural Commissioner Neumann attended a 10:30 a.m. service in the Chapel of Reconciliation at the Berlin Wall Memorial. Like Archbishop Zollitsch, Pastor Manfred Fischer also had in mind both the fall of the Wall and *Kristallnacht* in commemorating November 9. Fischer had therefore invited Ernst Cramer as the main speaker. A journalist and chairman of the board of the powerful Axel Springer publishing house, the ninety-six-year-old Cramer was, as he would emphasize in his address, "both German and Jewish" and thus could speak about both 1938 and 1989. Fischer sought to bring together these two dates and their different memory cultures and supporters at the Berlin Wall Memorial.[95]

Fischer had worked for over a year to find the right person to speak at the service. Once Klausmeier became the director of the Berlin Wall Foundation in January 2009, he joined Fischer in the search. It had not been easy. Most people involved in the Jewish community were quite reluctant to share November 9, fearing that more attention to the fall of the Wall would mean less attention to *Kristallnacht*. Indeed, Charlotte Knobloch, the president of the Central Council of Jews in Germany was critical that "joy about the twentieth anniversary of the fall of the Wall had displaced the commemoration of" *Kristallnacht* and urged that "a better way must be found in the future to commemorate both events appropriately."[96] Fischer and Klausmeier had contacted members of the Jewish community and the Centrum Judaicum in Berlin in winter and spring, but had not been able to find someone willing to speak on November 9, 2009.

It was Joachim Gauck, the former East German Protestant pastor and first chief of the Stasi Records Authority in united Germany, who suggested to Fischer that he approach Ernst Cramer. Fischer and Klausmeier wrote to Cramer, and he agreed to meet with them. In the early summer, the three men gathered in Cramer's office on the eighteenth floor of the Springer

---

[95] Interviews with Manfred Fischer, October 6 and 15, 2009.
[96] Charlotte Knobloch, "9. November 1938 darf nicht in Vergessenheit geraten," Pressemitteilung von Dr. h. c. Charlotte Knobloch, Präsidentin des Zentralrats der Juden in Deutschland, Zentralrat der Juden in Deutschland, Munich, November 9, 2009.

publishing house with a spectacular view overlooking the former border in central Berlin. Cramer had worked at Springer since 1958, when he began as deputy chief editor of the daily newspaper *Die Welt* and later rose to become chair of the board of Springer Publishing in 1981. The Axel-Springer-Haus had been erected between 1959 and 1965 directly up against the West Berlin side of the Berlin Wall, a few blocks from Checkpoint Charlie. When the border was closed and the Wall began to be erected in 1961, Springer had allowed a tunnel to be built under his construction site to help people escape from East Berlin. The high-rise building towering over the Berlin Wall opened in 1966 and – not coincidentally – was easily visible to people in East Berlin.

This history – as well as the history of the Holocaust, the fall of the Berlin Wall, and the nature of German memory culture – were all subjects of discussion among Fischer, Klausmeier, and Cramer. Fischer and Klausmeier wondered whether Cramer would say as others had that it was not possible for a Jewish German to celebrate the fall of the Wall. Yet Cramer told them that November 9, 1989 was in fact the happiest day of his life and he would give the anniversary address at the Chapel of Reconciliation.[97]

On the morning of November 9, 2009, Pastor Fischer opened the service with a deep sense of personal and national gratitude. So much of his life and that of his congregation has been connected in painful ways with the Berlin Wall, most significantly when the East German regime demolished the Church of Reconciliation. As Fischer noted in retrospect: "We could not have imagined that the demolition was a last tremor of a doomed regime."[98] Having the chance now to celebrate the fall of the Wall and to experience the significant local and national attention directed to the Berlin Wall Memorial Site, which he had labored for twenty years to create, was some sort of divine recompense.

Welcoming Cramer, Wowereit, Neumann, and other invited guests to the Chapel of Reconciliation, with crowds outside listening via speakers, was a profoundly moving moment for Fischer. As he declared,

> Twenty years ago today, anyone who tried to get to this place would have risked their life, since it was then in the middle of the death strip and thus on the edge of the world. Today it is located, as it was before 1961, in the center of Berlin. That we can experience reconciliation here today is only possible because of the magnificent fall of the Wall. The reconstruction of the Chapel from the ruins of the old church and the vibrant parish today show how people have taken back this death strip.[99]

---

[97] Interview with Manfred Fischer, October 15, 2009; and correspondence with Axel Klausmeier, May 30 and June 5, 2014.

[98] "Einführung, Pfarrer Manfred Fischer/Professor Ernst Cramer zum 20. Jahrestags des Mauerfalls, 09. November 2009 bei der Andacht in der Kapelle der Versöhnung," Archive, Versöhnungsgemeinde Berlin-Wedding.

[99] Ibid.

Looking back to the fall of the Wall, Fischer praised "first and foremost the civic activists" in the GDR "who behaved intelligently and with determination to seize the opportunity" in November 1989. He was always more of a proponent of civic action than state policy and noted, "The people with power in this world are not the men of history and definitely not the dictators."[100] Instead, he felt that the "motivating message" of the fall of the Wall was universal: "People can change things."[101]

This is what Fischer wanted all the visitors to the still developing and expanding Berlin Wall Memorial to understand. He felt a responsibility especially to "those who didn't experience it, we must explain it: it is not a fairy tale, it really happened. You can touch the Wall here, walk along the path of the border soldiers, you can feel history here. In this way we can know our origins and thus our responsibility." He believed this was essential for post-Wall generations of Germans and people of every nationality. With this sense of history and the importance of learning from it, Fischer turned to November 9, 1938 and introduced Cramer.

Describing the suffering he and other Jews endured under the Nazis but also his joy when the Wall came down, Cramer declared: "November 9, 1938 was the worst and most consequential November 9...and we must not forget it in all our joy about what happened on November 9, 1989." He was twenty-five years old when the "Nazi thugs" stormed into his family's apartment in southern Germany on *Kristallnacht*, "smashed my father's beloved cello and shattered my mother's small yet exquisite porcelain collection." The following day, Cramer himself was found "by Nazis in all sorts of uniforms." He was detained and sent to the Buchenwald concentration camp where he was interned for six weeks. In a reference to the victims of communism held at that site afterwards, Cramer told the guests in the Chapel of Reconciliation that he would "not speak more today about [Buchenwald], because I know that later, after 1945, many innocent people were taken to similar camps and that many died there, as they had then in Buchenwald. Suffice it to say: 'My time [there] was the worst period I have ever experienced'."[102] Publicly speaking both of the Jews under the Nazis and then others who suffered under the communists after the war in some of the same camps was a conscious effort to recognize that while Jews were the main victims of contemporary German history, they were not the only ones, an acknowledgment that Günter Nooke and others had fought for in recent years as described in Chapter 6.

---

[100] Ibid.

[101] Interview with Manfred Fischer, October 15, 2009.

[102] "Prof. Ernst Cramer zum 20. Jahrestag des Mauerfalls, 09. November 2009 bei der Andacht in der Kapelle der Versöhnung," http://xn–vershnnungsgemeinde-g3b.de/inhalt/gemeinde/mauer/rede09%20IVovcramer.htm. Excerpts from his speech were also published in Ernst Cramer, "Ein Schicksalsdatum im Lauf der Geschichte," *Welt*, November 9, 2009.

When Cramer could show proof that he had immigration papers, he was released, and in 1939 he immigrated to the United States. He studied at Mississippi State College and became an American citizen. When the Japanese attacked Pearl Harbor, Cramer enlisted in the army. He took part in the landings at Normandy in 1944 and found himself in his hometown of Augsburg with the US Army when the war ended in 1945. Cramer learned that his brother and parents had been killed in concentration camps and only his sister had survived. He never forgave himself that he had not emigrated sooner and gotten his family out of Germany.[103]

Cramer returned to Germany after World War II and lived in West Berlin since 1958. He witnessed the cementation of Germany's division with the erection of the Berlin Wall, and he longed for the unification of Germany on democratic, peaceful terms. That the Wall opened peacefully on November 9, 1989 was for him "a miracle of German history," as he told the assembled guests in the Chapel of Reconciliation.[104] It was the happiest day of his life: "It was a German experience that I had striven for with all my heart. When the people climbed up on the Wall, I must confess, I stood there watching with tears in my eyes."[105] Cramer thanked God and all the people who made the fall of the Wall possible, especially "the majority of people in the GDR who wanted freedom."

In contrast to other Jewish Germans who had not wanted the commemoration of November 9, 1989 to distract from what happened on November 9, 1938, Cramer made it clear, "We want to celebrate." He asserted: "Today we are primarily thinking back to...the bloodless revolution of November 9, 1989," made possible by the East German "demonstrators thirsting for freedom." He ended with a prayer for all who lost their lives at the Wall, for those who lost their houses at the Wall as the regime fortified the border, and for those who teach history to future generations.[106]

After the service, Cramer, Fischer, and others lit candles at the Kohlhoff & Kohlhoff memorial. The candles were meant both to honor the dead and to remember the important role the candle-holding demonstrators had played in the Peaceful Revolution. The ceremony ended with

---

[103] As cited by Mathias Döpfner in his obituary for Cramer, "Ein Mann, der mit 92 Jahren zu googeln began," *Welt*, January 19, 2010. Cramer had also been the main speaker in the Bundestag on the Day of Mourning the Victims of National Socialism, January 27, 2006. "Rede von Ernst Cramer," *Welt*, January 27, 2006.

[104] "Prof. Ernst Cramer zum 20. Jahrestag des Mauerfalls, 09. November 2009 bei der Andacht in der Kapelle der Versöhnung."

[105] Mathias Döpfner, "Ein Mann, der mit 92 Jahren zu googeln began," *Welt*, January 19, 2010.

[106] Author's notes from Cramer's speech, Chapel of Reconciliation, Berlin Wall Memorial, November 9, 2009.

the opening of the new visitors' center at the Berlin Wall Memorial, part of the expansion of the site set in motion with the *Gesamtkonzept*.

Speaking at the visitors' center, Wowereit, Neumann, and Klausmeier expressed gratitude to the East German civic activists of 1989 and emphasized the importance of educating young Germans about the history of the rise and fall of the Wall and of the East German regime. Wowereit declared: "We must keep the memory of the Wall and the division alive for future generations"[107] and "show young people that democracy can be developed."[108] The Berlin Wall Memorial had been hosting many groups of visiting high school students, and these numbers would increase in future years as would a focus on the site as a *Lernort* for *politische Bildung*.[109]

Throughout the day on November 9 at the Berlin Wall Memorial, there was major national and international media coverage of the events with journalists from the United States, United Kingdom, Russia, India, Israel, Colombia, South Korea, China, Uzbekistan, and many other countries coming to Bernauer Strasse. Seventeen television teams, twenty-three radio reporters, and thirty-two photo journalists were on site. Germany's *ARD-Tagesthemen* broadcast live from the observation deck. The front page of the *Washington Post* featured a picture of a former guard tower brought to Bernauer Strasse that week and placed in the rectangular section of the former border strip created by the Kohlhoff & Kohlhoff memorial. Walesa visited in the morning with a Polish television crew, and the mayors of Moscow and Paris were there in the afternoon. The Berlin Wall Foundation received nine million euros in project funds for 2009, which included 2.5 million euros for the visitor's center, and other funds to expand and improve the site as well as for conferences and publications.[110] The days of Manfred Fischer and his colleagues struggling for attention to be given to the site were long gone.

---

[107] Author's notes from Wowereit's speech, visitors' center Berlin Wall Memorial, November 9, 2009; and press release from the office of the Governing Mayor of Berlin, "9. November 2009: Berlin gedenkt der Maueropfer und weiht Gedenkstättenportal ein," November 6, 2009.

[108] G. Asmuth and P. Gessler, "Die Geschichte weitergeben: 20. Jahrestag der Maueröffnung," *taz*, November 10, 2009.

[109] Author's notes from Klausmeier's speech, visitors' center, Berlin Wall Memorial, November 9, 2009; and "20 Jahre nach dem Mauerfall wird Besucherzentrum eröffnet," press release, Stiftung Berliner Mauer, November 9, 2009.

[110] Stiftung Berliner Mauer, "Jahresbericht der Stiftung Berliner Mauer 2009," pp. 27–29; and conversation with Axel Klausmeier, November 9, 2009.

Bornholmer Strasse, Böse Bridge

The next major event of the day was hosted in the afternoon by Chancellor Merkel at the Böse bridge on Bornholmer Strasse, together with Mayor Wowereit and Bundestag President Norbert Lammert.[111] The ceremony was broadcast live on national television as politicians were joined by dozens of former civic activists and church leaders from the GDR as well as representatives of East German victims' groups, and former East Germans who had crossed the bridge on November 9, 1989.[112] The bridge and surroundings were again packed with people as they had been in 1989. More than 1,000 people gathered on the bridge itself.

Gorbachev and Walesa were special guests of the chancellor on the bridge (Figure 26) and were repeatedly thanked by the Germans for their roles in 1989. While Merkel no doubt did not intend for Walesa and Gorbachev to upstage the civic activists who were meant to be the focus of the event, this was somewhat the effect of including the former Soviet and Polish leaders. As Berlin's *taz* newspaper observed from the crowd's response on the bridge, "The biggest star of the day was...'Gorbi'."[113] Indeed, in a survey a few months before, when asked who contributed most to the success of the Peaceful Revolution, 62 percent of Germans said it was Gorbachev, more than the actions of the East German citizens.[114] The chancellor expressed deep gratitude to Gorbachev who "made it all possible, much more than we could have ever expected." Reflecting on her own experience, she also thanked Walesa for "the incredible inspiration" Solidarity was "for all of us," noting that "those who first crossed the border" on November 9, 1989 in Berlin "were not necessarily the ones who first set things in motion for its opening."[115]

---

[111] Although not ready in time for the twentieth anniversary, Wowereit would dedicate a "November 9, 1989 Square" the following year at the site. Next to the original sections of Wall still standing along the street, an outdoor exhibit space was created containing over-sized pictures and a description of the history at the site. Fifteen panels chronicle the hours between 9 a.m. and midnight on November 9, 1989. The panels also highlight the other important German ninths of November, including the declaration of a German Republic by Philipp Scheidemann in Berlin in 1918, Hitler's beer hall putsch in Munich in 1923, and the Nazis' attack on synagogues on *Kristallnacht* in 1938.

[112] dpa, "Fest der Freiheit, Eine bunte Mauer fällt," *Focus Online*, November 9, 2009.

[113] G. Asmuth and P. Gessler, "Die Geschichte weitergeben: 20. Jahrestag der Maueröffnung," *taz*, November 10, 2009. See also Nicholas Kulish and Judy Dempsey, "Leaders in Berlin Retrace the Walk West," *New York Times*, November 10, 1989.

[114] "Wird die historische Leistung der friedlichen Revolution im Herbst 1989 heute in der Öffentlichkeit gesehen als Leistung der ..." *Volkssolidarität Bundesverband*, July 2009, https://de.statista.com/statistik/daten/studie/30263/umfrage/meinung-zu-verantwortung-fuer-revolution-von-1989/.

[115] "Rede von Bundeskanzlerin Dr. Angela Merkel anlässlich der Veranstaltung mit Bürgerrechtlern/Zeitzeugen im Rahmen des 20. Jahrestages des Mauerfalls am 9. November 2009," Böse Bridge, Bornholmer Strasse.

Figure 26 left to right: Marianne Birthler, Mikhail Gorbachev, Angela Merkel, Joachim Gauck (behind Merkel's shoulder), Lech Walesa, Böse Bridge, Bornholmer Strasse, November 9, 2009
Source: Photographer: Steffen Kugler. Bundesarchiv, B 145 Bild-00207967.

Just as Sello with his exhibit on the Peaceful Revolution had wanted to "give people back their memories" of what life was really like in the GDR instead of remembering it nostalgically, so Merkel observed: "Sometimes one forgets now how many were not allowed to travel for years, how many had to sit in the prisons, how many children became victims. . . .But before the joy of freedom came, many suffered." Standing on the bridge where the former checkpoint had been and with a huge picture behind her showing rejoicing Berliners on the spot twenty years earlier, the chancellor spoke of "the long history of tyranny and struggle against tyranny" in the GDR and the "lost chances in life, fear and worry" endured by so many.[116]

Merkel expressed regret that since unification, "we took so long to recognize this type of injustice as such and to try to compensate for it in some

---

[116] "Rede von Bundeskanzlerin Dr. Angela Merkel anlässlich der Veranstaltung mit Bürgerrechtlern/Zeitzeugen im Rahmen des 20. Jahrestages des Mauerfalls am 9. November 2009," Böse Bridge, Bornholmer Strasse.

way."[117] The members of East German victims' groups joining Merkel for the occasion were no doubt gratified at this recognition. The anniversary of the fall of the Wall was an occasion not just to celebrate that happy day but also to reflect on the suffering and restrictions many East Germans had endured.

The chancellor invited Joachim Gauck to give the main speech at the gathering. As a pastor in the port city of Rostock on the coast of the Baltic Sea, Gauck had opened his church to people who were critical of the government and calling for reform and also to people who were trying to leave the country in 1989. He took part in the regular Thursday night protests in Rostock and gave increasingly political sermons and speeches in the fall and winter of 1989–90.

In his remarks on the bridge, Gauck remembered the East German people's urge for freedom in 1989 and their insistence that they deserved it when they told the SED leaders again and again, "*Wir sind das Volk!*" ("We are the people!") Gauck stated that this proclamation was the East German version of President Barack Obama's "Yes we can!" He remembered that although "in our part of Germany for fifty-six years, people had learned one thing: conform, be obedient, bow your head," they pushed themselves out of that habit and demanded freedom.[118] Following the speeches by Merkel and Gauck, the dignitaries, surrounded by the civic activists and others, walked across the bridge from east to west to commemorate the dramatic developments there twenty years earlier.[119]

The next stop for the dignitaries and other invited guests was a reception at Schloss Bellevue hosted by President Köhler. The president paid tribute to the brave East Germans and East Europeans, to Gorbachev, Kohl, and Bush, and to "a lucky stroke of fate that paved the way" for the dramatic events of 1989–90. In 1989, Köhler was living in Bonn and working for the West German Finance Ministry. Far from the action on November 9 in Berlin, the president told the assembled guests: "My wife and I. . .were still West Germans, and we marveled at the dancing on the Wall" and its transformation from "an edifice of fear" into "a site of joy." Jumping all too quickly over the fall of the Wall for some of the former East German civic activists in the room, Köhler spoke to the EU, US, and Russian leaders, "The trust of our friends and partners. . .brought us Germans reunification in freedom. In the name of all Germans, I say to you: thank you, this nation will not forget this."[120] While the occasion was the

---

[117] Ibid. See also Merkel's remarks about this in an interview in 2003, Merkel, *Mein Weg*, pp. 66–67.

[118] "Rede von Joachim Gauck am ehemaligen Grenzübergang Bornholmer Strasse zum 20. Jahrestag des Mauerfalls. Unser 'Yes We can!' heist 'Wir sind das Volk!'" November 9, 2009.

[119] The federal government devoted 600,000 euros for the event on the bridge at Bornholmer Strasse. Interview with Tilman Seeger, July 29, 2014.

[120] "Eine Epochenwende zu Freiheit und Demokratie," Ansprache von Bundespräsident Horst Köhler beim Empfang zur Feier des 20. Jahrestags des Mauerfalls am 9. November 2009 in Schloss Bellevue, Bundespräsidialamt.

twentieth anniversary of the fall of the Wall, the president actually spoke more about unification and the years since than he did about November 9, 1989.

German Pride and Joy at the Brandenburg Gate

The climax of the twentieth anniversary celebrations took place at the Brandenburg Gate in the evening. The Festival of Freedom featuring the more than 1,000 large painted *Dominosteine* had been kicked off by Mayor Wowereit two days before and would end with the ceremonial toppling of the Wall dominoes that night. Over the course of three days, an estimated one million people thronged the former path of the Wall around the Brandenburg Gate to see the Wall dominoes and the many ways people chose to commemorate the fall of the Wall in paintings on the *Dominosteine*.[121] Just as the Wall had cut off streets, so the mile-long area with the dominoes cut off traffic on some streets in central Berlin. There were only a few places one could cross, even on foot, offering a small reminder of how it had been with the real Wall.

Connecting the fall of the Wall in the official narrative with the East German people's striving for freedom, huge viewing screens around the Brandenburg Gate on the evening of November 9 carried one word: "*Freiheit!*" The breath of freedom so many had felt when the demonstration of October 9 in Leipzig was not put down was dramatically magnified when the East German people stormed – albeit peacefully – the checkpoints along the Berlin Wall a month later and pushed the guards to open the Berlin Wall. As the newly installed German Foreign Minister Guido Westerwelle noted at a gala event the evening before the grand celebrations in Berlin: "The Wall did not fall. . . .It was pushed down. By people, and in fact from East to West," due to their "love for liberty."[122]

With a crowd of 250,000 people gathered near the Gate and a live national television broadcast, the mayor, the chancellor, EU and world leaders, and prominent former East German dissidents, marked the occasion with a grand celebration lasting almost two hours. It was an evening full of symbolism and big gestures. The cool, rainy weather did little to dampen the spirits of the

---

[121] For the catalogue of all the *Dominosteine* and a description of the background and motivation for this ceremony, see Kulturprojekte Berlin, ed., *Dominobuch*. They also published a booklet at the end of the year describing all the key events of the twentieth anniversary celebrations and providing pictures, *20 Jahre Mauerfall. Dokumentation des Themenjahres 2009* (Berlin: Kulturprojekte Berlin GmbH, 2009).

[122] The Washington-based Atlantic Council hosted a gala ceremony on the evening of November 8 at the Hotel Adlon in Berlin, giving out "Freedom Awards" to mark the twentieth anniversary of the fall of the Wall. "Dankbarkeit für die Einheit Deutschlands," Auswärtiges Amt, Besuch Außenministerin Clinton, November 9, 2009, www.auswaertiges-amt.de/DE/Aussenpolitik/Laender/Aktuelle_Artikel/USA/091109-PKClinton_node.html.

speakers or the onlookers. Many people who had lived through the opening of the Wall were moved to tears. Young people who just wanted to party were there too. There was something for everyone: serious speeches to mark the event, music by the Berlin State Orchestra (*Staatskapelle*), as well as Bon Jovi ("We Weren't Born to Follow"), the German vocal quintet Adoro ("*Freiheit*"), and Paul van Dyk ("We are One"), and a fantastic finale with fireworks.

Opening the evening's ceremony was a concert by the *Staatskapelle* with Daniel Barenboim conducting. He chose one of the pieces from the free concert he had conducted for East Berliners with the (West) Berlin Philharmonic three days after the Wall opened as well as several others to fit the occasion in 2009.[123] Barenboim began the anniversary concert with music from Richard Wagner's opera *Lohengrin*. Wagner had composed the music during the 1848 revolution, which he had actively supported, a revolution that many saw as a distant relative of the Peaceful Revolution of 1989. Barenboim's next step in history was the Nazi period. He himself had been born in Argentina to Russian Jewish immigrant parents and chose Arnold Schönberg's 1947 piece, "A Survivor from Warsaw," to commemorate the Holocaust. To honor the fall of the Wall, one of the works Maestro Barenboim selected was the final movement, *Allegro con brio* (with great liveliness), of Beethoven's Seventh Symphony which he had conducted in Berlin at the 1989 concert.

The political leaders then took the spotlight. Escorted by young singers whistling the melody from Scorpions' hit song of 1990, "Wind of Change" and with pictures from the night of November 9, 1989 showing on giant screens, the German, European, and world leaders ceremoniously walked through the Brandenburg Gate from east to west. The image of so many world leaders together at the Brandenburg Gate was an extraordinary statement. It was a demonstration of the importance of the fall of the Wall not just to Berlin and Germany but for all of Europe and the world. The high-level participation in the event showed how much each of the leaders wanted to be associated with this epoch-changing event in world history.[124]

One also had the distinct feeling that the German leaders did not want to be celebrating alone at the Brandenburg Gate. Careful not to seize too much of the limelight and worry others about German national pride, they surrounded

---

[123] For information on the concert, see "Konzert zum 'Fest der Freiheit' am Brandenburger Tor: Daniel Barenboim und die Staatskapelle Berlin spielen Wagner, Schönberg, Beethoven und Goldmann," *KlassikInfo.de, News*, www.klassikinfo.de/NEWS-Single.54 +M50c8a9c6214.0.html.

[124] French president Nicholas Sarkozy even claimed he had been there when the Wall fell, although evidence later showed this not to be true. Reuters, "In France, a Clash of Memories and Media," *New York Times*, November 10, 2009; and David Francis and Dan Murphy, "At Berlin Wall Fall Celebration, Old Allies Ask Where Is Obama?" *Christian Science Monitor*, Global News Blog, November 9, 2009.

themselves at the Gate with their European neighbors and other world powers. Chancellor Merkel and Mayor Wowereit were cocooned at the center of the group of leaders walking through the Gate, hopefully dispelling any fears of a go-it-alone Germany. Unlike so many others on this historic anniversary, Merkel shied away from using the word "pride." Instead she spoke of being "glad" and "grateful" as she remembered the fall of the Wall as "one of the happiest moments of my life." She and the mayor of Berlin paid tribute to the role of other countries in the fall of the Wall and German unification. "Together we removed the Iron Curtain," said Merkel. She praised the "courage and irrepressible will of so many people in the former GDR" but also the "courageous engagement of our neighbors in the East" in Czechoslovakia, Poland, Hungary, and the Soviet Union. "The unification of our country would have been unthinkable without our Central and East European neighbors," Merkel declared.[125] This went some way toward diminishing the resentment in those countries for all the attention on the fall of the Wall, although nothing could fully eliminate it since global memory focused on the fall of the Wall and not on any other moment in 1989.

Mayor Wowereit also provided broader historical context for "movements for freedom in Eastern Europe," by "paying homage" to the 1953 uprising in East Germany, the Hungarian revolution of 1956, the Prague Spring of 1968, and the achievements of Solidarity in Poland.[126] He remembered "the many people killed at the Wall and the victims of the GDR dictatorship" and offered solidarity and respect for those East Germans who "had lost their jobs and their bearings" since the fall of the Wall. In addition, Wowereit and Merkel acknowledged the role of the Four Powers in the Cold War, thanking the United States, France, and Great Britain for supporting freedom and democracy in West Berlin and West Germany and thanking Gorbachev for not interfering with the opening of the Wall or stopping German unification.

British Prime Minister Gordon Brown's speech was the most eloquent of the evening. To huge cheers, he declared: "The whole world is proud of you. You tore down the Wall and changed the world. Because of your courage, two Berlins are one, two Germanys are one, and two Europes are one.... You showed that injustice is not the final word on humanity." Brown declared that the fall of the Wall and the unification of Europe showed that "history is moving toward our best hopes, not our worst fears."[127]

---

[125] "Rede von Bundeskanzlerin Dr. Angela Merkel im Rahmen des 'Fests der Freiheit' am 9. November 2009 in Berlin."

[126] "Rede des Regierenden Bürgermeisters Klaus Wowereit zum Fest der Freiheit," Pressemitteilung, Der Regierende Bürgermeister, Senatskanzlei, November 9, 2009.

[127] Author's notes on the speeches at the Brandenburg Gate, November 9, 2009; Nicholas Kulish and Judy Dempsey, "Leaders in Berlin Retrace the Walk West," *New York Times*, November 10, 2009; and "Berlin Wall 2.0," *Reuters Blog*, November 9, 2009, live.reuters.com/Event/Berlin_Wall_20?Page=10.

Berlin planners tried to offset the presence of all the leaders at the Gate by also featuring three former East German civic activists in the ceremony: Marianne Birthler, Roland Jahn, and Katrin Hattenhauer. But once the world leaders were invited and the focus of the evening was effectively broadened to include unification, it took great efforts to persuade the former East German civil activists to agree to participate. Indeed, many former dissidents wanted to boycott the event, which they believed would not focus enough on the Peaceful Revolution.[128] Moreover, many former East Germans were skeptical of official celebrations, since for forty years under communism (as previously under the Nazis) participation in such events was obligatory if one wanted to avoid direct or indirect punishment.[129]

The choice of emcee for the evening, the (West) German television personality Thomas Gottschalk, was criticized by many from both the east and the west for trivializing the commemoration. For more than twenty years, Gottschalk had been the host of the wildly popular show, *Wetten, daß . . . ?* ("Wanna bet that . . . ?") in which celebrities and audience members bet about whether regular people who appeared on the show could perform some crazy or complicated task. Having Gottschalk appear with people who had been imprisoned in the GDR and with heads of state seemed the height of incongruity but was no doubt part of the organizers' efforts to reach as many people as possible. It was under these conditions that the three former East German dissidents ultimately appeared at the Gate after the leaders had spoken.

Compared to the time given to the leaders of the Four Powers to speak, the appearance of Birthler, Jahn, and Hattenhauer, who were far more directly connected to the fall of the Wall, amounted to a sort of cameo appearance.[130] Kulturprojekte had consulted closely with Sello to choose speakers representing three sources of influence on the Peaceful Revolution of 1989: East Berlin

---

[128] Interviews with Wolf Kühnelt, January 25, 2010; Moritz van Dülmen, January 28, 2010; and Tom Sello, February 10, 2010. Bundestag Vice President Wolfgang Thierse also publicly expressed criticism that the role of the East Germans in the fall of the Wall was given insufficient recognition during the festivities. A live blog about the festivities on November 9, 2009 refers to an interview Thierse gave to Bayerische Rundfunk about this, "20 Jahre Mauerfall: So lief der Feiertag der Deutschen," *RP Online (Rheinische Post)*, November 9, 2009; and "Mauerfall-Feiern: Dominosteine und Politprominenz," DiePress.com, November 9, 2009.

[129] Interviews with Wolf Kühnelt, January 25, 2010 and July 3, 2014; Moritz van Dülmen, January 28, 2010; and Tom Sello, July 9, 2014.

[130] In fact, much press coverage of the event at the Brandenburg Gate, including blogs about the celebration, completely left out the appearance of the former dissidents: J. Oberländer, J. Haase, F. Klün, A. Sauerbrey, "Mauerfall-Jubiläum. 9. November: Der Live-Blog," *Tagesspiegel*, November 11, 2009; csi/spo, "20 Jahre Mauerfall. So lief der Feiertag der Deutschen," *RP Online*, November 9, 2009; Deanne Corbett, "World Leaders Commemorate Fall of Berlin Wall," *Deutsche Welle*, November 9, 2009; and AP, "Germany Wall Speeches," story no. 626277, *AP Archive*, November 9, 2009.

with Marianne Birthler who from a telephone at the Gethsemane Church had kept track of people detained by the Stasi and later was the second director of the Stasi Records Authority; Leipzig with Katrin Hattenhauer who was one of the founders of the Monday night demonstrations; and West Berlin with Roland Jahn. As a dissident in East Germany, Jahn's protests against the East German regime had so enraged the leaders that they had Stasi commandos capture him and forcibly put him on a train to the FRG, expelling him from the GDR.[131] Jahn then became a journalist in West Berlin where he privately helped and publicly highlighted protest movements against the SED regime, most famously when he aired the footage of the October 9, 1989 demonstration in Leipzig.

As a twenty-year-old, Hattenhauer had been imprisoned for months because she had stood on the street with a banner calling, "For an open country with free people."[132] Now an artist in a united and democratic country, her dream of 1989 had come true. She told the young people at the Brandenburg Gate: "Use your freedom; live your dreams!"[133] Roland Jahn described his difficult time in prison in the GDR due to his protests and became so choked up that he could barely speak.[134] With a clear implication of "better late than never," he noted that this was "the first time so many civic activists had been invited" to commemorate the fall of the Wall, referring probably both to the special seats for them in the VIP section at the Brandenburg Gate and to the ceremony on the bridge at Bornholmer Strasse.[135]

Birthler remembered life in the GDR as a "time when people were humiliated and surveilled."[136] Since the fall of the Wall and the demise of the East German regime, Birthler observed: "Every time I cross the death strip, my heart leaps." She also made sure people understood the correct chain of events in 1989 by reminding people that it was not the fall of the Wall that brought the GDR citizens freedom: "The revolution for freedom in the GDR had begun long before the Wall was breached. A people who won't allow itself to be suppressed anymore also won't allow itself to be caged in anymore."[137] In keeping with this spirit, the crowd was treated to two songs about the revolutionary days of 1989–90: the Berlin-based group Adoro sang Marius Müller-

---

[131] Author's interviews with Tom Sello, February 10, 2010; Wolf Kühnelt, January 25, 2010; and Moritz van Dülmen, January 28, 2010.

[132] Karoline Beyer, Joachim Fahrun, Sören Kittel, "Das Herz Berlins macht einen Sprung," *Berliner Morgenpost*, November 10, 2009.

[133] Sabine Höher, "Kopfnoten. Wenn sich einer die Freiheit nimmt: Katrin Hattenhauer," *Welt*, November 11, 2009.

[134] dpa, "Fest der Freiheit – Eine bunte Mauer fällt," *Focus Online*, November 9, 2009.

[135] "Zitate zum Mauerfall-Jubiläum," *B.Z.*, November 9, 2009.

[136] dpa, "Fest der Freiheit – Eine bunte Mauer fällt," *Focus Online*, November 9, 2009.

[137] Birthler's words at a press conference with Wowereit, Gorbachev, and Yunus earlier in the day on November 9, 2009: Beyer, Fahrun, Kittel, "Das Herz Berlins macht einen Sprung," *Berliner Morgenpost*, November 10, 2009.

Westernhagen's hit song from 1990, "*Freiheit*"; and Bon Jovi performed his new song dedicated to the Peaceful Revolution, "We Weren't Born to Follow."

For the highlight of the celebration with the falling Wall dominoes, however, the honor of starting the chain reaction was not given to East Germans who participated in the Peaceful Revolution. Instead the former Polish and Hungarian leaders, Lech Walesa and Miklos Nemeth, were invited to push over the dominoes at one end of the line to honor Walesa's leadership of Solidarity to victory against the Polish Communist Party and Nemeth's decision to open Hungary's border with Austria, both of which created cracks in the Iron Curtain. The presidents of the European Parliament and the European Commission were invited to topple the dominoes at the other end of the line in a reference less to1989 and more to the way Europe had united since the fall of the Wall and German unification and as a statement of German commitment to the EU. The Germans thus found a way to celebrate the fall of the Berlin Wall by embedding German history and politics in broader European history and politics, underscoring Germany's identity as a European power instead of a unilateral power.

As Gottschalk led the crowd in the countdown, "ten, nine, eight . . .," Walesa stood next to the domino he had sponsored. Painted by students studying Polish at a foreign language high school in Berlin, the *Dominostein* depicted the Polish flag and a hammer with the label "*Solidarnosc*" above the Brandenburg Gate and the Berlin Wall, indicating that a Polish hammer had been central to bringing down the Wall. The painting showed cracks in the Wall, and "*Es begann in Polen*" ("It began in Poland") was written on the Wall. Nemeth's *Dominostein* had been painted by Hungarian students at a high school in Budapest and depicted the two parts of Berlin and Germany growing together, with the words of Willy Brandt from November 10, 1989 written above them, "That which belongs together is coming together." With the countdown reaching zero, Walesa and Nemeth pushed over their dominoes and a whole series of Wall dominoes between the Reichstag and the Brandenburg Gate fell over in rapid succession, coming to a stop in front of the Gate. Standing at the Gate, Gottschalk then spoke with Gorbachev and former West German foreign minister Hans-Dietrich Genscher, both of whom had also sponsored dominoes. Genscher was particularly famous for having negotiated, in the fall of 1989, the release of thousands of East German refugees camped out at West German embassies in Prague and Warsaw and their transfer to West Germany.

The second, longer set of Dominosteine between Potsdamer Platz and the Brandenburg Gate was given a push by Jerzy Buzek, the President of the European Parliament (and a former Solidarity activist), and José Manuel Barroso, the President of the European Commission. The German drumming trio Stamping Feet accompanied the toppling of this set of dominoes, which suddenly stopped with one domino left standing in front of the Brandenburg Gate to represent all the walls in the world still to be toppled.

Figure 27 Falling dominoes at Brandenburg Gate, November 9, 2009
Source: Photographer: Wolfgang Rattay. Reuters.

The final domino had been painted by the artist Xu Bing of the Chinese Central Academy of Fine Arts. Xu Bing had first drenched the Styrofoam domino in cement so that it would be strong enough to remain standing when the other dominoes fell toward it. On the domino, Xu painted the text of an ancient Chinese poem about a former husband and wife who had been forced to separate and met again years later.[138] Xu Bing was not in Berlin for the celebration. Instead the South Korean artist, Ahn Kyu-Chul, who had also contributed a domino, spoke with Gottschalk at the Brandenburg Gate as the last domino was left standing. Ahn reminded the partygoers at the Gate, "This is to show that we're not here just to celebrate but to think about all the walls still left in the world." Muhammad Yunus, the winner of the 2006 Nobel Peace Prize, told Gottschalk and the crowd that "the wall of poverty still has to come down...too."[139] Buoyed up by their success in toppling a wall, the Berlin hosts wanted to send out a message to the world about all the other walls – whether physical or psychological – yet to be toppled.

[138] "'Das ist klare Pressezensur,' China will Mauerfall totschweigen," *n-tv.de* August 22, 2009; and DJ, "Now Here Is an Idea for People Looking for Chinese (Looking) Tattoos," *Fool's Mountain: Blogging for China*, foolsmountain.com, 13 November 2009.

[139] "Berlin Wall 2.0," *Reuters Blog*, November 9, 2009, live.reuters.com/Event/ Berlin_Wall_20?Page=10.

The closing song of the evening, the world premiere of "We are One," seemed to refer not just to Berlin and Germany but to the world as a whole. The song was composed by the German musician and DJ, Paul van Dyk. Growing up in East Berlin, van Dyk had listened to West Berlin radio frequently. He became a star in united Berlin. The crowd sang along to the catchy tune, "We can be as one/No more barriers/. . ./We are one." And with that, the final domino was toppled as fireworks jubilantly exploded all around and above the Brandenburg Gate. The politicians and assembled crowd applauded and cheered. Germany's leaders reveled in the moment enjoying the eyes of the world on them for something positive in their history. (Figure 27 and cover photo)

The Twenty-Fifth Anniversary of the Fall of the Wall, 2014

The dominant celebratory narrative of the Peaceful Revolution continued five years later for the twenty-fifth anniversary of the fall of the Wall, albeit consciously expanded to share agency in the fall of the Wall with others both inside and outside Germany. While the Germans had included their Central European neighbors in 2009 to recognize their role in helping to bring down the Wall, they did this in a more pronounced way in 2014. With the Poles and Hungarians continuing to assert that they had "removed the first bricks from the Wall," the Germans responded by embedding the fall of the Wall even more firmly in a broader European narrative in 2014.

The twenty-fifth anniversary was the first major Wall anniversary where both the chancellor and president were from the former East Germany. While Merkel had not taken part in the Peaceful Revolution of 1989, Joachim Gauck had been an active participant as the pastor of a Protestant church in Rostock. Although he had spoken at the Bundestag ceremony on the tenth anniversary of the fall of the Wall and at Bornholmer Strasse on the twentieth anniversary, Gauck would have a bigger role in 2014 due to his position as president.

In the spring of 2014, President Gauck announced that he would mark the twenty-fifth anniversary by joining his Polish, Hungarian, Slovakian, and Czech counterparts in traveling to key cities in those countries involved in the revolutions of 1989.[140] Each accompanied by ten people who were important actors in the revolutions in their country, between June and November 2014, Gauck and his colleagues visited each country on the anniversary of key revolutionary moments from 1989, starting in Warsaw on June 4 and including Leipzig on October 9 (Figure 28).[141] Gauck's

---

[140] "Gauck reist mit Amtskollegen in Städte der friedlichen Revolution," *Märkische Online Zeitung*, April 15, 2014.

[141] For Gauck personally, the first large demonstration in Rostock on October 19 was the turning point. Interview with Joachim Gauck, January 7, 2010.

Figure 28 Joachim Gauck (third from right) and his partner Daniela Schadt with (left to right) Czech President Milos Zeman, Leipzig Mayor Burkhard Jung, Polish President Bronislaw Komorowski, Slovak President Andrej Kiska, Hungarian President Janos Ader, Leipzig, October 9, 2014
Source: Photographer: Henning Schacht. Bundesarchiv, B145 Bild-00316023.

emphasis on Leipzig was mirrored by the decision of the German National Prize Foundation to award the 2014 prize to the "freedom movement in the GDR" and especially to people from the "Monday night demonstrations in Leipzig." The prize committee asserted that the winners "showed that each person can make history. The prize acknowledge[d] people whose revolutionary courage and non-violent methods caused the downfall of the GDR regime and the fall of the Wall."[142]

Reading Gauck's memoirs published in 2009, one could see the importance he placed on the role of the East German demonstrators in 1989, "In the end, out of our protest movement came a revolution. . . .Entirely without violence. . .the state order was destroyed by the people and replaced with a new system – even though no blood flowed and the protestors had banners and candles instead of weapons in their hands."[143] Just like Sello and so many others who took part in the protests of 1989, Gauck was convinced that the Peaceful Revolution was a central moment in German history and should be

---

[142] Deutscher Nationalpreis, www.nationalstiftung.de/nationalpreis2014.
[143] Joachim Gauck, *Winter im Sommer – Frühling im Herbst* (Munich: Seidler, 2009), p. 214.

more widely recognized and known about, including by young people.[144] He also remembered well how much he and others had been inspired by the Poles and Hungarians in the fall of 1989, and in 2014 he made it a point to express his gratitude. Gauck's approach to the twenty-fifth anniversary may be seen as an attempt to denationalize German memory of the fall of the Wall.

The Berlin Philharmonic followed President Gauck's example and traveled to Warsaw, Budapest, and Prague, performing Beethoven's Ninth Symphony with its "Ode to Joy" together with works by composers from those countries. The orchestra also gave a performance in the eastern German city of Halle (Saale), one of the many cities where people had taken to the streets in 1989. Each concert was streamed live on the Philharmonic's website.

The orchestra's celebration of the twenty-fifth anniversary began in Berlin on November 6 with Polish composer Karol Szymanowski's "Stabat mater" in honor of Solidarity's role in 1989 paired with Beethoven's Ninth. The program notes by Volker Tarnow for the concert elucidated an important connection between the Ninth and the fall of the Wall and German unification. At the end of World War II, parts of Beethoven's autographed copy of the Ninth Symphony were located in eastern and western Germany and in Poland. In 1977, Poland gave its part to the GDR. The signed work was thus divided by the Berlin Wall, with part of it in East Berlin and part in West Berlin. Only with German unification was the entire piece back under the same roof in united Berlin. The Philharmonic was not the only orchestra to play the piece in Berlin to mark the twenty-fifth anniversary. On the evening of Sunday November 9 at the Brandenburg Gate, Barenboim and the *Staatskapelle* performed the "Ode to Joy."

Along with President Gauck and the Berlin Philharmonic, Mayor Wowereit also embedded the city's celebrations more deeply in a European context, informing the press in March 2014 that "with our plans for the celebration of the fall of the Wall, we will remember. . .the European freedom movement of 1989 which radically changed the path of world history.[145]

The mayor pulled out all the stops for the celebration in 2014, as he had in 2009, declaring that the "theme of the year" for 2014 was "25 Years since the Fall of the Wall." A dedicated website, www.berlin.de/ mauerfall2014, provided information on many of the planned events. The tourism marketing branch of the government, "Visit Berlin," also created a website (mauer.visitberlin.de/en/). The federal government became involved earlier in the planning than it had in 2009 and launched a website as well (www.freiheit-und-einheit.de), which gave

---

[144] Interview with Joachim Gauck, April 6, 2004. Like many others from the East, Gauck preferred a monument to freedom as a way of commemorating 1989 instead of a national Freedom and Unity Monument. Interview with Gauck, January 7, 2010.

[145] Der Regierender Bürgermeister von Berlin, press release, March 2014 and press conference and press release, July 10, 2014.

information about both the historical events of 1989–90 and how they would be commemorated in 2014–15. As in 2009, officials announced that the Peaceful Revolution and the fall of the Wall were "symbols of hope for a world without walls." A new Berlin Wall app in English was introduced for the occasion, supplementing the previous app available only in German. The rbb television network broadcast historic material about the Wall and the day's festivities for twenty-five hours to mark the twenty-fifth anniversary.

The centerpiece of the anniversary celebrations in 2014 featured the release of 8,000 illuminated balloons along more than seven miles of the former border in Berlin, a so-called *Lichtgrenze* (border of light).[146] The image of balloons floating up into the sky instead of dominoes falling down was perhaps indicative of the diminished weight of the past German leaders felt on their shoulders since they had embraced the fall of the Wall as a central positive moment in their history, something that made them proud instead of ashamed. Indeed, the German news magazine *Der Spiegel* wrote in the summer of 2014 about "a new [German] lightness of being" and "how Germans are learning to like themselves."[147]

Just as each *Dominostein* in 2009 had been designed by an individual or group who also participated in the three-day-long event from November 7 to 9, so each balloon (illuminated, biodegradable spheres tethered to the ground by ten-foot poles) for the twenty-fifth anniversary had a sponsor (at no cost) who attached his or her own message to their balloon. The messages were meant to be connected to the history of the Wall or wishes for the future now that the Wall was gone. They were all published on a website devoted to the event, fallofthe-wall25.com. School classes, prominent individuals, companies, churches, and other institutions as well as regular people from Germany and around the world were again involved in creating their own message and (unlike in 2009 when only four people were invited to topple the dominoes) in releasing their balloon.

In keeping with the commitment of the Berlin government to using the anniversary to disseminate information on the history of the Berlin Wall, the *Lichtgrenze* had an educational mission. Surveys at the time showed that less than half of Berliners knew where the Wall had been and many young people

---

[146] For information on the *Lichtgrenze* and the twenty-fifth anniversary celebrations, see Kulturprojekte Berlin, press release "Das Jubiläumsprojekt 2014: Licht Installation entlang des ehemaligen Mauerverlaufs im Zentrum Berlins zum 9. November," September 19, 2013 (www.kulturprojekte-berlin.de/unsere-veranstaltungen/25-jahre-mauerfall.html); "Hunderttausende erwartet. Lichterkette zum Mauerfall-Jubiläum," *Berliner Morgenpost*, March 6, 2014; Kulturprojekte press release, July 10, 2014; press conference of September 8, 2014; and Moritz van Dülmen and Tom Sello, eds., *Mauergeschichten. Wall Stories*, trans. Büro LS Anderson (Berlin: Kulturprojekte Berlin GmbH, 2014), catalogue to accompany the Berlin Senate's project "25 Years Fall of the Wall. Wall Stories – LICHTGRENZE – Balloon Event."

[147] *Spiegel* staff, "The Bearable Lightness of Being: How Germans Are Learning to Like Themselves," *Spiegel*, July 17, 2014.

did not know much about what the Wall had meant to people while it stood. In addition to the balloons along the former border in central Berlin, there were large pictures of divided Berlin, historical markers at 100 locations, big screens showing footage and interviews from the time the Wall stood, information stands, guided tours, and viewing platforms at historically significant spots along seven miles of the former border, including at the Brandenburg Gate, Bornholmer Strasse, the Berlin Wall Memorial, Checkpoint Charlie, and the East Side Gallery. It all formed a kind of outdoor exhibit of the history of the Wall. Tom Sello was in charge of providing the historical information, working in cooperation with the Berlin Wall Foundation. The whole project was overseen by Kulturprojekte Berlin, as in 2009, and was funded with nearly two million euros from the lottery.[148]

The idea for the *Lichtgrenze* (Figure 29) paired with historical films and other information came from two brothers, Christopher and Marc Bauder, who had grown up in West Germany. Christopher was a media artist who created art installations using light and Marc was a filmmaker who had made several documentary films dealing with the history and suffering of people in the GDR. For years they had been brainstorming about a project to "show the Wall again," initially thinking of installing 43,000 balloons so that there would be one at every meter of the former border between East and West Berlin.[149]

After sharing their idea about the balloons with an enthusiastic Sello, the brothers then reduced the number of balloons and won the chance to create the main spectacle experienced by more than one million people from November 7 to 9, 2014. Christopher's illuminated balloons would be accompanied by Marc's film showing on screens along the Lichtgrenze. Marc worked in thirty archives to compile historic footage of interviews with people between 1961 and 1989 about the Wall. He divided them into topics such as "dreams," "escapes," and "life with the Wall." Together, the brothers tried to evoke a sense of what life had been like with the Wall.[150]

In addition to the public festivities along the *Lichtgrenze* over three days, there were also invite-only commemorations on November 9, 2014, at the Berlin Wall Memorial and later in the day at the Konzerthaus, both broadcast live nationally and by *Deutsche Welle* internationally. At Bernauer Strasse, Chancellor Merkel and other leaders attended a service in the Chapel of Reconciliation, laid wreaths at the monument to victims of the Wall, and opened a vastly expanded permanent exhibit at the Documentation Center.

Manfred Fischer had retired in early 2013 at the age of sixty-five, after serving as pastor to the Reconciliation community for thirty-eight years and

[148] Kulturprojekte Berlin, press release and press kit, July 10, 2014.
[149] Interviews with Christopher Bauder, July 23, 2014, and Marc Bauder, July 25, 2014.
[150] Press conference with Mayor Wowereit and Christopher and Marc Bauder at Radialsystem, Berlin, September 8, 2014.

creating, fighting for, and shepherding the Berlin Wall Memorial Site at Bernauer Strasse for more than twenty-three of those years. He was succeeded by Thomas Jeutner. Unlike Fischer, Jeutner had grown up in the GDR just outside of Berlin in Potsdam and then in a town further west near the border with West Germany. Hence, he had many personal experiences with the former border, including the Berlin Wall that was just down the street from his student living quarters in East Berlin where he studied theology, joined the civil rights movement, and wrote for the church newspaper. From his student quarters Jeutner could even see the tower of the Church of Reconciliation in the border strip.

On November 9, 1989, he and his wife were taking a walk near the Wall when they heard Günter Schabowski's press conference on someone's car radio. The following day, Jeutner and his very pregnant wife went to West Berlin for the first time, as fate would have it passing through a small hole in the Wall at Oderberger Strasse to Bernauer Strasse. Hence, his first steps in the West were on Bernauer Strasse. Jeutner and his wife walked to the border crossing at Invalidenstrasse, made their way to the KuDamm in West Berlin and then back across the fully visible layers of the death strip to East Berlin. Similar to the story told of Robert and Petra in the introduction to this book, Jeutner was very careful all day to shield his pregnant wife in the midst of the crowds. He would never forget either the glorious fall of the Wall or the deadly border it had been. Inspired by his work in those exciting times as a journalist for the church, Jeutner continued to work in media communications at churches in Greifswald and in Hamburg before succeeding Fischer as pastor at the Chapel of Reconciliation in 2013.[151]

To the shock of Jeutner, the congregation, and everyone who knew Manfred Fischer, the long-time pastor of the Reconciliation parish and memory activist died of a heart attack in December 2013, just months after his retirement. It had already been a significant adjustment for people at the Berlin Wall Memorial not to have the ever-active, creative Fischer in his old position anymore, but to lose him completely was a massive blow. The twenty-fifth anniversary of the fall of the Wall was the first major date connected to the Wall without Fischer there, and his absence was noted by everyone there that day.

The morning at the Berlin Wall Memorial began outside in the former death strip where Chancellor Merkel, Mayor Wowereit, and former Hungarian prime minister Nemeth placed roses between gaps in the original rear Wall (*Hinterlandmauer*) in memory of those killed at the border. Following a service in the Chapel of Reconciliation, a ceremony at the Berlin Wall Memorial

---

[151] Interview with Thomas Jeutner, November 5, 2018; transcript of interview with Jeutner conducted for the Berlin Wall Foundation by Lydia Dollmann, February 25, 2016; interviews with Jeutner aired in "28 Jahren vor der Mauer, mit der Mauer, nach der Mauer," rbb film, September 17, 2018; and Dirk Jericho, "Thomas Jeutner ist seit 2013 Pfarrer der Versöhnungsgemeinde," *Berliner Woche*, October 13, 2014.

visitors' center marked the completion of the final outdoor exhibit area of the expansion project at the Berlin Wall Memorial and the opening of the new indoor exhibit, "1961/1989: The Berlin Wall," replacing the old one focusing on 1961.[152] These were the final steps in implementing the *Gesamtkonzept* for remembering the Berlin Wall at Bernauer Strasse.[153] Between the Chapel of Reconciliation and the visitors' center, the chancellor and other guests walked along the stretch of Wall Fischer had fought so hard to preserve and that had been the beginning of the now vastly augmented historical site.

From Bernauer Strasse, Merkel and others made their way to the state ceremony hosted by the mayor at the Konzerthaus located on the historic Gendarmenmarkt. The ceremony featured two former civic activists from the opposition movement in Leipzig, Kathrin Mahler Walther and Stefan Müller, and a short film by Ansgar Hocke, "*Mauern sind nicht für ewig gebaut*" ("Walls are not built forever"). The film depicted the desire for freedom of the protest movements in Eastern and Central Europe in 1989 and how these inspired GDR citizens to go onto the streets calling for change and helping bring down the Wall.

Addresses by Mayor Wowereit and President of the European Parliament Martin Schulz emphasized not just what had happened in East Germany in 1989 but the European context of the revolutions of 1989.[154] Gorbachev was present for the ceremony and received a lengthy standing ovation when he arrived and again when the mayor thanked him for joining them. Walesa too was in attendance and given applause, although not as much as the former Soviet leader. Perhaps in recognition of criticism that it was not just the people who demanded change, but the East German authorities who acquiesced to and began to implement change, Wowereit also thanked "the people in positions of political responsibility who by their good sense and diplomatic skill contributed to a peaceful denouement" of the events in 1989–90.[155] This was a significant change from 2009.

---

[152] Axel Klausmeier, ed., *The Berlin Wall: Berlin Wall Memorial Exhibition Catalog*, trans. Miriamne Fields (Berlin: Ch. Links, 2015).

[153] The only part of the *Gesamtkonzept* still not completed is the creation of a Cold War Museum at Checkpoint Charlie on the site where the one-room Black Box Cold War exhibit stands. Investors have come and gone, and the city of Berlin remains unwilling to buy the expensive land. Rainer Klemke has retired from the cultural office of the Berlin government and as a private individual leads the efforts to create the museum. Andreas Austilat, "Klemkes Kampf um das Museum am Checkpoint Charlie," *Tagesspiegel*, August 24, 2018.

[154] The Mayor's foreword in the program book "remembered gratefully the courage of the men and woman in the GDR who rose up against the SED regime and went onto the streets," the victims of the Wall and the division, and also "the accomplishments of the movements for liberty in Central and Eastern Europe which prepared the ground for the change." Der Regierende Bürgermeister von Berlin, "Festakt des Landes Berlin anlässlich des 25. Jahrestages des Mauerfalls," Konzerthaus am Gendarmenmarkt, Berlin, November 9, 2014, program booklet.

[155] Ibid.

Figure 29 *Lichtgrenze* balloons, East Side Gallery, November 9, 2014
Source: Hope M. Harrison.

A scene from Beethoven's opera *Fidelio* closed the ceremony, performed by musicians from seven orchestras and choirs from eastern and western Berlin. Hungarian conductor Ivan Fischer told the audience that Beethoven's opera was a "fitting way to remember 1989," since it was "about liberation and unification" as represented by Leonore disguised as Fidelio successfully freeing her wrongfully imprisoned husband, Florestan, thus reuniting the pair.[156] Musicians performed as a flash mob the closing scene where Florestan is freed and he and Leonore embrace, "Oh God, what a moment!" As the orchestra played on stage, members of the choir popped up from seats throughout the hall and came in through various doors on both levels of the concert hall. The audience was surrounded by the glorious sound of Beethoven's opera.

Beethoven's music was played again a few hours later when Merkel hosted a party at the Brandenburg Gate for the release of the 8,000 balloons along the *Lichtgrenze*. As Merkel, Gauck, Wowereit, Walesa, Gorbachev, and Nemeth

---

[156] Program notes to Fidelio, ibid. For more on the twenty-fifth anniversary, see Hope M. Harrison, "Reflections from the Berlin Wall: Twenty-Five Year Later," blog for the International Spy Museum, Washington, DC., November 6-9, 2014, blog.spymuseum.org/reflections-from-the-berlin-wall-25-years-later/.

released their balloons to begin the dissolution of the seven-mile illuminated border in the center of the city, Daniel Barenboim conducted the Berlin *Staatskapelle* orchestra playing Beethoven's "Ode to Joy." Over the next few minutes, all of the balloon sponsors unlocked their balloons and they floated up into the night sky. The border was gone. Again.

In the following days, balloons and their messages landed all over Berlin and the surrounding area and as far away as Latvia and Poland. One of them landed six miles away in the backyard of Fischer's house where his widow found it. The message from an American student on the balloon said, "The fall of the Wall was one of the most significant events in modern history." Fischer's widow welcomed it as a sign from her husband.[157]

Lessons and a New Historical Narrative of the Wall and Founding Myth of the German Nation

After years of united Germany's *Erinnerungspolitik* focusing first on the Holocaust and World War II and later on victims of the Berlin Wall, the twentieth and twenty-fifth anniversaries of the fall of the Wall marked a decisive change in this approach by putting the "happy history" of November 9, 1989 front and center. Beginning in 2009 and continuing through 2014, German leaders used the memory of 1989 to create a new narrative or founding myth for united Germany: the nation was born from a peaceful, democratic revolution that toppled the Wall and then pushed for unification.[158] Aleida Assmann has posited that "since the 1990s, memory of the Holocaust has been anchored as the negative founding myth of reunited [Germany]."[159] The present work argues that this has been joined since 2009 by a positive founding myth, that of the Peaceful Revolution and the fall of the Wall.

The first unification of Germany in 1871 had been brought about "by blood and iron," following wars against Austria, Denmark, and France, creating the German Empire under Kaiser Wilhelm I and Otto von Bismarck. Following the Nazi defeat in World War II, the Four Powers effectively divided Germany into East and West, making Germany pay for the destruction of the Nazi regime and World War II. In 1989–90, however, the Germans via the East

---

[157] Email correspondence with Rudolf Prast, Berlin Wall Memorial Association, November 12, 2014. For a map of locations where balloons were found, see, fallofthewall25.com/ballon-gefunden.

[158] Former East German civic activists had long felt that, in the words of Tobias Hollitzer, the German "democratic tradition had been crowned by the successful and also peaceful revolution" which "is one of the most important spiritual-moral [*geistig-moralisch*] foundations of reunited Germany." Hollitzer, "15 Jahre Friedliche Revolution," *Aus Politik und Zeitgeschichte*, September 29, 2004.

[159] Aleida Assmann, *Das neue Unbehagen an der Erinnerungskultur* (Munich: C.H. Beck, 2013), p. 67.

German Peaceful Revolution and then with the support of those same Four Powers brought about the democratic, peaceful unification of their country. Democratic Germany's cooperation with its European neighbors then brought about the further integration of united Germany into Europe as well as the expansion of the European Union to Germany's east. Looking back on all of this in 2009 and seeing it through the eyes of so many people throughout the world who remained inspired by the fall of the Wall, the German leaders found the Peaceful Revolution was a unique, transformative moment in German history.

All nations look for key events in their past to hold up as defining moments in molding their collective national identity. In 2000 when Merkel became the chair of the CDU, she asserted, "If Germany can find its identity and stand by it, that would be good for democracy.... We must develop a sense of our history as a whole and then say, we are glad to be German."[160] In 2009, she and other leaders seemed to feel they had accomplished this. Any lingering hesitation among German public officials about whether to highlight the history of the Wall or not disappeared with the twentieth anniversary celebrations. The combination of the passage of time, the work of various memory activists in Germany, the positive view of the fall of the Wall compared to much darker moments in German history, and the worldwide resonance of the fall of the Wall all acted together to turn the tide and create large, high-profile celebrations on November 9, 2009 and 2014.

With the heavy weight of the Holocaust still exerting a shadow over the Germans and with the added weight of the forty years of communist rule in the East, Germans developed a new-found pride in their recounting of the Peaceful Revolution of 1989 twenty years later. After largely ignoring the leaders and followers of the East German opposition in 1989 for many years afterwards, German public officials now celebrated them as courageous German heroes who created the Peaceful Revolution.[161] In opening Sello's exhibit in 2009, Frank Walter Steinmeier had declared, "We need a common memory not for its own sake but a memory from which we can draw

---

[160] Kornelius, *Angela Merkel*, p. 90.

[161] The lack of a permanent home for the 2009–10 outdoor exhibit on the Peaceful Revolution initially did not quite match this commitment. Stefan Strauss, "Drei Etagen Widerstand," *Berliner Zeitung*, November 21, 2013. The federal government took a significant step, however, toward changing this, with the CDU-SPD Coalition Treaty of November 27, 2013. In the treaty, the parties pledged "to permanently secure" the outdoor exhibit and the Robert Havemann Society's Archive of the GDR Opposition. "Deutschlands Zukunft gestalten. Koalitionsvertrag zwischen CDU, CDU und SPD. 18. Legislaturperiode," p. 130, www.cdu.de/sites/default/files/media/dokumente/koalitions vertrag.pdf. The exhibit, "Revolution und Mauerfall," moved to a permanent home in the courtyard of the former Stasi headquarters on Normannenstrasse in Berlin-Lichtenberg in June 2016, revolution89.de.

direction."[162] By recasting the toppling of the Berlin Wall into a fundamental moment in all-German history, German leaders also hoped to foster a deeper sense of unity. They believed that recognizing the importance of what East Germans had done would make the latter feel more respected in united Germany and would inspire all Germans about their country's past and about the possibilities for the future.

On the anniversaries in 2009 and 2014, officials repeatedly spoke of lessons from the Peaceful Revolution and the fall of the Wall.[163] After all, drawing lessons from the history of the Wall was one of the key motivations voiced by politicians and historians in the 2004–6 discussions leading up to the creation of the *Gesamtkonzept*. German grappling with the history of the Holocaust has also emphasized drawing lessons from the past and created the model for doing this. The lessons emphasized in 2009 have been reiterated in political speeches on Wall anniversaries on August 13 and November 9 ever since.

These lessons fall into a variety of categories. First, and reminiscent of discussions about the *Gesamtkonzept*, German leaders emphasized the importance of teaching young Germans about the history of the Wall. This focus on the next generation learning about the history of the Berlin Wall was apparent with Kulturprojekte Berlin's outreach to over 500 school classes and almost 10,000 students to create the *Dominosteine* in 2009 and to schools and others in 2014 to sponsor balloons.[164] Politicians and many others felt it was essential that young Germans understand that not long ago, Germany and Berlin were divided by a deadly border. The director of the Berlin Wall Foundation, Axel Klausmeier, has observed that after honoring the victims, his second most important task is conveying the history of the Wall to the next generation, noting that 60–65 percent of the visitors to the memorial are younger than twenty-five.[165] The opening of a new visitors' center at the Memorial in 2009 provided more space for educational activities, and the expansion of the outdoor and indoor exhibits in 2014 added to what people could learn at the site. In 2006, Berlin's *Gesamtkonzept* for remembering the Berlin Wall highlighted the educational opportunities inherent in presenting the history of the Berlin

---

[162] "Rede des Bundesaussenministers und Vizekanzlers Frank-Walter Steinmeier zur Eröffnung der Ausstellung 'Friedliche Revolution 1989/90' am 7. Mai 2009 auf dem Berliner Alexanderplatz."

[163] Other countries in Central and Eastern Europe also used the twentieth anniversary to focus on the lessons of 1989. Susan C. Pearce, "1989 as Collective Memory 'Refolution'," in Lindsey A. Freedman, Benjamin Nienass, and Rachel Daniell, eds., *Silence, Screen and Spectacle: Rethinking Collective Memory in the Age of Information and New Media* (New York: Berghahn Books, 2014), pp. 213–37.

[164] Mortiz van Dülmen, "Vorwort," in Kuturprojekte Berlin, ed., *Dominobuch*, p. 13. See also p. 27.

[165] "Ein unbequemes Denkmal mitten in der Stadt. Interview mit Prof. Dr. Axel Klausmeier, Direktor der Stiftung Berliner Mauer," *Deutschland Archiv*, August 9, 2013.

Wall.[166] The Federal Memorial Plan (*Gedenkstättenkonzeption*) of 2008 made a similar commitment.[167]

Second, and closely related to the first, in the dominant narrative the existence of the Wall and of the SED regime – as with the far worse Nazi regime before it – showed the difference between democracy and freedom, on the one hand, and dictatorship, on the other. This is why it was essential for young people to learn about this history. Leaders argued that understanding the history of the Wall served as a charge for action in the present. In the words of Mayor Wowereit: "It is our common responsibility to keep the memory alive and pass it on to the next generation, to cultivate freedom and democracy and to do everything so that such injustice never occurs again."[168] *"Nie wieder"* ("Never again"), a proclamation long applied to learning from the Holocaust is now also applied to the Wall and the SED regime. Foreign Minister Westerwelle asserted in 2011 that the "lesson of the Wall for us as convinced democrats is to fight against political extremism having a place in Germany."[169] To ensure the present and future would not repeat the past, "Freedom and democracy must be defended anew every day.... .Freedom is not to be taken for granted."[170] This is something that older Germans are particularly fervent about and nearly every German speaker at the anniversary events emphasized this.

Accordingly, just as East German activists learned how powerful they could be when they acted together to change things and overcome a repressive regime and its Wall, so united Germany's leaders asserted that citizens must remain actively engaged in defending democracy in their country. Werner Schulz declared in Leipzig on October 9, 2009: "Our future is also decided by our dealing with the past.... .[T]he generation that came after the fall of the Wall...should also learn how to overcome fear and learn civic courage" and should learn the importance of "being engaged for freedom from violence, for peace, democracy, social justice, and cultural diversity."[171] Leipzig's Mayor Jung emphasized: "Historical memory gives us a charge for our behavior in the present and future." German leaders used the history of the Berlin Wall to appeal to all Germans to get involved in governing the country instead of just being passive bystanders. Indeed, Joachim Gauck would go on to write a book,

[166] Thomas Flierl, ed., "Gesamtkonzept zur Erinnerung an die Berliner Mauer: Dokumentation, Information und Gedenken," June 12, 2006, p. 35.

[167] Unterrichtung durch den Beauftragten der Bundesregierung für Kultur und Medien, "Fortschreibung der Gedenkstättenkonzeption des Bundes. Verantwortung wahrnehmen, Aufarbeitung verstärken, Gedenken vertiefen," Deutscher Bundestag, Drucksache 16/9875, June 19, 2008.

[168] Mayor Wowereit, speech at the Berlin Wall Memorial, August 13, 2011.

[169] Guido Westerwelle, speech, January 11, 2011, www.auswaertiges-amt.de/DE/Infoservice/Presse/Reden/2011/110111-BM_Mauerausstellung.html.

[170] Mayor Klaus Wowereit, speech at Berlin Wall Memorial, August 13, 2012.

[171] Werner Schulz, "Was lange gärt wird Mut," Festakt "20 Jahre Friedliche Revolution," Gewandhaus Leipzig, October 9, 2009.

Freiheit. Ein Plädoyer (*Freedom: A Plea*) about the ways freedom brings responsibility to be civically engaged.[172]

The third lesson drawn by policymakers and others from the fall of the Wall was that "walls can fall" in general and that, therefore, there is hope for others to fall as well. "What seemed impossible can become possible." German leaders then took this a step further in maintaining that their experience of the fall of the Berlin Wall gave them a responsibility to help bring down other real and metaphorical walls in the world. In opening the *Fest der Freiheit* in 2009, Mayor Wowereit exhorted: "Let's tear down the walls that are still standing!"[173] At the Brandenburg Gate on November 9, he called on world leaders to work together to tackle poverty and climate change and to rid the world of nuclear weapons.[174] In a similar spirit, Chancellor Merkel declared that the good luck of the Germans and Europeans "obligates us to solve the problems of our times," including the securing of peace, liberty, prosperity, and justice and protecting the environment and human rights all over the world.[175]

Finally, the fourth lesson leaders drew was connected to German identity, anchored anew as a nation formed from a democratic Peaceful Revolution. Leipzig's Mayor Jung observed in 2009 that German history "has given us Germans little occasion for democratic celebrations. . .[F]or a long time, democracy in Germany was not capable of achieving a majority and was even scorned. Exactly because of this, we have every reason to celebrate. . .the first non-violent and successful revolution in German history." This historical lesson was one of Germans as good and peaceful democrats.[176]

In Merkel's third term as chancellor beginning in 2013, the increased attention given to the importance of the Peaceful Revolution and the fall of the Berlin Wall for German historical identity was reflected in the coalition treaty between the CDU, CSU, and SPD. The treaty noted that German "consciousness of freedom, justice and democracy is marked by the memory of the Nazi reign of terror, Stalinism and the SED dictatorship, but also by positive experiences of democracy in German history."[177] The latter part of

---

[172] Joachim Gauck, *Freiheit. Ein Plädoyer* (Munich: Kösel Verlag, 2012).

[173] Author's notes at Mayor Wowereit's opening ceremony, November 7, 2009; and Jens Anker and Birgit Haas, "Die Welt feiert Deutschlands Einheit in Berlin," *Berliner Morgenpost*, November 7, 2009. Note that the title of the newspaper article is "The world celebrates Germany's unification in Berlin," not "the fall of the Wall."

[174] Der Regierende Bürgermeister, Senatskanzlei, "Rede des Regierenden Bürgermeisters Klaus Wowereit zum Fest der Freiheit," Pressemitteilung, November 9, 2009.

[175] Rede von Bundeskanzlerin Dr. Angela Merkel im Rahmen des "Fests der Freiheit" am 9. November 2009 in Berlin, November 9, 2009.

[176] Burkhard Jung, "Rede des Oberbürgermeisters der Stadt Leipzig," Festakt, "20 Jahre Friedliche Revolution," Gewandhaus Leipzig, October 9, 2009.

[177] "Deutschlands Zukunft gestalten. Koalitionsvertrag zwischen CDU, CDU und SPD. 18. Legislaturperiode," November 27, 2013, p. 91, www.cdu.de/sites/default/files/media/dokumente/koalitionsvertrag.pdf.

this statement about "positive experiences" appeared for the first time in such a government document and clearly came from the change of view about German history that took hold on the twentieth anniversary of the fall of the Wall. To emphasize this change, the chancellor herself spoke to a high school history class about the Berlin Wall and the Peaceful Revolution so as to "strengthen the students' understanding of traditions of freedom and democracy in German history."[178]

The new narrative of 2009 emphasized that Germany was not just a nation of Nazi and then communist perpetrators and victims; it was also a nation of heroes who demanded freedom and democracy and peacefully brought down the Berlin Wall and the East German *Unrechtsstaat* along the way to German unification. Germans could hold their heads high, knowing that they were part of a community of nations with democratic revolutions as their founding moment.

---

[178] Florentine Anders, "Kanzlerin Angela Merkel gibt Unterricht an Berliner Schule," *Berliner Morgenpost*, August 13, 2013. The quote is from her spokesman, Georg Streiter.

∼

Conclusion: Memory as Warning

After years of putting the memory of the Wall aside, followed by a period of focusing on the victims of the Wall and finally on proud celebration of the brave and peaceful East German people who pushed open the Wall, the official narrative as well as its contemporary relevance changed again in the wake of the 2015 refugee crisis in Germany and the resulting rise of right-wing, sometimes violent, extremism in Germany. The lessons of the Wall that politicians had repeated every year at commemorative rituals on August 13 and November 9 about the importance of standing up for democracy, freedom, and civil rights, lessons that had come to feel rote and formulistic, suddenly became urgent and tinged with panic. Now politicians used memory of the Wall as a warning, a plea for holding fast to democratic principles and behavior. The fact that as of February 2018 the Wall had been gone for longer than it had stood for twenty-eight years did not make its history any less important or relevant.

The Refugee Crisis

In the summer of 2015, waves of refugees fleeing wars and violent conflict in Syria, Iraq, Afghanistan, and elsewhere crossed by land or the Mediterranean Sea north into Europe, with hundreds of thousands entering Germany in the first eight months. Faced with Hungary's plans to close its borders by building a fence against the influx,[1] a very different Hungary than the one that had opened its borders in 1989, Chancellor Merkel announced on August 31 that she would accept the refugees: "Germany is a strong country.... .We have achieved so much. We can handle it." ("*Wir schaffen das.*")[2] In early September, she went to a refugee reception center in Berlin where she met

---

[1] Robert Samuels and William Booth, "Hungary Begins Mass Arrests," *Washington Post*, September 15, 2015. See also www.bbc.com/news/world-europe-34131911.
[2] Die Bundesregierung, "Sommerpressekonferenz von Angela Merkel im Wortlaut," August 31, 2015; Tina Hildebrandt and Bernd Ulrich, "Angela Merkel: Im Auge des Orkans," *Zeit*, September 20, 2015; Björn Hengst and Sandra Sperber, "Flüchtlinger am Münchner Hauptbahnhof: Start in ein neues Leben," *Spiegel*, September 6, 2015; and Heather Horn, "The Staggering Scale of Germany's Refugee Project," *The Atlantic*, September 12, 2015.

with refugees and even allowed them to take selfies with her, pictures that went around the world and led to even more refugees flooding into Germany.[3]

Merkel passionately defended her open-border policy against criticism: "If we have to start excusing ourselves for showing a friendly face in emergency conditions, then this is not my country. . . .I will say it again and again, we can handle it, and we will handle it."[4] Merkel believed that welcoming the refugees and not erecting walls against them was the right thing to do and that Germany could afford to do it both economically and politically. Indeed, she was following through on the confident 2009 impulse to help others facing walls of their own. Remembering the brutality of the Berlin Wall and then the wonder of its peaceful fall, the chancellor and many others viewed the notion of building new walls in Europe (or indeed leaving Europe, as voters in the United Kingdom supported with the Brexit vote in 2016) in response to the refugee crisis with great sadness and shock.[5]

In 2016, Wolfgang Schäuble, Germany's finance minister at the time, justified Merkel's policy on refugees, arguing that Germans were fueled by "a moral imperative not to make refugees pay the price for Europe's inability to take effective action" to help them. Although he rejected a reporter's question about whether Germany's approach to the refugee crisis was motivated by a desire to compensate for guilt about the Nazi past, Schäuble also declared: "I do admit on the other hand that the Germans have this need now and then to realize that we too can be good people, as when we welcomed the world as our guests in the 2006 World Cup. In September [2015], when we gave refugees a warm welcome. . ., this may be connected in some way with the fact that the German people, we do not really like ourselves too much, and understandably so."[6] This was an extraordinary statement by a senior politician who went on to become the president of the German Bundestag in 2017.

The impact of the weight of history on the German sense of national identity to which Schäuble alluded seemed to have been lifted in an important way with the festivities surrounding the twentieth and twenty-fifth anniversaries of the fall of the Wall in 2009 and 2014. Fortified in the newly-found belief that the new united Germany had been born from Germany's first successful democratic revolution, which also brought down the Berlin Wall,

---

[3] Thomas Kröter, "Angela Merkel besucht Flüchtlinge: Selfies mit der Kanzlerin," *Berliner Zeitung*, September 10, 2015.

[4] Hans Monath, "Angela Merkel rechtfertig Flüchtlingspolitik: 'Dann ist das nicht mein Land'," *Tagesspiegel*, September 15, 2015.

[5] On the creation of new walls and fences in Europe, see Jon Stone, "The EU Has Built 1,000km of Border Walls since Fall of Berlin Wall," *Independent*, November 9, 2018; and Kim Hjelmgaard, "Trump Isn't the Only One Who Wants to Build a Wall. These European Nations Already Did," *USA Today*, May 24, 2018.

[6] Patrick Wintour, "Germany's Refugee Response Not Guilt-Driven, Says Wolfgang Schäuble," *Guardian*, March 3, 2016.

German political leaders seemed to hold their heads higher, feeling that their history was not solely defined by violence and moments of shame. As Bundestag MP Eckart von Klaeden had observed years earlier, the East German Peaceful Revolution "freed our nation from the stigma of never having won our own liberty."[7] Germany was not just a country of perpetrators and victims; it also had heroes. In addition to the "memory of the Holocaust as united Germany's negative founding myth,"[8] Germans now had a positive founding myth, something to be proud of, to openly celebrate, and not shy away from.

During the refugee crisis of 2015–16 and since then, however, the jubilant celebrations in Berlin for the twentieth and twenty-fifth anniversaries of the fall of the Wall seem like distant memories, and the actual fall of the Wall in 1989 even more so. One particular moment of the ceremony at the Brandenburg Gate on November 9, 2009 has turned out to be far more relevant than the Germans could have imagined at the time. As the Wall dominoes toppled over and the crowds cheered, one final *Dominostein* was left standing to represent all the walls in the world still to fall. The organizers had in mind both literal examples such as the divide between North and South Korea and less tangible examples such as walls between rich and poor in the world. They certainly did not anticipate that the open borders of Europe would start to close in a matter of years and that xenophobic groups in their own country, led by the *Alternative für Deutschland* (AfD) and the even more xenophobic, nationalistic PEGIDA (Patriotic Europeans against the Islamization of the West), would lash out against refugees in need of safe haven and against the politicians who supported them.

Between 2015 and 2016, more than one million refugees entered Germany, overwhelming the system and leading ultimately to a backlash of right-wing, anti-Muslim, xenophobic nationalism as well as increasing criticism of the chancellor herself.[9] Even while majorities of Germans supported Merkel's policy initially and volunteered in all sorts of ways to help the refugees with medical care, housing, clothing, and German language tutoring, the AfD took advantage of voters' fears about the influx and moved further to the right, leading it to become the country's third most popular party in September 2017's federal elections. With 12.6 percent of the vote, the AfD entered the

---

[7] Eckart von Klaeden, Deutscher Bundestag, Plenarprotokoll 14/199, November 9, 2001, p. 19511.

[8] Aleida Assmann, *Das neue Unbehagen an der Erinnerungskultur* (Munich: C. H. Beck, 2013), p. 67.

[9] Cynthia Kroet, "Germany: 1.1 Million Refugee Arrivals in 2015," *Politico*, January 6, 2016. On the refugees in Germany, see also "Zahlen zu Asyl in Deutschland," *Bundeszentrale für politische Bildung*, October 1, 2018; Bundesamt für Migration und Flüchtlinge, *Das Bundesamt in Zahlen 2016* (2017); and "10,6 Millionen Ausländer in Deutschland," *Tagesschau.de*, April 12, 2018.

Bundestag for the first time. The party was particularly popular in the former east where nearly 22 percent of the voters supported it, although people all over the western part of the country (where in fact the party was founded in 2013 by Euroskeptics who did not want to bail out Greece or anyone else in the eurozone crisis) also cast their ballots in favor of the AfD. In the party's strongest base in the eastern state of Saxony, it garnered 27 percent of the votes. Saxony was also the home of PEGIDA, which held right-wing Monday night demonstrations in Dresden, a dark historical twist on the East German Monday night peace prayers and demonstrations for democratic change in Leipzig.

National polls in the fall of 2018 put the AfD second only to the CDU and ahead of the SPD.[10] The AfD's success in the 2018 polls was likely fueled by the killings of two Germans by immigrants in Chemnitz and in Köthen, both in the east. In August, two immigrants from Syria and Iraq killed a German man in Chemnitz, Saxony, and in September two Afghan immigrants killed a German man in Köthen, Brandenburg. In the wake of the killings, there were right-wing, often violent protests involving thousands marching through the streets of Chemnitz and elsewhere, many making the Nazi salute. Large counter-protests were also held.[11] This all made headlines throughout the country and put most politicians, to say nothing of the police, on edge. The political establishment seemed to be in shock and to feel let down by their own people. Leaders had reveled between 2009 and 2014 in the feeling of pride that democratic, peaceful German citizens had brought down the Wall and helped unite Germany. They believed and hoped that Germany was beyond the ghosts of the past, that Germans were finished with doing bad things and having angry, violent mobs on the streets and with representation in parliament. Since 2015, however, they are faced with old worries again: *Are ugly, xenophobic, racist attitudes gaining traction? Is this really our country?* The majority of German politicians became profoundly concerned that citizens of the country that perpetrated the Holocaust and built and manned the Berlin Wall had not learned more from German history. There was also a chance that the heroic, proud narrative created in 2009 could be used in a more aggressive way by nationalists in the AfD.

---

[10] Dietmar Neuerer and Michael Stahl, "AfD steigt im ARD-Deutschlandtrend erstmals zum zweitstärksten Partei auf," *Handelsblatt*, September 21, 2018. See also www.wahl recht.de/umfragen/; and https://dawum.de/AfD/. By 2019, polls showed the AfD in third place behind the CDU and the Greens but ahead of the SPD. http://www.wahlrecht.de/ umfragen/forsa.htm. On the rise of the AfD, see also Philipp Adorf, "A New Blue Collar Force: The Alternative for Germany and the Working Class," *German Politics and Society* 36, No. 4 (Winter 2018), pp. 29–49.

[11] Johannes Grunert, "Der Abend an dem die Rechtsstaat aufgab," *Zeit*, August 28, 2018; Helena Ott, "Rechte Gewalt: 'Das ist wie eine Welle'," *Süddeutsche Zeitung*, September 20, 2018; and "Friedliche Demonstrationen in Köthen – doch anderswo kommt es zu Gewalt," *Focus*, September 16, 2018.

The intensive work of *Erinnerungspolitik* and *politische Bildung* that German leaders supported for decades suddenly appeared to have failed (at least among a significant portion of the population) in creating the kind of democratic, tolerant German citizens they had hoped for. With the thirtieth anniversary of the fall of the Berlin Wall approaching, and with a sense that "historically important anniversaries . . . offer the chance to make visible the . . . national self-image of Germans," political leaders seemed to be afraid of some of their own citizens and colleagues and began pleading with them to remember and not repeat the past. The federal government also increased funding for *politische Bildung*, with more than one million euros in 2017 being devoted to memorial sites connected to learning about and from German history in Berlin, such as the Berlin Wall Memorial. The director of the Berlin Wall Foundation, Axel Klausmeier, argued that the rise of right-wing extremism made the foundation's mission of fostering commitment to freedom and democracy even more imperative. In the fall of 2018, he asserted that "contending with the sharpening political discourse and a crumbling grasp of democracy must be at the center of educational work on *Erinnerungspolitik*." In his view, the thirtieth anniversary of the fall of the Wall in 2019 offered "a tremendous opportunity to identify again in detail the values of 1989, democracy and freedom, in contrast to those forces which reject a cosmopolitan, diverse society."[12]

Klausmeier has had direct experience with these forces, since the Marienfelde Refugee Camp memorial and museum he also oversees in Berlin has been increasingly a target of right-wing ire. The site includes temporary housing for recent refugees, and in 2017 the museum opened a special exhibit about contemporary refugees, called, "After escape: how we want to live" (*"Nach der Flucht. Wie wir Leben wollen"*). While the permanent exhibit there focuses on the East Germans who came to the West Berlin refugee camp after fleeing the GDR, the more recent additional exhibit includes interviews with Syrian, Afghan, Iraqi, and Chechen refugees about why and how they fled their countries as well as their experiences since arriving in Germany and what they hope for in Germany.

Groups supporting the AfD have become such a regular, aggressive presence at the museum that tour guides employed there receive special training about how to respond to "provocative questions" by people visiting the site who have "populist, racist" views. Right-wing visitors insist that they want to see *German* history at the site, *not* the history of non-Germans, and they make it clear that they are not happy that Muslims are housed there.[13]

---

[12] Deutscher Bundestag, ed., "Schlußbericht" Enquete-Kommission "Überwindung der Folgen der SED-Diktatur in Prozess der deutschen Einheit," *Materialien der Enquete-Kommission "Überwindung der Folgen der SED-Diktatur in Prozess der deutschen Einheit,"* Band I (Baden-Baden: Nomos Verlag, 1999), p. 626. The quotes from Klausmeier are from "Klausmeier: Populismus stellt Gedenkstätten vor neue Aufgaben," *chrismon, das evangelische Magazin*, October 3, 2018.

[13] Ibid.; author's interview with Maria Nooke, June 20, 2017; and correspondence with Axel Klausmeier, October 6, 2018.

Other Germans, however, hold very different views about the recent refugees. For example, some people who fled East Germany for West Germany, including those whose first stop was the refugee camp at Marienfelde, have viewed it as their duty to help the new immigrants. In September 2015, in honor of the twenty-fifth anniversary of German unification, *Die Zeit* published interviews with twenty-five former East German refugees about why they were helping the new refugees. The series was entitled, "Because we know what it was like" ("*Weil wir wissen, wie es war*").[14] As former East Germans who risked their lives to escape across the border, they expressed their empathy with and sympathy for the recent refugees who had to make heart-wrenching decisions to leave their homes and then endured an anxious, risky journey with uncertain outcome – experiences the former East German refugees knew all too well. They also felt that as hard as it was for them to adjust to their new lives in West Germany, having left so much behind, it was far harder due to cultural and language differences for the recent refugees to make this adjustment. Thus, these refugees needed and deserved even more help.

Just as most of the recent refugees are young men, so were most of the people who escaped from the GDR. As Michael Schwerk, one of the former East German refugees put it, "When I see [these] young men today. . ., I see myself."[15] The former refugees also remembered how much it meant to them when at the end of their grueling journey, they received help in West Germany. They decided to help the new refugees. In the words of one of the former refugees from the GDR, Christian Bürger, "We Germans are a nation of immigrants. My parents fled from Silesia to Saxony. I fled from Prague via Saxony to Bavaria. Who knows what would have happened to me or my parents if no one had taken us in."[16] Members of the AfD would no doubt respond: *Yes, but you are German; the current refugees are not German nor are they Christian. They do not belong here.*

One of the former East German refugees featured in *Die Zeit*, Hartmut Richter, was imprisoned for five years in the GDR for helping people escape and decided to speak out in favor of helping current refugees. He explained that he tells his "story [about his experiences in the GDR] so that Germans will understand why people flee from unjust regimes today."[17] The message about the difference between freedom and the lack thereof that policymakers, experts, and officials at the Berlin Wall Memorial have long emphasized as the essence of understanding the Wall, is precisely what, in Richter's view, connects the experience of East German refugees with the contemporary refugees. As Klaus

---

[14] Anna Hänig, Julius Lukas, and Martin Machowecz, "Flüchlingen: 'Weil wir wissen wie es war'," *Zeit*, September 10, 2015.
[15] Michael Schwerk, ibid.
[16] Christian Bürger, ibid.
[17] Hartmut Richter and Christian Bürger, ibid.

Wowereit's successor as mayor, Michael Müller, also of the SPD, observed in 2018, "There are always more people who are ready to pay with their lives for freedom."[18] In his sermon on the twentieth anniversary of the fall of the Wall in 2009, Catholic Archbishop Robert Zollitsch had insisted that such people must be helped, warning: "There are potential wall builders everywhere, also today. . . . It is our duty now to help others who live in tyranny."[19]

In the context of increasing instances of hostility to refugees as well as political pressure to tighten up regulations regarding refugees, Mayor Müller used the anniversary of the erection of the Berlin Wall in August 2018 to insist in deep emotional tones: "Our answers to the experience [with the Wall] are openness, tolerance and readiness to help, also and precisely for people in need. These are our lessons from our past and thus we must reject new wall projects like the intention to create fortress Europe. We have experienced it: it doesn't work. We must find other, better, humane solutions."[20] A group of protestors in Berlin's neighboring city of Potsdam, the capital of Brandenburg, agreed. With slogans like, "No one flees for no reason," and "Rescuing people at sea is not a crime," they gathered outside Potsdam's "Office for Foreigners," demanding that the authorities stop sending refugees back home. The demonstrators maintained that, "Commemorating those people killed at the Wall and on the inner-German border must also be a warning about the current approach to refugees."[21]

Yet as election results, demonstrations, and violent incidents against refugees have shown, there are many Germans, especially (but not only) from the east, who are hostile to the refugees and to Merkel's government for supporting them. They feel that the German government has not done as much as it should or as they had hoped to help people from the former GDR or to understand them. Many eastern Germans also assumed that Merkel, herself from the east, would prioritize their interests more and became increasingly disappointed that, in their view, she has not done this.[22] They believed that the finances and political attention that have been devoted to the recent refugees should be devoted to them instead. Indeed, the eighteenth anniversary of

---

[18] Der Regierende Bürgermeister, Senatskanzlei, "Müller zum 13. August," press statement, August 10, 2018; and "57. Jahrestag Mauerbau: 'Niemand hat die Absicht, eine Mauer zu errichten'," *Berliner Zeitung*, August 13, 2018.

[19] "Mit meinem Gott überspringe ich Mauern," Predigt des Vorsitzenden der Deutschen Bischofskonferenz, Erzbischof Dr. Robert Zollitsch, beim ökumenischen Gottesdienst anlässlich der Gedenkveranstaltung "20 Jahre Mauerfall" am 9. November 2009 in Berlin. Pressemitteilungen der Deutschen Bischofskonferenz, www.ekd.de/download/ 091109_pm296_predigt_zollitsch.pdf.

[20] Der Regierende Bürgermeister, Senatskanzlei, "Müller zum 13. August," press statement, August 10, 2018; and "57. Jahrestag Mauerbau: 'Niemand hat die Absicht, eine Mauer zu errichten'," *Berliner Zeitung*, August 13, 2018.

[21] Anna Köhler, Sophie Skeisgerski, and Robert Jurkschat, "Gedenktag des Mauerbaus in Potsdam. 'Seebrücke statt Seehofer'," *Potsdamer Neueste Nachrichten*, August 13, 2018.

[22] Martin Machowecz, "Angela Merkel: Die Entfremdung," *Zeit*, October 7, 2018.

German unification in October 2018 was marked by a backdrop of growing east-west tensions within the country, with many observers arguing that extremist right-wing hostility to refugees in the east (especially given the relatively fewer refugees placed in the east than the west) was a result of the continued economic lag of the east behind the west and more generally due to insufficient attention being paid to what east Germans had faced since unification. The period approaching the thirtieth anniversary of the fall of the Wall was increasingly used as a moment to take stock of the experiences and treatment of East Germans since then.

The State of German Unity or Disunity

The 2018 "Report on the State of Unity" by the German government announced that there were still relatively higher levels of unemployment in the east (although it was at an all-time low at 7.6 percent) than in the west (5.3 percent) and that the average income in the east was 15 percent lower than in the west. The differences in both measures continued to narrow, but there were not many signs of economic growth in the east, which had seemed to stagnate. It was also still the case that almost no major German companies were based in the east and hence were not providing jobs there. Demographic realities of not enough young people to support the older people in the east contributed to ongoing economic challenges as well.[23] The east-west problem, however, seemed to go beyond these basic facts to something more psychological.

Suddenly in the fall of 2018 and continuing into 2019, there were widespread public discussions about how people from the east had never been given the proper respect for the difficulties some of them had faced since unification: losing their jobs after unification, sometimes not able to find a new one, figuring out how to adjust to capitalism, and living in a system dominated by West Germans who saw the East Germans as second class citizens.[24] Some German leaders had previously recognized the challenges east Germans had encountered since the fall of the Wall and unification, but their words clearly had not stemmed the growing tide of dissatisfaction. Speaking in Leipzig on the twentieth anniversary of the peaceful demonstration of 70,000 East Germans, President Köhler had declared in what seemed eight years later to be quite prescient words:

[23] Der Beauftragte der Bundesregierung für die neue Bundesländer, *Jahresbericht der Bundesregierung zum Stand der Deutschen Einheit 2018* (Berlin: Bundesministerium für Wirtschaft und Energie, August 2018), p. 31. On economic differences between eastern and western Germany, see also the study by the Leibniz-Institut für Wirtschaftsforschung Halle, "Vereintes Land – drei Jahrzehnte nach dem Mauerfall," March 4, 2019.

[24] Sarah Mahlberg, "Die Stimmung war ratlos bis stinkig," *Süddeutsche Zeitung*, October 3, 2018; and Cordula Eubel, "Westdeutsche pflegen ähnliche Klischees über Ostdeutsche und Muslime," *Tagesspiegel*, April 2, 2019.

Almost everything changed in the eastern states after 1990, while for West Germans much afterwards remained for years as it was before. The vast majority of East Germans have successfully mastered this fundamental change in their living conditions, this rupture in their own biographies. This is an achievement that is still recognized much too little and from which people should draw lessons.[25]

Similarly, on the fiftieth anniversary of the erection of the Berlin Wall in 2011, President Wulff had spoken about ongoing challenges with unification and with East Germans not feeling respected, including for the lives they lived in the GDR and how they had to adjust to life in united Germany afterwards.[26] In 2018–19, however, there was a new sense of urgency about east-west divisions no doubt due to the rise of right-wing extremist behavior and the strength of the AfD, which many believed was fueled by frustration with the results of unification in the east.

The national Unity Day ceremony, which rotates each year among the federal states, was held in Berlin in October 2018, with Mayor Müller and Bundestag President Schäuble going out of their way to address eastern concerns in their speeches. The ceremony at the *Staatsoper* opened with Daniel Barenboim conducting the overture to Beethoven's *Fidelio,* yet Beethoven's music about the triumph of justice and liberty was not enough to counteract the worried, beseeching tone in speeches by Müller and Schäuble.

The mayor opened his remarks by remembering the twenty-eight years – or 10,315 days, as he pointed out – the Wall stood, representing the lack of democracy and freedom. Müller seemed to want to remind people of how bad things could get when those values were not defended. On the other hand, to those in the audience at the *Staatsoper* and watching live on television who were perhaps worried about current developments in Germany, Müller tried to foster optimism. He reminded people that the message of the fall of the Wall was: "The impossible can be possible! It's worth it to fight for freedom." Referring to the slogan of the day's celebration, "*Nur mit Euch!*" ("Only with you!"), the mayor emphasized that only by all of them working together could they achieve real unity and preserve democracy by defending the core values of the rule of law and tolerance against the old currents of nationalism and racism. In the face of threats to longstanding values of inclusion, tolerance, and democracy, he urged his fellow citizens, "Don't be silent!"[27]

---

[25] Horst Köhler, "70,000 Herzen," Festakt "20 Jahre Friedliche Revolution," Gewandhaus Leipzig, October 9, 2009.

[26] Christian Wulff, "Schätzen und schützen wir die Freiheit," Berlin Wall Memorial, August 13, 2011, www.bundespraesident.de/SharedDocs/Reden/DE/Christian-Wulff/Reden/2011/08/110813-Gedenkveranstaltung-Mauerbau.html.

[27] Der Regierender Bürgermeister, Senatskanzlei, "Rede des Bundesratspräsidenten und Regierender Bürgermeisters Michael Müller auf dem Festakt zum Tag der Deutschen Einheit, 2018," October 3, 2018.

Pointing out that Germany's difficulties were "not a question of east vs. west," the mayor spoke of how much the eastern Germans had to adjust to since 1990, including concerns about their daily livelihood when, for example, 200,000 industrial jobs were lost in Berlin soon after unification. He pointedly asserted (and was applauded for it): "We recognize what you've been through. We know there are still problems. We must help. As Minister President of a state in the center of eastern Germany, I see this as my responsibility." He vowed to persuade more companies to move to the east and create jobs there. "Otherwise all of society is threatened." He also urged people not to forget that many good things had been accomplished in the eighteen years since unification.

Schäuble, who himself had negotiated the terms of the Unification Treaty in 1990 as Kohl's interior minister and who became Bundestag President in 2017, got right to the point in addressing concerns of people in the east in his speech on October 3, 2018: "Not just the years of division, but also the years of unity have left their traces. In private and professional life. Among these are fulfilled desires and realized dreams, but also disappointments suffered by the loss of employment, a sense of home, trust in oneself and in others." In recognition that anxiety about the present and future was affecting people throughout the country (and likely contributing to the growth of the far right), Schäuble observed that, "With globalization, we all are experiencing what became daily life for many east Germans after unification. This creates unease." While historians such as Martin Sabrow had long argued that a comprehensive understanding of the GDR would require looking at the "everyday life" (*Alltagsleben*) of the citizens and not just at the government's means of repression via the Berlin Wall and the Stasi,[28] nearly thirty years after the fall of the Wall, political leaders were realizing that they also needed a better understanding of and empathy for the "daily life" of east Germans not only in the GDR but in united Germany as well. Yet Schäuble exhorted Germans not to waste the "second chance" they had been given at unification, clearly having in mind that the Nazi regime ruined the first chance.[29]

Perhaps not finding the common tie most likely to inspire people, the Bundestag president pointed out that eastern and western Germans were united by the Nazi past and that German "identity comes from looking at our past. Our country became what it is today, because it found the courage to confront its past. It was never easy, but we had the will and the strength to do it. That created international trust in us and gave us the luck of a 'second chance' with unification." He insisted that Germans "must not waste this or ignore our historical responsibility...to liberal democracy which is fragile and challenging." Schäuble

---

[28] Martin Sabrow, Rainer Eckert, Monika Flacke, et al.,eds., *Wohin treibt die DDR-Erinnerung? Dokumentation einer Debatte* (Göttingen: Vandenhoeck & Ruprecht, 2007).

[29] Deutscher Bundestag, "Rede von Bundestag President Dr. Wolfgang Schäuble am 'Tag der Deutschen Einheit', in Berlin," October 3, 2018. See also AP, "Germany Celebrates 28th Anniversary of Its Unification," *Washington Post*, October 3, 2018.

spoke of "old certainties which are faltering" and defended liberal democratic values of nonviolence, diversity of opinion, tolerance, mutual respect and protection of minorities.

At a time when leaders of the AfD had been quite critical of Germany's regular expression of shame and guilt about the Nazi past, Schäuble's emphasis on learning from this past was unlikely to appeal to AfD supporters. Indeed, in June 2018 party leader Alexander Gauland had called the thirteen years of National Socialism "bird shit" compared to Germany's long, "glorious" and "successful history."[30] Even before that, there had been so many taboo-breaking statements by AfD leaders about the Nazi past that the Green Party brought a motion to the Bundestag in February 2018 calling for a discussion about "Democracy and Memory Culture in Germany in Light of Attacks by Right-Wing Extremists."[31] The discussion occurred in the Bundestag on February 23 with the overwhelming majority of parliamentarians condemning the AfD for its approach.[32] Given that Gauland's remark on "bird shit" came months later, however, clearly the AfD approach had not changed.

The sense of crisis in German society evident in the addresses by Schäuble and Müller was also palpable at the 2018 national Unity Day church service in the Berlin Cathedral attended by political leaders and other invited guests. Archbishop Heiner Koch centered his sermon on the fundamental importance of the capacity to learn and to learn from history, especially mistakes in history. At a time of increasing polarization in society and in politics, he lamented that "too few of us seem ready to learn from others" and instead "surround ourselves with people who think as we do, providing no opportunity for learning." Koch began his sermon remembering the devastation of World War I, which ended nearly a century earlier and concluded with an admonishment: "We must never stop learning. Never stop." The comparison between the growing nationalism and internal tensions of 2018 regarding German domestic and foreign policies and those that played out in World War I was not lost on anyone. He beseeched his fellow citizens to live by the slogan of the day's unity celebrations in Berlin: "Only with you!" ("*Nur mit Euch!*") Only with the participation of all people living in the country could Germany achieve success and internal unity.[33]

---

[30] Maria Fiedler, "Alexander Gauland und der 'Vogelschiss'," *Tagesspiegel*, June 2, 2018.

[31] Bündnis 90/Die Grünen Bundestagsfraktion, press statement, February 20, 2018. www .gruene-bundestag.de/presse/pressemitteilungen/2018/februar/gruene-beantragen-aktuelle-stunde-demokratie-und-erinnerungskultur-in-deutschland-angesichts-rechtsex tremistischer-angriffe.html.

[32] Deutscher Bundestag, Plenarprotokoll 19/15, additional agenda item 6, "Aktuelle Stunde auf Verlangen der Fraktion Bündnis 90/Die Grünen: Demokratie und Erinnerungskultur angesichte rechtsextremistischer Angriffe," February 23, 2018, pp. 1289–1307.

[33] Archbishop Heiner Koch, "Predigt von Erzbischof Dr. Heiner Koch aus Anlass des Ökumenischen Gottesdienstes zum Tag der Deutschen Einheit am 03. Oktober 2018

Bishop Markus Dröge similarly declared that only with everyone working together – "eastern and western Germans, young and old, rich and poor, immigrant and native Germans" – would German unity finally be realized.[34] Schäuble shared the concern that "we are not listening to each other. It won't work if we don't. Diversity is a value. We need it."[35] The minister of the cathedral, Michael Kösling, dismissed the congregation at the end of the service with the directive or perhaps a plea, "Go in peace! Interact with each other! Listen to each other!"[36]

There was little sense of unity on the Day of German Unity in 2018, and the more the politicians declared their optimism that Germany could handle the challenges and overcome the divisions, the more their fears of precisely the opposite came through. British Prime Minister Gordon Brown's enthusiastic conclusion in 2009 that the fall of the Wall and the unification of Europe showed that "history is moving toward our best hopes, not our worst fears" seemed like a voice from another world, a different time.[37] German leaders were more worried than proud, more anxious than brimming with confidence in their desire to help bring down other walls. Perhaps it was not just concerns about rising costs and debates over the best design and location for the long-planned Freedom and Unity Monument that had prevented it from being constructed so many years after the Bundestag had pledged to do so.[38]

The collection of important historic anniversaries in November 2018 added to the sense of all that could go wrong and had gone wrong in German and European history: November 9 was not just the twenty-ninth anniversary of the fall of the Wall but also the eightieth anniversary of *Kristallnacht*; and November 11 was the centenary of the end of World War I. German history policy and memory culture went into overdrive with

im Berliner Dom," October 3, 2018, www.domradio.de/sites/default/files/pdf/20180303nurmiteuchkochpredigt.pdf.

[34] Bishop Markus Dröge, "Eröffnung im ökumenischen Gottesdienst zum Tag der Deutschen Einheit," October 3, 2018, www.ekbo.de/fileadmin/ekbo/mandant/ekbo.de/1._WIR/06._Bischof/Gru%C3%9Fworte_und_Vortr%C3%A4ge/181003_Gru%C3%9Fwort_Bischof_Dr%C3%B6ge_Tag_der_Deutschen_Einheit.pdf.

[35] Deutscher Bundestag, "Rede von Bundestag President Dr. Wolfgang Schäuble am 'Tag der Deutschen Einheit', in Berlin," October 3, 2018. www.bundestag.de/parlament/praesidium/reden/017-571556. See also AP, "Germany celebrates 28th anniversary of its unification," *Washington Post*, October 3, 2018.

[36] Michael Kösling's words of dismissal, Berlin Cathedral, October 3, 2018, static4.evangelisch.de/get/ccd/ooQbrSjdO7ELs6ZxpXT9gkOg00209330/download.

[37] Author's notes from Gordon Brown's speech, Brandenburg Gate, November 9, 2009; and "Berlin Wall 2.0," *Reuters Blog*, November 9, 2009.

[38] As of June 2019, there was still no start date for construction of the monument, with the latest twists being delayed construction of the subway underneath the site and accusations of plagiarism against the authors of the winning design. Ralf Schönball, "Plagiatsvorwurf gegen Entwickler der Einheitswippe," *Tagesspiegel*, May 10, 2019; and Reinhart Bünger, "Einheitsdenkmal wird zum Jubiläum nicht fertig," *Tagesspiegel*, June 8, 2019.

countless events and widespread media reports on both the crimes perpetrated by the Nazis against Jews on *Kristallnacht* and the mass destruction and casualties brought on by Germany in World War I.

To emphasize the importance of remembering history and learning from it, the Peace Prize of the German Book Industry, traditionally bestowed on the last day of the Frankfurt Book Fair, was awarded in October 2018 to the scholars Aleida and Jan Assmann for their significant work on memory culture. Speaking on the occasion, the chair of the German Publishers and Booksellers' Association Heinrich Riethmüller called the Assmanns "path-breakers of an intelligent and enlightened memory culture" and described their works as "foundations for how a modern society can learn from the past so as to be able to live in peace and freedom."[39] Speaking in November at the Ryke Strasse Synagogue in Berlin to mark the eightieth anniversary of *Kristallnacht*, both Chancellor Merkel and Josef Schuster, President of the Central Council of German Jews, referred to the prize awarded to the Assmanns and noted "the fundamental importance of memory work" and *politische Bildung*; knowing about history and drawing lessons from it.[40]

In the face of so much worry about contemporary developments in Germany between east and west and between Germans and refugees, on the twenty-ninth anniversary of the fall of the Wall in November 2018, President Frank Walter Steinmeier at the Bundestag and Axel Klausmeier at the Berlin Wall Memorial sought to inspire more optimism among Germans about their past and future. Delivering the main address at the parliamentary ceremony on November 9, Steinmeier highlighted the 100th anniversary of the establishment of the first German parliamentary republic, the Weimar Republic, as it became known. He lamented that this history "is treated as a stepchild in German memory culture" and that German *Erinnerungskultur* pays far more attention to the end of the Weimar Republic with the Nazis' assumption of power than to the beginning of the Weimar Republic. The German president argued eloquently and passionately about changing the German approach to this history.[41]

Steinmeier called for bringing the "courageous women and men...of the Weimar democracy...out of the shadows of the history of the failure of the

---

[39] Heinrich Riethmüller's comments can be found at www.friedenspreis-des-deutschen-buchhandels.de/445651/?mid=1532297.

[40] "Rede von Bundeskanzlerin Merkel auf der Zentralen Gedenkveranstaltung zum 80. Jahrestag der Reichspogromnacht am 9. November 2018, Ryke Strasse Synagogue, Berlin," www.bundeskanzlerin.de/bkin-de/aktuelles/rede-von-bundeskanzlerin-merkel-auf-der-zentralen-gedenkveranstaltung-zum-80-jahrestag-der-reichspogromnacht-am-9-november-2018–1548196. See also the speech by Josef Schuster, President of the Central Council of German Jews.

[41] "Rede von Bundespräsident Frank-Walter Steinmeier bei der Gedenkstunde zum 9. November 2018 im Deutschen Bundestag in Berlin," www.bundespraesident.de/Shared Docs/Reden/DE/Frank-Walter-Steinmeier/Reden/2018/11/181109-Gedenkstunde-Bundestag.html.

Weimar democracy" and also for remembering the East German "women and men who poured onto the streets in the autumn of 1989." He spoke about the crimes of *Kristallnacht* and the Holocaust and referred to "the ambivalence of November 9 in German memory." Maintaining that Germans "can be proud of the traditions of freedom and democracy without averting our eyes from the abyss of the Shoah," he assured his fellow citizens: "Yes, we can allow ourselves to trust this country, even if – or indeed because – these two things form part of it." This trust in themselves as Germans was evident in 2009 but had come under fire since 2015.

The president urged, as previous German leaders had, that his compatriots pay more attention to the positive side of German history: "I would like us to devote more attention. . .and more financial resources to the places and protagonists of the history of our democracy [as opposed to the non-democratic moments]. On behalf of our Republic's identity, we should invest in more than merely royal crypts and princes' palaces!" Making oblique references throughout his speech to the rise of right-wing, anti-democratic forces in Germany, Steinmeier concluded by urging all Germans to "be brave!" and "dare to demonstrate the hope and republican passion of those days of November 1918 in our own era. Let us dare to say once again with conviction: long live the German Republic! Long live our democracy!"[42] The Bundestag chamber filled with applause when the president finished speaking.

A few hours later at the Berlin Wall Memorial on Bernauer Strasse, Klausmeier hosted Mayor Müller and other dignitaries as well as students from Germany, France, Norway, and Switzerland for a commemorative ceremony. Klausmeier consciously put young people at the center of activities at the memorial for the twenty-ninth anniversary of the fall of the Wall. At both the outdoor and indoor ceremonies on November 9 and on the evening before, it was high school students who spoke about or demonstrated their work on the history of the Wall. Outside at the *Hinterlandmauer* on Bernauer Strasse, French students performed a song and spoke about their studies on the Berlin Wall, and inside the Chapel of Reconciliation, the focal point of the ceremony was a short film featuring a dance about the Wall that had been choreographed as a senior thesis project by a student from Switzerland, Leonie Kuhn. Following the film of the dance, Pastor Thomas Jeutner interviewed Leonie about her studies on the Wall and her integration of both violent and joyous aspects of the Wall's history into her choreography. An event the evening before in the visitors' center at the Berlin Wall Memorial had also featured Leonie as well as students from Germany who had performed plays, conducted interviews, and constructed exhibits about the history of the Wall.[43]

---

[42] Ibid.

[43] "Mauerfall – verdammt lang her? Projekte junger Menschen zur Geschichte der Berliner Mauer," presentations and discussion at the Berlin Wall Memorial, November 8, 2018.

The dramatic history of the Wall continues to be of great interest to students and so many others. By giving students such an active role in the commemorative activities at the Berlin Wall Memorial, Klausmeier sought to highlight its status as a key educational site (*Lernort*) and to recognize the efforts of students to engage with this history. Praising "the freedoms achieved through the Peaceful Revolution," the director emphasized that "at a time of growing populism everywhere, the defense of freedom and democracy is still incredibly relevant." Klausmeier redoubled his commitment to the Berlin Wall Memorial "as a *Lernort* about open-mindedness to the world, tolerance and respect as well as standing up against any form of exclusion."[44] Seeing these attitudes expressed by young students was a sign of hope for the future. Klausmeier was inspired by these young people, as Steinmeier was by those who created the Weimar Republic and the Peaceful Revolution.

The Thirtieth Anniversary of the Fall of the Wall

The contemporary dynamics of growing east-west tensions and conflicts between the far right and others presented challenges for those planning the thirtieth anniversary celebrations of the fall of the Wall in 2019. Tensions over views about the fall of the Wall in 2019 were reminiscent of the discordant atmosphere on the fortieth anniversary of the erection of the Wall in 2001, with both serving as examples of the capacity of commemorations to divide rather than unite. Elections to the European Parliament in May and in three eastern German states in the autumn of 2019 (Saxony, Brandenburg, and Thuringia), were also sources of concern to those involved in planning for the thirtieth anniversary.[45] In addition to the much sharper political mood in Germany and in Europe in 2019 as compared to in 2009 or 2014, some former East German civic activists who were previously lauded as heroes had now joined the far right.[46] This all complicated placing the focus of the thirtieth anniversary on the people who made the East German Peaceful Revolution.

On the one hand, the prevailing atmosphere of anxiety made political leaders and the organizers of the commemoration reluctant to engage in the same kind of mass festivities that marked the twentieth and twenty-fifth anniversaries of the fall of the Wall. The triumphant emphasis on the heroic Peaceful Revolutionaries in

---

[44] "Erinnerung an den Fall der Berliner Mauer vor 29 Jahren," November 9, 2018, press statement, Berlin Wall Foundation.

[45] Jana Hensel, "Selten zuvor wurde über so viel Zukunft entschieden," *Zeit Online*, January 1, 2019 The results of the EU elections in Germany nearly recreated the former east-west dividing line. Julian Stahnke, Julius Tröger, and Sascha Venohr, "Gespaltenesland," *Zeit*, May 27, 2019.

[46] "Vera Lengsfeld spricht bei AfD-Bürgerforum," *n-tv*, September 14, 2017. See also Markus Decker, "DDR-Bürgerrechtler auf rechten Abwegen," *Frankfurter Rundschau*, May 31, 2018.

2009 and 2014 was insufficient for acknowledging – to say nothing of overcoming – the challenges many east Germans had faced since the fall of the Wall and unification. The favored "happy" state narrative established in 2009 about the fall of the Wall clashed with the increasingly expressed disillusionment felt by many in the east. This disillusionment with the transition away from communism was not confined just to Germany; post-communist challenges were experienced elsewhere particularly by older generations who missed the guaranteed employment and low prices under communism in Central and Eastern Europe and Eurasia, also fueling the rise of nationalistic parties.[47]

On the other hand, most leaders in Berlin as well as the planning committee of Kulturprojekte Berlin (with former civic activists strongly represented by Tom Sello and Marianne Birthler) still believed that the peaceful fall of the Wall was worth celebrating and that the message of the power of people standing up for freedom and democracy was one that bore reiterating, especially given the growing popularity of the AfD and right-wing sentiment.[48] Indeed, two and a half years before the thirtieth anniversary, all of the major political parties in Berlin's House of Representatives (except the AfD, which was not invited to join in the motion) urged advance planning for the "thirtieth anniversary of the Peaceful Revolution" and cooperation with Berlin's partner cities, "especially in Eastern Europe, Warsaw, for example." They sought to emphasize the importance of developments in East European countries and in East-West détente as key contexts for the fall 1989 demonstrations in East Germany, the toppling of the Wall, and German unification. The parliamentarians proposed that significant buildings and sites connected with developments in 1989 should be highlighted and explained, since "many people [now] live in Berlin who did not experience 1989 or did not experience it in Berlin. Moreover, many tourists come to Berlin looking for sites [connected to] the division and reunification. Berlin should present its history for all of these people in 2019."[49] As Manfred Fischer and Helmut Trotnow had understood thirty years earlier, future generations of Germans and tourists (including today's generations) needed to see authentic historical sites such as the Berlin Wall combined with explanatory exhibits to be able to understand this history.

[47] In her comparison of 2009 twentieth anniversary commemorations across the region, Susan C. Pearce found similarities in the "cynicism and divisiveness" over post-1989 developments: Pearce, "1989 as Collective Memory 'Refolution': East-Central Europe Confronts Memorial Silence," in Lindsey A. Freeman, Benjamin Nienass, and Rachel Daniell, eds., *Silence, Screen, and Spectacle* (New York: Berghahn, 2014), pp. 213–38. See also Ireneusz Pawel Karolewski and Roland Benedikter, "Neo-Nationalism in Central and Eastern Europe," *globale-e*, March 16, 2017.

[48] See, for example, the interview with Tom Sello by Uwe Rada, "Bürgerrechtler über 30 Jahre Mauer Fall. 'Ich mag keine einfachen Erklärungen'," *taz*, March 3, 2019.

[49] Antrag der Fraktion der SPD, der Fraktion der CDU, der Fraktion Die Linke, der Fraktion Bündnis 90/Die Grünen und der Fraktion der FDP, Abgeordnetenhaus von Berlin, Drucksache 18/0247 Neu, April 5, 2017.

In the plenary debate in the House of Representatives about the thirtieth anniversary plans, the AfD representative Martin Trefzer criticized the other parties not only for leaving his party out of the planning but also for the assumption that "the historical judgment of the meaning of the anniversary was completely unambiguous."[50] Andreas Otto of the SPD insisted that they had purposely not included historical judgment in their motion, since they hoped the Senate's plan would have "a variety of events, ideas and perhaps even interpretations." Indeed, in Otto's view, "thirty years is a relatively short period of time for a final multi-faceted assessment."[51] Deputy Mayor and Senator for Culture, Klaus Lederer of *die Linke*, however, ventured more of an optimistic verdict about the significance of the Peaceful Revolution and the fall of the Wall, maintaining that the motion put forward by the SPD, CDU, *die Linke*, Bündnis 90/Die Grüne, and the FDP "clearly was directed at celebrating the victory of democracy and human rights."[52]

Finding the right approach to the anniversary was the job of Kulturprojekte Berlin and its director Moritz van Dülmen, as it had been in 2009 and 2014. In coordination with the Senate, Van Dülmen created a planning committee that included representatives from the Berlin Wall Foundation (Klausmeier and Klaus-Dietmar Henke), the Havemann Gesellschaft, the Federal Foundation for Reappraising the SED Dictatorship (the *Stiftung Aufarbeitung* led by Anna Kaminsky), the Berlin State Commissioner for Reappraising the SED Dictatorship (a post Tom Sello had assumed in 2017), the Holocaust Memorial (due to the *Kristallnacht* anniversary sharing the same date), the Maxim Gorki Theater (which had taken on a leading role in combating the rise of the far right), Rundfunk Berlin Brandenburg, the Senate's cultural department, and Berlin's tourism office as well as Marianne Birthler.[53]

Kulturprojekte began the process of deciding what to do for the thirtieth anniversary by carrying out an informal opinion survey in Berlin in the winter of 2017–18, speaking to about 100 people on the street in different parts of the city and with various experts, historians, artists, and politicians, Germans (of both German and Turkish background) and non-Germans. The survey included questions directed at attitudes toward the fall of the Wall, the current situation in united Germany, and whether the anniversary of the fall of the Wall should be celebrated and if so, how. The results of the survey were

---

[50]   Martin Trefer, Abgeordnetenhaus von Berlin, Ausschuss für Kulturelle Angelegenheiten, Inhaltsprotokoll, 12. Sitzung, Öffentliche Sitzung, November 6, 2017, p. 7.

[51]   Andreas Otto, ibid.

[52]   Klaus Lederer, ibid., pp. 8–9.

[53]   Phone conversation with Julia Wachs of Kulturprojekte Berlin, February 1, 2018, and email correspondence, April 19, 2018; interview with Moritz van Dülmen, November 14, 2018. See also the memo from Torsten Wöhlert of the Senate department for culture and Europe to the chair of the budget committee, "30 Jahre friedliche Revolution," 1609, November 29, 2018. This memo requested ten million euros for the thirtieth anniversary commemorations.

compiled in a "mood board" and assessed by the members of the planning committee.[54]

The survey showed that the "achievement of unity makes people grateful. . .and disillusioned." The views of the people who were interviewed fell into four basic groups: those who were bitterly disappointed since 1989 (people from the east and people who had immigrated to the west, i.e., Turks); those (the majority) who were indifferent about the fall of the Wall; those who favored a differentiated approach to the celebration; and those who encouraged a celebration believing Germany has much to be proud of (a view only expressed by people from other countries, including Poland, the United States, and France). The groups had very different ideas about how the thirtieth anniversary should be approached.

Leaving aside the indifferent group and the most optimistic group (which included only non-Germans), the results of the other two groups were the significant ones for planning purposes. The embittered group ranged from wanting more focus on uniting Germans and Turkish immigrants to calling for kicking out all foreigners and refugees and then perhaps being ready to celebrate. Those in favor of a differentiated approach recommended a celebration be combined with open discussion about ongoing challenges and with measures to educate young Germans about the history of the Wall and democratic values. Given that all of these sentiments were widely expressed on a regular basis and the subject of much media coverage, the survey results held no great surprises. They did emphasize, however, the need to tread carefully if the anniversary planners wanted to reach as many people as possible.

Van Dülmen was fully aware that the combination of an SPD-*Linke* ruling coalition in the Berlin government (which would be under particular pressure to remember the history of the Wall and the role of the Peaceful Revolutionaries in its fall lest the coalition leaders be accused of downplaying the East German communist past) and the certainty that the world's eyes would again be on Berlin for the anniversary put him and the city of Berlin "under great pressure to respond to all of this and do something." He believed that abdicating the opportunity to present something big for the thirtieth anniversary due to east-west tensions within the country would get the same response people generally feel when they say, "really, I don't need you to give me any Christmas presents," and then don't receive any. After all, as van Dülmen asserted, "ninety-nine percent of people have a positive view of November 9. They remember it with goosebumps. November 10 or 11 or October 3 is a different story, but November 9 has a positive strength. It was a moment of hope and is still worth celebrating. People still think it is amazing that it all worked out peacefully."[55]

---

[54] Phone conversation with Julia Wachs of Kulturprojekte Berlin, February 1, 2018, and email correspondence, April 19, 2018.

[55] Interview with Moritz van Dülmen, November 14, 2018.

Both the Senate's cultural department as well as van Dülmen expected significant global interest in the anniversary as there had been in 2009 and 2014 and endeavored to make the event as international as possible both in terms of the intended musical performances and the audience. Already a year in advance of the thirtieth anniversary, van Dülmen traveled abroad to line up international participation, including multiple trips to the USA, sometimes accompanied by Berlin's tourism director.[56]

In the lead-up to the thirtieth anniversary, politicians and planners were stuck in a bind. It was clear that, in spite of their efforts in 2009 and 2014 to establish a new "positive" founding myth of united Germany being born out of the Peaceful Revolution and the fall of the Wall, this narrative was being severely challenged as was a sense of German unity. Yet the politicians and planners still favored this narrative and still sought to disseminate it, backed by historical details of 1989, to create a united German memory culture. They were caught between wanting to unite and educate people around the Peaceful Revolution narrative and knowing that the level of eastern frustration in 2019 made such an approach problematic and that therefore other views and life histories needed room for expression. Hence, they developed a two-pronged strategy.

Following in the tradition of Germany's open grappling with difficult aspects of its past, the planners decided to host a variety of events that would cast a more "differentiated view" on the GDR in the fall of 1989, looking at the hopes, desires, and demands people had then instead of just assuming they all wanted to tear down the Wall and join West Germany.[57] This approach would take into account the majority in the east (62 percent) who felt in 2009 that society had become *more* unjust instead of *less* since the demise of the GDR and the vast majority in 2019 who did not see themselves as the main beneficiaries of German unification.[58] A survey of 18–29 year olds in early 2019 found that the majority of young people in the east felt that it still mattered whether one is from the east or the west, with the obvious implication that people from the east faced greater barriers to advancement than those in the west.[59] Creating commemorative events on the fall of the Wall that included these perspectives marked an important change, since most of the

---

[56] Ibid.; and memo from Torsten Wöhlert of the senate department for culture and Europe to the chair of the budget committee, "30 Jahre friedliche Revolution," 1609, November 29, 2018.

[57] Stefan Strauß, "30 Jahre Mauerfall," *Berliner Zeitung*, February 13, 2019.

[58] Jörg Schönenborn, "Die Angst um die Arbeitsplatz wächst: ARD-DeutschlandTrend, November 2009," *Tagesschau*, November 5, 2009, www.tagesschau.de/inland/deuts chlandtrend/deutschlandtrend942.html ZDF, "Suche nach der Einheit: Umfrage zur `ZDFzeit'-Doku mit Joachim Gauck, ZDF Presseportal, April 5, 2019.

[59] Rainer Faus and Simon Storks, "Im vereinten Deutschland geboren – in den Einstellungen gespalten? OBS-Studie zur ersten Nachwendegeneration," Otto Brenner Stiftung, February 25, 2019, www.otto-brenner-stiftung.de/wissenschaftsportal/informa tionsseiten-zu-studien/obs-studie-zur-ersten-nachwendegeneration/.

influential memory activists with regard to the Wall have been either from the West or from the East German opposition, not from the ranks of those who felt they had lost out since the fall of the Wall.

In a press conference in February 2019, announcing details of the thirtieth anniversary plans, including the ten million euros devoted to it, Cultural Senator Lederer pointed to the need for an "appropriate commemoration" and a more nuanced view of the events of 1989 and their results. He highlighted four focal points of the thirtieth anniversary plans taking into account four different groups of people: respecting those who have lost out with unification and have "broken biographies"; commemorating victims of the Wall and the SED regime; remembering the "heroes of the Revolution" about whom "one can be confidently proud"; and considering the nationalistic tendencies that were unleashed with German unification from the perspective of people who have emigrated to Germany – i.e., the refugees the AfD has been so hostile to – and acting against such nationalistic tendencies.[60] Lamenting that, "Openness, diversity, understanding, growing together and dialogue are not exactly on the offense," Lederer gave the impression that the anniversary would be marked by fewer fireworks and more quiet commemoration.[61] As a memo from his department outlined for the budget committee of the House of Representatives in November 2018, Lederer and his colleagues hoped to cover all bases, making the commemoration "simultaneously local and international, participatory and emotional, remembering and warning."[62]

The plan aimed to satisfy several groups of Germans with very different views on 1989 and an international public and media that expected a big celebration featured many and varied activities. Hence, the planners organized a six-day festival from November 4 to 10 consisting of more than 100 events: exhibits; film, light, and sound installations projected onto screens or large buildings to bring back the atmosphere of November 1989; discussions and seminars, including about the difficulties faced by some east Germans as well as others such as Turks, Syrians and others since the fall of the Wall; poetry slams; films; plays; virtual and augmented reality experiences; and musical performances. These would take place in locations that were important in 1989 and 1990. Planners intended the city to become a "huge history workshop" that would highlight key sites in the "Path of the Revolution" (thus maintaining the Peaceful Revolution narrative). The story of that revolution would be embedded in the Central and East European context of 1989 and in memories

---

[60] Ronald Berg, "Es war nicht alles gut," *taz*, February 14, 2019.

[61] Harry Nutt, "Weniger Feuerleuchten, mehr stilles Gedenken," *Berliner Zeitung*, February 13, 2019.

[62] Memo from Torsten Wöhlert of the Senate department for culture and Europe to the chair of the budget committee, "30 Jahre friedliche Revolution," 1609, November 29, 2018, p. 3.

and developments over the thirty years since then, including the erection of new walls in Europe.[63]

Axel Klausmeier took seriously the importance of including new voices with other narratives about the fall of the Wall. For November 9, in addition to the usual official ceremony, he planned public roundtable discussions featuring Turkish immigrants in Berlin speaking about their experiences with the fall of the Wall and in the years since. He also created a new position at the Berlin Wall Memorial focusing on outreach, including to immigrant groups whose voices had not been heard in discussions about the fall of the Wall and its impact. Following on from the Berlin Senate's commitment to viewing the fall of the Wall in the context of the revolutions of 1989 in Central and Eastern Europe, Klausmeier planned to involve young people from those countries in projects developed under the slogan, "My Europe, Our Common Europe."[64]

In place of the large group events with falling dominoes in 2009 and rising balloons in 2014, the 2019 celebrations would be more loosely structured around the slogan "Music Knows no Borders," featuring performances by professional and amateur musicians from Germany, Europe, and beyond throughout the week at multiple sites connected to the Peaceful Revolution and the fall of the Wall. [65] These would culminate in large-scale performances on the evening of Saturday November 9, 2019, at a small number of major sites along the former border such as the Brandenburg Gate and the East Side Gallery. The Senate's cultural department believed that a wide variety of musical events and genre would "offer a nearly ideal chance to integrate Berliners and international partners" into the celebrations, as would a special thirtieth anniversary smartphone app. The organizers expected to have a synchronized musical performance on all the stages in the early evening around the time of Günter Schabowski's famous press conference, to be followed by big-draw performers in concert at three sites, "such as classical music at the Brandenburg Gate and rock or pop music at *Mauerpark* or the East Side Gallery."[66] Songs were a part of the opposition movement in Germany in the fall of 1989 and most famously in the "Singing Revolution" in Estonia, Latvia, and Lithuania in the late 1980s and early 1990s. Since then,

---

[63] Gerlinde Schulte, "Siebentägiges Festival zur Feier des Mauerfalls," *Berliner Morgenpost*, February 14, 2019; "So soll 30 Jahre Mauerfall in Berlin gefeiert werden," *B.Z.*, February 13, 2019; Ulrich Zawatka-Gerlach, "Route der Revolution," *Tagesspiegel*, May 20, 2019; and memo from Torsten Wöhlert of the Senate department for culture and Europe to the chair of the budget committee, "30 Jahre friedliche Revolution," 1609, November 29, 2018, p. 3.

[64] Conversation (by phone) with Axel Klausmeier, May 2, 2019.

[65] Interview with Moritz van Dülmen, November 14, 2018; and correspondence with Axel Klausmeier, October 6, 2018.

[66] Ulrich Zawatka-Gerlach, "Route der Revolution," *Tagesspiegel*, May 20, 2019; and memo from Torsten Wöhlert of the Senate department for culture and Europe to the chair of the budget committee, "30 Jahre friedliche Revolution," 1609, November 29, 2018, pp. 2–4.

music has also been a fundamental part of marking the fall of the Berlin Wall on important anniversaries. This has been particularly the case, as we have seen, with Beethoven's Ninth Symphony and *Fidelio*, but there have been other examples as well, including the hit song from 1990 by the German rock group Scorpions, "Wind of Change," whose melody accompanied the German and international leaders for their walk through the Brandenburg Gate in 2009, and David Hasselhoff's "Looking for Freedom," which he sang at a concert at the Gate on New Year's Eve in 1989.

Federal plans for the thirtieth anniversary lagged significantly behind the Berlin plans. Only in the fall of 2018 did a representative from the federal finance ministry, Armgard Wippler, present some quite low-key proposals to the Bundestag's committee on tourism. These included activities in the so-called Green Belt along the former inner-German border such as bike tours, an exhibit of works by thirty contemporary artists in the Martin Gropius museum in Berlin, a traveling exhibit on "30 Years of Developing the East" sponsored by the Federal Commissioner on the New (eastern) States, and a lecture series on the revolutions in Central and Eastern Europe between 1989 and 1991 sponsored by the *Stiftung Aufarbeitung*. Wippler told the Bundestag committee members that there were no plans "for the kind of spectacular event like the *Lichtgrenze*" with the balloons in 2014.[67]

The tourism committee members were quite critical of the thin list of activities to mark an event "so deeply connected to peace and freedom." They urged Merkel's government to develop plans "with international resonance" and did not hide their hope that the report represented "only the very first steps" of planning. On the financial side, they observed that anniversaries as important as this one usually included a variety of options to involve tourists but that these options had not yet been developed. A representative from *die Linke* expressed the view that the anniversary should not just focus on SED-repression and the Stasi but should show "respect" for how much the eastern Germans have accomplished during and since 1989.[68]

Merkel herself began the thirtieth anniversary year with a video podcast commemorating the last known victim of the Berlin Wall, Winfried Freudenberg, who was killed in March 1989 when the hot air balloon he was using to escape crashed and killed him on landing in West Berlin.[69] Merkel told viewers, "This fall we will remember thirty years since the fall of the Wall, but we must not forget that many people lost their lives trying to get across the Wall."

[67] Deutscher Bundestag, Tourismus Ausschuss, "Kritik an Planungen zu Einheits-Jubiläen," *Heute im Bundestag, Nr. 752*, October 10, 2018.

[68] Ibid.

[69] Angela Merkel, "Im Gedenken an die Maueropfer," February 23, 2019, www.bundesre gierung.de/breg-de/mediathek/merkel-gedenken-an-letztes-maueropfer-1583416. For more information about Winfried Freudenberg, see chronik-der-mauer.de/en/victims/180604/freudenberg-winfried.

Yet as it turned out, Merkel's government had not created a line item in the budget for the thirtieth anniversary commemorations of the fall of the Wall and German unification in 2019–20, leading to a very embarrassing and tardy request for sixty-one million euros for "unexpected need" in April 2019.[70]

Two possibilities came to mind about why the government forgot this essential step in a country that has long devoted great attention and resources to commemorations of major historical events, such as the fall of the Wall anniversaries in 2009 and 2014. One was that perhaps Germany was becoming more "normal" in its memory policy (*Erinnerungspolitik*), namely by not being so focused on it. However, given Schäuble's prominent role in the Unity Day ceremony in 2018, that seemed unlikely. The other more likely possibility was that with Chancellor Merkel's impending departure brought on by growing internal criticism of her in the wake of the refugee crisis, officials were distracted by internal jockeying for power in the post-Merkel period.

In 2018, the CDU/CSU-SPD coalition government had formed a commission, or at least appointed the commission head, former minister president of Brandenburg, Matthias Platzeck of the SPD, to oversee plans for the 2019–2020 thirtieth anniversaries. Platzeck apparently drafted some ideas in the summer of 2018, but he and his plans came under fire from the CDU Bundestag members in the east who feared that he would focus more on contemporary dissatisfaction in eastern Germany than on the historical events of 1989 and 1990 and would not devote sufficient attention to former civic activists or the Peaceful Revolution. They feared that this "history would be rewritten" by the SPD.[71] For its part, the SPD worried that if the CDU was in charge of the commission, they would make the commemorations into "a Kohl party" focused on the leaders and ignoring the people.[72] In early 2019, the coalition parties were still arguing about who should lead the commission and what the message of the anniversary celebrations should be, although they did agree to create a two-euro commemorative coin for the thirtieth anniversary of the fall of the Wall.[73]

In April 2019, Merkel's cabinet finally created a plan for the anniversary, or more accurately, a strategy for developing a plan for federal commemorations during the year between November 2019 and October 2020. The government announced that Platzeck would indeed lead a planning commission of twenty-two people, ranging in age from their thirties to their seventies. Christian Hirte of the CDU, serving as the Federal Commissioner for the East, was named the deputy director of the commission, which was tasked with proposing plans for

---

[70] Frank Jansen, "Stimmungstest vor Einheitsfeiern," *Tagesspiegel*, May 6, 2019.

[71] "30 Jahre Mauerfall: Ost-CDU unzufrieden mit Platzeck als möglichen Chef der Gedenkkommission," *Spiegel Online*, February 27, 2019.

[72] Anne Hähnig, "Einigkeit und Recht und Streitigkeit," *Zeit Online*, March 4, 2019.

[73] "Nun doch: Bundesregierung feiert 30 Jahre Mauerfall," *Münzen Woche*, February 28, 2019.

the thirtieth anniversaries by the middle of August, just three months before the Wall anniversary. Eighty percent of the commission members were born in the east. Half of them were politicians in parties connected to the ruling coalition, namely the CDU, CSU, and SPD (including six Bundestag members and two minister presidents of German states),[74] and the other half were non-politicians, including professors, actors, and business people.[75]

Some of the commission members had been civic activists in the GDR, including Maria Nooke, Andreas Otto, and Platzeck himself. Platzeck, it should be noted, as a member of the freely elected East German Volkskammer in 1990, had abstained in the vote on the Unification Treaty. He was critical of the fast-track plan for unification by West Germany's absorption of the East German states via Article 23 of the West German *Grundgesetz* instead of via Article 146 whereby representatives from both German states would create a new constitution together. Thus, Platzeck was not someone who had wanted unification at any price, no doubt one of the reasons the CDU was critical of him as the commission's chief.

The focus of the commission was to be on meeting, over the following four months, with people in the east in a series of citizens' dialogues (*Bürgerdialog*) geared toward "strengthening consciousness of what has been achieved [in the east over the previous thirty years], but also to discuss the existing challenges." It seemed that the government wanted to emphasize all the ways in which conditions in the east had been improved since the fall of the Wall and unification but also give citizens the chance to ask questions and talk about their concerns. At these sessions, the commission members were tasked with gathering information to guide them on three matters: how to approach the anniversaries; how to learn "from the experience of social change for future transformation processes"; and whether the government should implement the proposal made by Platzeck and backed by Interior Minister Horst Seehofer

---

[74] The *Linke* and the Greens were critical that they were not included in the "Commission on Thirty Years since the Peaceful Revolution and German Unity" and thus that the views of those who voted for them would not be represented. "Linke und Grüne kritisieren Seehofer wegen Einheitsfeier," *Zeit Online*, May 8, 2019; and Markus Decker, "Ostbeauftragter weist Kritik der Opposition an Einheits-Kommission zurück," *Landeszeitung* (Lüneberge Heide), May 8, 2019.

[75] Die Bundesregierung, "Deutsche Einheit: Leistungen zeigen, Verständnis fördern," April 3, 2019. See also "Kein ostdeutsches 'Disneyland' – Union stoppt Platzecks Pläne zur Einheitsfeier," *Welt*, May 5, 2019; and Tilo Gräser, "Zentrum 'Aufbruch Ost' statt 'DDR Museum' – Kommission plant Jubiläen von 1989 und 1990, *Sputnik News*, May 6, 1990. An open letter to the government by more than fifty former East German civic activists called for adding more civic activists and victims of the SED regime to the commission and starting the commemorations on October 7 in Leipzig. "Offener Brief zum 30. Jahrestag der Friedlichen Revolution am 9. Oktober 2019," Berlin and Leipzig, May 29, 2019. www.havemann-gesellschaft.de/beitraege/offener-brief-9-oktober-30-jahre-friedliche-revolution/

to create a new center in the east dedicated to gathering and disseminating information about the experiences of east Germans since the fall of the Wall and unification.[76] The chancellor herself began by hosting a *Bürgerdialog* in the former eastern city of Schwedt in late April.[77]

For his part in the thirtieth anniversary celebrations, President Steinmeier decided to follow in the footsteps of his predecessor, Joachim Gauck, and invited his counterparts from Poland, Hungary, the Czech Republic, and Slovakia to join him for the November 9, 2019 celebrations in Berlin.[78] Perhaps he hoped that the experience would inspire, for example, Hungary's Viktor Orban to remove the fences he had erected against immigrants on the country's southern border. Certainly inviting right-wing leaders with ties to the AfD to participate in the celebrations could be seen as a risky strategy and one that focused on the events of the past and not the realities of the present.

Germany and Wall Memory after Thirty Years

At the end of the second decade of the twenty-first century, the Germans are not the only ones discussing the impact of the rise and fall of walls. In recent years, many others in Europe as well as Donald Trump's America and Benjamin Netanyahu's Israel have erected, extended, or strengthened walls or fences, arguing as East German leaders did that this was necessary for national security and that it was part of their sovereign right as a nation to control their borders.[79] Even with the fundamental difference that the Berlin Wall was directed internally not externally, the German experience shows the high costs walls bring with them: the lengths people will go to in order to get past them, the way they can divide families, the impact guarding the walls can have on those at the border in the short- or long-term, as well as the financial and moral costs of walls. The Germans after all are still grappling with the history and effects of their Wall, thirty years after its fall, and devoting millions of euros each year to the process. Understanding the history and effects of the Berlin Wall, therefore, is relevant not just to Germany but to others as well.

Memory of the Wall was not officially welcomed by many German leaders or society for a long time. Yet this work has endeavored to show that memory of the Berlin Wall is now a fundamental part of German *Erinnerungspolitik*

---

[76] Die Bundesregierung, "Deutsche Einheit: Leistungen zeigen, Verständnis fördern," April 3, 2019; and dpa, "Seehofer unterstützt Idee eines Zentrums 'Aufbruch Ost'," *Süddeutsche Zeitung*, May 6, 2019.

[77] Dpa, "Bürgerdialog in Brandenburg. Merkel: Stadt und Land 'immer weiter auseinander'," *ZDF heute*, April 30, 2019.

[78] Dpa/zdf, "30 Jahre Mauerfall – Steinmaier lädt Präsidenten ein," April 1, 2019.

[79] Kim Hjelmgaard, "Trump Isn't the Only One Who Wants to Build a Wall. These European Nations Already Did," *USA Today*, May 24, 2018.

especially on key anniversaries. The fall of the Wall and German unification have changed German memory policy, first by adding a new set of victims and then a new set of heroes coupled with a new narrative about German identity. Many German memory activists have played important roles in the thirty-year project of making the history of the Berlin Wall matter to political leaders and visible and understandable to Germans and to people from all over the world who come to Berlin. Manfred Fischer, Helmut Trotnow, Rainer and Alexandra Hildebrandt, Rainer Klemke, Thomas Flierl, Tom Sello, Gabriele Camphausen, Maria Nooke, Michael Cramer, and Axel Klausmeier are among the memory activists from east and west, from civil society and the government, who have had the greatest impact on preserving and commemorating the Wall for posterity and creating spaces where the public can learn the history and reflect on its lessons for the present.

There are no simplistic ways of dividing the memory activists between east and west or among political parties to understand their approaches to remembering the Wall. They have represented a variety of political parties, officially or unofficially, including the CDU, the SPD, the Greens, and the *Linke*. Günter and Maria Nooke, Flierl, Sello, and Gauck were from the east, while Fischer, Klemke, Rainer Hildebrandt, Trotnow, Camphausen, Cramer, Klausmeier, and van Dülmen were from the west. Alexandra Hildebrandt was from Soviet Ukraine. Flierl is a particularly interesting figure, since he was from the east and was part of the ruling SED instead of the civic opposition as Sello, the Nookes, and Gauck were. Yet as Berlin's cultural senator in the mid-2000s, Flierl ultimately played a fundamental role in anchoring the memory of the Wall in Germany with his *Gesamtkonzept*, arguing against some of his own party colleagues at times while also coming under fire from conservatives and former victims due to his party affiliation.

These memory activists have not all backed the same narrative, and some of them, particularly at the Berlin Wall Memorial, have gone out of their way to present a variety of information in a straightforward manner for others to put it all together and create their own narrative of the history of the Wall. Victims, perpetrators, and heroes have all been reflected in narratives on the Wall. While more public attention has been directed to the victims and heroes than to the perpetrators, there has been steadily increasing recognition – in historical research, films, and photo exhibits – that the experiences of border soldiers in particular were an important part of the history of the Wall and need to be included in depictions of that history.[80]

German discussions about the Wall and more generally about the GDR have tended more toward black and white views than toward a more nuanced

[80] On recent calls to modify the overemphasis on the experience of victims in the GDR so as to also consider the experiences of perpetrators, see Christine Wahl, "Nur aus der Opferperspektive können wir die DDR nicht verstehen," *Tagesspiegel*, March 14, 2019.

approach. This has been clear in descriptions of the GDR as an *Unrechtsstaat* or a dictatorship[81] as well as in the heroization (especially since 2009) of people who were in the opposition that created a Peaceful Revolution and toppled the Wall. There is still insufficient attention to the people in positions of power who gave up that power – and the Berlin Wall – peacefully, and there is scant discussion of the impact on events of people who fled the GDR in 1989. A critical view of role of the West before and after the fall of the Wall has also generally not been part of official *Erinnerungspolitik*. This began to change on the eve of the thirtieth anniversary with calls from *die Linke* and the AfD for a government commission to investigate the role of *Treuhand*, the government organization formed to privatize property in the east after unification, in creating so much unemployment and dislocation in the east. Scholars at the Institute for Contemporary History had already been studying *Treuhand* before the issue became politicized in advance of state elections in 2019.[82]

The Berlin Wall Memorial (Figure 30), which started as just one block and was created over many years with great effort by Fischer and his colleagues, always wondering whether they would be successful or not, attracted over one million visitors in 2018. In addition to that popular site stretching along seven blocks and the Marienfelde Refugee Camp Memorial Museum, as of 2019 the Berlin Wall Foundation also oversees the Günter Litfin memorial guard tower, the Berlin Wall walking and biking trail (*Mauerweg* and *Radweg*), the information site at the Brandenburg Gate train station, the BlackBox Cold War exhibit at Checkpoint Charlie, and, as of 2018, the East Side Gallery. This is an extraordinary success story, which even the confident, energetic Fischer probably could never have dreamed of when he started trying to save some of the Wall as a memorial at the end of 1989.

There is no single narrative that can fully capture the complexity of the Wall. Was it the representation of a regime that did not value democracy or freedom? Was it a manifestation of the broader Cold War confrontation between East and West and a method for stabilizing that conflict? Was it a place where mostly anxious young men fulfilled their obligations to their

---

[81] For a fascinating discussion about the possibility that a narrative focusing on the GDR as a dictatorship was created so as to justify devoting attention to studying and remembering it instead of just the Nazi period, see Simone Rafael, "'Der Recht Rand der DDR-Aufarbeitung.' Keine Gleichsetzung von Verbrechen des Nationalsozialismus und der DDR," *Belltower News*, February 25, 2019. The same article asserts that this kind of approach has distracted people from paying attention to the fact that, for example, only 5 percent of Stasi employees were engaged in repression against dissidents, while the vast majority of people in the Stasi were involved in matters related to the economy, www.belltower.news/der-rechte-rand-der-ddr-aufarbeitung-keine-gleichsetzung-von-verbrechen-des-nationalsozialismus-und-der-ddr-81479/.

[82] Reuters, "Linke will neuen U-Ausschuss zur Treuhand," *Tagesspiegel*, April 19, 2019; and Georg Ismar, "Die AfD entdeckt die Treuhand für den Wahlkampf," *Tagesspiegel*, May 2, 2019.

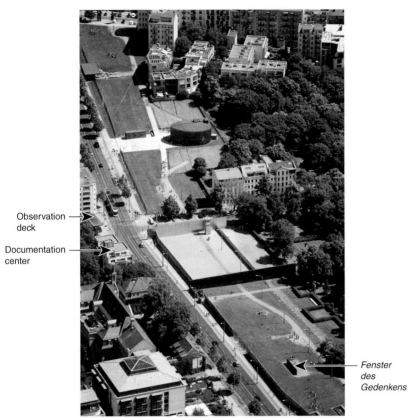

Observation deck

Documentation center

Fenster des Gedenkens

Figure 30 Central section of Berlin Wall Memorial showing former patrol route (through grass), oval-shaped Chapel of Reconciliation (center top), Kohlhoff & Kohlhoff Memorial (middle with guard tower), Documentation Center, Observation Deck, and *Fenster des Gedenkens*
Source: Photographer: Dirk Laubner. Stiftung Berliner Mauer-19.

country? Was it a means for the East German leaders to preserve their power? Was it a violation of the basic human right of freedom of movement? Was it a reality that many people on both sides came to accept in one way or another? It was all of these things.

Germans still do not agree on many aspects of the history of the Wall: why it was built, who bears primary responsibility for its erection and whether building the Wall was justified; whether the deadly border regime at the Berlin Wall was a violation of human rights or a justified defense of the regime; why the Wall fell; and whether the consequences of its fall, particularly German unification, have been more beneficial or detrimental. The indoor and outdoor exhibits at the Berlin Wall Memorial like the photography exhibits of the Wall in the 1960s by Arwed Messmer and Annett Gröschner present a variety of perspectives, leaving it to the viewer to formulate their own view of the Wall. The judges in the Wall trials also acknowledged the salience of multiple perspectives.

Politicians and those who had personal experience with the Wall and the East German regime tend to adopt one or more of the narratives as "the truth." Some memory activists do as well. The current narrative of the Wall subscribed to by most German leaders puts them in a kind of paradox. They feel that as representatives of a "democratic memory culture," they must highlight the ways in which they see the Wall as representative of the undemocratic, *Unrecht* East German regime that limited the freedom of its citizens by walling them in and shooting them if they tried to escape. But in their insistence that this is the only justified way to view the Wall and the former GDR they narrow the sphere of discourse and alienate parts of the population.

Just as a dominant narrative or narratives about the Wall have evolved over the past thirty years, so they will continue to evolve as contemporary circumstances change and result in different kinds of questions being asked about the past. This will also surely be the case when those who lived with the Wall are no longer available to share their memories. It may be that the current dominant narrative of the Wall will become more popular as those in the older generation who criticize it pass on. As a 2011 survey of Berliners showed, three-quarters of the population who came to Berlin after the Wall was toppled judged the erection of the Wall as unjustified,[83] and with every passing year, the post-Wall population grows.

On the thirtieth anniversary of the fall of the Wall throngs of German and international visitors will make their way to Berlin and its sites connected to the Wall, including the Brandenburg Gate, Checkpoint Charlie, the East Side Gallery, and the Berlin Wall Memorial. On Bernauer Strasse, they will walk along the original segments of the former internal and external Walls with the Corten steel columns filling in the spaces where the Wall no longer exists. They will visit the Kohlhoff & Kohlhoff memorial to victims of the Wall and the division as well as the *Fenster des Gedenkens* with its pictures of people killed at the Wall. They will step inside the Chapel of Reconciliation with its loam walls used in the hope of healing the wounds from the division and the lethal border. They will climb to the top of the observation platform to gain a broader view of the former path of the Berlin Wall.

In the former death strip and in the Documentation Center, visitors will learn about those who sacrificed their lives attempting to escape across the Wall, those who lived with the Wall, those whose service at the Wall made it

---

[83] Regine Zylka, "Mauerbau war damals richtig," *Berliner Zeitung*, August 3, 2011; and Nina Apin, "Mauerbau hat immer noch Fans," *taz*, August 3, 2011.

lethal, those who called to bring it down, and those who took home pieces as souvenirs. They may also attend some of the anniversary discussions with people who have critical views of the fall of the Wall and developments since then, not a perspective portrayed originally at the site, but one that Fischer would have agreed deserved a place there, since he understood that efforts to remember and understand the past take place in a constantly shifting present.

This book has demonstrated the variety of ways in which memory activists have exerted influence on how the Berlin Wall has been remembered in public spaces and in public ceremonies over the past thirty years. It has also investigated the ways public officials have integrated Wall memory into a sense of national identity, culminating in their embrace in 2009 of the Peaceful Revolution and fall of the Wall as a new founding myth of united Germany, a myth facing new pressures thirty years after the fall of the Wall. Drawing on the model of the East German citizens taking to the streets in 1989 to demand freedom of travel across the Berlin Wall, free elections, freedom of assembly, and other core parts of a democratic polity, German leaders and others have called for civic activism in the face of challenges to democracy brought about by forces of intolerance in recent years. At a time of growing polarization in Germany and elsewhere, we must all hope for and contribute to the success of such activism. As Manfred Fischer frequently enjoined his colleagues at the Berlin Wall Memorial: "We can never sit still and think our work is finished. We must keep confronting new challenges or we won't matter."[84]

---

[84] Author's phone conversation with Axel Klausmeier, May 2, 2019.

SELECTED BIBLIOGRAPHY

Primary Sources

Archives

Abgeordnetenhaus von Berlin
Allied Museum
Berliner Philharmoniker Digital Concert Hall
Bundesarchiv (BArch)
Deutscher Bundestag
Landesarchiv Berlin (LAB)
Robert-Havemann-Gesellschaft (RHG)
Senatsverwaltung für Wissenschaft, Forschung, und Kultur, Berlin (SWFKB)
  Gedenkstätte Berliner Mauer (GBM)
Stiftung Berliner Mauer
Stiftung Deutsches Historisches Musem (DHM)
Versöhnungsgemeinde Berlin-Wedding

Published Collections of Documents

Deutscher Bundestag, ed. *Materialien der Enquete-Kommission "Aufarbeitung von Geschichte und Folgen der SED-Diktatur in Deutschland"* (12. Wahlperiode des Deutschen Bundestages). 8 Bände in 18 Teilbänden. Baden-Baden: Nomos Verlag, 1995.

Materialien der Enquete-Kommission "Überwindung der Folgen der SED-Diktatur im Prozeß der deutschen Einheit" (13. Wahlperiode des Deutschen Bundestages). 15 Bände. Baden-Baden: Nomos Verlag, 1999.

Marxen, Klaus and Gerhard Werle, eds. *Strafjustiz und DDR-Unrecht: Gewalttaten an der deutsch-deutschen Grenze. Dokumente.* Band 2. Compiled by Toralf Rummler and Petra Schäfter. Berlin: De Gruyter Recht, 2002.

Sabrow, Martin, Rainer Eckert, Monika Flacke, et al. *Wohin treibt die DDR-Erinnerung? Dokumentation einer Debatte.* Göttingen: Vandenhoeck & Ruprecht, 2007.

*Interviews, Conversations (in Berlin and in person unless
otherwise noted), and Email Correspondence*

Kani Alavi, January 14, 2010; November 15, 2013 (phone)
Andreas Apelt, July 19, 2007
Yadegar Asisi, February 9, 2010
Christopher Bauder, July 23, 2014
Marc Bauder, July 25, 2014
Hans-Dieter Behrendt, July 8, 2014
Monica Geyler von Bernus, July 18, 2007
Marianne Birthler, March 24, 2004; July 7, 2014
Hans-Otto Bräutigam, March 13, April 24, May 29, 2004; December 21,
    2009
Heinz Buri, July 25, 2007
Gabriele Camphausen, July 25, 2007; December 15, 2009; September 11, 2018
    (email); November 6, 2018
Michael Cramer, July 20, 2007; November 28, 2009
Gabi Dolff-Bonekämper, January 12, 2010
Moritz van Dülmen, January 28, 2010; November 14, 2018
Rainer Eckert, September 23, 2009 (Leipzig)
Roland Egersdörfer, July 22, 2014
Franziska Eichstädt-Bohlig, November 19, 2004
Rainer Eppelmann, March 26, 2004; April 20, 2010
Bernd Faulenbach, September 12, 2013 (Washington, DC)
Manfred Fischer, October 6 and 15, 2009; March 16, 2010; August 17, 2011;
    September 27, 2012
Thomas Flierl, November 26, 2009
Christian Freiesleben, July 19, 2004; February 8, 11, and 15, 2010
Joachim Gauck, April 6 and November 22 (phone), 2004; January 7, 2010
Georg – (name has been changed), November 9, 2014; June 25, 2018
Gunthart Gerke, July 31, 2014
Wieland Giebel, January 27, 2010
Ruth Gleinig, January 27, 2010
Peter Goralczyk, March 22, 2010
Gregor Gysi, April 15, 2004
Jörg Hackeschmidt, July 7, July 8 (email), July 29, 2014
Volker Hassemer, July 17, 2007
Klaus-Dietmar Henke, December 22, 2009; January 27, 2010
Hans-Hermann Hertle, July 25, 2007; January 27, 2010; November 15, 2013
Alexandra Hildebrandt, November 10, 2004; June 4, 2008; July 24, 2014
Stephan Hilsberg, November 22, 2004
Irmtraud Hollitzer, September 25, 2009 (Leipzig)

Jens Hüttmann, January 10, 2010

Thomas Jeutner, November 5, 2018

Barbara Junge, July 4, 2014

Ingeborg Junge-Reyer, November 22, 2004

Rainer Just, March 16, 2010; June 26, 2018; September 7, 2018 (email); November 16, 2018

Anna Kaminsky, January 19, 2010

Sven Felix Kellerhoff, January 8, 2010

Axel Klausmeier, July 20, 2007; June 5, 2008; December 19, 2009; January 13 and September 6 (email), 2010; July 10, 2012 (phone); November 13, 2013; July 23 and August 25 (email), 2014; December 9, 2015 (Haverford, PA); June 21, 2018; July 30, August 1, September 11, October 6, 2018 (email); May 2, 2019 (phone)

Rainer Klemke, November 24, 2004; July 5, 2005; July 9, 19 and 27, 2007; June 2, 2008; December 18, 2009; January 25, 2010; August 2, 2011; November 15, 2013; January 6 (email), January 9 (email) and July 3, 2014; June 19, 2017

Silke Klewin, November 4, 2009 (Bautzen)

Hans-Ulrich Klose, May 29, 2008; August 1, 2011

Helmut Kohl, February 11, 2004

Thomas Krüger, November 4, 2013

Werner Kuhn, November 11, 2004

Wolf Kühnelt, January 25, 2010; March 26 and April 8, 2014 (email); July 3, 2014

Eberhard Kuhrt, July 24, 2014

Holger Kulick, October 11, 2018 (email); November 6, 2018

Mechthild Küpper, February 22, 2010

Simone Leimbach, July 3, 2014

Jürgen Litfin, August 1, 2014

Ulrich Mählert, January 7, 2010

Lothar de Maizière, April 6, 2004; April 22, 2010

Georg Mascolo, October 7, 2013 (Washington, DC)

Markus Meckel, April 2 and November 23, 2004; March 25, 2010; November 13, 2013

Hans Misselwitz, March 16, 2004

Hans Modrow, March 29, 2004

Petra Morawe, July 7, 2014

Knut Nevermann, March 29, 2010

Günter Nooke, November 25, 2004

Maria Nooke, July 5, 2005; July 23, 2007; April 15, 2010; June 20, 2017; April 28, 2018 (email)

Gerd Nowakowksi, July 28, 2014

Susanne Olbertz, March 29, 2010 (phone)

Ulrike Poppe, April 23, 2004
Rainer Prast, October 31, 2018
Jens Reich, April 22, 2004
Siegfried Reiprich, July 27, 2007
Matthias Reuschel, July 13, 2014
Robert and Petra – (names have been changed), December 15, 1991;
    April 14, 1992; and with Petra on June 26, 2018
Thomas Rogalla, January 11, 2010
Mario Röllig, July 30, 2014
Robert Rückel, June 4, 2008
Martin Sabrow, February 12, 2010
Gerhard Sälter, July 23, 2007; November 5, 2018
Günter Schabowski, April 19, 2004
Christoph Schaefgen, March 26, 2004
Wolfgang Schäuble, May 26, 2004
Günther Schlusche, July 19, 2007; June 5, 2008; February 8 and March 4,
    2010
Leo Schmidt, November 12, 2013
Peter Schneider, August 1 and 12, 2011
Jens Schöne, November 14, 2013; July 4, 2014; June 19, 2017
Richard Schröder, April 19, 2004
Rolf Schwanitz, May 25 and November 23, 2004
Tilman Seeger, July 29, 2014
Tom Sello, February 10, 2010; July 9, 2014
Uwe Spindeldreier, August 7, 2014 (phone)
Holger Stark, September 15, 2013 (Washington, DC); July 4, 2014
Ulrich Stark, July 24 and 30, 2014
Holger Starke, November 5, 2009 (Dresden)
Hans-Joachim Stephan, November 6, 2009 (Radebeul)
Carl-Ludwig Thiele, November 11, 2004
Wolfgang Thierse, February 3, 2010
Daniel Trepsdorf, November 5, 2009 (Dresden)
Helmut Trotnow, October 5, 2007 (San Diego); March 17, 2010; August 9 and
    November 7 (email), 2011
Wolfgang Ullmann, March 23, 2004
Burkhart Veigel, March 23, 2010
Julia Wachs, February 1, 2018 (phone); April 19, 2018 (email)
Rainer Wagner, April 30, 2010 (phone)
Martina Weyrauch, March 25, 2004
Manfred Wilke, July 23, 2004; March 16 and 19, 2010
Hans-Jochen Winters, May 11, 2004
Klaus Wowereit, February 10, 2010
Joachim Zeller, March 24, 2004

Autobiographies, Memoirs, Broadcast or Published Interviews, and Other Publications by Primary Actors

Baumgarten, Klaus-Dieter. *Erinnerungen: Autobiographie des Chefs der Grenztruppen der DDR.* Berlin: edition ost, 2008.

Birthler, Marianne. *Halbes Land. Ganzes Land. Ganzes Leben: Erinnungen.* Munich: Hanser Berlin, 2014.

Camphausen, Gabriele and Manfred Fischer. "Die bürgerschaftliche Durchsetzung der Gedenkstätte Berliner Mauer." In Klaus-Dietmar Henke, ed., *Die Mauer: Errichtung, Überwindung, Erinnerung.* Munich: Deutscher Taschenbuch Verlag, 2011, pp. 355–76.

"The Fall of the Berlin Wall: Memories of Musicians of the Berliner Philharmoniker." Berliner Philharmoniker Digital Concert Hall, November 7, 2014.

Flierl, Thomas. *Berlin: Perspektiven durch Kultur. Texte und Projekte.* Ute Tischler and Harald Mueller, eds. Theater der Zeit Recherchen 45. Berlin: druckhaus koethen GmbH, 2007.

Führer, Christian. *Und wir sind dabei gewesen: Die Revolution, die aus der Kirche kam.* Munich: Taschenbuchverlag, 2010.

Gauck, Joachim. *Freiheit. Ein Plädoyer.* Munich: Kösel Verlag, 2012.

Winter im Sommer – Frühling im Herbst. Munich: Siedler, 2009.

Geipel, Ines. *Generation Mauer: Ein Porträt.* Stuttgart: Klett-Cotta, 2014.

Gysi, Gregor and Hans Modrow. *Gysi und Modrow im Streit-Gespräch: Ostdeutsch oder angepasst.* Berlin: edition ost, 2013.

Hensel, Jana. *After the Wall: Confessions from an East German Childhood and the Life that Came Next,* trans. Jefferson Chase. New York: Public Affairs, 2004.

Hildebrandt, Alexandra. "Die Freiheit verpflichtet. Das Freiheitsmahnmal am Platz Checkpoint Charlie." In Ingeborg Siggelkow, ed., *Gedächtnis, Kultur und Politik.* Berlin: Frank & Timme, 2006, pp. 79–121.

Horn, Gyula. *Freiheit die ich meine: Erinnerungen des ungarischen Aussenministers, der den eisernen Vorhang öffnete.* Hamburg: Hoffmann and Campe Verlag, 1991.

Jahn, Roland. *Wir angepassten: Überleben in der DDR.* Munich: Piper, 2015.

Keßler, Heinz. *Zur Sache und zur Person.* Berlin: edition ost, 1996.

Keßler, Heinz and Fritz Streletz. *Ohne die Mauer hätte es Krieg gegeben: Zwei Zeitzeugen erinnern sich.* Berlin: edition ost, 2011.

Klausmeier, Axel "Ein Memorialort neuer Prägung. Die Erweiterung der 'Gedenkstätte Berliner Mauer' an der Bernauer Strasse." *Deutschland Archiv* 42 (5/2009), pp. 892–900.

"Die Gedenkstätte Berliner Mauer an der Bernauer Strasse." In Klaus-Dietmar Henke, ed., *Die Mauer: Errichtung, Überwindung, Erinnerung.* Munich: Deutscher Taschenbuch Verlag, 2011, pp. 394–406.

Interview with Klausmeier carried out by Clemens Maier-Wolthausen. *"Ein unbequemes Denkmal mitten in der Stadt. Interview mit Prof. Dr. Axel*

Klausmeier, Direktor der Stiftung Berliner Mauer." *Deutschland Archiv* August 9, 2013.

Klausmeier, Axel and Gerhard Sälter. "Der Sophienfriedhof in Berlin-Mitte als Gegenstand der Erinnerungspolitik." In Christian Dirks, Axel Klausmeier, and Gerhard Sälter, *"Verschüttet": Leben, Bombentod und Erinnerung an dieBerliner Familie Jaschkowitz. Judische Miniaturen*, Band 110. Berlin: Hentrich & Hentrich und Centrum Judaicum, 2001, pp. 51–78.

Klausmeier, Axel and Leo Schmidt. "Mauerrelikte." In Klaus-Dietmar Henke, ed., *Die Mauer: Errichtung, Überwindung, Erinnerung*. Munich: Deutscher Taschenbuch Verlag, 2011, pp. 342–55.

Klausmeier, Axel and Günter Schlusche, ed. *Denkmalpflege für die Berliner Mauer*. Berlin: Ch. Links, 2011.

Klemke, Rainer. "Das Gesamtkonzept Berliner Mauer." In Klaus-Dietmar Henke, ed., *Die Mauer: Errichtung, Überwindung, Erinnerung*. Munich: Deutscher Taschenbuch Verlag, 2011, pp. 377–93.

"Between Disappearance and Remembrance: Remembering the Berlin Wall Today." In Anna Kaminsky, ed., *Where in the World Is the Berlin Wall?* Berlin: Berlin Story Verlag, 2014, pp. 246–59.

Leo, Maxim. *Haltet euer Herz bereit: eine ostdeutsche Familiengeschichte*. Munich: Wilhelm Heyne Verlag, 2011.

Merkel, Angela. *Mein Weg. Angela Merkel im Gespräch mit Hugo Müller-Vogg*. Hamburg: Hoffmann und Campe, 2004.

Nooke, Maria, ed. *Mauergeschichten von Flucht und Fluchthilfe: Begegnung mit Zeitzeugen*. Berlin: Ch. Links, 2017.

Richter, Peter. *Dresden Revisited: Von einer Heimat, die einen nicht fortlasst*. Munich: Luchterhand Literaturverlag, 2016.

Schmidt, Horst. "Vater eines Maueropfers. Sie morden wieder auf Befehl." In Roman Grafe, ed., *Die Schuld der Mitläufer: Anpassen oder Widerstehen in der DDR*. Munich: Pantheon, 2009, pp. 145–50.

"Kaltblütiger Mord. Bericht des Vaters von Michael Schmidt," 1991. www .chronik-der-mauer.de/todesopfer/171662/horst-schmidt-kaltbluetiger-mord-bericht-des-vaters-von-michael-schmidt-1991

Veigel, Burkhard. *Wege durch die Mauer: Fluchthilfe und Stasi zwischen Ost und West, 3. Auflage*. Berlin: Edition Berliner Unterwelten, 2011.

Wowereit, Klaus. . . . *und das ist auch gut so. Mein Leben für die Politik*. Munich: Karl Blessing Verlag, 2007.

Newspapers, Radio, and Television

3sat
ARD
Badische Zeitung
Berliner Morgenpost

Berliner Zeitung (and *Berlin Online*)
Bild
B.Z.
Deutsche Welle
Deutschlandradio
Deutschlandfunk
Economist
Focus
Frankfurter Rundschau
Frankfurter Allgemeine Zeitung
Handelsblatt
Independent
Los Angeles Times
Märkische Allgemeine Zeitung
Mitteldeutsche Zeitung
Neue Osnabrücker Zeitung
Neue Zeit
Neues Deutschland
New Yorker
New York Times
Phoenix
Rheinische Post (*RP*)
Rundfunk Berlin-Brandenburg (*rbb*)
Sächsische Zeitung
Semper Magazin
Spiegel
Süddeutsche Zeitung
Tagesschau
Tagesspiegel
taz
VOX
Wall Street Journal
Washington Post
Welt
ZDF
Zeit

Exhibits, Exhibit Catalogues, and Related Sources

Asisi, Yadegar. *Die Mauer. Das Asisi Panorama zum geteilten Berlin.* Foreword by Hope M. Harrison. Berlin: asisi Edition, 2012.

The Berlin Wall – Memorial Site and Exhibition Center Association, ed., *Berlin Wall Memorial Site, Exhibition Center and the Chapel of Reconciliation on Bernauer Strasse*, trans. Tom Lampert. Berlin: Yaron Verlag, 1999.

Cramer, Michael. *Berliner Mauer-Radweg*. Berlin: Esterbauer, 2001 (and expanded, revised 8th edition in 2016 with waterproof paper to carry while biking).

Cycling, Skating, Hiking along the Berlin Wall Trail, Germany. Berlin: Esterbauer, 2003.

Deutsch-Deutscher Radweg. Berlin: Esterbauer, 2007.

Europa-Radweg Eiserner Vorhang, 3 vols. Berlin: Esterbauer, 2009.

van Dülmen, Moritz and Tom Sello, eds., *25 Jahre Mauerfall 2014. Mauergeschichten. Wall Stories*, trans. Büro LS Anderson. Berlin: Kulturprojekte Berlin GmbH, 2014. Catalogue to accompany the Berlin Senate's project "25 Years Fall of the Wall. Wall Stories – LICHTGRENZE – Balloon Event."

Gröschner, Annett and Arwed Messmer. *Aus anderer Sicht: Die frühe Berliner Mauer*. Berlin: Hatje Cantz, 2011. Catalogue to accompany exhibit.

Exhibit, "Aus anderer Sicht: Die frühe Berliner Mauer." Unter den Linden 40, second floor, Berlin. August 5-October 3, 2011.

Inventarisierung der Macht: Die Berliner Mauer aus anderer Sicht. Berlin: Hatje Cantz, 2016. Catalogue to accompany exhibit.

Exhibit, "Inventarisierung der Macht: Die Berliner Mauer aus anderer Sicht." Haus am Kleistpark, Berlin. May 27-August 21, 2016.

Hildebrandt, Alexandra, ed. *German Post-War History in Selected Articles by Rainer Hildebrandt 1949–1993*. Foreword by Hans-Dietrich Genscher. Berlin: Verlag Haus am Checkpoint Charlie, 2002.

Hildebrandt, Rainer. *Es Geschah an der Mauer: Eine Bilddokumentation des Sperrgürtels um Berlin (West), seine Entwicklung vom "13. August" 1961 bis heute mit den wichtigsten Geschehnissen*. 15th expanded ed. Berlin: Verlag Haus am Checkpoint Charlie, 1986.

Klausmeier, Axel, ed. *The Berlin Wall: Berlin Wall Memorial Exhibition Catalog*, trans. Miriamne Fields. Berlin: Ch. Links, 2015.

Kulturprojekte Berlin GmbH, ed. *Dominobuch. Geschichte(n) mit Dominoeffekt*. Berlin: Kulturprojekte Berlin GmbH, 2009. Catalogue to accompany the Berlin Senate's project "Dominoaktion zum 20. Jahrestag des Mauerfalls."

Kulturprojekte Berlin GmbH, ed. *"Wir sind das Volk!" Magazin zur Ausstellung Friedliche Revolution 1989/90*. Berlin: Kulturprojekte Berlin GmbH, 2009. Catalogue to accompany Peaceful Revolution exhibit, Alexanderplatz, 2009.

Kulturprojekte Berlin GmbH, ed. *20 Jahre Mauerfall. Dokumentation des Themenjahres 2009*. Berlin: Kulturprojekte Berlin GmbH, 2009.

Kulturprojekte Berlin GmbH, ed. *Berliner Zukünfte. Darstellung und Bilanz – Perspecktiven und Visionen*. Berlin: Kulturprojekte Berlin GmbH, 2009.

Möbius, Peter and Helmut Trotnow, eds. *Mauern sind nicht für ewig gebaut. Zur Geschichte der Berliner Mauer*. Berlin: Propyläen, 1990.

Starke, Holger, ed. *Keine Gewalt! Revolution in Dresden 1989*. Dresden: Sandstein Verlag, 2009. Catalogue to accompany exhibit at Stadtmuseum Dresden.

Verein Berliner Mauer – Gedenkstätte und Dokumentationszentrum (Gabriele Camphausen, Maria Nooke) ed. *Die Berliner Mauer*, trans. Mariamne Fields. Dresden: Michel Sandstein Verlag, 2002. (includes 1999 "Grenzblicke: Werkschau des Dokumentationszentrums Berliner Mauer" and 2001 "Berlin, 13. August 1961: Eine Austellung zum 40. Jahrestag des Mauerbaus")

Films, Novels, Plays, Recordings, and Musicals

Barenboim, Daniel. *Das Konzert: November 1989*. Sony Classical CD. 1989.

Bechtel, Clemens (producer). Lea Rosh, Renate Kreibich-Fischer, and Clemens Bechtel (dramaturgy). *Staats-Sicherheiten*. 2008.

Beethoven/Barenboim. *Fidelio*. Warner Classics CD. 1999.

"The Berlin Celebration Concert." Beethoven, Symphony No. 9, Bernstein. Schauspielhaus, East Berlin. December 25, 1989. www.youtube.com/watch?v=IInG5nY_wrU

Bernstein, Leonard. *"Ode an die Freiheit." Bernstein in Berlin. Beethoven Symphony Nr. 9*. Deutsche Grammophon (CD). 1990.

   Ode to Freedom. Beethoven: Symphony Nr. 9. Medici Arts (DVD). 2009.

Brussig, Thomas. *Helden wie Wir*. Frankfurt am Main: Fischer Taschenbuch Verlag, 1998.

Candaele, Kerry. *Following the Ninth: In the Footsteps of Beethoven's Final Symphony*. Battlehymns Productions. 2013.

Egger, Urs (director). Stefan Kolditz (screenplay). *An die Grenze*. ZDF and ARTE, 2007.

Frank, Hans-Joachim (director). Jörg Mihan (dramaturgy). Hans-Hermann Hertle (idea and historical consultant). *Das Ende der SED. Die letzten Tage des Zentralkomitees der SED*. Performed by theater 89. 2012.

Fromm, Friedemann (director). Marc Müller-Kaldenberg and Regina Zielger (producers). Annette Hess and Friedemann Fromm (screenplay). *Weissensee*. ARD. 2013–2018.

Grass, Günter. *Im Krebsgang*. Göttingen: Steidl, 2002.

Hirschbiegel, Oliver (director). Bernd Eichinger (director and screenplay). *Der Untergang (Downfall)*. Constantin Film, 2004.

Huber, Florian (director and screenplay). *Wenn Tote Stören. Vom Sterben an der Mauer*. NDR and ARD. 2007.

Schmidt-Sondermann, Volker (director). Thomas Gaevert and Volker Schmidt-Sondermann (screenplay). *Tödliche Grenze – Der Schütze und sein Opfer*. ZDF, 2015.

Schneider, Peter. *The Wall Jumper: A Berlin Story*, trans. Leigh Hafrey. Chicago: University of Chicago Press, 1983.

Waller, Ulrich (producer). Thomas Brussig (screenplay). *Hinterm Horizont. Das Berlin-Musical über das Mädchen aus Ostberlin mit den Hits von Udo Lindenberg.* Berlin: Stage Management, 2011.

Weinert, Stefan (director, screenplay, producer). *Die Familie.* The Core Films, 2014.

Secondary Sources

Ahonen, Pertti. *Death at the Berlin Wall.* New York: Oxford University Press, 2011.

"Anniversaries," a Forum. *German History* 32, no. 1 (2014), pp. 79–100.

Apelt, Andreas H., Robert Grünbaum, and Jens Schöne, eds. *Erinnerungsort DDR: Alltag– Herrschaft – Gesellschaft.* Berlin: Metropol, 2016.

Ashworth, G. J. and P. J. Larkham, eds. *Building a New Heritage: Tourism, Culture and Identity in the New Europe.* New York: Routledge. 1994.

Assmann, Aleida. *Erinnerungsräume: Formen und Wandlungen des kulturellen Gedächtnisses.* Munich: Beck, 1999.

Der lange Schatten der Vergangenheit: Erinnerungskultur und Geschichtspolitik. Munich: Beck, 2006.

Geschichte im Gedächtnis. Von der individuellen Erfahrung zur öffentlichen Inszenierung. Munich: Beck, 2007.

Das neue Unbehagen an der Erinnerungskultur: Eine Intervention. Munich: Beck, 2013.

Der europäische Traum. Vier Lehren aus der Geschichte. Munich: C. H. Beck, 2018.

Assman, Aleida and Sebastian Conrad, eds. *Memory in a Global Age: Discourses, Practices, and Trajectories.* New York: Palgrave Macmillan, 2010.

Assmann, Jan. *Das kulturelle Gedächtnis: Schrift, Erinnerung und politische Identität in frühen Hochkulturen.* Munich: C. H. Beck, 1992.

Bagger, Thomas. "The World According to Germany: Reassessing 1989." *The Washington Quarterly* 41, no. 4 (Winter 2019), pp. 53–63.

Beattie, Andrew. *Playing Politics with History: The Bundestag Inquiries into East Germany.* New York: Berghahn Books, 2008.

Behrens, Heidi and Andreas Wagner, eds. *Deutsche Teilung, Repression und Alltagsleben: Erinnerungsorte der DDR-Geschichte.* Leipzig: Forum Verlag, 2004.

Berger, Stefan. "Former GDR Historians in the Reunified Germany: An Alternative Historical Culture and Its Attempts to Come to Terms with the GDR Past." *Journal of Contemporary History* 38, no. 1 (2003), pp. 63–83.

Betts, Paul. "The Twilight of the Idols: East German Memory and Material Culture." *The Journal of Modern History* 72 (September 2000), pp. 731–65.

Boym, Svetlana. *The Future of Nostalgia.* New York: Basic Books, 2001.

Browning, Christopher R. *Ordinary Men: Reserve Police Battalion 101 and the Final Solution in Poland.* With a new Afterword. New York: Harper Perennial, 2017.

Browning, Christopher R. interviewed by Ephraim Kaye, "An Interview with Christopher Browning." Shoah Resource Center, The International School for Holocaust Studies, Pacific Lutheran University, Tacoma, Washington, March 1997.

Brummer, Arnd, ed. *Vom Gebet zur Demo. 1989 – Die friedliche Revolution began in den Kirchen.* Frankfurt: Hansisches Druck- und Verlagshaus, 2009.

Carrier, Peter. *Holocaust Monuments and National Memory Cultures in France and Germany Since 1989: The Origins and Political Function of the Vel' D'Hiv in Paris and the Holocaust Monument in Berlin.* New York: Berghahn Books, 2005.

Clarke, David and Ute Wölfel. *Remembering the German Democratic Republic: Divided Memory in a United Germany.* New York: Palgrave Macmillan, 2011.

Colomb, Claire. "Requiem for a lost *Palast.* 'Revanchist urban planning' and 'burdened landscapes' of the German Democratic Republic in the new Berlin." *Planning Perspectives,* 22 (July 2007), pp. 283–323.

Connerton, Paul. *How Societies Remember.* New York: Cambridge University Press, 1989.

Cooke, Paul. *Representing East Germany since Unification: From Colonization to Nostalgia.* New York: Berg, 2005.

Cubitt, Geoffrey. *History and Memory.* New York: Manchester University Press, 2007.

Dennis, David B. *Beethoven in German Politics, 1870–1989.* New Haven: Yale University Press, 1996.

Deutz-Schroeder, Monika and Klaus Schroeder. *Soziales Paradies oder Stasi-Staat? Das DDR-Bild von Schülern – ein Ost-West-Vergleich.* Stamsried: Druck und Vögel, 2008.

Dolff-Bonekämper, Gabi. "Sites of Hurtful Memory." *The Getty Conservation Institute Newsletter* 17, no. 2 (Summer 2002), pp. 4–10.

Dorgerloh, Annette, Anke Kuhrmann, and Doris Liebermann. *Die Berliner Mauer in der Kunst: Bildende Kunst, Literatur und Film.* Berlin: Ch. Links, 2011.

Eley, Geoff. "Feature: After 1989 – the Unease of History: Settling Accounts with the East German Past." *History Workshop Journal* 57 (2004), pp. 175–201.

Enders, Judith C., Mandy Schulze, and Bianca Ely, eds. *Wie war das für euch? Die Dritte Generation Ost im Gespräch mit ihren Eltern.* Berlin: Ch. Links, 2016.

Fahlbusch, Jan Henrik and Alissa King. "Towards the 'Renationalisation' of Historical Memory? Tendencies of Commemoration Practices in Contemporary Germany." *Humanity in Action* 6 (December 2004), pp. 38–42.

Feversham, Polly and Leo Schmidt. *Die Berliner Mauer heute/The Berlin Wall Today.* Berlin: Verlag Bauwesen, 1999.

Fisher, Marc. After the Wall: *Germany, the Germans and the Burdens of History.* NY: Simon & Schuster, 1995.

Flix, *Da war mal was. . . Erinnerungen an hier und drüben.* Hamburg: Carlsen, 2009.

Francois, Etienne, Kornelia Kończal, Robert Traba, and Stefan Troebst, eds. *Geschichtspolitik in Europa seit 1989: Deutschland, Frankreich und Polen im internationalen Vergleich.* Göttingen: Wallstein Verlag, 2013.

Francois, Etienne and Hagen Schulze, eds. *Deutsche Erinnerungsorte*. Munich: Beck, 2001.

Frank, Sybille. *Der Mauer um die Wette Gedenken: Die Formation einer Heritage- Industrie am Berliner Checkpoint Charlie*. New York: Campus Verlag, 2008.

"Competing for the Best Wall Memorial: The Rise of a Cold War Heritage Industry in Berlin." In Konrad H. Jarausch, Christian F. Ostermann, and Andreas Etges, eds. *The Cold War: Historiography, Memory, Representation*. Berlin/Boston: Walter de Gruyter, 2017, pp. 267–82.

Friedrich, Jörg. *The Fire: Germany in the Bombing War, 1940–45*, trans. Allison Brown. New York: Columbia University Press, 2008.

Gillis, John R., ed. *Commemorations: The Politics of National Identity*. Princeton: Princeton University Press, 1994.

Grafe, Roman. *Deutsche Gerechtigkeit: Prozesse gegen DDR-Grenzschützen und ihre Befehlsgeber*. Munich: Siedler, 2004.

Grafe, Roman, ed. *Die Schuld der Mitläufer: Anpassen oder Widerstehen in der DDR*. Munich: Pantheon, 2009.

Haase-Hindenberg, Gerhard. *Der Mann, der die Mauer öffnete: Warum Oberstleutnant Harald Jäger den Befehl verweigerte und damit Weltgeschichte schrieb*. Munich: Wilhelm Heyne Verlag, 2007.

Hacker, Michael, Stephanie Maiwald, Johannes Staemmler, et al., eds. *Dritte Generation Ost: Wer wir sind, was wir wollen*, 3rd revised and expanded edition. Berlin: Ch. Links, 2013.

Halbrock, Christian. "Weggesprengt: Die Versöhnungskirche im Todesstreifen der Berliner Mauer 1961–1985." *Horch und Guck*, Special Edition, 2008.

Halbwachs, Maurice. *On Collective Memory*, trans. Francis J. Ditter Jr. and Vida Y. Ditter. New York: Harper Colophon, 1980.

Harrison, Hope M. *Driving the Soviets up the Wall: Soviet-East German Relations, 1953–1961*. Princeton: Princeton University Press, 2003.

Ulbrichts Mauer: Wie die SED Moskaus Widerstand gegen den Mauerbau brach, trans. Karl-Dieter Schmidt. Berlin: Propyläen, 2011.

"The Berlin Wall and Its Resurrection as a Site of Memory," *German Politics and Society* 29, no. 2 (Summer 2011), pp. 78–106.

"Die Berliner Mauer an der Bernauer Strasse als ein Ort des Erinnerns, 1989–2011," *Jahrbuch für Historische Kommunismusforschung*. Berlin: Aufbau Verlag, 2011, pp. 281–97.

"From Shame to Pride: The Fall of the Berlin Wall through German Eyes," *The Wilson Quarterly* (November 4, 2014).

"Berlin's *Gesamtkonzept* for Remembering the Berlin Wall." In Konrad H. Jarausch, Christian F. Ostermann, and Andreas Etges, eds., *The Cold War: Historiography, Memory, Representation*. Berlin/Boston: Walter de Gruyter, 2017, pp. 239–66.

Heidenreich, Ronny. "Eine Mauer für die Welt. Inszenierungen außerhalb Deutschlands nach 1989." In Klaus-Dietmar Henke, ed., *Die Mauer:*

Errichtung, Überwindung, Erinnerung. Munich: Deutscher Taschenbuch Verlag, 2011, pp. 440–55.

"From Concrete to Cash: Turning the Berlin Wall into a Business." In Anna Kaminsky, ed., *Where in the World Is the Berlin Wall?* Berlin: Berlin Story Verlag, 2014, pp. 268–81.

Henke, Klaus-Dietmar, ed. *Revolution und Vereinigung 1989/90: Als in Deutschland die Realität die Phantasie Überholte*. Munich: Deutscher Taschenbuch Verlag, 2009.

Henke, Klaus-Dietmar, ed. *Die Mauer: Errichtung, Überwindung, Erinnerung*. Munich: Deutscher Taschenbuch Verlag, 2011.

Henseler, Thomas and Susanne Buddenberg. *Tunnel 57: A True Escape Story*. Berlin: Ch. Links, 2013.

Hertle, Hans-Hermann. "The Fall of the Wall: The Unintended Self-Dissolution of East Germany's Ruling Regime." *Cold War International History Project Bulletin* 12/13 (Fall/Winter 2001), pp. 131–40.

Die Berliner Mauer – Monument des Kalten Krieges. The Berlin Wall – Monument of the Cold War, 1st edition. Berlin: Ch. Links, 2007.

Chronik des Mauerfalls. Die dramatischen Ereignisse um den 9. November 1989, 11th expanded edition. Berlin: Ch. Links, 2009.

Hertle, Hans-Hermann and Maria Nooke, eds. *Die Todesopfer an der Berliner Mauer 1961–1989. Ein biographisches Handbuch*. Berlin: Ch. Links Verlag, 2009.

Hertle, Hans-Hermann, and Maria Nooke, eds. *The Victims at the Berlin Wall 1961–1989. A Biographical Handbook*. Berlin: Ch. Links Verlag, 2011.

Heß, Pamela. *Geschichte als Politikum: Öffentliche und private Kontroversen um die Deutung der DDR-Vergangenheit*. Baden-Baden: Nomos, 2014.

Hoffmann, PM and Bernd Lindner. *Herbst der Entscheidung. Eine Geschichte aus der Friedlichen Revolution 1989*. Berlin: Ch. Links Verlag, 2014.

Huyssen, Andreas. *Twilight Memories: Marking Time in a Culture of Amnesia*. London: Routledge, 1995.

"The Voids of Berlin." *Critical Inquiry* 24, no. 1 (Autumn 1997), pp. 57–81.

Present Pasts: Urban Palimpsests and the Politics of Memory. Stanford: Stanford University Press, 2003.

Institute für Kulturpolitik der Kulturpolitischen Gesellschaft, ed. *Jahrbuch für Kulturpolitik 2009. Thema: Erinnerungskulturen und Geschichtspolitik*. Essen: Klartext, 2009.

Jarausch, Konrad H. "Beyond the National Narrative: Implications of Reunification for Recent German History." *German History*. 28, no. 4 (2010), pp. 498–514.

Jarausch, Konrad H. ed. *United Germany: Debating Processes und Prospects*. NY: Berghahn, 2013.

Jarausch, Konrad H. and Michael Geyer. *Shattered Past: Reconstructing German Histories*. Princeton: Princeton University Press, 2003.

Jarausch, Konrad H. and Martin Sabrow, eds. *Verletztes Gedächtnis. Erinnerungskultur und Zeitgeschichte im Konflikt*. New York: Campus Verlag, 2002.

Jarausch, Konrad H., Christian F. Ostermann, and Andreas Etges, eds. *The Cold War: Historiography, Memory, Representation*. Berlin/Boston: Walter de Gruyter, 2017.

Jelin, Elizabeth. *State Repression and the Labors of Memory*, trans. Judy Rein and Marcial Godoy-Anativia. Minneapolis: University of Minnesota Press, 2003.

Jones, Sara. *The Media of Testimony: Remembering the East German Stasi in the Berlin Republic*. New York: Palgrave Macmillan, 2014.

Jordan, Jennifer A. *Structures of Memory: Understanding Urban Change in Berlin and Beyond*. Stanford: Stanford University Press, 2006.

Kaminsky, Anna, ed. *Where in the World Is the Berlin Wall?* Berlin: Berlin Story Verlag, 2014.

Kaminsky, Annette, ed. *Orte des Erinnerns: Gedenkzeichen, Gedenkstätten und Museen zur Diktatur in SBZ und DDR*, third revised and expanded edition. Berlin: Ch. Links, 2016.

Kansteiner, Wulf. *In Pursuit of German Memory: History, Television, and Politics after Auschwitz*. Athens: Ohio University Press, 2006.

Klausmeier, Axel and Leo Schmidt. *Wall Remnants – Wall Traces: The Comprehensive Guide to the Berlin Wall*. Berlin/Bonn: Westkreuz Verlag, 2004.

Kleßmann, Christoph. "Der schwierige gesamtdeutsche Umgang mit der DDR-Geschichte." *Aus Politik und Zeitgeschichte* (May 26, 2002).

Klinge, Sebastian. *1989 und wir: Geschichtspolitik und Erinnerungskultur nach dem Mauerfall*. Bielefeld: transcript Verlag, 2015.

Knischewski, Gerd and Ulla Spittler. "Remembering the Berlin Wall: The Wall Memorial Ensemble Bernauer Strasse." *German Life and Letters* 59, no. 2 (April 2006), pp. 280–93.

Koposov, Nikolay. *Memory Laws, Memory Wars: The Politics of the Past in Europe and Asia*. Cambridge: Cambridge University Press, 2018.

Kornelius, Stefan. *Angela Merkel: The Chancellor and Her World*. London: Alma Books, 2013.

Kowalczuk, Ilko-Sascha. *Endspiel: Die Revolution von 1989 in der DDR*. Munich: C. H. Beck, 2009.

Kramer, Jane. *The Politics of Memory: Looking for Germany in the New Germany*. New York: Random House, 1996.

Kundnani, Hans. *The Paradox of German Power*. New York: Oxford University Press, 2015.

Kuzdas, Heinz J. *Berliner Mauer Kunst. Mit East Side Gallery*. Berlin: Espresso, 1990/1998.

Ladd, Brian. *The Ghosts of Berlin: Confronting German History in the Urban Landscape*. Cambridge: Belknap Press of Harvard University Press, 1995.

"Center and Periphery in the New Berlin: Architecture, Public Art, and the Search for Identity." *PAJ: A Journal of Performance and Art*, No. 65 (2000), pp. 7–21.

Landwehr, Achim. "Mein Jahr mit Luther. Thesen zur Geschichtskultur," mein jahrmitluther.wordpress.com/category/thesen-zur-geschichtskultur/.

Lebow, Richard Ned, Wulf Kansteiner, and Claudio Fogu, eds. *The Politics of Memory in Postwar Europe*. Durham: Duke University Press, 2006.

Levi, Primo. *The Drowned and the Saved*. New York: Simon and Schuster, 2017.

Light, Duncan. "Gazing on Communism: Heritage Tourism and Post-Communist Identities in Germany, Hungary and Romania." *Tourism Geographies* 2, no. 2 (2000), pp. 157–76.

Lindenberger, Thomas. "Ist die DDR ausgeforscht? Phasen, Trends und ein optimistischer Ausblick." *Aus Politik und Zeitgeschichte* 24–26 (June 3, 2014).

Loeb, Carolyn. "Planning Reunification: The planning History of the Fall of the Berlin Wall." *Planning Perspectives* 21 (January 2006), pp. 67–87.

Lowe, David and Tony Joel. *Remembering the Cold War: Global Contest and National Stories*. New York: Routledge, 2013.

Ludwig, Andreas. "Musealisierung der Zeitgeschichte: Die DDR im Kontext." *Deutschland Archiv* 10 (October 5, 2011).

Macdonald, Sharon. *Memorylands: Heritage and Identity in Europe Today*. New York: Routledge, 2013.

Macmillan, Margaret. *The Uses and Abuses of History*. London: Profile Books, 2009.

Magofsky, Benjamin. *Berliner Mauer und Deutsche Frage im Bundesrepublikanischen Spielfilm, 1982–2007*. Hamburg: Diplomica Verlag, 2009.

Maier, Charles S. *Dissolution: The Crisis of Communism and the End of East Germany*. Princeton: Princeton University Press, 1997.

  The Unmasterable Past: History, Holocaust, and German National Identity, with a New Preface. Cambridge: Harvard University Press, 1997.

Major, Patrick. *Behind the Berlin Wall: East Germany and the Frontiers of Power*. New York: Oxford University Press, 2010.

Mathew, Nicholas. *Political Beethoven*. New York: Cambridge University Press, 2013.

Maurer, Jochen. *Dienst an der Mauer: Der Alltag der Grenztruppen rund um Berlin*. Berlin: Ch. Links, 2011.

  Halt – Staatsgrenze! Alltag, Dienst und Innenansichten der Grenztruppen der DDR. Berlin: Ch. Links, 2016.

Maurer, Jochen and Gerhard Sälter. "The Double Task of the East German Border Guards: Policing the Border and Military Functions." *German Politics and Society* 29, no. 2 (Summer 2011), pp. 23–39.

Mawil. *Kinderland*. Berlin: Reprodukt, 2014.

McAdams, A. James. *Judging the Past in Unified Germany*. New York: Cambridge University Press, 2001.

Mellon, James. "Urbanism, Nationalism and the Politics of Place: Commemoration and Collective Memory," paper presented to the annual Canadian Political Science Association conference, 2006. www.cpsa-acsp.ca /papers-2006/Mellon/pdf

Meyen, Michael. *"Wir haben freier gelebt": Die DDR im kollektiven Gedächtnis der Deutschen.* Bielefeld: transcript, 2013.

Mitchell, Gregg. *The Tunnels: Escapes under the Berlin Wall and the Historic Films the JFK Whitehouse Tried to Kill.* New York: Crown, 2016.

Moore, Anne Elizabeth and Melissa Mendes. "How Two-Thirds of the Berlin Wall Ended up in the U.S." *Wilson Quarterly* (Fall 2014).

Müller, Jan-Werner. "Just another *Vergangenheitsbewältigung?* The Process of Coming to Terms with the East German Past Revisited." *Oxford German Studies* 38, no. 3 (2009), pp. 334–44.

Niven, Bill. *Facing the Nazi Past: United Germany and the Legacy of the Third Reich.* New York: Routledge, 2002.

Niven, Bill, ed. *Germans as Victims: Remembering the Past in Contemporary Germany.* New York: Palgrave/Macmillan, 2006.

Nooke, Maria and Hans-Hermann Hertle, eds. *Die Todesopfer am Aussenring der Berliner Mauer 1961–1989/The Victims at the Berlin-Brandenburg Border, 1961–1989*, trans. Mariamne Fields. Berlin/Potsdam: Center for Civic Education of the Federal State of Brandenburg, 2013.

Nora, Pierre. "Between Memory and History: Les Lieux de Memoire." *Representations* 26 (Spring 1989), pp. 7–25.

Olick, Jeffrey K. *The Politics of Regret: On Collective Memory and Historical Responsibility.* New York: Routledge, 2007.

The Sins of the Fathers: Germany, Memory, Method. Chicago: The University of Chicago Press, 2016.

Olick, Jeffrey K., ed. *States of Memory: Continuities, Conflicts, and Transformations in National Retrospection.* Durham: Duke University Press, 2003.

Vered Vinitzky-Seroussi, and Daniel Levy, eds. *The Collective Memory Reader* New York: Oxford University Press, 2011.

Oplatka, Andreas. *Der erste Riß in der Mauer: September 1989 – Ungarn öffnet die Grenze.* Munich: Paul Zsolnay Verlag, 2009.

Packer, George. "The Quiet German: The Astonishing Rise of Angela Merkel, the Most Powerful Woman in the World." *The New Yorker* (December 1, 2014).

Pakier, Malgorzata and Bo Strath, eds. *A European Memory? Contested Histories and Politics of Remembrance.* New York: Berghahn Books, 2010.

Paul, Gerhard. "Von Psychopathen, Technokraten des Terrors und 'ganz gewöhnlichen' Deutschen. Die Täter der Shoah im Spiegel der Forschung." In Gerhard Paul, ed., *Die Täter der Shoah. Fanatische Nationalsozialisten oder ganz normale Deutsche?* Göttingen: Wallstein Verlag, 2002, pp. 13–89.

Pearce, Susan C. "1989 as Collective Memory 'Refolution.' East-Central Europe Confronts Memorial Silence." In Lindsey A. Freeman, Benjamin Nienass, and

Rachel Daniell, eds., *Silence, Screen, and Spectacle: Rethinking Social Memory in the Age of Information*. New York: Berghahn, 2014, pp. 213–38.

"Who Owns a Movement's Memory? The Case of Poland's Solidarity." In Anna Reading and Tamar Katriel, eds. *Cultural Memories of Nonviolent Struggles: Powerful Times*. New York: Palgrave Macmillan, 2014, pp. 166–87.

Rathje, Wolfgang. *"Mauer-Marketing" unter Erich Honecker. Schwierigkeiten der DDR bei der technischen Modernisierung, der volkswirtschaftlichen Kalkulation und der politischen Akzeptanz der Berliner "Staatsgrenze" von 1971 – 1990*, 2 vols. Berlin: Ralf Gründer Verlag, 2006.

Reuth, Ralf Georg and Günther Lackmann. *Das erste Leben der Angela M.* Munich: Piper Verlag, GmbH, 2013.

Richter, Sebastian. "Die Mauer in der deutschen Erinnerungskultur." In Klaus-Dietmar Henke, ed., *Die Mauer: Errichtung, Überwindung, Erinnerung*. Munich: Deutscher Taschenbuch Verlag, 2011, pp. 252–66.

Roll, Evelyn. *Die Kanzlerin. Angela Merkel's Weg zur Macht*. Berlin: Ullstein, 2009.

Rosenberg, Tina. *The Haunted Land: Facing Europe's Ghosts After Communism*. New York: Vintage Books, 1996.

Ross, Corey. *The East German Dictatorship: Problems and Perspectives in the Interpretation of the GDR*. New York: Oxford University Press, 2002.

Rottman, Gordon L. *The Berlin Wall and the Intra-German Border, 1961–89*. Oxford: Osprey Publishing, 2008.

Rudnick, Carola S. *Die andere Hälfte der Erinnerung: Die DDR in der deutschen Geschichtspolitik nach 1989*. Bielefeld: transcript Verlag, 2011.

Sa'adah, Anne. *Germany's Second Chance: Trust, Justice, and Democratization*. Cambridge: Harvard University Press, 1998.

Sabrow, Martin. *Zeitgeschichte schreiben: Von der Verständigung über die Vergangenheit in der Gegewart*. Göttingen: Wallstein, 2014.

Sälter, Gerhard. *Mauerreste in Berlin. Relicts of the Berlin Wall*, 2nd rev. ed., trans. Mariamne Fields. Berlin: Verein Berliner Mauer Gedenkstätte und Dokumentationszentrum e.V., 2007.

Grenzpolizisten: Konformität, Verweigerung und Repression in der Grenzpolizei und den Grenztruppen der DDR 1952 vis 1965. Berlin: Ch. Links, 2009.

Sarotte, Mary Elise. *1989: The Struggle to Create Post-Cold War Europe*. Princeton: Princeton University Press, 2009.

The Collapse: The Accidental Opening of the Berlin Wall. New York: Basic Books, 2014.

Saunders, Anna. *Memorializing the GDR: Monuments and Memory after 1989*. New York: Berghahn, 2018.

Saunders, Anna and Debbie Pinfold, eds. *Remembering and Rethinking the GDR: Multiple Perspectives and Plural Authenticities*. New York: Palgrave Macmillan, 2013.

Savage, Kirk. *Monument Wars: Washington, D.C., the National Mall, and the Transformation of the Memorial Landscape.* Berkeley: University of California Press, 2009.

Schmidt, Leo. "Die universelle Ikonisierung der Mauer." In Klaus-Dietmar Henke, ed., *Die Mauer: Errichtung, Überwindung, Erinnerung.* Munich: Deutscher Taschenbuch Verlag, 2011, pp. 456–68.

Schmidt, Leo and Henriette von Preuschen. *On Both Sides of the Wall: Preserving Monuments and Sites of the Cold War Era.* Berlin/Bonn: Westkreuz-Verlag, 2005.

Schneider, Peter. *Berlin Now: The City after the Wall,* trans. Sophie Schlondorff. New York: Farrar, Straus and Giroux, 2014.

Schöne, Jens. *The Peaceful Revolution: Berlin 1989–90: The Path to German Unity,* trans. E. F. S. Zbikowki. Berlin: Berlin Story Verlag, 2009.

Schroeder, Klaus. *Die veränderte Republik: Deutschland nach der Wiedervereinigung.* Munich: Bayerische Landeszentrale für politische Bildungsarbeit, 2006.

Schroeder, Klaus and Jochen Staadt. *Die Todesopfer des DDR-Grenzregimes an der innerdeutschen Grenze, 1949–1989: Ein biografisches Handbuch.* Frankfurt am Main: Peter Lang, 2017.

Schuerer, Ernest, Manfred Keune, and Philip Jenkins, eds. *The Berlin Wall: Representations and Perspectives.* New York: Peter Lang, 1996.

Schultke, Dietmar. *"Keiner kommt durch": Die Geschichte der innerdeutschen Grenze und der Berliner Mauer.* Berlin: Aufbau, 2008.

Schwartz, Barry. "Commemoration." In James D. Wright, ed. *International Encyclopedia of the Social and Behavioral Sciences,* 2nd ed., vol. 4. New York: Elsevier, 2015, pp. 235–242.

Schwartz, Simon. *drüben!* Berlin: avant-verlag, 2009.

Siegmund, Jörg. *Opfer ohne Lobby? Ziele, Strukturen und Arbeitsweise der Verbände der Opfer des DDR-Unrechts.* Berlin: Berliner Wissenschafts-Verlag, 2002.

Siggelkow, Ingeborg, ed. *Erinnerungskultur und Gedächtnispolitik.* New York: Peter Lang, 2003.

Stuhler, Ed. *Die letzten Monate der DDR.* Berlin: Ch. Links, 2010.

Suckut, Siegfried and Jürgen Weber, eds. *Stasi-Akten zwischen Politik und Zeitgeschichte: Eine Zwischenbilanz.* Munich: Olzog, 2003.

Till, Karen E. *The New Berlin: Memory, Politics, Place.* Minneapolis: University of Minnesota Press, 2005.

Tilmans, Karin, Frank van Vree and Jay Winter, eds. *Performing the Past: Memory, History, and Identity in Modern Europe.* Chicago: Amsterdam University Press, 2012.

Trotnow, Helmut. "Sag mir, wo die Spuren sind. . . Berlin und der Umgang mit der Geschichte der Berliner Mauer." In Bernd Faulenbach, Franz-Josef Jelich, eds., *"Asymmetrisch verflochtene Parallelgeschichte?" Die Geschichte der*

Bundesrepublik und der DDR in Ausstellungen, Museen und Gedenkstätten. Essen: Klartext, 2005, pp. 157–66.

Ullrich, Maren. *Geteilte Ansichten: Erinnerungslandschaft Deutsch-Deutsche Grenze.* Berlin: Aufbau Verlag GmbH, 2006.

Vaizey, Hester. *Born in the GDR: Living in the Shadow of the Wall.* New York: Oxford University Press, 2014.

Verheyen, Dirk. *United City, Divided Memories? Cold War Legacies in Contemporary Berlin.* Lanham: Lexington Books, 2008.

Vinitzky-Seroussi, Vered. *Yitzhak Rabin's Assassination and the Dilemmas of Commemoration.* Albany: State University of New York Press, 2009.

Vollnhals, Clemens, "Die strafrechtliche Ahndung der Gewalttaten an der inner-deutschen Grenze." In Klaus-Dietmar Henke, ed., *Die Mauer: Errichtung, Überwindung, Erinnerung.* Munich: Deutscher Taschenbuch Verlag, 2011, pp. 241–251.

Ward, Janet. *Post-Wall Berlin: Borders, Space and Identity.* New York: Palgrave Macmillan, 2011.

Whitehead, Anne. *Memory.* New York: Routledge, 2009.

Wilke, Manfred. "Die Bundesregierung will die Erinnerung an die SED-Diktatur konzeptionell neu ordnen." *Deutschland Archiv* 38, no. 3 (2005), pp. 438–42.

Williams, Paul. *Memorial Museums: The Global Rush to Commemorate Atrocities.* New York: Oxford University Press, 2007.

Wingenfeld, Heiko. *Die öffentliche Debatte über die Strafverfahren wegen DDR-Unrechts: Vergangenheitsaufarbeitung in der bundesdeutschen Öffentlichkeit der 90er Jahre.* Berlin: Berliner Wissenschafts-Verlag, 2006.

Winter, Jay. "Remembrance and Redemption." *Harvard Design Magazine* 9 (Fall 1999), pp.1–6.

Remembering War: The Great War Between Memory and History in the Twentieth Century. New Haven: Yale University Press, 2006.

Sites of Memory, Sites of Mourning. Cambridge: Cambridge University Press, 2014.

Wittlinger, Ruth. "Collective Memory and National Identity in the Berlin Republic: The Emergence of a New Consensus?" *Debatte: Journal of Contemporary Central and Eastern Europe* 14, no. 3 (December 2006), pp. 201–212.

German National Identity in the Twenty-First Century: A Different Republic After All? New York: Palgrave Macmillan, 2010.

Wolfrum, Edgar. "Neue Erinnerungskultur? Die Massenmedialisierung des 17. Juni 1953." *Aus Politik und Zeitgeschichte* 40–41 (September 29, 2003), pp. 33–39.

Wüstenberg, Jenny. "Conflicted Memories: Germans Struggle to Adequately Commemorate the East German Dictatorship." *American Institute for Contemporary German Studies Advisor* (August 31, 2006).

Civil Society and Memory in Postwar Germany. New York: Cambridge University Press, 2017.

Yang, Daqing and Mike Mochizuki, eds. *Memory, Identity, and Commemorations of World War II: Anniversary Politics in Asia Pacific.* Foreword by Akira Iriye. Lanham: Lexington Books, 2018.

Young, James. *The Texture of Memory: Holocaust Memorials and Meaning.* New Haven: Yale University Press, 1993.

Zeruvabel, Eviator. *Time Maps: Collective Memory and the Social Shape of the Past.* Chicago: University of Chicago Press, 2004.

Zeruvabel,Yael. *Recovered Roots: Collective Memory and the Making of the Israeli National Tradition.* Chicago: University of Chicago Press, 1995.

Zubok, Vladislav M. *A Failed Empire: The Soviet Union in the Cold War from Stalin to Gorbachev.* Chapel Hill: University of North Carolina Press, 2007.

"With His Back Against the Wall: Gorbachev, Soviet Demise, and German Reunification." *Cold War History* 14, no. 4 (Oct. 1, 2014), pp. 619–45.

INDEX

444